FILIPPO BRUNELLESCHI

EUGENIO BATTISTI

FILIPPO BRUNELLESCHI

the complete work

RIZZOLI
NEW YORK

Design Diego Birelli

The photographs were expressly made by Paolo Monti

April 1982

Translated from the Italian, *Filippo Brunelleschi*, by Robert Erich Wolf
Text revised by Eugenio Battisti and Emily Lane

First published in the United States of America in 1981 by

RIZZOLI INTERNATIONAL PUBLICATIONS, INC.
712 Fifth Avenue/New York 10019

Printed and bound in Italy.

LC 78-68509
ISBN 0-8478-5015-3

Contents

To the memory of Elena Caciagli, the cherished pupil whose generosity, intelligence and devotion made it possible for me to start my seminars on Architecture at the University of Florence.

Foreword and acknowledgments

*Here then are those things about which you
asked me to write. Not, mind you, that I wish
to affirm anything whatsoever to be just so and
not otherwise. It is certain that these matters
of history are such precisely because they
possess not a shred of certainty; it suffices
that they be at least not lacking in verisimilitude,
which is something halfway between the fiction
of fable and the certainty of truth.*

COLUCCIO SALUTATI, in a letter

Whatever our acquaintance with Brunelleschi, in point of true knowledge of the man and his works we are currently in a kind of "third age". Between the great nineteenth-century works of erudite exploration and today's approach there was something of a dark age during which, in some respects, we came to know not more but less: certain works, the Rotunda of S. Maria degli Angeli, the lantern of the Old Sacristy, were destroyed, every scrap replaced with new materials; and measured drawings and data were arbitrarily contrived or copied, unthinkingly, from inaccurate nineteenth-century sources. Still, there was progress: in the study of the relationships between the culture of the man himself and that of the political and philosophical circles of his time, in the ever increasing ability to define the broader importance of some of his ideas in domains such as perspective and architectural designing and drawing, and in such concepts as the importance of experimentation and the nobility of intellectual values. Then too, fundamental monographs and studies on the painting and sculpture of his time created something like a concave form into which, as a working hypothesis at least, the architect and what he did could somehow be fitted and take on meaningful shape.

The original commission for this book came from Italian Radio and Television, who wanted to present it as a gift to participants in an international competition held in 1975. The illustrated text was published in that year. A second part, including the Chronology, further comments, and notes, was added when the book was published commercially a year later, in 1976; no changes to the illustrations could then or now be made. I agreed to do the book under those conditions because I was at the time associated with the School of Architecture at the University of Florence, and was attempting, with the help of intelligent and generous assistants and former students, to transform the classes in History of Architecture from lectures into a kind of workshop. We were already investigating Quattrocento architecture, especially visiting buildings, studying their incongruities, and making measured drawings. I spoke in my original Preface of this now unbelievable atmosphere of enthusiasm and frantic activity: there was no spot in Florence without groups of students, both Italian and Greek, taking measurements or photographs, and the final versions of the drawings for publication were normally presented to me about 3 a.m. at Florence railway station, as I was constantly commuting between Rome, where my library is, to Milan, where my publisher was. This is not the usual way to prepare a scholarly work; but there were advantages. A good example is the discussion of the various phases of construction at S.

Lorenzo, elaborated through endless different hypotheses and checked at each stage by a new visit to the building and new measured drawings. In some cases, the research involved spending weeks and months inside the building itself, as for the dome of S. Maria del Fiore.

Now, thanks to a publisher of exceptional good will, this new, English, edition goes far beyond the original. The text has been thoroughly revised in relation to the new material added since 1976; it has been checked and where necessary corrected; a number of important new facts and documents are included; and I have tried to take account of all the important contributions to Brunelleschi studies up to the summer of 1979. In 1977 came the sixth centenary celebrations of Brunelleschi's birth, which produced a plethora of new information, interpretations and clashes of opinion. The book — perhaps of particular interest because it consists essentially of an examination by Italians of the buildings themselves, of the original documents, and of the ideas of foreign scholars, at one time German, now mostly American — thus contains a profusion of material, and plenty of loose ends. But it was not meant to be a final statement.

Much has been achieved in various fields, but much still remains to be done. The technical enquiries concerning the statics of the dome of Florence Cathedral have until now been inconsequential. The image of Brunelleschi is still stereotyped and associated with only a few buildings, most of which were not built under his direction. And the largest group of measured drawings — obviously not without their faults — is still that presented by my own assistants and students to the Accademia Nazionale di S. Luca and the Berenson Library at I Tatti in 1977.

There are, nevertheless, encouraging signs for the future. More scientific restoration or conservation of several of the works is yielding new and essential information on their fabric and how they were built. Corrado Bozzoni and Giovanni Carbonara have produced an excellent bibliography, published in two volumes in 1977 and 1978 by the Istituto di Fondamenti dell'Architettura, Department of Architecture, University of Rome, containing 2,132 items. Brunelleschi's political career has been documented year by year, from September 1418 to 1432, by Diane Finiello Zervas (1979). Our understanding of his technical ingenuity in both hydraulics and fortification has been extended — in the former by the topographical study of the dams built in an attempt to flood Lucca (see Chapter 11), and by knowledge of the aqueduct at Assisi (deduced by Bozzoni and Carbonara from a statement by Pietro Farulli[1]), which was later improved and still feeds an original fountain in front of the Cathedral; and in the latter by Gustina Scaglia's attribution to Brunelleschi of the Torre del Marzocco at Livorno, and by Professor J.R. Hale's new appreciation of his defensive system at Pisa. An extremely new field of research is Brunelleschi's activity as supervisor in the mining district of Volterra and the marble quarries of Campiglia Marittima and Carrara.

Finally, a few observations on organization. The book is composed of three elements: a biographical chapter with appended chronology and notes, incorporating all the information I was able to collect up to the time of finalizing the text; chapters, again with notes, on particular buildings and projects, forming a catalogue of Brunelleschi's works, discussing previous interpretations and putting forward new hypotheses; and the illustrations with their captions, sometimes extended. I have tried to provide a general survey that will be useful to students and a reference book for scholars. Particular care has been taken in translating the original documents in Latin and Italian, normally inaccessible to the foreign reader because of their difficulty. This was a long, tiring and frustrating job, especially for Dr Wolf, whom I want to thank specially. Inevitably the translation is also an interpretation, and as such will be challenged and discussed by scholars. I feel a personal responsibility for the decoding of several ambiguous passages and I remain sometimes uncertain.

In the research and preparation of the material in the book I have been aided by a host of friends, colleagues and assistants whom I list not by order of rank or seniority but instead all together, informally: Gino Anzivino, Pier Luigi Bandini, James H. Beck, Amedeo Belluzzi, Renzo Beltrame, G. Caprioli, Beppe Cruciani, Marco Dezzi Bardeschi, P. Mazzoni, Guido Morozzi, Alessandro Parronchi, Carlo Pedretti, Howard Saalman, Silvano Salvadori, the late Professor Piero Sanpaolesi, and G. Verga.

To Professor Lucia Gai I am particularly indebted for her generous contribution to the discussion of Brunelleschi as sculptor, as I am also to the advanced students and assistants whose names appear with their contributions. The work of making new measured drawings, begun a few years earlier under the direction of Professor Carla Pietramellara and my assistant Franco Luchini, became an organized programme during the academic year 1974-75. The findings were subjected to continual review and checking, often even during the process of measurement, and always with direct verification on the monuments themselves. Architectural drawings are like the scholar's transcription of manuscripts: they require unremitting alertness to possibile flaws in reading or interpretation. One may regret a lack of graphic uniformity and some disparity in methods (the drawings were not redrawn by the original publisher), but we nonetheless now have an alternative to the diagrams of Geymüller, which were often oversimplified and at times incorrect, and we have something like twice the information.

Seminar groups were led by Franco Luchini and Carlo Bertocci (Foundling Hospital, Barbadori Chapel, S. Lorenzo, the pulpit in S. Maria Novella), Francesco Quinterio (Palazzo di Parte Guelfa, S. Spirito, the Cathedral exedrae, works outside Florence), Giordano Conti (fortifications in the Pisa region especially, chapels outside Tuscany influenced by Brunelleschi), and Giovanni Degl'Innocenti (perspective, Masaccio's *Trinity*). Structural problems of the Pazzi Chapel and S. Lorenzo, particularly the systems of roofing and vaulting, were studied by Riccardo Pacciani and Massimo Baldi.

An independent research group, organized by the students themselves, took on the arduous job of surveying the Cathedral dome. Their Study Group was guided by Elio Rodio, Pierangelo Scatigna, and Giovanni Themelis, and a considerable number of other students helped in the measurements.

Invaluable help was given by the personnel of the Archivio di Stato in Florence. In the hunt for hard-to-find bibliographical material I was aided by Janet D'Alberto, Pina von Henneberg, Louise Henning and Corrado Bozzoni. My research was much facilitated by the splendidly accessible Pattee Library of Pennsylvania State University, by the cordiality of Professor Hellmut Hager of that university and the support of its Institute for the Arts and Humanistic Studies. A small grant from the University of Florence helped towards acquiring indispensable materials for the measured drawings of the dome.

The final version of this book would not have been possible without the generous understanding, broad culture and solid learning of a young friend, Dr Riccardo Pacciani, to whom I owe several stimulating suggestions and occasionally sharp criticisms, and enough challenging questions to require another book to answer. His unstinting collaboration in the many problems of the translation greatly facilitated that thorny undertaking.

EUGENIO BATTISTI

8

Introduction

Now that so much visual and documentary material on Brunelleschi has been brought together in a single volume and systematically arranged, we find ourselves faced with something unexpected. As page follows page the traditional image of the man that one finds in hundreds of general works on the Renaissance, appearing as a precise, well-defined point of reference whose nature is taken for granted, begins to fade, as in a poorly developed photograph. In some areas what we see is so very different from that textbook image that we might be tempted to think that words distort the facts they are meant to express; but then we find on close examination that the supposedly objective plans, drawings and measurements that are traditionally used, and the photographs from Alinari, are equally untrustworthy. And the reason is the same in both cases: subjective interpretations, the products of particular historical moments, have been handed on as factual evidence from book to book, and from teacher to teacher, gradually losing their meaning and superimposed like successive paintings by different artists on a single canvas. This is why I believe that our first task is to X-ray that confused picture and examine each "layer" of interpretation.

Between Brunelleschi's time and our own there have been basically four different ways of looking at the architect. All but the first have taken into account only a selection of his work, ignoring various minor jobs and everything that was chiefly technical in nature.

The first interpretation of Brunelleschi is clearly stated by an unusual marginal note on a notarial act of 1444: there Filippo, who was acting as a witness, was described as "homo magne industrie" (a man of great enterprise), endowed with "vertute perfecta" — *virtus* in this context clearly referring to his technical ability to erect the dome of Florence Cathedral. A similar note is struck in the epitaph of 1446 below his bust in the Cathedral and in the inscriptions that accompany his tomb [2, 3]. (For a non-churchman to have a bust so displayed was itself an unusual honour.)[1] The epitaph speaks of Brunelleschi as a most famous architect, and the tomb and wall inscriptions further describe him as one whose counsel was sought everywhere, a man of exceptional ingenuity in solving difficult problems or, indeed, in recognizing their existence, and the inventor of machines of enormous innovative importance for the future — machines which made it possible to substitute intelligence for brute force, and meticulous execution for physical effort and improvization (a point demonstrated by the very small number of accidents among the workers engaged in raising the immense dome of the Cathedral). Brief as these Latin inscriptions are — one of them by no less a figure than the humanist papal secretary Carlo Marsuppini — they give us a portrait in the round, with complexities and contradictions that are confirmed by documents and by drawings derived from Brunelleschi's machinery. The man that emerges is even more like Leonardo da Vinci than is commonly thought.

The second view of Brunelleschi dates from a few decades after his death. It is connected with a new emphasis on what we might call the ideological significance of his style and with praise of him almost entirely as an architectural designer. It is the product of a time when geometrical design, order, symmetry and simplicity in plan were becoming the common patrimony. For this interpretation, the chief document is a biography attributed to Antonio di Tuccio Manetti, who will be referred to in these pages simply as the Biographer (see below, pp. 13-14). Penned under the influence of the writings of Alberti, this biography also reveals how much the humanists in the late Quattrocento had begun to accept the architect as their legitimate counterpart. In the words of the Biographer (f. 295v), Brunelleschi is said to have revived "that manner of building that is now called' in the Roman fashion' and' in the Antique fashion', which nowadays is so eagerly imitated... since before him everything was German [i.e. Gothic] and what is called 'modern' ".

If we replace "manner" with "style" we already have the slogan: Brunelleschi, Creator of the Renaissance. Not that the Biographer can be held responsible for that oversimplification. His chief concern was to distinguish clearly between the initial project and the alterations made during execution, noting each punctiliously and deploring them in almost all the buildings mentioned. Since he explicity invited the reader to take these modifications into account and to go back to the initial designs, the Biographer was not so much fostering a myth as attempting to defend, documents in hand and with what are obviously his own recollections of visits made as a youngster to building sites — perhaps in the company of the master or of his faithful assistants — the figure of Brunelleschi as he really was. Not very successfully, though.

To help in understanding the climate of the 1480s in which, we think, the Biographer was writing — forty or so years after the death of Brunelleschi, at a time when S. Spirito and S. Lorenzo were nearing completion and the Pazzi Chapel had been built (but who can say how faithfully those projects were carried out?) — one can turn to the simple, grandiose and solemn structure of S. Maria delle Carceri in Prato. This church by Giuliano da Sangallo (begun in 1484, built as high as the lantern by 1492), with a ground plan which was originally absolutely symmetrical and an elevation based on the exact repetition of forms all around both exterior and interior, appears at once as a geometrical model of the centrally-planned church, and can serve as metaphor of how the figure of Brunelleschi was transformed in this second phase of interpretation. Refined down or simplified as regards the outward technical, symbolic, perhaps even political aspects, his personality was reduced to three canonical roles: as Neo-Platonic worshipper of pure geometrical forms, as reviver of the Antique art of building, and, together with Donatello and Masaccio, as leader in a general aesthetic and cultural renewal of Classicizing and archaeological character.

What is more, with the Biographer and others who acclaimed Brunelleschi as prime mover in the renewal of the arts that took place in Florence, there was a paradoxical inversion of the values traditionally associated with the terms "ancient" and "modern". "Ancient" took on a fully and culturally discriminating positive significance, while "modern" became the opposite, and in equal measure negative, pole.[2] Disregarding the civic and cultural fervour which, we shall see, was the impetus for everything Brunelleschi undertook in architecture, disregarding too the historical contingencies that favoured or impeded his efforts, observers came to think of his art as the fruit of some arcadia, his programme an escape towards some impossible Golden Age. True, the antithesis between "ancient" and "modern" was accompanied by that between "Roman" and "German", but the terms of comparison were really too general, and even absurd, if one thinks of the position of Florence in relation to Europe as a whole, with which it had the good fortune to be linked by a number of bonds, including even those of kinship. To be meaningful the antithesis should have been between "Tuscan" and "Lombard", though even that formulation risks oversimplifying the wealth of tendencies — including anti-Classical movements — present in Florence in Brunelleschi's time. In any case, there is the fact that, successfully and utterly faithfully, he carried further a substantially Gothic structure in Florence (S. Maria del Fiore) and was a paid consultant to the Opera or Board of Works of Milan Cathedral, which suggests that his forte was as much dialogue as polemic.

Unfortunately, by the time the Biographer was writing, the civic fervour of Florence was a memory that it was useless and even dangerous to celebrate. Public opinion was crediting Brunelleschi with all the work on the dome rather than with a leading role in its execution. Even Brunelleschi's wealth of archaeological investigations, richly imaginative and wide-ranging, became reduced to a system of rules and solutions ready to be printed in handbook form. It is curious that the writers of the late fifteenth century say nothing about, for instance, the sociological motivations behind the great urban schemes projected or realized by Brunelleschi, such as the system of piazzas, in part porticoed like Roman forums, that he introduced or suggested at key points in Florence (at SS. Annunziata, S. Lorenzo, S. Spirito) in association with institutions or churches whose tutelage and administration were in the hands of either the city itself or the population of a particular quarter, thereby providing for numerous social and collective functions, which would otherwise have been centralized in the Piazza della Signoria, to be carried out locally with full autonomy.

The third view of Brunelleschi is the romantic one. It took up the already oversimplified attitude of the late fifteenth century and through Vasari turned that into even more of a myth, and made it apply not only to the architecture of Florence in contrast to that of Italy as a whole but also to that of the entire peninsula in contrast to all the rest of Europe, forgetting among other things that it was only at Pescia, Pistoia, Prato, Bologna and Castiglione Olona in northern Lombardy that there was anything that could properly be attributed to the school or direct influence of Brunelleschi; forgetting too that this influence often showed itself late and was therefore more the product of a revival than of any continuity. The same is true of the notion of perspective: first propounded around 1425, it received its theoretical formulation only much later, in the 1470s and 1480s, at the hands of Piero della Francesca, and later of Luca Pacioli, who was responsible for diffusing the knowledge of perspective more widely, and for a new wave of interest. In the meantime perspective had become part of the practical equipment of artists and had been expounded by Alberti, Filarete and Ghiberti.

The nineteenth century then schematized the figure of Brunelleschi historically and at the same time, in an attempt to document his works, redrew them on straight and symmetrical lines, simplifying his system of proportions or inventing particular interpretations of it (looking for the Golden Section, etc.). Curiously, at the very time when nineteenth-century Tuscan scholars were picking holes in the attribution of S. Lorenzo to Brunelleschi, the major historians, such as Guasti and Fabriczy, using many hitherto unknown documents, were dramatically extending the coordinates within which his personality was to be defined. But this serious research unfortunately had no significant critical consequences.

Currently there is a wealth of hypotheses and analyses which in a few years, in all likelihood — despite the banalities of the sesquicentennial celebrations of 1977 — will lead to a general review and revision of all the data and to a definitive monograph (presumably by Howard Saalman). On the historical-critical level interest has been focused, excessively perhaps, on three themes: Brunelleschi's relationship with Antiquity, perspective, and proportions. All three had been discussed, in the most precise manner, by the Biographer. We have already noted what he said about the first; concerning perspective he praised the master because "from him was born the rule which is the basis for everything of the sort done from his time forward"; and, in the matter of proportions, he

gave thought to rediscovering... the musical proportions... [and] saw the way of building of the Ancients, and their symmetries [ornaments], and he felt he could recognize [as in human anatomy] a certain order of limbs and bones as very clear and evident... the which he studied since it appeared to him very different from what was being used in his times. [ff. 297r, 299r-v]

Nonetheless, the subtle paths and lengthy studies of his archaeological research and the distinctive and novel solutions that he proposed for various problems of statics and practice remain hypotheses that cannot be documented: nothing survives to give direct evidence of that research; not even a fragment has come to light, or at any rate been identified, of those "strips of parchment cut off when they square up the pages" (cuttings of sheets bought from parchment-makers or bookbinders, no doubt long narrow strips) on which, the Biographer explains (f. 299v), Brunelleschi and Donatello noted the measurements that they themselves had made of the elevations of Roman monuments:[3] "And thus where they could conjecture the measurements of the space between base and base, or the heights from foundations and plinths to the roofs of buildings, they wrote them down... with arabic numerals and letters of the alphabet that Filippo used [as a code] for himself." This would mean identifying the proportions of various elements by letters and measurements (more or less as Leonardo Benevolo has done for the architectonic elements of S. Spirito: see *fig.219*), anticipating the practice commonly recommended in architectural treatises of the sixteenth century. Measurements were taken in *braccia* (singular *braccio*, "arm's length"), a unit which varied at different times and in different places but was roughly about 58 cm or just under 2 ft, and *once*, about 2 cm or 1 in.[4]

In the matter of perspective (which will have a chapter of its own) it is important to know what the state of research was in Brunelleschi's lifetime. The effect provoked by distance — the changes in apparent size of objects and persons in relation to the position of the viewer, so that a man seen close up appears three or four times taller than one at the end of a piazza — was already well known in the Middle Ages and much discussed by theorists of optics. Also known, and already applied though with some uncertainty, was the effect of convergence of parallel lines, such as the sides of a straight street, with increasing distance: today we speak of vanishing towards a point in infinity, and as illustration we commonly refer to railway tracks, which seem not to run forever parallel but to meet in the distance in a much elongated triangle. The specific problem faced at the time of Brunelleschi was to find a theoretical and practical system for representing another effect, that which in our railway example makes the sleepers or cross-ties appear to become closer and closer together the greater the distance, according to a law of proportion of such complexity as to defy its formulaic use by painters, accustomed to geometry rather than mathematics. In addition, Brunelleschi studied the relationship between the dimensions of the real subject and its reproduction to scale on the basis of the effective distance from the viewer.

Thus, what Brunelleschi achieved in the study of perspective was so very specific that one can understand why the principles he discovered were applied only tentatively and gradually and, at the outset at least, almost exclusively in Florence, almost as if their understanding required personal contact and first-hand explanations. It is very probable that those studies were reflected in the architectural designing of Brunelleschi and others, but no one has yet been able to show just how. Certainly perspective space is a completely measured space artificially reconstructed, but in two dimensions only, whereas architecture calls for a space measured in three dimensions according to independent drawings correlated among themselves but not necessarily in accord with the laws of perspective. It is highly relevant that precisely at this time pictorial — that is, perspectival — representations of architecture came to be mistrusted and condemned as deceptive and worse than useless, because ineffective in giving the necessary data concerning the size of the various elements.

In any event, it is only in the church of S. Spirito that we can look for any application of perspective to architecture, since there alone the ground plan survives in the form Brunelleschi intended. In S. Lorenzo not even the transept reflects the original measurements and disposition; the nave was built after Brunelleschi's death, and the side chapels opening off the aisles, proposed in 1434, were not built until the 1460s to 1480s, and then to a modified design. In S. Spirito, however, besides a succession of effects like wings in a theatre, we still see a highly calculated effect of scansion in the columns and a continuous articulation of the spaces which flow into one another without interruption [205]. But this kind of description is only a metaphor. What we really need is to understand the principles of design that created those effects. In the meantime, we had best limit ourselves to the notion that perspective may indeed have entered into play there, but only as what Argan has called an "essentially critical method or process applied to the spatial fact of the architecture, reducing it to a proportional system or imposing some reasonable order on it, aiming to substitute a rational conception, one therefore historically motivated, for an irrational conception of space".

The matter of the use of proportional systems is even more uncertain: the proof is that once all the measurements had been taken of certain buildings by Alberti it was no longer possible to derive a module from them. (And, besides, what Alberti wrote in his treatise on architecture only confirms the futility of all simplistic attempts at establishing elementary proportions in works of the Renaissance.) The data presented in these pages — again with the exception of S. Spirito — give grounds for even more scepticism and, we hope, for ruthlessly honest

verification. Some writers still persist in finding the Golden Section, in, for example, the ground plan of the Pazzi Chapel — a structure that had to be fitted in, like wooden panelling, between existing medieval walls! The wonderfully simple portico of the Foundling Hospital is based on the tenfold repetition of a module of 10 *braccia* (from the centre of one column to the next), but there is immediately a second rhythm: the height of each column (base, capital and impost included) corresponds to the diameter of the arch. Yet this system of cubes surmounted by a hemisphere is inserted, so to speak, between column and column and is evidently only the iceberg-tip of a complex if not downright enigmatic system (see Chapter 3, note 10). Wittkower, moreover, in one of the books that were gospel for my generation, taught that we must look not for modules but for progressions, thus linking the harmonic system of Renaissance architecture, which certainly goes back to Brunelleschi, with musical polyphony and not only monody.

The use of Antique elements that can be codified and universally repeated, of perspective, and of proportional systems, has the same abstract quality as some of the most valid "conceptual" experiments of our own day, and this can lead us to overstate Brunelleschi's approach to architectural design as something lucidly and perennially complete and self-contained. Yet what he did achieve was nothing less than a genuine revolution which gradually and persistently made its way from Florence to all of Italy, then to the rest of Europe and the farthest outposts that Europe colonized or influenced. Imitation of Antiquity ceased to be a matter of symbols or ideology and, instead, provided a typology and a grammar: one need only think of the later theory of the orders with its codification into a body of exemplary proportions in accord with certain fundamental characteristics such as solemnity, elegance, and so on. Perspective, once an uncertain and approximate makeshift, was elevated to an exact science with precise and easily learned rules that made it possible to lay out usable spaces exactly measured in scale with the viewer and with the architecture and persons viewed, which meant that the same logic, proportions, and order could prevail in the real world and in the world created by the imagination.

And so, all things considered, we find there is an historical Brunelleschi but also a Brunelleschi beyond and outside time, and they cast light on each other. In this book we shall be delineating the key traits of the former, but with the hope that they may help too towards a better understanding of the latter, more universal, figure.

1 Brunelleschi and his world

What we know of Filippo Brunelleschi is less than half of his life and of his works. Not until 1418 do we get our first clear glimpse of him as an architect, and by then he was over forty. By then, too, we find him caught up in an extraordinary number of undertakings — not only the dome of the Cathedral but also projects for the Foundling Hospital, the Palazzo di Parte Guelfa, and the Old Sacristy and then the transept of S. Lorenzo. His patrons are at the top of the political and economic hierarchy, and his style very consciously expresses a political and cultural ideology. The obscure man suddenly becomes a public figure, regularly chosen for political office, whose proposals are given the broadest discussion, first rejected by everyone but a handful of supporters, then generally and enthusiastically exploited in their most readily applicable aspects. He was praised not only for the archaeologizing style of his works — what his contemporaries called his "muramenti alla romana" — but also for his solutions to problems of technique and internal organization and his numerous contrivances invaluable in both peace and war: machines to hoist weights or transport persons, city walls, embankments, aqueducts, temporary dams, shallow-draught boats for navigating the Arno, even musical instruments (he tried to improve the volume of the organs in the Cathedral by a new system of pumping air). His counsel too was much sought after: as early as 1424 he was in demand for the remodelling of fortifications, mostly in the Valdarno and Siena regions, and these brought him such fame that he began to be called on, as consultant at least, by Milan (for the Cathedral and castle), Ferrara, Mantua, Rimini, and Pesaro, places where considerable evidence of his activity survives but still awaits proper study.

Remarkable light is cast on the figure of Brunelleschi by a biography of uncertain authorship that has survived in three copies (one of them Florence, Biblioteca Nazionale, Cod. Magliabechiano II, II, 325). All are incomplete and break off suddenly while discussing the work at S. Spirito, so that there is no mention of the exedrae of 1439 around the Cathedral dome, the Pazzi Chapel, the pulpit of S. Maria Novella, or the trips to Rimini and northern Italy. It is safe to conclude that the original manuscript was never finished. The author, whom we shall call the Biographer, is not known. The attribution to Antonio di Tuccio Manetti (1423-97), who copied the manuscript, is accepted by most scholars, though the language strikes me as unlike that in the *XIV Huomini Singhulari in Firenze dal MCCC innanzi*, which is more securely attributed to Manetti and in which the architect is spoken of with equal accuracy. (Manetti's text — Florence, Biblioteca Nazionale, Cod. Magliabechiano XVII, 1501 — is reprinted in an appendix). The Biography can be dated to shortly after 1482, thus more than three decades after the death of its subject in 1446.[1] Another biography of later date, though no less trustworthy, is the *Libro di Antonio Billi*, of about 1516-20 (Florence, Biblioteca Nazionale, Cod. Magliabechiano XIII, 89: also reprinted at the end of this book).

The anonymous Biography is one of the most reliable documents in all the history of architecture. It springs from seven different elements: (1) first-hand examination of drawings and models, almost always specifying the type of designing procedure used by Brunelleschi (verbal explanation, drawings, wooden models), and thus, by implication, just how difficult it was for the later executants of his work to respect his intentions; (2) examination of changes in programme, with detailed analyses and comparisons between the original projects and the works as realized, together with explanations (unfortunately concerned more with personal than with economic and practical motivations) as to how and why such modifications took place; (3) genuine archive documents, especially for S. Maria del Fiore and its dome but also for most of the major undertakings; (4) personal contacts with the master ("he was an architect of our city and in my day, and I knew him and spoke with him"); (5) first-hand experience of the optical instrument with the representation of the Baptistery devised by Brunelleschi to demonstrate perspective ("and I have had it in my hand and seen it many times in my day and can give first-hand testimony concerning it"), and direct acquaintance with the other small panel representing the Piazza della Signoria ("it being something marvellous to see what appears in it together with everything the eye takes in in the place"); (6) a deliberately didactic approach designed to teach the reader to distinguish with precision the architectural grammar and syntax developed by Brunelleschi — though only from the time when he revived "that manner of building that is now called 'in the Roman fashion' and 'in the Antique fashion' which nowadays is so eagerly imitated" — espressed clearly and with a use of remarkably specialized terminology; and finally (7) acquaintance with the technical side of building as well as a good knowledge of the history of the local architecture.

All these things suggest a man of extraordinary curiosity and culture, who was in contact with the entire Florentine artistic world and was himself able to read Latin and to express himself in an elegant fashion.

In what he himself terms a long digression on the origins, splendour, and decadence of architecture — obviously inspired by Vitruvius, Pliny and perhaps already by Alberti — the Biographer gives us the earliest essay of the sort in the vernacular. In it he espresses the idea of a slow progress from Greece to Rome, then a decline associated with the economic, political and cultural deterioration resulting from the barbarian invasions, a decline interrupted only briefly by Charlemagne, who is credited with making use of architects from Rome "lacking in skill through lack of practice, but building in that manner simply because they were born among those things and had never seen any other". This first return to Antiquity in Italy was then cut short, pressure from the North fostering instead the Gothic style, which lasted until the time of Brunelleschi. In this extremely lucid excursus we find a fully conscious distinction between *tradition*, as represented by the architects who were still active in Rome and were shipped off by Charlemagne to places like Florence, and *return to Antiquity*: a dramatic and deliberate opposition on the part of a man who had already seen something other and *new* and could therefore take a critical position with respect to the Gothic and the Classical styles alike.[2]

The Biography is generally arranged chronologically, which suggests that it may have been based on a book of memoirs or a journal by Brunelleschi himself, similar to that left by Ghiberti. When he is discussing individual buildings, however, the Biographer starts with the design and then traces the complete history of a work, even beyond Brunelleschi's death, before returning to the chronological sequence for the design stage of the next project. The practice is the same as that followed in a modern monograph, to avoid fragmenting the analysis of a particular work by dividing it up over a number of years. The effect in the Biography is to interrupt the chronology; but one might well argue that where an architect was not also the contractor in charge of building the significant date as far as he is concerned is the date of design.

1. The great dome of the Cathedral of S. Maria del Fiore, a Marian crown which still dominates all Florence.

The facts and dates of the Biography, as they are checked against the monuments themselves, are increasingly recognized as reliable.[3] In addition to that information, the many rewarding critical insights of the Biography and its thoughtful use of language — which includes invaluable specific terminology for problems of technique, projecting, design, and execution — make it an exceptional portrait of Brunelleschi. The chief areas not illuminated by it are Brunelleschi's visits to Rome, his experiments in perspective, and other similar activities not connected with particular architectural undertakings or which occurred before 1418-19. As for the critical judgments, they may have been written down from conversations and probably visits to the building sites in the company of Brunelleschi himself: in Mariano Taccola's account of his interview with Brunelleschi [9] the architect gives him good counsel concerning the wisdom of concealing one's intentions so as to forestall criticism and plagiary, and this same advice is found in a passage in the Biography.[4]

Certainly without this important source, much drawn on by Vasari, historians would have lacked the most detailed and precise analytical instrument concerning the problems of architectural design to have come down from the Renaissance. It is surprising that scholars have only recently begun to make systematic use of this remarkable first-hand account, which is also a direct outcome of the deep concern with history, the scholarly capability, and the critical acumen of humanist Florence at its most vigorous moment.

If we know a considerable amount about the mature Brunelleschi, the long "prehistory" of the master appears singularly mysterious, beginning with his journeys to Rome. An early visit, before his participation in the competition of 1401 for the Baptistery doors, would account for otherwise inexplicably precise quotations from Classical sculpture in his relief plaque [21]; another visit is likely before 1417; and one can posit a third at the start of the 1430s if one accepts the hypothesis of some serious modern historians. None of these visits seems to have been long enough to arouse in him, in addition to a respect for archaeologically correct mouldings and an initial interest in the orders, that sensuous love for materials (travertine, precious marbles, massive masonry, heroic dimensions even in ornamental elements, intense feeling for plastic form) that was later to characterize Alberti, or which, in the guise of polychrome decoration imitated from the Cosmati, had become a kind of badge sported by the fourteenth-century Tuscans to show what they had learnt from their trip to Rome. The real purpose of Brunelleschi's journeys to Rome seems to have been, rather, to bring Florentine Classicism back to its origins, to purify it further, in a sense to de-materialize it.

Mysterious and unexpected too is his behaviour as an architect-sculptor. For all his superior ability to design architectural profiles in three dimensions and to conceive interiors and exteriors in unified fashion as if they were intended to be seen in an axonometric projection, in his buildings he did his best to exclude or at least to limit the role of any other art. Sculpture, above all, he confined within an architectonic framework or exploited in the form of sophisticated and highly skilled craftsmanship to shape architectural elements. But perhaps there is a subtler aspect to this. Brunelleschi was in fact a goldsmith-sculptor and, according to the Biographer, he exhibited all the skill of a miniaturist in his perspective views. Considering too the naturalism of his work in silver on the Pistoia Altar [10-17], it almost seems as if we must assume some dramatic crisis midway in his career that made him prefer to forget

all his early works in a different style, even architectural works like the headquarters and residence of the officials of the Monte (now destroyed or no longer recognizable), the most important financial organization of the city, which he projected, designed and built (as *capomaestro*, or master of the masons' yard) and about which the Biographer says (f. 297r): "In the matter of hewn stones, the way of treating them in his day was not to his liking and he could not accept it, and for that reason he used them differently; and that manner that he was to use later he did not yet know, because he adopted it only after having seen the ancient masonry of the Romans."

The almost complete silence concerning everything preceding the commission for the dome is broken only in the case of his studies in perspective and archaeology, of two pieces of sculpture, and of the relief plaque for the competition for the Baptistery doors — very little for twenty years of activity. The silence seems suspect, intentional even. Where was he all those years? Outside Florence or even outside Italy? In the service of one of the anti-popes, as goldsmith perhaps? It is a disturbing fact that only after the healing of the schism in 1417 do we find him back home in Florence, now set on making himself the unrivalled cultural leader in the field of the visual arts.

Another mysterious factor, and one that might explain much more than imagined hitherto, is the economic and political situation of his father (notary of the Signoria in May-June 1400), an employee of the Dieci di Balìa, what we would call today the War Ministry, for whom Brunelleschi senior bought mercenaries, the soldiers of fortune indispensable to the Florentine wars, seeking them out wherever they were to be found of good quality, better equipped, and of course at a good price. The Biographer tells us of Ser Brunellesco di Lippo Lapi (f. 295v):

he was throughout his life concerned with matters having to do with the soldiery, generally with all the captains and *condottieri* we had during his time and especially with the most important amongst them, and he acted as their agent [*procuratore*] and solicited and drew their appropriations and pay: a loyal and trustworthy person and in whom many placed their confidence. And he had the everyday task of serving them in their affairs, arms, clothing, silverware, and horses, and whatever else they might chance to need wherever they might be. He was much employed... in going to find such fighting men and fetching them here, sometimes from Germany, sometimes from France, sometimes from Britain, and sometimes from Flanders and other such places, because generally in those times in Italy they used mostly fighting men from across the Alps and those for the most part were lords in their own houses.

The documents confirm some of those voyages, and in view of the architectural importance of Germany, France, England and Flanders one cannot but wonder if perhaps the young Filippo did not sometimes accompany his father, and wonder too what ideas of Europe he may have gleaned from those foreign contacts before settling down to make proud show of his Florentine and Roman nationalism. And who can say where he went to learn the far from easy art of making clocks and carillons with multiple intermeshing gears moved by counterweights which the Biographer mentions as another of his talents? That art, at any rate, he put to good use in his construction machinery and theatrical machinery, which for decades remained the marvel of his contemporaries and was even used by Leonardo when, working with Verrocchio, he had to hoist the crowning globe of the Cathedral lantern into place at an otherwise impossible height of 114 m (374 ft) above the ground.[5]

Let me counsel further that you do everything possible to secure commissions only from the leading citizens, they being generous and much devoted to this sort of thing. And this because work done for the ordinary sort of persons of low rank is looked down on for precisely that reason. Have you not thought how much it profits you in winning fame to have the support of the most influential personages to whom you propose your services? For my part — besides the fact that virtually all of us, for no reason I myself can grasp, when we rely on the opinion and counsels of powerful individuals are, in consequence, reputed by most people to be wiser than we really are — I am of the opinion that the architect should have at his disposition, conveniently to hand and in plentiful supply, everything he might need to carry through his task, something which very often the less prosperous feel less need of for the simple reason that they have less means of having it.

That is Alberti speaking, in *De re aedificatoria*, Book IX. His shrewd advice seems to have taken into account the experience of Brunelleschi as well.

Suddenly, or almost so, in 1418, while his name was regularly chosen in the public elections, Brunelleschi set about to make himself a mirror of the splendour of the most elevated cultural and economic oligarchy of Florence, assuming a position which was decidedly unusual even among the most noted masters of his time, including Donatello. Thus he took to acting almost exclusively as adviser and executor for public bodies such as the major Arti (guilds), the Parte Guelfa (the Guelph faction, made up of wealthy nobles conservative in policy), the Monte (the communal income tax agency), and other financial institutions. Moreover, by far the greater number of the works he designed thenceforth had a civic function, insofar as they were sponsored or administered by the commune, even in the cases of S. Lorenzo and S. Spirito. This meant that his dealings were with decidedly bureaucratic organizations whose representatives were elected by councils, held office for a limited term, and were obliged to defend their decisions in open assemblies or at least before their fellow-members. This civic function obviously became even more important when Brunelleschi concerned himself with fortifications and, like any mercenary captain, had to face criticism for his failures.

If all of this made his position far from comfortable and always risky, and entailed interruptions and modifications in many of his works, yet that perennially precarious situation seems to have been perfectly congenial to him: he made the greatest efforts, often with a notable spirit of sacrifice and with considerable patience (despite his notorious fits of envy, hatred and intolerance), to achieve and hold it, repeatedly entering into the principal public competitions for commissions. There is no reason to doubt that what attracted him above all was the grandeur — economic as much as artistic — of undertakings under that sort of patronage. The Opera of S. Maria del Fiore may have had its administrative deficiencies, but it was certainly never parsimonious. All the preparatory experimentation for its commissions was well paid or else subsidized in the form of generous reimbursements of expenses. Moreover, all discussions and disputes were public, and that meant violent, merciless, head-on.

It is interesting to observe how, compared with these public commissions or with undertakings which, though private, were public in character (the Old Sacristy, for instance), private patronage showed itself less open to both experimentation and grandiose conceptions. The relationship between Brunelleschi and Cosimo de' Medici (here singularly pragmatic and more moderate) over the rebuilding of S. Lorenzo,

marked by conflict and by parings-down in expense and scope, shows that in choosing public patrons the architect was guided by very precise tactical and economic motives.

An essential consequence of this fact is that his style, instead of being bound up with the wishes of an individual client and therefore varying according to the whims of different personalities, became linked to the special type of construction made possible by a state enterprise: once everything had been worked out perfectly, it could be repeated with only minor variations. S. Lorenzo and S. Spirito are twins in many respects in spite of the changes imposed on the former, and the Old Sacristy and the Pazzi Chapel resemble each other in structure, plan and decoration. The style, moreover, made use of a corpus of themes which were also not individual but, so to speak, public. It evoked an ancient Roman way of thinking and being and was the immediate and direct corollary of the public-oriented approach of Coluccio Salutati and Leonardo Bruni, so much so as to be describable in their terms.[6]

It was certainly not by chance that in 1419 Brunelleschi presented a model for the Cathedral dome in collaboration with Donatello and Nanni di Banco. The latter was the earliest and most systematic representative of an archaeologizing Classicism up to the time of the Porta della Mandorla of the Cathedral, which he was forced by unknown pressures to redesign in the Gothic style. If anyone was equipped to join Brunelleschi on his study trip to Rome at the start of the century it was certainly Nanni, though the sources do not mention him. His desire to recover the Antique past was, so to speak, total, both iconographic and stylistic, a desire that was shared by Brunelleschi.

Such interests and enthusiasms were, we know, not limited to artists. Among the humanists the one most interested in architecture, even to the point of virtually posing as a commentator on Vitruvius, was Niccolò Niccoli, of whom Guarino wrote ironically as early as 1413:

Who could fail to burst into laughter at the sight of this man demonstrating his understanding of the laws of architecture? Look at him stretching out his arms, showing us ancient buildings, poring over the walls, diligently explaining the ruins and half-collapsed vaults of the ruined cities, telling us how many tiers there were in the ruined theatres, how many columns have fallen and how many still stand, how many feet wide the foundations, and the height to which the tips of the obelisks soar.

That sort of analysis, based on the manuscript tradition of Vitruvius, an author known and used in Florence already by Boccaccio in the preceding century, obviously entailed a visit to an archaeological site, which may have been Fiesole.[7] Other humanist texts described the Roman heritage surviving in Florence itself — something of which today, with a more careful analysis of the Baptistery and with the excavation of S. Reparata and the exploratory digging in the Piazza della Signoria, we can at last have a rather better idea. Probably such associations of Florence with a Roman past were made by Brunelleschi himself, who was, after all, a leading factor in the civic pride voiced by Leonardo Bruni in his *Laudatio* of the city of Florence. Then too, besides his own explorations in Rome Brunelleschi could have gathered archaeological information of the most varied provenance from one of the most original men of learning of the Quattrocento, the inveterate traveller and passionate antiquarian Ciriaco Pizzicolli d'Ancona, who, as Fasolo has pointed out, made repeated visits to Florence.

The relations between an intellectual like Brunelleschi and his time are many and subtle and often difficult to grasp. But for the first half of the Quattrocento there may perhaps be more information than scholars

2. Brunelleschi's tomb slab, as it was found during excavations of S. Reparata, the old Cathedral of Florence, under the south aisle of S. Maria del Fiore. The epitaph reads: "CORPUS MAGNI INGENII VIRI PHILIPPI BRUNELLESCHI FIORENTINI", referring to him not as an architect but as an "ingenious" man, i.e. a man of mechanical genius. That distinction comes out even more strongly in the epitaph in the Cathedral composed by the Chancellor, Carlo Marsuppini, and inscribed in monumental Roman characters with all the elegance of humanist epigraphy: "D. S. QUANTUM PHILIPPUS ARCHITECTUS ARTE DAEDALEA VALUERIT CUM HUIUS CELEBERRIMI TEMPLI MIRA TESTUDO, TUM PLURES MACHINAE INGENIO AB EO ADINVENTAE DOCUMENTO ESSE POSSUNT. QUA PROPTER OB EXIMIAS SUI ANIMI DOTES, SINGULARESQUE VIRTUTES, XV KAL. MAJAS MCCCCXLVI EJUS B. M. CORPUS IN HAC HUMO SUPPOSITA GRATA PATRIA SEPELLIRI IUSSIT." (Just how eminent Filippo was in the arts of Daedalus is shown by the wonderful dome of this very famous temple, and by the many machines invented by him with ingenuity. And because of the excellent qualities of his soul, and his exceptional abilities, his well-deserving body was buried in this ground on 15 May 1446 by order of his grateful fatherland.)

There could have been an even more apt tribute. A resolution by the public authorities, only recently discovered, proposed that marble plaques should be set up on the wall above his tomb, depicting his projects for the dome and presumably also the machines used in constructing it. The scheme, which would have provided us with invaluable information, was never carried out.

3. Marble bust by Buggiano, Brunelleschi's adopted son (Florence, Museo dell'Opera del Duomo). In this portrayal executed at his own expense, the architect appears in a somewhat idealized, Roman guise; but the association between sitter and sculptor makes one believe that the image is true to life.

4. Detail of a group portrait of artists and theorists attributed to Uccello by Vasari, but now thought to be a work of his school (Paris, Louvre). Other figures in the group are Giotto, Uccello himself, Donatello, and the mathematician Antonio di Tuccio Manetti. Brunelleschi appears younger than in the bust (though Antonio Manetti, born in 1423, is depicted as already adolescent); and while the portrait is more stylized, it was almost certainly based on a sketch from life.

5. Woodcut from Vasari's *Lives*, Venice, 1568: the best-known portrait, based on the Uccellesque panel [4].

6, 7. Death mask (Florence, Museo dell'Opera del Duomo). Examination of Brunelleschi's skeleton showed that he was short, but had above average cranial capacity; Vasari, writing over a century later, was correct in speaking of his "insignificant appearance" and "low stature".

For Brunelleschi's tomb and appearance see note 1 to the Introduction.

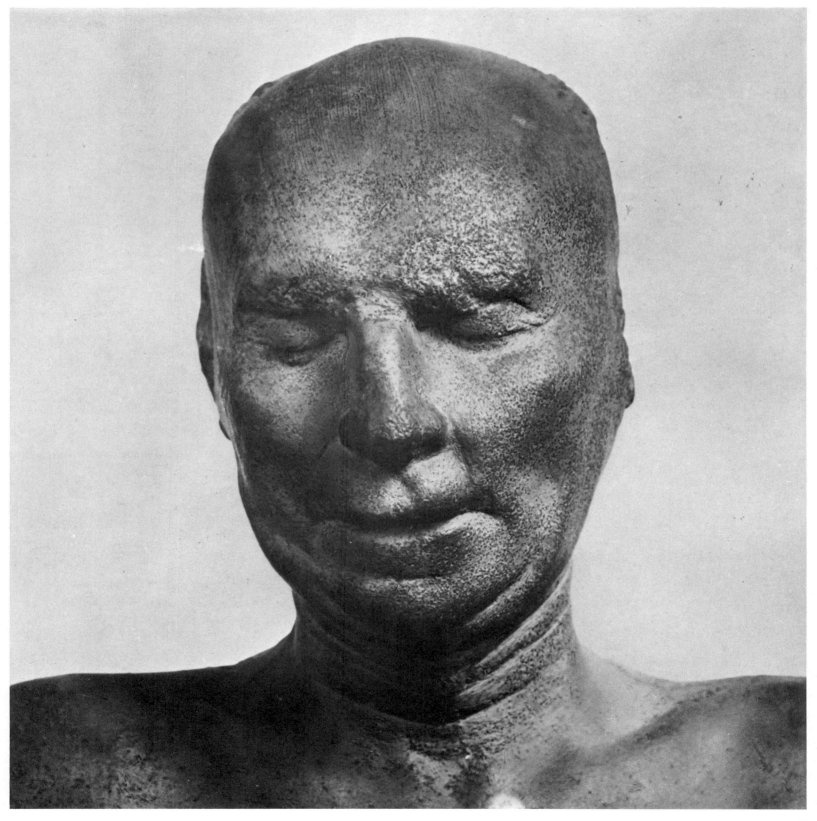

8. Pictorial map of Florence by Pietro del Massaio Fiorentino (Paris, Bibliothèque Nationale, MS. lat. 4802, f. 132v) — schematic but selective, and remarkably aware of the new style introduced by Brunelleschi and Michelozzo.

At the lower left is the Foundling Hospital; above its loggia, facing right, there is as yet no upper storey [32]. Just beyond is S. Maria degli Angeli, without Brunelleschi's Rotunda, whose walls remained low. In the centre the Cathedral appears (with its old name, S. Reparata): the exedrae are not built, and the lantern is not the one executed. Below and right of the Baptistery is S. Lorenzo, with its medieval tower and nave, shown with a portico on the façade; Brunelleschi's transept appears next to a dome that was planned, but not executed. Slightly above and right of centre, by the Loggia dei Lanzi, is the unfinished Palazzo di Parte Guelfa, a wooden roof over half its new walls. Across the Arno is S. Jacopo, where Brunelleschi built the Ridolfi Chapel; then S. Spirito, with a projected (but at the time unbuilt) dome, doubtless copied from a model by Brunelleschi; in the centre beyond the river S. Felicita, with the Barbadori Chapel; and above it the bulk of the Palazzo Pitti, formerly attributed to Brunelleschi.

have been willing to put together. The view of Brunelleschi as major representative of the high capitalist bourgeoisie of Florence, on the basis of commissions received from the Silk Merchants' Guild, the Wool Merchants' Guild, and the Parte Guelfa (an interpretation particularly well presented by Antal and Argan), can be confirmed, we have seen, by his continuous participation in the government of the city as well as other commissions: as one instance, in 1427 he was called in to advise on the placing on the Palazzo del Saggio in the Mercato Nuovo of the coats of arms of the Università dei Mercanti, the tribunal controlling banking and mercantile activity.[8] Brunelleschi was himself, by middle age, a relatively wealthy man.[9] But even when we have accepted the thesis of a relationship of class as well as of social order, we still need to define the links with those more restricted groups or even individuals who had power to make decisions but nonetheless represented only one sector of public and private life in the city. And it is here that further research may produce surprising and significant results.

Then too, the relations between Brunelleschi and the society in which he lived must have existed on different levels and with differentiated functions. His religious ideas, at least as we can read them in the basilicas deliberately based on Early Christian examples, had links with the Christian scholarship of Ambrogio Traversari who, as Prior of the Camaldolese Order, was instrumental in getting Brunelleschi to design an oratory for that order in which he could experiment with the decidedly unusual feature of a centralized plan. Quite different motives impelled him to accept, or seek, the task of organizing the fortifications and assault and defence measures during the unhappy campaign against Lucca — a task which brought him only discredit and probably forced him into a brief exile from Florence. From a human standpoint the various measures he took to avoid accidents on the job during the construction of the Cathedral dome are difficult to reconcile with the harshness of the man who, according to an undocumented story, dismissed all his workers as soon as they showed signs of unrest and then hired them back at lower pay. (The documents published by Guasti indicate only one death among the dome workers, and the man was suspected of drunkenness, but they represent a selection only and it may be that on this point the nineteenth-century archivist was deliberately elusive.) Likewise his alacrity in plunging into the midst of the melée with the aim of securing public commissions, and thence honours and profit, contrasts strangely with his absolute refusal to make any compromise whatsoever, an intransigence whose final result was all too often his removal from control, subsequent drastic alterations to his designs, and even the suspension or cancellation of many of his projects. In the matter of income tax returns, he was several time delinquent. In short, with Brunelleschi in particular every oversimplification seems to end up in distortion and downright confusion of the facts.

When we compare events in Brunelleschi's life with wider historical events we must also beware of oversimplification. Between the acquisition of Pisa in 1406 and that of Livorno in 1421 Florence enjoyed a period of exceptional prosperity; yet Brunelleschi's appointments coincided not with this general prosperity but with the effective dictatorship of Rinaldo degli Albizzi, initiated in 1417. During this time Brunelleschi received two crucial commissions: a hospice for abandoned infants, in 1419, and a sacristy that was connected with the overall remodelling of S. Lorenzo, certainly designed around 1419-20, though begun only in 1421. In the same period work started on the dome of the Cathedral, an undertaking that continued for years with perhaps occasional interruptions. In 1423 Florence made ready for war with Filippo Maria Visconti of Milan, who was considered a mortal threat, and engaged mercenary captains who in the next year were defeated in Romagna or, like Carlo Malatesta, went over to the Milanese. It took the most strenuous diplomacy to secure a very costly Venetian intervention, which in 1427 resulted in the defeat of the Milanese by Carmagnola and, a year later, in a peace treaty. During that time Brunelleschi absented himself from the work on the Foundling Hospital, to go off and direct some task of fortification at Lastra a Signa and Malmantile; the programme for S. Lorenzo ceased to be a public undertaking and in consequence was later taken over once and for all by the Medici; and, after the peace, Brunelleschi went to Milan.

In 1430 there was the Florentine attack on Lucca which proved in every sense disastrous: Brunelleschi concentrated on a very elaborate attempt to create an artificial flood which, however, did all the wrong things, and the Florentine army was defeated.[10] Then, with the defeat at Imola in 1434, Florentine territory itself was threatened by Niccolò Piccinino in the service of the Visconti. The funds Pippo Spano had intended for the construction of the oratory of S. Maria degli Angeli had to be used for the war, and the unfinished building became a walled kitchen garden. Only after the Florentine victory at Anghiari in 1440 did architectural activity begin again, on S. Lorenzo and S. Spirito.

Meanwhile the economy of the city had suffered greatly. It was no longer possible to find private citizens who could pay for large chapels in S. Lorenzo, nor could public funds be found to carry through the demolition necessary to open a piazza in front of S. Spirito. The economic decline of the city went along with the growth of the Medici's political leadership. They were entrusted with collecting tithes for the Holy See and continued to carry out that function regularly, thereby channelling an enormous amount of money into their own banks and getting from it, as one would expect, rather more than adequate interest. The malicious remarks of certain citizens that Cosimo had built S. Lorenzo with the Pope's money (thus, paradoxically, returning the money of the Church to its church) is in a sense confirmed by the fact that Cosimo financed the undertaking not with capital (which, after all, need not have been his own) but with interest alone. Significantly, in spite of all his connections with large public projects Brunelleschi was excluded from these later Medici commissions, whether residences or churches. True, he had completed his work for the Cathedral only with the most strenuous effort and in a decidedly vexatious climate of competition, but with the snuffing out of the republican spirit, the reintroduction (though not on a regular basis) of the practice of choosing men for major offices by lot rather than vote, and the institution of the Balìa, his name disappeared from the list of citizens chosen for public offices after 1433. As architect Brunelleschi came to be more eulogized than discussed, transformed into a myth, so that until his death there was no room for any other master alongside him.

An even more significant relationship, this one personal, has been brought to light by Creighton Gilbert: that between Brunelleschi and the humanist statesman Gregorio (Goro) Dati, who had voiced his political programmes in his celebrated *Istoria di Firenze* which records events from 1380 to 1405.[11] As consul of the Silk Guild, Dati was one of

9. Manuscript containing a conversation between Brunelleschi and Mariano Taccola (Munich, Bayerische Staatsbibliothek, Cod. lat. 197, f. 107v).

This extremely rare example of a transcribed conversation was probably written down immediately after it took place in Siena (Taccola was known as "the Archimedes of Siena"). Though the conversation was certainly in Italian, it was ennobled by being translated into Latin. From it one gets a picture of Brunelleschi's quick temper and sweeping contempt for the incompetent, the irredeemably ignorant and the stupid (his solution is to dispatch them all to the battlefield).

The date of the conversation is unknown, but it must have been after 1433. Brunelleschi could have passed through Siena around 1436 or 1440, or again in 1446, when he was working on fortifications and canals for Pisa, and visiting quarries and mines. Certainly the discussion is concerned with the Pisa area. His experience as a builder of aqueducts, mentioned here, is documented in Assisi, but has not been studied. Taccola's manuscripts are an invaluable source of illustrations of the machinery invented by Brunelleschi, which Taccola could have seen in action in Florence.

"Pippo de Brunelleschi of the magnificent and powerful city of Florence, most highly esteemed, famous, and endowed by God with many virtues, especially in architecture and in designing, a most shrewd creator of buildings, spoke to me in Siena in these terms out of the kindness of his heart: 'Do not tell everybody about your ideas but speak only to the few who understand and appreciate science, because putting yourself about too much and explaining your own inventions and actions is just squandering your own talent. There are many who love to listen only in order to criticize those who do new things and to contradict what they make and say, so as to prevent them from being heard in high places and by the right authority.

And after a few months they will go about saying the same things or writing them down or putting them into their own drawings, and they will boast with utter presumption of being themselves the inventors of the very things they had first scoffed at, and will not hesitate to appropriate the glory belonging to others. And there are thickheaded and ignorant types who, whenever they hear of some new idea or invention that they never thought of before, will at once call the inventor crazy and his theories ridiculous. "For God's sake, shut up," they say, "or everyone will think you're a fool." But don't be browbeaten by those who speak ill of you out of envy and ignorance to waste the talents God has given you. Pursue them, exercise them in such a way that you will be held wise by the wise, through your virtue and your mind. One cannot reveal to all and sundry the secrets of the waters of the sea, the rivers, and the constructions to be built in them, but only to an appropriate gathering of men of science, philosophers, and masters expert in the mechanical art, who may then resolve on everything necessary for constructing and building these things. Everyone, whether cultivated or ignorant, wants to know about the subject under discussion, but the cultivated man grasps what one is saying about a work or building and understands something of it, either in part or wholly, but the ignorant and incompetent take in nothing at all of it, and when one attempts to explain, and they still do not understand, they immediately fly into a rage out of sheer ignorance, because they would like to make it appear as if they grasped the point and yet are unable to do so. And so they induce other ignorant individuals to go along with their backbiting and to heap slander on those who do know something. So you are taking a great risk when you open your mouth at all in the presence of such utter blockheads and people who know nothing, and [even more] when you speak of aqueducts, of conduits which water is forced through under pressure either upward or downward, either above or below ground, and of constructions built above or below the surface of the sea or of fresh water. Those who do understand these things are to be most greatly prized, but much more you should flee from the ignorant, and the ignorant who have thick heads are good for nothing but to be sent off to the wars. The specialists should be elected to the Council, because they bring honour and glory to the Republic. Amen.' "

the Operai or wardens of the Foundling Hospital in 1419-20, right at the start of the work there, and it is therefore probable that it was he who appointed Brunelleschi as architect in charge. Dati held the same position again in 1422-23. As Gonfaloniere in 1428-29 he saw to the raising in the Mercato Nuovo of a column, ceded by the Operai of the Cathedral to the Uffiziali delle Torri, on which Donatello was to place a statue personifying Abundance, and he was also among the promoters of the renovation of S. Spirito.

The luxurious bronze tomb by Ghiberti for Leonardo Dati, General of the Dominican Order, was paid for by a source outside the monastery, which may have been his brother Gregorio. Lorenzo Lenzi, the probable donor of the fresco by Masaccio in S. Maria Novella, had twice been a fellow-consul of Gregorio in the Silk Guild as well as Gonfaloniere when Gregorio was Prior. Further, the third wife of Gregorio was Ginevra Brancacci, whose dowry was administered by her cousin Felice Brancacci, who commissioned the famous frescoes by Masaccio and Masolino in the Carmine. Felice was commander of the Florentine fleet constituted in 1421, the year in which Brunelleschi turned his interests to navigation and obtained a patent for a flat-keeled boat to transport marble on the Arno between Pisa and Florence. It is of course possible, as Gilbert remarks about certain of these relationships, that personalities of such importance for the history of art were brought into close contact only because the world in which they lived was so small, in size and population, but it seems more likely that all these relationships of patronage, with their interconnections, were the result of very deliberate choices, of a true political and aesthetic ideology in which people outside this close circle also came to participate, either following the lead of friends or imitating their better choices.

2 Goldsmith and sculptor

The young Brunelleschi had been given a literary and mathematical education fitting him for a profession such as his father's, which at the time could be considered "liberal", and had a very comfortable financial base to start with. Once he had decided not to follow his father as a civil servant a number of possibilities were open to him: since he had doubtless already begun to learn drawing, one was to enroll in the Arte degli Speziali, the Apothecaries' Guild, and practise painting. That art however seems to have had few charms for him, if we can judge from the fact that he virtually banned frescoes from his buildings, like Alberti preferring reliefs which were of course polychrome. In all the sources there is only one mention (and that very vague) of a painting by him, other than the two small panels showing the Baptistery and the Piazza della Signoria in perspective, and these were primarily architectural notations executed with the skill of a miniaturist. In any event, as Frederick Hartt has pointed out, painting in the Early Renaissance was chiefly a matter of private commissions and restricted to traditional religious subjects, and therefore not likely to attract a young man avid for innovation.[1]

If from the start he had been interested in stone sculpture or architecture, he should have enrolled in the Ars Magistrorum, the guild specific to those pursuits. He would thereby have escaped a series of difficulties dramatically evident in the documents. In 1434 he was arrested for not belonging to the proper guild: this was immediately countered by an illegal act smacking of blackmail — the arrest of the protesting guild's consul by the Arte della Lana, the Wool Guild, who were responsible for the work being done on the Cathedral and for whom the presence of Brunelleschi on the scaffolding was indispensable. The disadvantage for Brunelleschi in belonging to the Ars Magistrorum would presumably have been that it was a secondary guild dependent on the others for major commissions, this despite the fact that sculpture and architecture were the arts in which a stylistic revolution was first and most effectively making itself felt, and that this guild was responsible for carrying out the ambitious projects being promoted by the major guilds.

The solution he opted for, enrolment in the Arte della Seta, the Silk Guild, which included goldsmiths, metalworkers and bronzeworkers, underscores his interest in inter-media artistic operations. It now seems that he was already active as an apprentice about 1392 and that he became master in 1398, his official matriculation being delayed until 1404, perhaps to take advantage of a large discount in the admission fee.[2] His membership of the Arte della Seta, and perhaps his father's connections and friendships as well, brought him into contact with the economic oligarchy of the city. It was surely not by chance that his first important public commission, the Foundling Hospital, came from the same guild to which he belonged, with the resultant paradox that he was twice elected by the guild as its representative in the Opera in charge of the undertaking, so that in a sense he was administering himself.

Early years; the Silver Altar at Pistoia
by Lucia Gai

In 1401, the year of the competition for the second doors of the Baptistery, the Florentine scene still gave little clear sign of the splendid artistic flowering so soon to come.

The new "virtue", one both active and contemplative, that went by the name of *humanitas* was as yet restricted to very few learned men,

writers, and philosophers, who were taking up again the never truly broken thread that linked them, through the Middle Ages, to Classical thought. What matters in our context, though, is that among those leaders of culture there was a clear awareness that a different position was accruing to the *litterae* who had quitted the *hortus conclusus* of medieval science to assume an active political role within the *civitas*. It was with the highest awareness that Coluccio Salutati, Chancellor of the Florentine Republic, wrote in those years: "God has made you not for yourself but for others; in the same way as all things visible were made for man who is the end of all physical things, so too man is for man".[3]

In art too, in those same years, there was a clear symptom of the change in values: in the prologue to his *Libro dell'arte* Cennino Cennini hailed painting, considering it as the second worthiest of human activities after science, since painting unites the skill of the hand with creative thought. Yet the Florentine artistic situation itself was as yet poor in ideas and stagnating in a banal repetition of Late Gothic formulas. Society itself showed a formalistic taste, with a very marked predilection for the merely illustrative and a reliance on impoverished simplifications of the profound human experiences towards which Giotto had pointed at the start of the Trecento.

In the works commissioned at the close of that century one finds all too clearly a widespread and disheartening conformism in the figurative language and in all varieties of artistic activity. As early as the 1350s there was an awareness of the distressing decline: in a well-known novella by Franco Sacchetti the last word in a gathering of late Giotto followers and adherents of Orcagna, where art is the subject of discussion, falls to Taddeo Gaddi who, with due melancholy, affirms that while the skill of Florentine painters remains secure, "that art today has failed and is failing".

Poor in ideas and mediocre in form is now we might describe painters like Andrea Bonaiuti, Giovanni del Biondo, Niccolò di Pietro Gerini and the rest of that numerous company of minors and minimums (no wonder Giovanni da Milano remained isolated in Florence); nor can one say more for the sculptors who were content to carry on within the set lines of a respectable craftsmanship, sometimes taking over inappropriate suggestions from painting: think of Giovanni d'Ambrogio, Niccolò Lamberti, Pietro di Giovanni and many others like them, often anonymous, some of them from Lombardy, with the barren crudeness of mere stonecutters.

The goldsmiths too in the second half of the Trecento can be situated roughly within the borders of the Orcagnesque style, its decorous linguistic structure occasionally disturbed by expressionistic influences from beyond the Alps. But in this field the evidence in Florence is scarce and full of gaps. True, there is the large silver antependium from the Baptistery altar (now in the Museo dell'Opera del Duomo), commissioned in 1386 and after[4] from various goldsmiths — Betto di Geri, Leonardo di Ser Giovanni, Cristoforo di Paolo, Michele di Monte — and completed in the next century by more energetic protagonists of the Florentine Renaissance. There is also a large number of enamelled, engraved or embossed processional crosses, pyxes, chalices and patens, but they are often without a sure attribution and sometimes even of uncertain provenance. Classical motifs were used by Giovanni d'Ambrogio (active 1391-96), who worked on the Porta della Mandorla of the Cathedral, and we know that German and North Italian sculptors were active in the city. But little survives from which to reconstruct credibly the stylistic tendencies and principal exponents of the goldsmith's art in

Florence in the last third of the Trecento, the very time during which artists like Ghiberti, Brunelleschi and Donatello were born and had their training.[5]

Of Donatello, about ten years younger than Brunelleschi, we at least know that he served his apprenticeship with Ghiberti. But for Brunelleschi there is only a blank, except what Vasari tells us, and this he drew from the anonymous Biographer. As Vasari has it, the young Filippo was placed by his father "with a friend of his" — presumed to be Benincasa Lotti — to learn the art of the goldsmith, and quickly proved capable not only of mounting "fine stones better than an artisan of long experience in that craft" but also of mastering completely the techniques of niello and embossing, a statement Vasari supports by citing the "half-length figures in silver of two prophets placed at the top of the altar of St James in Pistoia, and considered to be very beautiful, which were done by him for the Opera of that city", and also "works in low relief in which he showed such great understanding of that craft that perforce his ingenuity [ingegno] went beyond the limits of that art".

Despite the attribution of the figures on the Silver Altar in Pistoia Cathedral to Brunelleschi by Vasari, despite too the significant fact that the attribution is confirmed in the Biography,[6] not all art historians have accepted it. A problem was pointed out in 1810 by Ciampi, who first published excerpts from the documents having to do with the later, fifteenth-century phase of the work on the Silver Altar.[7] From the documents it appears that two separate contracts for the decoration were drawn up within just over a month, the first on 31 December 1399, the second on 7 February 1400. Among other provisions, the iconographic programme was slightly modified, and there was also some concern with saving on silver so as to cut down expenses (see below, notes 9 and 10). The trouble arises from the fact that the first document specifies that part of the work is to be entrusted to a certain "Pippo da Firenze", while in the second the name is spelled out as "Pippo di ser Beneencasa da Firenze".

Ever since those documents were published scholars have been divided into two camps, one willing to disregard the family name "Beneencasa" and arguing for the attribution of at least the two prophets to Brunelleschi, the other doubting his authorship not so much on stylistic grounds as because of the variant on the name in the documents. Thus the small group of recent studies, resulting from the major exhibition of 1950, when the Silver Altar was shown after restoration and not yet reassembled, ranges from the firm assertion of an even more extensive role for Brunelleschi (Sanpaolesi, Ragghianti) to a rather more prudent and circumscribed critical position (Marchini, Steingräber).[8]

Admittedly the documents do reveal a somewhat tangled skein of commitments on the part of the goldsmiths, some not carried through at all, and this is the more difficult to explain because of the strange silence when it comes to certain phases of the work and, even more, certain extremely important changes in the second contract.

To understand what follows, one must have clearly in mind the original structure and position of the altar. Located in a chapel at the end of the right aisle, its left side (as we view it) is towards the chancel and the main body of the Cathedral — and thus more important — while its right side is towards the adjacent sacristy. It consists of two distinct parts, a high reredos dating from the thirteenth and fourteenth centuries, which rises from the altar table, and the altar itself with its front and two end panels signed and dated 1316. The ensemble has no less

than 628 figures in relief and in the round. The parts that concern us here are the left and right sides of the reredos.

As called for in the iconographic programme, each of the sides of the reredos was to have two half-length prophets in low relief surmounted by two full-length Doctors of the Church in higher relief, and these were to be topped in turn by two half-length Evangelists in low relief. However, we do not know for certain which figures were to go where, nor even the original organization of the architectural elements framing them. What we do know is that a change was made in the initial arrangement: the evidence for this comes from the documents and also from the wooden support with its niches and frames that was brought to light during the restoration.[9]

There are good reasons for believing that if, as I think, Brunelleschi began the part assigned to "Pippo" and worked on it during February, March and April and into the first days of May 1400, he did not complete it, for the documents refer to much less worked silver for his part than for the other, and an inventory of 1401 describes the altar in an unfinished state.[10] The right side of the reredos was only completed much later, by a mediocre goldsmith from Pisa.

This is not the place to discuss all the probable hypotheses, a task reserved for another publication. For the present, with contracts that are not wholly reliable and have many gaps, it is preferable to set aside the quest for documentary certainty and to explore instead the tenuous thread of stylistic and iconographical analysis which, because of formal differences, may produce rather more concrete results.

The character of the stylistic language used by Brunelleschi should be deduced from the only piece of metal sculpture known for certain to be his, the cast bronze panel for the Baptistery doors competition of 1401 [21]. Though Ghiberti writes that his victory was uncontested, the Biographer recounts the scornful refusal of Brunelleschi to collaborate on the door with his rival as proposed by the Opera of the Cathedral. Vasari seems to incline towards the first version, enhancing his account with anecdotes. Be that as it may, from the conflicting stories given in fifteenth-century sources one cannot make out just why Brunelleschi subsequently abandoned the goldsmith's art, as he seems to have done. His competition panel itself may tell us more. In his panel [20] Ghiberti undeniably gave proof not only of an excellent technique and thorough command of composition but also, more important, showed himself the only one capable of carrying out the project in true relief. As a Gothic goldsmith knowing all the tricks of his trade, he exploited the optical device of a continuous line flowing from figure to figure: the relief itself is worked out in function of light thought of as a liquid and undulating pictorial medium, and because Ghiberti was also a painter he was particularly attentive to all the recent innovations in form from beyond the Alps. Then too he had the goldsmith's taste for small-scale surfaces treated elaborately and ornamentally, with everything reduced to decorative rhythm and virtuoso technique. Vasari observed,

the work as a whole had design [disegno] and was very well composed; the figures in that manner were lithe and made with gracefulness and in very beautiful poses; and it was finished off with such diligence as to seem not cast nor polished by iron tools but, rather, with a mere breath.

In comparison, the panel by Brunelleschi [21-24] strikes one as awkward, without unity of vision: the scene of the sacrifice breaks down into isolated, almost jerky episodes; the figures are elastic and tense, with not the slightest concession to Gothic elegance in their poses; their movements are brusque, their gestures incisive, without formal graces. Only with strain do they fit into the cramped quatrefoil shape, which acts as a highly contrived stop to the three-dimensionality that suffuses and dominates the composition. It was, however, precisely through such a grandiose feeling for space that (the small dimensions of the plaque notwithstanding) Brunelleschi achieved a monumentality of style disproportionate to the purpose for which the panel was intended: one simply cannot imagine other similar plaques arranged with this one in a traditional decorative composition like that of the earlier doors by Andrea Pisano, which were the model to be followed by all three contestants.

While Ghiberti articulated his figures easily in an integrated relationship with the background, which thus became their necessary complement, meaning that his forms could only be conceived in terms of low relief, Brunelleschi let it be seen how uncomfortable he was with a technique fundamentally based on embossing. He was already no longer a goldsmith — that is, a modifier of surfaces — but rather an architect of spaces.

The treatment of space in his panel is nonetheless still "ingenuous", an early essay in those studies in perspective for which he became famous. The sacrificial altar — virtually a domestic hearth despite the attempt at an archaizing bas-relief on its front — is still conceived and constructed with the optical schemes of the Trecento, and the entire spatial articulation of the plaque seems the result of an emotional revival of the space of Giotto. Nor is it accidental that there are allusions to that master in the browsing ass and the solid and realistic profile of the angel. Still, the forms do not impose themselves in the manner of Giotto, with the tranquil power of solid masses. At this point in his career at least, Filippo felt the corporeal structure in terms of a tense impetus and violence deeply akin to the exacerbated but very human energy of Giovanni Pisano, counterbalanced perhaps by the profound Classical wisdom of another Pisano, Andrea: the solid figure of Abraham is revealed and set in motion by the coiling drapery furiously whipping back against the sapling that clings to the rock. The boy at the far left pulling a thorn from his foot, seated in precarious equilibrium and almost pushed out of the picture by the large, calm form of the donkey, is a quotation from Antique sculpture (the *Spinario*) that reopens the problem of just when Brunelleschi first went to Rome.[11]

We see then that in 1401-02, while Ghiberti with all the sureness of a highly cultivated professional showed himself oriented towards a particular Gothic Classicism less Italian than Northern and quite without innovations foretelling the Renaissance, the young Brunelleschi was seeking his own way and meanwhile passionately cramming quotations into his relief plaque with the enthusiasm of a self-taught artist. Giotto, Giovanni and Andrea Pisano, the Antique, and, not least, "Nature": these were his *auctores*. This visual culture staking everything on ardour and instinct, this eye and mind alert to the masters of the tradition that had true and universal things to say about man, were destined to transform themselves very soon into a high capacity for self-consciousness and design which would be lucidly focused in architecture as a concrete representation, through its structure, of the *humanitas* but also of the *divinitas* of a mankind renewed.

It is at this point that Brunelleschi shows himself to have achieved already, through deep meditation, a concept of *humanitas* in some respects different from that of the men of letters. The humanists were proposing a new model of man whose ideal setting was nonetheless that of the *civitas*, and for this the models to be followed arose with spontaneous consistency out of the Classical tradition of the Oratores. But Filippo overleapt this first and too bookish dimension of the Renaissance, sought the living substance of Man, what we can almost call his fundamental structure, the universal dimension which is that of the alternation of hopes, fears, passions, needs in the perpetual *drama* which is history. It was by that path that he regained the sense of the divine as consciousness of the infinite in the face of the finite but also, on the other hand, the feeling for tradition and the Antique as capable of recreating the logic of the succession of human facts and values, in accord with the concept of *historia magistra vitae*.

Which is why there is no mistaking the art of Brunelleschi, even as a goldsmith. It bears the mark of man's place — space — and bears too the suggestion of the third dimension as an element necessary to the image. Not for him the formal tendencies of his great friend Donatello, where an extremely powerful feeling for plasticity, understood as an acute and tensely contracted awareness of the matter artistically formed, results in an emptying out of the surrounding space, which thereby becomes a negative value.

For these reasons, and despite the reservations of illustrious scholars, I hold that other figures on the Silver Altar in Pistoia, as well as the two prophets mentioned by the Biographer and by Vasari, are to be attributed to Brunelleschi.

According to the contract of 1399 the goldsmith "Pippo da Firenze" and his Pistoian guarantors were to be responsible for the side towards the chancel, including full-length figures of St Gregory and St Augustine and paired half-length figures of St Luke and St Matthew. The other team, whose goldsmith was Domenico da Imola, was to deliver the side towards the sacristy, with representations of SS. Jerome, Ambrose, John and Mark. The new contract of February 1400, however, for reasons that are still unknown, changed the allocation. The side towards the chancel was given to Domenico da Imola, with figures of SS. Jerome, Gregory, John and Mark; and the side towards the sacristy, with figures of SS. Augustine, Ambrose, Matthew and Luke, was entrusted to "Pippo di ser Beneencasa". As we know the scheme was never completed.

The postwar reassembly of the reredos did not take into account the evidence of the documents. On the left side are the two prophets presumed (on the basis of the second contract) to be by Brunelleschi [14-16], surmounted by St Jerome [11] and St Gregory [10]; above is St Augustine [12] in a Gothic surround, topped by a seated Evangelist who is difficult to identify [17]. On the right side, from bottom to top, are two half-length prophets, St Justus of Canterbury and St Ambrose [13], St Leonard, and the Evangelist Mark — all except St Ambrose by the later Pisan goldsmith Piero d'Antonio.

Now the figures of SS. Jerome and Gregory, though assigned to Domenico da Imola and clearly executed according to the prescriptions of the second contract as full-length figures in relief (" di tucta figura, di mezo rilevo"), are not both by the same hand. The St Jerome [11] is a small masterpiece of fragile Ghibertian grace, in its characteristic counterbalancing pose almost an incunabulum of the distinctive *déhanchement* of the figures on the second doors of the Florentine Baptistery. The St Gregory [10] seems a more uncertain work, by a goldsmith incapable of suggesting a body beneath the drapery, with as a result an unstable and exaggerated pose, extremely weak hands in awkward gestures, and the head set most uncomfortably and rigidly on the bust.

Scholars have for a long time been uncertain about the identification of the other two figures mentioned in the contract of 1400.[12] There are no clear iconographical elements in them or the other figures of the altar (except for SS. Justus and Leonard, which are not relevant since they were added later), though among the full-length figures the one looking abruptly upwards, pen in one hand and open book in the other, is almost certainly Augustine [12]. That the other figure [13] is Ambrose is less certain because of the absence of the standard attributes, but it is not impossible that over the years the mitre and crozier have been lost. If so, these would be the two sainted Doctors the documents say were assigned to "Pippo da Firenze". Stylistically, however, they cannot be by the same hand. The St Augustine [12] is a splendid autograph work of Brunelleschi: look at the overwhelming instinct for space confirmed even in the remarkably solid body; at the capacity — unique at the time — to reject the Gothic stylistic repertory, with its rhythmic attitudes and sinuous *contrapposto*, and to reveal, with dazzling clarity, the naked, powerful simplicity of bone and muscle, perfectly balanced beneath the drapery. This St Augustine lives, like architecture, in the relationship between structure and space. The St Ambrose, however, is in a different idiom, articulated in the calm decorum of a Gothic pose somewhat up-dated by reference to Classical exemplars, and though not, I believe, by the same hand, is akin to the St Jerome [11], which is more agile and svelte, and is therefore in all probability to be related to the very earliest manner of Ghiberti.

As for the two splendid prophets [15, 16] and the seated Evangelist [17] (difficult to identify in the absence of attributes), these can surely be given to Brunelleschi because of the unmistakable stamp of his personality, with its capacity to create space around his figures and to dissolve the real limits of their small format. But striking above all is the heroic grandeur of the two prophets, the philosophical spirit breathing life into them, recovering through a visionary passion the magnitude of the ancient seekers after truth, made sublime by the sculptor's stylistic reference to the ennobling splendour of the Classical era. Here for the first time Brunelleschi tried out what he was to do in the Baptistery plaque. In these figures he attempted a new moral dimension, brought into being with an exceptional precocity the heroic language of the art of the Early Renaissance, introducing in the *imago* the *humanitas* of the philosophers and men of letters.

What is certainly an essay in the manner of Giovanni Pisano, arrived at through direct acquaintance with the pulpit in S. Andrea at Pistoia, here takes on a new fullness, within the framework of a dramatic narrative. No longer do we see Giovanni's fiercely violent pathos, which conditions the form even to the point of grotesque distortion, and stems from the conviction that the distance separating man from the infinitely superior Divine is transcendental.[13] For Brunelleschi too the drama is born out of the presence of divinity within man, possessing him entirely: for him too the dialogue with "truth" is entirely inward, that is, the relationship can only be prophetic. But that truth when restored to man himself bridges the gap that was the source of medieval anguish, wins back a Classical fullness and stability, and proclaims the Renaissance religious optimism with its assertion of man as the dwelling-place of God.

In the prophet on the right [14, 15], the one straining upwards, there is the same impetuous élan as in the St Augustine [12], the same intensity of gesture as in the Abraham of the Baptistery plaque [21]. The high relief uncompromisingly brings out the robust structure of the body around which the drapery is wrapped with utter naturalness; in the facial features the modelling obtained by the technique of *sbalzo*, or repoussé, is extremely sharp, thanks to the use of the burin; the hands, all tendons and bone, are of an impressive realism, with the dry veins of old age moulded in relief by the lost-wax method. No less passionate, locked in himself as if in a visionary harshness, the prophet on the left, listening to the voices within him, is articulated with a sculptural power whose progressive quality is still a matter for marvel today [14, 16].

The feeble curved and pointed quatrefoils decorated with floral motifs clearly speak of another hand, indicated too by the crudeness of their relation to the contours of the figures, yet they cannot destroy the grandiose feeling of space that surrounds the prophets.

To Brunelleschi must be given also the seated Evangelist writing in a book on his lap, his gaze lost in the distance [17]: here again the truth is inward, does not come from outside. Here too the structure, grasped with astonishing sureness and a maturity anticipating the later developments of Renaissance statuary, possesses a spatial quality entirely like that of the Baptistery relief, even if in comparison with that work it seems formally to belong to a later date in the Quattrocento, as some have suggested; but the throne is not in perspective and has no more depth than Trecento space. The expression of the Evangelist is weaker than that of the prophets, as if the finishing touches with the burin had been interrupted. This is so especially in the face, in the insufficiently articulated bone structure beneath the skin, and in the flowing beard whose lowermost curls do not conceal the rounded-off edge of the piece of silver acting as a support.

So much, then, to suggest that the young Filippo did not have time to complete his work, though we shall never know why. We can only conjecture that, seeking refuge in Pistoia in a time of plague [14] and taking his first steps there as an architect of forms, when the peril diminished in the first months of 1400 he left: for Rome? In 1401 he was in Florence, competing against others for the Baptistery doors; but the Renaissance had in reality already been born with Brunelleschi a year earlier, in Pistoia.

Details of the Silver Altar of St James, in Pistoia Cathedral.

12. Brunelleschi: St Augustine (?).

13. Unknown artist: St Ambrose (?).

14. Brunelleschi: two prophets.

Bruno Bearzi, the restorer, analysed the technique used for the Silver Altar (Micheletti and Paolucci 1977, pp. 19-22): the sculptures are made of "sheets of silver of considerable thickness, cupelled, embossed, and finished off with the chisel. The titre of the silver is quite high, equivalent to 962. Only the hands are cast; all the other elements ... were realized with the much more sophisticated technique of embossing. The heads in particular are made up of two symmetrical halves, the front and the back. ... Where the join between embossed and cast parts left unpleasant gaps, as for example in the wrists of the seated Church Father or the left sleeve of the St Augustine, Brunelleschi soldered on additional silver sheets in such a way as to simulate drapery. All the sculptures were fire-gilded. It appears that the mantles, beards, hair, and decorations of the garments were gilded."

15, 16. Brunelleschi: prophets, on the Silver Altar of St James in Pistoia Cathedral.

17. Brunelleschi: Evangelist, from the Silver Altar of St James in Pistoia Cathedral.

The competition relief for the Baptistery doors

Although Brunelleschi's relief of *Abraham and Isaac* for the competition of 1401 has given rise to an innumerable host of commentaries, not least because of its usefulness as a teaching tool to explain the difference between Brunelleschi as forerunner of the mature Renaissance and the more tradition-bound Ghiberti, its interpretation has by no means been exhausted. Lucia Gai has already examined some of its stylistic peculiarities in connection with the Pistoia Altar, and Bruno Bearzi has argued that technically as well the two works have features in common. Let us now look more closely at the style and technique of the competition plaque.[15]

The *Commentarii* of Ghiberti give us a first-hand account of the competition though, understandably, not without personal bias. No one, unfortunately, has ever found the written report signed by the thirty-four members of the commission, or their delegates, which awarded the victory to Ghiberti and explained the choice. This would have been dated at the close of 1402 or the start of 1403 when both finalists were in their mid-twenties.

According to Charles Seymour all the advantages in the competition were apparently on the side of Brunelleschi: Ghiberti was away working in Pesaro, he was an illegitimate child and not well off, and he had begun his career as a painter.[16] The Krautheimers on the other hand suggested that one of the reasons behind the choice of Ghiberti, other than the technical aspects we shall consider below on the basis of their findings, may have been that the members of the sponsoring guild, the merchants' Arte di Calimala, were more widely travelled, hence more cosmopolitan, hence more appreciative of Late Gothic art.[17] The decisive factor must, however, have been technical, as we shall see.

Iconographically, the subject of Abraham and Isaac is complex and rich. The episode of Abraham, constrained by obedience to God to prepare the sacrifice of his son and to carry it out in a solitary place, is clearly a prefiguration of the Crucifixion. Isaac, like Christ, carries the wood for his own sacrifice, and the binding of Isaac is associated with the Passion of Christ. The scene is linked to images of salvation and, from the Byzantine period onwards, is a symbol of the Eucharist. The episode can also be seen as an anticipation of the sacrament of baptism, in association with the vigils of Easter and Pentecost, and, according to the principle of concordance between the two Testaments laid down by Gioacchino da Fiore, Abraham is the type of John the Baptist. This suggests that the new doors of the Baptistery were intended to be devoted to a system of symbolic biblical parallels. But this particular episode, touching as it does family affection and in particular the difficult relationship between father and son, offered in itself a dramatic theme of personal import to every viewer, one used later in the theatre by a friend of Brunelleschi, Feo Belcari, for precisely that reason.

Let us imitate the unknown persons who laid down the precepts for the artists, underlining in the story those narrative and scenic elements that had to be included. We shall then examine in what ways the story was interpreted and modified.[18]

18, 19. The Sacrifice of Isaac, illustrated in Italian fourteenth-century Bibles: below, the Hamilton Codex in Berlin (Staatliche Museen, Kupferstichkabinett, MS. 78 E 3, f.4); bottom, a manuscript in Vienna (Österreichische Nationalbibliothek, Cod. 1191, f.11).

OVERLEAF

20. Ghiberti: *The Sacrifice of Isaac*, gilt bronze competition panel for the Florence Baptistery doors. (Florence, Museo Nazionale del Bargello)

21. Brunelleschi: *The Sacrifice of Isaac*, gilt bronze competition panel for the Florence Baptistery doors. (Florence, Museo Nazionale del Bargello)

22. Brunelleschi: detail of *The Sacrifice of Isaac* [21]: heads of the Angel, Isaac and Abraham.

23. Brunelleschi: detail of *The Sacrifice of Isaac* [21]: ass and servant.

And God said, *Take now thy son, thine only son Isaac, whom thou lovest, and get thee into the land of Moriah; and offer him there for a burnt offering upon one of the mountains which I will tell thee of.* And *Abraham* rose up early in the morning, and *saddled his ass, and took two of his young men with him, and Isaac his son*, and clave the wood for the burnt offering, and rose up, and went unto the place of which God had told him. *Then on the third day Abraham lifted up his eyes, and saw the place afar off. And Abraham said unto his young men, Abide ye here with the ass; and I and the lad will go yonder and worship, and come again to you.* And Abraham took the wood of the burnt offering, and laid it upon Isaac his son; and he took the fire in his hand, and a knife; and they went both of them together. And Isaac spake unto Abraham his father, and said, My father: and he said, Here am I, my son. And he said, Behold the fire and the wood: but where is the lamb for a burnt offering? And Abraham said, My son, God will provide himself a lamb for a burnt offering: so they went both of them together. *And they came to the place which God had told him of; and Abraham built an altar there, and laid the wood in order, and bound Isaac his son, and laid him on the altar upon the wood. And Abraham stretched forth his hand, and took the knife to slay his son. And the angel of the LORD called unto him out of heaven, and said, Abraham, Abraham*: and he said, Here am I. And he said, Lay not thine hand upon the lad, neither do thou any thing unto him: for now I know that thou fearest God, seeing thou hast not withheld thy son, thine only son from me. And Abraham lifted up his eyes, and looked, and beheld behind him *a ram caught in a thicket by his horns: and offered him up for a burnt offering in the stead of his son*. [Genesis 22:2-13]

In addition to these "historical" elements, the tale imposed on the competing artists certain other narrative or stylistic qualities, most notably an elevated pathos, a search for variety in types and gestures, and a certain degree of archaeological imitation.

In the matter of iconographical representation, all possible types were already present in the tradition. Isaac clothed or nude, standing or kneeling or seated; a bush or a tree or some other feature in the background.[19] In the two competition reliefs that survive we find exactly the same elements: the young Isaac, nude, on an altar (in clear allusion to the liturgical significance of the episode), the father with knife in hand stayed at the very last instant by the angel, two servants with the ass referring to the journey or to the congregation of the faithful, rocks to indicate the mountainous setting, and a ram as surrogate offering appearing miraculously, this too a symbol of Christ.

Comparing the reliefs to representations in Trecento Bibles [19], including the Hamilton Codex [18], which may possibly already have been in Florence about 1400, we find that there are differences: there Isaac is not a Classical nude but fully clothed, and, more significantly, the angel does not merely point to the ram but brings it to Abraham. In the reliefs the ram appears merely as a symbol. While this would make the story more difficult for the uninstructed to grasp, it does shift the emphasis to the human sacrifice, interrupted at the crucial moment when the knife is about to plunge into the flesh and when the moral drama of father and son has reached its climax. Frederick Hartt has observed that the extreme tension and sudden swift resolution, unexpected and unforeseeable, have striking parallels with the ever more rapid accumulation of victories and strength on the part of the enemies of Florence, dispersed miraculously by the sudden death from plague of Giangaleazzo Visconti on 3 September 1402.

Another distinctive feature of the reliefs is that Abraham, invested with the divine command, becomes a frenzied enemy of his son, something like a prophet possessed. It is interesting in this connection that the story of Abraham and Isaac is also the theme of one of the most famous religious dramas of the Quattrocento, composed around 1440 by Feo Belcari, who — according to the *Novella del Grasso Legnaiuolo* (see Chapter 16) — was a close friend of Brunelleschi, and that he emphasizes the human side, Abraham's doubts and the injustice of God.[20]

In the competition panels the two sculptors used the prescribed programme each in his own way, and organized the narrative in singularly different terms. That both panels were contest-pieces is clearly shown by the striving for originality that appears even in minor details and by the archaeological approach revealed in numerous Classical references. Above all, as Krautheimer and Argan have both sensed so lucidly, in the relief by Ghiberti [20] "the gesture is hesitant, does not express will but only intention, and the angel is still distant in the sky", whereas in that by Brunelleschi [21] "Abraham has decided on the sacrifice, is resolved to carry it through, but his will is contested by that of the angel: from that conflict arises, and in that conflict is concluded, the dramatic action." Argan points out,[21]

The *story* of the Brunelleschi takes much less time. The actions of the figures are simultaneous. ... The forces collide ... Ghiberti *describes* the space in a succession of planes and episodes; Brunelleschi *constructs* it with the simultaneity of the movements, the dynamic equilibrium of their opposition. ... Brunelleschi eliminates natural space, makes a void; within the void he constructs a new space with the bodies, the gestures, the action of the persons.

Brunelleschi's officiant-protagonist, strikingly tall and compact, is in fact caught up in a deed which is not only violent and aggressive — look at the hand seizing the throat of Isaac — but paroxysmal, whipping his entire body into action as revealed in the agitated folds of the drapery. His movement is indeed swifter than that of the wind bending the tree on the mountain top around which, swept by two diverse forces, a flap of his mantle wraps itself: between physical movement and willed movement, it is the latter that dominates. The readiness of Abraham to perform the command is further marked by the V formed between his body, as it bends to the act, and the contour of the rock which meets his form at its base but diverges markedly as it rises.

Brunelleschi's Isaac is small and fine-bodied: in his last moment of unawareness he writhes, with no dignity but that of his handsome body naked to his father's aggression; with Ghiberti the reciprocal relationship is noble, almost ceremonial. The body of the boy in Brunelleschi's plaque is contrived and deformed anatomically, while Ghiberti's nude, with eyes raised to heaven, is a virtuoso exercise in modelling. Then too, Brunelleschi drew from Antiquity dynamic suggestions for the gestures of his figures, most of them in unusual poses. With Ghiberti the angel seems only just appearing on the scene, as yet is neither heard nor seen; with Brunelleschi the celestial messenger hurtles forward energetically against the wind and, instantly aware that it would be useless to call out, struggles with the patriarch, now determined on his victim, and is able to arrest him only by seizing the murderous arm [22]. Less happy, and rather forced, is the gesture of the angel's other hand pointing downwards at the ram. The animal itself looks jammed in between the cusp of the frame and the acute angle of the bent leg of Isaac and is intent on extricating itself from the thicket with the aid of a hoof.

Ghiberti tells the story following the normal direction of reading, ordering it elegantly from left to right with the journey, the ascent of the mountain, the beginning of the sacrifice, the intervention of the angel, and, still unseen by the protagonists, the ram on a tall peak. The land-

scape is only slightly characterized, but on the ground lie Isaac's garments which introduce, almost subliminally, another episode, the ritual preparation for the sacrifice, within a narration rendered slow and fragmented by the separateness of its various parts. The whole could be reproduced perfectly well in six photographic details, and because the climax coincides with the final episode there would be almost no need for an overall view.

As conceived by Brunelleschi, however, the action is co-ordinated not by time but by the structure of the quatrefoil panel itself. Major and minor personages are wedged symmetrically into its lobes, while Abraham with his excessive height, whence his hieratic, sacerdotal dignity, is inserted obliquely, on the edge of the vertical axis. The servants, both copied from Antique models [23, 24], make up two pendants, neatly balanced on either side of the conspicuous browsing donkey, and the altar is almost exactly in the centre of the plaque. Most of all, the possibility of replacing Isaac with the ram is so well brought out by their physical contact that the happy conclusion of the story comes as no surprise. In the topmost, divine, portion of the plaque the drapery of the angel in flight is repeated in the opposite direction by the whirling mantle of Abraham: Isaac is thus caught between two diverse and opposed tensions. Argan rightly observes that "the time is single and determined, just as the space too is single and determined". The impression of simultaneity, it should be noted, is accentuated by the fact that all the elements are contiguous and in contact with each other, whereas with Ghiberti they are disjunct or side by side. Brunelleschi also introduces such additional details as the sapling high up on the rock and — minutiae of a man inclined to overdo things — the blazing logs in the altar-hearth and its ornamentation depicting an unidentified but probably pre-Christian scene.[22]

There are other curious differences, minor but significant, between Ghiberti's and Brunelleschi's interpretations. The bleak mountainous site, dramatized by Ghiberti with a lizard, is shown as less arid by Brunelleschi, who depicts not only a bush (indispensable to the story) but also a tree. In both reliefs Isaac has his hands bound behind his back, and in Ghiberti's his feet too may be tied. Ghiberti correctly places the victim directly on the fire; Brunelleschi makes the altar a kind of pizza oven where at the best the boy would be in for a slow cooking. Both altars are ornamented with notable dignity and plastic richness, thus attributing to Abraham, presumed to have made it, the skills of a goldsmith and sculptor. Though swift and agile in his movements, as shown by the flying draperies, Abraham does not stay his course to look at the angel; at the most, Isaac is just about to. The ram is obviously caught in the thicket in the Ghiberti relief and accepts its plight; in Brunelleschi's, it tries to disengage itself. Because the actions of the waiting servants have no direct narrative function, they can be treated in quite different manners. Ghiberti has them in dialogue, almost as if in a reference to the *Bucolics*; Brunelleschi stresses physical actions suggestive of the arduous journey and fatigue and hunger, and isolates their figures at either side of the ass in the centre (they even overlap the frame), thereby dramatically training his light on a humanity crushed by sweaty toil and daily needs and incapable of sharing in act or word.

As Krautheimer has pointed out, the victory obtained by Ghiberti with the final commission before 25 March 1403 was due also to technical considerations. From the analysis made by Bruno Bearzi while restoring it, we know that the plaque by Brunelleschi was not cast in a single piece but consists of a platform about 5 mm (3/16 in.) thick throughout on which various parts were bolted or soldered, the largest piece comprising the rocks, ass, ram, altar, perhaps Isaac, Abraham with the rock behind him, and the left arm of the angel, while the two servants, the angel, and the tree on the rock at the right were cast separately and individually fixed to the base.[23]

Ghiberti, on the other hand, cast separately only the figure of Isaac together with the left arm of Abraham and part of the rock in the background. The back of his panel reveals the same fluid unity as the relief itself. This is true especially of the rock on the left, which is hollowed out together with the figures of the servants and the ass and is connected with the altar. The lower part of the body of Abraham is similarly hollowed out, whereas the nude Isaac, unlike the angel, is entirely in the round. The faults in casting pointed out by Bearzi to Krautheimer are clearly visible, especially in the front legs and the head of the ass. The soldering of the body of Isaac perhaps consolidates bolts attaching it to the ground. But for all this one would need a more detailed restorer's report with precise diagrams and macrophotographs.

The major stylistic differences in the general layout of the competing reliefs prove to be strikingly bound up with the different technical means used by the two artists. The textural richness of Brunelleschi's plaque is due to chiselling as well as engraving. Bearzi has pointed out that the technique used here and in certain figures on the Pistoia Altar is identical [12]. All Brunelleschi's casting is solid, not, like Ghiberti's, hollow. It has been suggested that he chose to have separately-cast figures so that he could use the chisel on the background;[24] but one would guess that his more old-fashioned method would be harder to correct in case of error. However that may be, Ghiberti's panel would have been more resistant to time and weather, and it certainly used less material. Brunelleschi's plaque weighs 25.5 kg (56 lb) as against the 18.5 kg (41 lb) of Ghiberti's, a difference which, Bearzi has estimated, would have called for an extra 600 *libbre* (1 *libbra* = 12 oz, so 450 lb or 104 kg) for the entire door, adding 60 florins to the cost in raw materials alone.

personal style. For this reason the Crucifix impresses us as more intentional and deliberate than those by Donatello, with an inherent square-hewn monumentality and a certain feeling of lack of vitality, a sense of something grown numb and unyielding. Donatello oscillates between Classicism and realism; here there is neither one nor the other. The two men went such separate ways that we can only echo Janson's comment on Vasari's famous anecdote explaining this Crucifix as having been done in competition with Donatello's in S. Croce: the two works are so dissimilar in style that, without Vasari, no one would ever have thought of comparing them. I see no resemblance either to the magnificent Crucifix in the church of Bosco ai Frati near Florence, which Parronchi attributes to Donatello.

As Lisner has observed, the modelling of the body is in the convention of marble or bronze statuary rather than that of woodcarving, and partly on the basis of a passage in Vasari she supposes that Brunelleschi may first have made a model in terracotta. The treatment of the limbs and thorax undoubtedly reflects the new interest in Classical sculpture, and was conceived in function of a dignity of the image that can be called Stoic. The Classical influence is accentuated by the absence of a loincloth [25], though one was added later in the form of a cloth soaked in plaster [27], with the obvious aim of suggesting a greater realism in the image itself. The representation of the Crucifixus as a nude figure, already seen occasionally in Trecento art, became more common after the second decade of the Quattrocento, and is one of the elements that suggest an approximate dating. The recent cleaning of the S. Maria Novella Crucifix has shown that the "expressionistic" quality of the ribcage area was due merely to dirt, and has consequently invalidated comparisons with German sculpture. Brunelleschi's Crucifix has been variously dated, some scholars seeing it as a youthful work, and others placing it as late as 1430-40.

Investigations of the measurements and proportions of the Crucifix show that, with both height and breadth an identical 1.70 m (5 ft 6 7/8 in.), the Crucifixus is a *homo quadratus*. A simple modular system based on the *braccio* was applied throughout: the circumference of the head taken at the outermost points of the hair comes to one module; the face is 1/2 module long and 1/4 wide; the torso from the hollow of the windpipe to the groin measures one module; the legs are divisible into two equal sections of 3/4 module each; and the hands and feet are 3/8 module. The volume of the torso varies proportionally from 1 1/2 to 1 1/3 to 1 1/4 module.[26]

The Crucifix in Santa Maria Novella

The only large sculpture by Brunelleschi that survives is the Crucifix in S. Maria Novella. The fact that unlike everything else by him it is in wood, the difficulty in pinning it down chronologically, and the traditional comparison with similar works by Donatello all drastically limit the possibilities of interpretation.[25] The anatomical treatment of the thorax [27] is more like what Donatello was doing before he went to Padua than it is like his bronze Crucifix for the church of the Santo there, which probably reflects a more direct contact with the medical studies for which the University of Padua was famed. Also compared to Donatello it is less Gothic (that is, less fluid) and more discontinuous, and though the relief of the ribs is rendered dramatically the thorax is a virtually rectilinear block. The lack of unity in the Crucifix has much in common with the impetuous simultaneous combination of diverse elements in the relief for the Baptistery doors, but since that disunity does not fulfil an aesthetic or narrative function it seems more a constant in a

The School of Brunelleschi; lost and attributed works; other sculptors

Brunelleschi probably never abandoned sculpture entirely, even if he was forced to limit himself to giving models and guidance to some trustworthy collaborator like his adopted son Andrea Cavalcanti, usually known as Il Buggiano (from the name of the village near Pistoia where he was born in about 1412), or to making use of him to execute commissions awarded to himself. Buggiano at times appears indistinguishable from Brunelleschi; at times he surpasses his master; occasionally he proves merely a mediocre artisan, though this must be due not to personal factors but to the different types of collaboration involved.

In 1434 — when Brunelleschi fell into political disgrace — Buggiano made a sensational flight to Naples, whence he and the money with

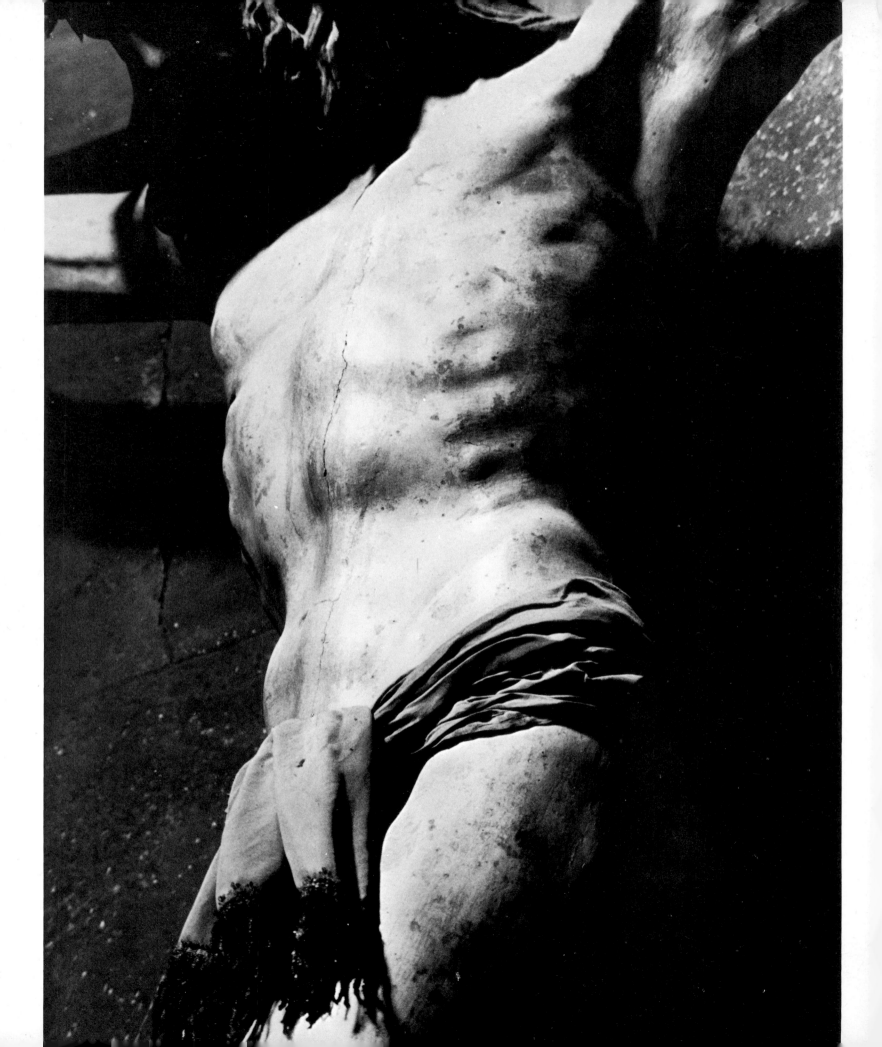

27, 28. Brunelleschi: details of Crucifix of polychromed pearwood, before restoration; the loincloth has now been removed. (Florence, S. Maria Novella)

handy whenever major commissions were scarce. Often Brunelleschi himself was active in the workshop while at the same time busying himself with seeking out commissions, and at other times he lent a hand when special difficulties or problems arose. The most interesting example of such collaboration, other than that which produced the sarcophagus of Giovanni d'Averardo (di Bicci) de' Medici and his wife, along with the well, lavabo and altar in the Old Sacristy [65, 68], is the pulpit with spiral staircase suspended from a pier in S. Maria Novella [322]. For this commission from Andrea di Donato Rucellai in 1443 Brunelleschi prepared a highly complicated wooden model, perhaps the highest manifestation of his geometrical subtlety. All these works of what we can call the School of Brunelleschi are marked by extreme experimentation, thanks in part to their relatively small size, but there were large-scale architectural experiments as well, such as the sumptuous Cardini Chapel in S. Francesco at Pescia [108].[27]

To judge Brunelleschi as a sculptor one would need more than these few works, and one would especially like to have the "painted wooden statue of St Mary Magdalen, in the round, slightly less than life-size and very beautiful" which, the Biographer goes on to tell us, burned in the church of S. Spirito in 1471. It would doubtless have provided a striking comparison with Donatello's *Magdalen* for the Baptistery. Brunelleschi is said to have collaborated with Donatello in 1411 on a statue of St Mark for Orsanmichele, and was due to work with him again, apparently as a metalworker, in 1415-16 on a trial sculpture for the Cathedral now thought to have inaugurated the revival of Classical terracottas. A tabernacle at Orsanmichele has been attributed to him; it dates from *c.* 1423-25, and Arnaldo Bruschi has suggested that it may represent the first reappearance of a correct Classical pediment. Brunelleschi may have decorated the niche at Orsanmichele in which the figure of St Peter stands, and the Cross of the Pisans, executed some time between 1424 and 1436, has been ascribed to him. His advice was apparently sought in 1426 on a tabernacle for S. Jacopo in Campo Corbolini, and again in 1427 the Tribunale della Mercanzia consulted him on the placing of their coat of arms in and on the façade of the Palazzo del Saggio. Other works that have been attributed to him at various times include a small plaque in the Louvre showing the miracle of the woman possessed and a wooden Crucifix in S. Giorgio Maggiore in Venice.[28]

Brunelleschi's relations with the other leading sculptors of his time are not well documented. We know that he was a friend of Donatello, with whom he might have been in Rome, perhaps even before 1401, and who in 1409 (?) was a co-conspirator in the trick played on the "Fat Carpenter". They worked together in 1430 on the attempted flooding of Lucca. The conflict that exploded between them at the Old Sacristy was probably due more to decisions made by the patrons than to the artists; and indeed the Biographer reports that the walls flanking the altar recess, later decorated by Donatello, were long left rough and unplastered. Similarly, I doubt that Brunelleschi's tempestuous relationship with Ghiberti can be ascribed only to personal antagonism. Their quarrel was perhaps soon resolved, because when work began on the Cathedral dome their collaboration was close and their respect apparently mutual.

Paradoxically, the sculptor who seems closest to Brunelleschi spiritually is Luca della Robbia, but this resemblance is based on a late work left unfinished (and completed no one knows how), the Pazzi Chapel [231], which may have been the result of a revival of the Brunelleschian manner rather than of any continuity.

which he had absconded were brought back through intervention at the highest diplomatic levels: it was Pope Eugenius IV or his Apostolic Abbreviator Leon Battista Alberti who wrote to Queen Giovanna of Naples about the rather embarrassing escapade. But the young man was more than an aide or partner to the master, functioning rather as his *alter ego*, maintaining a domestic workshop which no doubt came in

3 The Foundling Hospital

We are so accustomed to the architectural style of Brunelleschi and the interpretation of Antiquity that he initiated that it is easier for us to describe what was done badly before him or at the same time than what he himself achieved. Of Ghiberti, for instance, Krautheimer observed:[1]

It would seem that all these architectural elements, whether pseudo-antique or genuinely *all'antica*, Ghiberti employed without much consistency, intermingling them with Late Gothic forms. Even when genuinely antique, capitals, bases, shafts, and entablatures are not woven into a system in which everything tallies and results in what the ancients, as well as those who in the fifteenth century consciously strove to revive the architecture of antiquity, called an "order". No relation has been evolved between membering and wall, between supporting and supported parts. No axial network has been developed to hold in place the entire design of the structure. And no general concept of the principles and properties of the architecture of the ancients underlies the architectural designs of Ghiberti prior to and around 1420.

The first work to effect that miracle and, what is more, to exemplify it in a way that would make it clear to everyone, was the Foundling Hospital, the Ospedale degli Innocenti. It was also Brunelleschi's first public commission and one that proved awkward, his employment lasting only long enough for him to lay the foundations, raise the main walls, finish off the basement with a cryptoporticus beneath the cloister walks, and leave his unmistakable mark on the lower part of the front facing the piazza, the famous loggia [41].

Few architectural ensembles are as simply and clearly laid out as this hospice [30]. Occupying an entire long side of a rectangular piazza (originally merely an unorganized open space in front of the church of SS. Annunziata), it catches the eye and invites the viewer to enter its long high portico. This arcade must have presented a singular contrast to the ordinary buildings around it, with its impressive arches, each about 8 m (26 ft) in height and over 5 m (16 ft) in breadth, something like the size of a modest two-storeyed house of the time. In a city just beginning to aspire to straight streets and uniform façades it presented the rare sight of a unified front more than 71 m (233 ft) in length — later extended — and with an alignment so precise as to have no need of a margin of error, an edifice which furthermore was so costly, despite the use of common materials for most of it, as to call for an expenditure between 1419, the year of its foundation, and June 1427 of no less than 2,809 florins, 12,268 *lire* and 1 *quattrino*. (The architect, for all his labours, was paid a mere 55 florins.) Where Florentine buildings normally had straight and flat stone or plastered fronts, here there was a most elegant distinction between the weight-bearing structures (pilasters, columns, arches, and the architraves separating the storeys) and the walls: the former elaborate indeed (though the soft and perishable *pietra serena* would be inexpensive to carve), the latter of utter simplicity and designedly divided into homogeneous and continuous geometrical fields. An occasional expedient — painting the arches between the vaulting bays in the loggia to look like real stone [40] — could easily be overlooked. Anyone technically minded could only marvel at how such broad arches could, from the start, do without tie-rods: in fact there were ties incorporated into the shallow domical vaults of the loggia, though evidently not without difficulty since the first vault promptly came apart.

Despite its innovations the building struck a familiar note. In its elegance and in other features it recalled surviving Florentine Romanesque monuments, though for their luxury of marbles and decorative inlays it substituted something more sober but also more systematic and unusual: a precision of design hitherto unknown, probably based — to everyone's surprise — on drawings done to scale and perhaps squared up for enlargement, drawings which were more specific than any wooden model but nonetheless required complicated explanation from the architect in person. Accustomed to constructing arcades like this on the basis simply of the height of the columns and their interval, the workers objected to Brunelleschi's punctilious instructions. Worse, he was often away from Florence, working on fortifications or other public buildings. In 1423 he had to be called back from Pistoia (where he went again in the summer of 1424) to organize the work on the loggia; later a worker had to be sent to plead with him to provide a model and form for the "unframed roundels", and came away with the answer — certain to make the stonecutters sweat over their compasses — that these were to be fitted in exactly between the curves of the arches and the architrave. The roundels, originally concave like shells, were in 1487 arbitrarily filled by Antonio della Robbia with glazed terracotta medallions of infants in swaddling clothes [42, 44]. Originally the sole conspicuous decoration on the façade was to be the coat of arms of the all-powerful Arte della Seta, the Silk Guild, to whom on 19 May 1294 the body known as the General Council of the Florentine Population had delegated responsibility for the care of abandoned infants (*innocenti*), a duty the guild took on promptly though initially in existing hospitals, first that of S. Gallo, then that of S. Maria della Scala.[2]

The documents provide a chronology,[3] and show that the work went quite slowly, through a number of phases [31-37] — though it was not interrupted by the wars and the related economic crisis of 1429-32, for in that period an additional 7,236 *lire* and 2 *quattrini* were spent. Thus, while the orphanage was founded in 1419 it was not until 5 February 1445, at about eight o'clock in the morning, that the first foundling was furtively abandoned in the wheel set up for that purpose. Because it was a girl she was baptized with the names of Agatha, saint of the day, and Smeralda, a poetic appellative which may, emerald being associated with the muse of song, have been an allusion to the type of education and potential occupation proposed for the children.[4] In time the population of "innocents" grew, despite the enlightened practice of entrusting the great majority to foster parents and retaining in the institution probably only the difficult cases and the older children being trained for some trade. A record of 25 August 1643 shows that two centuries later there were 1,091 children in foster care, 28 nursing infants in the hospital, 21 wet nurses, 642 babies, children and women of all ages, 98 other children, 40 priests and other ministrants, the prior, and an additional 25 infants sent to S. Gimignano.

A small city in itself therefore, carefully built and diligently administered through wars and economic crises by an intelligent bureaucracy not shirking even such unpopular decisions as that of playing havoc with the project of Brunelleschi only eight years after the foundation in order to meet new practical needs: in 1427 they seized the opportunity to purchase another plot of land alongside the loggia to the south and called on Gherardo di Giovanni for plans for an annex to be built there. With the same practical spirit they added or transformed rooms, though at no time did the need for more space become dramatic.

Precedents for hospitals fronted by a loggia are not lacking: examples nearby are that of S. Matteo in Florence, dating from the end of the fourteenth century, and the one in Lastra a Signa of 1406, attributed by some to Brunelleschi himself. In any case the arrangement derived naturally from the need to protect the entrance of a building which combined convent, church and living quarters, set side by side and each with its own door, and which therefore required an especially long portico whose dimensions, obviously, must depend on those of the interiors behind it as well as allowing for future expansion.[5]

Nonetheless the loggia of the Foundling Hospital can only be termed monumental, and its impressive dignity was more than was required by its practical functions or even by the desire to confer greater nobility on those functions. It became nothing less than a symbol, one expressing above all the high social position of those who commissioned and administered the institution. This is true of the inner arrangement as well [30]. The central door leads to the cloister [49], in its way a second piazza whence visitors can make their way to the various administrative offices. Flanking it are the church and the main ward, equal in size and each with its own large door to the loggia. The ward serving as dormitory for the children was known as the *abituro*, a word now implying the humblest of dwellings, here belied by the splendid trussed ceiling made of beams brought from Pratomagno by river along the Arno [48]. The service corridors are around the central courtyard and on the central axis and probably gave on to small side streets. At the two ends of the façade other doors, the sixth and seventh, led to other premises or to stairways to the upper storey. As in a machine or well-constituted republic, every part fulfils its function without interfering with the others. There is not even an optical connection: the windows of the church, like those of the ward, are too high to permit a glimpse of the cloister, and from it only blank walls are seen.

For the inhabitants, however, the isolation of the parts is broken by the most ingenious system of passageways at ground and semi-basement levels [30b,c]. All the original portions, except the loggia, are two-storeyed. Beneath the church and the ward are very large rooms with low vaults supported on piers [47], designed to serve as respectively the refectory and the workroom where the boys, required to remain in the hospice to the age of eighteen, could be trained in crafts and other trades. These rooms, exactly the same size as the church and ward above, received their light from two deep courtyards on the side away from the piazza. They are connected by a genuine barrel-vaulted cryptoporticus running beneath the cloister walks and lit, probably then as now, by small windows at pavement level [49]. Two stairways, one alongside the small room of the *camerlengo* (the bursar) now occupied by the porter, the other next to the council room and archives, lead down to semi-basement rooms [30c] from which one can proceed along the axis of the building to a point beyond the cloister, crossing a kind of internal street that connects other cellar rooms and finally emerges in the garden. Although the women's cloister, an annex designed to house mothers, was laid out later, in 1437, and does not follow Brunelleschi's plan, it uses the same system of circulation and adds considerably to the semi-underground area as well as making it possible to enter it from the sides.

The plan of the Foundling Hospital has certain features which were applied a few years later to the palaces of Florentine patricians: a large square court treated like a cloister, with arcades; a staircase placed no longer in the courtyard but inside the building; a central axis that runs from the middle of the façade to the garden in the rear; two symmetrical rooms for custodians at the start of that passageway to protect it [30d]. The Villa della Petraia [50], which the Biographer somewhat uncertainly attributes to Brunelleschi, has a similar cryptoporticus around three sides of the courtyard.[6]

29. The Foundling Hospital, from the pictorial map of Florence by Pietro del Massaio Fiorentino [8]. The loggia faces right, with the church and ward running back from it. In the lower right corner of this detail is SS. Annunziata, facing the piazza.

The majestic façade of the Innocenti, the refined execution, and a new overall design for internal communications and services, all suggest a political programme intended to bring credit to the sponsors. As it took shape the Hospital assumed the role of an instrument of state, taking in those infants "quorum patres et matres contra naturae jura sunt desertores" (deserted by their parents contrary to the law of nature), and while performing this traditional charitable service also sought to give it a specialized and improved function. The great economic oligarchy of Florence, impelled by the crisis to identify themselves with the fortunes of their city though the interests at work were really what we would call multi-national, turned to large public works in an effort to salvage the dignity of a capital whose population was seriously in decline: from a maximum of 95,000 inhabitants it had plunged rapidly to 90,000 in 1338, 76,000 in 1347, 54,747 in 1380, and 37,225 in 1427. (This was still better than Pistoia and Prato, which lost about two-thirds of their population.) Despite public-minded measures, population in Florence finally reached a level of only 40,000.

The new structures in the city — including the great new churches of S. Lorenzo and S. Spirito — far exceeded the urgent needs of the moment, but in a sense they were auspicious omens of a hoped-for but scarcely possible future city. There was also, at least in the case of the Hospital, from which every suggestion of traditional ecclesiastical and aristocratic architecture was eliminated, a desire for an autonomous administration of good works. The funds in fact came from Francesco Datini, a wealthy merchant of Prato who had a branch establishment in Florence and had already founded a hospital in his own city. When he transformed most of his house in Prato into a charitable institution Datini had explicitly declared his intention that

47

it should be and remain a kind of charitable centre [*ceppo*], granary, and private house, and not religious, in no way subject to the Church or ecclesiastical offices or ecclesiastical prelates or any other ecclesiastical person, so that it can in no way be reduced to something else but will remain always for the poor and wholly for the use of the poor of Jesus Christ and their nourishing and perpetual support.

Then too the humanists, from Coluccio Salutati to Leonardo Bruni (the latter in this period Chancellor of the Republic), sought inspiration for a progressive alternative solution in Classical law and philosophy. One wonders whether in organizing the ensemble of the Foundling Hospital with its nursery, boarding school, trade school, social centre and hospital, the administrative heads were thinking of a passage in the *Republic* of Plato (if only as cited by Ambrogio Traversari):

They will begin by sending out into the country all the inhabitants of the city... and will take possession of their very young children, who will be unaffected by the habits of their parents; these they will train in their own habits and laws, I mean in the laws which we have given them; and in this way the State and constitution of which we were speaking will soonest and most easily attain happiness, and the nation which has such a constitution will gain most. [VII, 540-41, Jowett translation]

Here they would find the clue to transforming an evil into a good by taking advantage of the violation of nature on the part of the begetters of the "innocents" to replace those unworthy individuals with a superior "law of reason" (see above, note 2).

Piazza della SS. Annunziata

As with all such experiments, propaganda was needed for the new ideas to seep down to the city and the local districts. Since those ideas probably also had to do with a better way of rearing children, of controlling them in their play and introducing them into social relations, the ideal agents for spreading the new pedagogy would be the nursing mothers and wet nurses living in or connected with the Hospital. Its site, though distant from the commercial streets and major arteries (and chosen for the simple reason that the land, used only as a garden, was cheap), had the advantage of neighbouring on a great pilgrimage sanctuary, the church of SS. Annunziata, which was also the scene of civic manifestations and religious spectacles [*30a, 38*]. Indeed, work on the Hospital and on the church was correlated and often under the direction of the same master masons; and it even seems as if the Hospital planned to extend a connecting wing to the church, or at least to be in some way architecturally related to it, its own axis being at right angles to that of the church nave. With two sides thus determined and a straight street, the Via de' Servi, running from the Cathedral and offering itself as axis for a piazza, a regular open space was bound to be laid out.[7] The geometrical scheme, however, must have been skilfully worked out in advance. Moreover, the very broad stairs in front of the Hospital, doubtless occupied then as now by loungers as if on the tiers of an amphitheatre, implicitly lent a theatrical character to everything in the vicinity. The term is intentional, because not only are the loggia steps like seats in a Roman amphitheatre, an image reinforced by the presence of arcades with Classical pilasters, but in the church itself a mystery play (which made use of an aerial ropeway, lights and fireworks) was presented at least as early as 1439. Today the Piazza della SS. Annunziata is still a traditional place for the few folk festivities that can survive in a city where every square is a jam-packed open-air garage.

The piazza acts as an extension or, as it were, a gigantic atrium to Brunelleschi's loggia and confers on it a unique function while at the same time providing a link with the city for the "innocents", preventing the feeling that they were outcasts from society, sunk in the depths of misery. Seeing the loggia at noon and in the early afternoon with students and tourists sprawling on the stairs or visitors (still too few) on their way to the splendid small museum in the Hospital, one cannot doubt the social importance of this work. In this context it is interesting that Alberti, in Book VII of his treatise on architecture, speaks of the necessity of employing uniform structures and porticos, preferably symmetrical, to ornament especially crossroads, forums and theatres, places he in fact equates: "In reality the forum is nothing other than a more spacious crossroads, and the place for spectacles is simply a forum surrounded by tiers and benches." That equivalence of functions holds perfectly for the Piazza della SS. Annunziata: a place to pass through or linger in where urban life, though slower here and more peripheral, is nonetheless active and conducive to sociable gathering. In his Chapter VI Alberti follows Plato in the *Republic* in urging that places be set aside where nurses can gather, because "I believe that the children would be healthier for being in the open air, and the nurses would maintain a more fitting deportment out of pride in themselves, and being among so many others all engaged in the same surveillance, would be less negligent". Moreover, "an elegant portico, that would have that function, would also serve the heads of families for strolling about or sitting in or resting after their meal or for meeting on business matters". Thus the Hospital, whose primary task was to distribute the foundlings among families or with wet-nurses, instead of being a place of shame to be shunned became a lively gathering point, with a portico much larger than was needed merely to lead into the church and cloister and ward — a loggia ingeniously transformed into setting, stage and stalls for that great theatre which is a busy city square.

Construction of the Hospital

Besides the usual material, such as stones from the river, the construction of the orphanage and its loggia called for what the documents refer to as a large quantity of *conci*, hewn stones, and these had to be absolutely identical and regular, almost as if in anticipation of the idea of mass-produced prefabricated elements. For that purpose many models were required, and these could not be merely of *rape grosse*, the turnip-like root used by Brunelleschi to make models of the stones in the Cathedral dome: they had to be made accurately in clay or wood. To mount and fit the stones together, long and difficult explanations were necessary. Called elsewhere by the wars and urgent need for fortifications, Brunelleschi had to settle for overall drawings and models of details, explaining what he wanted in person to the workmen and those left in charge. When he returned he found that his design had not always been carried out. It seems, however, that the stonecutters did not make too many errors, evidently having had better guidance than the masons: as we know, one of them was sent to Pistoia to obtain advice and drawings to go by.

The Biographer gives a detailed account of the building of the Foundling Hospital, and of the alterations made to Brunelleschi's design, which is worth quoting almost in full (ff. 307v-308r):

continued on page 58

30. Plans of the Foundling Hospital.
a) Schematic plan of the Hospital and Piazza della SS. Annunziata as they are today (from Klotz 1970). The piazza is in fact an irregular trapezoid in form (see note 7).
b) Plan of the semi-basement level, prepared during the restoration project. To the left of the central cloister is the church, to the right the ward, and beyond it, the women's cloister. The cryptoporticus passages are indicated by darker shading.
c) Diagrammatic plan of the semi-basement level. In this conjectural reconstruction a symmetrical layout has been worked out on the basis of existing structures, and the service corridors have been completed. The courtyards which light the large vaulted rooms below church and ward are shown as gardens. The plan of this level indicates that the women's cloister was not part of the original project.
d) Plan of the ground floor before the recent restoration, which, among other things, cleared the ward of the later internal partitions shown here. For a bird's-eye-view of the Hospital, see [266].

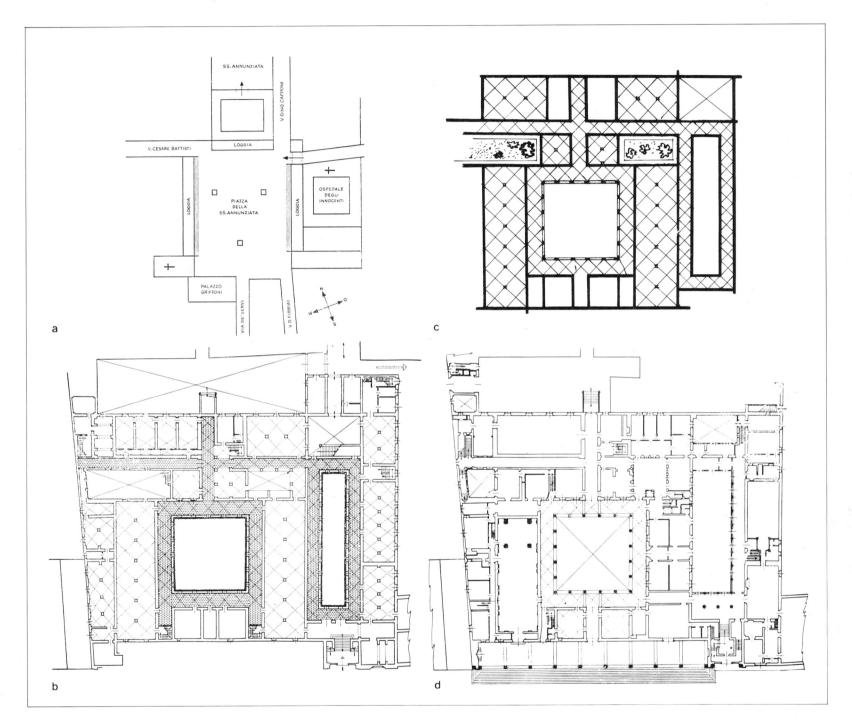

Phases in the construction of the Foundling Hospital, analysed by Franco Luchini. (1 cm = 1.87 m; 1 in. = 15 ft 7 in.; 1 Florentine *braccio* = *c.* 0. 5836 m = *c.* 23 in.: see note 4 to the Introduction.)

31. State of the building in 1424.

This is the latest date at which Brunelleschi supervised the construction in person, at least according to the documents examined (see the chronology in note 3). His first documented leave of absence took him to Pistoia, whence he had to be called back in September 1423. On 21 July 1424 he was again in Pistoia when he had to be called on for advice, probably for the construction of the vaults (carried out in September of that year), which did not yet include herringbone masonry.

The first vault on the left (probably the first to be built) is different from the others: it has no crown or internal cavities, and it seems that the circular iron tie-rod used elsewhere was not inserted here or else broke. Cracks in the vault are visible even from outside.

The steps up to the loggia were not yet built, and the basement wall on which the loggia rests had no openings, since the underground rooms received light and air from the internal courtyards (called, in fact, "cortili dell'aria").

The foundations of the loggia consist of pyramidal stone piers beneath the columns, and, between them, smooth stones from the bed of the Mugnone [*32*].

There were openings for five large doors and ten windows, five of which were later blocked. The two wings at the sides, though part of the original project, may not yet have been built.

32. State of the building in 1427.

In this year Brunelleschi's name disappears from the documents: the last payment of his salary was made on 29 January, and on 1 May the name of Francesco della Luna appears, to remain until 1430.

The ground plan was U-shaped, comprising the façade range, church and ward.

The façade range had 10 columns, 4 pilasters (2 at each end), 10 roundels between the 9 arches, and architrave and cornice 122 *braccia* long, 3 large doors within the loggia, a door at each end, at piazza level, between the pilasters on the outer wall, and 2 small doors in the ends of the loggia.

The church was roofed, and the walls of the ward had been built.

The foundations of the central cloister had been constructed but not the cloister itself.

The vaults of the loggia were covered by a rough temporary roof (with wooden frame, gutter tiles, and flat tiles) supported by 26 slender brick pilaster strips on the side of the wall with the eaves and 31 similar pilaster strips for the rest of the roof itself.

The frames of all the doors and windows had been made between 30 April and 4 May 1426.

The stairs, consisting of 7 steps, had been built from the right end to beyond the door of the ward.

33. State of the building in 1445.
On 25 January 1445, the Foundling Hospital was formally opened.

The façade had been extended to the south (right) side as commissioned on 15 May 1430.

The façade above the loggia, comprising the upper storey with its windows, had been built in 1439.

The coat of arms of the Arte della Seta, over the door at the far right, had been installed in 1439.

By this date the alterations to Brunelleschi's project condemned by the Biographer had already taken place (see below).

34. State of the building in 1488.
Since the Biographer's life of Brunelleschi was written in the 1480s, this is the situation he would have had in mind when he denounced a number of omissions or errors committed by Francesco della Luna in completing the work.

The steps had been completed in 1457, and a fresco over the door to the church was painted in 1459.

35. Reconstruction of Brunelleschi's original design for the Foundling Hospital, based on the Biographer's criticisms of the completed building, analysed by Franco Luchini. (1 cm = 4.03 m; 1 in. = 33 ft 7 in.)

The "frieze that runs above the arcade of the loggia", plain in the façade as completed, is here shown on the model of that in the Old Sacristy of S. Lorenzo [65].

The "architrave" and "two windows" were probably meant to be more elaborate, but cannot be reconstructed without further evidence.

The "small pilasters that should have risen from the cornice serving as window sill and which were designed to support the [upper] cornice" are drawn from three sources: the Palazzo Rucellai in Florence, the Ducal Palace in Urbino, and the circular building in the third panel from the bottom on the right-hand wing of Ghiberti's Doors of Paradise.

The upper cornice should have been higher, "where the eaves of the roof are now", and may have been a complete entablature.

The roundels above the columns of the loggia were intended to be blank, with smooth concave backs.

Other incorrect features in the façade as built are the extra bay on the right, and the architrave carried downward like a frame at both ends.

36, 37. Elevation and plan of the façade as built. (1 cm = 2.37 m; 1 in. = 19 ft 9 in.)

38. The loggia of the Foundling Hospital (right)
and the Piazza and façade of SS. Annunziata.

39. Section of the loggia and upper storey of the
Foundling Hospital. (1 cm = 1.13 m; 1 in. = 9 ft
5 in.)

40. View inside the loggia.

And among other things, since I will begin with the first things he did in Florence, he was requested to build the loggia of the Foundling Hospital by the Guild and University of Por S. Maria [i.e. the Silk Guild] who are patrons of it and have charge of it, for which loggia a drawing alone sufficed, without a wooden model, and this he made. And for what was requested from him for that space lying above the loggia and for a single bay on either side of the loggia between two fluted piers of hard sandstone, he supplied them with the drawing precisely measured on a reduced scale of small *braccia*. That drawing, in elaborated form, is still in the meeting hall of the consuls of that guild and contains various and very excellent architectural solutions the reasons for which few grasp. Also he gave explanations in person to the master masons and stonecutters as well as to certain citizens, heads of the guild, and Operai deputized for this matter, because he was obliged to absent himself elsewhere for a while. Returning from there [he found that] the loggia had been erected in the form it has at present [the Biographer is mistaken], which caused Filippo great displeasure because in many respects they had gone astray. Certain among those Operai, in their arrogance deeming themselves no less authorities than Filippo, had made it that way under the impression that Filippo would praise them, or, should he not praise them, that they could defend themselves by claiming that what they had done was good. Which is why, when Filippo condemned certain things one of the men in particular, the very one who had erred most, undertook a defence. There are major errors, some of them obvious, and they show differences from the design Filippo had left, so that they could be seen by someone setting out to track them all down: one is in the frieze that runs above the arcade of the loggia; another is in the architrave, and in two windows; and the small pilasters that should have risen from the cornice serving as window sill and which were designed to support the [upper] cornice, which cornice should have been where the eaves of the roof are now. Likewise too there is an additional wing built beside the façade to the south, which is visible from the front along the face of the loggia, in which he violated the proportions laid down by Filippo, and this in addition to the error of building this additional wing at all; and here there is an architrave which bends downwards and extends all the way to the plinth of the building. In short, all these errors are only the result of sheer presumption on the part of one who had things like that done on his own authority. And when that individual came to defend himself Filippo indicted him of everything so thoroughly that the man simply did not know what to say, and it is only fair not to give the name of the man in question. But to introduce defects into, and remove, things by such men [as Filippo] is nothing less than great presumption. And in the works of Filippo it has been learned from experience in the long run, and often, that nothing could be altered without lessening their beauty, increasing their cost, and in large part weakening the buildings and making them less functional.

When checked against the documents this account proves almost entirely reliable. On 1 May 1427 Francesco della Luna did indeed take over the direction of the work at the Foundling Hospital, though his responsibility may only have been administrative.[8] The motive of the architrave bending down at right angles to become a pilaster [36] is taken from the attic storey of the Baptistery. To the man justifying his choice of model Brunelleschi is supposed to have said: "There is only one thing wrong with that building, and you had to imitate that"[9].

The architectural incongruities complained of are departures that violated the system of proportions (it is thought that the length of the façade was originally meant to be the same as the diagonal of the cloister), medievalisms like the bent architrave at the right, a decrease in the height of the upper storey, and poor alignment of the columns in the cloister. These errors so excited the scorn of the faithful Biographer that he refused even to discuss the internal arrangement of the building. An excess of loyalty perhaps, because what was done can in fact be considered a miracle of respect for a minutely detailed architectural plan such

continued on page 64

41. Piazza della SS. Annunziata, looking towards the church and the Foundling Hospital. The character of the open space is set by Brunelleschi's loggia and its arcaded imitations, built in the sixteenth and seventeenth centuries.

42. The compositional geometry of the façade of the Foundling Hospital, with roundels touching the arches and architrave. (1 cm= 96 cm; 1 in. = 8 ft.)

43. One of the two surviving original capitals of the loggia. (The others were replaced in the nineteenth century; see note 11.)

44. Detail of the façade.

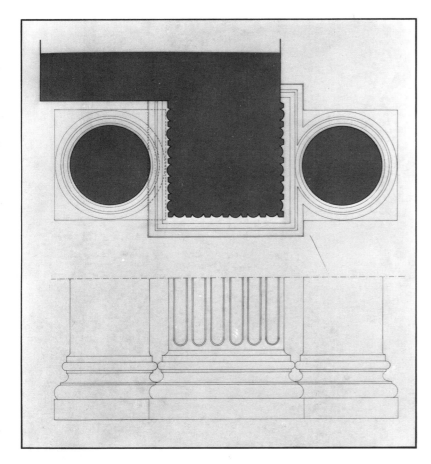

as had perhaps never been seen in Florence, and one can only regret that the replacement in the nineteenth century of most of the columns of the loggia prevents one from checking the precision of their original disposition, and makes it difficult to determine whether a module was used. (Recent restorations too have not been above criticism.)[10]

To realize a design like this a new system of marking-out had to be used, involving a grid of cords coming off an axis such as is described by Alberti in Book III:

In laying out the foundation we use the system of tracing lines, called axes, in the following manner. From the midpoint of the front façade of the building to that of the rear façade we trace a line in whose exact middle we plant a spike in the ground; there we make another line crossing at right angles according to the rules of geometry. Everything to be measured will be brought into relationship with those two lines. In this way everything works out perfectly: parallel lines are easy to make, the angles can be defined with precision, the parts turn out properly shaped and correctly related to one another.

We are immediately aware of that exactness in laying out the plan when we see in foreshortening the long façade or the colonnade of the loggia described by Alberti as "a wall pierced by numerous apertures" [*38*]. One cannot but marvel at the rigidity of the straight line staked out in this manner which so markedly contrasts with the crooked lines of the streets that continue at either side of the Hospital. To ensure that the lines thus established would be followed in the actual execution, new working methods proved necessary, including even rest breaks to compensate for the unwonted concentration and precision demanded of the workers. Here is Alberti again, in Book IX:

In any case one will have to see to it that the latter [the labourers] always make correct use of the plumb line, marker, and square. When the time is right building can go on, then be interrupted, then taken up again when ready; use only pure, sound, unmixed, solid, genuine materials, disposing them in the most appropriate, convenient and efficacious manner, and distributing them in the right and proper places so that they stand upright, lie flat, or are inclined, with the front uncovered and the sides covered or vice versa, according to what their characteristics or functions require.

The Tuscan Renaissance style is so often seen as a local phenomenon, that is to say as the product of tradition as much as or more than revolution, of a deliberate return to early Tuscan architecture, that in looking at the capitals of the Foundling Hospital loggia we tend to minimize their novelty. For, while they are not precise replicas of Classical capitals, they nevertheless show a special knowledge of earlier capitals or of Vitruvian principles. (Obviously we can only speak of the two surviving originals, those on the second and eighth columns from the left [*43*], particularly in the matter of their decoration, some small parts of which have been repaired in plaster.) In the three tiers of superimposed leaves and volutes there is a rhythm of increased energy rounded off decisively in the volutes, which assume a tight and precisely geometrical spiral form. In the centre, where two volutes meet, they are not foreshortened with false perspective as in late Classical and medieval examples, but project, and can thus be almost as large as those at the corners. The basket-like shape of the capitals clearly shows that Brunelleschi knew the legendary origin of the Corinthian order, as recounted by Vitruvius.[11]

The construction of the Hospital must have been envisaged in two major phases [*31-32*]. During the first, which could extend over several decades, the loggia was to remain only one storey high, which meant

47. One of the large vaulted semi-basement rooms of the Foundling Hospital, undoubtedly part of Brunelleschi's original design, seen after restoration. We are looking at half the room: the central row of square piers is on the right (see the plans, *fig. 20b,c*).

48. The timber ceiling of the ward, after restoration. The 14 beams and 28 brackets, all of walnut, were ordered from the carpenter Nanni di Bartolomeo di Lucca in 1426.

that the doors at the sides would have been used only as service entries. Instead of adding to the sides, as was later done on the right [*33*], the only extensions considered initially would have involved duplicating the building in depth beyond the internal transverse passageway. It does seem highly unlikely that the central cloister would not have been enclosed by buildings on all sides and that there would have been no plan for at least two symmetrical rooms like those at the entrance to have been built at the opposite end of the central axis. The two courtyards below ground level, needed to give light and air to the large underground rooms [*30c*], were laid out in relation to a transverse passageway running from the centre to the two sides, a true internal street with, in a sense, the same axial function as the loggia on the exterior. By way of that central "crossroads" one could arrive at a second building, itself presumably around a cloister.

Punctilious as always, the Biographer does in fact speak of two phases, but only for the loggia. The first involved a design for which a drawing was sufficient. Only later did the architect supply another design for "that space lying above the loggia and for a single bay on either side of the loggia between two fluted piers of hard sandstone": this meant the entire storey above the loggia, realized in 1439, and the wings on either side, which are in fact marked off by fluted stone piers or pilasters. The second drawing, "in elaborated form", was still to be seen in the late fifteenth century in the meeting hall of the consuls of the Arte della Seta, and it is to it that the Biographer refers with characteristic precision. The drawing must have been prepared well before the second stage of building began: it is difficult otherwise to explain how there could be an explicit reference to the original design for the upper storey of the Foundling Hospital [*35*] in Ghiberti's "Doors of Paradise" for the Baptistery, whose casting was completed in 1436.

49. Cloister of the Foundling Hospital, looking towards the façade range and the church. The columns and arches were erected in 1445 on foundations which were being dug in 1426. The narrow windows just above ground level light the cryptoporticus passages below. The cloister was later given an upper storey, which partially blocks the windows of both church and ward — windows which are themselves fourteenth-century in style.

50. Schematic plans of the basement and ground floor of the Villa della Petraia. (See note 6.)

Around three sides of the courtyard at basement level (upper plan) runs a cryptoporticus, lit by windows placed high up. The clearer organization of the part to the left of the courtyard, at both basement and ground levels, suggests that some remains of the original Brunelleschian building may survive there. The area under the tower has not yet been investigated. (1 cm = 5.26 m; 1 in. = 43 ft 10 in.)

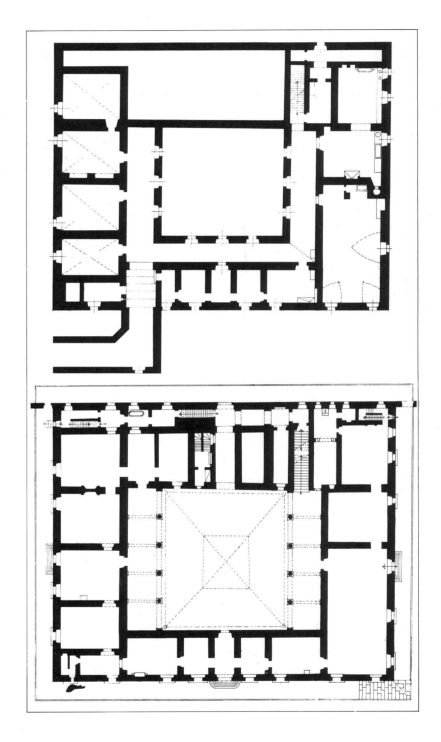

4 The Palazzo di Parte Guelfa and Florentine private palaces

Another significant involvement, this time even more political than social, came about for Brunelleschi when the Parte Guelfa, the Guelph faction, commissioned from him a new assembly hall and two adjoining rooms.[1] In the complex vicissitudes of the city the Guelphs had come to represent the merchant class in its highest echelons and therefore constituted the most influential group of notables. In 1419 Leonardo Bruni drew up a new statute (which was at the origin also of this undertaking by Brunelleschi), based on a truly noble ideal of liberty in the domestic affairs of the city as well as in its external relations — a domestic freedom that was meant to go along with parity of rights for the entire citizenry and thus with a certain social equality, and an external freedom that called for maintaining a state of military superiority, offensive and defensive, possibly by means of a national militia. Humanist ideology contrasted Florence with Milan, a city dominated by a lord who was not elected or subject to any controls or removable; but this ideology also scorned those men of letters and Churchmen who, like Petrarch, preferred a solitary life to involvement in civic matters. (In this they somewhat anticipated the present-day insistence that intellectuals should be directly involved in the running of the state.) In the language and theme alike of the early fifteenth century one can recognize the desire to equate the mercantile and lay nobility of the day with the citizenry of Florence's noble past.

These concepts, now familiar thanks to the studies of Eugenio Garin and Hans Baron (and subject to some criticism and discussion), also imply a change in the functions attributed to public architecture and, by analogy, to private commissions, in accord with a process that reached its peak under the government of Albizzi and of Bruni but had begun already in the late Trecento. Boccaccio in his *Filoloco*, for instance, applies words like "grand", "magnificent", "sublime", "excellent", "noble" and "splendid" not only to human and divine beings but also to buildings: we find "the greatest temple", "the noblest sepulchre", "lofty" and "great" palaces. As Georg Weise observed, "it seems... characteristic that from the grandeur and magnificence of the buildings the 'magnanimity' of those who constructed them should be deduced, a judgment in fact adopted throughout the Renaissance and Baroque. Everything having to do with the Classical ambiance is great and majestic." Those qualities were immediately transferred to those who make use of such constructions. It was precisely Bruni, as Weise points out, who in his description of the Roman gate and bridge at Rimini used categories easily applicable also to the new monuments of Quattrocento Florence and adjectives which were in fact applied to them. The gate is "sublimis ac magnifice lapide quadrato et diligenti artificio perpolita" (magnificently sublime and perfected with squared stones and diligent skill), and the bridge is "ex marmore ornatissimus ac pulcherrimus" (in marble and highly adorned and beautiful).

This same notion of grandeur is found in the documents referring to the financing of the work on the palace for the Guelph party: it is being erected "to the honour and dignity of that party" ("pro honore et exaltatione dicte inclite partis"), but also "to the honour not only of that party but of the entire Florentine Republic"; and it is essential "to the dignity and honour of that party that the edifices begun with such magnificence in view be completed" ("ad decus et honorem dicte partis quod edificia pro ejus magnificentia incoata perficiantur"). One is inevitably reminded of Alberti, who wrote that "we are erecting great buildings so as to appear magnanimous and powerful to those coming after us", and suggested that every citizen should aspire to "an increase

in beauty and great dignity for himself, his family, posterity, the city".

For such a solemn task, with all its political overtones and economic difficulties, Brunelleschi opted for an impeccably pure and unornamented structure. Our only information as to what Brunelleschi designed comes from the Biographer (f. 308v):

And then, the Palace of the Parte Guelfa having been begun when he was away from Florence, the side looking towards the street called Porta S. Maria being already up with its walls raised above the ground to within about two *braccia* from the sill of the main windows, and built to that point and carried out by traditional masters [though] among the best in the city in those times, it was decided that he should complete it and [this meant] both the audience chamber and the corridor from the old hall and also the new hall; and to judge by what was done and by what was devised for both the exterior and the interior, anyone with good taste can easily judge the level of beauty that would have been attained had it been completed.

Brunelleschi expressed in the simplest and most effective manner the function of the council chamber on the upper storey, by huge windows some 5.5 by 2.5 m (almost 18 by 8 ft) surmounted by roundels 1.5 m (5 ft) in diameter; he regularized the plan of this upper storey visually, and treated it almost like a pavilion raised on piers above the fourteenth-century rooms and streets beneath it [51-53]. What he conceived floats, as it were, on that medieval structure, and thus on an earlier tradition, but is also explicitly separated from it by means of a large cornice that acts less as a division between storeys than as a kind of very high base course, so that all the part below it, including its shops, becomes something like a podium. Although the plan is not regular and symmetrical, as can be seen in the drawings done specially for this book [53], the effect is of a remarkable symmetry and homogeneity. It is interesting too that there are no Classical references or, to be more precise, no archaeological ornaments: the corner pilasters were designed for the simplest bases and capitals, like those of the Palazzo Medici-Riccardi, and whatever striving for prestige there is in the building is summed up in its perfect mouldings, impeccably accurate stonework, and fine general proportions.

A date prior to 1427 seems the most likely for Brunelleschi's rebuilding.[2] The Biographer explains that he did not choose to make a model here, but "got along with drawings only, and by word of mouth from time to time told the stonecutters and stone-layers what they had to do" (f. 311v). The palace was never completed to his design, and indeed even before the final abandonment of work his scheme had been modified — as at the Foundling Hospital, and apparently by the same person.[3]

Although the bases of the large corner pilasters are not very readable today [51, 56], the earliest photographs show that they had a Classical form of which Geymüller was able to draw the profile. The pilasters moreover are in the same plane as the wall below: the corner between them continues, but so to speak in negative, the colonnette below, and this indentation resolves the problem of the junction of two pilaster strips by leaving them unfused and independent. In the same spirit the junction of the walls in the *salone* is marked by a slender "positive" segment of pilaster [58]. Portoghesi, in his study of Borromini, suggested that we have here an anticipation of the Baroque treatment of the corner. The upper termination of this arrangement, which is almost a giant order but which projects so little from the wall, remains problematical.

The type of window may have been derived from the palace depicted in the background of a sarcophagus like that of the Apostles (now in the

continued on page 74

51. The Palazzo di Parte Guelfa (left) and Palazzo dell'Arte della Seta, as they appeared after surrounding buildings had been destroyed by the Germans in the Second World War.

52. Elevation of the Palazzo di Parte Guelfa and neighbouring buildings, with some decorative elements reconstructed. (1 cm = 2.58 m; 1 in. = 21 ft 6 in.)

53. Plans, with the adjacent buildings. (1 cm = 13.40 m; 1 in. = 111 ft 8 in.). The street frontage shown in *figs. 51* and *52* is at the left. (a) Ground floor, pre-Brunelleschi; (b) first floor, with the great hall or council chamber shaded in grey; (c) second floor.

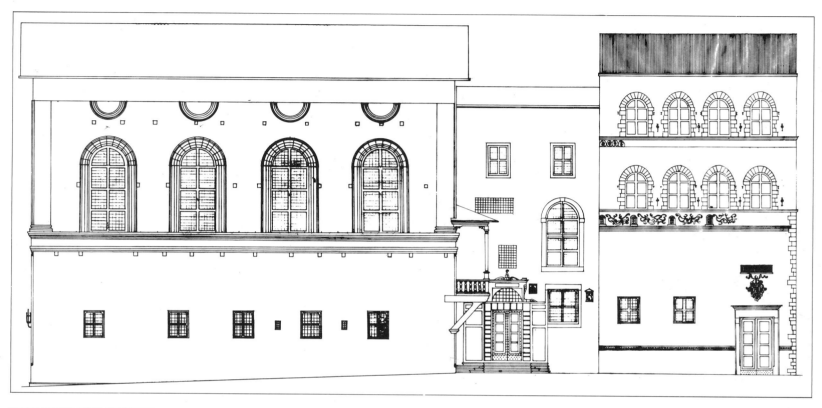

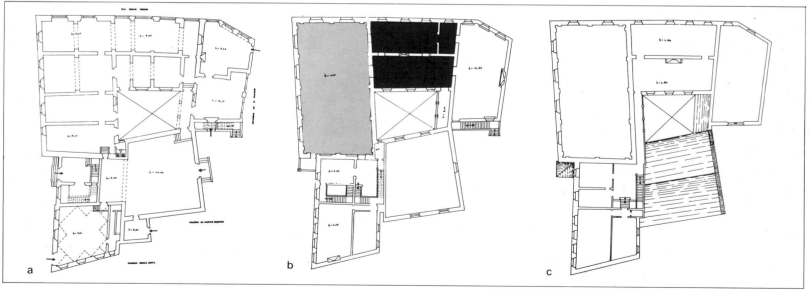

a b c

54, 55. The large windows of the Palazzo di Parte Guelfa, above the main cornice which marks the beginning of Brunelleschi's work. The oculi were originally open.

56. Treatment of the corner of the Palazzo di Parte Guelfa. Brunelleschi's pilasters, above the cornice, frame a spur which carries on the line of the colonnette below.

Vatican Grottoes),[4] a prototype which may also have served for the portals of the Medici and Gondi Palaces in Florence.

The interior, unfortunately, virtually defies judgment today, and cannot even be properly documented photographically. The original furniture has vanished; it consisted of tiers of benches which probably rose to the bases of the pilasters (as suggested by the black line in the drawing, 58).[5] A splendid sixteenth-century ceiling cuts down the height of the hall, having been wedged in between the windows and the roundels above them which were intended to be open and a source of light [58, 59]. Here, in the context of the tradition of solid walls with only sparse openings that prevailed in both medieval and Renaissance Italy, we find the surprising fact that this council hall was intended to be totally open to the light coming from two directions, from the sides and above. In a sense this double source is a rhetorical figure, that is an "amplification" which is paradoxically the opposite of Brunelleschi's treatment of the naves of his churches, where illumination from the sides is extremely limited and what light there is enters from above so as to exclude all reference to earthly things. From the hall of the Palazzo one can see the city, indeed one dominates it, because of the height of this upper storey — something true also of the upper storey of Orsanmichele, which was the precedent that Brunelleschi looked at and then redesigned. Thus political life is identified with openness, clarity and rationalism, whereas religious life, though it is controlled and protected against devotional superstitions, nevertheless remains within the ambit of psychological privacy, of suggestion, of an uncertain hovering between reality and mysticism.

The hall with its two rows of windows and giant angular pilasters is in effect double-storeyed, and as such was imitated, though with poorly designed window openings, in the Palazzo Farnese in Rome, in the corner *salone* on the left side of the façade by Antonio da Sangallo and Michelangelo.

The Classical fluted pilasters which, according to the most convincing interpretation, were to have risen to the ceiling [59], stand on an elevated podium, thus making room for the tiered benches reserved for the principal hierarchies of the Parte. These pilasters were probably the work of Maso di Bartolomeo, who was paid for them in 1452 when an attempt was made to resume building — though only on the interior — after an interruption (see below). For their design he could have looked at precedents by Brunelleschi rather than specific drawings; indeed, he may simply have imitated the Pazzi Chapel [231] with some simplification. Had these pilasters extended above the roundels they would have constituted, like the corner pilasters on the outside of the building, an embryonic giant order [59d]. Their capitals, to be consistent with other solutions by Brunelleschi, would have supported a monumental architrave, thus giving the hall something of the appearance of the contemporary painted architecture by Andrea del Castagno in the hall of the Villa dei Carducci at Legnaia, which may slightly predate the resumption of work in the Palazzo di Parte Guelfa. With this division by pilasters the long wall facing the windows would have offered surfaces suitable for large frescoes or tapestries or a display of numerous coats of arms. The idea that the interior was intended to have frescoes comes from what we know of the old hall, which had Giottesque wall paintings, and also from a comparison with the chapel in the Palazzo Medici-Riccardi, the Florentine interior closest to it in style.

Work was interrupted for the usual reason, war, but also, more specifically, because of the confiscation by the Republic of the capital,

57. External elevation of the end wall of the hall. The carved bases of the pilasters, now almost entirely weathered away, can be made out in old photographs. (1 cm = 86 cm; 1 in. = 7 ft 2 in.)

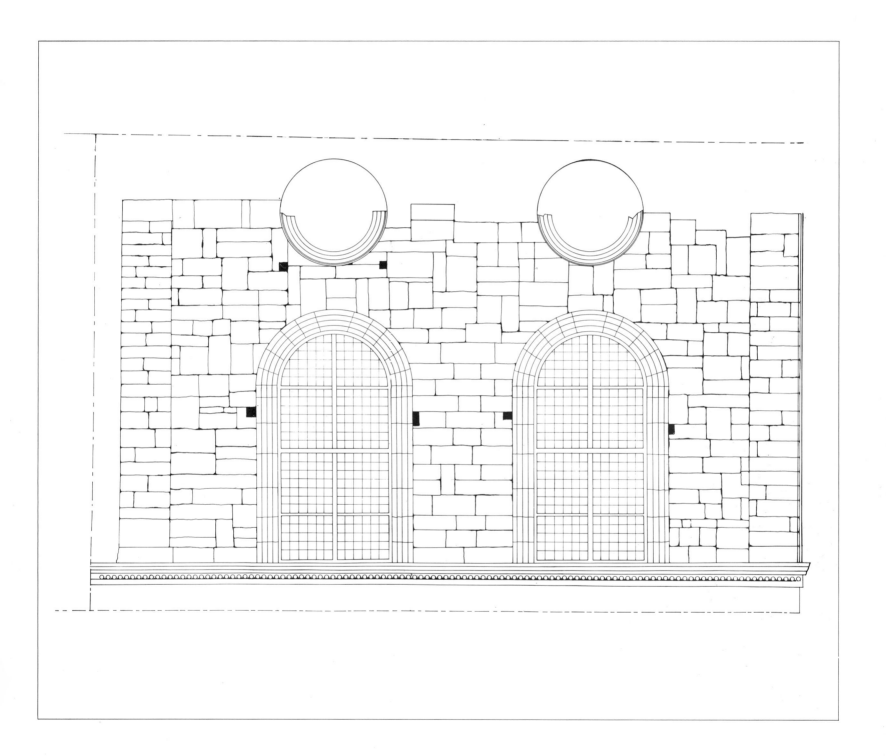

58. Plan and partial elevations of the hall in the Palazzo di Parte Guelfa. The black lines below the pilasters indicate not the floor level (shown by the door) but the top of wooden panelling or tiers of benches. It seems that the pilasters were originally gilded. (1 cm = 1.67 m; 1 in. = 13 ft 11 in.)

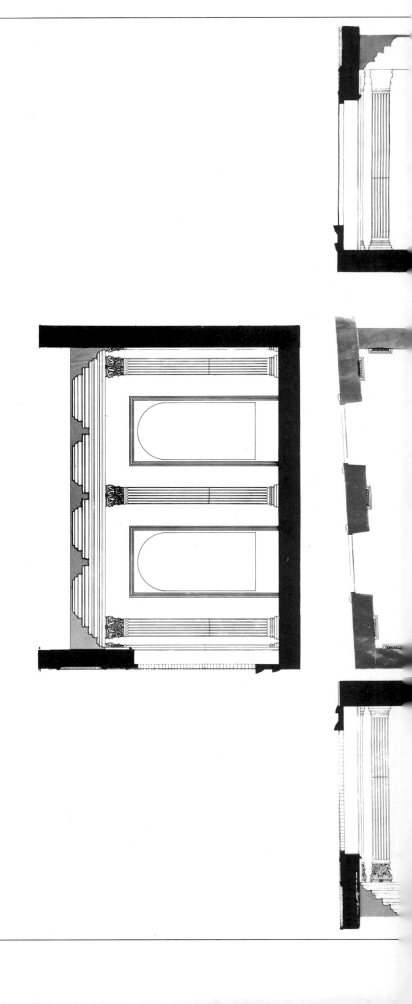

or rather the income, invested in the Monte. The major guilds would seem to have had fiscal loopholes not available to the Guelph faction. Apparently around 1442-45 a certain amount of liquid capital again became available, and work briefly resumed, but by then the activity of the Parte Guelfa was declining; their programme of freedom and civic responsibility had grown out of date and without the practical means — collective consensus — for bringing it into being.

That the work on the palace was broken off for political reasons is explicitly stated by the Biographer (f. 309r): "This edifice was left unfinished, those governing the city deeming it more expedient to take something away from the prestige of that organization than to add to it. That decision has been persisted in ever since." The "ignominy that ensues from initiating a building and then being unable to carry it through to completion" thus became a perennial shame.

Brunelleschi and Florentine private palaces

In view of his ambition to work on a large scale, to transform the city in monumental fashion, and to give it a new character through a consistent modern style of the most noble antecedents, one is tempted to credit Brunelleschi with the invention of the new type of Florentine palace that arose in the Quattrocento and which, as Ackermann has well observed, marked the definitive end of the Tuscan tradition of controlled town-planning based — as in other more strictly ruled parts of Europe — on medieval communal laws that "severely restricted the height, placement, overhangs, and general design of private houses and palaces in order to gain a uniformity that may be appreciated still in the streets of Siena. The new palace style violently disrupted communal controls to substitute an aesthetic of unrestrained individuality for one of conformity." Towering above the streets and the low houses, the new type of palace (in reality, a camouflaged fortress) raised by the Medici or the Pitti or the Strozzi family represented in a brutal but certainly frank manner the ambitions of a small and arrogant economic oligarchy competing with the guilds for the control of the state, indifferent to the city in that their income was not from local sources but from international markets and banking commissions, and eager not for military conquests but for diplomatic pacts: in short, palaces not unlike the skyscrapers of Chicago or New York whose remote ancestors they were and many of whose defects they anticipated.

Significantly, as private and not public entrepreneurs — and thus not accountable for particular political and social problems — these magnates surpassed in economic power and sometimes in prestige the community that was their home base: they had no need to persuade public officials or trade unions but could simply, as necessary, buy them off. Understandably, these palaces seldom bothered with a grandiose *salone* for assemblies but concentrated on apartments reflecting the wealth and status of the owners. Neither did the commercial and administrative organization of the families, run from above as it was and anything but unified, give rise to any architectural forms of its own.

Highly expensive, if only because of the cost of acquiring land in the city centre and on the outskirts (about five minutes' walk from the centre), the new palaces represented an imposing feat even in their designing, which was based on giant wooden models and certainly on consultation with several architects. The material used was remarkable too: their rusticated ashlar made them rather more akin than was politically advisable to the Palazzo Vecchio, which they in fact set out to rival

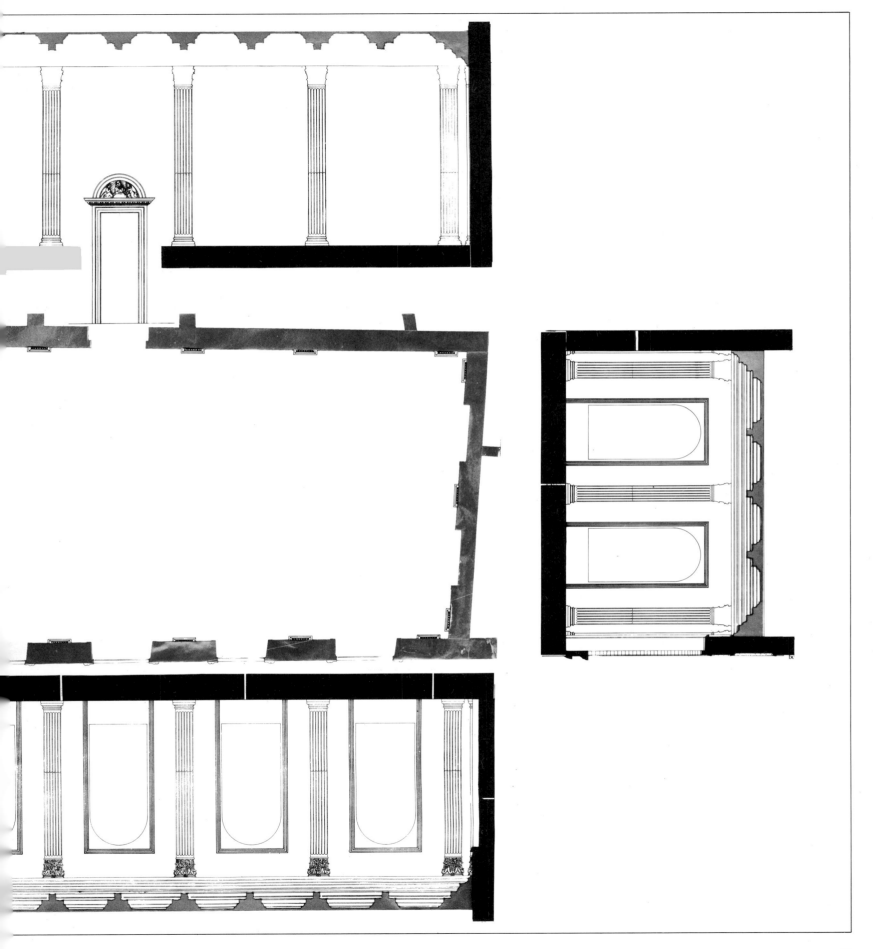

59. Conjectural reconstructions of the interior of the hall in the Palazzo di Parte Guelfa: (a) with pilasters supporting arches enclosing the oculi, as proposed by M. Salmi; (b) schematic drawing showing the volumetric relationships, and including the inner frames of the windows which may not be original; (c) without the pilasters, which were completed — and perhaps only introduced — after Brunelleschi's death; (d) with a giant order of pilasters extending up to a flat roof above the oculi. Note the lack of space for a ceiling between windows and oculi.

and which was therefore the obvious though tacit point of reference. Such stonework gives the impression of power intended to endure until kingdom come, and because it really required special skill and care it was only by gross hypocrisy that it could be justified — as it was — as involving less work and expense than the usual hewn stone.

The construction of these large palaces went along with the process of reunification of the families whose members had previously lived in separate houses, as one sees in the lists of property holdings of the Medici and Strozzi. Thus, at least as concerned housing, there was a reversal in the trend especially marked in the latter half of the Trecento towards breaking up businesses and families so as to prevent the entire firm from going under in the event of collapse or crisis in a single sector.

That reunification coincided also with the drift of the Florentine economy towards the manufacture and sale of luxury goods such as silks woven with gold threads, and also perhaps with the attempt to replace the waning political and military power of Florence with a new prestige as what we would call a "tourist centre", exploiting the many foreigners and outsiders visiting it. The new monumentality in architecture followed, and perhaps resulted from, the introduction in 1427 of the general *catasto*, the tax on movable and landed wealth, which by taking into account part of the expenditures for both private and religious constructions — which were regularly registered and scaled according to importance — and by training the public light on private wealth with severe fiscal controls, was rendering pointless the previous camouflage and false modesty when it came to building. Further, it is a verifiable fact that the new type of construction came into being only when stable conditions of military and political peace had been re-established, and therefore only in the last years of the life of Brunelleschi; also that the initiative came from a very few magnates: Cosimo de' Medici beginning in 1446, the Pazzi who did not begun their palace until 1462, the Strozzi from 1489 on. Which means that none of these monuments can go back to designs and models by Brunelleschi: Cosimo rejected his project, according to the Biographer; and the Pazzi and Strozzi must be excluded for the simple reason that the land on which their palaces were built had not yet been acquired in his time, and no one is likely to have an architect design a palace without any idea of where and, worse, when it can be built.

If anywhere, traces of his ideas can perhaps be discerned in that intermediate type of merchant's house, which appears, for example, in the backgrounds of the frescoes by Masolino and Masaccio in the Carmine and which perpetuates a medieval type but makes it more regular, with an axis marked by a central doorway and an odd number of windows and with cornices which clearly divide the storeys and also designate their different functions (traditionally commercial on the ground floor, residential for the *paterfamilias* on the first floor, domestic for the women, children and servants on the third floor), and with improvements in the courtyard and the stairways, which came to be no longer in the courtyard, open to the sky, but incorporated in the building proper. Nothing however permits us to suppose that the façades of these buildings were already decorated with simple superimposed orders, as in the Palazzo Rucellai, the earliest Florentine example, which itself seems to be a version of the Palazzo Piccolomini at Pienza, and thus perhaps not by Alberti, as has always been thought.[6]

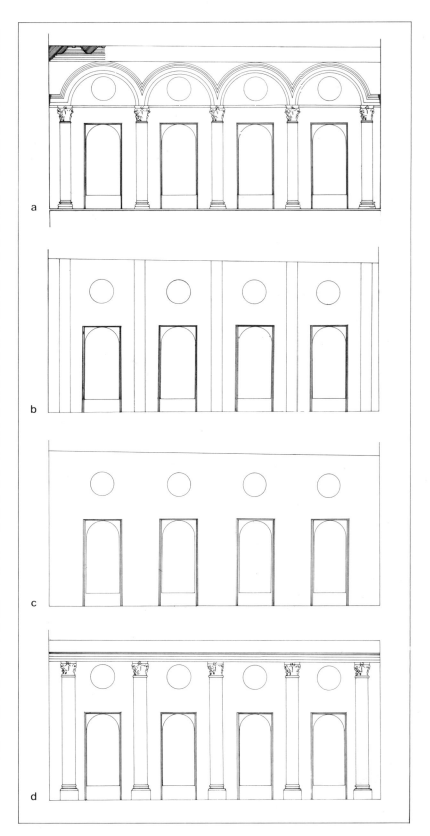

5 The Old Sacristy of S. Lorenzo

The history of the church of S. Lorenzo is so complex and discontinuous (see Chapter 9) that a separate analysis is required for its Old Sacristy — which in any case, like the later Pazzi Chapel, is a self-contained structure with an independent plan, elevation and style. It is also the building by Brunelleschi with the most intact interior. As a commission it represented a private contribution, by Giovanni d'Averardo de' Medici — Giovanni di Bicci — within a programme of public character.[1]

Recent investigation of the foundations has revolutionized traditional thinking about the building, and it is now clear that the Old Sacristy reflects three phases of building.[2] It was first projected as a cube, and the foundations laid accordingly. That the date of commencement was 1421 can be presumed from the act of foundation of the new transept on 10 August of that year; the date of completion, 1428, was found to be incised on the lantern of the dome.[3] At a later date foundations were laid for an altar chapel or *scarsella* and two flanking service rooms. The chronological relation of the upper part of these extensions to the square sacristy is uncertain, but the *scarsella* at least was built before 1434. Their construction involved alterations to the end wall of the sacristy. The building was said to be complete in 1440 and was used for a meeting then, but a poem of 1459 refers to it as still under construction.[4] Finally, some time after 1459, the entire sacristy was recased to unify it with the transept.

When newly built the little building was quite isolated. It was joined neither to the dilapidated monastery nor to the venerable church of S. Lorenzo, a famous basilica with an atrium, originally consecrated by St Ambrose himself and rebuilt in the eleventh century. Its appearance before the fifteenth-century reconstruction was completed is known from a remarkably detailed image in the Rustici Codex (Florence, Biblioteca del Seminario), where the Old Sacristy appears at the left [176]. It is likely that the Old Sacristy had its own independent entrance, connected in some way with the newly planned transept.[5]

To understand its structure, which we now find hard to separate from that of the church, we must look at it from outside, beyond the Cappella dei Principi [64]. Though the sacristy is relatively small, seen from the ground it appears remarkably tall, almost like a tower, rising steeply above a high, fairly well lit basement comprising two chambers, one covered by a barrel vault, the other (which serves as an ossuary) by a vault resting on a central pillar. After the *scarsella* and the two service rooms had been built, the exterior was distinctly articulated: the end of the chapel was clearly delineated, like a Carolingian *sacellum*, with a pitched roof terminating in a triangular pediment, while the side rooms were lower and covered by lean-to roofs resting on the end wall of the sacristy, one of which has been discovered and appears unusually well preserved [76].[6] When the sacristy was altered to tie it in with the transept and with the chapel of the Medici Saints at the end of the transept, that articulation was obliterated and the structure encircled, as we see it now, with a cornice decorated with cherubs' heads and the gridiron of St Laurence [63].

Inside the building we find similar puzzles and incongruities, due partly to the addition of the *scarsella* and service rooms, and partly to the elaborate decoration by Donatello on the end wall, with which it is known that Brunelleschi was unhappy. Let us begin by considering the main domed space, imagining away Donatello's decorations. In its initial rough state, that is without the fluted angle pilasters, the interior would have looked very simple, with a concentration on essentials, and stylistically it would have been insignificant. To place a cupola on pendentives — disregarding for a moment the solution adopted for the cupola itself — was normal in Tuscan Romanesque, and in plan and dimensions the room is very similar to the Baptistery at Padua [67].[7] One might compare this box of bare walls with the wooden models or drawings that Brunelleschi gave to his workmen, and from which, for reasons explained by the Biographer, he almost invariably omitted all ornament:

After he had had a few years' experience of many things to do with architecture, it was Filippo's nature, or rather practice, to make the models [or drawings] needed for his buildings in such a way that there was little to be seen in them regarding the symmetries [architectural accents]: he cared only to show how the main walls were to be constructed and the correspondence between particular elements, without ornaments or the design of capitals or architraves, friezes, cornices, etc., because his own weapons were turned against him and he then suffered much annoyance and recrimination, his ideas being either misunderstood or claimed by others as their own. And for that reason the model for the Temple of the Angels [S. Maria degli Angeli], done in brick, was in that manner, as was that for S. Spirito.

Within the room, however, the architect by a stroke of genius introduced a complex rhythmic system of spatial divisions, of horizontal continuity from wall to wall, of an ascending movement from floor to ceiling first vertical and then curved, of contrast and opposition [65-68]. These are the "symmetries" to which the Biographer refers, to be distinguished for their nobility from the more elementary correspondences in the design.

Is there then no relation between structure and decoration? Is one merely applied to the other? Though decoration might not appear in the designs, the walls would have to be prepared for revetment in advance, and the interior of the Old Sacristy is so consistent in its language as to make one think that every slightest detail of the masonry was foreseen in function of it. If that was not the case then we are faced, paradoxically, with an even more interesting dialectic. Structure and ornamentation would be two independent and abstract spatialities, modifying each other reciprocally and jointly developing a space which would finally prove doubly defined and rationalized. At this point once again the Biographer comes to our aid. As we have seen, he identifies the second phase with the "symmetries", the recurrent and proportional elements which at one and the same time, as I see it, divide the space and unify it, rendering it homogeneous also by setting up consistently repeated symmetrical intervals, rhythmic cross-references, and echoes.

Certainly the decoration does not coincide with the supporting elements. No doubt this marks a break (and perhaps not for the better) with the Gothic system of design, in which, at least during a notable period of experimentation, structure itself became the real ornament. The pilasters in the Old Sacristy are there to support an entablature whose own purpose is only to divide the interior into two equal horizontal zones, the division coinciding with the springing of the arch of the *scarsella*. Unquestionably the mouldings have a "realistic" function in the sense that they protect the corners and strengthen the arches of the windows and that of the *scarsella*, but in the upper area they only outline — and surely in a more tenuous way than Gothic ribs — the course of the pendentives. The sole point where structure and decoration coincide is in the umbrella vault of the dome, as unusual as it is perfect in itself as a form. The vault is also, I must stress, the most Gothic — and therefore the most "modern", i.e. contemporary — element in the building, which otherwise can be read as entirely Antique, an imitation of a

60. Side elevation, section and plan of the Old Sacristy (by Sanpaolesi; see note 13).

The side elevation shows the service rooms and *scarsella* (on the right) as encased; they originally had separate roofs.

In the section and plan the service rooms and *scarsella* are on the left. The room to the right of the *scarsella* (above, in the plan), used to store candles and liturgical furnishings, now contains a staircase; that to the left serves for preparation of the mass. The plan also shows the well, fitted into the wall in the corner between the left-hand service room, the *scarsella* and the main room of the sacristy. The section indicates the two vaulted undercrofts below the main rooms and the extensions, separated by a thicker wall (see note 2).

(Elevation, 1 cm = 4.60 m; 1 in. = 38 ft 4 in. / Section and plan, 1 cm = 3.87 m; 1 in. = 32 ft 3 in.)

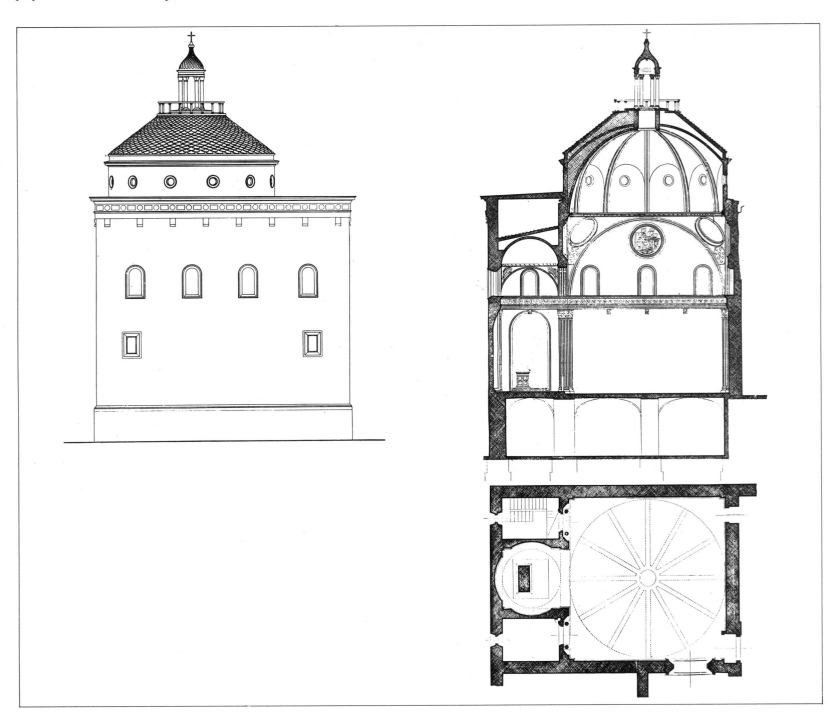

61. Axonometric projection. (1 cm = 4.31 m; 1 in. = 35 ft 11 in.)

62. Elevation, section and plan of the lantern. (The present one is entirely restored.) The Ionic capitals of the balustrade are based on those beside the windows of the Baptistery. The spirally-fluted roof is a reference to the Holy Sepulchre, and has also been compared to Islamic pinnacles (see note 14).

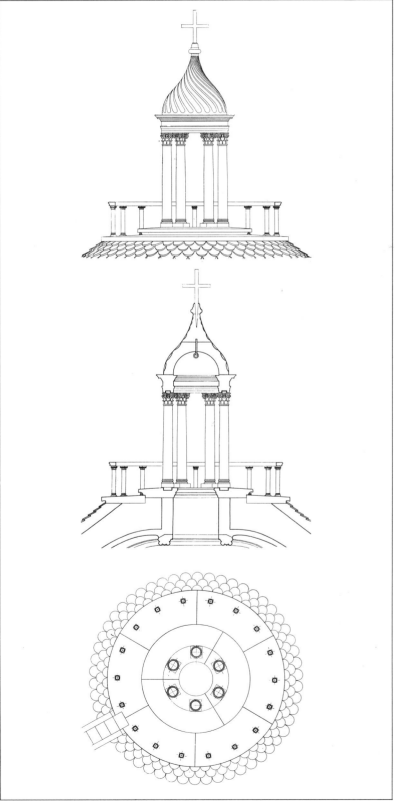

63. View of the Old Sacristy (left) and transept end above the Chapel of SS. Cosmas and Damian, showing the cornice and frieze of angel heads and gridirons − now much weathered − added, after the walls had been raised, to unify sacristy and chapel. (See also *figs. 178, 179.*)

64. End view of the Old Sacristy. The middle window, lighting the *scarsella* (*opposite*), is in its original position. Above it, a pitched roof covered the *scarsella*, while to the left and right the service rooms were covered by lean-to roofs at a lower level, running at right angles (i.e. from front to back). The side windows of the *scarsella* and the windows of the sacristy above Donatello's doors thus received light directly.

65. Interior, looking towards the *scarsella*. The doors to the service rooms, and the panels surrounding them, are by Donatello (see note 11). Of this end wall in its original state a poem of 1459 commented, "he who gazes long at it thinks himself blinded".

Late Empire *sacellum* and an archaeological exercise in the use of the Classical orders.

The cupola of the Old Sacristy was certainly built during Brunelleschi's lifetime, the date on the lantern being 1428. It is of the type known as *a creste e a vele* ("with crests and sails"), that is rib-and-web or umbrella [78]. It not only makes a splendid crown for the Sacristy, a kind of plan of the floor turned upside down which calls to mind the incommensurate beauty of the heavens, but has striking constructional features. It is built with a system of large ribs joined at the centre by a ring which supports the small lantern. It thus resembles Gothic construction, and in fact the same system is found in the apse of Milan Cathedral: one need only double that to obtain a circle (something that was done at Milan later to produce the design of the inner ceiling of the *tiburio* or lantern). Each segment is itself a vault, with a curved cell resting on the ribs as if on walls. The structure is thus quite light but extremely strong; and the webs are made even lighter and stronger by being covered, under the roof, with hollow clay pots, as in the Early Christian buildings in Ravenna.[8] Unlike a hemispherical dome, it allows the insertion of round or pointed windows in each segment, those oculi which are such an important factor in the lighting of the room.

This type of dome seems particularly well suited for covering medium-sized interiors, and may have been used in the Barbadori Chapel in S. Felicita (see Chapter 6) or the now destroyed Ridolfi Chapel in S. Jacopo sopr'Arno.[9] It is in no way related to herringbone construction. Brunelleschi may well have learnt the technique from a visit to Milan or northern Europe or Spain. It is not uncommon in Gothic buildings, and suggestions that Brunelleschi's source was Roman or Islamic seem to me unnecessary.[10]

Aside from its structural interest, Brunelleschi's umbrella dome design − particularly as seen here in the Old Sacristy − has a virtually miraculous power of co-ordination. Through its agency the various elements of the building assume a dramatic unity, in a slow but solemn and tightly focused ascending movement which can also be read in reverse as irradiation downwards.

It is certain that the Old Sacristy was Brunelleschi's very first ecclesiastical building, and in it one already finds the complex grammatical and syntactic elements of his style exhibited with the highest degree of awareness. Certain key qualities appear that were to recur throughout his work: a feeling for the interplay of geometrical forms such as the square and the circle; an interest in proportion; a preoccupation with the measurable, through the deliberate limitation of the visual field by small-scale elements; a concern with overall co-ordination, so that one is everywhere convinced of an absolute coherence between the parts and the whole, and between interior and exterior (though the latter was never fully realized); and finally a commitment to the correct use of archaeological features, both in their details and in the way they are combined. A number of other principles are also perfectly clear: the use of a restricted range of colour, here white and grey, with originally, perhaps, gilded pilasters and graffiti in the dome; the definition of the interior by means of diversified light concentrated in the upper and middle zones and disposed in a circle; the exploitation of a homogeneous shell to express isolation and enclosure as distinct from openness and variety; and finally the suggestion, through a complete and consistent system, of a calm, rational devotion, unaffected by mysticism and passionate *élan* but not renouncing symbolism.

The Old Sacristy was designed with such a feeling for mirror-image

66. Diagram of the Old Sacristy, showing the decorative system superimposed on the structure.

67. The Padua Baptistery, similar in plan and elevation to the Old Sacristy (from Bettini; see note 7).

68. The main room of the Old Sacristy, seen from the *scarsella*. The altar-table in the centre covers the tomb of the founder and his wife. Note how the present entrance door is awkwardly placed in the corner, cutting through the pilasters: the original entrance may have been where the

monument by Verrocchio now is, on the right. The upper windows were blocked when the transept and Chapel of SS. Cosmas and Damian were constructed.

High up on the right-hand wall is a small round window covered by a glazed wooden frame (not visible here). It lights a secret room (perhaps reached by an inner staircase that no longer survives), which may have been used for the safekeeping of documents and money, as in the sacristy of SS. Annunziata.

and symmetry that we scarcely notice that the entrance is now through a quite inappropriate door in a corner. (The original door may in fact have been where the Verrocchio monument now is. Keys and locks for the new door were only paid for in 1442.) A solemn ternary rhythm completely absorbs us. Nevertheless the three purely architectonic bare walls stand in contrast to the very elegant fourth side with the altar in which, prior to the intervention of Donatello, the only ornamental element was the arch. Here there is a very marked change in rhythm. The other three walls are characterized by an extraordinary equilibrium, horizontal in orientation, realized by the entablature with the frieze of cherubim which, from the start, must have been conceived in association with the other horizontal line of the wooden cupboards and benches for the chapter, a horizontalism accentuated by the marble altar-table over the marble sarcophagus of Giovanni di Bicci and his wife — the sarcophagus by Buggiano, the altar perhaps by Brunelleschi himself.

On these walls are superimposed three systems, which are progressively more decorated. The lowest is characterized only by horizontal lines, the second by the round-headed windows, the third by complete circles isolated in the wall but tangential to the circular cornice of the dome and seeming almost to hover above the viewer. On the altar wall, conversely, as in a gigantic Palladian window, the focus is vertical and concentrated in the lower part, with its very fine openwork balustrade inspired by Early Christian models and its elegant altar. The vertical emphasis is accentuated by powerful pilasters, which seem even more massive because one inevitably compares them with the abbreviated pilasters in the four corners of the room and the even more minimal ones in the *scarsella*. The insertion of a roundel in the exact centre of the triumphal arch on the end wall, touching its mouldings, confirms this vertical thrust. Unfortunately this centripetal and ascensional tension is dispersed laterally by the grandiose reliefs and monumental doors of Donatello with their pediments and Ionic columns so foreign to the architectonic system of Brunelleschi. The Biographer (f. 310v) records that Donatello came on the scene "with great haughtiness and arrogance, without asking anyone's opinion and without himself conferring with Filippo".[11]

This is perhaps the moment to examine the later additions to the original square room, to look at the character of the *scarsella*, and to see how it and Donatello's work may have modified Brunelleschi's original design.

Without being able to examine the internal structure of the upper walls it is impossible to say definitely what stage construction had reached when the *scarsella* was added, together with the lateral service rooms. We know that the cupola of the sacristy was complete in 1428, and that the *scarsella* existed by 1434. Its altar is dated 1432. That year, by the Florentine calendar, would run from March 1432 to March 1433, so that the date corroborates the attribution of the altar to Buggiano, to whom payment for "an altar" and "other works" for private patrons is recorded in Brunelleschi's tax return for 1433. It is impossible, however, to regard that as a conclusive date for the *scarsella*, since the altar may have been transferred (perhaps from the chapel of the Medici Saints) at a later date. Other attempts at dating the *scarsella* have been made on the basis of the astronomical painting on its vault, and an examination of the outer walls.[12] These studies are inconclusive, and their importance has diminished with the recent discovery of a document providing a *terminus ante quem* of 1434. It is just possible that the

continued on page 97

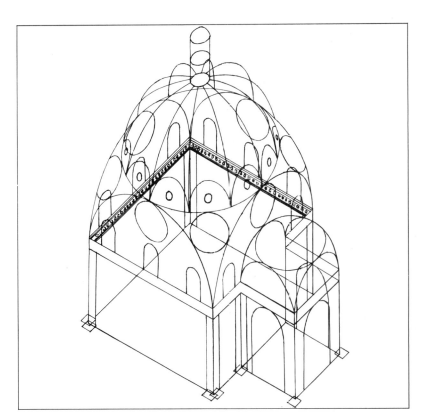

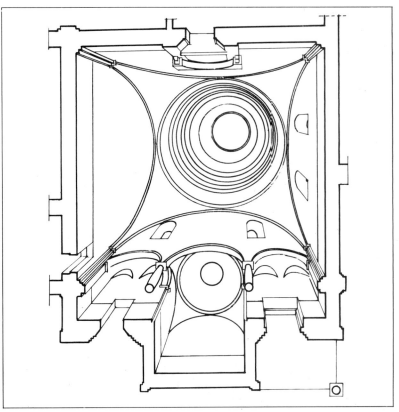

69. Looking up in the *scarsella* of the Old Sacristy.

70, 71. Details of the curved walls of the *scarsella*.

72. The rib-and-web dome of the Old Sacristy, showing the oculi in the webs. These were filled with ornamental bronze grilles and glass, paid for in 1451-53. Also visible here are the eight roundels that touch the mouldings of arches, pendentives and dome.

73. Looking up at the entrance wall [*68*] and dome of the Old Sacristy.

74. Looking up at the altar wall and dome.

75. The drum of the old Sacristy dome. The *pieta serena* frames of the oculi
have been restored.

76. Remains of the lean-to tiled roof that originally covered one of the service rooms (see note 6).

77. View inside the present roof-space, showing the dome of the *scarsella* and, on the back wall, the outline of the original pitched, tiled roof which rested directly on that dome.

78. Structural system of a rib-and-web dome (drawn by Alberto Rossi). In the Old Sacristy it is impossible to examine the space below the roof, so the model here is the Pazzi Chapel — virtually identical, though built after Brunelleschi's death.

79. Sketch of the astrological decoration on the dome of the *scarsella* (see note 11).

80. The domes over the main room and the *scarsella*. Note the difference between the apparently similar cable mouldings round their bases.

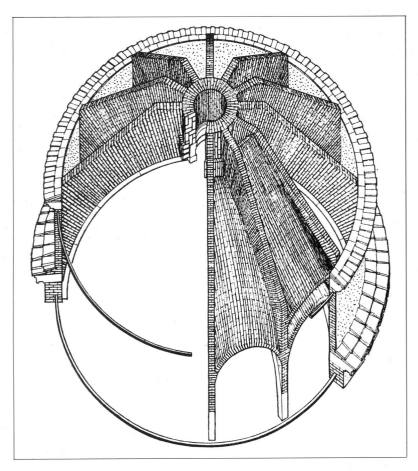

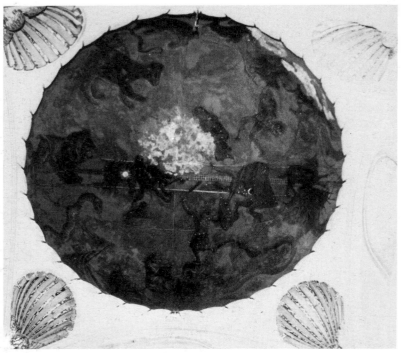

81. The entire decorative system of the dome and pendentives over the main room of the Old Sacristy.

enormous sum allocated for the funeral of Giovanni di Bicci, who died on 20 February 1429, may have included something towards acquiring more land in order to enlarge the sacristy. In that case, the square domed building would have stood to its full height before construction of the *scarsella* and side rooms began.

Various discrepancies certainly suggest that the decoration of the *scarsella* was carried out independently. The module of 2 *braccia* which, it has been suggested, governs the sacristy does not apply to the measurements of the *scarsella*, even in the form of a half-module of 1 *braccio*.[13] The decoration of the domes is slightly different: whereas the ring at the base of the large cupola shows a large smooth ovolo motif imitating something like sailcloth tightly tied, in the similar moulding around the small cupola the cloth looks as though it is creased. The architrave of the main room seems to be cut into on either side of the triunphal arch to take the architrave of the *scarsella*, whereas one might expect the latter to be cut to fit. Nevertheless, the stylistic unity is admirably maintained.

Going into the *scarsella*, we find a space which in many ways repeats the disposition of the sacristy as a whole: cupola on pendentives, large horizontal architrave, and an upper stage described in curves. It is also independent and distinctive, though clearly articulated by the mouldings that outline the three curved recesses — recesses which act like curved lenses to focus the attention of the viewer on the tiny space where the mass is celebrated. This triple-niche pattern is of key significance both structurally and symbolically. Like the spirally-fluted lantern on top of the main dome [62] it goes back to the Holy Sepulchre, and the identification is confirmed by the fact that here, as in other funerary *sacella*, the profile of the three niches is derived from a single circle.

Similar symbolic intentions may lie behind the construction of the two side rooms, of which the one on the left with well and lavabo serves for the preparation of the mass, while the one on the right is used to store liturgical furnishings.[14] After their creation and the raising of their lean-to roofs some time after 1459 an essential element was lost which must have given much more emphasis to the process of "focusing" that we have considered in the main sacristy. Originally light came in directly through all the windows in the end wall, and not only from the end window of the *scarsella*: the illumination on the other three walls was distributed in an extremely regular, widely-spaced rhythm, but on this end wall the rhythm suddenly accelerated, and light was intensified with an almost Baroque effect. This dazzling illumination, together with the rich materials of the sacristy and the Medici tomb in the centre, is celebrated in a poem written in 1459 to celebrate the visit of Pius II to S. Lorenzo (see Chapter 9), which thus provides a *terminus post quem* for the alterations.

The Biographer is decidedly uniformed about the early phases of construction of the Old Sacristy, but he does tell us what the walls left and right of the *scarsella* arch looked like, at least until after the return of Donatello from Padua: they were "addentellate" — "jagged", or keyed to receive decorative masonry — "with nothing but the opening

and the relieving arch at the top". This could be read as support for Beppe Cruciani's suggestion that the openings which now contain reliefs by Donatello were originally windows to the outside.

In any event, neither the horizontal nor the vertical triadic rhythm of the other walls is violated on the end wall and indeed it is so insistent as to confirm the dedication of the chapel to the Trinity. The cupola, radiating out into twelve segments, each lighted through its own oculus, expresses the idea of apostolic illumination — twelve pentecostal flames dominated by the broad central eye. Because of this the sacristy has all the character of a council chamber and more particularly, because of its luminosity, resembles a chapter house of the type associated with English cathedrals, though those are polygonal in plan. Another fundamental symbolic element is the insistence on the number 4, not because the ground plan is a perfect square but because the symmetry of the overall disposition and the surprising spatial function of the pendentives with roundels inserted into them impel the viewer to a continuous orientation towards the four corners of the world, as do also the roundels containing representations of the Evangelists on the four walls, whose skilful and even three-dimensional perspective creates angular penetrations within the space, an effect reinforced by the pendentive roundels with their accentuated curve.

Adding all this up we have a symbolism based on 3 that creates a movement which is both ascending and circular; we have a symbolism based on 4 which develops in the corners; and we have a vertical radiation, expanding through the ribs of the cupola with its twelve cells, and thereby relating the symbolism of 4 to that of 3.[15] This is all brought about without the slightest inconsistency or difficulty, and indeed creates a sense of equilibrium that is worthy of an Antique building. The protective and delimiting enclosure goes along with a permeability of the structure to light, which is not without accents, and is proportionally reduced in intensity, serving a symbolic purpose itself.

Apart from the symbolism, explicable theologically, and the calculated use of light resulting from a thoughtful study of optics, the impression given by the Old Sacristy arises from a particular system of architectural designing: the use of drawings of the plan, elevation and section all represented to the same scale. It is the method in everyday use today. But though documents show that an architect from Bologna in 1390 already knew how to work to scale and also how to draw an elevation from a plan and to correlate the two types of drawing on a single sheet, Brunelleschi seems to be the one who applied the method in a concentrated, revolutionary way. A key concept behind the technique is the difference between a representation of architectural space produced intuitively and with the aid of psychological suggestion, and a representation based on measurements, that is exclusively rational, methodically planned and set down on paper, such as to be easily consulted as a guide both to realizing the actual construction and to controlling the quality of its technical execution. The architect's manner of drawing, which must convey accurate explanation and information, is thus radically different from that of the painter.[16]

6 The Barbadori Chapel in S. Felicita

The church of S. Felicita, which lies on the south side of the Arno, is curiously enough the backdrop for the cruel joke played by Brunelleschi on the "Fat Carpenter" (see Chapter 16), and it may be that the commission to build a new chapel there dedicated to the Virgin Annunciate came to the architect through the good offices of the prior or some common friend. At the same time he is said to have begun a palace for the Barbadori, which was left unfinished for technical reasons or because of the exile of the patrons in 1434.[1]

The chapel — known also as the Capponi Chapel, and famous for its paintings by Pontormo — presents difficult problems to the architectural historian. Though the Biographer describes it, no documents have come to light, and some scholars have doubted the attribution to Brunelleschi. Further, the building as we see it today is no more than a poignant fragment of the fifteenth-century structure.

The Biographer tell us (f. 308r) that Brunelleschi

was assigned to make in his manner that small chapel in S. Felicita in the corner on the right as one enters by the main door, which [chapel] was a novelty at the time and very beautiful. And then too he made the marble holy water stoup on that side of the stairs of the said chapel, and all of it, chapel and stoup alike, were new and uncommonly fine and aroused admiration in all men of understanding and natural good taste.

This very novelty, of a style based on the Antique, could definitely explain certain incongruities and naïveties.

In 1487 the chapel passed to the Paganelli family and in 1525 it was acquired by the wealthy banker Ludovico di Gino Capponi, who commissioned from Pontormo the *Deposition* altarpiece, and in fresco an *Annunciation* on the end wall (inside the front wall of the church), the four Evangelists in roundels in the pendentives of the dome, and in the dome God the Father with four patriarchs.[2]

In 1589 the dome was destroyed during the creation of Vasari's long corridor linking the Pitti Palace and the Uffizi, when the chapel was used to support a loggia. Then in 1735, together with the whole church, it was remodelled in a sober classical style by Ferdinando Ruggieri, who built a new dome and refaced the walls, increasing the splay of the window between Pontormo's *Annunciation* figures.[3] The present stone cornice does not match the one depicted by Pontormo. Our only clues as to the chapel's original character are its plan, and the corner piers, capitals and altar that happily survive.

In its design the Barbadori Chapel constituted a kind of independent aedicule, with a cupola resting on walls on three sides and on a pillar on the fourth (perhaps as a demonstration of the possibility of constructing lightweight vaults supported on relatively fragile uprights), closed off by an iron or bronze grille whose attachments survive. As an architectural conceit it may derive from the loggia in which the Annunciation is traditionally depicted as taking place. It belongs to — and may indeed have created — a particular type of chapel dedicated to the Virgin, which is located either against the façade wall or at the beginning of the nave and is thus independent and isolated.[4] A famous example is the freestanding shrine in SS. Annunziata, and a similar aedicule occurs in S. Francesco at Pescia.

The contrast between this elegant classical structure and the fourteenth-century church must have been odd indeed, and did in fact strike contemporaries. The biographer says that it "aroused the admiration of all men of understanding and natural good taste", and there are striking similarities between it and two pieces of painted architecture — in the *Trinity* by Masaccio in S. Maria Novella [*101-103*] datable about

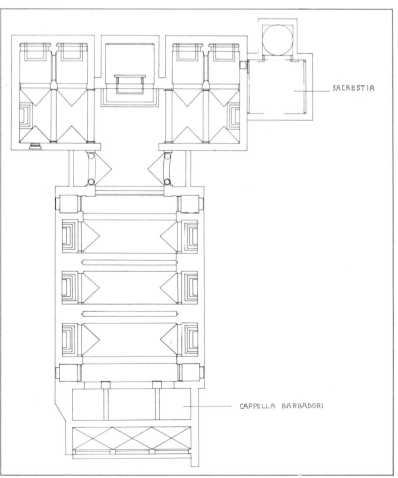

OPPOSITE

82. The church of S. Felicita, from the map of Florence by Pietro del Massaio Fiorentino [8].

83. Plan of S. Felicita: the main Quattrocento features are the Barbadori Chapel and the sacristy.

84. Plan of the Barbadori Chapel as it is now (1 cm = 58 cm; 1 in. = 4 ft 10 in.). The compound piers at the corners, indicated in solid and dotted lines, are features of Brunelleschi's original design.

85. Conjectural reconstruction of the original plan (to the same scale).

86. Elevation of the chapel as it is now, looking towards the altar (to the same scale).

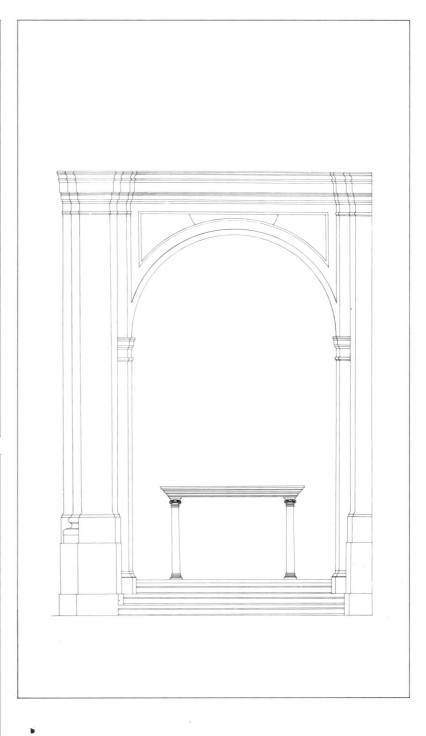

99

87. Internal elevation of the wall to the right of the altar in the Barbadori Chapel. The present vault is indicated by the heavier dark-line, the probable original dome by the semicircle above. (1 cm = 58 cm; 1 in. = 4 ft 10 in.)

88. Conjectural reconstruction of the original elevation, looking towards the altar. Unlike the reconstruction proposed in *fig. 87*, an architrave is here suggested above the Corinthian capitals of the major order. (To the same scale)

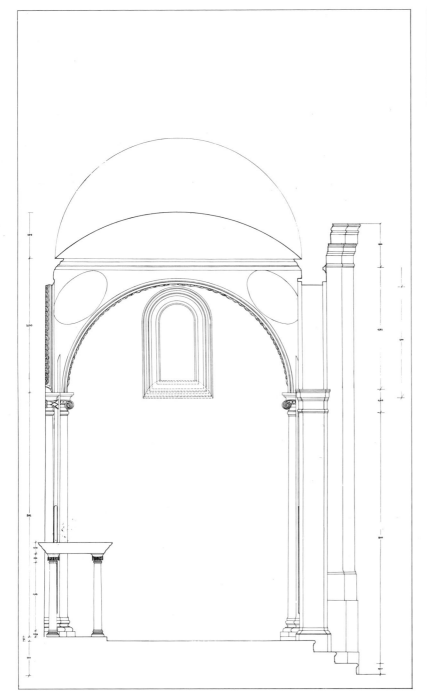

89. Conjectural reconstruction of the dome, with an architrave above the Corinthian capitals, and a window inserted in the tympanum. (1 cm = 46 cm; 1 in. = 3 ft 10 in.)

90. Conjectural reconstruction of the dome, with an architrave but no window. Though the illumination would be reduced, the overall design is more convincing. (To the same scale)

1425-28, and in an *Annunciation* at Castiglione Olona attributed to Paolo Schiavo, where it becomes an open portico.

Surviving features of the chapel are, as has been said, its plan, corner piers, capitals and altar. The plan is perfectly square, the length of the sides being about 4 m (13 ft), or about 7 *braccia*. The piers consist of half-columns attached to a square core in such a way that two adjacent half-columns frame a pilaster form reduced to a slender stone arris. The combination of column and pilaster occurs also at the end of the loggia of the Foundling Hospital [88]. There the two are simply juxtaposed, as if the architect wished to keep them independent of each other, only lessening the space between them and making their upper tori touch while partially merging the lower tori [45]. In the Barbadori Chapel, conversely, the elements are fused to make a sort of compound pier. The solution may be seen as either more mature or more traditional, i.e. Gothic, in inspiration.[5]

The capitals belong to two orders, the upper ones Corinthian, the lower ones Ionic (both with Doric bases). Two characters are thus united, according to Vitruvius's typology (IV,1), the former "slender and florid", the latter "moderated" between "severity and delicacy" and therefore particularly appropriate to Juno and Diana, goddesses noted – like the Virgin – for chastity and virtue.[6] The two orders occur also in the niche of Donatello's *St Louis*, completed about 1423.

The altar is supported on slender colonnettes with Ionic capitals of a different type, derived from those flanking the windows of the Baptistery.[7] Other furnishings included the holy water stoup mentioned by the Biographer and a mosaic with the portrait of Alessandro Barbadori, both lost in the seventeenth century.[8]

The original character of the upper part of the chapel is extremely problematical. The walls were investigated in 1938 by R. Niccoli, who observed that the reduced corner pilasters extend upward beyond the level of the Ionic capitals, only to break off unevenly at different heights. From this he concluded that Brunelleschi intended an entablature, pendentives, and a dome. Among other fragments Niccoli found a pediment and medallions decorated with a shell, painted in gold and blue.[9] The use of colour, which occurs elsewhere in the work of Brunelleschi and Alberti, must have given the chapel an appearance of lavish splendour far different from what its Classicizing elements alone would suggest.

The reconstruction here [88-90] is based on the belief that the interior and exterior of the chapel were coherently related, and that the corner pilasters would have ended in abbreviated capitals below an architrave of the same depth as the one outside. Above this there would have been the dome, perfectly round and without openings. It seems impossible for any sort of window, whether elongated or round, to have been fitted into the space between entablature and dome [89], and the resulting dim light may explain the extraordinarily luminous and brilliant colours used by Pontormo. The dome would have rested on pendentives and would have been rimmed by a stone ring, which has survived, cut down in diameter, in the present dome.[10]

In the absence of documents, and the presence of so many unclear features in the building itself, its attribution and dating (Brunelleschi or, perhaps, Buggiano? before the Old Sacristy, contemporary with it, or several years later?) remain the subject of argument and uncertainty.[11]

7 Experiments with perspective

There are several interesting links between the Barbadori Chapel and Masaccio's *Trinity* in S. Maria Novella [*103*], a painting which leads us naturally into the subject of Brunelleschi and perspective. It marks the moment when perspective was first used correctly on a monumental scale and throughout the composition, and it is generally agreed that it was Brunelleschi who was responsible — obviously only in the preparatory phase of Masaccio's cartoon. Its so-called "errors" are by no means as egregious as some have supposed. The unusual coupling of Corinthian and Ionic occurs in both the painting and the Barbadori Chapel (and in the cloister of the Foundling Hospital); and the vault of the painted *sacellum* in which the Trinity appears to stand conforms to a type of geometrical perspective invented — according to the Biographer and all other sources — by Brunelleschi (it was to serve as a model for painters of any ingenuity for the next two centuries, and was given a theoretical basis by Piero della Francesca). Finally the dates fit: true, 1425 for the Masaccio depends on late sources and circumstantial evidence, but nothing much is changed if we allow it to be somewhat later and nearer to 1428 when the artist died in Rome. The year 1425, however, has a special charm, for it was in that year that Brunelleschi was Prior of the district of S. Giovanni; on the standards and coats of arms of that district the Baptistery had to be depicted; and it was the Baptistery that Brunelleschi chose for his first experiment in perspective, a pure abstract shape, like a Neo-Platonic form, with — as one comes out of the Cathedral and sees it frontally — two oblique sides with their own vanishing points, a challenging technical complication.

Why did Brunelleschi embark on the study of perspective? The question is a large one, but it points towards another, even larger: why did Brunelleschi's experiment become the basis for a change in our whole conception of space, initiating a "way of seeing" that was to hold sway in the West right up to Impressionism — indeed, up to Cubism? (In somewhat the same way, his use of the Classical orders could be said to initiate a "way of building", a way of visualizing structure and decoration, that was to last right up to the days of steel, suspension and pre-stressed concrete techniques.)

By means of experiments sometimes involving the use of drawing, anthropologists have been able to compare the feeling for space characteristic of the West with that of numerous other cultures, both primitive and advanced, and have confirmed (what indeed the history of art already taught us) that in some the natural tendency is towards two-dimensional representation (e.g. Chinese painting and a good deal of modern art) and in others towards three-dimensional (e.g. Greek and Hellenistic sculpture, the mature Renaissance, the Baroque). Not that these are mutually exclusive. They can alternate or even co-exist. In Italy, a decisive shift from two- to three-dimensionality came with Giotto, slackened in the second half of the Trecento but regained its momentum precisely when Brunelleschi was carrying out his experiments.[1]

But what Brunelleschi did was something new. In representing, say, an architectural view, he was no longer content merely to make it convincing. He wanted a mathematical demonstration that it was correct, and he wanted the spectator to be critically aware of that demonstration. With a formula that could serve as the most apt and comprehensive definition of the Renaissance itself, the Biographer (f. 297v) observes that "from him came the rule which constitutes the foundation for everything of that sort done ever since. And his merit is much more because we do not know whether those ancient painters of hundreds of years ago, who are believed to have been good masters, ... were

acquainted with it and applied it with understanding." In other words, yet another science of the remote past is recovered: there are, after all, Roman wall-paintings with perfect geometrical perspective [*91*]. Nevertheless, "even if they did do it by rule, that is, scientifically, as he did it, for I do not call what is done without rule scientific, still anyone who could have taught him it had been dead for hundreds of years, and there are no written explanations of how to do it, or if there are no one can understand them." Classical scholarship, therefore, was not enough: the whole chain of experimentation through which the Ancients had found their way had to be re-traversed creatively.

The perspective formula or rule for which Brunelleschi was searching was in effect a corollary to something that was already well understood. He knew enough about optics to have no worries about visual angles, the relation between the apparent height of an object and the viewer's distance from it, or the laws of proportion that can be derived from that relation. He must, too, have had an interest in trigonometry, which is a form of applied optics. Lines drawn from the eye of an observer to the top of a tower and to its base form a triangle (with the tower as the third side). The closer the observer approaches the tower, the greater will be the angle subtended by it at his eye [*93*]. Some theorists were trying to establish the optimum angle for vision in such a case, but what concerned Brunelleschi in this first experiment of his was to work out how that effect of real perception could be imitated in order to bring about a perfect illusion of reality. He did this by studying the relationship between the distance of an observer from an object — the Baptistery — and the distance of an observer from a *painting* of that object. In other words, he shifted the problem from reality as perceived by an observer to the laws that *create* "reality" *for* an observer.

Let us now read the Biographer's description (f. 297v), which is admittedly not easy to follow, but is as closely argued as a geometrical theorem:

About this matter of perspective, the first thing in which he displayed it was a small panel about half a *braccio* square on which he made a picture showing the exterior of the church of S. Giovanni in Florence. And he depicted in it all that could be seen in a single view; to paint it he took up a position about three *braccia* inside the middle door of S. Maria del Fiore. The work was done with such care and accuracy and the colours of the black and white marble were so faithfully reproduced that no miniaturist ever excelled him. In the picture he included everything that the eye could take in, from the Misericordia as far as the corner and the Canto de' Pecori on one side to the column commemorating the miracles of St Zenobius as far as the Canto alla Paglia and all that could be seen beyond it on the other. And for what he had to show of the sky, that is, where the walls in the painting stand out against the open air, he used burnished silver so that the actual air and sky would be reflected in it and the clouds also, which were thus seen moving on the silver when the wind blew. Now, the painter had to select a single point from which his picture was to be viewed, a point precisely determined as regards height and depth, sideways extension and distance, in order to obviate any distortion in looking at it (because a change in the observer's position would change what his eye saw). Brunelleschi therefore made a hole in the panel on which the picture was painted; and this hole was in fact exactly at the spot on the painting where [in reality] the eye would strike on the church of S. Giovanni if one stood inside the middle door of S. Maria del Fiore, in the place where Brunelleschi had stood in order to paint the picture. On the picture side of the panel the hole was as small as a bean, but on the back it was enlarged [through the thickness of the panel] in a conical shape, like a woman's straw hat, to the diameter of a ducat or slightly more [i.e. 2.3 cm]. Now, Brunelleschi's intention was that the viewer, holding the panel close to his eye in one hand, should [turn the picture away from himself and] look [through the hole] from the back, where the hole was wider. In the other hand he should hold a flat mirror directly opposite the painting in such a manner as to see the painting reflected in it. The distance between the mirror and the other hand [holding the panel] was such that, counting small *braccia* for real *braccia* [i.e. measured in the same scale as that which obtained between the painting and the real thing], it was exactly equivalent to the distance between the church of S. Giovanni and the place where Brunelleschi was assumed to be standing when he painted it. Looking at it with all the circumstances exactly as described above — the burnished silver, the representation of the piazza, the precise point of observation — it seemed as though one were seeing [not a painting but] the real building. And I have had it in my hand and looked at it many times in my days and can testify to it.

A text, as one sees, that calls for some elucidation. Brunelleschi depicted the Baptistery and piazza, whose visual limits the Biographer specifies, as if viewed from a point 3 *braccia* (roughly 1.75 m, or 5 ft 8 in.) inside the middle doorway of the Cathedral, with the door jambs serving as a frame. The finished painting had to be looked at in a special way, through a small hole in its back and looking at its reflection in a mirror [98, 100] (a reversed image, of course). To complete the illusion, instead of a painted sky there was a reflecting surface on which, when the wind blew, one saw the clouds scurrying past. It is my hypothesis that in this way one could place or remove the mirror at will and ask the participant in the experiment whether he was looking at the Baptistery itself or a painted image. The fact that he could sometimes not be sure, was for Brunelleschi proof that his perspective theory was correct.

Summarized in this way, the difficulties of the experiment can easily be overlooked. Some of them emerge only when one tries to repeat the experiment (as a group of enthusiastic students recently did, under Giovanni Degl'Innocenti). Certain points, however, are fairly straightforward, and we may examine them in the light of the later and clearer perspective theory. In the first place, Brunelleschi's experiment is extremely artificial, even if under ideal conditions it produces a genuine *trompe l'oeil*. The eye, indeed both eyes, are reduced to a single point, the apex of the triangle or visual cone. For realistic reasons it is supposed moreover that the viewer's eyes are at a normal height above ground level, say about 1.75 m or 5 ft 8 in. or so. He must stand immobile in the axis of the doorway, at an equal distance from both lateral door jambs. The reason for this was explained (perhaps even on the basis of Brunelleschi's panel, which seems to have entered the Medici collection [2] and was no doubt often tested by artists) by Leonardo da Vinci:

If you wish to depict a thing close up with the effect given by natural things, your perspective will certainly appear wrong, with all those errors of proportion and awkward proportions one expects in a poor work, if the person viewing its perspective does not place his eye at the proper distance, height and position predetermined by you in painting your perspective. Wherefore a window should be made the size of your face, or simply a hole through which you should look at that work, and if you do this it is certain beyond doubt that your work, if well provided with shading and light, will give the effect of the real thing and you will not be able to make people believe that the things in it are painted.

The panel with a hole serving as optical focus or viewfinder corresponding to the eye indicates also that Brunelleschi was perfectly aware that all horizontal lines at right angles to the viewer converge by perspective towards a point in infinity.

Here we come to another element which at first sight seems more likely to complicate the experiment than to simplify it. This is the use of the mirror (which, by the laws governing reflection, has to be precisely half the size of the panel). The main reason for introducing the mirror seems to have been that only by this means — by making the eye look *through* the picture — could the eye be placed exactly at the vanishing point of the picture. The spot which marks the vanishing point in the picture is physically the same as that from which the eye sees both picture and reality. Since this vanishing point could not in fact be shown in the picture, as it was hidden by the large octagonal bulk of the Baptistery, it became all the more necessary to pinpoint it as precisely as possible.

This painstakingly achieved equivalence of eye and vanishing point raises an interesting possibility. One of Brunelleschi's reasons for setting up the experiment might have been to supersede the old medieval theory of optics, according to which rays emanating from the objects seen converge upon the eye. As noted above, by the use of the mirror Brunelleschi manages to make this point of convergence physically the same as the vanishing point of the perspective by placing the eye at a specific point in the picture itself. The old theory saw the picture as an open window, the rays converging from every point towards the eye; Brunelleschi's theory — which could be demonstrated either with a mirror or a geometrical drawing — reversed that idea, with perspective lines converging on a vanishing point at the furthest distance from the eye.

Another reason for introducing the mirror might have been that by reversing the image left-to-right it would confirm the exact symmetry of the perspective, though of course this is only apparent when the object depicted is, like the Baptistery, itself symmetrical.

Thus a number of reasons can be adduced to prove the usefulness, if not the indispensability, of the mirror in this experiment. The Biographer, however, does not dwell on the point but states absolutely unequivocally that the experiment consisted above all in moving the mirror forward or backward, closer to or farther from the eye, until a certain optimum position is reached which will correspond in scale — presumably according to the units on a marked-off ruler on which the mirror can slide back and forth — to the distance between the eye of the viewer and the central façade of the Baptistery.

In order to correlate (1) the distance between the mirror and the picture and (2) the distance between the observer and the object (i.e. between a point inside the Cathedral door and the Baptistery), the pictorial representation has to be to scale. Brunelleschi must have made careful measurements of the distances involved and reduced them all to a pre-established scale on his panel. Moving the mirror back and forth had the same result as altering the lens on a camera, the field becoming larger or smaller. I think it more than probable, therefore, that the aim of the device was to demonstrate that a picture had to take into account not only the relative sizes of the objects represented and their relationship to one another, but also the height above ground from which they are assumed to be viewed and the distance between them and the viewer. Only in this way can the effect of reality be recreated. In other words, the experiment showed how the relationship of objects to one another varies according to the relationship of the viewer to those objects.

The experiment has been repeated using a camera as well as the eye in conjunction with the mirror, and the accuracy of the Biographer's account has been confirmed beyond cavil.[3] The picture panel that corresponds to the real view proved to be, as he said, 1/2 *braccio* square, with the base equivalent to about 26.8 cm and the height to about 31.8 cm (slight modifications depending on variants in the height of the horizon, i.e. the eye-height of the observer), and the visual angle of about 45 degrees. Under those conditions the picture came out exactly in the scale of 1:75, the real distance of the viewer from the Baptistery was 60 *braccia*, and that between the picture and the mirror was perfectly in scale at slightly less than 1 *braccio* (35 cm).

Any attempt to reconstruct Brunelleschi's train of thought in devising this experiment runs into two kinds of difficulty. The first has to do with the interpretation of the documentary sources, and is almost resolved; the second is exclusively theoretical, and presents many problems. Various treatises existed, going back to Classical writers like Euclid and Ptolemy, in which these problems were expounded, and many of them were illustrated with diagrams. So far Brunelleschi's own sources have been deduced only in the most general terms. We need to know far more exactly which method he used in each case, and how he carried out his measurements in practice.

The choice of the piazza of the Baptistery as the object of his first experiment in perspective is particularly problematical. Though it is possible to reconstruct the layout of the piazza in Brunelleschi's time, it is still hard to understand how the perspective of the buildings surrounding it could be seen converging upon the central vanishing point as the Biographer says it did. But presumably, on the basis of the present alignments, the effect of foreshortening was obvious enough. Now, the orthogonal lines of the roofs and of the sills converging on the vanishing point (though that was hidden by the Baptistery) were, as we have seen, made — by the use of the mirror — to coincide with the visual rays converging on the eye of anyone looking through the peephole of the panel. From the central door of the Cathedral the Baptistery is seen as a solid with three faces visible, the side ones foreshortening rapidly towards the left and right because of the obliquity of their ground plan. To us, with our modern approach to perspective, it seems natural to suppose that at least one of Brunelleschi's aims was to demonstrate how these two oblique walls, produced to infinity, would form converging visual lines leading from the picture plane to two equidistant lateral vanishing points. Anyone with pencil, paper and ruler can confirm that the sides of the piazza would converge upon one point in the middle, and the two oblique walls upon two others — all on the same horizontal line. By a corollary that was also perhaps known already to Tuscan artists of the time, if the horizontal lines of the oblique walls are produced not away from but towards the viewer, they will meet not at a point but at a vertical axial line, like the spine of a fish. Both solutions are possible. And the way that the building is divided into a chequerboard of blacks and whites must have been helpful in measuring distances and proportions with the eye alone.

In spite of Brunelleschi's apparent mastery of this construction involving two lateral vanishing points (by means of which an oblique object such as a cube can be shown in correct foreshortening) — a technique that any child can understand today — it is a fact that very few examples of it exist in Italian fifteenth-century painting. Oblique bodies are still extremely rare. Construction by means of lateral vanishing points is almost exclusively used for depicting areas of pavement or ceiling in foreshortening, as with Paolo Uccello.

Indeed, in painting after Brunelleschi one finds no sign of the solution of problems of perspective that his experimental city view certainly suggested. Nor can it as yet be said just how much he anticipated the

approach to perspective of the next century, which was nevertheless aware of its debts to him. This is true even of Piero della Francesca, who was singularly timid in his use of lateral construction points.

The great problem lay elsewhere. There are two co-ordinated phenomena involved in perspective vision. One is the convergence towards a single vanishing point of the parallel lines at right angles to us or to the surface of the painting (thus, the standard example of the railway tracks); the other is the decrease in size of the various elements with increasing distance (as in a row of telegraph poles).

The simplest way to grasp this problem is to draw a series of elements parallel to a picture surface: cross-ties of a railway or, even better, the horizontal sides of a regularly square-tiled pavement whose longitudinal sides converge towards the central vanishing point. If those small pavement squares are identical, one sees that with increasing distance the transverse parallels become increasingly close to each other. If such squares are applied with the same regularity to walls (e.g. majolica tiles), their height likewise would appear to diminish regularly. The mathematical formula for this graduation is highly complex, nor is there any simple way to apply it. Thus artists were obliged to proceed by geometrical construction to obtain these results rather than calculating them algebraically (impossible at that time and difficult even today). Only within a generation of our own day did Erwin Panofsky, following suggestions put forward by Raoul Butt, manage to deduce the correct formula after centuries of inexact approximations. The solutions arrived at by Quattrocento artists were as inexact as the rest, though Giotto and Ambrogio Lorenzetti, surprisingly, got nearer to the truth.

Yet there is a very simple trick that resolves everything and in the best possible way, because it is not theoretical but practical. The first clear explanation of it is given by Serlio (Book II), and I therefore reproduce his account, but there is no doubt that Serlio derived it from earlier practice. I give first his own words and then a paraphrase in modern terminology:

It happens often that the architect wishes to show both the exterior and the interior of an edifice, for which purpose a sure and quick device is to have first rendered the entire ground-plan of the edifice in perspective and then actually to draw out from it those parts of the elevation that he wishes to be seen, leaving the other parts not visible, letting the plan stand for the rest of the edifice; whence, wishing to put a plan into perspective, to do it well it will be necessary first to make that plan in proper form and after that to foreshorten it in perspective. In order to make this method of construction easier to understand, I have drawn out an entirely transparent building [94]. Once you have become familiar with this, it should be possible to do much more complex drawings in perspective. My example does not require much explanation, since it is very simple and straightforward. Thus, I have drawn in proper form all the lines that lead from the corners and sides of the walls on the ground-plan. The bottom line signifies the closer limit of the area you wish to represent in foreshortening and the upper line the horizon. Above this I have chosen where to put a line that stands for the farthest limit of the square and have closed the foreshortened square there. I have then drawn the two diagonal lines, and these will show where to place all the columns and pilasters in such a manner that you cannot possibly fail.

In other words: draw a square (a plan) and subdivide it vertically into, say, five equal parts; then extend the vertical lines to a vanishing point (a). What we have now is a perspective representation of the plan. Now mark the line that is going to be the top of the picture (ef). Draw a diagonal line on the plan (cb), then carry the same diagonal line into the perspective (be). Where it intersects the verticals both on the plan and on the perspective, draw horizontals (refer now to the drawing on the

91. Schematic analysis of a rare example of Antique perspective painting, a fresco on the south wall of the Room of the Masks, in a house of the Augustine period on the Palatine Hill in Rome (by Gioseffi).

92. Conjectural diagrammatic reconstruction of Brunelleschi's small panel depicting in perspective the Piazza della Signoria in Florence (by Gioseffi). The construction seems to have involved a number of vanishing points, but how they would have been worked out in practice is not known.

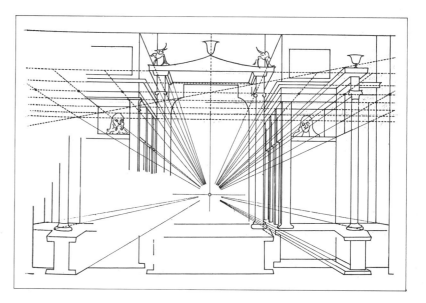

right in *94*). Whereas the horizontals on the plan are at equal intervals, those on the perspective will be closer and closer together.

In depicting the Baptistery one can furthermore turn the picture on one side and, treating the frontal façade as plan, put the two oblique flanks into foreshortening and thereby render the whole with very great precision. Indeed, the frontal façade will almost automatically give all the information needed.

Since Brunelleschi had to start by measuring the piazza, taking all the measurements of the Baptistery, calculating the visual field, and establishing exactly the position of the viewer, he already had in hand the elements for laying out in plan and thence reducing to perspective the buildings on the piazza and in particular the octagon of the Baptistery.

Various sources, none going directly back to Brunelleschi, inform us about this method which so far we have deduced only from his general situation and from the conditions in which he realized his perspective panel. In one of his three manuscript treatises, which seems to have been fairly widely known, Piero della Francesca gives the geometrical explanation of the method by the use of Euclidean rules and shows how to foreshorten quite complex bodies beginning with a ground plan. The lateral vanishing point — recognized as a point as far from the centre of the perspective composition as the viewer is assumed to be from the surface of the picture — is used only for verification, and is actually useful in distinguishing whether the geometrical form rendered in foreshortening is an oblong or a square. Piero's treatise, *De prospectiva pingendi*, is an exercise of extreme subtlety, containing instructions on how to resolve exceptional problems which were actually dealt with in painting only rarely in the Quattrocento, and then only late; which seems to indicate that the ability to use this method in constructing perspectives was not very widespread.

As we have seen, a simplified form of this method was still being presented by Serlio in the sixteenth century, and I quote him the more readily because he himself indicates that this system of working from a squared plan to foreshortening was peculiar to architects.

Two other methods are possible, though both are more complex and require numerous operations, whereas the one described above is quick as well as accurate. One [*95a*] is to simulate the foreshortening of a pavement or ceiling directly, without going through the process of drawing out the plan and using that as a guide. Here one treats the area to be depicted as a triangle, the base of which is divided into exactly equal parts (C, H, I, D); from these points draw lines converging on a central vanishing point (A) and others converging on a lateral vanishing point (B). Where the diagonals intersect with the orthogonal lines (E, F, G) draw horizontals, which turn out to be proportioned in the same way as in the first method. The disadvantage here is that only relatively simple geometrical shapes can be rendered in perspective; it would certainly not work for complex architecture which requires an elaborate plan often squared up to a very large scale.

A third method was proposed by Alberti [*95b*]. It is identical with the second method except that the lines that converge upon the lateral vanishing point intersect a vertical (RB) and mark on it where the intervals of the horizontals should fall. The same system can be applied to a ground plan with the advantage of being able to make the line of intersection fall wherever desired [*96*]. In a sense this third method unites the advantages of the others, but we have no schemes exemplifying it in the Quattrocento for complex architectural constructions.

This is as far as we can go with any certainty. Beyond this we shall be lost in a maze of conjecture, and I therefore forebear discussion of Brunelleschi's second perspective panel, which showed the Palazzo Vecchio and Piazza della Signoria [92]. In it the Palazzo was shown as a parallelepiped, with two oblique sides of different design, so that the picture must have been drawn with a much broader visual angle and must inevitably have used lateral vanishing points.

With this we have come full circle to Masaccio's *Trinity* [103] in S. Maria Novella, a church for which Brunelleschi produced at least two works, the wooden Crucifix already discussed (Chapter 2) and a pulpit that stood precisely in front of Masaccio's painting (Chapter 13). As the sole surviving work connected at least chronologically with this initial experimentation with perspective, the fresco offers a key to the methods used. Its execution moreover was extremely carefully calculated, and the painter used all possible means to ensure accurate transfer of the cartoon (on which the perspective was worked out) to the wall, among them separate cartoons of details, perforation of the full-size cartoon which was then dusted with powdered charcoal in the usual way, grids incised into the plaster, circles traced with compasses, and so on [105]. Despite this, Joseph Polzer and the group of students working with Giovanni Degl'Innocenti were able to demonstrate a number of small discrepancies between the perfect realization and the actual execution. This emerged particularly in the painting of the illusionistic vault, but the deviations are so small that they did not prevent the group from working out the precise point from which the fresco was designed to be viewed — a distance of 8.942 m (29 ft 4 in.) (rather than the 5.80 m or 19 ft arrived at by Sanpaolesi) — as well as the desired eye-level, which turns out to be 1.74 or 1.75 m (5 ft 8 1/2 or 8 7/8 in.) above the pavement [101]. The system used to lay out the perspective of the vault corresponds to that given theoretical formulation later by Piero della Francesca, Serlio and others. The complexity of the chamber depicted quite certainly required that it should first be drawn in both ground plan [102] and elevation, and in all probability by an architect.[4]

Brunelleschi's introduction of a scientific method of perspective is a fascinating and far from exhausted subject. I began this chapter by stressing its cultural and even anthropological significance. Masaccio's *Trinity* can serve as a paradigm to show its effect upon religious art. That art, in order to represent the relationship between God and man, has to be both hierarchical and hieratic. In the Middle Ages the distinction was signalled by size — divine persons were simply made larger than human ones, so that for instance Christ's spiritual superiority is immediately obvious. But as soon as perspective, with its attendant spatial realism, is introduced, serious difficulties begin to arise. Figures closer to the viewer are required to be larger than those further away. In this case the chief character would become the skeleton in the immediate foreground, while Christ is set well back into the painted chapel. How is this problem to be solved? Masaccio was obliged to reformulate the sacred event in quite different terms. For the old hierarchy of dimensions he substitutes a new hierarchy of levels, of complexities and of symbolic values. The skeleton — an impressive *memento mori*, highly dramatic in its effect — is actually reduced in size, from what would be natural to a modest 1.60 m (5 ft 3 in.). From this statement of the physical human condition, transitory and wasted away in the decomposed cadaver, we ascend to the civic and ancestral nobility of the two donors; thence to the dignity of sainthood in Mary and John; then to Christ raised aloft on the cross, and still further back the Dove of the Holy Spirit, and finally God the Father. The theological superiority of the upper part of the fresco is signalled by the rich ornamentation of the vault and the purplish arch. In a Trecento picture the progression from a physical to a spiritual level would have been intuited almost at a glance; but here — a foretaste of the true Quattrocento — the viewer is obliged to give it his conscious attention. Moreover the abandonment of symbolic attributes and distinctions, in order to express the devotional structure purely through the location of the persons within the architectural framework, was to have a further very important consequence: a condition of virtual parity between the human and the divine that was almost without precedent in any earlier art.

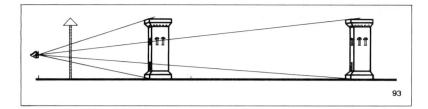

93. Variation in the apparent height of a tower relative to its distance from the viewer, calculated according to the angle subtended by the tower at the eye. The effect is measured on the vertical arrow which stands for the picture-plane.

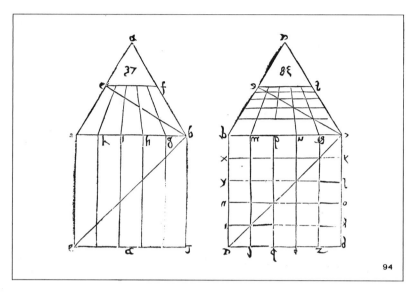

94. Foreshortening of a ground plan by means of diagonals (from Serlio). In the first diagram the lines perpendicular to the viewer are made to converge towards the vanishing point (a), and a diagonal line is established for the square in both plan and foreshortening.

In the second figure, horizontal lines are added where the diagonal intersects the verticals, forming small squares; lines drawn at the corresponding points of the foreshortened square permit the rendering of the squares in correct proportion.

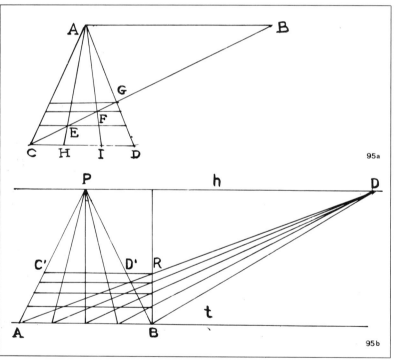

95a. Foreshortening of a plan by the use of a lateral construction point (the vanishing point). While this has the advantage of not requiring the laying out of a plan, obviously it cannot serve for complex constructions which would inevitably require a detailed plan.

95b. Construction by means of a lateral vanishing point according to the method suggested by Alberti. The lines converging on point D (in foreshortening) are those which, in plan, converge on P; the graduated succession of the horizontals in foreshortening is determined by the points where these lines intersect the vertical R-B.

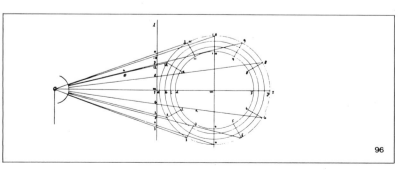

96. Foreshortening of a ground plan, in this case circular, by cutting across the lines converging on a vanishing point with a transverse line. The system is similar to that in *fig. 95b*, except that the object is viewed frontally.

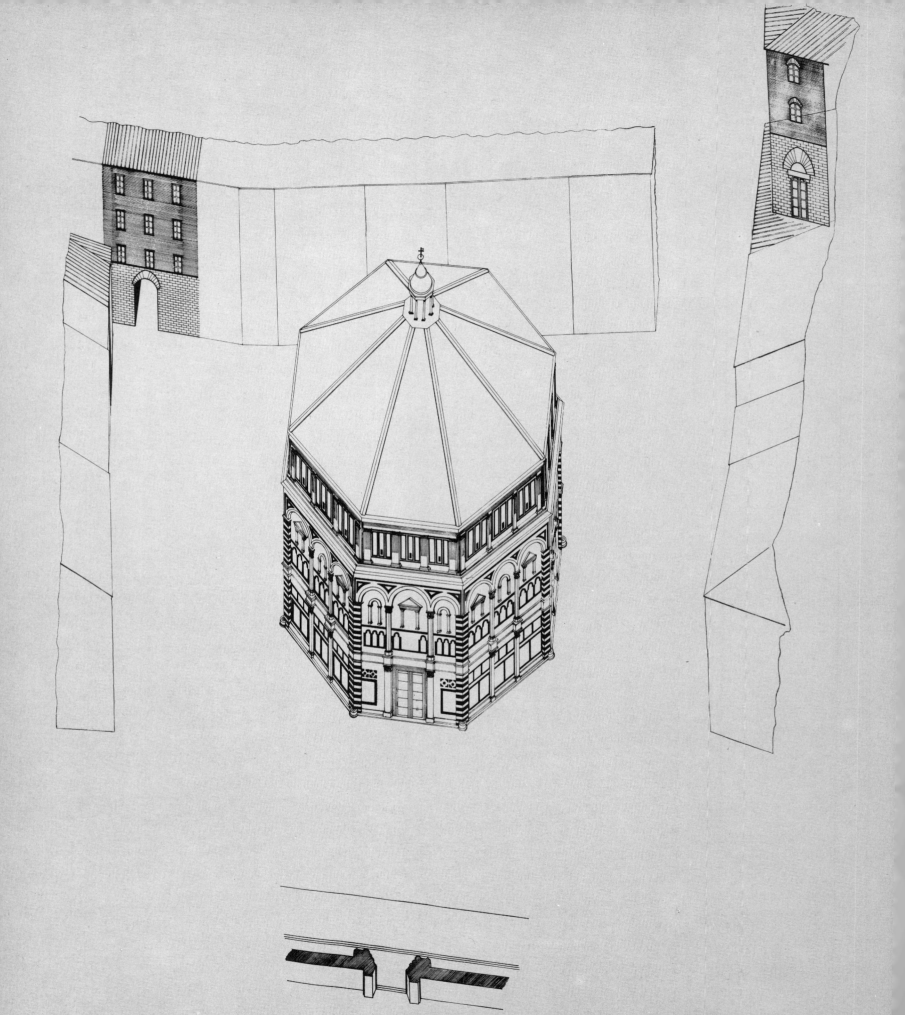

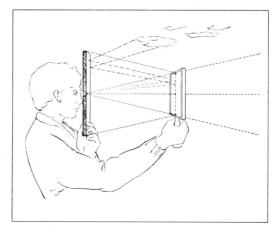

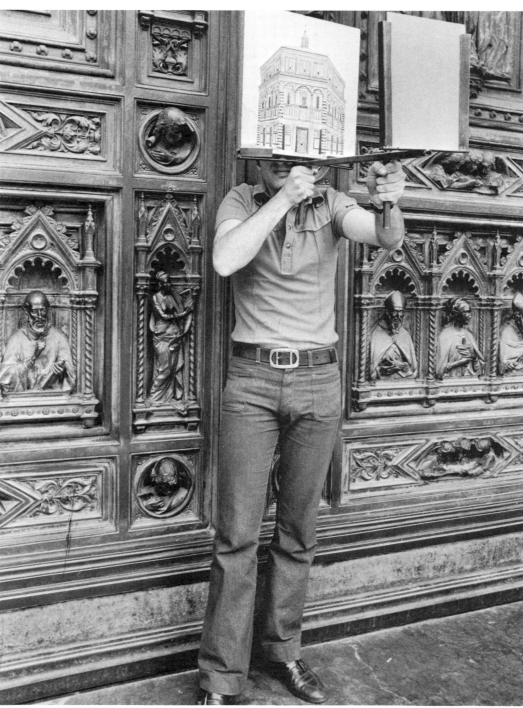

97. Schematic representation of the Baptistery and the piazza around it with the viewing point situated in the middle of the central door of the Cathedral (by Parronchi).

To establish the perspective according to the method in *fig. 94*, based on the ground plan, would have required no fewer than thirteen operations: (1) measurement of the entire piazza; (2) measurement of the distance point; (3) construction of a panel of the correct format; (4) subdivision of the panel, probably by means of small checkerboard squares, into the small units of measurement known as *piccoli palmi*, i.e. a scale of 1:75; (5) preparation of a proportionate squared-up ground plan of the piazza and Baptistery; (6) preparation of an elevation drawing of the Baptistery based on precise vertical measurements; (7) construction of the foreshortening of the visible oblique sides of the Baptistery by working from the plan, with the verticals in the correct graduated succession; (8) construction of their vanishing points in relation to the horizontal elements; (9) construction of the foreshortening of the sides of the piazza; (10) reversal of everything thus constructed from left to right, and execution of the final painting; (11) perforation of a hole corresponding to the vanishing point of the lines; (12) construction or provision of a flat mirror of the right size (half that of the painting); and finally (13) contrivance of a movable connection between mirror and painting by means of a marked-off ruler or measuring rod. The resulting illusion is thus the product of a very high level of technical expertise. (1 cm = 4.53 m; 1 in. = 37 ft 9 in.)

98. Diagram of the optical instrument used by Brunelleschi to render the Baptistery in perspective. The painting is on the left, the mirror on the right. The "sky" area in the painting is of a polished material that would reflect real clouds.

99, 100. Brunelleschi's experiment reconstructed. The upper picture shows the viewer looking through the hole in the painting at its reflection, with the actual Baptistery beyond. The lower picture shows the apparatus; the viewing hole (in the part of the painting showing the Baptistery door) coincides with the vanishing point of the perspective on the horizon, hidden in reality by the Baptistery.

The viewer is shown here in front of the central door of the Cathedral: Brunelleschi intended him to stand some 2 m (6 ft 7 in.) inside, and at the level of the old floor, lower than at present.

101. Diagram showing the position from which Masaccio's fresco of *The Trinity* in S. Maria Novella [*103*] was intended to be viewed, at a distance of 6.12 m (20 ft 1 in.). The exactness with which this can be calculated is due to the extremely precise way in which the vault in the painting is foreshortened [*107*].

102. Ground plan of the chapel depicted in Masaccio's fresco.

103. Masaccio: *The Trinity*, fresco in S. Maria Novella, Florence. (Many areas of the fresco have been completed by restoration: compare *fig. 105*.)

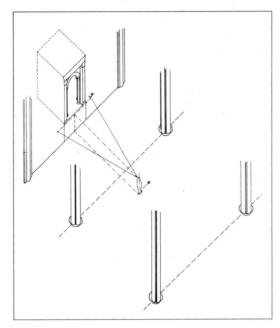

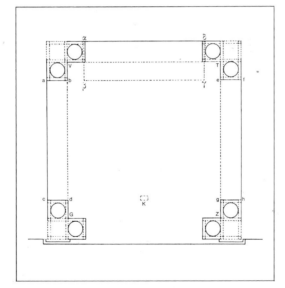

Renaissance methods of perspective construction by Giovanni Degl'Innocenti

To represent architecture on a flat surface, Quattrocento artists had several methods at their disposal, some using optical instruments, others geometrical procedures.

The simplest optical instrument is the mirror, known to have been used by Flemish artists for the depiction of interiors. The mirror must be clamped rigidly to an easel or other support 1.70 m (5 ft 6 7/8 in.) high. The artist then looks through a fixed viewfinder, and paints directly on to the mirror the basic lines of his subject, or at least the main reference points. A pane of transparent glass was sometimes substituted for the mirror, since the reflection of the artist's own face and hand made it difficult for him to look and paint at the same time. Leonardo describes this method thus: "You should have a pane of glass as large as a royal half-folio, and fix it firmly before your eyes, that is, between your eye and the thing you wish to depict, and then you take up a position with the eye at 2/3 *braccio* from the glass, fix your own head with some device so that you cannot move it, shut or cover one eye, and with the brush or pencil or chalk draw on the glass what you see beyond it, and then polish it down with sandpaper and dust it off over [transfer it to] good paper and paint it as you wish."

We drew the Baptistery in this way, using both mirror and glass. Renaissance paints, according to Cennini's formulas, adhered perfectly to glass when used with the correct binding medium (milk of figs). When glass rather than mirror is used, the drawing is not only much easier to do but much more precise. It is reasonable to suspect that curved mirrors were used only as a kind of wide-angle lens to encompass a very large scene that would exceed the normal angle of vision; it would have been very difficult to paint on them.

The *velo*, a network of string used to subdivide the scene into a grid of small squares, gives almost the same result as the pane of glass, but the image cannot be transferred directly, and there is more room for error in the perspective.

However, we can be certain that for his experiment Brunelleschi used neither mirror, glass, nor grid. Filarete, a quite reliable source (who in fact gives us the earliest correct diagrams of perspective), writes: "Lippo di ser Brunelleschi of Florence founded the procedure of working out this method [of perspective], in which there was truly something ingenious, subtle, and beautiful; by rational procedures he constructed what you see when you look in a mirror": Brunelleschi deduced by reason — by geometrical demonstration — what is normally caught by a reflecting surface. Filarete, writing decades before the Biographer, is already commenting on Brunelleschi's formula of rational construction rather than mere copying. Thus the mirror, as

used by Brunelleschi, served only for confirmation and not as the means of executing a view.

As regards optical instruments, it has recently been suggested that Brunelleschi may have used an astrolabe, a plumb-line, and a mason's level (at the time, dependent simply on a plumb) to find the exact position of the points of the Baptistery that he wished to depict in exact scale on his perspective panel.

If one uses either the pane of glass or the astrolabe, and takes up the position specifically indicated by the Biographer, the resulting panel would work out to be a square of about 1/2 *braccio*, i.e. 1:75, whereas using a mirror it would be only half as wide.

The other system – the "rational procedure" – was used in almost all Quattrocento paintings involving elaborate architecture as a setting or background. It called for a series of complex preparatory steps and, to all practical purposes, was much like the modern system of projection by means of ground plan, elevation, and sometimes section for every building depicted. We tried out this principle as well, using not only our observations of the piazza as it is today but also what is known of Florence as it was in the past: as a result, we detected many inaccuracies in the conjectural reconstructions made by previous historians.

One way of constructing perspective rationally on the basis of ground plan is by using a simple diagonal [94]; a very extensive investigation during seminars over three years showed this to have been the method most commonly used. Another is by means of a lateral vanishing point [95a] (or two vanishing points if the building, like the Baptistery, has oblique sides), from which lines are drawn that are either taken all the way to the base line or, a third technique, stop at an arbitrary line [95b, line R-B]. The first and second methods give the same results, but the third differs slightly, and was found in none of the Quattrocento painted perspective analysed by our students.

Since Brunelleschi's panel of the Baptistery does not survive, we cannot say which method of construction he used, but our experiments indicate that he could have used all three.

104. The architectural organization of Masaccio's *Trinity*, without the figures.

105. Diagram of the *Trinity* fresco showing the sections painted day by day, together with the tracing grid and geometrical devices used by Masaccio and his assistants in transferring the cartoon to the wall. (In this drawing, by the Istituto del Restauro of the Soprintendenza in Florence, missing areas which had to be restored are shown in grey: compare *fig. 103.*)

106. Entrance arch of the chapel depicted in Masaccio's *Trinity*. The design shows similarities with the Barbadori Chapel [88] and the Cardini Chapel in S. Francesco at Pescia [108]. (1 cm = 25 cm; 1 in. = 2 ft 1 in.)

107. Perspective reconstruction of the vault in the fresco, drawn according to the method suggested by Piero della Francesca, which may be that used by Masaccio. (1 cm = 44 cm; 1 in. = 2 ft 9 in.)

108. Cardini Chapel in S. Francesco, Pescia, completed in 1451, and attributed to Buggiano.

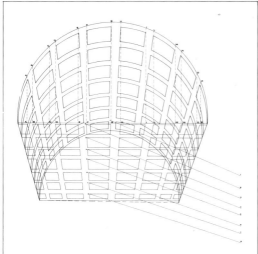

8 The dome of S. Maria del Fiore

The dome of the Cathedral of S. Maria del Fiore stands apart from all Brunelleschi's other works.[1] In some respects it can be adequately discussed only in the context of the great Gothic cathedrals, since only there can one find significant terms of comparison. Paradoxically, here, more than in any other of his undertakings, his choices were conditioned by decisions previously taken by other men and by factors over which he had no control, but his solution was original and unforeseen.

The idea of covering the crossing of Florence Cathedral with a single huge dome goes back to at least 1357.[2] Its form and dimensions were settled in 1367, and were thereafter regarded as sacrosanct.[3] Up to the end of the fourteenth century it was assumed that a gigantic scaffolding would have to be built inside the church to support the centering for the dome.[4] The problem of the centering continued to be one of the main preoccupations of those responsible for the work, but indeed the whole project was almost unprecedented in scale and difficulty. It was to be one of the largest domes in the Western world — roughly equal to the Pantheon and far larger than the dome of Hagia Sophia (which is a little over two-thirds the size of the Pantheon). It was, moreover, to renounce all those forms of external buttressing used by Byzantine and perfected by Gothic architects, and to concentrate all the lines of stress within the building itself, without even transverse tie-rods. The solution to the problem was to lie in the use of a double shell, and it is beyond question that the basic models were the baptisteries of Florence and Pisa, both of which have double shells.[5] In the event, Brunelleschi also solved the problem of the centering. In Alberti's words, the dome "was made without any recourse to trussing or a great quantity of timber", that is, without fixed centering or wooden supporting scaffolding during its construction. Its weight has been estimated by Prager and Scaglia as over 25,000 tons, excluding the lantern.[6]

Just how early Brunelleschi became connected with the work at the Cathedral is not known with certainty. As far back as 1409 he may have advised on the round windows in the drum on which the dome was to be raised. The following year, as we read in the published documents, he was paid 10 *soldi* — virtually nothing — for "a bushelful of bricks" loaned to the Cathedral Opera, a quantity not sufficient for a small model but perhaps serving for samples of a special type of brick. The only other known connection concerns a project for sculpture in 1415 to be done together with Donatello and for which he obtained an advance which, however, he was asked to repay in 1416 for default. Only in 1417, on 19 May, did he receive a sizeable payment — 10 florins, an amount equivalent to what he would receive for a year's work designing the Foundling Hospital. This was "for his labour in making designs and for exerting himself for the Opera in the matter of the main dome", a task we know to have concerned the problem of the scaffolding or centering for the huge dome.

This document happens also to be only the second one (the first relates to the advice he gave in 1412 on the façade of Prato Cathedral) that refers to Brunelleschi explicitly as an architect; curiously, the Biographer has nothing to say about it. The following year, by an adjudication of 31 August 1418, those "designs" were translated into a large brick model whose construction was diligently watched by delegates of the master masons of the Opera in order to check on its feasibility or otherwise.

This model, as we shall see, seems to have been Brunelleschi's trump card, for it apparently won him the victory, though it was a victory that had to be shared with Ghiberti.[7]

What, then, was the situation facing Brunelleschi when he took over, and what were the problems that he had to solve? As we have seen, the breadth, height and curvature of the dome had already been decided in 1367, presumably by a committee of eight masters and painters who, among other things, called for a gigantic drum, with a height of almost 10 m (33 ft), to be built between the crossing and the dome. The construction did in fact respect this ordinance, which was guaranteed by the vow imposed on the builders that "the dome is to be 72 *braccia* across, the height of the dome from the vault to the ground 144 *braccia*". In modern measurements this means 41.976 m (182 1/2 ft) in diameter and 83.95 m (309 1/3 ft) from the apex to the ground. The diameter as measured in 1941 was virtually that (41.98 m), but the height calculated from the photogrammetric measurements of 1969 was 86.66 or 86.79 m, denoting a difference of about 3 m (9 ft 10 in.) between stipulated and actual height. This difference is due entirely to the further raising of the drum in 1420, to allow room for a circular gallery around the outside.

The height of the dome from the ground was thus, by a very simple type of proportion, to be double its diameter. If one considers that the apsed ends of the choir and transepts were also to measure 72 *braccia*, it is clear that the intention (discounting subsequent modifications to the drum) was to superimpose an imaginary cube, into which the dome would fit, on the other cubes of the base. There was moreover an intentional reference to the diameter of the Pantheon, which is 42.70 m (140 ft 1 in.) — an explicit statement that the Cathedral of Florence was to rival the great monument of Rome. Since the dome was to be octagonal, it would be constructed according to geometrical principles. As Braunfels has shown, the basis was a circle with a diameter of 78 *braccia*, which involved working with fractions or recurring decimals. Perhaps for this reason, the sides of the octagon as built vary between 16.40 and 17.42 m (53 ft 9 3/4 in. and 57 ft 2 in.) — a serious drawback when it came to actually constructing the walls.

Apart from geometrical considerations, there was a symbolic intent, at least in the choice of the height. According to Revelation (21:17) the wall girdling the celestial city measures "an hundred and forty and four cubits", which is why that measurement is found in at least thirteen Early Christian and Byzantine churches. In the exedrae around the base of the Florentine dome there is the further symbol of the shell, a decorative element of the Temple according to biblical prophecies; and in fact the Cathedral itself with its aisles unroofed was to do duty as the Temple of Jerusalem in a painting now in Philadelphia (Johnson Collection), which is attributed to the School of Masaccio or, currently, to Francesco d'Antonio. But the dominant symbolism of the dome is the exclusively Marian theme of the crown: in the earliest documents the dome was referred to allusively as the "garland". Compare the strikingly similar canopy in the form of a dome on a drum over the Madonna and Child on the exterior of the church of Orsanmichele [110].[8]

Once the model for the dome was approved and the solution for the centering was found, the problems that remained were wholly technical, and these can be divided into various groups: those connected with establishing correct measurements — an endless and extremely difficult task; the provision of special scaffolding for the workers and of serviceable machinery for hoisting, especially when the vault would begin to close in and the scaffolding would have to be entirely suspended on the inside from the structure as it was actually being built; and the solution of various problems of statics that arose to ensure stability. The latter

109. The Cathedral as depicted in Pietro del Massaio Fiorentino's map of Florence [8].

110. Tabernacle of the Physicians and Apothecaries' Guild at Orsanmichele (Via Lamberti façade), attributed to Simone Talenti. This baldacchino over a figure of the Virgin takes the form of a dome on a drum, and shows clearly the symbolic identification of a dome with a crown.

had necessarily to be largely based on practical experience, since no specific theory so far existed (that had to wait until the eighteenth century), though obviously ideas could be drawn from other fields such as geometry, the writings of Archimedes, shipbuilding, even carpentry and barrel making (see below, note 27).

But the realization of the dome involved more than solving technical difficulties. It was a masterpiece of administrative organization, and the fact that it exists at all makes it a symbol of the power of the Arte della Lana, the Wool Guild, responsible for it.

The attitude of the Florentines is perfectly clear. It was based on a strong sense of, and respect for, the traditions of the past. What had been decided on in 1367 was held to be subject to no modification whatever, and each new *capomaestro* had to swear to abide by it. Instead of resorting to foreign consultants (even if only to reject disdainfully whatever they might suggest, as happened at Milan) the Florentines relied solely, or almost so, on their fellow-citizens, stimulating them in every manner to pool their ideas. Here tradition and parochial pride or even chauvinism (*campanilismo* in Florence, where Giotto's belltower sets the note) were proudly linked, however much such an attitude was at odds with the city's international-minded approach to business and truly world-wide market capacity. Thus at one and the same time there was narrow exclusiveness and eager stimulation. Everything was done to encourage the citizenry to formulate hypotheses, discuss them, test them out in models, discuss them all over again in small and large assemblies, co-ordinate them into a serviceable final proposal, and finally designate the persons to carry it through (always in the service of an already established programme). A model for the scaffolding had been presented by Matteaccio di Leonardo prior to 4 August 1418, but would seem to have been rejected outright, for on 19 August a public competition was launched. This permitted everyone, without regard for any of the limitations imposed by the individual guilds, to submit models or designs for the centering, scaffolding or construction machinery at any time during the month of September, with a closing date extended first to 12 October, then to 22 October, and finally to 12 December. Contestants were promised that they could present their ideas and problems to a friendly and trustworthy audience (" et bene et gratiose audietur") and receive compensation for any work done and, in the case of acceptance, a reward of a full 200 florins.

As we have seen, Brunelleschi had already been paid in 1417 for his collaboration in working out certain technical problems of the dome. Now, before 22 October, he submitted to the adjudicators a small-scale model realized in masonry. One of his workers had begun to be paid as early as 1 September, which tells us that he must have settled on his project between 19 August (when the competition was launched) and 30 August, since on the following day a commission of four Operai was named to observe and check on its construction. Brunelleschi was not without rivals: at least seven masters, some from "foreign places" like Pisa and Siena, submitted models. Among the numerous participants one is known to have come up only with a model for a windlass.

To go by the published documents, Brunelleschi seems to have been given special consideration when it came to examining for feasibility. His model was under observation during its construction, but this seems to have been intended only to demonstrate a new masonry technique; and no doubt for this reason he was called on later to make a wooden model concentrating on the gallery round the dome and the lantern. Subsequently he made a wooden model (paid for on 11 and 12 August

115

111. Andrea di Buonaiuto (Andrea da Firenze): *The Church Militant*, fresco in the Spanish Chapel of S. Maria Novella, Florence, *c.* 1366-68. The Cathedral appears here as it was envisaged before Brunelleschi's time, with a higher nave and a drumless dome.

1419) for the lantern as well, evidently to answer various questions to do with style, and with this he made a brave show, having it gilded and topped off with a tiny banner bearing the lily of Florence. Almost certainly this was not a wooden model of the dome itself, since that existed already, having been made in 1417 (and approved on 21 May of that year) by the carpenters Andrea di Giovanni and Manno di Benincasa, perhaps with the advice of Maestro Giovanni dell'Abaco.

The four Operai had received their final payment on 19-23 December 1418, so by the close of that year the Opera already had a good general idea of what to expect. The following year was devoted to working out details, and the documents for that period show few names of architects and artists.

Late in 1419, however, an important administrative change took place. On 15 November four eminent citizens were elected, among them Simone di Filippo of the Strozzi family, "pro constructione cupule" — "to build the dome" — and charged with arriving at a final decision. Filippo, together with Nanni di Banco and Donatello, presented another model in masonry for which he was partially paid on 29 December 1419, and which was presumably the one that won him the commission together with Ghiberti. Ghiberti seems to have done very little in the way of practical experimenting: for his models he had made use of workmen for a mere 16 working days, as against the 89 1/2 required by Brunelleschi. On 16 April 1420 the committee examined all the material, drawings, models, samples, and so on, and recommended the official appointment of Brunelleschi and Ghiberti together with Battista d'Antonio, a man who already held a high position in the Opera. However, because Ghiberti was paid 300 *lire* for the work done on his model and Battista d'Antonio received 180 as a regular *capomaestro* for the Opera, while Brunelleschi got a mere 30 *lire* and 15 *soldi* for his model of the lantern and the gallery around the dome, one can deduce that at that point, at least in the matter of the designs, the hierarchy of payments for models corresponded to the tasks actually assigned. When Brunelleschi came to the fore, it was doubtless because of the technical innovations, first in the method of building without centering — put to the test in his model of 1418 whose construction was followed step by step by a commission of technicians — and then in the contrivance of machinery to hoist the building materials to the dizzying heights where the work went on.

Highly specific norms for the dome were arrived at which thereafter were modified only in minor details, and these were set down in 1420 in a document that has survived in versions that are almost identical but extremely difficult to interpret because of the terminology used.[9]

In March 1422 the original document was supplemented by a second resolution,[10] and in January 1426 by a third.[11] Committees to supervise the work were regularly elected. That of 1423 included a Rucellai and that of 1426 a Barbadori, both families at one time or another patrons of Brunelleschi.

What were the extent and the limits of Brunelleschi's authority? It is known beyond doubt that there was dramatic tension between him, the other members of the committee, and the authorities presiding over the building of the dome. Despite this, the way in which the work was administered was singularly different — more of a group effort — from the procedure in other church undertakings, even those that were yet more grandiose and involved yet more people.[12] It corresponds, in fact, to the basic approach of the public government in Florence which was rigorously oligarchic but based on assemblies, public bodies in which a

continued on page 122

112. Florence, seen from the Bellosguardo hill to the south. The dome of the Cathedral dominates the scene: its scale proclaims its political importance (and the economic power of the guild that commissioned it, the Arte della Lana), and also the immense difficulty of such a building project, even in the form envisaged in the fourteenth century [111].

113. The drum and dome seen from the campanile. The whole composition is so confident and consistent that some writers have attributed the bold and inspired design of the drum to Brunelleschi as well.

119

114. Looking from the dome of the Cathedral over the city of Florence: a foreshortened view of one side of the dome, photographed from the level of the second exterior gallery. The relationship with the city directly below the gallery is highly dramatic: the houses and palaces appear completely out of scale, not only because of the height (something already known to Gothic architects) but also because of the compact dimensions and the bulk of the huge terracotta tiles.

115. The dome from the city: seen from Via dei Servi the "magnificent and swelling" dome (in the Biographer's words) almost seems designed to close an axial vista. But from any point in the city it overwhelms everything around it, making even the campanile look small.

121

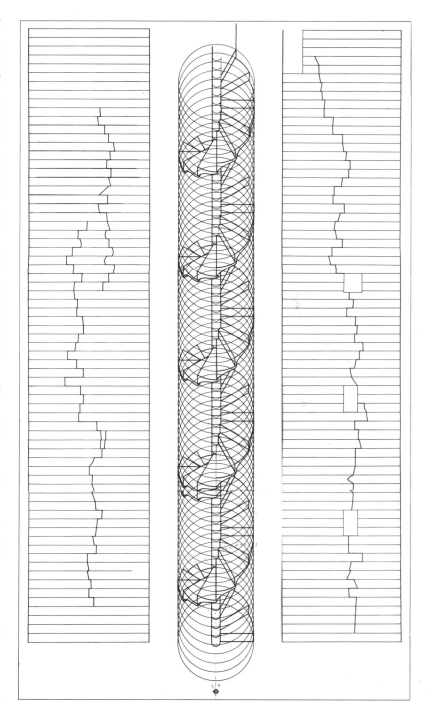

Brunelleschi too had his part and his say. Comparing this with the lot of Giovanni Pisano and what he himself wrote in the pathetic and touching epigraph on his pulpit in the cathedral of Pisa, I think one cannot agree with Heydenreich when he says of Brunelleschi that "by actively defending and carrying out his own, personally conceived design in the face of the Duomo building commission, he was also defending, perhaps for the first time in history, the standpoint of the solely responsible architect against the anonymous authority represented by the Operai." [13] For one thing, that collegial authority was in no way anonymous, and it acted on decisions taken prudently and with full awareness of what was involved; for another, Brunelleschi sought always to demonstrate that what he was doing did not violate those decisions but, on the contrary, realized them fully, with due economy and with technical improvements. Moreover, at least in some instances, the compromises suggested from above seem to have resulted in an improvement and not a worsening of Brunelleschi's project: see the deliberations concerning the exedrae and the lantern.

Only in a second phase, and then because he had so fully proved himself, was his right to authority confirmed and a position of definite leadership granted him. But this gives no grounds for a general judgment on the earlier situation. Indeed, in the findings presented here there seems to be at least partial confirmation of the thesis put forward by Sanpaolesi in 1936, which at the time aroused a general outcry, that at the start there was an intimate collaboration between Ghiberti and Brunelleschi (to whom, now, must be added the master mason of the Opera del Duomo, Battista d'Antonio, whose role was even more important in practical matters).[14]

Whatever the nature and extent of the collaboration, clearly the chief characteristics of the upper third of the dome, where Brunelleschi had a freer hand, beginning with the system of access by means of stairs in the middle of each of its segments, are visibly different from those of the earlier parts.[15]

Work on the dome lasted from 1420 to 1436. We know the dates for the beginning and end exactly. On 7 August 1420, a barrel of red wine and a *fiasco* of Trebbiano (a good white wine from the Romagna, evidently reserved for the architect and his close collaborators), along with baskets of melons, were sent up the spiral staircase of the drum, or lifted with machines. The year 1430 was engraved upon the plaster at the height of the upper circular walk. And on 30 August 1436, the whole enterprise was brought to a triumphant conclusion when 72 *lire*, 12 *soldi* and 6 *denari* were appropriated

for divers expenditures... made by order of the Opera to the trumpeters and pipers who played; and bread and wine and meat and fruit and cheese and macaroni and other things to give to the masters and ministers of the Opera, and to the canons and priests of the church, for the festivity and benediction... and to give and present them to the Bishop of Fiesole who went up into the dome to bless it.

Already during the winter Pope Eugenius IV had sent a golden rose, and before the work was entirely finished, being himself present in Florence, had re-consecrated the basilica on the feast of the Annunciation in the month of March. A not very well known description by Giannozzo Manetti gives us an idea of the unusual pomp: a wooden gangway a thousand paces long, raised above the ground and lined with poles bedecked with flowers and perfumed herbs, led to the Cathedral which, both inside and outside, was the setting for a magnificent display of heraldic, civic and pontifical pageantry. The main altar, erected in the centre of the vast interior, overflowed with reliquaries and fine liturgical

117a. Cross-section at the level of the level of the holes made for scaffolding beams, 53.85 m (176 ft 8 in.) from the ground. The holes (visible in *fig. 119*) are about 1 *braccio* (*c.*59 cm, or 2 ft) square; they originally ran through the drum but are now only about 3 m (10 ft) deep, so they could serve only for the interior.

Resting on this level, at the base of the dome, is a ring of stone blocks about 3 m (10 ft) high, which are joined together by lead strips in special grooves. At intervals, this ring is pierced by passageways [*149*]. Of the segments numbered here, 1 is above the nave, while 4, above the Loggia del Grillo, is the one specially measured and studied for this book.

117b. Conjectural reconstruction of the working platform constructed inside the dome, supported on beams inserted into the holes in the drum [*136*]. (1 cm = 5.36 m; 1 in. = 44 ft 10 in.)

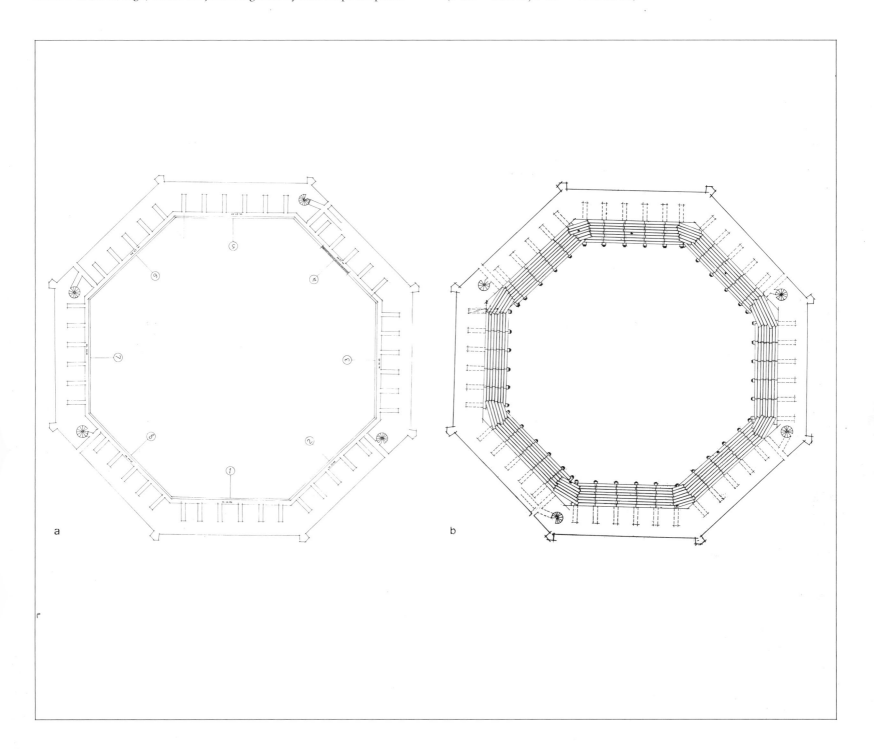

a

b

objects from the goldsmiths' workshops. The interminable varicoloured procession entered the church — the boys were clad in green or red and there was a crescendo of status, splendour and richness from the lay nobility of famous lords like Sigismondo Malatesta to the supreme dignitary of all, the Pope in person — and finally, when Eugenius had climbed the steps to the altar, the chorus burst forth in a splendid motet by Guillaume Dufay.[16]

Technical problems and solutions

The enormous dimensions of the building made it difficult to take reliable measurements with measured cords stretched from one side to the other of the empty space of the drum: elasticity and tendency to sag introduce considerable imprecision, as has been proven experimentally. Those dimensions also made it impossible to raise a giant wooden pole that would serve as an optical sighting point at the centre.

The key to the whole enterprise was the precise calculation and measurement, first of the base of the dome and then of each layer as it rose in a gradually narrowing sequence, according to a rule for the curvature of the shells known as the "acute fifth" (see below). In the event it was managed with a few minor errors but on the whole with remarkable accuracy, as photogrammetry has shown. Giovanni Battista Gelli (1498-1563) tells us that in order to work out the horizontal measurements, Brunelleschi had a large area of the river bank levelled off along the Arno below Florence, and drew on it, full-size, the plan of the dome, perhaps at various levels — probably at the levels of the stone chains or circular galleries, but certainly at points related to the successive upward shifts of his scaffolding and platforms [146].

For the elevation and curvature we fortunately have a unique drawing by Giovanni di Gherardo da Prato, who was assistant and deputy for Ghiberti from 1420 to 1426, which shows how the "acute fifth" ("misura del quinto acuto negli angoli"), established as the norm for the curvature, was constructed geometrically [141-143]. In this method (known already to Villard de Honnecourt) the diameter of a semicircle is divided into five equal parts and the farthest point from the segment under construction is used as pivot for the compass still set at the same radius as used for the semicircle, in this case the corners of the octagon.[17] To check if the segment under construction was in fact following that curve, triangulation with cords could be carried out, though this required correcting errors resulting from flexions in the cords with instruments specifically devised for that purpose. It may however have been safer to use wooden centering or temporary frames, which are in fact mentioned in the documents. According to the official instruction, once a certain height was reached the giant ribs at the corners were to be built as in Gothic cathedrals before building the infilling webs, but it seems that this was not done. The preparation of the required materials called for special precision since those elements had to fit like pieces of a jigsaw puzzle, and we know that Brunelleschi used all sorts of materials to make models to show what he wanted (even *rape grosse*, a sort of large turnip!). The stone chains [135], similarly, had to have their components specially shaped.

Alberti, who is the richest source of glosses on Brunelleschi's architecture, explains in *De re aedificatoria* how a dome may be constructed without centering:

The spherical vault [on a circular plan], unique among vaults, does not require centering because it is composed not only of arches but of superimposed rings; and you cannot imagine just how much those two elements turn out to be

continued on page 130

124

119. View down from the base of the lantern showing the octagonal drum pierced by oculi and framed by the second and third internal galleries. Below is the first internal gallery, running across the piers. At the bottom, left of centre, is the high altar, with the chancel behind it; in the central pier is the entrance to a former sacristy; on the right, the right arm of the transept. The dome segment in the centre, above the Loggia del Grillo, is the one specially studied.

120. The junction of two segments of the dome at the level of the third internal gallery.

121. The meeting between the dome and the drum with its large round windows, seen from the third internal gallery.

122. A *stella*, or star of pulleys worked by a winch, in use at the Tempio Malatestiano, Rimini. Miniature by Giovanni da Fano, in the *Hesperis* of Basinio (Oxford, Bodleian Library, Canon. Class. Lat. 81, f. 137r).
123, 124. Two drawings of a medium-duty hoist used on the ground or on scaffolding, showing details of a gear system that would maximize force. From the *Zibaldone* of Buonaccorso Ghiberti (Florence, Biblioteca Nazionale Centrale, MS. BR 228, ff. 102, 103).

Brunelleschi's fame owes as much to his inventions of machinery as to his architecture. He introduced several innovations derived from clockmaking, such as overdrive transmission (to facilitate winding the extremely long and heavy hopes used in hoisting) and changeable gears (allowing rapid reversal of direction or change in speed). From documentary evidence we can even work out the number of teeth on the cogwheels, and the machines' approximate capacity.

interconnected, in countless junctions both at right angles and at other angles, so that wherever one places a stone in the vault one finds that the stone belongs to many arches and rings. And once the rings have been built one above the other, and the arches in the same manner, even supposing that the construction might wish to collapse one simply cannot see in what part it could even begin to do so, especially because the stones all gravitate with equal weight and force towards a single centre. ... In constructing a dome it seems to me much preferable to follow the same procedure as that used in bonding the stones of a wall to one another, interlocking each ring with the one above and below it, and similarly each arch with the one to its left and right. This is especially to be recommended when one does not have a sufficient quantity of pit-sand at one's disposal [to make cement], or where the structure is going to be exposed to coastal gales or southerly winds. [ed. Orlandi and Portoghesi, Book III, p. 244]

The arch or the vault erected using centering must be constructed rapidly and without ever interrupting the work; in one built without centering, on the other hand, work must stop for a while after almost every course [of stones or bricks], in order to give the materials used time to set and to avoid having the parts added last, when the preceding ones were still unsteady, come apart and collapse.

Even a polygonal dome, like that of S. Maria del Fiore,

can be erected without centering. ... Once one or more rings of stone have been put in position, when the mortar has set it will be useful to fasten to them light ties and braces that will support what centering is needed to hold the rings then built up above the preceding ones for the height of a few feet until they in their turn have dried; then, when those have set hard, that supporting centering can be moved up a certain number of rows in order to complete the next higher zone of the vault, and so on until the work is finished. [ibid., p. 246]

To construct his octagonal dome without centering Brunelleschi had to transform it into a circle both geometrically and structurally. It is probably to this operation that Alberti alluded when he said that a dome "a padiglione" on a polygonal plan can be built without centering on condition that "in its thickness a spherical vault is inserted ... In that case, however, there must be an extremely solid and an extremely close linkage between the weaker and the stronger parts." The simplest method would be to construct a circle inside the brickwork octagon by means of a series of stone or metal chains. But this is impossible here because neither shell is thick enough to accommodate a perfect circle. Only the ceilings of the passageways can possibly serve as active, continuous rings (see the deliberation of January 1426 (note 11), 2). What Brunelleschi could do, though, was to adopt an octagonal form with rounded angles, which seems to be the case with the second and third chains, according to the observations of Mainstone.[18] The low horizontal arches ("arcarecci") serve as a circular chain for the outer shell, and it is probable that bricks at an angle of 135 degrees were placed inside the gigantic spurs which give their support to the dome — spurs which, paradoxically, during the actual construction had to be themselves supported by the two shells. Since the aim was, in a certain sense, to carry out an operation exactly opposite to the squaring of a circle, the use of oblique vertical sections of masonry, incorporating bricks placed on end vertically in a herringbone pattern, had the effect of further subdividing the octagon [173, 282]. The static function of the herringbone system was affirmed (against contrary opinion) by Mainstone, who has now been joined in that view by P.A. Rossi.[19]

Examination of the masonry shows that as the dome rose the number of horizontal "rings" or parallel layers laid in one operation grew progressively less, proving that the builders waited for the mortar of one

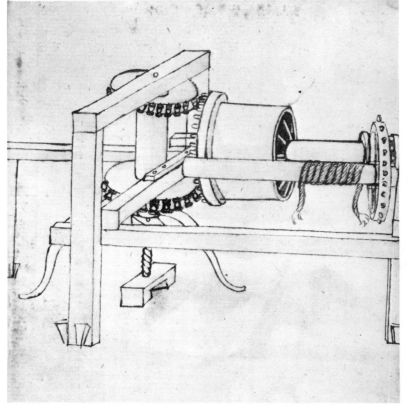

continued on page 138

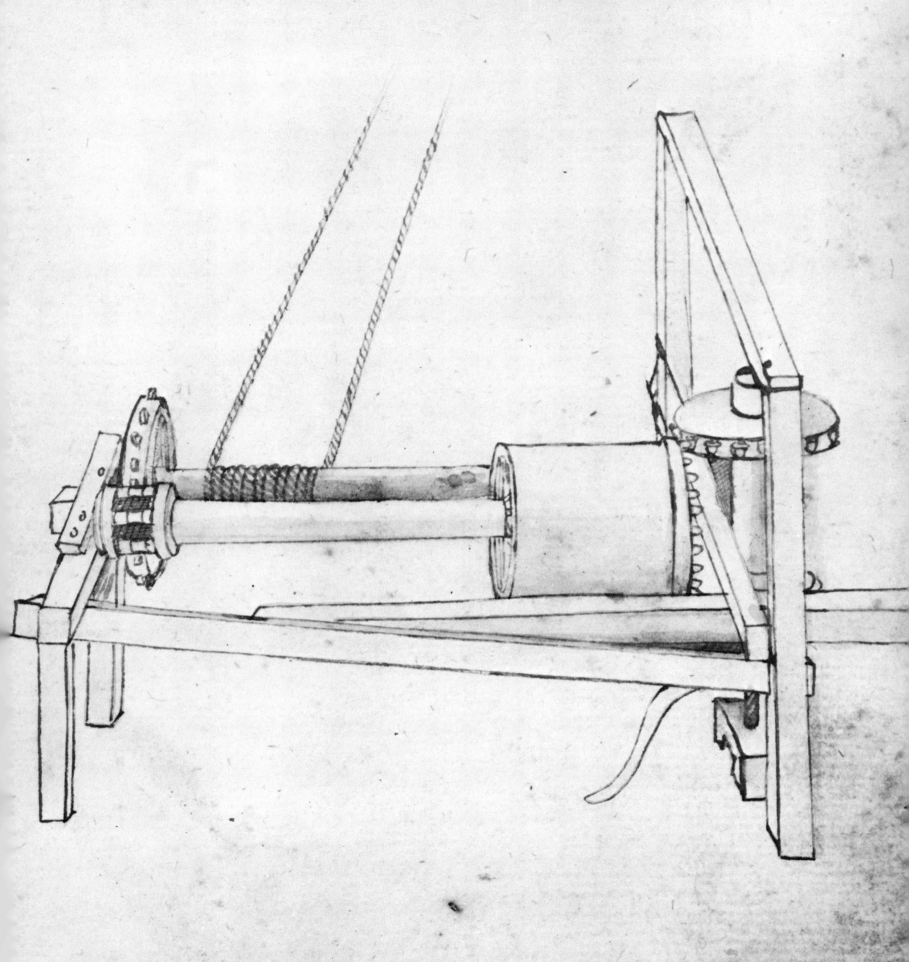

125. Model of a heavy-duty hoist used on the ground and worked by animals. They always go around in the same direction, but by moving the vertical gear drum from right to left the direction of the ropes lifting the weights can be reversed.

126. Model of a medium-duty hoist for rapid lifting. The ropes seen hanging here would have run up to the top of a *stella* or a scaffolding platform.

127. Machine driven by a vertical rotating shaft in which the direction of the movement can be reversed by raising or lowering the shaft which has an intermeshing gear. The shaft is moved by an endless screw.

128. Drawing of a heavy-duty hoist operated from ▷ the ground. The lower part shows the harness-fittings for animals, and wooden springs and connections devised to prevent sudden changes in the speed of the load. From the Sketchbook of Giuliano da Sangallo (Siena, Biblioteca Comunale).

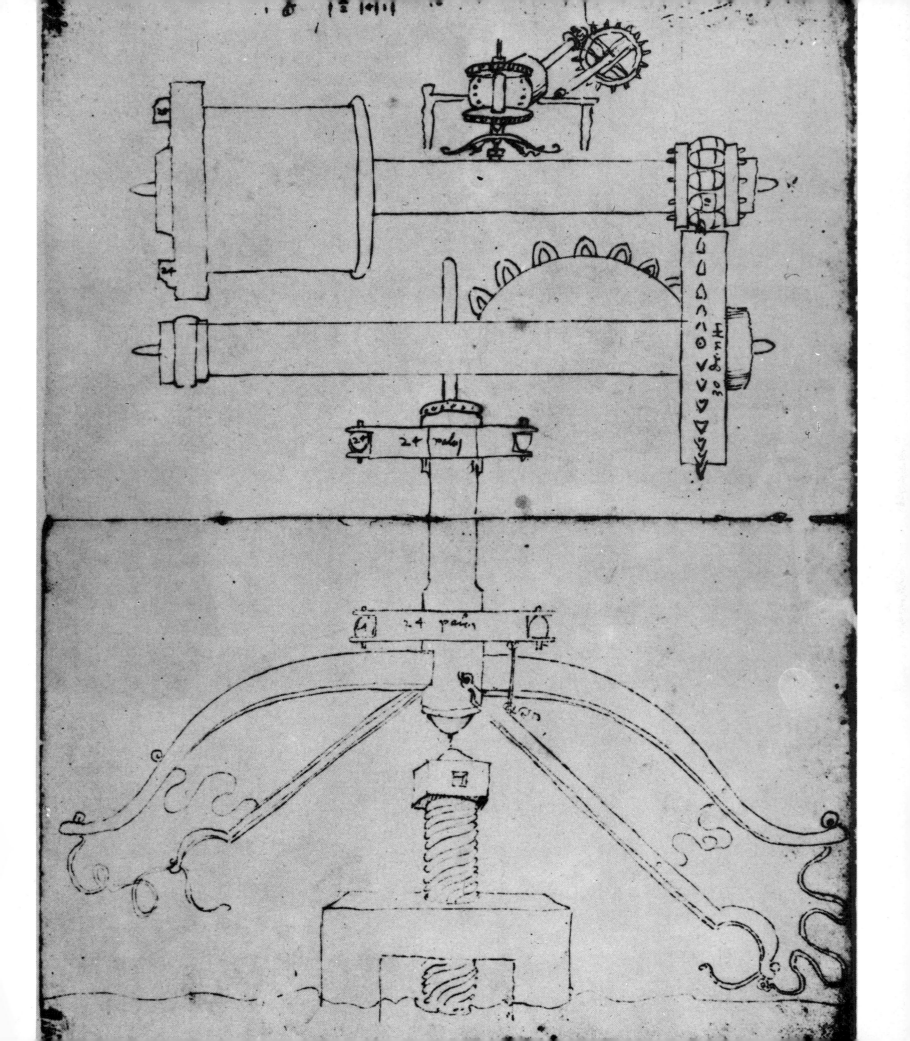

129. A pulley, probably one of the original ones, found in the exedra facing Via dei Servi. (Now in the Museo dell'Opera del Duomo)

130. A dovetailed tenon or lewis which, fitted into a mortise in a stone, ensured strong resistance and therefore a high degree of security. (Now in the Museo dell'Opera del Duomo)

131. Drawing of hooks used for the exact positioning of very large blocks. The load, hoisted to the correct height, was slowly rotated and lowered to the precise place designated. From the *Zibaldone* of Buonaccorso Ghiberti (Florence, Biblioteca Nazionale Centrale, MS. BR 228, f. 117r).

132. Construction equipment and ropes as formerly stored in the exedra facing Via dei Servi (now in the Museo dell'Opera del Duomo). Some things date from the fifteenth century; others are later but probably function in the same way as earlier types. In the upper right is a *gualandrino*, a safety belt tied to three guy ropes, worn by workers in particularly dangerous areas.

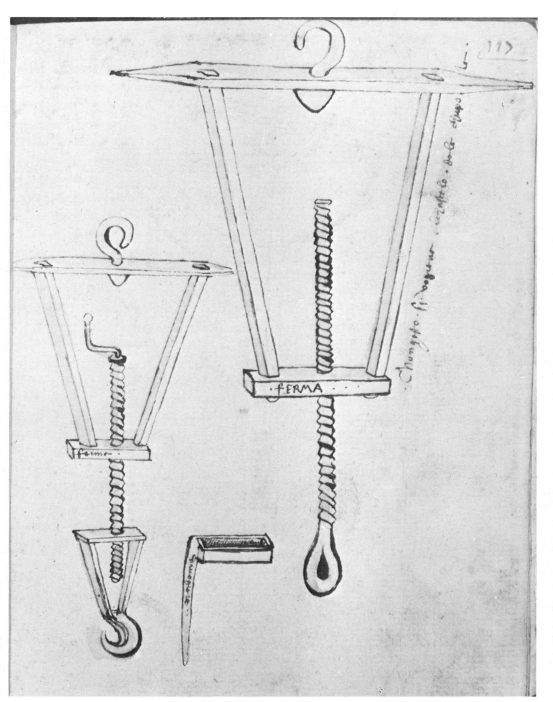

133. Pulley block found in the exedra facing Via dei Servi (perhaps post-Brunelleschi). With its two sets of wheels at right angles to each other it could be used to lift a weight and at the same time move it horizontally, to position it wherever desired inside the dome.

134. Pulley block in the exedra facing Via dei Servi (perhaps post-Brunelleschi). The wheels of different radius allow the force and speed to be geared down.

135. The system of chains inside the fabric of the dome (from Prager and Scaglia).

(a) detail of stone chains and iron ties on the exterior [139]; (b) stone chains of the upper levels; (c) stone chains of the lower levels; (d) detail of the lower stone chain and metal rod; (e) wooden chain, of chestnut and oak (see also *fig. 145*); (f) detail of a wooden chain.

Visible elements: 1, outer ends of the radial stone beams; 2, 3, outer and inner ends of the iron rods; 4, wooden chain; 5, metal rods fastening the wooden chain to the masonry; 6, connecting bars with mortise wedges; 7, 8, fillets and rivets joining two parts of the wooden chain.

Conjectural elements: 9, internal stone linking ring; 10-13, supplementary links; 14, metal clamps; 15, linking clamps; 16, metal rods with hooks on the outer face of the dome; 17, metal rods terminating in hooks on the inner face of the dome.

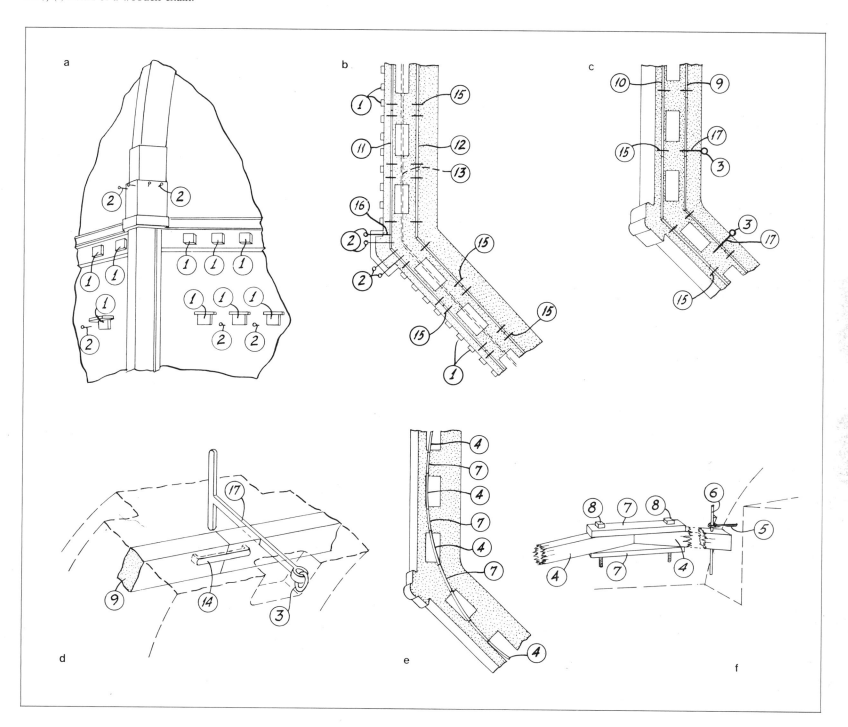

137

structural unit to be totally dry before beginning on the next. We can also recognize in the masonry places where a particularly long period elapsed between stages, presumably due to interruptions during the winter. Such indications are very visible in the hollow space between the two shells, especially on the inner surface of the outer shell [144]. To co-ordinate these "rings" Brunelleschi seems to have relied on taking only horizontal measurements, calculating that as the dome increased in height the sides of the octagon would become reduced in the right proportion, that they would maintain their alignment on the large corner ribs and would rise with the correct curvature as they decreased in thickness. So indeed it proved, and he even succeeded in correcting the considerable disparities of the base level of the drum, whose sides were already showing irregularities.

Seen from the outside, the dome appears to be a totally coherent and homogeneous structure. Nothing hints at the complex relationships and tensions within. In particular, the marble ribs that rise from the drum to the lantern, contrasting so vividly with the red tiles in between, seem to be almost an image of its vitality and strength.

These ribs are of primary structural importance — giant bridge-piers launched into the void to serve as guides and supports in the construction of the shells. Tapering as they rise towards the crown of the dome, they are very accurately disposed radially with respect to the geometric centre of the octagon of the drum, never deviating more than a metre from that centre.[20] The presence of a centre to which to refer was indispensable, and it is clear that both the vertical inclination and the radial disposition of the ribs were constantly checked against it as building went on. The plan laid out on the banks of the Arno could never have been more than theoretical.

The system used must have involved linear measurements with a measuring rod, triangulation with cords, and optical sightings to check the angles at which the sides of the octagon came together. The measurements to be used could have been worked out from analyses of the scale model in masonry constructed at the foot of the campanile. There was however another and more difficult co-ordination: the profiles of the external ribs have the shape of truncated pyramids, and the ribs converge almost exactly at the centre of the dome. How this was achieved is hard to say. It was not possible to place a sight vane except suspended at the centre of a star of cords, and these, because of their flexibility, could never be a precise guide. Equally improbable, in view of the distance, is that the sighting point could have been a central mark on the floor far beneath the dome, which would also require that the great angular ribs project considerably with respect to the inner wall of the cupola. The inner and outer shells seem to have been built virtually together with the ribs, and not later.

The vertical curvature of the dome presented further problems; it had to be regulated and checked by timber centerings and plumb-lines. The double shell greatly facilitated this procedure, since the inner shell provided support for building the other one: by placing the timber centering on the outer wall of the inner shell, the outer shell could be built with approximately the same inclination. From the drawings and measurements one actually sees that the curves of the two shells are roughly equal, so the same centering might have been used for both. To serve as a guide for the vertical curvature, the ribs at the corners seem to have been built first, together with vertical sections of herringbone brickwork that form walls or subsidiary "ribs" embedded in the masonry at right angles to the faces of the dome, linking the inner and outer shells at regular intervals. There are two of these internal ribs per side, dividing each of the eight sides into three sections. They are thinner than the main ribs and have a trapezoidal profile, but like the others they are oriented towards the centre of the drum. At each stage they seem to have been built up by a few courses of bricks before the intermediate webs were filled in. These webs themselves include bands of herringbone brickwork that become more dominant in the upper parts of the dome, until in the final ring they take over the masonry entirely.

At this point the question arises as to the practical purpose of the herringbone brickwork, which is visible wherever the plaster has peeled off or is worn away [157, 158]. Its origins are so obviously Near Eastern that one is tempted to speculate either that Brunelleschi had visited that part of the world or that foreign masons had been working in Tuscany.[21] True, herringbone masonry also occurs in small domes such as that of S. Spirito, where it forms a spiral winding gradually in upon itself. But at S. Maria del Fiore its function appears to be very much more complex. In the masonry of the webs it seems most probably to be a device for locking the courses in position in self-contained sections during the process of construction — an explanation that gains support from an account of the vaulting of domes without centering written three hundred years later by G.B. Nelli.[22] In the subsidiary "ribs" joining the two shells, it seems that the inclusion of courses of bricks set upright was intended to guard against the possibility of bricks slipping inwards (since they are inclined at the same angle as the dome itself). It is also possible that the oblique rows of projecting bricks were meant to facilitate the taking of sightings, in order to correct the alignment of the sides before the entire masonry ring was built. Finally, as in spherical vaults, they represent the miniature ribs on the inside that were recommended by Alberti.

The ribs that appear externally mark the corners of the octagonal dome, and continue the line of the pilasters of the octagonal drum beneath them; the others, of course, are visible only in the gaps between the two shells. Taken together the ribs can be considered as the material expression of the lines of force in the dome itself. Tapering upward towards the crown they also express a relationship between volume and function that recalls Gothic architecture. Equally Gothic is the way each separate element is shaped for its purpose. Brick was chosen instead of stone because of its lightness, its easily standardized forms and its ease of handling, but each brick is moulded for its position, taking account not only of its inclination towards the centre by the "acute fifth" but also of its position on plan as part of a circle.

The bricks were fitted in, so to speak, between the pre-established lines of the ribs, and their joining required special measures. When they came into contact with horizontal passageways or had to allow for intercommunicating doorways and therefore had to be adjusted to make corners, bricks of very specific type, shape and size are used, some even triangular in form, while in other cases there are wedge-shaped bricks or bricks shaped according to the angles of the octagon, with flanges to left and right to fit inside the masonry.

At regular intervals wedges were inserted which made it possible to obtain the three types of inclination — vertical, horizontal and radial.

The Biographer speaks of a number of expedients used inside the dome which have been partially confirmed only recently by the very extensive tests and electromagnetic investigations of the last few years. He also complains of several arbitrary changes.

continued on page 142

138

136. Conjectural reconstruction of the first step in constructing the dome, with scaffolding attached to the interior (see also *fig. 117b*).

137. Sketch of a scaffolding platform above the oculi.

138. Sketch showing the beginning of work on the exterior at the level of the circular gallery.

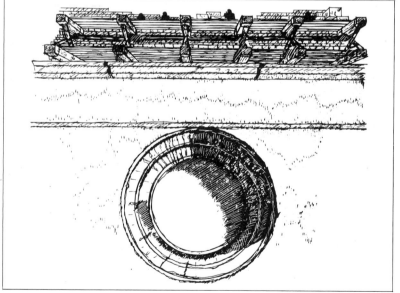

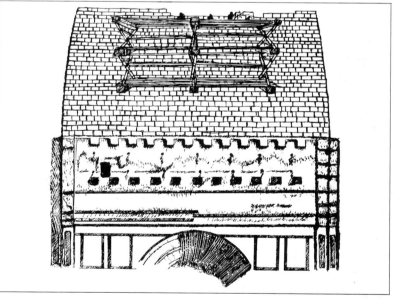

140

139, 140. Views of the undecorated part of the drum, showing the outer ends of the radial stone beams and iron rods (see *fig. 135*). The projecting stones above were cut away during the attempt to build a loggia.

141-143. The calculation of the curvature of the dome. Giovanni da Prato's drawing (*opposite*) shows how the "acute fifth" is produced. It is repeated in simplified form below. The internal diameter of the dome is represented by the line A-B, and a semicircle with its centre at C shows the height to which a round dome of those dimensions would reach. By drawing the curvature instead from two points, each 4/5 diameter away from the opposite side (D and E), two arcs are produced which meet at a point pronouncedly higher than that produced from C. Such was the theory.

In practice (*bottom*), Brunelleschi's equivalent of point E (and D) turns out to be not 4/5 but slightly over 5/6 from the opposite side, and to vary according to whether we measure the lower, middle or upper section of the curvature. For the first it is 5/6 + 1/4 *braccio*, for the second 5/6 + 1/3 *braccio*, for the third 5/6 + 1/2 *braccio*.

At the top of his drawing, upside-down, Giovanni da Prato shows a plan and section of the dome and drum to demonstrate the inadequacy of the lighting (see p. 260 and Chapter 12, note 46). (Florence, Archivio di Stato)

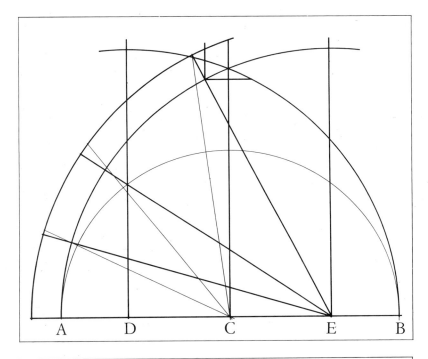

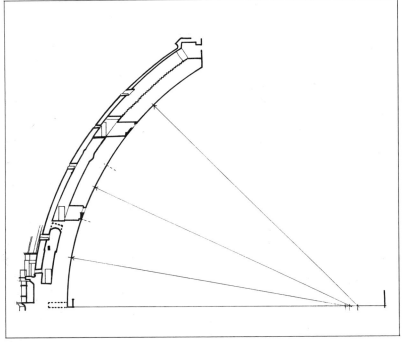

According to the Biographer, the original design for the exterior of the dome was modified, against Brunelleschi's wishes. The massive ribs at the corners were to have continued with the same measurements all the way up from the base of the octagonal drum. The Biographer comments: "up to the galleries from the ground, or from where it begins to show itself, it was the intention of the man who conceived it that it should look like a single member; to narrow its width makes it appear like two members, one above the other, of which neither one nor the other is pleasing" (f. 311v). Thus what was intended was much more massive ribbing that would embrace the vast dome in a more energetic manner, and the vestiges of this change in the programme are today easily discernible slightly above the gallery, which had been conceived a good deal higher than it is [1]. There are obvious discontinuities between the ribs and the drum, and the ribs are suddenly reduced in size.

Obviously this change in rib section did not entail a change in the basic form of the outer shell, though that is certainly rather more swelling and depressed than initially planned. The change in curvature, effected in several phases and amidst bitter polemics, was really fairly modest [142] and would certainly not significantly modify the form as conceived in the late Trecento. I cannot agree completely with Heydenreich's judgment: "The generation which planned it, however, lacked any means of giving its conception visible shape, and thus the dome of Florence Cathedral remains, actually and symbolically, what Alberti called it, the first work of the new style."[23]

There are no windows in the interior shell and only circular windows of moderate size in the drum. The result is to make the interior dark, giving an air of intimacy to the religious rites that take place beneath the dome, almost as if in a vast grotto. The effect was deliberate on the part of its builders, Brunelleschi in particular having declared himself in favour of stained glass rather than clear glass in the oculi of the drum, which he considered more as ornamental elements than as apertures. The various deputy commissions agreed with him and, for reasons of stability as well, rejected all proposals for apertures in the interior shell above the drum, including one by Giovanni da Prato for no less than twenty-four windows. Further, in the final closing of the dome Brunelleschi markedly reduced the opening for the lantern and thereby further limited the lighting from above, so that he was soundly condemned by Giovanni da Prato for making the dome not only dark but "murky and gloomy" (as it is still).

Throughout the Quattrocento in Italy there was a continuous argument between the advocates of light and dark churches. Light was given its theoretical justification by Pope Pius II, who explicitly spoke of religious symbolism and desired that the choir of the Cathedral in his town of Pienza be literally a *domus vitrea*, a "house of glass", in accord with the Marian attribute exalted by certain hymns and *laudi*. Darkness was forthrightly championed by Alberti, who considered the chief ornament of the altar to be the light of the candles and lamps and recommended that the architecture make a dark and atmospheric frame.

The discussions concerning the Florentine dome show that conflict of ideas to have been present already in the early Quattrocento. The enlargement of the round openings in the drum, with the result that the drum itself had to be built up higher in 1420 to allow space for attaching a circular gallery, was certainly done to obtain more light, and we know from the Biographer that Brunelleschi considered this an error. The stained glass in them, however, makes them less functional than they would otherwise be.

continued on page 150

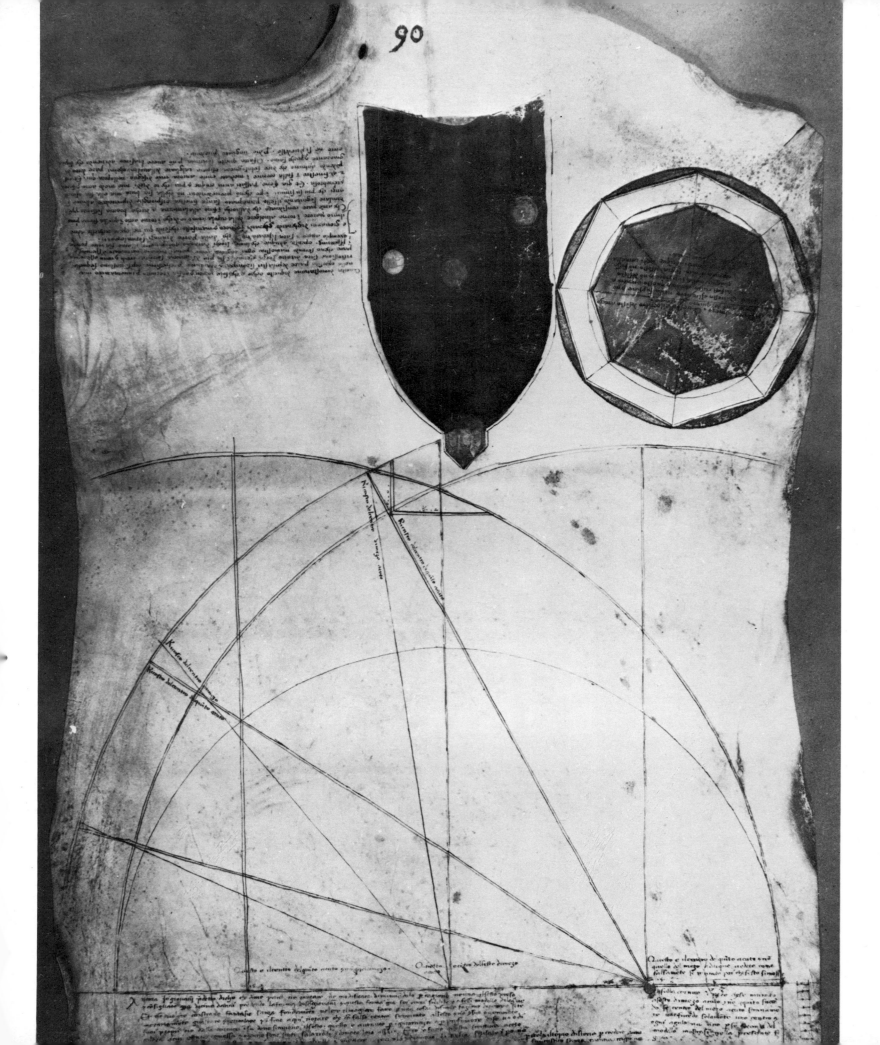

90

The interspace

A double-shelled masonry structure has two great advantages over a conventional roof: it is resistant to fire, especially fire caused by lightning, and it does away with beams, which deteriorate quickly and require constant inspection. Yet another advantage was pointed out by Alberti, who shows himself modern in his concern for the microclimate: "Then again, so that the parts in shadow remain fresh and cool, it will be useful to cover the roof with another roof and the walls with other walls; and the wider the space between them, the more the shaded parts will resist heat, so that an interior covered and surrounded in this manner will heat up less than others. In fact, the empty space left between the two walls has an effect almost identical with that of a single wall of equal thickness. Indeed, it has this advantage over the latter: the massive wall is slower to lose the heat accumulated in it by the sun and also retains longer the cold it has absorbed, whereas in the said double walls a moderate temperature is always maintained." (*De re aedificatoria*, ed. Orlandi and Portoghesi, Book X, pp. 976-79)

144. Section along the median vertical of the segment of the dome above the Loggia del Grillo. The section was made along the median axis rather than in the corners because only there could one measure directly the thickness of both outer and inner shells and the interspace. In any other radial vertical plane it would be difficult to pinpoint exactly the angle formed by that plane with that along the median vertical.

Our findings show that while the outer shell tapers upwards, with a thickness diminishing from 0.96 to 0.40 m (37 3/4 to 15 3/4 in.), the inner shell remains almost constant, with a reduction of only 22 cm, from 2.22 m at the bottom to 2.00 m at the top (7 ft 3 3/8 in. to 6 ft 6 3/4 in.). The width of the interspace, on the other hand, measured horizontally, increases from 1.22 to 2.60 m (4 ft to 8 ft 6 3/8 in.), to allow sufficient space for the workers to pass through.

For the floors, measurements were made utilizing pre-existing holes. While at the upper levels the floors show a slight inclination towards the exterior, the floor over the first internal passageway is inclined inward, following the radius of curvature of the dome at that point.

The passageways are pierced through the ribs. In the second and third passageways, particularly the latter, where the interspace is at a sharper angle, the shells are left intact and the outer corners of the doors at the top are nipped off at an angle. The amount cut back varies, in the second passageway [*157*] from 2 to 5 cm (3/4 in. to 2 in.), and in the third [*162*] from 10 to 15 cm (3 7/8 to 5 7/8 in.).

Notchlike indentations marking a change in curvature are present in the outer and inner shells. On the extrados of the inner shell there is one between the first and second passageways and another between the third and fourth, while on the intrados of the outer shell they were found between the first and second and the second and third passageways.

Between the second and third passageways, at the point where the curvature changes from the value of 5/6 diameter + 1/3 *braccio* to 5/6 + 1/2 there is an indentation in both shells aligned according to the radius of curvature at that point. This may indicate mistakes during the building process.

A significant alteration was made during the restoration of 1639, when a round-headed arch was inserted to reinforce the floor of the second passageway (see *fig. 152*).

0, scaffolding hole, base level for the measurements; 1, first passageway door; 2, second passageway door; 3, third passageway door; 4, fourth passageway, around the base of the lantern; 5, Loggia del Grillo; a,b, points where the curvature changes. (1 cm = 2.16 m; 1 in. = 18 ft)

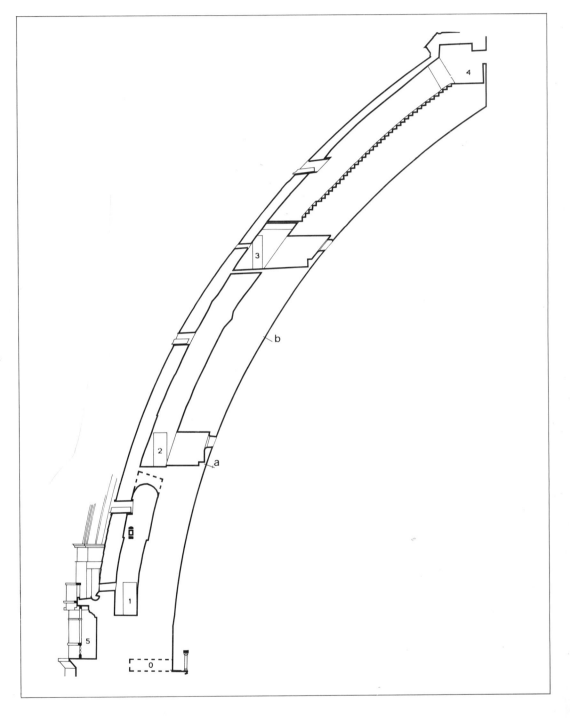

The stone armature of the dome
by the Dome Study Group
Above the stone base ring the dome is strengthened in both shells by other stone rings, or chains, composed of blocks joined together in pairs by metal clamps [135d]; not all the clamps could be checked, but they seem to have held remarkably well despite time, weather, and cracks in the stones. Some of the chains link the two shells and form a walkway, while others are entirely embedded in the masonry and are visible only occasionally in the internal passageways.

In each segment horizontal stiffener arches are visible (see also *fig. 173*). Their absence from the central area between the intermediate ribs has been variously explained: the space was left free for ladders; it was deliberately kept more elastic; or (something hinted at in Guasti's documents) the arches were built but then removed when the dome was completed, a procedure planned for the side sectors as well but not carried out there. An argument against this last explanation is that no traces of cutting away have been found in the masonry.

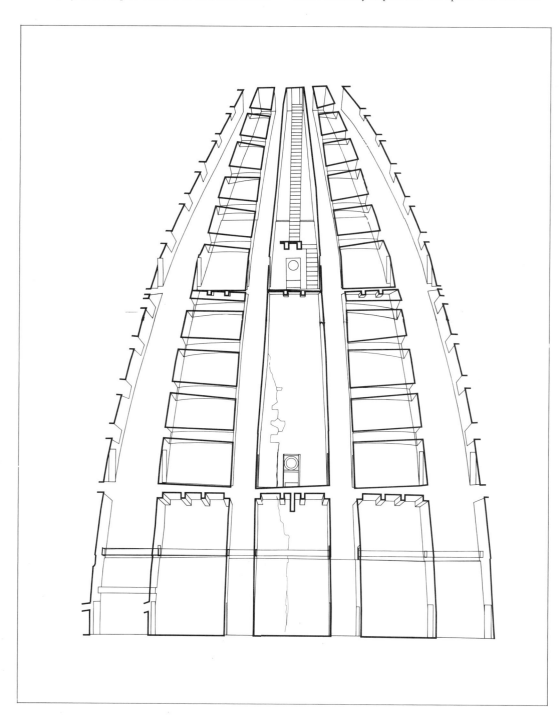

145. Elevation of the segment above the Loggia del Grillo, with the outer shell cut away, from the level of the first passageway to just above the top of the stairs (compare *figs. 173, 282*).

Measurements indicated that while the first passageway is almost perfectly level from left to right, the second and third have marked slopes and variations in thickness.

This drawing shows clearly the position and number of the almost-flat arches between the large ribs at the corners and the intermediate brick ribs. There are four between the second and third passageways and five between the third and fourth. Each of these arches has a double curve: its lower surface is arched, and its inner surface is concave, following the extrados of the inner shell [163].

In the centre there is a large crack which ends between the second and third passageways in the angle formed by the rib and the inner shell.

The corner rib on the left, above the door of the first passageway, is pierced from left to right by a small square opening [150], similar to the space occupied by the wooden chain [135], seen running through the web above it. An identical hole occurs in the rib diametrically opposite. Their purpose is unknown: they may have been intended for another wooden chain.

The ribs are regular in outline as far as the second passageway, but above that they show considerable changes in direction or corrections, particularly in the area of the passageways, which must have served as platforms to establish measurements. This is particularly noticeable from the third passageway upwards. (To the same scale as the section, *opposite*)

145

146. Horizontal sections of the segment of the Cathedral dome above the Loggia del Grillo at significant points; in each case the interior of the dome is to the left.
a) base level, 53.85 m (176 ft 8 in.) from the ground, with scaffolding holes and spiral stair
b) 3.20 m (10 ft 6 in.) above base level: first passageway, at floor level
c) 4.90 m (16 ft 7/8 in.) up: first passageway, at the level of the external light-holes and access to the upper part of the Loggia del Grillo
d) 7.90 m (25 ft 11 in.) up: first passageway, at the level of the wooden chain
e) 9.36 m (30 ft 8 1/2 in.) up: first passageway, at the level of the external oculi
f) 11.61 m (38 ft 1 in.) up: second passageway, at floor level
g) 11.46 m (47 ft 5 3/4 in.) up: second passageway, at the level of the arches linking the corner ribs and intermediate ribs
h) 18.93 m (62 ft 1 3/8 in.) up: second passageway, at the level of the external oculi
i) 22.86 m (72 ft) up: third passageway, at floor level
l) 24.16 m (79 ft 3 1/2 in.) up: third passageway, at the level of the external light-holes and the oculus in the inner shell
m) 25.33 m (83 ft 1 1/4 in.) up: third passageway, at the level of the stairway landing
n) 28.74 m (94 ft 3 1/2 in.) up: third passageway, at the level of the external oculi
o) 33.35 m (109 ft 5 in.) up: fourth passageway, at floor level
(1 cm = 3.03 m; 1 in. = 25 ft 3 in.)

147a,b. Arrangement of the rows of bricks of varying sizes in the outer wall of the inner shell, where the third passageway cuts through the corner rib (ringed on section i, *above*). The line along which the drawing was made is shown running through the passageway in the plan, *147b*.
    A similar part of the structure, but in the outer wall of the second passageway, appears in [*157*].
(1 cm = 63 cm; 1 in. = 5 ft 3 in.)

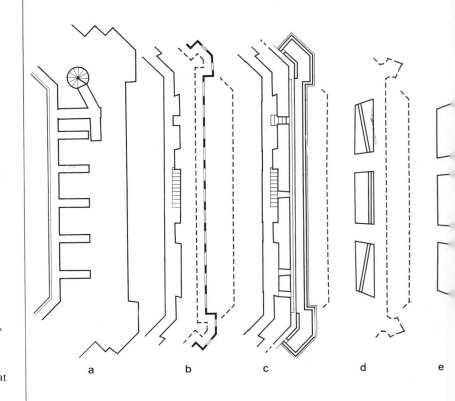

a   b   c   d   e

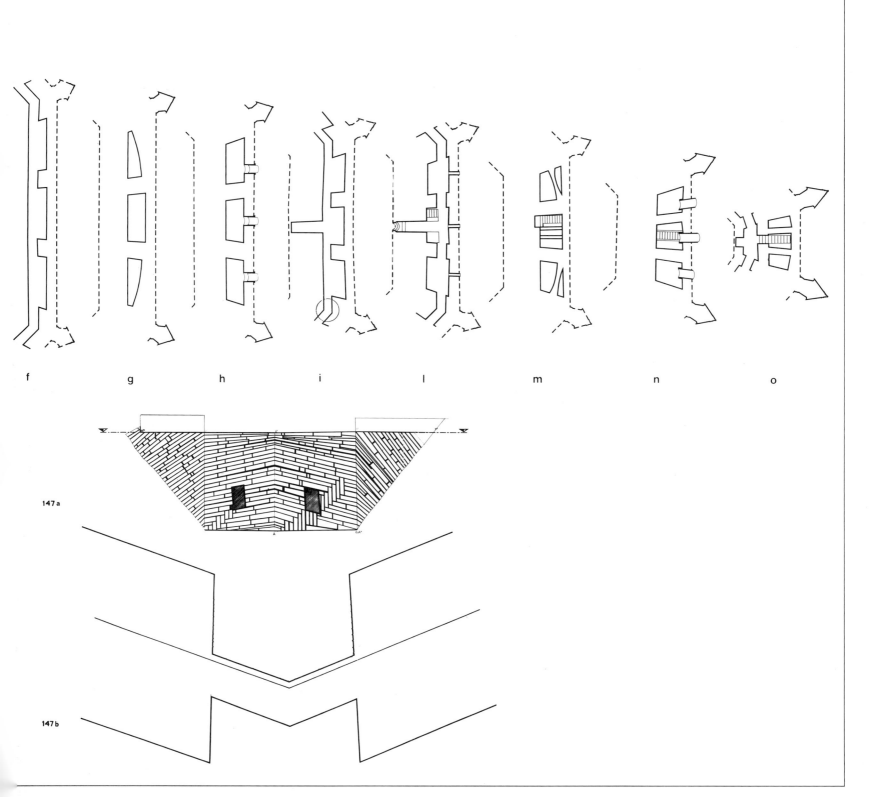

f g h i l m n o

147a

147b

148-170. Details of the Cathedral dome, climbing progressively higher. The sections are all of the segment above the Loggia del Grillo.

148. Median section of the segment, with the area between the first and second levels shaded.

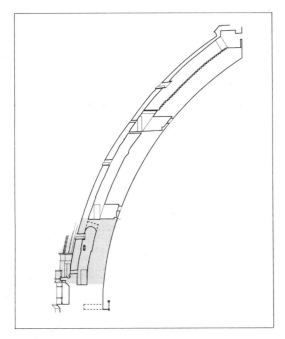

149. Passage through the stone ring at the base of the dome, between the topmost interior gallery and the Loggia del Grillo on the exterior.

150. The first passageway, where it runs through a main corner rib. Note the square hole pierced above the door (see *fig. 145*).

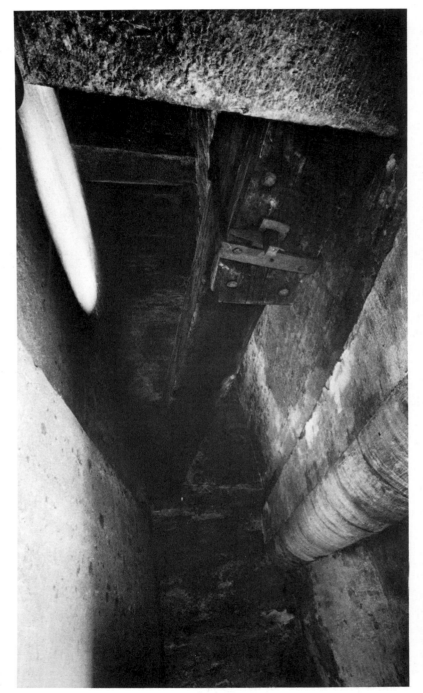

151. Looking up, where the wooden chain meets the corner rib. The chestnut beams of the chain are held together by a connecting element in oak, strengthened with iron [135f, 7].

The final result was a mystical, reduced illumination so that the choir, because of the distance from the lantern and its windows, is forever immersed in a kind of twilight, doubtless approved of by Alberti, who wrote in his Book VII: "Let the nave be not too sombre; but in the portion where the altar rises it seems to me better that solemnity should prevail over elegance".

The dome that we see now is very different from what was intended in the fourteenth and fifteenth centuries. Its inner face was meant to be adorned with mosaics, like the Baptistery, and this was so much a part of the plan that, during its construction, grooves were made to support the necessary framework.[24] On its exterior, the Biographer says, the large vertical ribs were reduced in size and the circular gallery not built, with grave aesthetic damage to the whole. However faithful the execution of the lantern, it too introduced substantial alterations (see Chapter 12). At least in the case of the drum, the modifications can perhaps be explained by a concern with connecting and harmonizing the dome with the nave beneath it. But the intention of Brunelleschi was that they be set off from each other sharply, almost as if the dome were an independent superimposed edifice, something like the later description of St Peter's in Rome as the Pantheon perched on a Roman baths building.

On the other hand, it is difficult even to imagine just what was intended for the double gallery, both covered and open, which was not built but for which the points of attachment remain. That there was no approved and binding project for it before the building of the dome seems to be demonstrated by the fact that it was possible to alter considerably the dimensions of the windows and thereby eat away that margin of space Brunelleschi judged indispensable for his supporting beams, which leads one to think, with Michelangelo, that the gallery would have been much higher and even deeper than the small stretch of it built in the sixteenth century.[25]

The scaffolding for the dome initially rested upon the top of the octagon of the drum. Long tree-trunks were forced into very deep holes already prepared at regular intervals to a distance of at least 3 m (10 ft) to provide support for a solid platform both inside and outside [136, 138]. It is almost certain that the building materials were piled up on the level open spaces where the solid exedrae were later erected. As the dome rose the same system of scaffolding would have been erected at each level — rings of wooden beams and planks projecting externally but providing support for a corresponding smaller ring inside. This system continued until the dome had reached two-thirds of its height. At that point the reasons, technical and economic, that had prohibited the use of ordinary scaffolding (i.e. scaffolding placed like a bridge across the whole space to be covered) no longer applied, and a large platform was built using the round openings left for that purpose in the outer shell.

Problems of structural design and of scaffolding were not the only ones facing Brunelleschi for which past experience gave little help. New machines had to be devised to hoist the material into place and new methods organized for transporting it to the site. Several illustrations of the hoisting machinery survive in the manuscripts of Mariano di Jacopo called Il Taccola, and other machines are known from drawings by Francesco di Giorgio and Giuliano da Sangallo, from the *Zibaldone* of Buonaccorso Ghiberti, and from sketches by Leonardo that either copied earlier drawings or analysed surviving machines. How much technical innovation we should ascribe to Brunelleschi himself is uncertain.[26] The invention of systems of winches with several pulleys (three,

continued on page 156

152. Looking up at the ceiling of the first passageway, past the dark line of the wooden chain. The arch supporting the ceiling was introduced during the restoration of 1639. In this photograph and the one opposite, the light comes from round windows in the outer shell of the dome.

153. Median section through a segment of the Cathedral dome, with the area between the second and third levels shaded.

154, 155. Stairs leading from the first to the second levels, passing through one of the brick subsidiary ribs. Note the inclination of the bricks in that rib, their courses tilted by a wedge built up on the stone foundation to the left of the opening. The stone beams of the ceiling (*below right*), which support the floor of the second passageway, are aligned towards the centre of the dome.

156. Second passageway, with openings pierced through the subsidiary ribs and, in the distance, through a corner rib. The brick courses tilt downward towards the centre of curvature of the dome, on the left.

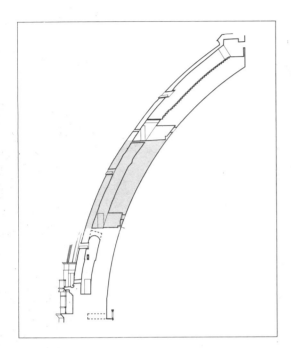

OVERLEAF

157. The second passageway, where it cuts through a corner rib. The inner wall of the outer shell, seen here, includes herringbone brickwork.

158. Herringbone brickwork in the inner face of the outer shell.

159. Landing where the stairs from a lower level (right) meet the passageway above. On the left, the inner shell; on the right, the outer, cut into to allow room for the stairs, and reinforced with stone.

160. Cracks in the inner face of the outer shell, below an oculus in the central section between intermediate ribs.

for example) was traditionally ascribed to Archimedes, and they must have been known in Tuscany, because Buschetto is praised for having raised the columns in Pisa using no more strength than that of a little girl.[27]

To transport marble down the Arno to Florence, Brunelleschi constructed a special barge at his own expense. Although held up to ridicule and irony as a "badalone", a do-nothing time-wasting folly, the boat did function but, because of shoals and sandbanks, was never able to push upstream beyond Empoli, some 34 km (21 mi.) or so from Florence.[28]

Brunelleschi's work on the dome of Florence Cathedral occupied sixteen years of his life, and during most of those years it must have been the project uppermost in his mind. Today his name is indissolubly linked to it, but at the time it was only gradually, and amid harsh rivalry and violent criticism, that it was identified as specifically the fruit of his genius. Only when the dome is finally closed do the documents begin to change in tone: the deputies no longer merely choose or accept the proposals of Filippo but praise him, reward him, declare openly that their esteem is no longer a matter or faith and belief but, instead, of true merit on the basis, they state explicitly, of what has been accomplished. This does not mean that their approval is not accompanied by critical judgments on the special value of the solutions proposed, by invitations to drop any resentments he might harbour against his adversaries, and by orders to make a place in his own project for improvements proposed by others during the public discussions.

The radical change in tone came about fundamentally because he had proved himself capable of resolving the difficult problem of completing the dome through its upper third, where it begins to close. This required the construction of suspended scaffolding on the interior, with difficulties clearly alluded to when the documents mention solutions, hoped-for but not yet specified, that would make possible the completion of the task. But the change in attitude was also preceded by a violent attack in 1426 which we can only think was directly incited by Ghiberti. From the documents it appears that this had to do with the change (a very slight one, as we have seen) that Brunelleschi made in the prescribed curvature of the vault and which was claimed to be an arbitrary violation of the contract. If Brunelleschi did raise the octagonal drum somewhat higher to allow for a double exterior gallery, this was compensated for by notable savings in materials through a slight lowering of the overall height, achieved by small deviations from the "acute fifth" criticized by Giovanni da Prato.

The final victory was his: the dome proved statically sound and solid, closed off by an extremely regular ring which, as the drawings and measurements show, neatly absorbed the inevitable differences and deformities in the structure below it. (The reason for the many cracks in it today is debated.[29]) The Florentines had been given the dome they had asked for; and its fame eclipsed all the other work that Brunelleschi did for the Cathedral.[30]

161. Median section through a segment of the Cathedral dome, with the area between the third and fourth levels shaded.

162. The third passageway, with openings pierced through the subsidiary ribs. As they go higher, the shells incline more and more steeply inwards.

163, 164. Stairs leading from the second to the third passageway. Note, on the left of the illustration *below*, three horizontal arches supporting the outer shell.

OVERLEAF

165. At the top of the third level, looking up. The intermediate ribs, on the left, are now much closer together. Between them is the straight stairway leading to the fourth level [*167, 173*]. For the round opening at the top on the right, see *fig. 169*.

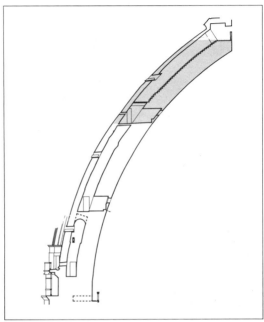

166, 167. Stairway between the third and fourth levels in the Cathedral dome, resting directly on the inner shell. At the top in the picture on the right is one of the oculi that light the interspace.

168. Median section through a segment of the Cathedral dome, with the fourth level shaded.

169. The fourth passageway, round the base of the lantern, with the outer shell on the right. Through the doorway one sees the inclined entrance to the stairway leading down to the third level. It is flanked by two round openings, which look into the interior of the church and into the interspace between the two shells [165].

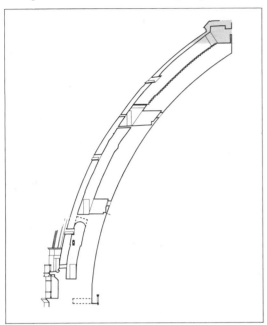

170. Herringbone brickwork in the fourth level, specially adjusted to give the correct inclination to the wall and stone slabs on which the lantern rests. On the right is the top of the stair down to the third level.

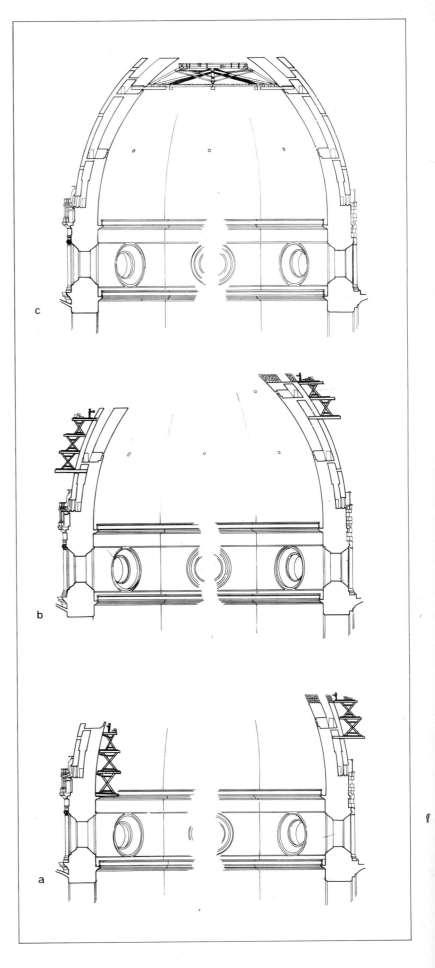

171. Conjectural reconstruction of the scaffolding used for the Cathedral dome. (For the sake of simplicity, the inclination of the brick courses towards the centre is not shown.)
a) The beam-holes at the base may have been used to support a platform and series of trestles on the interior (shown on the left), fixed to rings embedded in the masonry of the inner shell for that purpose [117, 135, 136]. These trestles would have been carried on up as far as height and the inclination of the shell allowed. As the dome began to curve inwards, it would naturally be easier to construct external scaffolding (shown on the right), using as base a platform resting on beams projecting from the external oculi of the first level.
b) At the height of the external oculi of the second level, a new base platform could be erected, on which trestles could be placed one above the other.
c) At the level of the third passageway, given the marked inclination inwards it may have been necessary to erect centering for the vault; the gap between the sides of the vault was at the same time much less than lower down, and from a base platform resting on beams inserted in the internal blind openings scaffolding could have been thrown right across the central gap [172].

172. Section and plan suggesting how the scaffolding and centering at the top might have been constructed (by Fabiano Gattari and Alfredo Vartolo). The base platform rests on beams inserted in the inner shell; the bridging scaffold supporting the centering is similar to that shown in a drawing in the Uffizi, which may reflect Brunelleschi's own ideas.

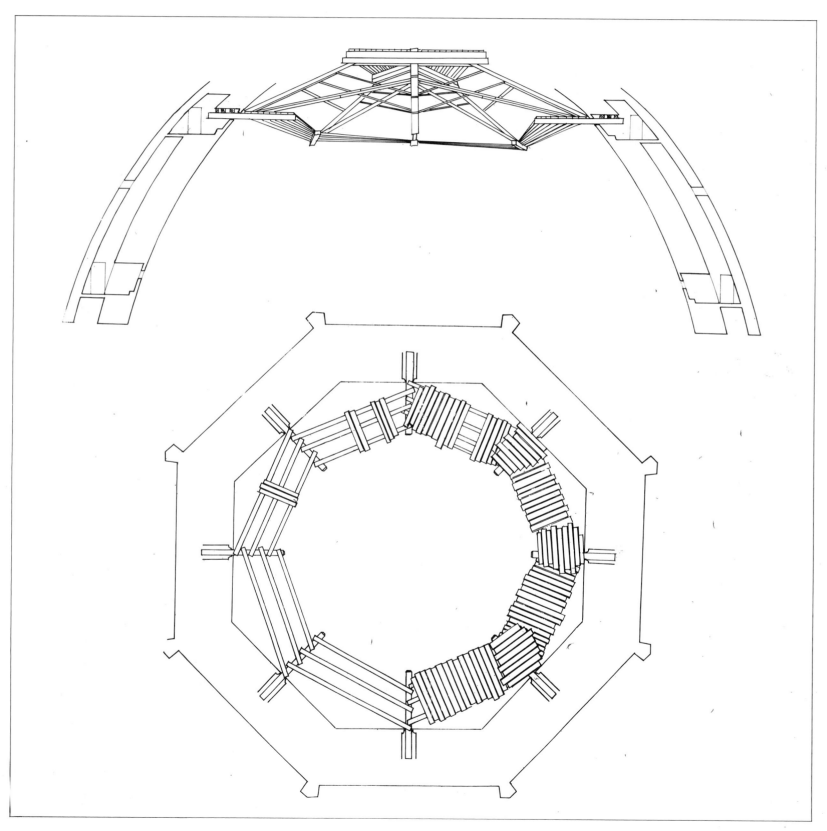

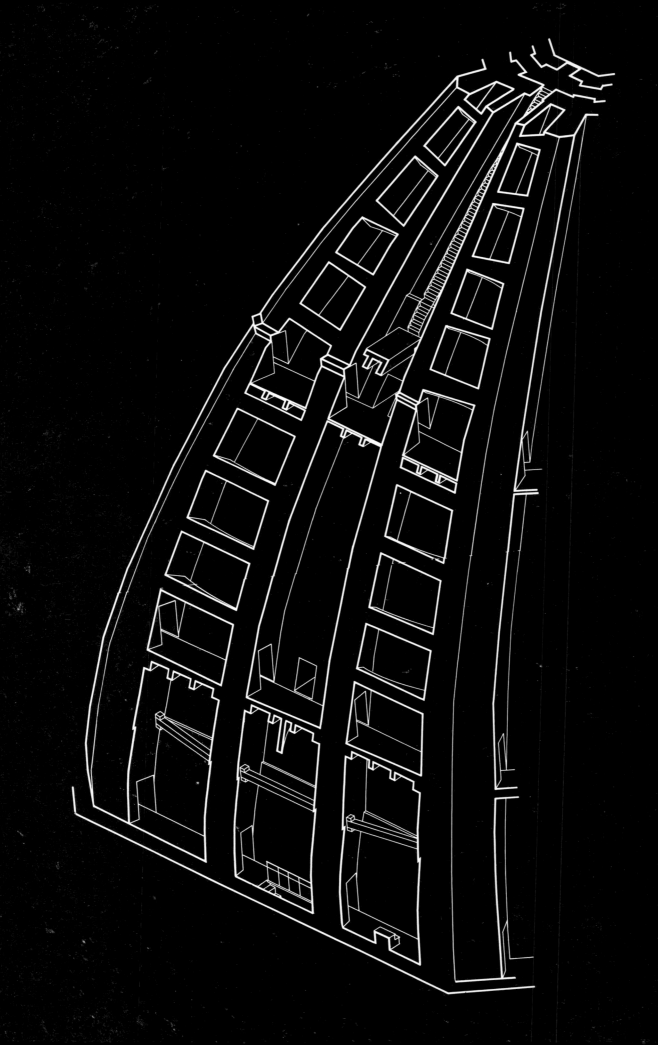

173. Axonometric drawing of the segment of the Cathedral dome above the Loggia del Grillo, with the outer shell transparent in order to show the internal structure, with main corner ribs, intermediate ribs, and horizontal arches (see also *figs. 144, 145, 282*). The wooden chain appears in the interspace between the first and second passageways. (1 cm = 1.91 m; 1 in. = 15 ft 11 in.)

174. Photogrammetric diagram of the inner face of the inner shell, made by the Istituto Geografico Militare in collaboration with the Engineering Department of the University of Florence. Contour lines indicate the curvature of the shell; also shown are cracks in the fabric, and parts of the fresco decoration. The measurement of the central area is incorrect, probably for technical reasons (1 cm = 2.10 m; 1 in. = 17 ft 6 in.)

OVERLEAF

175. Sunlight from the lantern streams down inside the dome. Note, on the right, the lines of hooks used to hold scaffolding [*171a*].

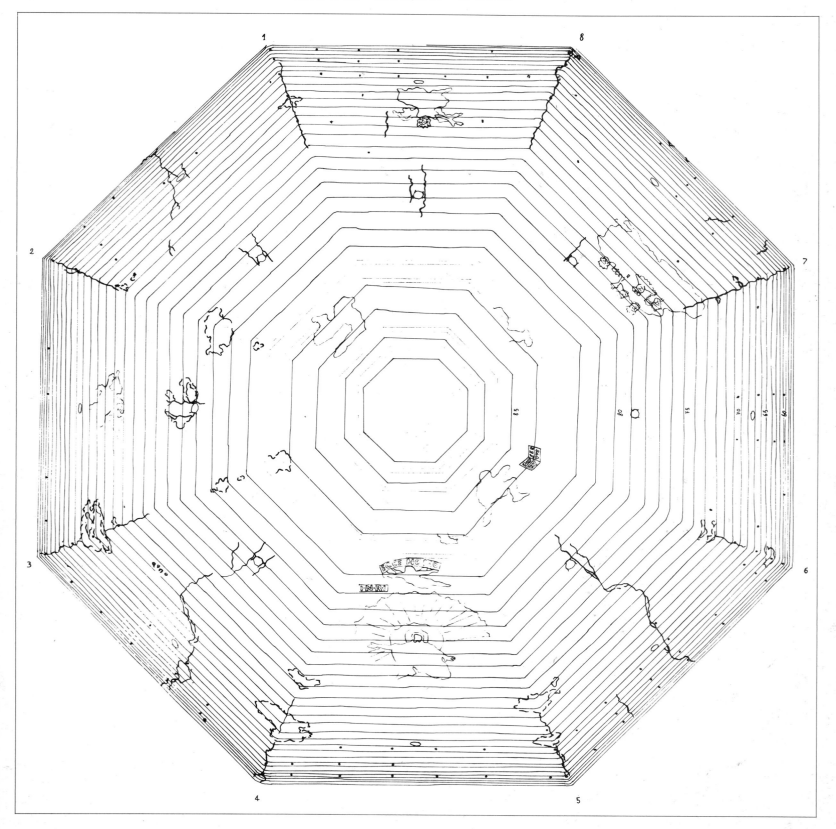

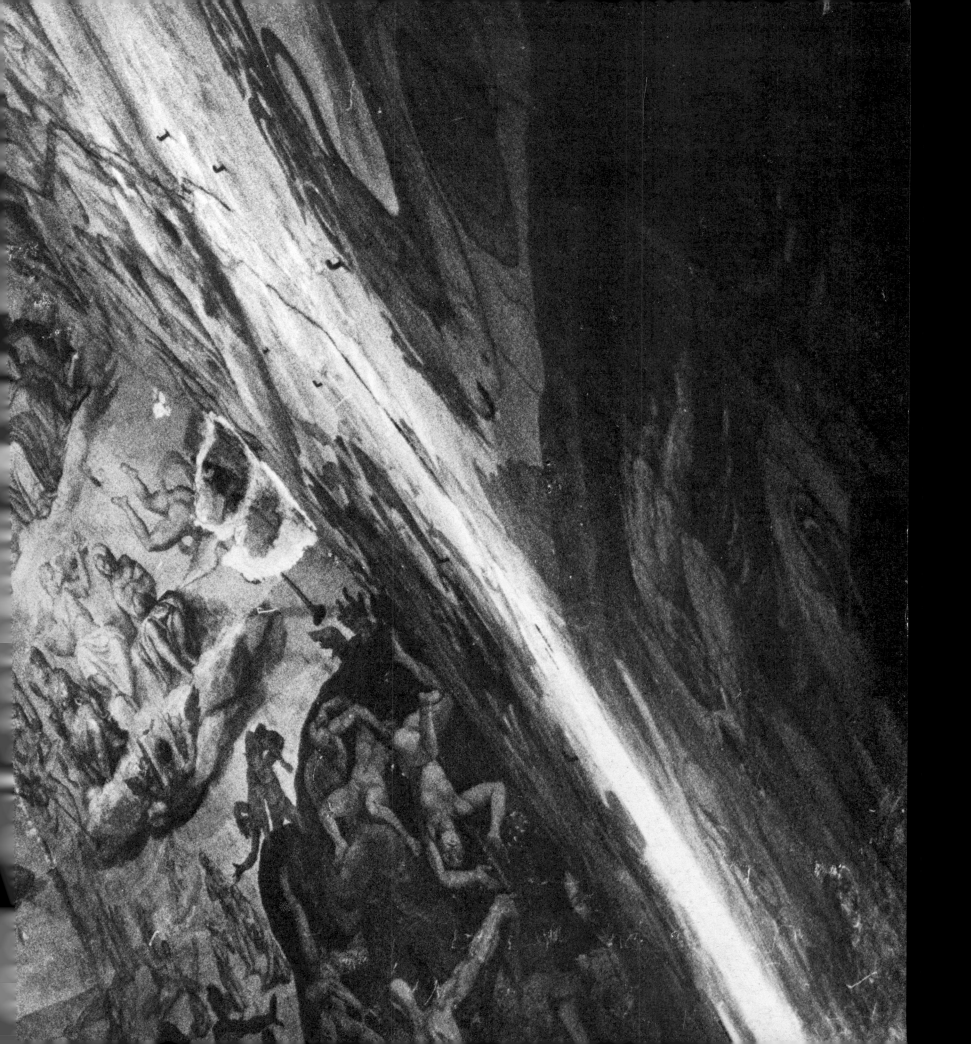

9 The basilicas of S. Lorenzo and S. Spirito

Background; town-planning

For all their differences in plan, the two famous basilicas in whose building Brunelleschi had a share, S. Lorenzo and S. Spirito, are so intimately related that it is only when discussed together that they reveal their true personality. Both were begun with the idea of simply extending and perhaps refacing an existing church and monastery that continued in use. As an economic operation they conformed to the precepts laid down by Giovanni Dominici (d. 1420) in his *Regola del governo di cura famigliare*:

Thus one's goods can be spent in erecting churches, monasteries, hospitals. ... And those charities are all of them good things done for God. ... But it displeases God that you should make for Him a church of dead stone and neglect that of live stone, to wit, man. Guard yourself well from the common vainglory which has much increased the number of dens of thieving scoundrels. If you do wish to spend great sums of money, I would rather counsel you to renovate a ruined and abandoned church or a hospital neglected through poverty, endowing them with whatever you can, than to build afresh; it will do greater honour to God to have one house which is sufficient than two in beggarly state; and you will have the greater reward from this since you will have less worldly fame lavished on you.

Subsequently, though, this programme of austerity and humility was superseded by an immense qualitative leap in style and magnificence, a project so far beyond the original modest scheme as to efface all memory of both the earlier building and the previous devout tradition — even at the cost of liturgical and organizational changes — in much the same way as the new St Peter's was to destroy every trace of its venerable predecessor. The new programme boldly ignored the further lesson of Dominici:

I take it for granted that, in so doing, you will build on [what] someone else [built] and their coats of arms will have the glory, and thus the name of the patronage will remain with the original patrons. And thus the right hand will not know what the left hand does, because your charitable deed will remain hidden; and the Good Lord who sees what is hidden will reward you in Heaven.[1]

So here, instead of restoration we find total replacement, along with the proposal — on the grounds of social aims, status interest and town-planning reforms — to make use of those religious structures as the focus for a general reorganization of the two city quarters to which the churches belonged. This was to involve extensive demolition of surrounding older buildings (accused explicitly, in the case of S. Lorenzo, of housing "meretrices et alii infames"), thus replacing the environment of a medieval society with piazzas of ambitious dimensions. In order to carry this through, it was necessary to take coercive measures such as expropriation decrees and transfer of some properties (in another project the houses of the Medici themselves were scheduled for demolition), projects and norms had to be established, property improvement taxes imposed, and daily indemnities paid to individuals assigned to such tasks.

The piazza of S. Spirito was initially intended to lie between the church and the bridge which leads to one of the principal thoroughfares of the city: it would become an extension of that street, re-orienting the life of the Lungarno towards the political and commercial centre. About this the Biographer says (suppl. MS, ff. xlviiir-xlixr):

And in discussing where to site the new church and, if it was agreeable to him [Stoldo Frescobaldi], when rebuilding it to make it face one cardinal point rather than another, Filippo persuaded him to turn the church round, placing the façade where the apse was [to the north] and desired that its piazza ... should begin with the Fondaccio [the first street parallel to the river, the present Via S. Spirito] and run towards the church, and that the front of the church should rise at the far end of that long space, or else the piazza should begin right at the river bank and thus make a seemly piazza, ... and indeed, had it been laid out in this manner the Friary would have lost nothing in the way of convenience and it would have proved more convenient for the rest of the city, and the front of the church would have faced in such a way that those coming to Florence from the Genoa coast would see it from the road, nor would it make the friars' quarters any less convenient, nothing would be disrupted, and all the dormitories and cloisters and refectories and chapter houses would have been conserved not the slightest bit less than in the present manner, and it would nevertheless still look out on the river.

Saalman has observed that the difficulties implicit in this project as regarded religious, adiministrative and political matters were so major and complex as to make it utopian. It was not unfeasible, however, since the authorities were prepared to go a long way in realizing such urban projects. In a recently discovered document of 16 March 1434 the Signoria, deeming itself in all ways responsible for

the elegance and magnificence of the city, seeing that the church of S. Lorenzo has been made grander in structure and ornament, and considering it fitting to enlarge in the same manner the piazza of that church, and keeping in mind that in the houses [marked for demolition] live persons not of honest life and unseemly in that place, in order to make provision for this [enlargement] decrees that all the houses, shops and warehouses, and every edifice whatever it may be and no matter to whom it belongs, that are on that piazza ... are to be destroyed and razed to the ground. And for the execution of this disposition an executive order is to be sent to the *capomaestri* and to the Operai of S. Maria del Fiore that they are to go and destroy and raze to the ground everything specified above.

To discourage any attempt at bribery the penalty for failure to execute this order was set at 100 or 500 florins. Another similar document concerning the same decision mentions consultations with the chapter of S. Lorenzo, and also with the notables of the quarter concerned in this slum clearance project (as we should call it), which would mean the Medici (though Cosimo was still in exile) and the owners of nearby palaces or of chapels in the church. The resolution was taken by secret ballot, though whether unanimously or by majority is not known, and everything indicates that, even though not immediately realized, the piazza began to take shape juridically at least.

At S. Lorenzo it is obvious that the undertaking was made possible by the private advantage that the Medici could get from it, in the matter of enlarging their own palace as well, and the same applied to the other major property owners in the district.[2] The fact that it was Brunelleschi who was assigned to see to the demolition of the houses along the north side of the church, in order to make room for a piazza of something like the present shape, was however in part mere coincidence, since his regular employer, the Opera del Duomo, carried out such public works at least as much as did the Ufficiali delle Torri traditionally responsible for them. Besides, he was already at work on S. Lorenzo, and presuma-

176. The old church of S. Lorenzo before 1459, from the Rustici Codex (Florence, Biblioteca del Seminario). Behind the church is the completed Old Sacristy, its dome appearing here like a crossing dome; on the right is one of the two chapels at the end of the transept. Neither transept nor aisles has side-chapels yet, and the crossing dome and upper part of the transept are still unbuilt. The tall campanile was subsequently demolished.

bly the projects under way required that the land be cleared of other buildings. An anonymous biography of Brunelleschi dating from the first half of the sixteenth century (Florence, Biblioteca Nazionale, Cod. Magliabechiano XVII, 17) speaks of an imposing project he presented for a new Medici Palace to be built directly opposite the façade of S. Lorenzo in such a way that "the door of the palace would face the door of S. Lorenzo" and "where the palace is at present was to be made into a piazza", which means that that square would have extended to the present Via Larga, created to the north of S. Lorenzo by a decree of 1434.[3]

Since, like its predecessor, the new S. Lorenzo was envisaged with a portico acting as an atrium but raised up and reached by a number of steps, the conjunction of the two new buildings would have created a decidedly theatrical ensemble, at least equal to that of the great piazza conceived for the opposite bank of the Arno, which, in its turn, would have necessitated a monumental façade for S. Spirito. The ambitious project, was, however, rejected by Cosimo, perhaps (as Isabelle Hyman suggests) because the union of palace and church would have signified a preponderance of political power with religious implications as well, since such a close connection between basilica and residence was the traditional prerogative of the bishop, or of the supreme civic authorities.

Here again, then, the rejection of a project by Brunelleschi prevented the solution of an existing urban problem. The Medici Palace soon proved inadequate: proposals were made either to move the family residence (to Via Laura) or to double its size, and finally it was abandoned for more regal quarters in the Palazzo Pitti.

Another factor in common between S. Lorenzo and S. Spirito is that their rebuilding was financed with the methods of modern capitalism. In both cases interest on bank or tax funds was appropriated: for the first, the interest on a very large sum deposited in the Monte; for the second, the revenues from the tax on salt. The financing was assured for a limited period, thus presuming a precise and rapid working programme and the hiring of extra labour. Personal contributions such as offerings on special occasions or bequests and the like seem to have been of only secondary importance and indeed, to judge by what happened at S. Lorenzo, precarious and not to be relied on.

The construction of these ambitious mountains of brick and stone, with their enormous dimensions still prominent in the townscape, coincided moreover with the suppression of the confraternities, which, by an order of 19 October 1419, were abolished within a mile of the city of Florence and forbidden to meet in churches or in public or private places under penalty of a fine of 1,000 florins. Their properties were handed over to the chapters, their headquarters converted into dwellings. The Laudesi of S. Lorenzo, who still submitted a tax declaration in 1427, were fined several times before their final suppression in 1432, when all their goods were forfeited to the chapter of S. Lorenzo. Such confraternities, which went back to the thirteenth century, had an important political and economic as well as religious function, and it was for this reason that they were suppressed.

The new religious architecture was, accordingly, exclusively a product of high-level planning, bureaucratic adroitness, a well-oiled banking administration, and an agreement between a very few money-aristocrats supported and encouraged by the political organs of the city. It was not by chance that later, at the time of Savonarola, S. Lorenzo became the eye of a cyclone, the centre of a protest movement, and once again associated with middle-bourgeois and lower-class groups such as the flagellants, the old Laudesi, and the like; nor that the church of S. Spirito, perhaps visited by Martin Luther on his travels in Italy, should be the prototype of that magnificent architecture typical of the Augustinians which during the Reformation was to lead, by reaction, to the burning and destruction of churches, and, indeed, to the proposal that worship should take place in people's houses, or outdoors, without any purpose-built structure.

Beyond these parallels, however, S. Lorenzo and S. Spirito are entirely unlike in their fabric. The former is very rich in moulded and sculptured ornamentation and was an extraordinary field for experiments in the integration of low and high relief with architecture, whereas the latter was built with humble materials of relatively modest cost. Although the columns in both are monolithic and required the greatest of care, those in S. Lorenzo are about 70 cm (28 in.) taller. The chief difference is in the almost total absence of carved mouldings in S. Spirito: thus the Biographer, though admiring the church and considering it rightly "something beautiful ... without peer in Christendom, even with the defects introduced there and tolerated by others", excluded expressly and emphatically from his positive verdict the materials in which it was built.

In both churches the original project did not provide for any ornamentation. At the most this might have consisted of low-relief decoration along the entablature above the arches of the nave, unless perhaps there was some thought of reserving that space for a long inscription, as in S. Bernardino at Urbino. The design of the chapels and their limited illumination were not such as to invite large altarpieces; in S. Spirito the altars were even placed so that the officiant would have to face the centre of the church, as in the Early Christian Church. No space was specifically designated, in the nave at any rate, for frescoes — in S. Lorenzo such spaces are, as it were, only fragments of the longitudinal walls — but the plaster would surely have been colour-washed, as we see in Fra Angelico's painting. The even lighting, even if filtered through stained glass, could not give rise to scenographic and picturesque effects, and it is highly doubtful that stained-glass windows were ever considered. In the Old Sacristy of S. Lorenzo, when Cosimo de' Medici paid for glass and bronze for windows in the dome, he did not have them filled with coloured glass, yet this was years after the work had been completed.[4] True, one can adduce the precedent of the extremely simple Early Christian and Romanesque previous church of S. Lorenzo, but more convincing and more susceptible to documentation is the hypothesis that behind this project may have been a tendency towards religious reform, highly intellectual in character.

S. Lorenzo[5]

With S. Lorenzo we come head on against the difficulties of unravelling the tangled skein of its history, aided by a complex but still incomplete series of documents.[6]

On 28 September 1417, in the presence of the Priors and the Gonfaloniere di Giustizia, Don Matteo Dolfini — only very recently elected Prior of S. Lorenzo — in order to avoid direct interference by the Pope in the nomination of successive priors who, according to the statute, were to be named only by the canons, petitioned for the protection of the city of Florence, its population and its magistrates, "to defend, to preserve and to enhance the said church or to increase it or any whatsoever of its goods and rights".[7]

continued on page 179

177. S. Lorenzo today. What looks like an outer aisle is in fact the row of side-chapels, built and encased after Brunelleschi's death, giving the exterior a blocklike, stepped effect alien to his style. A document of 1434 called for a row of independent rectangular chapels which would have had individual roofs at right angles to the aisles.

178. The low twin roofs of the Medici family double-chapel of SS. Cosmas and Damian, the oldest part of the new church. Above them is the transept-end, to the left the Old Sacristy.

179. The same area seen from further away, showing how the decorated cornice added to tie in the Old Sacristy, on the left, masks the independent roofs of the Medici double-chapel (see *fig. 63*).

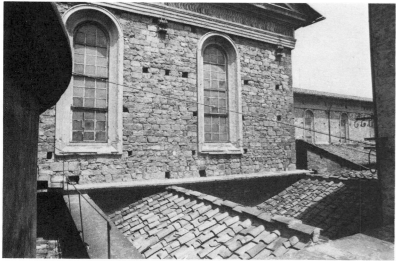

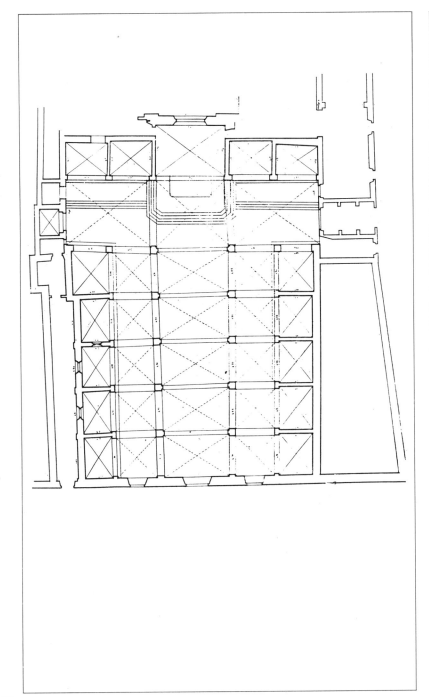

180. Plan of S. Trinita, a typical Florentine arrangement with chapels at the junction of nave and transept.

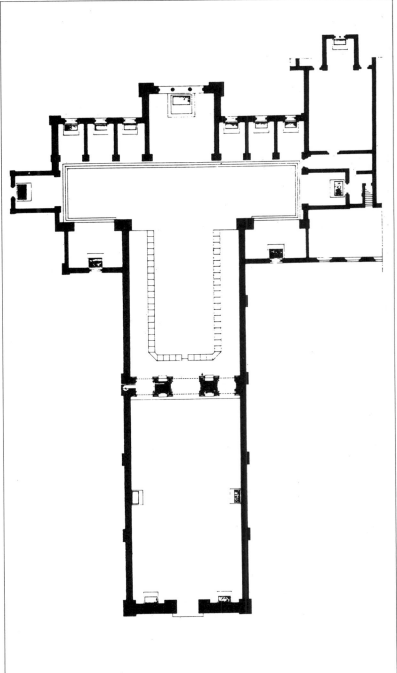

181. Plan of S. Maria del Carmine, Florence, as it was in 1439, with a similar disposition of nave, transept and chapels (by Lisi).

182. Plan of S. Lorenzo at basement level. The extensions to the Old and New Sacristies, on the left and right, have independent basements and are not shown. (1 cm = 6.17 m; 1 in. = 51 ft 5 in.)

183. Plan of S. Lorenzo at ground level. The transept chapels are as follows, clockwise from the chancel: Della Stufa, consecrated in 1461; Ciai (now Ridolfi), building in 1458; then a door which led to the street; then the Neroni (originally Ginori) double-chapel, finished in 1463; the Corsi Chapel, and, across the nave, the Chapel of the Operai (now Martelli), both a departure from the original plan for a deeper transept, after 1448/50; the Medici double-chapel of SS. Cosmas and Damian; and the Ginori and Rondinelli Chapels. (1 cm = 5.61 m; 1 in. = 46 ft 9 in.)

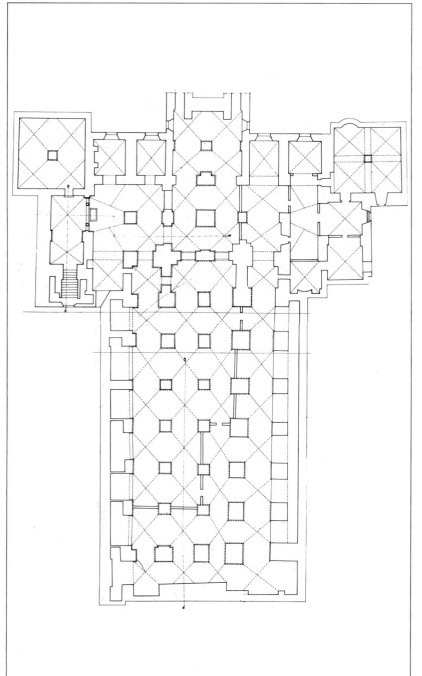

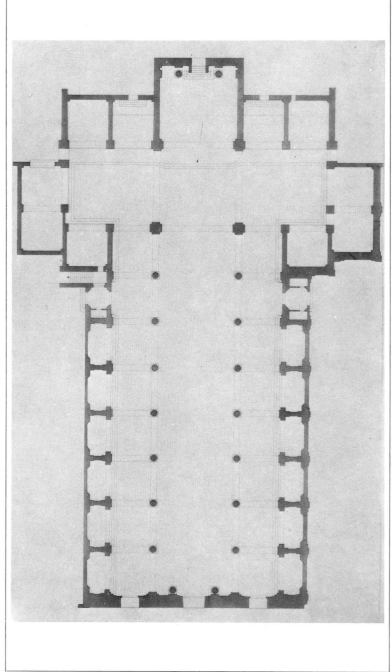

184. Measured plan of S. Lorenzo at ground level, without the Old and New Sacristies. (1 cm = 5.61 m; 1 in. = 46 ft 9 in.)

185. Plan of S. Lorenzo to show original roofing concealed beneath the present aisle roofs. The Chapel of the Operai, at the end of the left transept, and the two aisle bays following it have pitched roofs, as does the Corsi Chapel (balancing that of the Operai), where work seems to have been completed, with tiling, before the decision was made to cover aisles and chapels with a single roof. (To the same scale)

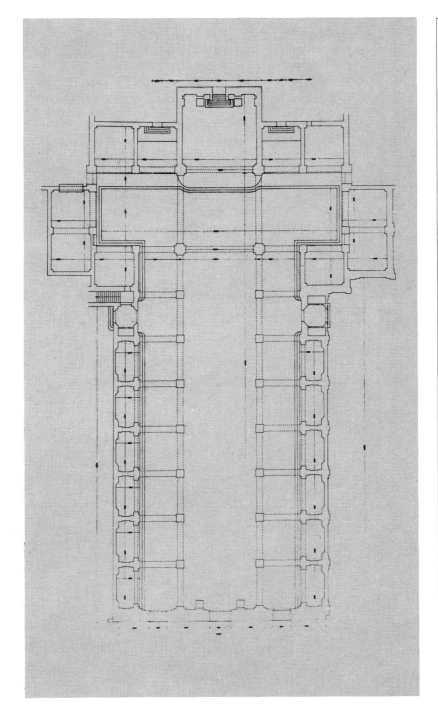

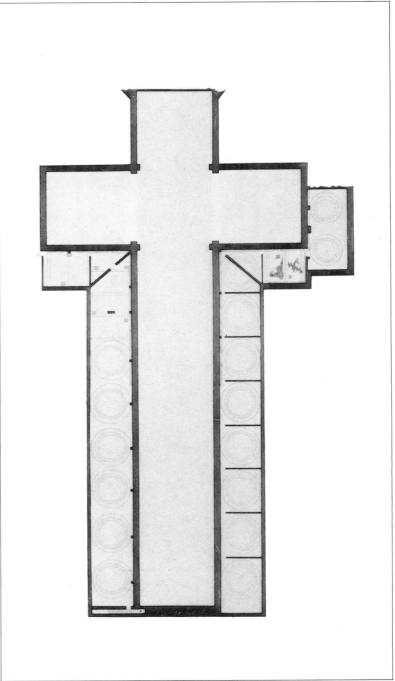

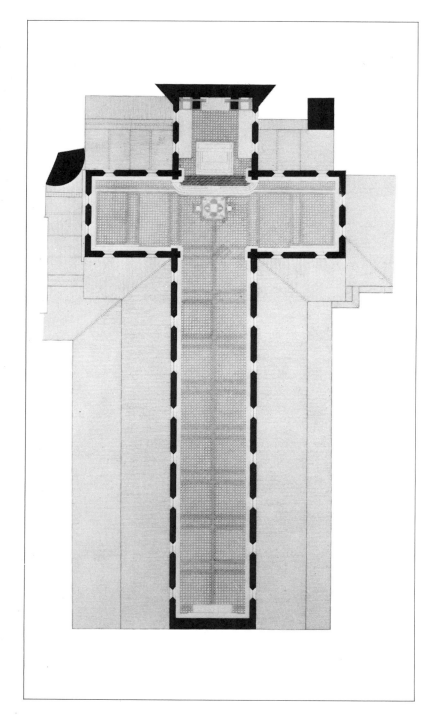

186. Plan of S. Lorenzo at the level of the internal gallery. The pitched roofs of the chapels at the ritual north, or left, end of the transept and along its ritual east side are still visible from outside. (To the same scale)

As a preliminary measure the new Prior had reformed the centuries-old constitutions and, with the addition of fourteen clauses, extended the custom of sermons to all Sundays in the year plus certain holy days, replaced offerings in kind by donations of money, and provided special concessions to canons intending to pursue theological studies, aiming thereby to establish the church and monastery as a cultural centre of distinction. One of the first acts to ensue from this was the permit requested on 22 December 1418 [8] and granted to expropriate gradually an extensive area — where the transept of the church now lies — with the intention of extending the Early Christian basilica on the ritual east side by the considerable length of 65 *braccia*, to a width of 110 *braccia* (38.78 by 65.626 m, or about 127 by 215 ft).[9] This meant demolishing a number of houses and absorbing a street (the Via dei Preti) and a small piazza near the belltower. The measurements more or less match those of the present structure if one includes also the Old Sacristy (without the *scarsella*) and allows for another chapel (again without the *scarsella*) at the right end of the transept where the New Sacristy was eventually built. The enlargement, according to the document of 1418, was to comprise "cappellis, sacristia, et aliis opportunis" (chapel, sacristy and other facilities), but the chancel would have projected much less than it does. There is no mention of demolishing the old church, which in fact remained in use until after 1465, so the date of 22 December 1418 cannot be taken as the start of work on a new church: the act only ordered the expropriation and demolition of the adjacent houses, a task to be carried out by the Ufficiali della Società delle Torri, the civil engineer corps of the time. Moreover, the registers of the Camerlenghi, the public bursars, furnish the first notices of demolitions, and these were not until 1422 and 1424, after the death of Matteo Dolfini.

Dolfini had, however, already taken steps to begin the project: after vespers on 10 August 1421, the Vicar, the Operai and the Masters went in procession to a piazzetta behind the ancient belltower, to the right of the present nave, and "each gave a blow with the mattock where the foundations were to be dug". This symbolic act was then celebrated with a supper of "pastry horns [*cialdoni*], peaches, fennel and shelled nuts".[10] Matteo Dolfini, unfortunately, died only a few months later, leaving the task of the new construction to Benedetto Schiattesi.

For his ambitious project the Prior of S. Lorenzo presumably drew inspiration from the Carmine and other fourteenth-century churches in Florence [180, 181], making alterations to the existing basilica and raising the new transept a good deal higher over a large vaulted crypt [182]. (The Old Sacristy was also built over a spacious undercroft.) Thus, when Brunelleschi — already responsible for the sacristy — was called in, the only variants possible were in the elevation. Saalman's suggestion that the plan of the transept was in no way due to Brunelleschi is certainly correct: everything was basically fixed; and the most he could have done was to extend the chancel in order to make room for the choir stalls. This happened later, however, as we shall see, and probably did not involve Brunelleschi.

Here again we can turn to the Biographer who, significantly, discusses the work in S. Lorenzo after, not before, that on the Foundling Hospital (f. 309r):

Thus likewise in the construction of the church of S. Lorenzo in Florence, begun by its parishioners, the Prior of the church at that time having made himself master of the works, the opinion being that he conceived it [the design] in the manner of the architects of those times, he had begun it with brick pillars; [but] Giovanni de' Medici, known as di Bicci, a man of repute and among the most

187. Schematic section across the transept of S. Lorenzo. (1 cm = 5.13 m; 1 in. = 42 ft 9 in.)

188. Simplified longitudinal section of S. Lorenzo. (1 cm = 7.78 m; 1 in. = 64 ft 10 in.)

189. Longitudinal section of SS. Apostoli, Florence. (To the same scale)

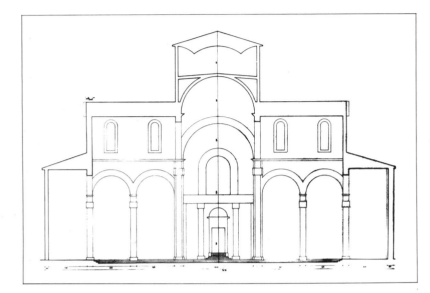

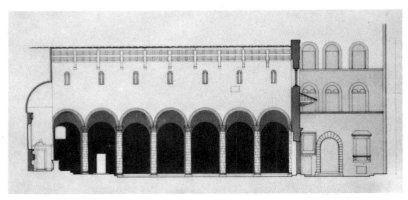

powerful in the city and wealthy, having undertaken to build a sacristy and a chapel, the which he had decided and arranged and promised on his own, and Filippo having started to work to his orders (Giovanni wishing to do something beautiful and lavish), he went to discuss [the general plan of the church].

The date of this consultation, which is crucial for the entire history of the church as well as for that of Brunelleschi, can perhaps be deduced from a jigsaw puzzle of documents and information. To start with, it would have to have been between December 1418 and 1429, the year in which Giovanni de' Medici died, and closer to the first date than to the second. With the death of Matteo Dolfini, and the need to decide in September 1424 who was to direct the project, steps were taken to elect the Operai who would be responsible for carrying on the work in progress. The names of those wardens are not known. It is also possible that advice was requested from the *capomaestri* at S. Maria del Fiore, and that is how Brunelleschi entered the picture (in view too of his success with the Old Sacristy) and came to be granted official powers and the right to discuss authoritatively what should be done and how, and to introduce essential modifications.

The Biographer leaves no doubt that the work was already well advanced. The Medici patron, he says, asked Brunelleschi "what he desired to do in the church and what he thought of what had been planned and built so far"; the architect's comments on the earlier work were diplomatic and vague, "always lauding and commending it; but if they should wish to do something more handsome and richer, he showed them a number of ways to do so" — that is, a number of possible designs (f. 309r). Certainly it was his suggestion that instead of octagonal pillars there should be supports of Classical form, and that architectonic decoration should be introduced. The Biographer explains (f. 308r-v):

This is why Giovanni, having met with others among the population, and because the design appeared to him very rich in worked stones [*conci*; another manuscript has *cornici*, cornices] and consequently more costly, being of generous nature he nevertheless came to the conclusion that the old fabric should be abandoned and torn down and that everything should be done according to one of the proposals of Filippo.

The phrase is somewhat ambiguous, but it seems probable that the "old fabric" to be torn down refers to some walls of the project initiated by Dolfini. Up to this point the intention had been to extend the Early Christian church, not to replace it.

The solution that was chosen involved adopting the designs for the transept but working out a new type of crossing to link the new work to the old church. Here is the Biographer (f. 309v):

And thus with both drawing and words the various arrangements for the church were explained, both in the transept arms and in the main body without the chapels as in the disposition divised by Filippo, on the basis of which Giovanni and the other citizens made their decision ... And Giovanni, to ensure that this would be done, confirmed all that he had offered at the beginning concerning the beautiful and large and ornate sacristy and chapel, [and declared himself ready to pay for] the chancel and even the entire body of the church that remained, except for the chapels and the walls above the chapels, which other citizens might want; and he ordered that Filippo make designs for this.

A number of interesting points emerge from this passage. According to the new project the transept would have chapels assigned to private patrons; the Medici were not yet interested in assuming patronage of the

continued on page 186

190. Looking up the nave of S. Lorenzo towards the altar.

191. Looking across the transept of S. Lorenzo, from the left to the right arm (the high altar is on the left). Only a small part of what one sees here — the far left corner at ground level — goes back to Brunelleschi's original scheme, and even that has been altered.

192. Looking from the left arm of the transept towards the façade: on the left is the aisle, with chapel openings, on the right the Chapel of the Operai (now Martelli). The nave chapels were not added until after 1460, but the project of 1434 (by Brunelleschi?) envisaged deep chapels opening off the aisles; and the Chapel of the Operai, though itself post-Brunelleschi, gives an idea of what those might have been like.

OVERLEAF

193, 194. Looking from the transept at the nave, aisles, and side-chapels. On the left of *fig. 193* is the Corsi Chapel, on the right of *fig. 194* the Chapel of the Operai.

On leaving the transept and entering the nave, one passes abruptly from a system of walled chapels to a system of open arcades, and from pilasters and piers to columns.

entire church; but their additional chapel — actually a double-chapel — because of its position beside the Old Sacristy would condition the form that the opposite arm of the transept should take, since symmetry would have to be preserved.

It should be said that if we take the Biographer literally it is because he is so well informed on everything to do with S. Lorenzo that one is led to think he must have learned about it from Brunelleschi himself, or his close friends, and indeed in one place (f. 310v) he gives Luca della Robbia as his source. Even where there is some ambiguity or historical incongruity in his text the archive documents confirm the general reliability of his information. Here, however, he was certainly wrong about one basic thing: nothing proves such a direct commitment by Giovanni, and the documents attribute this larger commitment to Cosimo, in 1442 (see below, note 16). But if we interpret the passage to refer to Giovanni's support for a new plan for the church, or even to a design presented by him for a transept well endowed with private chapels, that would help to explain why a new foundation ceremony (perhaps specifically to do with the Medici double-chapel) took place on 16 August 1425. It would also explain why the work on the church as a whole, which was still chiefly a public undertaking, was interrupted soon afterwards because of the wars,[11] whereas in the privately endowed Old Sacristy it continued undisturbed. Already in 1429 that building, together with the adjacent double-chapel, could be officially handed over to the church by Giovanni de' Medici, as at least legally completed and appropriately endowed.

In 1431 the new transept was a reality at least as a structural system, with chapels said to be "of equal dimensions and identical in style".[12]

The next date is 1434: an important document of that year has recently been discovered, which sheds new light on the original design for the chapels that were to open off the nave aisles, quite different from the present ones.[13] On 3 June a small group of private patrons declared their intention of building such chapels — perhaps already with the thought of completely replacing the old S. Lorenzo. The chapels were to be similar to those of the transept, already built or under construction. It appears that the chapel of Giovanni de' Medici had been roofed, since it is singled out to provide a model for an oculus to be made above the architrave over the entrance to each side chapel. The chapels were to open off the outer walls of the aisles, and to continue the decorative system of the transept, with pilasters, capitals, architrave, frieze and cornice. They were to be separated by pilasters projecting 1/4 *braccio* and to have an opening 6.565 m (slightly over 18 1/2 ft) high. Each chapel would consist of a smaller and rigorously proportioned chamber measuring 4.085 by 2.0425 m (roughly 13 ft 5 in. by 6 ft 8 in.). We must therefore suppose that the dividing pilasters would have been framed by strips of wall, whose width can be established as 90.165 cm (35 1/2 in.) on each side. Contrary to what Saalman maintains, the chapels must have been not rounded but rectangular: this can be deduced from the fact that their exterior is here decreed to be rectilinear. Moreover each chapel was to be independent, since the decree speaks of bases and cornices in the plural, not as single continuous elements. This means also that each chapel had its own independent roof and was separated from its neighbours by a gap.

For the interior of the chapels the decree prescribes corner ornaments in stone, as in the *scarsella* of the sacristy (which is called "new") [65]. Presumably these are the slender abbreviated corner pilasters found also in the transept chapels [200]. Continuity with the transept was to be ensured by two continuous steps and an interrupted one, which would circle the interior of the chapels. On that step in each chapel there would be an altar, which would rest on one central and four corner colonnettes. An interesting point is the prescription — identical to that made later by Pius II for his cathedral in Pienza — that painting was to be limited to a square altarpiece, the square format being an archaeologizing novelty, referred to as "all' antica" in later documents concerning pictorial commissions (though not commissions for S. Lorenzo).

Finally one must note a single incongruity in the document, the directive that the chapels to be added to the aisles should have the same height on the exterior as those in the transept. This is impossible, since to admit light to the oculi in the wall above them the roofs over these chapels had to be very much lower. What was probably intended was that their height should reach the large exterior cornice. Other than this error, one is struck by the lack of a clear binding definition of the ornamentation and form of the windows of the side chapels, even if one can take as valid the reference to what was done in the Old Sacristy and its "tribune", the *scarsella*.

One of the most interesting features of the document is the specificity of the architectural terms employed and the fact that they are mentioned not singly but in groupings: thus, pilaster, base and capital; architrave, frieze and cornice; base and cornice. Such precise terminology encourages me to think that behind this document there must have been a written proposal by Brunelleschi himself.

Evidently an architectural drawing existed and was the basis for the design of the side chapels when they were finally realized, in the 1460s to 1480s.[14] There were modifications, however: they were made broader, by reducing the strips of wall beside the pilasters and hollowing out the dividing walls between the chapels, and additional depth was acquired in the same manner; the third step was not continued around the interior of the chapels; the extremely simple and schematic decoration with abbreviated corner pilaster strips was eliminated; on the exterior a continuous single-slope roof was built the length of the aisles, and, consistent with this, the chapels were given a continuous common outer wall [177].

In 1440, complaining that for something like fifteen years — surely an exaggeration — everything had been at a standstill, a larger assembly of citizens decided that the high altar chapel (the chancel, or more precisely at this stage the area of the crossing), begun but left in disarray because of financial difficulties, should be consigned to any citizen or citizens of the parish of S. Lorenzo "in order to have it built and finished", conceding permission also to build in the high altar chapel and on any of its walls, and to have it completed in any way the new patron pleased.[15]

That decision marked the end of civic and ecclesiastical direction of the undertaking. The allocation to one or more private citizens was due partly to the poverty attendant on the war and a general fall in the standard of living, because of which, according to the document of 1440, it was difficult for both the Chapter and the city to survive, let alone to build or to finish the building tasks initiated. But it also reflects a general decline in civic spirit, something which the documents of the guilds, curiously enough, attest to much more specifically, or at least less ambiguously, than those of other bodies.

Then too the position of the Medici, by how represented by Cosimo, was curious. Significantly, in 1440 neither he nor his representatives

196. Detail of one of the crossing piers in S. Lorenzo.

197. Looking across at the right-hand side of the nave. Note the inconsistencies between the arches of the nave arcade and those of the chapels, added after 1470, when changes were probably also made to the decoration of the aisle walls.

took part in the solemn assembly called to re-launch the building programme, which proves that the family had assumed no other commitment beyond the sacristy and their double-chapel. As it happens, no one came forward to take on responsibility for the chancel and crossing area. But it was not until two years later, in 1442, that the Medici volunteered to be patrons, as the only wealthy family in the quarter with an interest in the project.[16] Up to that time there existed only extensive foundations, perhaps part of the walls, but not yet the raised floor of the presbytery, while at the left, standing out amidst these modern ruins, rose the sacristy endowed by the Medici, completed and with a large part of its interior decorated (though it is difficult to give a precise date to Donatello's work), and alongside it their double-chapel, vaulted and decorated inside and on the outside joined to the sacristy by a large cornice with reliefs adorned with cherubim and the gridiron of St Laurence [63, 179]. Unfortunately it is not possible to explore beneath the tiled roofs to discover whether the cupolas of the double-chapel were protected by a brickwork interspace like those of the Old Sacristy, but the roofs do show a characteristic double pitch which would have made the side view of S. Lorenzo much like that of S. Croce.

What the subsequent relations of Brunelleschi with Cosimo were is not known. But as a first step and certainly to lighten the financial burden Cosimo did decide to reduce the dimensions of the transept, narrowing it by almost one bay from east to west, and to displace the high altar and choir, originally intended to be in the crossing beneath the dome, into a projecting chancel.[17] The present depth of this space is about 12 m (39 ft) and corresponds to the area that would have been available in the crossing (as in S. Spirito [202]) had the transept not been reduced in size. The chancel appears on the exterior as a totally dissociated body, and indeed constitutes the third quasi-independent element in this unhappily modified ensemble. But it is inside that the trouble really arises, and irremediably. The second chapel at the end of the transept on the left is virtually cut off, leaving no more than the space required for a door should it be desired to close it off, thus ruling out the possibility of a door communicating with the monastery. On the opposite side it was necessary to give up the idea of a second sacristy in order to use the space for a door to the exterior.[18] The nonsensical consequences are numerous: there are, for example, false doors totally without function.

It is curious that such incongruities have been so little noticed, though many writers have made much ado about all sorts of "errors" in the church. This is because the critics have kept their eyes glued too much to the ground: Vasari, for one, snapped at "the columns set on the floor without putting beneath them a plinth which, by rights, should be as high as the level of the bases of the piers that stand on the steps [in front of the side chapels], so that seeing the pier shorter than the column makes the entire edifice look as if it were limping" [193, 194]. Yet the inability to harmonize the central supports with the noble steps that run all around the transept and would later be continued along the aisles is a most modest imperfection compared with the general confusion and defects in proportions, the more so since this was not the first but the second time Brunelleschi had attempted to fit a modern building into a traditional one.[19] Had the transept been deeper the dome would have been treated in a different way from what we see now, unless the chancel were given other dimensions. The windows at the ends of the transept would have been on the same axes as the chapels beneath them and therefore farther apart.

198. Detail of the pier between the left aisle of S. Lorenzo and the Chapel of the Operai; in the background, an abbreviated pilaster in the chapel.

199. The "eastern" wall of the left-hand transept, with the Ginori and Rondinelli Chapels; at the extreme right is the chancel. The plan of these chapels, with their dividing walls of Trecento type, probably goes back to a project pre-dating Brunelleschi's.

In 1445 further encouragement was given to potential private patrons. In response to the request of the Chapter, approved by the Bishop, "to be permitted to allocate and grant the sites of the chapels to whomever it pleases us or we deem fitting, in order that the church may be more rapidly brought to perfection and completion", the eight chapels envisaged by Brunelleschi were increased to ten by the addition of another two between transept and nave.[20] For this awkward solution, decided on when the piers supporting the dome had been in place ever since 1442 and therefore after all the details had been settled, the idea came from other Florentine churches. The junction with the nave is no less awkward than in, for example, the Carmine and S. Trinita [180, 181]. Inserted into these difficult spaces were on the left the Chapel of the Operai (under construction in 1447, still incomplete in 1450), and on the right that of the Corsi family (decided on only in 1448). On the exterior they looked like incongruous additions, with their roofs badly aligned. But there was reason for haste: Cosimo had agreed to pay for all the new work, but had committed himself for no more than six years.

To reconstruct in one's imagination the original plan of the transept, one must open up the terminal double-chapels inwards so that they face each other fully at opposite ends of the transept, and also shift the doors that now front the second (closed) chapels to make them balance the doors opening into the two sacristies, at the same time giving them the function not of a bit of stage scenery but of real passages to the exterior. The transept would thus be extended farther to the ritual west, gaining sufficient depth to house the choir, as in S. Spirito [202]. Minor modifications, such as the large niches over the doors, attributed by Saalman to Michelozzo, would in any case prove marginal with respect to the enhanced importance of the crossing. The design as we see it now seems to me maimed and stunted, and deserving of the same judgment that Brunelleschi pronounced on Michelozzo's project for the choir of SS. Annunziata: "It was designed by Michelozzo and in such manner as to be damned by Filippo, our Master, for several reasons: first of all because it was erected so close up against the church that there remains no proper crossing for the nave and the body of the church. ... And it does not work, either in itself or in relation to the whole, which is why this work is condemned in its entirety".[21]

If we look separately at the left arm of the transept of S. Lorenzo, the only part actually built by Brunelleschi, we find him intent on translating into modern terms the theme of the Classical basilica and conferring an unprecedented solemnity on the arches and chapels, each like a small church furnished with truly noble architectonic decoration [199]. (Only the capitals of the pilasters on the end wall next to the Old Sacristy are by Brunelleschi, according to Saalman.[22]) The design is reminiscent of the Badia at Fiesole — built too late to be by Brunelleschi but perhaps reflecting his ideas in a less compromised form than here [23] — or even of what Alberti did in S. Andrea at Mantua. The device of inserting a dosseret between capital and arch and extending it as an entablature could have been derived from the Portico of Pompey in Rome.[24] Brunelleschi may have intended to cover the entire transept with a grandiose barrel vault instead of the present flat wooden ceiling, a vault that would have been continued in the nave if, as the Biographer says, he was unhappy about having to design a plan with aisles rather than deep side chapels which would have continued the formal arrangement initiated in the transept.

Thanks to the documents assembled by Isabelle Hyman, the building history of the transept and the first three bays is now well established (see above, note 6). Shortly afterwards a further financial agreement had to be made, again with Cosimo, and with still other muddles and errors. In 1457 it was finally time to erect the dome: we know from a letter of 1 May of that year that Antonio Manetti Ciaccheri, who was in charge of the work, resorted to violence to prevent his project from being exposed to examination by outsiders, and the writer of the letter, Giovanni di Domenico da Gaiole, was twice given a trouncing for having said no more than that he was thinking of going to Cosimo and suggesting that the type of dome used in S. Spirito be adopted because in the long run "it would cost him less to demolish and re-do that tribune [the crossing] in the manner of Filippo, which is light, strong, well illuminated, and of good proportions, than to continue with this unfitting one". That letter fully bears out the criticisms of the Biographer and his warning not to mistake the nave, transept and crossing for work by Brunelleschi because "there is nothing in them of his excellence [onore]" but rather "numerous improprieties both in things necessary to the building and in defects in beauty both inside and outside".

Haste, at any rate, did make it possible to complete the enlargement "alla Romana" of the Ambrosian and Romanesque basilica by 1459, in time for the solemn visit of Pius II and Galeazzo Maria Sforza, Duke of Milan. On that occasion the church and its sacristy were celebrated in a poem which if not elegant in style does offer an appreciative reading of the building according to Quattrocento canons, with emphasis on certain elements which, because they have deteriorated or been replaced, we might be inclined to undervalue, among them the splendid way in which the predominantly horizontal rhythm of the bays concludes at the top in a ceiling painted in ultramarine with gilded decorations:

> Cercando in tutto 'l mondo le più ornate
> Chiese di Dio so che parrebbon brutte
> Quand'elle fosser poi paragonate
> Con San Lorenzo ch'ha le beltà tutte
> Eccelse, magne, degne e peregrine
> Fatte murar da Cosimo et construtte.
> La maggior nave ha il palco d'oro fine
> D'azzurro oltrammarino et pien di rose
> Lustranti come stelle mattutine.
> Non credo che mai più si magne cose
> Si facessero in chiese come quelle
> Degne, ammirande et sì miracolose.
> Veramente la volta delle stelle
> Non mostra più lucente o più serena
> Che in San Lorenzo queste cose belle.
> Da ogni banda è questa nave piena
> Di colonne d'un pezzo grosse e grandi
> D'una pietrina gentile et amena
> Con capitelli d'intagli ammirandi
> Occhi di pietre concie et finestrati
> Et lavori di vetro vi son pansi
> Et messi in volta vi sono gli altri lati
> Delle due navi e è ciascuna snella
> Di splendidi gentili et degni ornati.
> Un magno altare nella maggior cappella
> E dall'un lato è una sagrestia
> Che mai più non ne fu una sì bella
> Et si meravigliosa et sì giulìa
> Che chi la mira fiso par ch'abbagli

> Perchè per tutto par che sol vi sia.
> Evvi tanti gentili e begli intagli
> Di porfidi di vetri e vari marmi
> Ch'io non so chosa degna a che l'agguagli.
> Nel mezzo è il sepolcro suo che parmi
> Che di tanti ornamenti belli appaia
> Ch'io non saprei a dirgli da qual farmi.
> Di più fiorini che diciotto migliaia
> È già di questa sagrestia la spesa.
> Chi dicessi altro falsamente abbaia.
> Or pensa tu quel che verrà la chiesa
> Che rappresenta proprio un paradiso
> Quando fornita sia come l'è impresa.[25]

(Were one to seek out in all the world the most ornate churches of God, I know that they would seem crude indeed when compared to S. Lorenzo, whose beauties are all of the highest, greatest, most worthy, and rarest, as built and constructed by Cosimo. The nave has its ceiling in fine gold, with ultramarine blue and full of roses gleaming like morning stars. I scarce believe that things more peerless were ever done in churches than these which are so stately, admirable, and in truth miraculous. Truly the vault of the heavens shows no more lucent nor more serene than these lovely things in S. Lorenzo. In every bay this nave is full of columns hewn in a single piece, thick and tall, of a delicate and graceful stone, with admirable carved capitals, round windows of hewn stone with glass set into them, and the aisles are vaulted, and each is elegant with splendid, graceful and worthy ornaments. A high altar in the chancel, and to one side is a sacristy such that never has there been one so beautiful, and so marvellous is it and so festive that he who gazes long at it thinks himself blinded because there seems sun in all of it. And in it are so many lovely and beautiful inlays of porphyry, glass and diverse marbles that I can think of nothing worthy to which to compare them. In the middle is his [Giovanni de' Medici's] sepulchre which, methinks, is adorned with ornaments so many and beautiful that I do not know where to being in describing them. The expense of this sacristy has already gone beyond eighteen thousand florins. Who would say otherwise, rants falsely. Now think you what that church will become, which will look like a paradise when it is finished as it was undertaken.)

By 1470 at least part of the old church had been demolished. However splendid the nave that we see today [190], it represents another chapter in the architectural history of the church, following the death of Brunelleschi. The design seems taken over bodily from S. Spirito [205], enriched and much more decorated thanks to the wealth of the patron,[26] and not even properly related to its own outer walls. Those walls present another problem. The little chapels, already planned in 1434, as we have seen, were under construction on the cloister side in 1463-65, and were built on the right side in the 1470s and 1480s, after the demolition of the old nave. They block the windows of the corner chapels of the Operai and the Corsi family, which had been built earlier when the idea of chapels opening off the aisles had been given up. Their architectonic decoration repeats mechanically in half-size that of the transept, with a proportional deformation of the orders and a double grammar and syntax poorly reconciled with each other, as on the entrance wall of the chapels [197].[27]

I am not convinced by the suggestion that, in the process of building from the crossing towards the ritual west end, the side chapels were erected before the nave. A better explanation might be that the nave was planned to be one bay longer (using the two now-functionless

201. Fluting on the lower part of a pilaster in S. Lorenzo: a monumental treatment of *pietra serena*.

columns that flank the central door), and that these two end bays were to have had no side chapels, like the two bays next to the transept: the final bay was then given up and a façade erected, and only later was the last side-chapel added, which is shown by straight joints to be clearly not contemporary with the façade.

An idea of the external appearance of the new church as it was envisaged before the construction of the side chapels is given by a miniature in the Book of Hours of Laodamia de' Medici (London, British Library, MS Yates Thompson 30, f. 20v), which can be dated between 1502 and 1517, probably earlier rather than later. There one sees a façade in Renaissance style with a belltower (and next to it a piazza and the Medici Palace on the right). The accuracy of the representation is such as to suggest that it was copied from a project drawing or model. The famous drawings by Giuliano da Sangallo and Leonardo tell us nothing of the original design for S. Lorenzo.[28]

Let us then try to sum up the role of Brunelleschi in the church as we know it today. He began building the transept on foundations already partly laid before he came on the scene. His initial project was altered, with his consent, because of two related events: the political and economic crisis and the suppression of the confraternities, which eliminated possible patrons for larger chapels. The transept itself was modified after his death, however, when two chapels were added to its juncture with the nave, a change decided on only after deliberations in 1445. What of the nave? According to the Biographer (f. 309v), Brunelleschi "set about to build the church with nave and aisles only reluctantly, because to him that seemed something paltry". And he goes on to say (f. 310v), "the body of the church from the crossing to the façade, which is not in accordance with that transept, may be a handsome thing, but it introduces numerous improprieties both in things necessary to the building and in defects in beauty both inside and outside".[29]

Unfortunately we do not know the name of the architect placed in charge of the work after Brunelleschi had left, that is when work was fully resumed under Cosimo de' Medici, whose contract gave him the right to modify the previous project. It may have been Michelozzo, architect of the nearby Medici Palace, which was placed with the church under a largely unified administrative control.[30] Unity of administration does not necessarily mean unity of stylistic direction, but the same master workmen do turn up repeatedly in the accounts of both projects.

The subsequent building history concerns the New Sacristy and completion of the exterior, including a proposal for a loggia in front of the façade, but the façade remains unfinished to this day.[31]

Investigation of the chapel roofs
by Riccardo Pacciani

Through observation and direct examination of the structures above ground and in the spaces between ceilings and roofs tangible proof has been found of the variations, second thoughts, and abrupt modifications that marked the anything but simple and straightforward process of building S. Lorenzo. We have already seen in Chapter 5 what can be learnt by exploration of the roofs of the Old Sacristy. From the terrace produced by the encasing of the *scarsella* and service rooms one can see that the roofs of the adjoining double-chapel of SS. Cosmas and Damian [*178, 179*], as well as those of the nearby Ginori and Rondinelli Chapels, are pitched in the manner typical of Gothic religious architecture. The line of these roofs doubtless had its rationale in the way they harmonized with, and were integrated into, the much broken-up and, so to speak, empirical line of the roofs of the neighbourhood whose image was surely present, consciously or not, in the conception of the original project. The view of that line from below is blocked, however, by a quite high frieze of *pietra serena* on the encasing wall around the Ginori and Rondinelli Chapels and another of terracotta with reliefs of cherubs' heads and the gridiron of St Laurence around the Medici double-chapel [*179*]. This latter frieze, with its overt function of stressing the formal compactness of the entire structure, might be attributable to Brunelleschi himself or his closest collaborators since the same technique is found in other buildings known to be by him, but this hypothesis cannot immediately be verified. The frieze may have been intended to integrate or closely connect the new church with the Early Christian basilica and the Old Sacristy in a project envisaged but never carried through.

Even a superficial inspection of the spaces beneath the roofs now accessible [*185*] raises a number of problems of attribution and chronology to which the only possible responses for the present consist of plausible and, in some cases, contradictory hypotheses. The Chapel of the Operai (now Martelli) is covered by a hemispherical dome of brick (in which it has not been possible to determine whether herringbone brickwork was used, as in the chapels of S. Spirito), which is in turn covered by a ridged roof or, more accurately, the brickwork supporting structure of a ridged roof which however shows no vestiges of tiles nor any imprint of them in the plaster. The apex of the dome on the inside is not the same as the ridgeline of the structure immediately above it but is, instead, aligned with the axis of the window above it, evidence that the dome was built later. The presence of small drainage channels for rainwater suggests that the work was laid out and brought almost to completion on the model of the preceding chapels and that the various interruptions and resumptions resulted in more and more shifts and readjustment of the alignments.

Questions of this sort are even more numerous as regards the covering of the bay where the transept and left aisle meet. Here we find the same technique of roofing, with the difference that the direction of the ridge line (again complete as a brickwork structure but with no trace of tiles) is at right angles to that of the Chapel of the Operai. The space covered is moreover larger: measurements at floor level have shown that this bay is wider than those preceding it and more markedly wider than the others along the nave aisle. The alignment of the axes of roof and window is respected, but here there is no trace of drainage channels. The covering of the bay adjoining the door to the cloister is smaller than the one before it though of identical structure and orientation. At the third bay from the transept, and therefore adjoining the Aldobrandini Chapel, the large cornice in roughly worked stone that already ran along the wall above the Chapel of the Operai breaks off. That a large cornice was intended for the exterior is shown by the fact that the lower surface of the stone blocks is grooved for rain drainage. The interruption occurs precisely above the third column of the nave, at the point where the old basilica was joined to the new construction. There too the double-roofing of the bays stops, and to the end of the aisle there are only domes without a pitched masonry structure over them. Doubtless when the work reached this phase it was finally decided to cover the aisles with a single-slope roof which extended over the roofs already in place and completely modified the exterior appearance of the church.

The coverings of the bays of the right aisle are very similar to those of the left aisle, with simple brickwork domes and no intermediate roof.

Here too, at the level of the third column of the nave the heavy stone cornice stops.

Of all those observable in the spaces beneath the roofs, the covering of the Corsi Chapel (built after 1448-50) appears to have been carried furthest. Besides drainage grooves it has the double-roof found in the bays of the left aisle, but here on the outer surface of the pitched roof, or more precisely in the plaster covering the ridgeline, there are imprints of tiles. The stone cornice runs around three sides of the chamber (this may by part of the unfinished plan to cover the pediments of the chapels with a large cornice, an attempt already noted for the Chapel of SS. Cosmas and Damian) and, supported on a stone wall, partially blocks access to the compartment containing the domes over the Neroni family double-chapel at the end of the right transept adjacent to the New Sacristy. This is evidence that the Corsi Chapel was built before the others in the same aisle and the adjacent double-chapel in the transept.

The pitched roofs of the Della Stufa and Ciai (now Ridolfi) Chapels on the ritual east side of the right transept are directly visible on the exterior, further confirmation that the ensemble of the transept was built earlier than the aisles.

S. Spirito[32]

Bernini was certainly not mistaken when he showed his pupils S. Spirito, "saying to them: this is the most beautiful church in the world". Juvarra, too, when he visited the church in 1714 made a drawing of it on which he noted: "For me, this is very beautiful architecture. ... I have examined it and find it very beautiful."[33]

At S. Spirito, as at S. Lorenzo, the building history is complex and was much affected by administrative and economic crises. The church had already once been enlarged, between 1269 and 1301 or 1308 (this was the building that burnt in 1471). The idea of rebuilding it on a yet larger scale goes back to a public votive act in 1397, intended to commemorate the Florentine victory over the Milanese at Governolo near Mantua.[34]

Funds began to be gathered, witness a bequest made in 1411 (or 1421?) for a chapel in the new building.[35] Subsequently various attempts must have been made to establish a firm financial basis for the undertaking, and about 1428 — when the nationalist-minded Gregorio Dati headed the city administration — five Operai were appointed and Stoldo de' Frescobaldi was named *provveditore* or superintendent. We know this from the Biographer (f. 312v), though he is for once rather vague.[36] It would appear, however, that no decision had as yet been taken as regards an architectural project if on 19 January 1434 Stoldo and Piero di Ghirigoro d'Andrea, both residents of the S. Spirito quarter and wealthy men, were given absolute power to collect funds and make plans. This was the very time when S. Lorenzo was being given up as a public undertaking. In April 1436 " the men of the S. Spirito quarter and the friars of that monastery, meeting together several times concerning the decision that work should begin on the edifice of the church to be made anew and more magnificent, appointed six Operai", again wealthy men of the neighbourhood.[37]

It seems likely that between 1434 and 1436 Brunelleschi made a model, though one not showing the dome or the façade.[38] Work then seems to have stopped.[39] In 1440, however, came the victory at Anghiari, and after the peace on 23 April 1445 four-fifths of the salt tax finally began to be paid over to S. Spirito, supposedly to continue for the next twenty-five years. On 5 April 1446 the first of five columns contracted for at 150 florins was brought to the worksite, and a second was finished and consigned on 25 January 1447.

The fire in 1471 (started, as we shall see in Chapter 14, by careless-ness during a religious drama) proved a new spur for the collection of special funds and for proceeding with the work more energetically.[40] In 1472 there were further payments for columns as well as for capitals and other decorative elements. Much activity in carving and sculpting is documented for 1473 and 1475, and in 1477-78 the aisles were vaulted and the piers to support the cupola were erected according to a model by Salvi d'Andrea based on summary indications from Brunelleschi. In 1479 the building was roofed, an attempt was made to co-ordinate the arcade and clerestorey levels of the nave, and there was discussion and approval of the model of the dome made by Salvi d'Andrea on the basis of Brunelleschi's model, which he was to follow "as much as possible". In 1482 it was decided to reject Brunelleschi's design for a façade with four doors, which documents show had already been begun:[41] the committee's decision was implemented in a model by Salvi d'Andrea, and given formal approval in 1486.

We have already seen how nothing came of the brilliant town-planning proposal for the church to face a piazza open to the river; but in other respects S. Spirito was one of the few buildings in which Brunelleschi was allowed a virtually free hand (even if ambitions and expenses had to be tailored to fit reality), and which was carried through with some degree of fidelity, at least in the ground plan and up to the level of the arcades.

Brunelleschi, who entered the picture at the precise moment when work at S. Lorenzo was blocked, was well aware of what he was about when he proposed that instead of a limited number of costly large chapels there should be a series of niches, forty in all, which would run right round the church, eliminating all contrast between nave and tran-sept: both are lined by an uninterrupted succession of columns and vaults, and perhaps even the inner wall of the façade was intended to have niches.[42] Nor is there any sort or ambiguity or difficulty with proportions: every element is standardized, every space equal, every-thing disposed inflexibly on a grid which is itself based on the simplest unit of measurement.[43] The exterior was originally intended to reflect the interior, with the niches of the chapels bulging out through the wall and independently roofed like so many towers in a curtain wall [223, 224].[44] By about 1469, however, when only the right transept arm and the right side of the chancel had been built up, it was decided to encase the entire undulating surface in a conventional straight wall with a single-slope roof [223]. Evidence for this comes from exploration of the roof and wall space [222] and from the observation of incongruities in the chapel windows [227, 228].

Other incongruities, to which Francesco Quinterio will also be draw-ing our attention, include the failure of the arcade to touch the entabla-ture above it [216] and, a more serious fault recognized by Renaissance writers like Antonio Billi and Antonio da Sangallo the Younger, the awkward section of the crossing piers which is responsible for the asymmetrical vaults in the four bays where nave, transept and chancel meet [214].

Looking at the arcade [205], however, one cannot praise too highly whoever it was who erected the columns and arches with complete respect for the wishes of Brunelleschi as far as they could be read in his

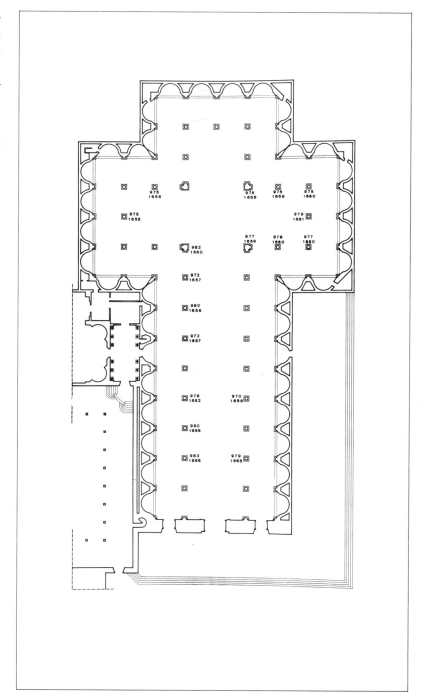

model and learned from his own explanations. It seems incredible that the first column was not raised until eight years after his death, yet the document is perfectly clear:

I record here that on 23 May 1454, a Thursday, at 22 hours [at that time of year, probably about 6 o'clock in the evening], the first column in a single piece was raised in the new church of S. Spirito, this being the column in the middle closest to the [high altar] chapel, and I was present at that laborious task and so can certify it with my own hand. I, Bianco di Ghinozo di Cancellieri di Doffo, woolmaker in Via Maggio.

For these monolithic columns wooden models were presumably required, as at S. Lorenzo, as well as complicated systems of transport and scaffolding to raise them, since they are about 7 m (23 ft) high, only slightly less than in S. Lorenzo. There are thirty-three of them (one more would have completed a loggia inside the façade), whereas in the Medici church, so much richer in carved ornamentation, there are only fourteen plus two inside the main door. In S. Spirito more than anywhere else columns are proved to be the finest ornament a church can have. They are, moreover, not a passive element, not objects in and for themselves. The circle of their shafts is echoed throughout the ground plan and in the half-columns along the walls that support the vaults and frame the chapel niches. Seen in perspective [45] they seem to increase in number and give something of the effect of a mosque, an impression suggested also by the way in which what should be the end walls curve in and bend, creating shadowy, scenographic zones which, in part because of their dim illumination, seem even farther away.

This is in fact the only interior based on rectangular components in which one can evaluate the system of lighting that Brunelleschi intended for his religious buildings — moderate and from above. At human height there are only thin vertical strips of light, whereas the dominant light shines down from above into the nave and aisles, making a clear separation between the terrestrial and spiritual domains. This upper illumination is concentrated in the centre, to attract the faithful from the four corners towards the ceremonies in the choir at the crossing, with an effect similar to that of chapter houses, creating a sense of psychological concentration rather than of mere physical confinement between four walls.[46]

Interior and exterior elevations of S. Spirito
by Francesco Quinterio

"He felt that he had made a church according to his intention as regards the composition of the building." Thus the Biographer (Suppl. MS, f. xlix v) in reporting the artistic result and personal satisfaction of Brunelleschi at having been able to design the church of S. Spirito precisely as he wished and in what must have been a very short time, thanks to the thoroughly understanding patronage of the S. Spirito quarter and the notable gentlemen living there, neither showing the stubbornness he had had to face over the Cathedral dome nor calling for a reduction in the programme, as Cosimo de' Medici had over S. Lorenzo and the family palace, destined never to be built.

But the Biographer continues:

And certainly if it had not strayed from the model [or design] given by Filippo, according to which a few chapels were begun and a part of the walls raised in his lifetime, it would have been something beautiful which, leaving aside the material used, would have been without peer in Christendom, even with the defects introduced there and tolerated by others.

The documents give us the names of those "others", of the *capomaestri* who did the damage and of those who permitted it — the *capomaestri* of higher degree, with the approval of the respectable Operai and "the most well-reputed architects".[47] And so this church is another of those buildings which the historian must try to re-integrate mentally, along the lines of Brunelleschi's grammar and syntax.

The ground plan offers the only certain point of departure. The concept behind it is clear, as is its organization, and it is extremely easy to reconstruct its general form since the alterations were limited to the exterior facing, unanimously condemned ever since the *Libro di Antonio Billi*. (The Biography breaks off just where it speaks of the arbitrary modifications to S. Spirito.) The only unknown data in the plan are the possibility of four niches in the façade wall and the position of the crossing piers.

Taking the ground plan as given and complete, we may try to work out what the architect had in mind for the interior elevation. The first order is known: column, base, capital and impost up to the springing of the arch have a relationship with the impost (which here acts as entablature) of 7:1, with the whole equal to a height of 16 1/2 Florentine *braccia* (16 1/3 had it respected the module more rigorously). We know that a few days before Brunelleschi's death one of five columns ordered from the quarry, and unquestionably designed in dimensions and details by the master himself, was brought to the site. Eight years were to go by before that column could be raised in the ambulatory of the right-hand transept arm, but we may consider the arrangement of the lower order to be faithful to Brunelleschi's original designs and intention.

We cannot be so certain about the proportions of the second order, represented by the four piers that support the dome and by the continuous entablature around the nave, transept and chancel. It is precisely here that the problem comes to a head, with the question of whether the nave was meant to be covered by a flat ceiling or a barrel vault. For this second order Benevolo proposes two solutions, one proportional, the other modular proportional. It is a curious fact that both hypothetical solutions work out to be lower than what we actually have: comprising base, pier, capital and entablature, that has a height of 28 1/4 *braccia* as against the 25 2/3 *braccia* of the proportional hypothesis and the 27 5/12 of the modular proportional scheme. (To grasp this, it must be remembered that the first of Benevolo's solutions takes over the proportion of the first order, with the entablature equal to 1:7, while the second is obtained by laying out five times vertically the module of 5 1/2 *braccia* that governs the entire ground plan [204] as well as the elevation of the first order.)

Why then was the second order heightened? We can be sure that by the time the builders were ready to raise the first pier of the crossing the entire right transept arm, including chapel niches and aisle, had been built up probably to arcade level. Exploration of the interspaces of the walls of the niches shows that on the exterior these were already completed, with all the finishing touches, along the entire right end of the transept, but not yet around the chancel [203a]. It was when that point was reached that it was decided to conceal the succession of apses on the exterior behind a straight wall [222, 223]. Even supposing that such a mutilation might have been necessary for technical reasons, the entire exterior elevation — and the interior as well — was irremediably compromised. To cover the protruding niches it was necessary to use a narrow single-slope roof coming off the outer wall of the nave at a very much higher point than would have been reached by the small

continued on page 206

203. S. Spirito (drawings by Benevolo).
(a) Plan above the level of the aisle vaults. Low dividing walls between the transept aisle vaults [221, 223] are shaded in grey. It is also clear how the original chapel-niches off the aisles are encased and covered by continuous straight roofs.
(b) Ground plan with detailed measurements.
(c) Longitudinal section.
(1 cm = 7.59 m; 1 in. = 63 ft 3 in.)

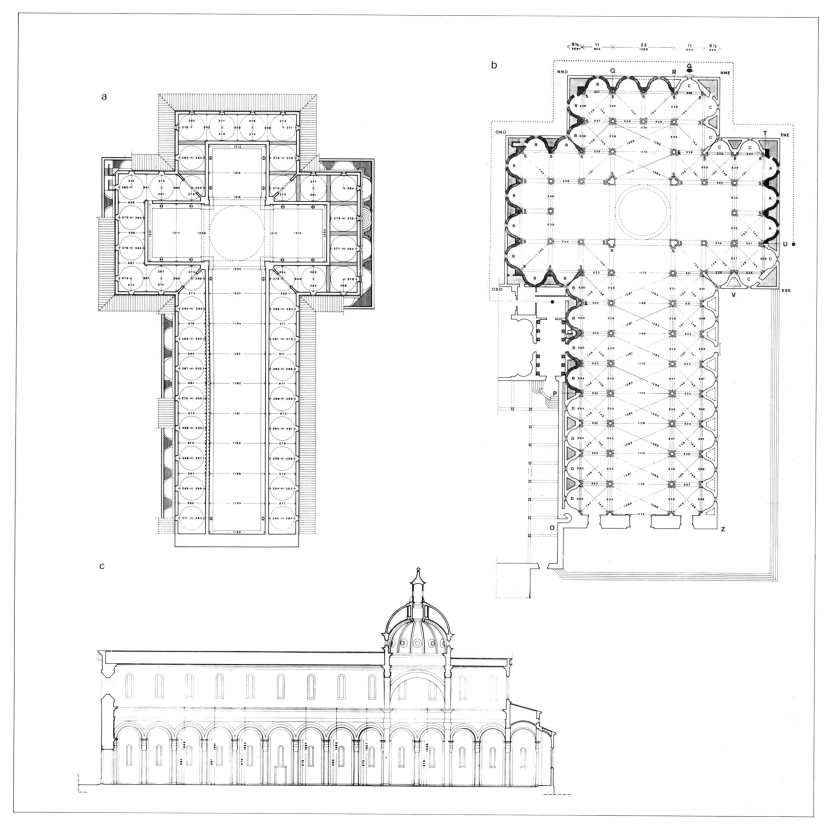

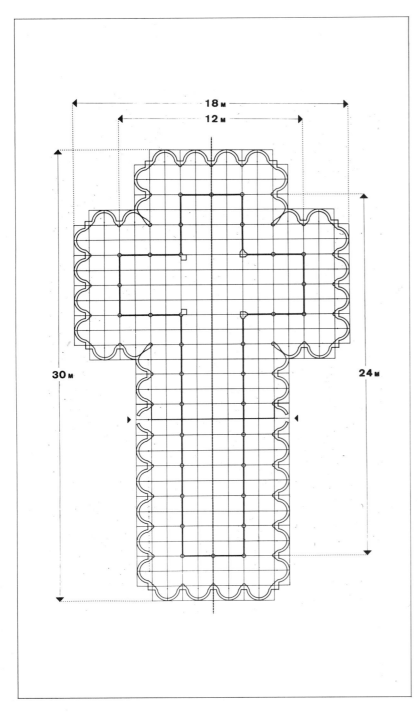

204. Modular plan of S. Spirito, drawn by Benevolo, on the basis of a unit of a half-bay or 5 1/2 *braccia*. The aisle and niches are carried across the façade, as in a drawing by Giuliano da Sangallo (Rome, Vatican Library, Cod. Barb. Lat. 4424, f. 14v), and the two left-hand crossing piers are shown as in a drawing by Antonio da Sangallo (Florence, Uffizi, Gabinetto dei Disegni e Stampe, 900).

205. S. Spirito, looking from the end of the nave towards the high altar in the crossing.

207. View across the left transept arm towards the nave. The high altar, in the crossing, is on the left.

209. The crossing dome of S. Spirito as it is (right) and as Brunelleschi probably intended it — more pointed in section, covered by a pitched roof, and rotated so that a rib is in line with the central axis of the elevation.

The drawing on the right shows the end wall of the nave, with a large round window.

210. One of the crossing piers.

211. The crossing with its dome, the chancel (top) and the two transept arms (left and right).

semidomes that were probably originally intended. The side aisles in their turn were covered by a similar lean-to roof which rises very high, to a level directly beneath the cornice that runs along the sills of the upper windows. This series of causes-and-effects, already pointed out by Sanpaolesi, resulted in an even higher alignment for the upper tier of windows. With this we have arrived at the truly problematical zone of the upper part of the nave.

We know that before it was decided to conceal the apses on the exterior (with the consequent alteration and excessive height of the roofs) one arm of the transept and part of the chancel were built up to a certain height. But between those two bodies, and precisely at their junction, there is one of the problematical crossing piers. Because it was not customary to begin colonnades or bays at any arbitrary point of the perimeter of a building under construction but rather at a specific point — here the transept — from which they would be continued progressively along the entire perimeter, it is safe to conclude that the idea of increasing the height of the entire order was already being entertained, *in pectore* at least, before it was decided to wall up the apses on the outside. As a proof of this we find an additional archivolt of smooth stone encircling the moulded archivolt used for all the arcades of the interior [216]. It is hard to decide whether this is a device introduced by Brunelleschi. Without this band the arcades would be less marked, but we can unhesitatingly say that the slender blank strip of wall that separates the top of the arcades from the entablature above them is scarcely coherent, if not actually contrary to Brunelleschi's syntax. This is the first arcade by him not to touch the architrave, and indeed the distance between the two mouldings is indefinite, weak, lacking in any proportional or modular basis.

This heightening of the upper part of the nave can be explained either by the change in the exterior to which we have referred or by the intention to build a barrel vault. But a barrel vault would have reduced the height of the central space and, what is more, would have made clerestorey windows virtually impossible. Without such upper windows there would have been only two openings in each end wall, that is, in the two transept arms, the chancel and the façade, and these would have been much smaller than they are now and compressed, if not cramped, between the cornice of the entablature and the arch of the vault [209 left, 224a]. One can imagine the paltry effect of such dwarf windows seen from a distance (consider the length of the vistas in S. Spirito), tacked on to an entablature and immediately above the extremely tall and slender window openings in the niches of the transept and chancel.

Another possibility for illuminating a barrel-vaulted nave would have been a round window in each end wall, of the sort adopted forty years later by Salvi d'Andrea for the front wall alone, which may go back to an early idea of Brunelleschi's [209 right]. But this is entirely unacceptable, because a single large circular window forces the eye to a single sightline which, by nature, must be axial and frontal, and this would be contrary to the bilateral symmetry that characterizes the church as a whole.

Raising the entire upper register, which meant lengthening the uprights and widening the frieze, may have suggested the idea of stilting the vault above the level of the cornice, with the advantage that the pairs of windows could fit more comfortably into the end walls [224b].[48]

If however a flat ceiling was planned from the outset, even without raising the upper walls there would have been no problem in accommodating all the clerestorey windows. But in that case other problems

continued on page 219

206

212. The left side of the nave of S. Spirito, showing the smooth bands of *pietra serena* added around the arcade mouldings, and the gap between them and the upper entablature.

213. The crossing arch, awkwardly dying into the wall.

OVERLEAF

214. Corner bay behind the crossing pier at the junction of the left-hand nave aisle and transept aisle. These four bays have unequal diagonals.

215. The right-hand nave aisle of S. Spirito, looking towards the façade.

216. Continuity and alignment of spaces between the nave, aisle and chapels.

217. Elevation and section of chapels at the end of the transept in S. Spirito
(By Benevolo. 1 cm = 1.06 m; 1 in. = 8 ft 10 in.)

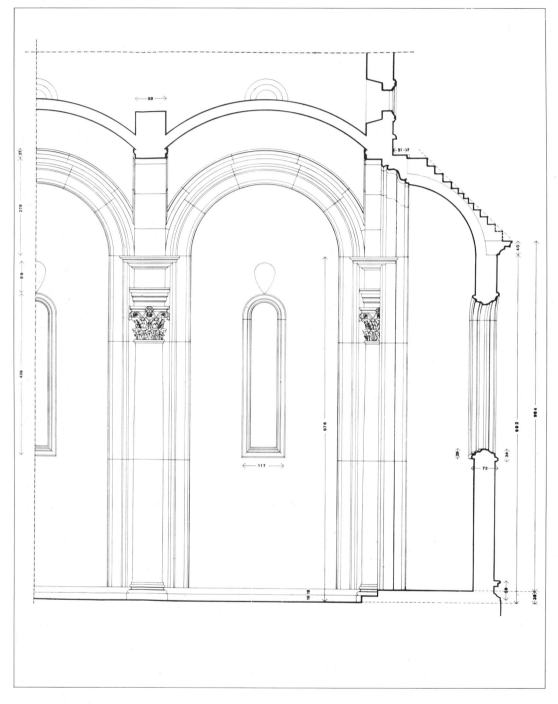

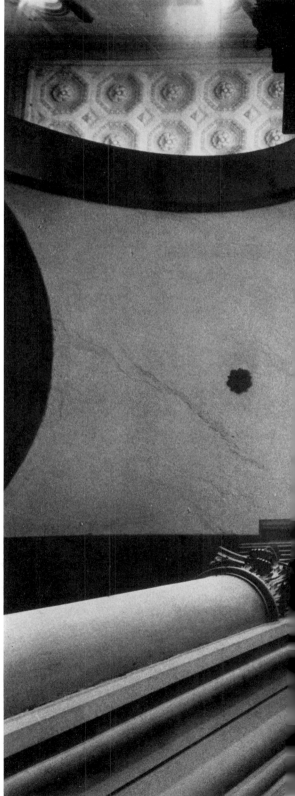

219. Section of an aisle bay of S. Spirito at the crossing, with a chapel on the right. Note how the attached demi-column of the crossing pier leads to the arch being narrowed. (By Benevolo. 1 cm = 1.33 m; 1 in. = 11 ft 1 in.)

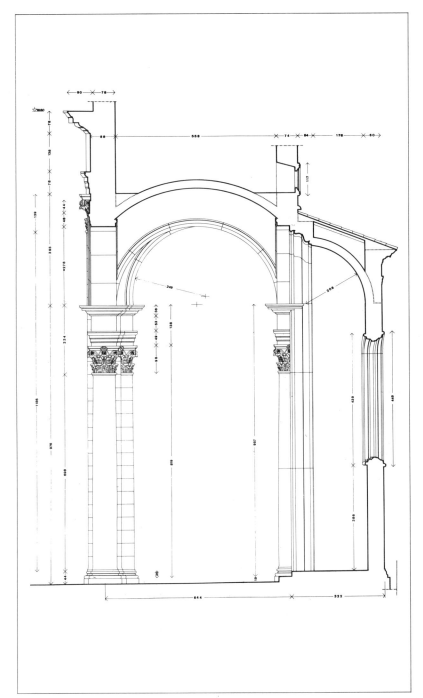

220. The domical vaults of the aisles, seen in the roofspace.

221. One of the low dividing walls, between the aisle vaults, whose function is still mysterious.

222. *Right* One of the chapels, seen from the roofspace, showing its original semicylindrical exterior, later encased in a straight wall (right).

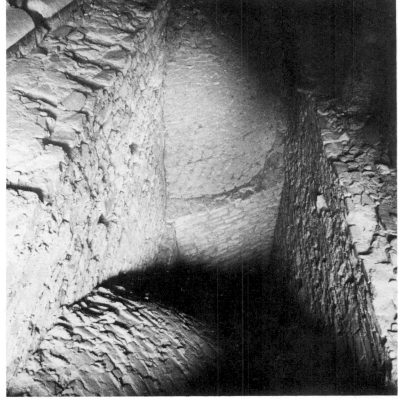

223. Axonometric drawing of two bays, showing the semicylindrical chapels and their encasement, and the dividing walls between aisle bays. It has been conjectured here that the latter are supported on brick arches. (By Benevolo. 1 cm = 1.03 m; 1 in. = 8 ft 7 in.)

224a,b. If S. Spirito had had a high barrel vault it could not have had tall clerestorey windows (a), unless the vault had been stilted (b).

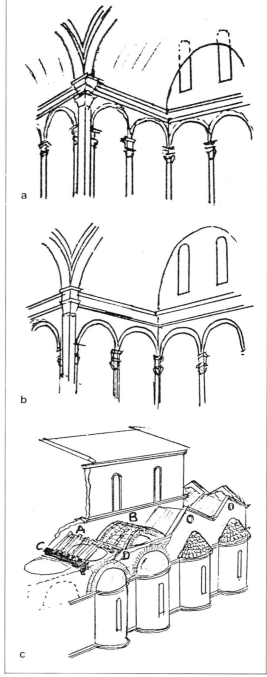

224c. Conjectural reconstruction of the original appearance of the aisle and chapels. The chapel apses are covered with tiles. The aisle bays are roofed independently, either on rafters (A) or on hogback vaults (B), in either case resting on the low crosswalls (C,D). The suggested exterior, with gables decorated with roundels, is based partly on S. Croce.

225a. Plan of the arrangement of the chapels at the transept end in S. Spirito, showing the curved walls inside straight walls.
(By Benevolo. 1 cm = 1.58 m; 1 in. = 13 ft 2 in.)

225b. Exterior elevation of the chapels, with modular analysis in terms of a unit of 5 1/2 *braccia* (numbers are in *braccia*) and suggested reconstruction of the roofs, by Benevolo. (To the same scale)

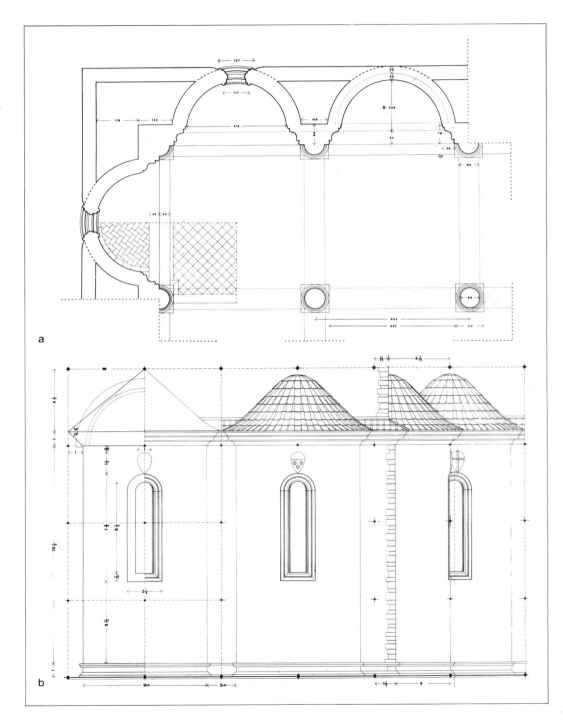

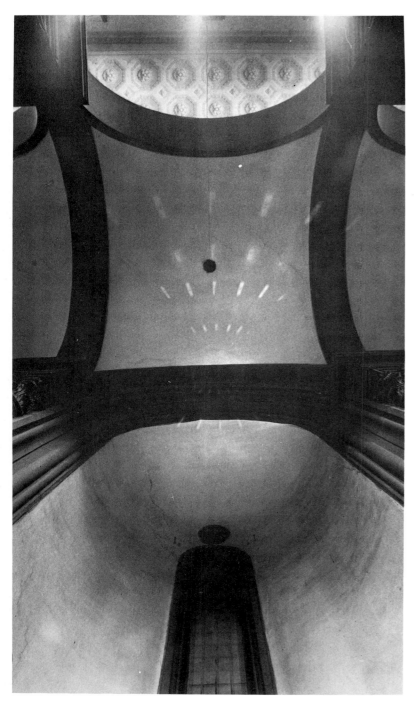

226. A chapel and aisle bay, seen from below.

would have appeared. The very marked projection of the cornice supporting a service catwalk around the church, as in S. Lorenzo, would have concealed almost all of the lower part of the windows, and in fact the elevation as we see it today is still confused, since the windows are confined above the cornice as if in a zone that has nothing to do with us below. It should be kept in mind that on the exterior a cornice connects all the sills of the tall windows and formerly served as a drainage channel above the sloping side roofs. This was a matter of particular concern for the Operai when the time came to roof the nave: they instructed that "the model be followed, along with the cornices that go outside above the roof". Various examples, above all that of S. Lorenzo, encourage one to think that the original plan called for a flat ceiling. The confusion is probably due to a chain of misunderstandings of Brunelleschi's project.

Consideration of the piers and crossing arches leads to the problem of the dome. As we know, the existing one was executed not by Brunelleschi but by Salvi d'Andrea, on the basis of Brunelleschi's model: the Operai stressed, when approving the new model presented by the *capomaestro*, that the dome should be built "without departing in form from that of Filippo but following it as much as possible". Yet even if the model left by Brunelleschi was fairly sketchy, as is likely, it would certainly not have been hemispherical as is the dome we see now. There are several reasons for this. The first is contextual: the shape of the chapel semidomes suggests that the crossing dome should have been more pointed, and the lean-to roofs of the aisles indicate that it should have had a sloping roof rather than the outer dome that it now has [209]. Another reason is historical: the more pointed form of dome had been used by Brunelleschi for the Old Sacristy [60] and could very well have been used again on a large scale for a church. This form, moreover, was used by Giuliano da Sangallo, who admired and learned from Brunelleschi, for the dome of S. Maria delle Carceri at Prato in 1485, a time when the dispute over the number of doors for the façade of S. Spirito, in which Giuliano was involved, was at its height. The Prato dome, which is furthermore a rib-and-web dome in twelve sections like that of the Old Sacristy, can thus be taken as *a posteriori* confirmation.

Another modification seems to have been made in the laying out of these twelve ribs and segments, which in S. Spirito are justified both theologically and in geometrical and compositional terms: theological because the Holy Spirit descended to enlighten — illuminate — the twelve Apostles; geometrical because three ribs should come down above the crossing arches to emphasize a double partitioning, framing the oculi in pairs when seen from the nave, chancel or transept arms [209 *left*], while each of the remaining four ribs would be related to one of the pendentives and its blind roundel. Thus the dome was undoubtedly intended to have twelve segments and oculi, but not as we see it now: Salvi d'Andrea rotated the design and made not a rib but an oculus coincide with the apex of each crossing arch [209 *right*].

There remains the question of the exterior. Variant solutions for the niches have been proposed by Sanpaolesi and Benevolo, but they have not touched on the roofing, particularly that of the aisles. Numerous explorations of the most important parts of the church have revealed over the years that in the space beneath the roofs of the aisles there are low walls resting on the arches between the bays [203a, 221, 223]. What is strange is that these low walls, which are no higher than the tops of the shallow domes over the aisles, are found along the right transept and flanking the chancel and not elsewhere. They have been

227. One of the chapel windows at S. Spirito. Its curved sill, and the indentations left and right of it, are the only vestiges of the original curved wall.

228. The collision between two chapels at the corners is wittily marked by twinned windows.

taken as further evidence for a barrel vault — rudimentary buttresses which would have been repeated all around the church at regular intervals matching the bays of the aisles and serving to check the outward thrust of the large vault. This should no longer be regarded as certain, and it is truly baffling to guess what purpose could be served by all these buttresses disposed at right angles to each wall-face. What thrust would they control? That of the end walls? Certainly not, because those walls would have reacted to compression without any thrust we can imagine. On the end walls these supplementary buttresses would have fulfilled the purely aesthetic (and superfluous) function of marking off the bays. In preparing this book, however, we looked more closely at S. Lorenzo, built at the same time as S. Spirito, and found some low walls that take the thrust of small hogback vaults of the same sort as those discovered beneath the roof of the Pazzi Chapel [232] and which doubtless served as covering over the shallow domes of the aisles. Those small vaults, whose outer surface is straight-sided, almost resembling a pitched roof, may very well have been considered for S. Spirito as well. They derive from a perfect and authentically Florentine model, S. Croce, where each bay of the aisles is covered by a pitched roof at right angles to the outer wall. This theory is a synthesis of those put forward by Sanpaolesi and Benevolo, taking from the former the idea of the pitched-roof configuration (though not extended over the chapel niches), from the latter the idea of a gable of undeterminable height covered by a pitched roof which, in turn, could have had slopes that were straight and supported by rafters, as in S. Croce, or curved and resting on very small vaults, as in the first projects for S. Lorenzo and the Pazzi Chapel. (For these forms see [224c].)

As for the nave, if it was intended to have a barrel vault then three types of roof would have been possible, even if we are unable to say how Brunelleschi usually handled roofing (except for the apses of the Cathedral). The first type is a barrel vault visible on the exterior, but this is unthinkable. The second is a hogback vault such as that found at the Pazzi Chapel [232], which has a barrel vault inside. The third type is a pitched roof with flat slopes ("the model is to be followed, along with the cornices that go outside above the roof"), though naturally at a lower level than the present pitched roof. The only question then would be whether buttresses were planned for the exterior or whether they were ruled out in favour of niches in the upper register in place of windows, as in the reconstruction by Sanpaolesi. The latter does seem the most probable if a vault was actually considered.

Covering the nave with a flat ceiling inevitably entailed the pitched roof that we see today, with no difference other than the height of the line of the eaves. In Brunelleschi's model that line (which may or may not have been marked by an entablature like the one now existing) must have come lower than at present. That would also avoid an excessive increase in height of the square base that supports the drum and cupola.

Unfortunately we have nothing to go on for a reconstruction of the façade and portico. But neither did the "respectable citizens" and "most reputed architects" who in 1486 condemned the church of S. Spirito to follow the ancient pattern of the façade with three doors.

In 1977-78 the exterior of S. Spirito was subjected to a drastic restoration, in the course of which some original elements were obscured and others were removed altogether.[49]

10 The Pazzi Chapel

What has traditionally been considered the culmination of the art of Brunelleschi, the Pazzi Chapel in the first cloister of S. Croce, proves now, on the basis of what documents are known, of recent investigations of the fabric and of dates found on the plaster, to be instead an ambiguous and much altered work, on the one hand very different from everything we know by the master, on the other hand imitative of his work, and too undemandingly tuned to the trend that Florentine taste took on after his time and which led to countless imitations.[1]

The chapel is substantially a replica of the Old Sacristy, transformed from a square to an oblong plan by extra bays at the sides (compare *60* and *65* with *230* and *231*). This plan was, we shall see, largely dictated by the presence of medieval walls. The front displays a splendid portico, inspired by triumphal arches like that at Civita Castellana:[2] its design, however, is completely autonomous and nothing to do with Brunelleschi. Behind that portico, we now know, is the original façade, punctuated by four windows — a truly extraordinary idea that breaks up the usual homogeneous compactness of a front wall. These windows lead us to the decoration of the interior, through the first of a series of almost pedantic displays of symmetry, for on the wall facing the entrance are four sunk panels corresponding to them in shape. These panels below roundels are continued on the end walls; and on these end walls we find repeated, on a slightly reduced scale, the motif of the arch framing the altar recess or *scarsella*. In that arch and in the entrance wall there are blocked circular windows. Pilasters punctuate the walls and support a main cornice, below which the decorative language is Brunelleschian, even including his idiosyncratic abbreviated pilasters in the corners. Above the cornice, however, the end bays are covered by very short barrel vaults, which are emphasized, too conspicuously, by heavy mouldings and a flat decoration of coffers with central rosettes. To find anything similar one must look not to Brunelleschi but to his followers, and stylistically the ornamentation of this upper part must postdate his death. This obvious effort at monumentality was accompanied by a schematization and in some elements an unabashedly literal replication of solutions arrived at earlier, so much so as to make one think of a direct copy. The umbrella dome [*78*] is very close to that of the Old Sacristy, and the spirally-grooved roof of the lantern, apparently erected after the seventeenth century, simply repeats that of the Old Sacristy [*62, 229*].[3]

These problems and doubts stated, we can look at the essential documents and dates on the building.

The Biographer is silent. Since his manuscript has come down to us incomplete, we can argue that this work dates from late in the architect's career and that its description, accompanied no doubt by an analysis of the errors due to unskilful executants, may have been planned for the final pages which have not survived or were never written. Vasari, who whenever possible followed the Biographer faithfully, had to make use of the short but detailed and precise biography included by Antonio di Tuccio Manetti in his *XIV Huomini Singhulari in Firenze dal MCCC innanzi*. Even there the chapel is given only the briefest mention: "He built the chapter house of the Pazzi in the first cloister of S. Croce in Florence." This could, of course, be an interpolation by someone who had read the Biographer and, by some association of ideas, advanced this attribution at a point in the text dealing with commissions from private citizens, after the Old Sacristy and the Barbadori Chapel.

The documentary information comes almost entirely from tax declarations by members of the Pazzi family listing expenses met or to be met.[4] Andrea dei Pazzi's returns of 1430 and 1433 indicate that in 1429 a contract was drawn up between him and the chapter of S. Croce for the rebuilding of their chapter house, which was to serve also as a funerary chapel. If Brunelleschi drew up his project then, it would have been contemporary with S. Spirito.In 1433 Andrea cancelled the earlier pledges, interest on which would have yielded about 682 florins, and replaced them by two installments totalling about 11,120 florins. By 1442 another 4,005 florins would have been earned in interest. In that year the same principal, rounded up to 12,000 florins, was committed for another six years, to yield a further 2,880 florins in general interest. The principal remained constant. In the tax declaration of 1446 we read that building was still going on, and that in addition to the main capital the Pazzi were directly contributing hundreds of florins each year.

While the increased sum committed in 1433 would indicate that greater expenses were in the immediate offing, the way in which the funds that Cosimo de' Medici had similarly deposited in the Monte were used for S. Lorenzo, together with various other reasons, suggest that the date when work would actually begin was postponed, perhaps until about 1443. This may be confirmed by the fact that not until the declaration of 1446 is there mention of further sums to be paid out personally each year. Yet more money must have been set aside for the building subsequently, since it was only completed some fifteen years later. One would also like to know whether the interest from the Monte was paid out regularly or held back in times of economic difficulties, as happened in the case of other projects such as the Rotunda of S. Maria degli Angeli.

The date 10 May 1443 was found written on one of the lower walls of the chapel.[5]

The next important document is the mention in the *Diario* of the notary Ser Recchio di Domenico Spinelli (as transcribed by Dal Migliore) that on 7 January 1444 Pope Eugenius IV "took his midday repast in the said S. Croce in the chamber that Andrea dei Pazzi has had made above the chapter house that is under construction, and remained there until the evening at one hour" (approximately 6 o'clock our time at that season). If we interpret correctly the phrase "sopra al Capitolo di nuovo fatto", this chamber must have been at the level of the upper storey of the monastery, above (not to the right or left of) the chapter house, perhaps using the scaffolding as temporary flooring and with an equally temporary roof thrown up over the walls. (It should be remembered that at least three of the walls existed before the Pazzi rebuilding began.) This would imply that the dome and vaults did not yet exist.

In 1447 Antonio dei Pazzi was brought before the law in Rome for having attempted to buy and export to Florence pieces of Antique porphyry from a religious building. The Florentine Signoria defended him: "desirous of adorning a very beautiful sacristy of theirs [the Pazzi], and finding these items of porphyry for sale, he purchased them because he did not believe this to be dishonest, especially since he desired them for a sacred and not a profane place..."[6] It seems that he was unsuccessful: the porphyry visible today in the altar of the Pazzi Chapel is relatively insignificant. It is most likely that what Antonio was purchasing on impulse was columns; and that he was doing so in 1447 argues a somewhat cavalier attitude to the original decorative scheme for the chapel.

229. The Pazzi Chapel, S. Croce. The portico was added long after Brunelleschi's death, and contrary to his intention.

230. Plan and longitudinal section of the Pazzi Chapel.

In the plan, two-thirds of the walls are medieval – the left arm (top) and the left wall of the *scarsella*, and the whole right-hand wall including the sacristy; only the entrance wall and the walls creating a square *scarsella* and adjacent sacristy, and thus a symmetrical right arm, are new.

In the section, the walling of the area shaded in grey was probably completed by the time of Pope Eugenius IV's visit in 1443. (1 cm = 2.14 m; 1 in. = 17 ft 10 in.)

231. The interior, looking towards the *scarsella* and right arm.

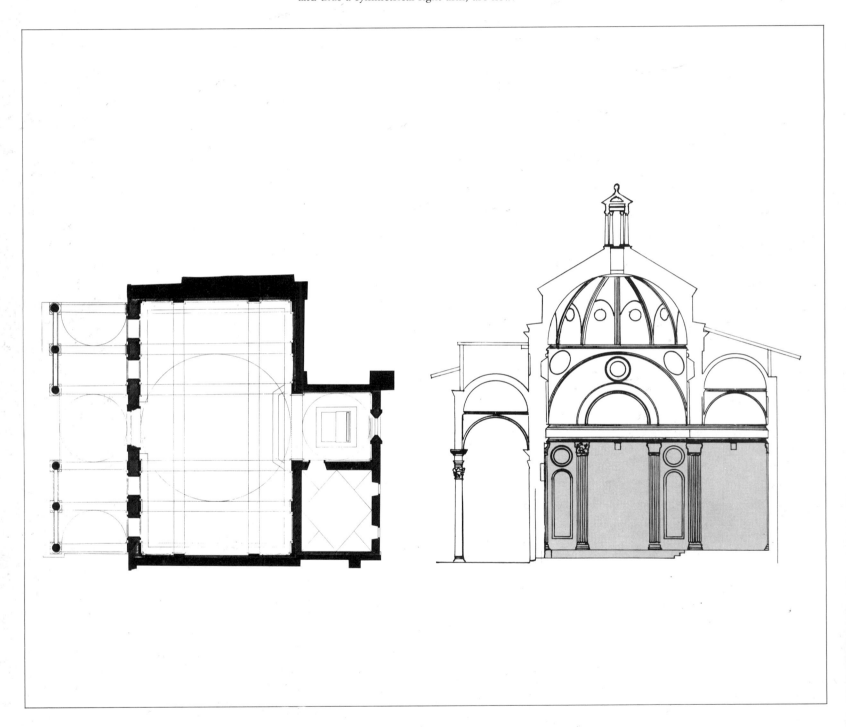

232. Cut-away perspective views of the Pazzi Chapel as it is now, seen from the front (top) and from the back. Note the blocked circular windows above the arch leading to the *scarsella* (bottom left) and on the original façade wall, above the dome of the portico; that wall also shows keying for marble revetment. Individual hogback roofs are indicated under the present roofs. (Drawings by P.A. Rossi)

233. Detail of the *scarsella*. When this photograph was taken, the carved roundels of Evangelists and Apostles had been temporarily removed.

The next date is 11 October 1459, found painted in fresco on the base of the drum of the main cupola, marking the completion of that cupola and the vaults over the side bays.

Similarly, the completion of at least the lower part of the atrium is indicated by the date 1461, scratched on the cupola above the central door.

Finally in 1478, when the Pazzi family were driven out of Florence because of their conspiracy against the Medici, one of their creditors was Giuliano da Maiano, who claimed payment for 1,800 *lire*, due to him for work on the chapel among other things.

What, then, in this famous chapel, can we ascribe to Brunelleschi? The handsome umbrella dome is a close copy of that in the Old Sacristy, which was completed before 1428, and it is hard to imagine that Brunelleschi would have made it quite so similar, with no evidence of his growth and change in the intervening years. He surely would have had something else in mind by then — after all, the architects completing his work in both S. Spirito and S. Lorenzo showed themselves no longer able to understand his intentions. While the symbolism of the dome and the sculptural roundels is a legitimate subject for discussion, it may not tell us much about Brunelleschi. The round-headed windows and panels, on the other hand, may be closer to him.[7]

Several changes in the design have been detected. The front wall was prepared for revetment, probably in marble, indicating that the present atrium cannot have been foreseen in the original plan, and this is further proved by the fact that the cupola at the centre of the portico blocks a round window in the upper part of the inner façade. A corresponding round window in the wall above the altar is also blocked, showing that the *scarsella* was intended to have a lower vault. The vaults of the end bays were originally directly covered by curved tiles and slabs, resting on a hogbacked extrados of brick, as they had been in the Old Sacristy (and in Alberti's S. Andrea at Mantua), to emphasize the cruciform shape of the interior.

Even the interior decoration in *pietra serena* is difficult to evaluate. We have seen that Brunelleschi as a matter of policy seldom indicated ornamental details on his models or drawings. It is not impossible that the accentuated verticalism and broken horizontal rhythm are late peculiarities of his style. However, the decorative system seems much closer to works by Giuliano da Maiano. Michelozzo may have been the designer who took over from Brunelleschi (and who knows how much responsibility Brunelleschi had?), for he built the library and other monastic buildings adjacent to the chapel, but in 1453 he was replaced and drastic changes were made to his programme.[8]

What we may attribute to Brunelleschi is the plan. Medieval walls already marked out the two ends of the room, and half the altar space. What Brunelleschi did was to regularize the arrangement, and establish a modular system based on extremely simple relationships: the two lateral bays, for example, are each half as wide as the central compartment.[9] The medieval walls were lined with new masonry,[10] and new walls were constructed, including the façade. There Brunelleschi was free; and by piercing it with four windows he made it a mere diaphragm, a wall of light, as the altar wall of the Old Sacristy would have been before the *scarsella* and service rooms were added.

It is likely that Brunelleschi would have organized the structure in quite a different way from what we see today, stressing the cruciform nature of the plan, and the tension between narrow and broad spaces, between forward and lateral movement. Forget the dome, for a mo-

234. The Pazzi Chapel, looking towards the *scarsella* and left arm.

ment. Instead one would have had the contrast between the broad, barrel-vaulted arms and, running at right angles, a narrow nave, extending in one direction to a porch of a single bay only, and in the other to the small sanctuary, presumably intended to be covered with either a domical or a tunnel vault.

The system of ornamentation, which now places the emphasis on the lateral extensions, was intended, I believe, to operate in the contrary direction, that is entirely towards the altar. The elegant fluted pilasters give equal emphasis to the *scarsella*, the pendentives which lead up to the dome, and the corners: instead of bringing out the masterly grafting of the two forms that actually intersect, they call attention to the difficulty of handling this intersection. It was to be left to brilliant masters like Giuliano da Sangallo, in S. Maria delle Carceri at Prato, to liberate the butterfly from the chrysalis, to reveal the effectiveness of a symmetrical Greek-cross plan. And it was Ventura Vitoni, in the atrium of the Madonna dell'Umiltà at Pistoia, who successfully grasped the robust monumentality inherent in tunnel vaults as well as the lesson of how the various members as used by Brunelleschi could convey force, energy, and a sense of solemnity.

My assessment of the Pazzi Chapel is largely negative in its conclusions: I need hardly say, however, that it is entirely subject to revision if and when those many key matters that are still obscure become clear.

11 Military works, I: Lucca, Milan, Pisa, Vicopisano and Rimini

Although Brunelleschi's activity as a builder of fortifications and towers is quite well documented, a great many official papers in the archives of the Florentine Opera del Duomo are still, unhappily for history, unexplored and unpublished, and the constructions themselves, after having been studied and discussed at the start of this century, have been almost forgotten.[1]

Brunelleschi's involvement came through three channels: like other *capomaestri* of the Cathedral he was expected to carry out military work, to be funded by the Opera and regarded as the Opera's own projects; the Arte della Lana and other guilds for which he was consultant were charged by the commune with such tasks; and he himself took part directly in military ventures or was in contact with the most famous *condottieri* of the time. It was what he did at Vicopisano in particular that ensured his fame in this branch of architecture. But long before that he was sought after for designs or advice, even for installations distant from Florence and for warlords potentially or in fact enemies of his city.

There is a hint in his interview with Mariano Taccola [9] that he despised war and the military, but his presence on the battlefield is attested at least once, during the attempt to direct an artificial flood against Lucca. Taccola's illustrations may include some of Brunelleschi's designs for the military engines he is said to have devised for transportation, hoisting, scaling walls, and attacking towers. The situation is obscure because we have no drawings certain to be by him, and because the study of his fortresses has only recently been undertaken. However, his specific competence in fortification is directly confirmed by the two fifteenth-century biographies that speak of him, and by the documents of the Opera del Duomo published by Fabriczy. The fortifications that survive are imposing in scale, and he seems to have been responsible also for residential layouts, river dams, canalization, drainage systems and aqueducts.[2]

We can at least put together a chronological list of his military works, according to the date of their commissioning and, when it is known, of the missions that he undertook, usually on horseback and with one or two companions.

1423 September: Brunelleschi in Pistoia (for fortifications, or for the new hospital?)
1424 September: in Pistoia (for fortifications, or for the new hospital?)
25 September: Brunelleschi is to go to Pisa for fortifications
25/26 September: work to begin on the fortress-villages of Lastra a Signa and Malmantile (see Chapter 15)
1426 new fortifications decreed for Pisa: Brunelleschi goes to Pisa several times in connection with this task
1427 February: work under way in Pisa
28 February: estimate ratified for the work done at Lastra
1428-1432 some time during this period Brunelleschi is called to Milan for consultations on the castle and Cathedral (and suggestions for military machinery?)

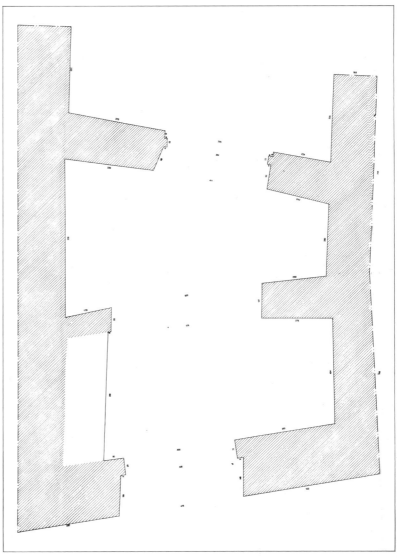

Fortification of the Porta del Parlascio, Pisa.

235. Plan of the existing bastion, extending northward from the city wall (bottom line); the fifteenth-century works are encased in the centre [*240e*]. (1 cm = 9.50 m; 1 in. = 79 ft 2 in.)

236. Plan of the central part of the bastion, associated with Brunelleschi. The gate into the city is at the bottom. (1 cm = 1.44 m; 1 in. = 12 ft)

237. The south, inner, side of the gate. (1 cm = 47 cm; 1 in. = 3 ft 11 in.)

Sections of the fortification of the Porta del Parlascio, Pisa.

238. From the east (1 cm = 1.52 m; 1 in. = 12 ft 8 in.)

239. From the north. (1 cm = 1.27 m; 1 in. = 10 ft 7 in.)

1430 war with Lucca; Brunelleschi builds a dam to flood the battlefield or the city itself

1431 February: mission to Castellina, Staggia and Rencine

1432 to Ferrara and Mantua (according to Vasari perhaps for work on dikes)

1435 May and June: decision concerning the Porta del Parlascio at Pisa
28 June: Brunelleschi to go to Pisa
29 July: deliberations on the castle of Vicopisano

1436 January: inspection trip to Pisa and Vicopisano
April: second trip to Ferrara and Mantua

1438 28 August-22 October: Brunelleschi in Rimini for the castle and possibly for other fortifications in Romagna

1440 23 March: inspection trip to Vicopisano and Pisa for the Porta del Parlascio
17 May: Cittadella Nuova to be built in Pisa
13 June: mission to Pisa for the Cittadella Nuova; work under way at the port of Pesaro, whose defensive La Torretta is attributed to Brunelleschi by Vasari

1444 8 January: contract for fortifications in Pisa, witnessed by Brunelleschi
16 September: mission to Pisa to heighten the embankments of the Arno near Porta S. Marco [3]

1444-1446 barrier against flooding of the Arno at S. Giovanni in Val d'Arno (referred to in a letter by Antonio di Tuccio in 1476).

The earliest documented fortifications by Brunelleschi date from 1424, and it was probably because of them that he was forced to relinquish control over work at the Foundling Hospital. In that year the Opera del Duomo of Florence was made responsible for strengthening the fortifications of Lastra a Signa and Malmantile (see Chapter 15).

Lucca

During the Florentine siege of Lucca in 1429-30 Brunelleschi was involved in what proved a disastrous plan to flood the plain around the city by channelling the waters of the Serchio into a canal that entered Lucca, and building a dam some 8 km (5 mi.) long to hold the water thus built up.[4] When Brunelleschi was sent with his plan to Neri di Gino Capponi, commissioner for the Florentine army, Capponi "made fun of it, praying his companions first to go and have a look at it with their own eyes, either all together or by pairs, and then to make up their minds". Capponi was in any case opposed to the strategy imposed by the Dieci di Balìa, which called for a direct assault on the city without first conquering the castles in the countryside; but he was not wrong about Brunelleschi's scheme: "The Lucchese ruined the point of entry of the water and the weir in the Serchio, and the dam simply fell apart."[5] The Lucca debacle hastened the defeat of the party of Rinaldo degli Albizzi, with whom, politically at least, Brunelleschi was linked, and it made the architect the subject of attack and ridicule.[6]

Milan

A more prestigious commission than the fortification of the Signa area, according to Antonio Manetti's *XIV Huomini Singhulari*, involved consultation or designs for the new castle in Milan — obviously during a period of truce between that city and Florence, thus between 1428 and 1432. Brunelleschi may have been responsible for raising fortifications against the Milanese and their allies during the campaign of 1424-28, in

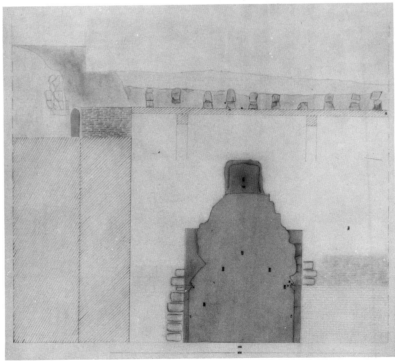

which case Filippo Maria Visconti could already have appreciated his talents. The castle of Milan, which included a separate dwelling for Maria Allobroga, second wife of Filippo Maria, was destroyed between 1447 and 1449. From research by Cristina Vitali it appears that the sloping walls below street level along the old moat were remarkably regular and had a revetment of granite slabs. That castle, with modifications, was the model for the subsequent reconstruction.[7] It was probably during the same visit that Brunelleschi gave advice to the Opera del Duomo of Milan, which was faced with a crisis over work on the ambitious lantern-tower, the *tiburio*. Whatever Brunelleschi did in Milan, he left a legacy of key ideas that were to turn up again in the work and writings of Francesco di Giorgio, Leonardo, Giuliano da Sangallo and Bramante, who in all probability took into account his designs and have perhaps handed on to us their essential principles.[8] From that voyage to the north, in exchange, Brunelleschi must have drawn a more moderate attitude towards the Gothic tradition, of which he appreciated at least the articulation and the geometrical complexity of the forms.

Pisa

After Florence, it was Pisa which most engaged his services, and for three separate undertakings. On 16 August 1426, he was assigned to heighten the walls of the Vecchia Cittadella because the sand dredged from the bed of an adjacent watercourse (either to deepen the channel for navigation or to forestall flooding) had accumulated and formed a dike of almost the same height. Brunelleschi's task consisted of raising and extending the curtain wall.[9] Later, in May and June 1435, he began the work of "building, completing, and fortifying" the Porta del Parlascio along lines proposed by the Florentine military commander in Pisa and other officials, to be finished within a year. The three-storeyed fortress erected over a medieval gate was reinforced with iron chains in 1440, still to designs by Brunelleschi. In the mid-sixteenth century it was almost totally demolished by Grand Duke Cosimo I, with the excuse that it had been damaged by an earthquake, and replaced by a bastion [235-240].[10]

Brunelleschi's third job in Pisa was even more important: the creation of the Cittadella Nuova, decided on in 1440, perhaps as a result of a new site visit and report by Brunelleschi himself. Three years were allotted for its construction. The fortress was to consist of a wall battlemented on both sides, at least 4 *braccia* thick and of sufficient height, running from the fort of S. Marco along the bank of the Arno to the Ponte della Spina, with a tower to defend that bridge and others where suitable, "secundum quod iam designatum est". The bridge and a gateway included in the fortress, known as the Porta alle Piagge, were to be fortified.[11] Little of this exists today, least of all in the form built by Brunelleschi, although one does get the impression that fifteenth-century sections survive here and there. In 1495, when Pisa was liberated by Charles VIII of France, the Cittadella Nuova was largely demolished, partly by the Pisans themselves, showing that such strongholds were viewed by the citizenry as hated instruments of military oppression. In 1509 a new citadel was designed by Giuliano da Sangallo.[12]

Associated with the fortifications of Pisa was the creation of a fortified harbour at Livorno, including a tower, the Torre del Marzocco, formerly attributed to Ghiberti but now ascribed to Brunelleschi.[13]

Vicopisano

The impression that Brunelleschi's fortifications include no significant technical innovations is reinforced by the most celebrated of them, that of Vicopisano, which defended a vital point on the Arno, at the time still flowing close by [241-257]. Work began in January 1436. The keep lies at the centre of a large enclosure with moderately thick walls (obviously not designed to resist artillery), ingeniously disposed in typi-

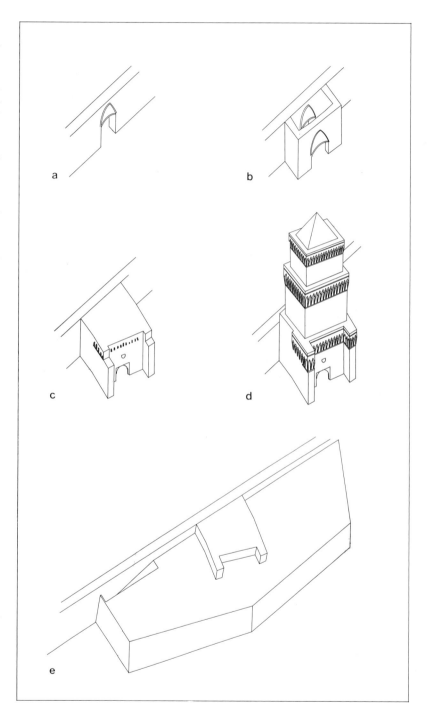

241. Plan of the town of Vicopisano. The Rocca or keep with its tower appears above and to the right of the centre, as a grey square with a black square in one corner. It is linked by a straight line — the curtain wall — to a gate-tower on the right edge of the town. (1 cm = 59.10 m; 1 in. = 492 ft 6 in.)

242. View of the keep from above, with the tower (upper left), open courtyard, and forebuilding (left). (1 cm = 5.89 m; 1 in. = 49 ft 1 in.)

243. Plan of the keep, tower and forebuilding at first floor level. (To the same scale)

cal medieval manner around a point of high ground. It consists of a hollow square block with at one corner a tower of perfect geometrical form and the remarkable height of 31 m (102 ft). The keep is connected by means of a walkway along a stretch of freestanding wall with a gate-tower in the outer curtain.[14]

The tall central tower can only be entered from the inner courtyard [256, 257], so to reach it a foe must first penetrate the walls of the keep. Those walls and the tower have battlements of the same type, with simple crenellations and a wall-walk and machicolations above a corbelled arcade. Though in very poor state, with some parts crumbling away, the battlements still give some idea of their appearance in the Quattrocento. Each side of the tower has one or two windows, probably for observation, and in the lower part there are also large slits for firearms at the height of a man. The interior of the tower [255] is still in excellent state (it was restored at the end of the last century by Leopoldo Feer, its proprietor at that time), except for the top storey where the vault leaks and the bricks used in it are crumbling. The original stairways linking the storeys have disappeared, except for a few stone and brick steps remaining at the start of the fourth, fifth and sixth storeys, and have been replaced with wooden stairs.

Both tower and keep walls are built of large blocks of stone, though with bricks for the battlements and parapets of both. From a reading of the various materials used for the tower, and from an examination of its walls at different levels (with projections ranging from 5 to 10 cm, or 2 to 4 in.), it is possible to identify a number of building periods. Other evidence — traces of a batter at the base of the tower, and of a blocked up window in its west side — increase one's conviction that Brunelleschi's work was inserted into an earlier Pisan fortification, and that what he should be credited with at Vicopisano is the renovation of the castle as a whole and the construction of the tower from the level of the keep wall-walk to its summit.

The keep is linked to the Torre dei Silvatici at the foot of the hill by means of a curtain wall as high as the keep walls, with crenellations and machicolations constructed in the same way. This wall was connected to the keep by a drawbridge, of which the only evidence now is the space into which it fitted on the keep wall. Technical problems presented by this junction obliged Brunelleschi to make another site visit in 1440. This curtain wall provided a swift and safe passage from the central command post to the outer circle of walls at the foot of the hill, thus expediting the dispatch of orders, troops, and arms to the protected wall-walk running right round the castle. Another tower stood against this inner curtain wall, but it is in such ruinous state that one cannot say whether it was built at the same time. The curtain wall has no gunloops or arrowslits, so defence must have depended on the two major towers. The Torre dei Silvatici, which is directly attached to the stretch of linking wall, is the only tower in the outer walls to have crenellations and machicolations from which projectiles could be dropped.[15]

According to the Biographer (f. 312r ff.), who can be taken as particularly reliable here since Vicopisano was a late work, Brunelleschi's drawings and models in wood and clay were highly praised by the leading specialists of the time, among them the Florentine military commander Niccolò Gambacorti, who "much admired such ingenuity and such industry", and Francesco Sforza himself. This favourable judgment was handed down on 29 July 1435 by a special commission of the Dieci di Balìa, set up to solicit authoritative outside opinions before work at Vicopisano began.

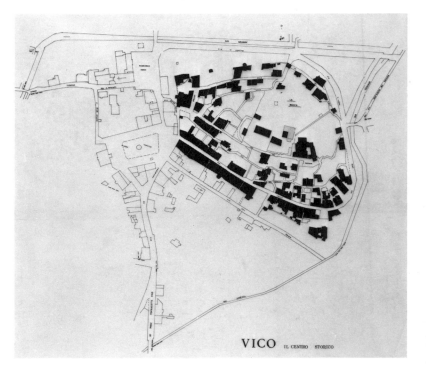

VICO IL CENTRO STORICO

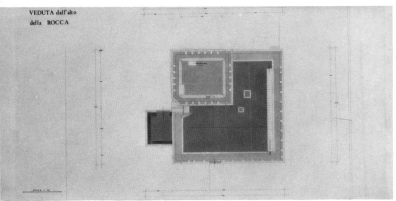

VEDUTA dall'alto della ROCCA

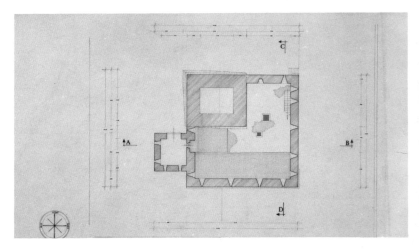

Vicopisano tower and keep. (1 cm = 4.42 m; 1 in. = 36 ft 10 in.)

244-246. North, west and south elevations.

247. Section along A-B in the plan [243].

248. Section along D-C in the plan [243].

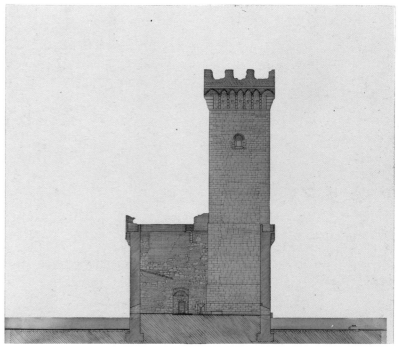

249. East elevation of the forebuilding, tower and keep of Vicopisano. (1 cm = 1.19 m; 1 in. = 9 ft 11 in.)

250. The tower and, below it, the machicolated curtain wall leading down to the Torre dei Silvatici.

251a,b. Transverse and longitudinal sections of the tower of Vicopisano, and plans at the second, third, fourth and fifth levels. (1 cm = 4.33 m; 1 in. = 36 ft 1 in.)

252. General view of the curtain wall leading to the keep and tower.

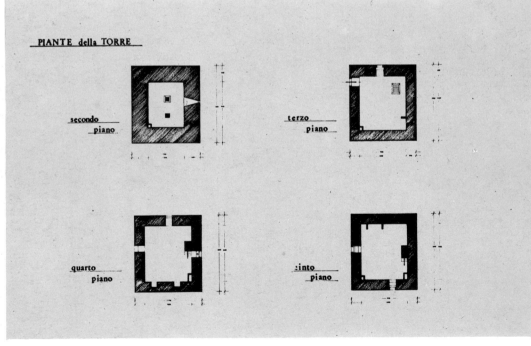

OVERLEAF

253. The tower, from inside the keep.

254. Machicolations of the curtain wall.

255. A room in the tower of Vicopisano.

256, 257. The cantilevered stairway that leads from the keep courtyard to the tower. (The vertical brick supports are modern.)

258. Model of the Castello Sismondo at Rimini, based on the fresco by Piero della Francesca (*opposite*) and the actual building. (Model made by U. Barlini, under the direction of P.G. Pasini)

259. The Castello Sismondo, depicted in Piero della Francesca's fresco of Sigismondo Malatesta kneeling before his patron saint, in the Tempio Malatestiano, Rimini.

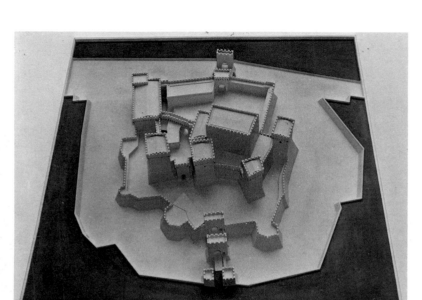

Although cannon had begun to be depicted in manuscripts about 1325, and were first used in the field in Italy in 1331 (at the siege of Cividale), there are no indications that in Brunelleschi's time the Florentines considered them a significant threat against which special defences were necessary. Paradoxically, while Italy in general showed itself little concerned with the technological development of this formidable new weapon, it was a Venetian woman living in France, Christine de Pisan, who about 1410 pointed out the inadequacy of contemporary fortification and recommended, among other things, the installation of defensive artillery "on platforms projecting from the fortress walls, thus anticipating the bastion by almost a century".[20] In Renaissance Italy neither Alberti nor Filarete speaks of artillery, and Taccola mentions only mines (on them and on artillery see also Chapter 15). Only Fontana, who was with the *condottiere* Carmagnola from 1420 to 1432, was an enthusiast for firepower. Understandably, then, Brunelleschi simply continued the medieval system of rectangular walls defended vertically by towers in visual contact and interconnected rapidly and easily by passageways, a system offering protection from small projectiles, and made no attempt at a new approach with strongly reinforced walls, concealed emplacements, and horizontal extensions affording no main target for heavy missiles.

The type of geometrical organization based on right angles which Brunelleschi used even in the most difficult topographical situations was to prove most vulnerable to the improved firearms, so that, soon after they were built, the essential fortifications had to be replaced entirely by defences using platforms and more markedly projecting spurs. One need only turn the pages of Francesco di Giorgio's treatise to see the difference in arrangement, though he too retained an optimistic faith in geometry as a defensive aid (ideologically at least), and displayed it boldly and persistently. In that respect, the lesson of Brunelleschi was not lost in fortifications. And, had the need existed at the time, there is no doubt that his knowledge of optics would have enabled him to make enormous innovations in both offensive strategy and defence.

Rimini

As a result of the commission's praise, Brunelleschi was invited to Rimini to advise Sigismondo Malatesta on one of the most celebrated castles in Italy — the Castello Sismondo, commemorated on a medal by Matteo de' Pasti and later in a fresco by Piero della Francesca — as well as other strongholds.[16] He was in Rimini from August to October 1438, probably accompanying Duke Sigismondo through Romagna from Rimini to Montefiori, Fano, S. Giovanni in Marignano, Cervia and Cesena. Antonio Manetti states categorically that Brunelleschi designed the castle at Rimini [258-265], which was certainly an entirely new creation from the ground up, something proclaimed by the numerous inscriptions formerly on its towers. Comparison with Malmantile [343-346], Staggia [352-355], and Vicopisano, its immediate predecessors, seems to confirm that its central nucleus and gateway were Brunelleschi's work. The strong battered bases to the towers, enclosing shock-absorbing clay, are a remarkably progressive feature: that they are original is proved by Piero's fresco [259], and particularly by his perforated transfer pattern. That fresco, and the medal, are our only documents for the skyline of the castle, since its towers were lopped off in 1625 to provide modern artillery emplacements. The restoration now in progress, begun under the direction of the late Professor Piero Sanpaolesi, has brought to light extensive and elegant living quarters.[17]

Some of the fortifications at Pesaro have been attributed to Brunelleschi, but this seems unconvincing.[18]

From the documentary evidence, more than from the actual remains, it appears that Brunelleschi's military work in general responded to precise and specific requirements. What those were is difficult to determine without a general campaign of surveying and excavation, and a comparison of all the relevant chronicles and histories and the writings of military theorists from ancient times through the Middle Ages[19] right up to Giovanni Fontana, whose manuscript in Munich contains discussions of military affairs that may date from around 1430.

CASTELLVM · SISMVNDVM · ARIMINENSE · M · CCCC · XL · VI

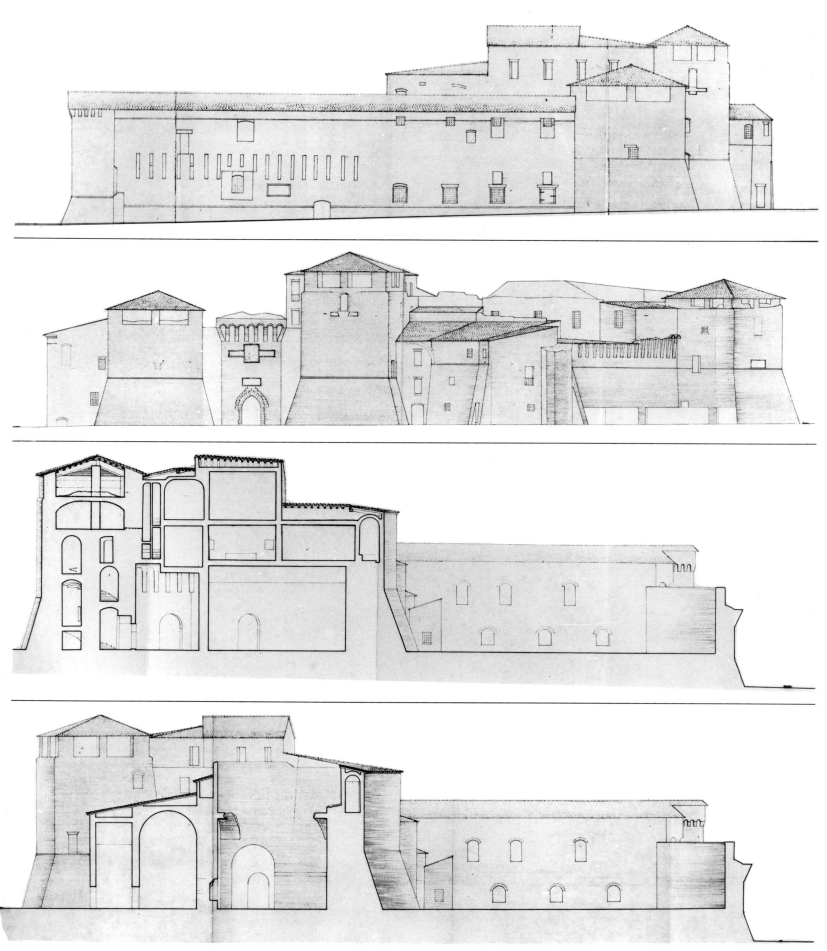

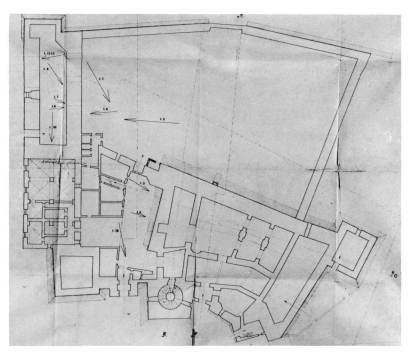

260-263. Elevations and sections of the Castello Sismondo at Rimini. (By S. Cumo and M. Mori)

264, 265. Plans of the Castello Sismondo at ground (top) and upper levels. The entrance is between the two towers at the bottom left. (By S. Cumo and M. Mori)

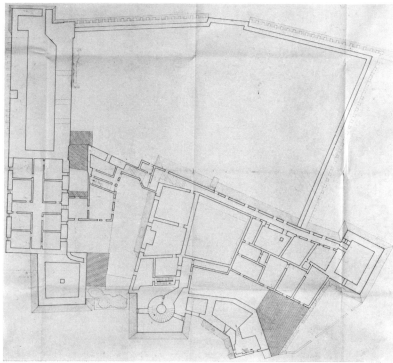

12 Late works: the Rotunda of S. Maria degli Angeli and the lantern and exedrae of Florence Cathedral

The design of S. Maria degli Angeli dates from 1434-36, the Cathedral lantern from 1436 and the project for the exedrae from 1439. All three embody a profound change that affected Brunelleschi's architecture in his last years.[1] The causes of this change have been variously surmised — a more refined knowledge of geometry, new contacts with the Gothic world, or with archaeology, or the influence of the young Alberti (who may have visited the Cathedral dome as it was being built). At any rate, Alberti comes close to defining the new style when he speaks (in *De re aedificatoria*, VI) of "mingling elements of similar proportions, straight lines with curved lines, lights with shadows", trying new ways and "extracting something new, as if from the conjunction of masculine and feminine elements", with a preference for the feminine.

Each of the three projects is in its way unique, but they share certain characteristics. The plan is based on alternations of concave and convex, the elevation presents an ingenious integration of buttressing and structure, and the masonry itself is hollowed out in such a way as to give it maximum lightness. The dynamic function of the arch is applied horizontally, so as to make it possible to resist great forces with minimum weight and to distribute those forces by centrifugal radiation. One can almost speak of a return to the use of Gothic flying buttresses, but with the experience of Classical Antiquity as guide.

The Rotunda of S. Maria degli Angeli

The Biographer devotes much space to S. Maria degli Angeli and assures us (f. 309r) that

although it is entirely in the Antique manner inside and out it has rare and subtle inventions in what one can see as it stands now, because he attempted new and beautiful things; [Brunelleschi] was able to remedy difficulties that normally entailed considerable inconvenience. He introduced new methods and saved a great deal of money. There anyone who put his mind to it and really looked into it would find many surprises and have good reason for marvelling at all sorts of things.

Unfortunately we are very far from being able to enjoy these "surprises" or even from seeing what the Biographer saw, given the heavy restoration of the building. Aside from the various attempts at conjectural reconstruction on the basis of surviving copies of drawings and the Rustici Codex [267, 268], discussion has turned mostly on its possible sources, which some claim to be chiefly medieval and others Classical.

The historical background to this building is known in its essentials. It was initiated by Pippo Spano,[2] the Tuscan *condottiere* Filippo Scolari, who in 1426 had received two legacies, each with the condition that he build a Camaldolensian monastery.[3] Pippo himself, however, died in the same year, and after many complications the two legacies became vested in the merchants' guild, the Arte di Calimala, and were pooled to build a single structure, an oratory at the Camaldolensian convent of S. Maria degli Angeli.[4]

At the head of the Florentine Camaldolensians at this time was Ambrogio Traversari, and he must have become the leading spirit in promoting the new building. Famous as a humanist, he was noted among other things for his studies on the early Church Fathers and for a biography of St Ambrose attributed to him.[5] On 2 April 1434, 5,000 gold florins were deposited for the erection of an "Oratory of the Scolari at the [monastery of the] Angeli", and what had begun as a private project assumed the character of a public undertaking.

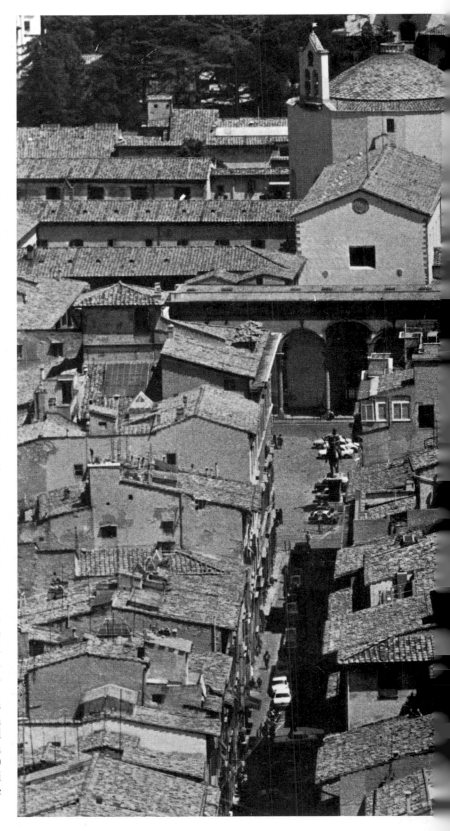

266. The Rotunda of S. Maria degli Angeli (bottom right), seen from the dome of the Cathedral. Behind it is the Foundling Hospital, and to the left is SS. Annunziata, with its large rotunda, perhaps partly modelled on that of S. Maria degli Angeli.

267. The monastery of S. Maria degli Angeli, with the Rotunda attached to its outer wall (bottom right), illustrated in the Rustici Codex (Florence, Biblioteca del Seminario).

268. Drawing probably derived from the original plan for the Rotunda, perhaps sixteenth-century (Florence, Uffizi, Gabinetto dei Disegni e Stampe, 1949A).

269. Plan of the Palatine Chapel, Aachen, a famous medieval prototype for an octagon within a sixteen-sided polygon.

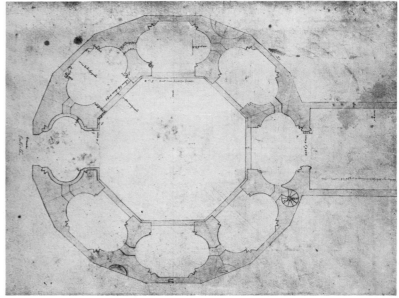

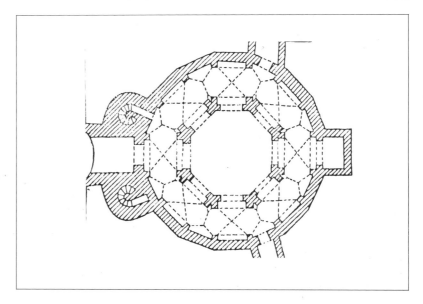

At this point an interesting development occurred. No sooner had the funds become available and the designing begun than, in the autumn and winter of 1435-36, Ambrogio Traversari was sent first to the Council of Basel, and then to Vienna and Budapest as ambassador to the Emperor Sigismund, with the assignment of bringing about a fusion of the Greek and Roman Churches (though really, practically speaking, to consolidate the position of the latter). Now, an octagon which on the exterior becomes a sixteen-sided polygon is not unknown in the architecture of the Holy Roman Empire: it is the plan of the venerable Palatine Chapel in Aachen [269]. How this could have come to be among the ancient monuments studied by the Florentine architects of the early Quattrocento is not known but, curiously enough, the case is not without parallel: one could cite, again without being able to account for it, the resemblance of the conical cupolas of the Old Sacristy and Pazzi Chapel to the Carolingian abbey of Centula in northern France. But there may have been another independent source for the Rotunda of S. Maria degli Angeli: the philological patristic studies of Traversari himself, who was a friend of Manuel Chrysoloras and acquainted with Greek as well as Hebrew.

The Emperor Sigismund enters the story of S. Maria degli Angeli at more than one point. As the patron of Pippo Spano he was ultimately responsible for the two legacies, and in 1431 he had actually come south and had himself crowned King of Italy in Milan and then Holy Roman Emperor in Rome in 1433. Sigismund visited Lucca and Siena, where he was triumphantly welcomed, but not the Guelph Florence, although commercial relations between that city and Hungary were highly active (at least between 1412, when Antonio Fronte of Florence set up a financial society in Buda to concede credit to the State, and 23 May 1439, when the anti-feudal and anti-patrician movement sacked and destroyed the houses of the Italian merchants in Buda.[6]

Brunelleschi was commissioned to design the oratory of S. Maria degli Angeli and a contract was signed early in 1434 (see p. 256). Building seems to have begun immediately.[7] As conceived by Brunelleschi the chapel would have constituted a sort of huge tabernacle at the corner of the extremely simple monastery, whose plan can hardly be deciphered today amid the chaos of the State University which occupies the site. To give an imposing position to the new oratory it was necessary to take in part of a public thoroughfare.[8] The designing and construction must have gone quite rapidly if the height of the building as it stood until 1934 (i.e. about 5 m or 15 ft) had been reached by 1437 when, because of the second war with Lucca, funds consigned to the Monte were forfeited and never returned. In that same year, moreover, the Emperor Sigismund died, and Ambrogio Traversari died two years later.[9]

A large number of drawings of the Rotunda survive which enable us to reconstruct Brunelleschi's intentions in some detail,[10] and it will be advisable to discuss these sources before trying to assess the final form and significance of the building.

It is entirely probable that the monastery itself possessed a series of original drawings presented by Brunelleschi for approval, and perhaps a wooden model as well (modello can mean both things).[11] Others must have been in the archives of the Arte di Calimala which was responsible for the work, but no trace or record of these is known, whereas there are various references to the model or designs in the monastery. According to the Biographer (ff. 309r, 311r), a modello existed but had been lost. It seems to have been quite basic: "there was little to be seen regarding the

270. Measured ground plan of the Rotunda. (1 cm = 1.97 m; 1 in. = 16 ft 5 in.)

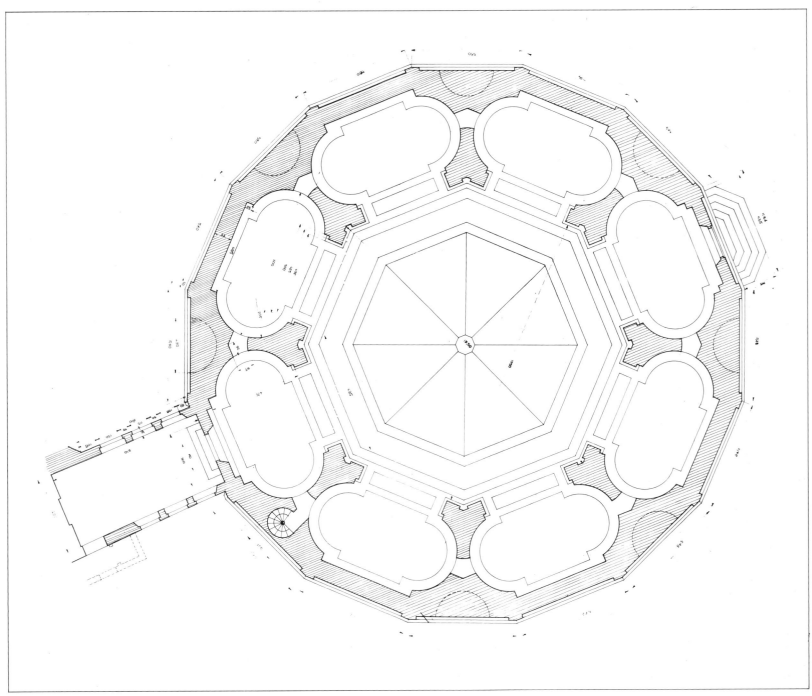

Geometrical construction of the Rotunda by Riccardo Pacciani

The Rotunda is the most notable example in Brunelleschi's work of a design determined by the compass. Given the outer circumference one can construct the sixteen-sided polygon, and the internal octagons can be drawn from a series of concentric circles. Thus the exterior walls form the sixteen-sided polygon; the outer walls of the

passages between chapels mark an octagon, and their inner walls follow a circle inscribed in that octagon, while the major piers mark the corners of another inner octagon.

More complex means are needed to follow the curvilinear course of the niches and the profiles of the vertical elements in the chapels. By dividing the overall diameter into sixty-four equal parts and drawing the corresponding concentric circles one

can fix references from which many structural elements of the chapels can be traced. If the circumference is then divided into sixty-four equal parts this gives the module for the outer polygon (i.e. four per side).

Still undetermined is the geometrical construction of the niches and of the triangles, each with one of the sixteen outer sides as its base, which enclose the supporting piers.

251

271. Elevation of the Rotunda of S. Maria degli Angeli after the 1937 reconstruction. (1 cm = 1.82 m; 1 in. = 15 ft 2 in.)

272. Section of the Rotunda in its present state. The intended height of the piers is shown in faint outline.

273, 274. Conjectural reconstructions of the interior and exterior, based on drawings and the description by Fortunio. The interior shows two solutions for the decoration and windows. The exterior shows several possible variants: niches and windows of the same size (right); pediments fronting roofs over the chapels (left) or purely decorative; the dividing pilasters extended up or stopping at the cornice.

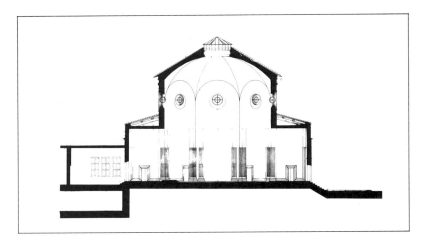

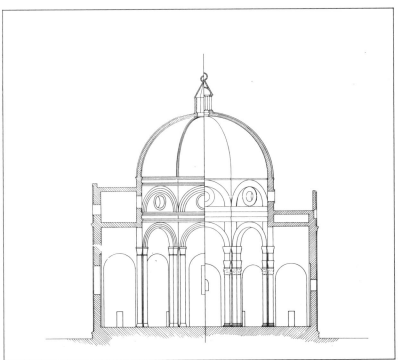

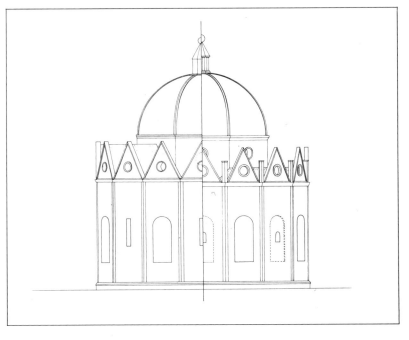

symmetries [architectural ornamentation]: he [Brunelleschi] cared only to show how the main walls were to be constructed and the correspondence between particular elements without ornaments or the design of capitals or architraves, friezes, cornices, etc."

There are, however, at least twelve drawings, mostly from the sixteenth century, that reproduce the ground plan of the Rotunda,[12] together with a long written description by Agostino Fortunio. The earliest and most detailed of these is the one by Giuliano da Sangallo in the Barberini Codex (Vatican Library, Cod. Barb. Lat. 4424), which has been assigned to a date before 1494 (that is, before the pages of the manuscript were enlarged, since much retouching was done because of that operation). The drawing is to scale, which makes it even more exceptional, and is probably a fair copy of an earlier drawing, perhaps Brunelleschi's original project. It raises a number of difficult questions — in particular there are discrepancies between the measurements on it and those of the actual building — but is on the whole certainly the most authentic source for the Rotunda.[13] Finally, there is the long and detailed account by Agostino Fortunio of 1579:[14]

The fabric of the temple was admirable because there was a drawing by Filippo Brunelleschi, the illustrious architect. He wished to construct the temple in such manner that the lower part would present an octagonal form of such size that the span between one wall and the other was 29 *braccia*, and from corner to corner 31, with in each wall a concave *sacellum*, that is a chapel, 10 1/4 *braccia* wide. In the width of these was opened an access between chapels with a doorway of about 1 1/2 *braccia*. The building was to extend to a height of 46 1/2 *braccia* from the ground to the oculus of the lantern. The chapels make a marvellous spectacle with columns and pilasters of 10 3/4 *braccia*, rising 22 *braccia* from the level of the floor to the summit. For the exterior it was the intention of the ingenious architect to divide each side into two faces, that is, into sixteen parts altogether, so that it would look almost, if not completely, like a round building. In every second face he left an empty niche, for greater beauty. From the ground to the eaves of the chapels the height is 22 *braccia*, then it rises with moderate slope as far as the second eaves [of the cupola], which is about 35 *braccia* above the base, whence the outer part of the dome rises with moderate slope to the lantern. The master adorned his construction also with splendid cornices, blank roundels and windows, parts that rise and descend, as can be seen from the model. The main door of the church faces the east, the choir and chapels face the west, with a spiral stairway from which one can walk all around the edifice and which rises to the left of the doorway. And you can see to what point the construction was taken: its height is about 18 *braccia*, though unevenly erected and incomplete, and in every part shows an admirable art; the pilasters and columns are refined works in *pietra serena* and *pietra tenera*.

Fortunio evidently based his account on one or more measured drawings very similar to the one by Sangallo.[15]

For the elevation there are also graphic sources. The exterior is pictured in a drawing in the Rustici Codex [267].[16] It shows the cupola covered with tiles like the apses of the Cathedral, triangular pediments masking the vaults over the chapels, as at S. Croce (perhaps these are the "parts that rise and descend" mentioned by Fortunio), and dividing pilasters which however extend upward above the roofline and stop. These cannot be read as spur buttresses in console form like those of the Cathedral lantern. The pediments do not seem to be intended to reproduce Classical forms faithfully, though they probably allude to them, as Arnolfo di Cambio had done earlier. The drawing is remarkably precise, though it does not show the alternation of niches and windows in the outer wall, and is further proof that a wooden model must have existed or at least sketches derived from one. Nonetheless, not all writers agree on its credibility.[17]

275, 276. Looking up in the Rotunda of S. Maria degli Angeli as it is today. The whole internal facing of the walls was renewed or inserted in 1937, but one can nevertheless see how some of the original spaces were arranged.

278. Pilasters meeting at an obtuse angle.

277. A flat modern ceiling over one of the chapel niches, which can be read as a kind of inverted ground plan.

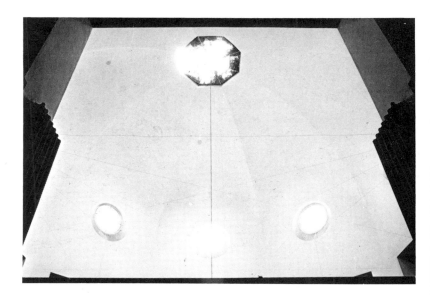

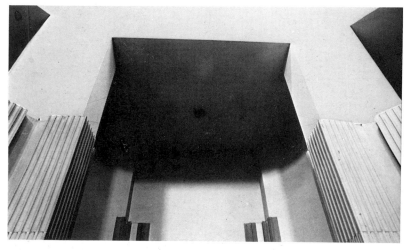

279. Pilaster bases.

280. Base of an abbreviated corner pilaster.

For the interior elevation the most reliable document known so far is a late fifteenth-century drawing in Florence (Biblioteca Laurenziana, Cod. Ashburnham 1828, App., f. 85), first published in 1962.[18] This too seems to be derived from a model.

In our reconstruction [273, 274] we have tried as far as possible to reconcile the information from the Sangallo drawing, the Ashburnham drawing, the view in the Rustici Codex, and the description by Fortunio, keeping in mind also what has been learned from the investigations into the original covering of the chapels in S. Lorenzo and S. Spirito. Most helpful of all was the Ashburnham drawing, which moreover seems to combine two views, one representing the octagonal cupola with its lantern seen from the outside, and the other from below the large cornice giving a remarkably correct view of the interior.

Still unsolved is the problem of possible external buttresses springing from the top of the large walls dividing the chapels and which would have had the same function as the spurs that support the lantern on the Cathedral dome [290]. Proof of their presence may be implied in the Biographer's eulogy (f. 309r): "difficulties that normally entailed considerate inconvenience ... were here remedied ... and it is of such durability and ingenuity [precisely] because of the difficulties that occurred in it". Yet Brunelleschi may have had the skill and cleverness to contain the thrust entirely through an interior structure.[19] Equally difficult to interpret is the expression used by Fortunio when he seems to speak of a structure growing homogeneously from the height of the eaves above the chapels on the exterior to the cornice of the large central octagon, rising "with moderate slope" ("cum honeste penderet"). Yet he says nothing of corner buttresses or consoles, and this is a strange omission in such a detailed analysis made on the basis of scale drawings of the ground plan and elevation.

Brunelleschi's motives for reviving the centralized plan have been much debated.[20] Because of the political and economic relations between Florence and Eastern Europe, one might posit some influence from Byzantine central-plan buildings, passed on by means of drawings. The importance of Traversari for this commission, even if his influence was only indirect, is stressed rightly by Miarelli Mariani,[21] who also makes the fascinating suggestion that the oratory may have served in addition for public or solemn assemblies of the academy of Greek and Latin founded by that scholarly ecclesiastic. Some confirmation of that possible function might be the fact that, more than a century later, Grand Duke Cosimo I seems to have had the idea of completing the Rotunda as the seat of the newly founded Accademia del Disegno.[22]

This aside, we have no direct testimony as to the possible specific uses of a central-plan edifice at the time Brunelleschi designed this oratory except for the traditional function of baptistery,[23] nor is there mention of any association with the monuments in the Holy Land. What Wittkower has to say about the centralized church in the Renaissance and, in particular, its association with the cult of the Virgin remains unsurpassed but nonetheless does not solve our puzzle.[24] Although the oratory is octagonal, like numerous votive chapels dedicated to the Madonna in the Quattrocento, because the entrance door occupies one side there are seven chapels; Zander has rightly pointed out the symbolic relation of this number with the seven virtues of the *Speculum Beatae Virginis*, the seven grades of perfection of the *Itinerarium mentis in Deum*, and the seven gifts of the Holy Spirit, that is, the *Sacrum Septenarium*.[25] But lacking any precise liturgical reference, I think we must give considerable weight to what we can learn from the official

contract between the Arte di Calimala and the monastery of S. Maria degli Angeli cited below, which is also the first to enlighten us on the liturgy envisaged in such an unusual building.

The Rotunda of S. Maria degli Angeli has been interpreted in two quite opposite ways. According to the first, propounded by the Biographer (f. 309r), it is "entirely in the Antique manner inside and out". This idea has obviously given support to those who (especially during the celebrations of 1936) made much of the Classicism of Brunelleschi or, better, of his "archaeologism", though so far without being able to adduce convincing affinities.[26] Another case for contact with the monuments of Rome was put forward by Heydenreich for this oratory as well as the Cathedral lantern.[27] One immediately thinks of the so-called Temple of Minerva Medica, of certain structures in Hadrian's Villa, and of sepulchral shrines, even though these may have been altered in later reconstructions and drawings. Similar central-plan buildings which occur in the drawings of archaeologically-minded architects

281. A doorway in the Rotunda of S. Maria degli Angeli: the lintel is the only surviving original piece of ornamental stonework.

282. Wooden model of the lantern of Florence Cathedral, before flood damage and subsequent restoration (Florence, Museo dell'Opera del Duomo). The lower part seems to be an original model for the closing of the dome, showing the massive corner ribs, the subsidiary ribs, and the straight staircases in each segment [173]. The date of the upper part is uncertain: it may have been made in the seventeenth century, as a guide for repairs (see note 44).

of the Renaissance are, however, of late date, highly imaginative, and not identifiable.[28] Rather than some small temple, Brunelleschi is likely to have studied the Basilica of Maxentius, with its vault-supporting pylons and its articulation by niches.

But against this Classical interpretation there is another, now more widely accepted, which can be called Neo-Gothic. Heydenreich himself, Gori-Montanelli, Burns, Klotz, Bruschi and Manieri have all related this central-plan building to late medieval structures such as the apsed choir and transept-ends of Florence Cathedral. This interpretation proves particularly fascinating if one considers the function of the small round temple (the *tempietto*) as tabernacle, its Marian symbolism, and the character of the spurs, almost like flying buttresses, that support the Cathedral lantern. The similarity is also striking between the design here and the later apsidal plan of the Gothicizing Cathedral of Pienza.[29]

It was once thought that no provision had been made for a separate sanctuary, and that the high altar would have been in the middle (as in the rotunda built some years later onto SS. Annunziata). The choir was seen by many scholars as a later and incongruous addition. But it is now clear that it was in fact requested in the contract of 1434 and was intended to serve also to connect the oratory with the existing monastery, perhaps by way of the Cappella de' Nobili. The difficulties in joining a choir to this octagon, conceived as an isolated form in itself, have been well analysed by Miarelli Mariani, though I think they were the consequence of the dual nature of the commission, which came from both the Arte di Calimala and the monastery.

Actually, many of the perplexities as regards not only the choir but also the ground plan, arising from the sixteenth-century and later drawings, disappear on an attentive reading of the contract drawn up between the Arte di Calimala, as executors of the testaments of Andrea and Matteo, and the monastery and signed sometime between 14 February and 14 April 1434.[30]

After repeating that the funds will not stretch to two new foundations, and recalling the reduction conceded by Martin V (see above, note 4), the consuls stipulate the construction of

a single oratory under the title and name of St Mary the Virgin, Mother of our Lord Jesus Christ, honourable and devout in the manner, quality and form and in the various parts and ornaments and other things of the sort, according to what will please and appear good to the consuls of that guild who will be in office at that time and to whom it will be entrusted.

The choice of design therefore seems to remain entirely in the hands of the consuls in office or those persons they might delegate to that task. But then it goes on:

And in that oratory and parts of it are to be placed in visible position, painted and carved coats of arms and insignia of that guild as well as of the family of the Scolari. And in that oratory is to be made and should be made a fitting choir with grille, altar, and other appropriate things according to the desire of the hermits [the Camaldolensian term for their members] of that monastery. The choir is to be entirely enclosed and without exit according to the form and customs of the hermits, and to the dimensions that they require.

Thus, paradoxically, we have two different projects, arbitrarily combined, entrusted to two different administrative authorities and associated with two dissimilar functions. The drawings that have come down to us lacking the choir either derive from an intermediate stage in the design, before the order had given their approval, or are simplifications. The choir was to have been enclosed and "without exit" which, if I understand it rightly, means not preceded by a chancel arch.[31]

283-285. Measured drawings of the wooden model of the lantern of Florence Cathedral [282]: elevation, ground plan, and view from above. (From Sanpaolesi; drawn by L. Capecchi)

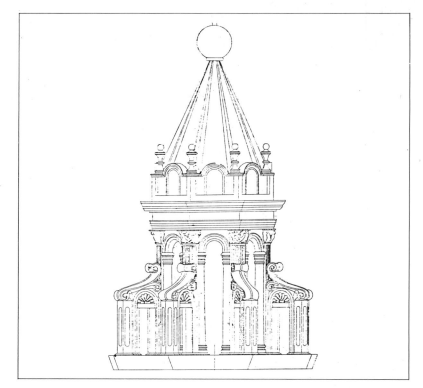

The design of the Rotunda of S. Maria degli Angeli is subtle and avant-garde, consistent with the high cultural level of the monastery, which was one of the major centres of humanism in Florence and therefore in Europe. In opposition to the recently constituted humanist Studio, the Camaldolensians called for a new concept of a "civil" regime in which, in theory at least, the public and private weal would coincide. Traversari himself, however, favoured the most rigid absolutism and violently opposed the anti-papal would-be democratic Council of Constance whom he called a band of criminals. Perhaps then it is not by chance that to modern eyes the Rotunda would have resembled a small fortress, nor is it irrelevant that it would have been a masterpiece of erudition and a challenge, indeed a prophecy, in humanistic terms.

That the structure was recognized to be exceptional is in any case shown not only by the numerous drawings made of it and by the care with which they were preserved and later made known, but also by the clear signs of its influence almost from the moment it was conceived.[32]

The history of the building since work stopped in 1437 can be briefly told. Fortunio, writing in 1579, mentions a proposal by Grand Duke Cosimo to complete it, but nothing came of this because of the opposition of the monastery (see above, note 14). New projects were probably drawn up at that time, and there may have been a revival of interest in central-plan structures.

The shell of walls was given a provisional covering in 1503 with a simple wooden roof, but this collapsed in 1600 and was not replaced.[33] A century and a half later, Richa could only lament in his Lesson XII that "what had been built of the temple was so totally damaged that soon everything will be knocked down". The idea of transforming it into the seat of the Accademia del Disegno had come to naught.[34] From 1808 to 1844 and again from 1867 the building belonged to the Hospital of S. Maria Nuova, which at one point handed it over as a studio to Enrico Pazzi, the sculptor of the monument to Dante in Piazza S. Croce.

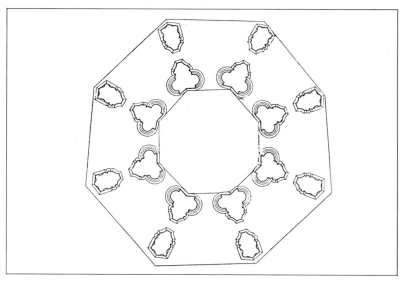

After having been occupied by two other sculptors, Mancini and Aloisi, in 1919 it was taken back through eviction and at that time some demolition work was done to clear the interior spaces. The ground plan made then and published by Linacher[35] proves beyond a shadow of doubt that the one produced by Stegman and Geymüller, which has become the standard always referred to, was largely conjectural, since the interior was divided by partitions. A few photographs taken in those years show that there was serious but not irreparable damage to the walls, exposure to the weather having eroded the *pietra serena*.

A report on the notorious reconstruction done in the 1930s was published by the architect responsible, Rodolfo Sabatini, in 1935. Siebenhüner, who observed the work in progress, nevertheless assured Paatz that the replacement of the elements was done in the most correct and honest manner. First-hand documentation, mostly unpublished, concerning the large-scale alterations between 1934 and 1940 was assembled by Miarelli Mariani and was also studied by Bencivenni.[36]

The lantern of Florence Cathedral

From documents and from the fresco in the Spanish Chapel [111], which shows the dome crowned by a remarkably well proportioned octagonal lantern, we know that this method of finishing the building was already envisaged in the project of 1367. In 1432 it had apparently

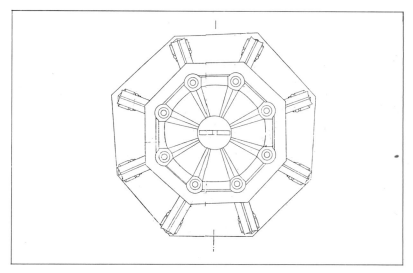

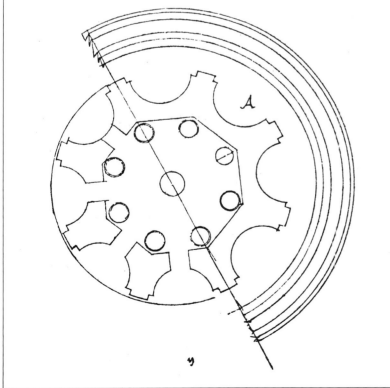

286. The lantern, seen in a drawing attributed to Giuliano da Sangallo (Lille, Musée des Beaux-Arts).

287. Plan of a circular Roman building at Hadrian's Villa, from a drawing which belonged to Leonardo da Vinci (Cod. Ambrosianus, *Le Rovine di Roma*, f. 57r; from Pedretti). The niched polygon suggests the plan of Brunelleschi's exedrae on the Cathedral (see *fig. 308* and p. 278).

been assumed that Brunelleschi would be responsible for the whole design including the lantern, but the final form was certainly not settled at that time and four years later it was decided to hold another competition.[37]

The discussion preceding it, and the vicissitudes of the contest itself, can be reconstructed in some detail through the records of payments made to Brunelleschi's assistants and to other competitors.[38] Brunelleschi won fairly easily, though the arguments were so fierce and the atmosphere so acrimonious that one of the conditions specified in writing was that he should make his peace with the other contestants. We know in detail the reasons for Brunelleschi's model being chosen in the assembly of 31 December 1436,[39] but it is by no means easy to translate them into the language of today. The chief concerns were functional more than aesthetic: Brunelleschi's design was judged to be stronger and more watertight than the others. It looked stronger perhaps because of the buttressing, and more solid because of its compact masonry made up of large single blocks laid horizontally and envisaged as being sealed at the top by immense consoles made of marble monoliths; while at the same time it would be light in weight since the thrusts were well distributed, the structure was very open, with many voids between the solids, and the structural elements would themselves be in part hollow. The solid blocks were partly hollowed out so that when they were juxtaposed — a task demanding the utmost accuracy — they could be fixed together with mortar poured into the interstices. The large windows would be protected from rain, but especially the covering cone (which for centuries now has rested on the original wooden frame) would be virtually sealed and would not normally permit water seepage; and there may also be an allusion to some ingenious system of draining off the water so that it would not stagnate on the broad cornice.

Preparation probably began immediately, but as the documents show, the practical difficulties were numerous. There were problems over the supply of marble.[40] And, even more important, as with the dome itself, the problem of devising machinery for lifting and positioning the heavy marble blocks was almost as demanding as the design of the structure. Up to a certain point the hoisting could be done from inside by a central windlass (something like the large winding apparatus used in constructing the dome), but the greatest care had to be taken to reduce as much as possible the risk of the blocks swinging back and forth. For the final stage, however, the material had to be dragged up on a kind of cableway running along the outer curve of the outer shell, which had not yet been covered by roofing. Once the perilous height of more than 90 m (some 300 ft) was reached, the blocks (which were too heavy to be carried by one or two masons on the narrow scaffolding, where the slightest sudden movement could result in a plunge to death) would have been placed mechanically one above the other with meticulous exactness, some set into one other, some cemented, with their hollowed-out cores carefully fitted together. Here Brunelleschi gave further proof of his technical genius, inventing an apparatus to hoist and position the blocks which was activated by an endless screw of wood, something like the mechanical arm now used for handling radioactive substances, which could move the weights horizontally, vertically, or from side to side as needed [*292*].[41] All of these operations were quite faithfully documented in drawings, some even by Leonardo.

This very flexible positioning mechanism and the other hoisting apparatus, according to a later drawing which is perhaps a copy, were contained in a monumental wooden tower resting on the closing ring of

259

288. Section and elevation of the lantern of Florence Cathedral. (From Sanpaolesi, drawn by L. Capecchi)

289. Plan of the lantern and view from above. (From Sanpaolesi, drawn by L. Capecchi)

290. The lantern. The size of the people shows how unexpectedly large it is.

the dome which had platforms and crane arms projecting both outwards and inwards [291]. On the outside it was supported by vertical beams set into the holes made for that purpose (now covered by tiles) and extending into the space between the shells of the cupola. On the inside it almost entirely covered the octagonal opening, leaving only a narrow passage for the blocks of marble hoisted up by a *stella*, that is a winch suspended from a pyramid of beams held rigid by ropes. Three types of lifting mechanisms can be made out in the drawing: one with a cantilever, at the left, which must have projected a good way and therefore required its own elaborate scaffolding; another a kind of sledge pulled by two ropes [295]; and the third a large central windlass presumably operated from the ground by means of extremely long rope cables.[42] Some iron and bronze pincers, as well as ropes long enough for the windlass, still exist and could be seen in one of the exedrae until their recent removal to the Museo dell'Opera del Duomo.

In the drawing [291], which we believe shows the situation of the work some years after Brunelleschi's death, it looks as if the volutes of the lantern buttresses had just been put into place: this cannot be, however, for their position is higher, corresponding to the second tier of the scaffolding at least. The scaffolding as shown here is not high enough to carry the construction to completion; and in fact a note at the top duly advises that to put the globe in position (which was not done until 1472) "it will be necessary to erect another scaffold about twelve *braccia* in height".

The drawing is skilful in its perspective and selects the elements to be emphasized as plainly as a diagram in a technical manual. But at that height not a *stella* but something like the rotary crane used for building the cone [293, 294] must already have been functioning, since it was devised to draw up the blocks of marble through the centre of the lantern. This entire machine revolved on wooden or bronze cylinders. Making use of the same platform equipped with cylinders, virtually a system of ball bearings, this rotating crane could be replaced when the work was at an advanced stage by a specialized stone-positioning crane, of which we have a diagrammatic drawing [292] as well as a representation in the general view of the scaffolding [291]. This took in its grasp the marble block that had been brought to the topmost platform and slowly raised it, by an endless screw mechanism, which a worker seated at the top of the scaffolding turned with a crank. To prevent the block from swaying back and forth, the endless screw was held rigidly in place by two wooden beams running vertically in grooved channels. Once the stone reached the maximum height it was moved horizontally by another endless screw until it reached the position into which it should be lowered. A counterweight on the opposite side, also regulated by an endless screw, prevented the whole thing from toppling over. These manoeuvres had to be controlled from above, and, as the drawing [291] correctly shows, there were stairways right up to the top of the scaffolding. An added advantage of the system was that the entire surface of the lantern could serve as base and platform: materials could be stockpiled there, and numerous masons could work at the same time. It should be remembered that all this equipment was enormous: even the gold ball at the top of the lantern [290] is big enough for a man to stand up in.

Brunelleschi died in 1446, when the lantern could have progressed not much further than the bases. The direction of the work was taken over first by Michelozzo, then by Manetti Ciaccheri (who had been paid for the wooden model), and finally by Rossellino. These men supervised

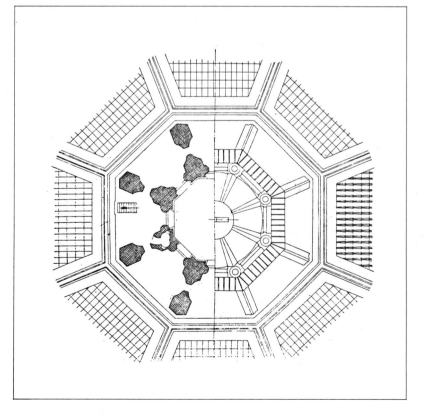

continued on page 266

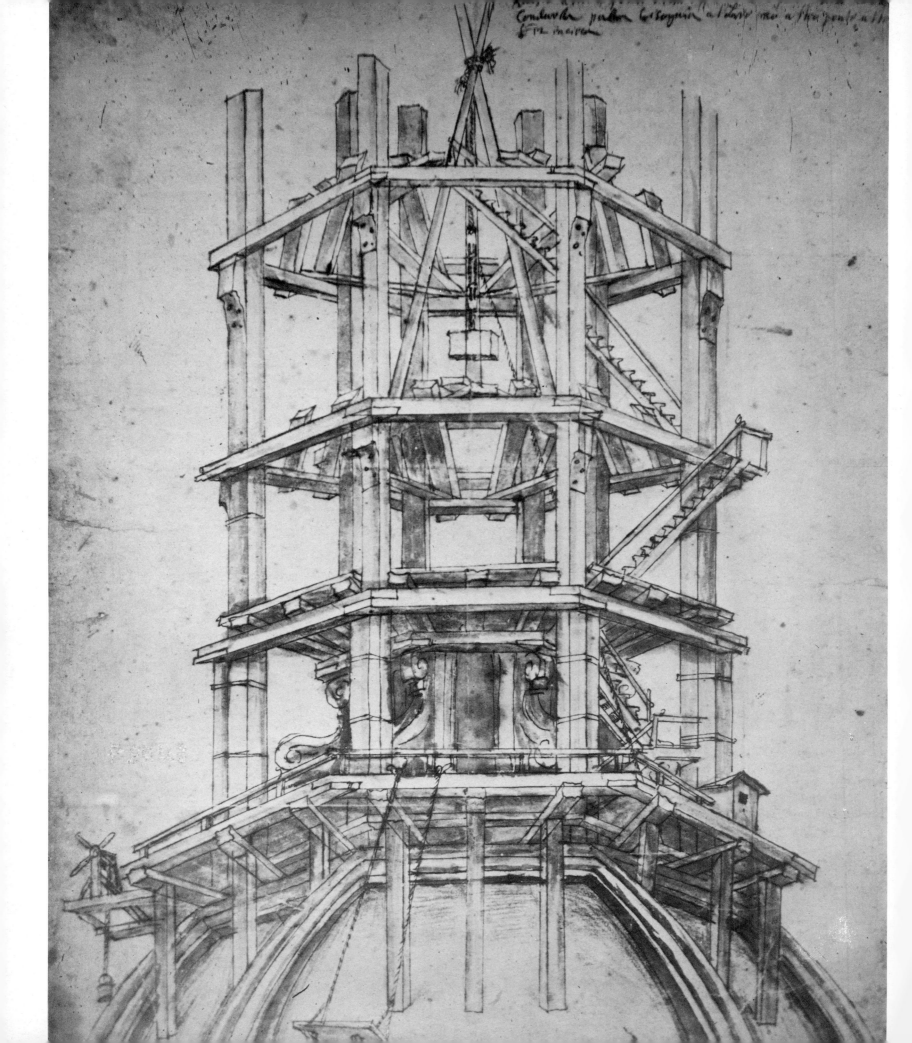

291. Drawing recording scaffolding and cranes used for the Cathedral lantern (Florence, Uffizi, Gabinetto dei Disegni e Stampe, 248A).

292. Stone-positioning crane, movable vertically, horizontally or from side to side; from the *Zibaldone* of Buonaccorso Ghiberti (Florence, Biblioteca Nazionale Centrale, MS.BR 228, f. 106r).

293. Crane revolving on rollers on a circular platform, used to build the cone; from the *Zibaldone* of Buonaccorso Ghiberti (f. 105r).

294. Detail of the mechanism of a revolving crane; from the *Zibaldone* of Buonaccorso Ghiberti (f. 104r).

295. "Sledge" used to slide building materials along the outer shell, as rebuilt and altered (Florence Cathedral).

OVERLEAF
296. Interior of the lantern.

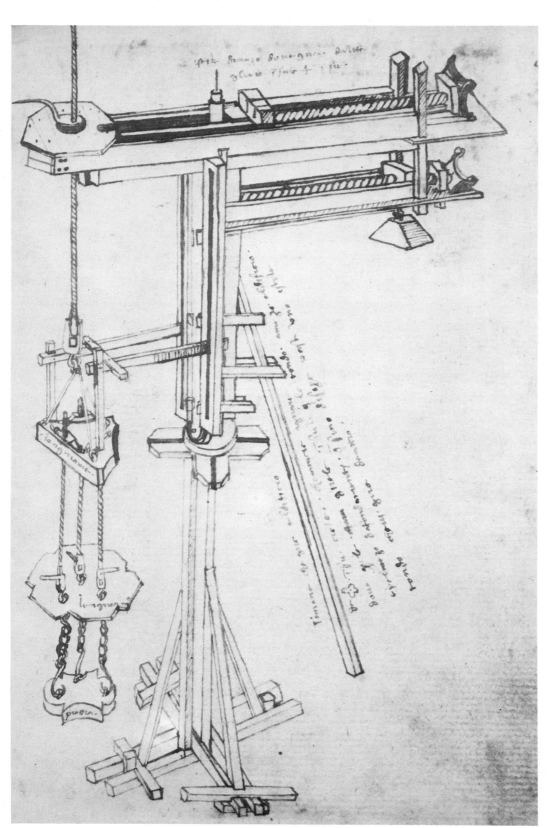

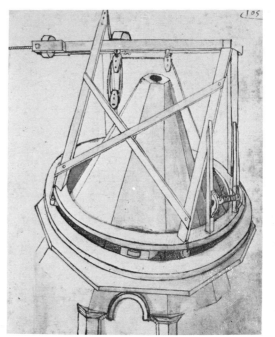

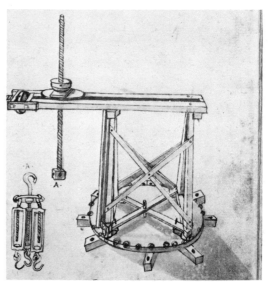

the completion,[43] and although certain ornamental features owe something to them in their details (more profuse and florid, less geometrical), Brunelleschi must have envisaged such decoration. The Biographer (ff. 310v-312v) makes it clear that the wooden model, though in many respects only approximate, contained all the ornamentation, including that on the large volutes. Such a wealth of detail was exceptional, but not sufficient to guide those executing the work after the death of its inventor, the obstacle being that "he who built the model did not make plain all of its secrets, hoping to deal with them one by one, when they came up in the building process, and to have them executed carefully and correctly". Thus Brunelleschi seems not to have indicated the type of ornamentation for the lintels of the openings in the buttresses, so they were simply left plain [282]: "those marbles above the uprights of the small doorways in the buttresses beneath the volutes not being in fact in the model, are not in the lantern, because at that point Filippo was in the other world". In this particular case, though, since special deliberations were required to decide on the symbolic flowers (connected with the Virgin) of the volutes (strictly *viticci*, vine tendrils), whose profile does not match up with the shell-niches, it may well be that the failure to define the architraves was not Brunelleschi's but rather that of the theologians who were consultants for the Opera del Duomo.

It is not certain that the wooden model which we see today is really the one paid for in 1436 or a faithful copy of it, or a later model depicting the lantern as built. Whatever its date, I find plausible the suggestion that it was constructed on top of an original model showing the upper part and closing of the dome.[44]

The lantern, Argan has observed, is not so much a conclusion to as an interpretation of all the preceding work on the dome:

The lantern has two purposes — one *static* (because the dome consists of ribs coming together at the top, the lantern virtually serves as a keystone), the other *figurative* (on the exterior the lantern marks the vertical axis, giving an effect of centrality). Seen from the interior the lantern also has two functions: it serves to transmit light from the dome, and it serves as the point of convergence of the lines of perspective.

These various functions are fulfilled by means of a number of devices which are both stylistic and structural. The idea of building a lantern for static purposes stemmed from the Florence Baptistery (a model already in mind, the Biographer says, in the deliberations of 1420). There was also the Gothic theory of pinnacles, according to which a perpendicular weight reinforces a pier against lateral movement, though that theory cannot be applied unmodified to a dome, unless perhaps it was feared that it might open like the calyx of a flower and burst apart in all directions.

As the visual centre of convergence the lantern forms a focal point for the large outer ribs, in the same way as the octagonal ring of masonry on which it stands brings together the eight segments of the dome and thereby adjusts and reconciles the irregularities inevitably introduced during construction [288, 289]. The measurements done specially for this book show that the outer octagon at the end of the dome ribs, upon which one can walk, is almost unbelievably irregular, whereas the inner octagon below the windows of the lantern is perfectly regular, easily and elegantly finishing off that huge artificial mountain with all its bulges and asymmetries. This is true on the exterior as well, though now serious distortions are visible, due to the sinking of one of the piers. To the eye the continuity is emphasized by the white marble of the ribs

continued on page 277

298. The upper entablature inside the lantern of Florence Cathedral.

299, 300. Detail and general view of the ring around the base of the lantern, in the form of a giant entablature.

OVERLEAF

301. The windows of the lantern.

302. Window-head and pilasters inside the lantern of Florence Cathedral. The windows have a squeezed horseshoe shape and do not touch the cornice above, indicating a change to Brunelleschi's design (see note 45).

303. Window-head, pilasters and volutes seen from outside. The capitals of the columns are derived from capitals in the earlier Cathedral of Florence, S. Reparata.

304. Symbolic flowers and leaves on one of the volutes of the lantern of Florence Cathedral, designed by Antonio Manetti Ciaccheri and agreed in 1453.

305. The buttressing spurs of the lantern.

306. *Dante and his Poem*: this detail from Domenico di Michelino's fresco, painted about 1465 in S. Maria del Fiore, shows the Cathedral dome and one of the exedrae. The coloured marble facing of the drum has only reached the level of the exedrae (compare *fig. 113*).

Balancing the city of Florence here is the mountain of Purgatory. Brunelleschi himself was known as an interpreter of the *Divine Comedy*, and seems to have been interested in depicting its world (see Chapter 16).

which stand out against the red terracotta and would appear entirely convincing if we did not know that the design of the ribs differs from what Brunelleschi desired.

Minor but quite specific criticisms are made by the Biographer concerning "errors" in the upper part of the lantern, but it is often hard to say whether these are due to design decisions by Brunelleschi, to later alterations after his death, or to the stipulation imposed upon him to incorporate ideas from other models submitted in the competition.[45] They amount to very little compared with the energetic and truly dramatic sweep and curves of the lantern's forms and with the sheer genius of the invention of this optical instrument, equally effective from within and without, and, for all its precarious exposed position some 100 m (330 ft) above the ground, solid enough to resist any gale.

It is not without reason that I call the lantern an optical instrument. One of its essential elements is the long narrow windows designed to catch the light even when the sun is at its zenith and to direct it against the interior piers and masonry supporting the dome so that they act like mirrors [175]. Against this system Giovanni di Gherardo da Prato, who also argued against the curvature used for the dome, drew up a polemical memorandum accompanied by a drawing [143: the upper half, upside-down], claiming that this effect of refraction would be cancelled out by the enormous distance between the aperture admitting the sun's rays and the far depth of the church interior.[46] Probably it was in reply to this that Brunelleschi or his followers made the lantern windows more elongated than is usual, though when viewed from below and not from scaffolding (as is usual with documentary photographs) that elongation is automatically corrected and, by an effect of foreshortening, made to look fairly normal.

Around 1432 there was perhaps a discussion as to whether the oculus at the top of the dome should be octagonal or circular (as in the Spanish Chapel fresco [111]).[47] If the latter, the lantern would have been better connected with the cone and the ball at its top (planned from the start), but would have had to sacrifice the felicitous linkage with the eight large ribs. The dynamic ringlike function of the huge buttresses with their double volutes resting on arches would have been accentuated. On the other hand, the horizontal separation between windows and crowning cone would have been less in evidence, making it appear as if the constructional effort culminated in the large radial consoles and the vertex rose all by itself as an independent structure. This would also have been the impression when viewed from the Cathedral floor directly beneath it.

As for the basic plan of the lantern, a circular solution would have done little to modify the essential disposition and would have fitted better with the system of designing, which used both straight lines and curves but with a prevalence — most unusual before then — of curves. In plan, in fact, it is the compositional scheme of the contemporary Rotunda of S. Maria degli Angeli, only turned inside out — two systems of triangles with their vertices directed against the zone of major opposing force, as if to subdue it. In S. Maria degli Angeli this is internal (the thrust of the dome). Here it is external. The pilasters of the lantern strengthen it against wind, and the huge consoles brace it against the weight of its own upper part and hold it firmly against any tendency to move in a gale or to give way structurally.[48]

The townscape value of the lantern is almost incalculable. Crowning the greatest height of Florence it dominates the city, and its vast size makes it appear a virtual castle or tower. From its terrace one surveys

every corner of the city, and the compartments between the great buttresses are so many belvederes, each oriented towards an entirely different view of the valley of the Arno [290]. In a sort of inevitable sequence you move from one sector to another, at the same time enjoying two ever-changing landscapes, one architectural, made up of the structures and ornaments of the lantern itself, the other that of the roofs, monuments, spires, towers and hills of Florence. Curiously, at this altitude the dome below almost disappears, nor can the eye get any notion of its height and scale.

The compartments between the buttresses, made more spacious by the niches cut in the buttresses, each have an angle of aperture of 45 degrees (i.e. one-eighth of a circle). They are the end result of a set of possibilities within which the architect had little freedom to manoeuvre, since the buttresses had to be aligned with the large ribs of the dome. Yet this illustrates his feeling for space better than anything else he ever devised. The fact is, the angle he used in his experiments with perspective was also about 45 degrees. By the introduction of wings between the compartments, acting like the flats on a stage, the distant landscape is divided into finite sections and arranged more lucidly, as the Quattrocento thought the panoramas of Paradise would be. From the platform of the lantern the nearby architectural elements become reduced to a limited and, indeed, human measure (although the consoles themselves are 5.90 m, or 19 ft 4 in. high), and the tower of the lantern appears reduced, almost truncated in height, so that one is not overwhelmed.

The exedrae of Florence Cathedral

The four exedrae (also confusingly called aedicules or blind tribunes) were built by Brunelleschi at the base of the drum of the dome, in the angles between the four main directions of choir, transepts and nave.[49] The initial decision to build them dates from 27 February 1439,[50] and the twelve columns of the first one (that to the north-east, over the so-called Mass Sacristy) were contracted for on 20 March 1445.[51] This means that for that element at least there must have been a precise model by Brunelleschi himself, done in his last years.[52]

The intention seems to have been structural — to shore up the sides of the octagon before the lantern was placed on the top, at those points where it was not supported by the vaults of the three apses. Curved in both plan and elevation, the exedrae act statically like flying buttresses [309, 310].[53] Yet either they were not strong enough or there had been some miscalculation, for it is precisely in line with the exedrae that there are large vertical cracks which split the dome into four.

Visually the exedrae are important in forming part of a rhythmic alternation round the dome, set off from the octagon, and a necessary transition between the Gothic substructure and the (unbuilt) gallery round the dome, which would certainly have had Renaissance forms, and whose general structure and necessarily huge dimensions were envisaged from the start.

Stylistically the exedrae are probably the purest works that Brunelleschi ever created. They reveal an archaeological feeling for Roman forms that is worthy of Alberti. Contrasting with the older decoration of marble rectangles, which is rationalized if not yet completely Classical, they can be seen as the beginning of the next, more radical, phase of the

307, 308. Elevation and plan of one of the exedrae of Florence Cathedral, that to the south-east, facing Via del Proconsolo. (1 cm = 1.38 m; 1 in. = 11 ft 6 in.)

309. The exedra above the sacristy. The roofs of the apses of chancel and transept, left and right, were designed earlier by Brunelleschi.

architecture of humanism. With their broad niches culminating in stylized shells, they reflect a sublime geometrical severity, striking a solemn note of Marian or Apocalyptic symbolism which is echoed high above them in the lantern (though there the shell forms are more naturalistic and were not executed, or even designed in detail, by Brunelleschi).

Like the plan of the Rotunda of S. Maria degli Angeli, these exedrae can be drawn geometrically almost entirely by the use of the compass. Describe a circle; from it construct a decagon, using the method recommended later by Serlio; on the ten corners of the decagon describe ten small circles not touching each other; finally cut across these circles, but not across their diameters, to allow for wider and more open niches. Each exedra is slightly more than half such a niched decagon.

It will be noted that the curved exedrae are visually separated from the walls of the octagonal drum by subtly shifting their centres outwards, so that they are more than a half-circle in plan. This felicitous effect had been anticipated by Brunelleschi when he designed the roofs covering the three fourteenth-century apses of the Cathedral, at the ends of the choir and transepts [113]. The system there was decidedly unusual, but some light is shed on it by the documents.[54] Terracotta tiles were used, respecting the style of the rest of the building. The idea was approved in 1436 with two curious clauses that testify to the interest in the proposal and the fear that it might cost more than estimated: first a guarantee was demanded that the work would not require any repairs for twenty-five years, and second, the cost estimated by Brunelleschi was actually increased from 300 florins to 400, but with the proviso that Brunelleschi became liable to pay out of his own pocket any expenses in excess of that sum. These polygonal roofs give the impression of being isolated and not even touching the drum, an effect that makes the apses appear complete and independent structures. Probably the idea of topping them with a sort of stubby pinnacle, also in terracotta, came from Brunelleschi as well. The almost Islamic general profile of the roofs necessitated a highly skilful laying of the tiles as well as a considerable variety of shapes and sizes. The same was true for the conical roofs of the exedrae, especially because of the way they flare outward at the bottom.

Clearly, one explanation for the form of the exedrae is the architect's geometrical expertise, gained partly, no doubt, through the difficult studies necessary for maintaining and correcting proportionally the curve of the eight segments of the dome. But the influence of Classical models is equally evident, in particular certain features of Hadrian's Villa at Tivoli, which are typical of what has been called, not improperly, Late Antique Baroque: it was a style to be developed later by Leonardo, the master who perhaps learned most from these late works of Brunelleschi [287].

The effect of the exedrae is inspired and extremely unusual — boldly defined yet utterly homogeneous, thanks to the curving line that moves uninterruptedly from concave to convex and back again. Unlike most of Brunelleschi's designs, this one seems to have met with little opposition from the committee in charge. On 27 February 1439, it was decided that the exedrae were to be built "round in accord with the design and model of Filippo". On 8 March the committee seems to have changed its mind somewhat, though the justification is difficult to interpret: "pilastri dicano accordarsj più tosto alla forma tonda che a quella che seguita gli angoli" (literally, *pilastri* are said to go better with a round form than with one that follows the angles or corners). Now *pilastri* can

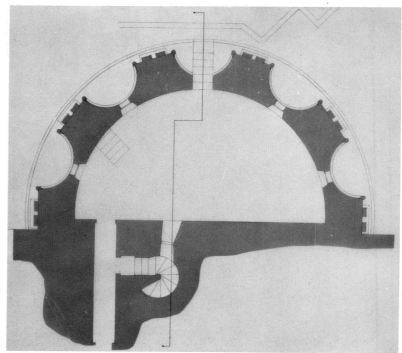

mean either columns or pilasters, but it would seem that the committee was opting for half-columns. The question appears to have been whether in shape the exedrae should take their cue from the octagonal walls of the drum to which they are attached, or whether on the contrary they should be made totally distinct entities, emphasizing their peculiar roundish forms. Half-columns were thought to achieve this better than

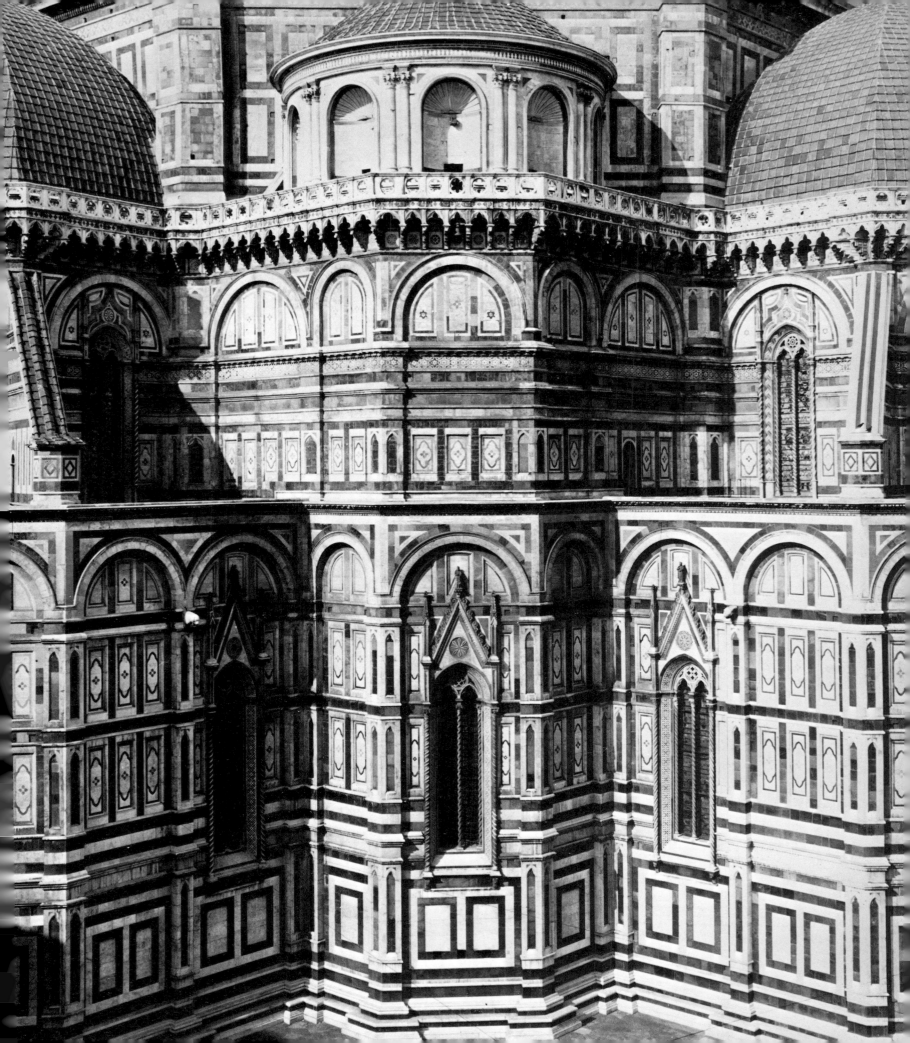

310. Section of the Cathedral exedra facing Via del Proconsolo, taken along the line shown in *fig. 308* to show the steps leading to the external gallery and, on the right, the windows between the exedra and the spiral stairway inside the drum. Note the difference in level between exterior and interior. (1 cm = 1.13 m; 1 in. = 9 ft 5 in.)

311. Section along the diameter of the exedra, as though seen through the wall from inside the drum. (To the same scale).

312. The exedra, from the side.

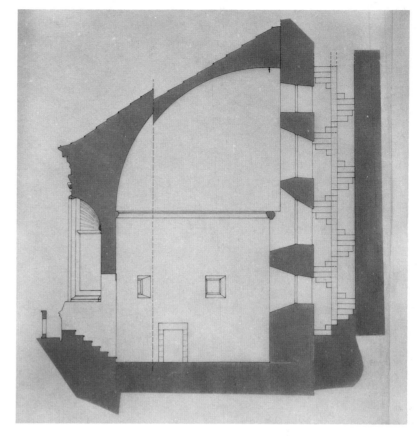

flat pilasters. Every niche is given flanking half-columns, and at the same time the independence of the exedra as a whole is further emphasized by setting a complete pair of half-columns at each end, so that it becomes a sort of separate rotunda. The motif of paired half-columns does not occur at Hadrian's Villa but, as Heydenreich observes, it was to become a special favourite of the sixteenth century.

The predominant character of these structures is one of ponderous circular volume, expressed particularly in the horizontal members. The fact that the exedrae were essentially massive buttresses endowed them with a kind of monumental simplicity; even the double capitals are carved out of a single block of marble [315]. Indeed, each element is a self-contained block. The shell, drastically stylized and made abstract, is neatly separated from the niche below it by a horizontal cornice; and the niche is outlined all the way round by a very emphatic band of green marble which makes it that much more telling at a distance.

Design and symbolism of the exedrae
by Riccardo Pacciani

During the work of measuring and surveying, it became clear that the impression of a direct correspondence between interior and exterior, which one gets from a hasty visit and from the drawings published by Geymüller, is completely wrong. The flooring inside, for instance, is at a much lower level than the base of the attached columns outside [310]. The fact that the plan is slightly more than a half-circle is no doubt partly due to the need to build the exedrae on existing spaces, but it also reflects a conscious decision to make them as conspicuous as possible.

With their play of alternating solids and voids, the exedrae constitute a decisive element in the complex interrelationship of forms that Brunelleschi established between the Cathedral and the city. Unlike anything in the Gothic project for the Cathedral, seen in the fresco by Andrea di Buonaiuto [111], the exedrae and the three polygonal roofs over the apses were deliberately set off from the compact organism of the drum — the exedrae in plan, the apse roofs in profile.

Despite the raising of the external base level of columns and niches, which helps to make the exedrae more readable from below, and despite the outlining of the niches with a band of dark green marble, the exedrae are inevitably overwhelmed by the dome above them — yet the true scale of the dome depends precisely on the contrast with these smaller structures below.

The shells at the top of the niches and the vase-shapes formed by inlaid marble in the frieze are symbols derived from the cult of the Virgin; but it is within the context of Early Renaissance theory about centrality and central-plan churches that the decoration of the exedrae takes on a deeper iconographic meaning, as part of the general "theme" of the whole Cathedral — the glorification of the Virgin. The church is both the image of the city and the reflection of the religious hierarchy. In the centre, above the altar in the crossing, the place where the divine is made manifest, rises the dome; the three apses that flank it are each covered by a quasi-domical roof; and the sacristies between them are crowned by the exedrae. It is not inside the church, within the religious experience as such, that one can grasp these simultaneously religious and formal structures and their rationale, but rather outside it, especially at the level of the many towers and roofs of the city [112]. And from that point also those urban and civil relationships on which the Renaissance form of the city is based assume their clearest visual embodiment.

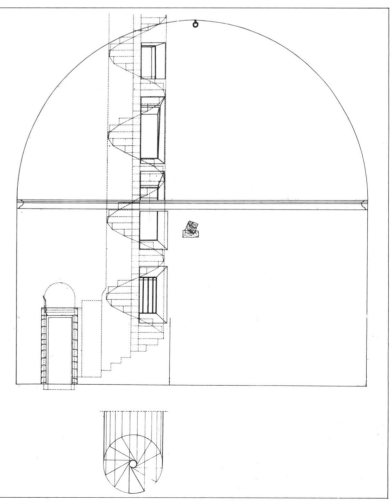

OVERLEAF: 313, 314. Stylized shells in the niche-heads.

315, 316. Monolithic coupled capitals, and coupled half-columns of one of the north exedrae on the Cathedral.

317. Drainage channel of one of the Cathedral exedrae. (The stones were all renewed during recent restorations.)

318. Bases of the coupled half-columns and lower part of a niche.

319. Door in one of the Cathedral exedrae, between the external gallery and the interior. The base level of the order is high above the actual floor level.

320. Interior of the exedra facing Via del Proconsolo. Windows lighting the spiral stairway appear on the left.

13 The pulpit of S. Maria Novella

The last documented work by Brunelleschi brings us round full circle to his beginnings, for it is virtually a work of sculpture: the pulpit in S. Maria Novella, suspended from a pier and reached by a spiral staircase.[1] On the last day of August 1443 Brunelleschi was paid a "large florin" (4.15 *lire*) for a wooden model.[2] The mediator for the commission was Fra Andrea di Donato Rucellai, admired as "a good mathematician" and "good and pleasant to converse with", who was acting in the name of "the family and men of the Rucellai house".[3] As so often with Brunelleschi's works, years went by before the pulpit was completed and installed. In 1448 a dispute between the Rucellai and the Minerbetti, who claimed to own the pier, was settled in favour of the Rucellai.[4] In 1453 Buggiano had finished carving the reliefs.

The visitor to S. Maria Novella too easily overlooks this pulpit, which is the first in a splendid series that includes those in S. Croce and the Badia at Fiesole. Certainly it is only by examining its design in detail that one becomes aware of the great intelligence with which it was conceived: it then begins to look like something from the pages of Philibert de l'Orme a century and a quarter later, or like a creation by one of those wizard-like stonecarvers of the Late Gothic and Mannerism in the North. The old Italian aversion to "German" art here became collaboration and love: the pulpit clings to the thirteenth-century composite pier like a liana, unfurls like a vine, blossoms from it.

The execution of the pulpit was in the hands of the stonemason and *capomaestro* Giovanni di Piero del Ticcia. He was also involved in the work on the lantern and exedrae of the Cathedral, appraised Donatello's pulpit in Prato, executed a memorial stone for Brancaccio Brancacci's daughter Lena, and worked with Brunelleschi on the fortifications of Pisa and Vicopisano and elsewhere. The S. Maria Novella document suggests quite close personal relations between the two men, and a partnership on commissions from private individuals. He contracted out the carving on the pulpit: decorative sculpture was commissioned from Giuliano di Nofri and Bartolo d'Antonio Bastranoli, and for the scenes from the life of the Virgin Buggiano was charged with making — evidently on the basis of a design already agreed on — "figures, houses, foliage and other ornaments pertaining to these narratives in marble". The panels were appraised to fix the price in February 1453.

The reliefs by Buggiano are mediocre, but they include bold attempts to make architectural settings emerge from the curved surface of the pulpit with correct perspective and convincingly straight lines, particularly in the baldacchino of the Presentation [329]. (For Buggiano see Chapter 2, note 27.)

The pulpit itself, in its placing in S. Maria Novella, also stands in a pivotal position. Next to it is Masaccio's *Trinity* [103]: Brunelleschi's splendid pulpit draws added attention to the fresco, and, in a sense, serves for both propaganda and devotion. And the next masterpiece to be added to the church would be the famous façade by Alberti — Alberti, who has been frequently quoted in these pages and used as a comparison to Brunelleschi and who, in fact, when that pioneering artist left the scene, took his place with the reverence of a disciple and the energy of a perfect pupil, determined to do something different, to surpass his master.

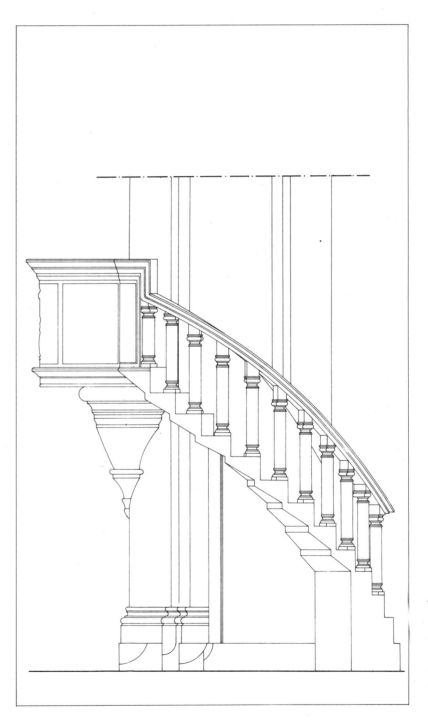

321, 322. Side elevation and view of the pulpit, by Brunelleschi and Buggiano. (Elevation scale: 1 cm = 31 cm; 1 in. = 2 ft 7 in.)

323. The pulpit of S. Maria Novella, from the front.

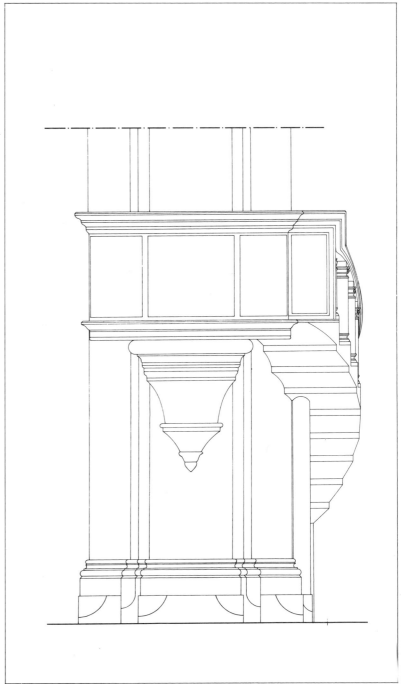

324. Front elevation of the pulpit. (1 cm = 31 cm; 1 in. = 2 ft 7 in.)

325. Side elevation of the pulpit. (To the same scale)

326. Rear elevation of the pulpit. (To the same scale)

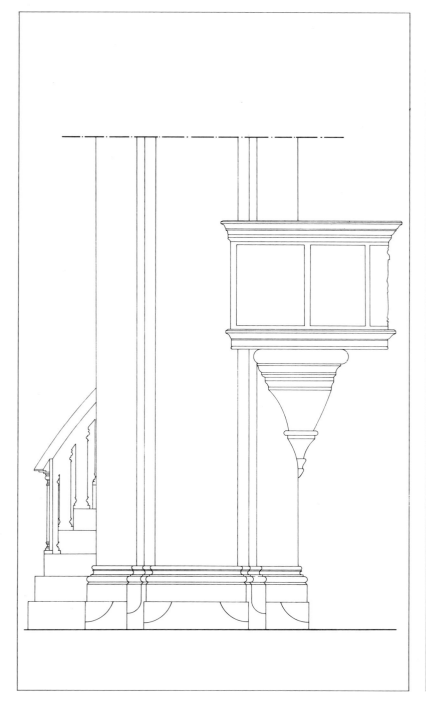

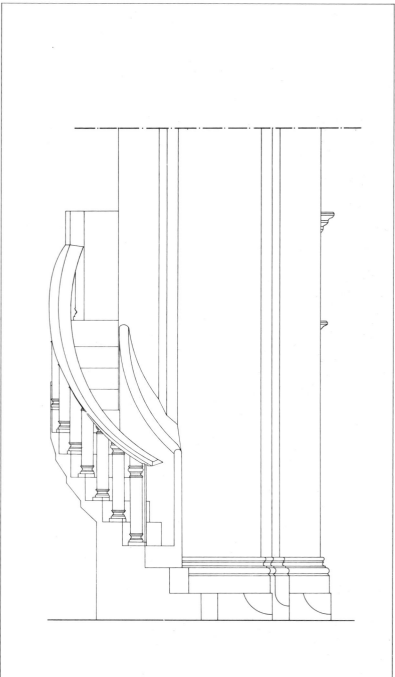

327. Sections and details of the pulpit of S. Maria Novella. (1 cm = 59 cm; 1 in. = 4 ft 11 in.)

328. The base of the pulpit.

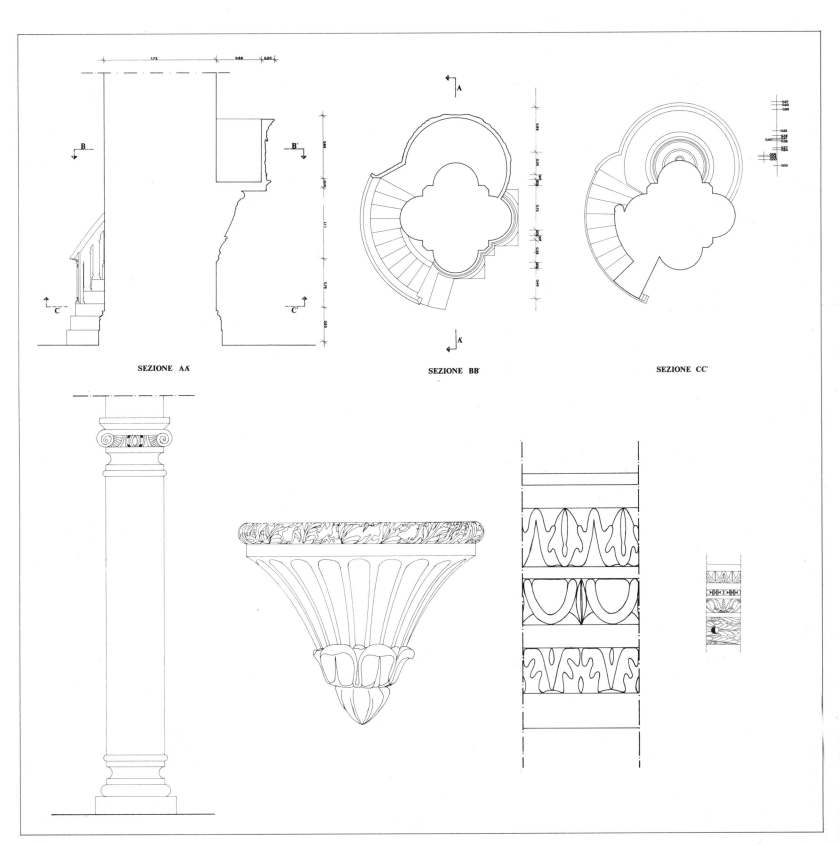

SEZIONE AA'

SEZIONE BB'

SEZIONE CC'

329. Buggiano: *The Presentation in the Temple*, on the pulpit of S. Maria
Novella. Note the rendering of an architectural setting in perspective — made
more difficult by the fact that the relief is convex — which is completely
successful when viewed from the right spot, as here.

330. Buggiano: *The Assumption of the Virgin*.

NT VERBVM DEI ET CVSTODVN

14 Theatrical machinery

Yet another of Brunelleschi's activities that was public and official in character was that connected with the religious drama of the church, the *sacre rappresentazioni*. These religious festivals were organized mainly in conjunction with solemn state or ecclesiastical visits to the city, and, more directly than is normally recognized, they anticipated the *trionfi* and scenic transformations of the Cinquecento.[1] The complex machinery necessary to achieve their effects was far beyond the resources and the expertise of the neighbourhood or parish, and this explains how Brunelleschi came to be involved in them. His work on the Cathedral dome had given him a wealth of useful experience, both in the hoisting of people and material and in the protection of life at high levels by means of safety belts.

Four churches, according to the documents, presented such *sacre rappresentazioni*: SS. Annunziata, S. Felice, S. Maria del Carmine[2] and S. Spirito. Once constructed, the mechanisms became permanent fixtures of the church. The performances of 1439, described to our good fortune in great detail by a Russian bishop, Abraham of Suzdal, were connected with the sessions of the Council in Florence, those of 1471 with the visit of Galeazzo Maria Sforza (though he left the crowds at the Carmine and S. Spirito waiting in vain for a glimpse of him), and there were others in 1494 associated with the sojourn of King Charles VIII of France.

Obviously both texts and machinery were improved and brought up to date from decade to decade, and we know that the machines made by Brunelleschi were later replaced by others having various technical improvements devised by Francesco d'Angelo, known as Il Cecca. These contrivances by which the characters were made to fly through the air in the midst of spectacular explosions of lights and fireworks were as much a source of terror as delight: Charles VIII came to the door of S. Felice but absolutely refused to enter (perhaps fearing murderers hidden in the crowd), and in a chronicle of S. Spirito for 1470 (1471 our style) we read that the festivity at the Carmine "was carried out... with great risk to the lives of many persons", and, more tragic, that "at S. Spirito, after the performance was over, those in charge of the festival went off without a thought for the danger of fire, so that at the fifth hour of the night in the top part of the tower of the apparatus fire broke out and, before anyone noticed, shot up so high that the flame set light to the roof of the church", which was largely destroyed and could not be used until the new one was built according to Brunelleschi's project. It was in that fire too that his statue of Mary Magdalen was lost.

Exactly how and how much the architect was involved in all these theatrical events is difficult to say: some minimize his role, others exaggerate it. Vasari connects him only with the contrivance at S. Felice; the Biographer makes no mention of that invention, his manuscript breaking off just before that very year; and contemporary descriptions that have survived praise the inventor but refer to him only as "a skilful Italian man".

The simplest apparatus seems to have been that in SS. Annunziata, described thus in a account traditionally ascribed to Abraham of Suzdal:[3]

When the time came for that great and marvellous spectacle, many people assembled in the church, silent, every eye fixed on the platform on the rood screen. Soon the curtains with the drapes fell, and on the magnificent chair alongside the couch one saw him who acted the part of the Virgin. All this was beautiful, marvellous, full of grace. On the same stage one saw four prophets, each with an inscription in his hand which contained the ancient prophecies of the birth and incarnation of Christ... Then they disputed together and each one tore up his own inscription and threw it away, whereupon they took other inscriptions and advanced to the front of the stage, saluted each other, each examined his own inscription, struck it with his hand, and argued with his neighbour... In that manner they carried on their argument for a half-hour or so. Then the curtains of the upper tribune were opened, making a noise like thunder, and the prophets scampered off. Above, on the tribune, one saw God the Father surrounded by more than five hundred burning lamps that revolved continually while moving up and down. Boys dressed in white representing angels were around Him, some with cymbals [*cembalo*], others with flute or harp, making a joyful spectacle of inexpressible beauty. After some time an angel dispatched by God descended on the two hempen ropes... to announce the Conception. The angel was a handsome youth dressed in a garment white as snow and decorated in gold, exactly as one sees the angels of Heaven in paintings. While descending he sang in a soft voice and held in his hand a small branch. The descent was contrived in this manner: behind him were two wheels invisible from below because of the distance, and two ropes ran around those wheels, while unseen persons up above made use of a very thin rope to make the angel descend and ascend.

After the ceremony of the Angelic Salutation a fire is sent forth from God and with the noise of thunder travels down the three ropes towards the centre of the stage where the prophets had been; a flame shoots up and sends out sparks in such a way that the entire church is quite full of them. The angel, while ascending, gives voice to jubilation, moves his hands this way and that, and beats his wings as if he were truly flying; fire comes down ever more abundantly and noisily from the upper tribune and sets ablaze the candles in the church though without burning the clothing of the spectators or doing them any harm. When the angel has returned to the point from which he descended the flame ceases and the curtains close again.

The description could not be more clear, and taking it as his starting point and combining it with a minute examination of the walls of the church, the architect Cesare Lisi was able to reconstruct the "miracle" in a remarkable large working model [*331, 332*].

Abraham's description and Lisi's reconstruction lead to some surprising conclusions. The fire that "with the noise of thunder travels down on the three ropes towards the centre of the stage... [and] shoots up and sends out sparks in such a way that the entire church is quite full of them" obviously represents the descent of the Holy Spirit interpreted as illumination, as luminous spirit pervading the earth and sanctifying it. Now, it was precisely on that point that a serious controversy had arisen at the Council of Florence in March 1439. The Orthodox interpreted the passage from John 15:26, "But when the Comforter [the Paraclete] is come, whom I will send unto you from the Father, even the Spirit of truth, which proceedeth from the Father", as proof that the Spirit emanated from the Father alone, whereas the Catholics, concerned also to emphasize the importance of the function of the Pope, tended to consider Father and Son as the dual source.[4] Surely, therefore, this sacred performance on 26 March 1439 was to celebrate the fact that agreement on the Eastern position had in principle been arrived at, so its importance went well beyond the merely scenographic virtuosity we can admire in the description.

The other very famous apparatus was that for S. Felice in Piazza, described by Vasari (1568, II, 375-76). Several drawings are associated with it, and it too has been the subject of reconstructions [*333-338*].

But I shall not begrudge the trouble to describe just how the contrivances of that machinery worked, especially because all of it has fallen to pieces and the men who could have told of it from their own experience are all dead and there is no hope of ever reconstructing it... Filippo for this purpose suspended a half-globe, something like an empty bowl or, better, a barber's basin turned upside-down, between two of the beams that supported the roof of the church. This half-globe was made of thin planks attached to an iron [framework shaped like a] star, which radiated out to secure the planks. The planks came together at the centre, which was the point of equilibrium; here there was a large iron ring from which the whole iron star supporting the half-globe radiated... At the base of its inner edge were fixed brackets just large enough for one person to stand on, and another iron strut, also on the inside, at the height of one *braccio*. On each bracket was placed a boy about twelve years old, and he was fastened in with the iron strut so that he could not fall even if he wanted to. When their cue came, these youngsters, twelve in all, having been arranged in this manner and dressed as angels with gilded wings and wigs of gold threads, took each other by the hand and waved their arms up and down, and it did appear as if they were dancing, the more so since the half-globe was constantly turning and in motion. Inside it, above the angels' heads were three circles or garlands of lights consisting of small lamps of a sort that could not spill over. Those lights seen from the ground really looked like stars, and the brackets, being covered with cotton wool, were like clouds.

Now, from the [central] ring, mentioned above, hung a very strong iron rod holding a second ring, to which was attached a thin rope which, as we shall see, reached down to the floor. This large iron rod had projecting from it eight [curved] arms or branches, which could revolve in an arc broad enough to fill the space inside the hollow half-globe. At the end of each arm was a flat area the size of a carving-board, upon which a boy of about nine could stand; each boy was firmly secured in place by an iron frame soldered to the upper part of the arm, but in such a way as to allow him to turn in all directions. By means of a small windlass that was gradually unwound, these eight "angels" supported on the iron rod were lowered from the interior of the half-globe to a point eight *braccia* below the level of the wooden beams holding up the roof, in such a way as to be seen but not to block the view of the angels around the rim of the half-globe. In the midst of this wreath of eight angels (which is what it truly was) there was a hollow mandorla in copper with numerous perforations holding small lamps fixed on pieces of iron in the form of a tube. When a spring was pressed down all these lights disappeared from view inside the copper mandorla, and when it was not pressed down the light shone out through perforations [335].[5] When the wreath of angels had arrived at the proper point, the small rope holding the mandorla was let out by another small windlass and it was lowered ever so slowly to the stage on which the play was being performed...

Within the mandorla was a youth about fifteen years old dressed as an angel... whereupon he stepped out of it and walked across the stage to where the Virgin was, saluted her, and spoke the tidings of the Annunciation. After which he went back into the mandorla, and the lights which had disappeared when he left it came back into view... It was drawn up again to the singing of the angels in the wreath and those circling about in the Heaven above, which made it all appear truly a Paradise, above all because besides that choir of angels and that of the wreath there was a God the Father just outside the half-globe surrounded by angels similar to those mentioned above and also supported by iron bars, so that the heavens, the wreath, the God the Father, the mandorla with its infinite lights, and the most sweet music all conspired to make a veritable representation of Paradise.[6]

For the true character of this spectacle we must again refer to symbolism, to the cosmological theories of the time. I consider the emphasis that Brunelleschi placed on movement, especially continuous movement, to be fundamental. It would also be of value to compare attentively the scheme of the various superimposed heavens with the studies he is said to have made of the cosmology of Dante in an attempt to determine from the poet's vision just what the distances are between the various parts of the cosmos. This was an idea which in Brunelleschi's own time was further elaborated by Ambrogio Traversari and subsequently by Antonio Manetti and Cristoforo Landino and which, in the next century, would interest great masters like Bramante and Michelangelo (see Chapter 16). Also, since the heavens were opened by "two large doors... sliding sideways on rollers in grooves" with a noise like thunder, this mechanism should be compared with numerous Quattrocento drawings for drawbridges or mobile bridges, for castles and other defensive works.

Much more simple, involving only a somewhat complicated vertical windlass, was the contrivance for the feast of the Ascension at the church of the Carmine [339-342], described thus by the Bishop of Suzdal:

A noise of thunder was heard, Christ appeared at the peak of the mountain, the sky opened and the Heavenly Father was seen suspended in the air in miraculous manner, wrapped in a dazzling light given forth by an infinite number of lamps. The boys representing angels moved around Him while a harmonious [instrumental] music and a sweet song sounded from a distance. Larger angels painted on the disk moved around in such a way as to appear living. From Heaven where God the Father was, there descended on the seven ropes a very beautiful and ingeniously formed cloud: it was round and surrounded by disks that revolved, and to right and left one saw two boys dressed as angels with golden wings. While the cloud was still descending Jesus took two golden keys and said to Peter, "Thou art Peter, and on this rock I shall built My church", and blessing him, consigned to him the keys. Upon which, with the aid of the seven ropes, He rose in the direction of the cloud, blessing Mary and the Apostles. It was a marvellous and incomparable sight. The ropes were set in motion by invisible contrivances made with the utmost skill, so much so that the person acting Jesus truly seemed to rise on his own, and without any sort of wobbling went up to a great height.

This obviously involved the use of complex systems for hoisting weights, and it is worth recalling that the hoists designed by Brunelleschi to lift materials were considered so safe that they were also used to raise the workers to the Cathedral dome.

The overall picture, deliberately kept general so as to give more space to the illustration of Cesare Lisi's reconstructions, gives us information about the technological context which supplements the basic studies by Prager and Scaglia. Beyond this, it demonstrates how much we need to broaden our ideas about the Florentine Quattrocento.[7] These *spettacoli* of Brunelleschi represent a new departure in the use of machinery on the stage, and may be considered as effectively reviving the Classical "deus ex machina". Very soon we find the same contrivances moving from the churches to the Classical festivals. The performances of Plautus's *Amphitryon* given at Ferrara in 1487 and 1491 involved building in the ceiling of a room a sky with planets that miraculously opened. And at Venice in the same century a performer — continuing the medieval tradition of flying personages but at the same time going far beyond it — flew from the sea to the top of the campanile of St Mark's and back to the loggia of the Ducal Palace, dressed as Mercury!

331, 332. Conjectural reconstruction of the theatrical devices used at SS.
Annunziata, Florence, for the feast of the Annunciation in 1439. God the
Father and angels appear in a gallery over the entrance door (left), in front of
a wheel of lights, and the Virgin sits opposite, on the rood screen (she is just
visible, haloed, at the extreme right). Between them the Angel of the
Annunciation flies on ropes. Three other ropes served for the descent of the
Holy Ghost as a fire from God. (Wooden model by Cesare Lisi)

333-338. Machinery for the *sacra rappresentazione* on the feast of the Annunciation at S. Felice in Piazza, Florence.

333. The mechanism by which the Angel of the Annunciation descended, held at the top and bottom. From the *Zibaldone* of Buonaccorso Ghiberti (Florence, Biblioteca Nazionale Centrale, MS. BR 228, f. 115v).

335. The mechanism for making lights appear and disappear in the mandorla around the Annunciant Angel: on the left is the complete mandorla, composed of a series of metal tubes containing candles, with cords hanging down to control the levers; to the right of it is a section of one of the tubes, showing the candle inside which would rise and shine out when the cord was pulled down;

above, detail of the winding mechanism operating two cords. From the *Zibaldone* of Buonaccorso Ghiberti, f. 115r. (For the drawing and its possible dating, see note 5.)

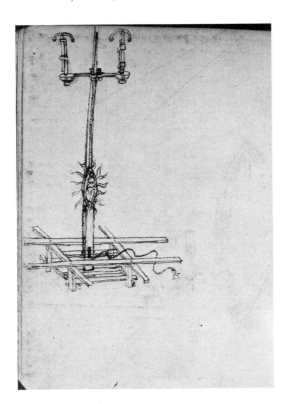

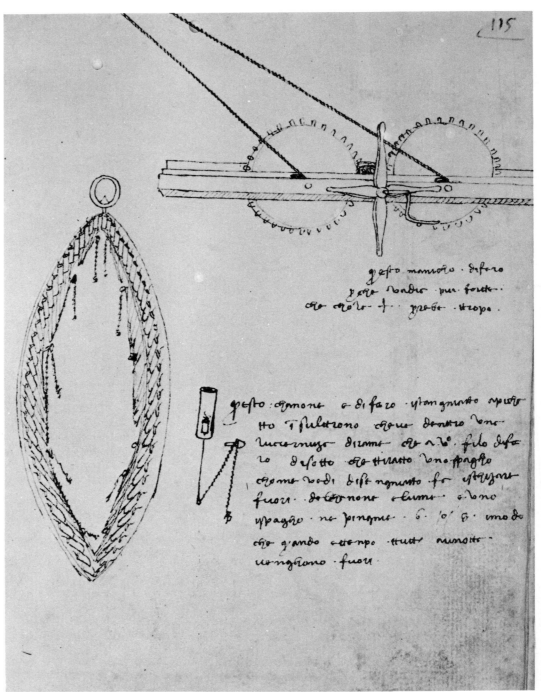

334. Conjectural reconstruction of the complete spectacle. At the top, God the Father and angels appear in an opening; behind them is the outside of the half-globe described by Vasari (see *fig. 336*); from it a framework supporting eight angels is lowered; and in the centre of that the Annunciant Angel descends. (Wooden model by Cesare Lisi)

336. Detail of Cesare Lisi's model, seen from the back in cut-away to show the winding machinery in the space below the roof. Behind the windlasses is the wooden half-dome containing twelve angels (who are visible only from below). The circle of eight angels and the Annunciant Angel are shown suspended below; the Virgin is seated in a loggia at the left.

337, 338. Details of the system used to make the wooden half-dome revolve. Cesare Lisi's model shows figures on a platform turning a handle, with the half-dome behind them, and the gearing with the platform removed.

339-342. Conjectural reconstruction of the spectacle at S. Maria del Carmine, Florence, for the feast of the Ascension in 1439. (Wooden model by Cesare Lisi)

339. The choir screen, with scenery and figures. Christ appears on the mountain-top at the right.

340. The machinery, with several windlasses, used to make the Ascension vehicle descend and rise again to heaven, where God the Father was surrounded by angels: a rear view of the apparatus shown in *fig. 342*.

341. The complete scene from the back. At the top left is heaven, from which the vehicle descends on ropes to Christ, standing on the mountain. The Holy Women and Apostles watch from below.

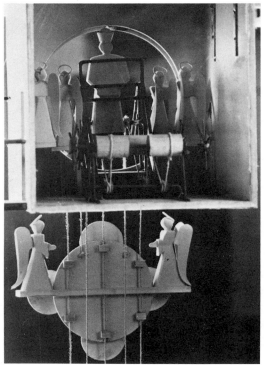

342. Heaven, and the vehicle on which Christ "ascended", seen from the front.

15 Military works, II: the Signa and Chianti areas

by Riccardo Pacciani

It is indeed my belief [wrote Alberti, going back directly to Vitruvius] that, if one inquires into who it was who defeated and caused to surrender all those cities right back to the most ancient times which in consequence of siege fell to the hands of the enemy, it will be seen that it was the architect. This is because the besieged could well make mock of the enemy army but were unable to hold out for long against the ingenuity of the inventions, the great bulk of the machines, the violence of the ballistic implements with which the architect had molested, oppressed, crushed them. On the other hand, it usually happens that the besieged themselves, to ensure their safety, deem it opportune to call to their aid the arts of the architect. If then the military campaigns of the past are called to memory, it will probably turn out that the greater number of the victories are to be attributed to the arts and skills of the architect than to the leadership and fortunes of the commander, and that the enemy was more frequently defeated by the acumen of the former without the arms of the latter than by the sword of the latter without the intelligence of the former. What is more, the architect is capable of winning victory with few troops and without enduring losses.

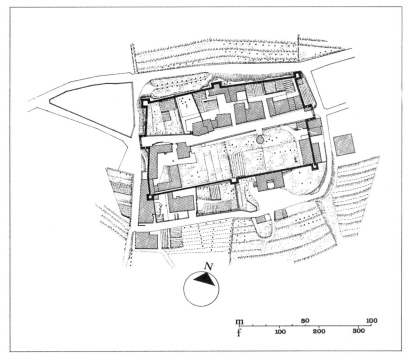

With this, Alberti offers us an effective introduction to one of the special roles that the new culture of the Renaissance allotted firmly to the architect, that of military organizer of the city and the surrounding territory.

In the medieval period that role had often been attributed to the architect-sculptor. But Brunelleschi was entrusted with something more: the task of redefining the form and reorganizing the face of the city and of the territory around it. He was a member of the Town Council in 1424 when the new work was decreed. Only Arnolfo di Cambio, probably, had so much responsibility concentrated in his own hands, and perhaps in no work more than in certain fortifications did Brunelleschi follow the models worked out in the cultural circle of his great predecessor. True, this could also have been a sign of the will of the new oligarchs — men who came to power by defeating the revolt of the Ciompi in 1378 and then survived unscathed the threat of Giangaleazzo Visconti — who, while draining all real content from the venerable communal institutions, were nonetheless reviving the myth of the Florentine commune on a formal level and a territory-wide scale.

The task of reorganizing two *terre murate* (planned walled villages), Lastra a Signa and Malmantile in the Arno Valley, was assigned by the Signoria to Brunelleschi, through the agency of the Opera del Duomo, between 1424 and 1426. The documents published by Fabriczy inform us of similar undertakings at Castellina, Rencine, and Staggia in the Chianti Valley on the main route to Siena.[1] From the standpoint of town planning these "new towns" constituted the most important and significant manifestation of the new relationships between agricultural, social and military control — extending even to a total redefinition of the landscape — that the commune of Florence had been attempting to institute for over a century with regard to the country areas.[2]

343-346. Malmantile: plan and air view, and the Porta Fiorentina (right, in the plan) and Porta Pisana (at the opposite end of the street).

The Signa area

The region of Signa, Lastra a Signa, and Malmantile was of particular importance for its strategic and economic position, and even more so after the difficult and by no means secure conquest of Pisa in 1406. The *mercatale* (country market town) and river port of Signa was the farthest inland point to which the Arno was navigable in summer as well as winter, and it controlled the flow of goods between Florence and Porto Pisano whose customs revenues as early as 1380 amounted to 300 florins. The nearby Lastra a Signa was the site of an extremely important bridge, up to the twelfth century the only one between Florence and Pisa. Cut by Castruccio in 1326, incorporated into a new system of fortifications in 1377, twenty years later it was attacked in vain by the Sienese troops of Giangaleazzo Visconti. Most probably the latter siege was responsible for a notable effort to reinforce the Signa area: on 14 April 1400, the Signoria decided that the *borgo* (village) of Lastra was to be fortified and that likewise "in burgo appellato Malmantile... fiant fortilitia". After the new war with the Visconti, which ended in defeat at Zagonara on 28 July 1424, the commune recognized on 25/26 September of the same year that the work of fortification at Lastra and Malmantile "had not been carried far enough for places of that sort to be, without grave risk, saved in time of siege" and ruled that the Operai of S. Maria del Fiore and other major building projects in Florence were to devote their efforts and funds to the task of "carrying to conclusion and completing the walls and buildings and the work on the wall of the fortifications of the site at Lastra, that is, in the villages of Lastra and Malmantile".[3] Two years later, when it seems the work had been completed, Brunelleschi and the chief of works Battista d'Antonio were assigned to come to an agreement with the "magistris concij Lastre" concerning the cost of the work done.

Like Arnolfo di Cambio to whom tradition — significantly — attributes the construction of the walled villages of 1299; like Giotto who was appointed "master and director of the work and building of the church of S. Reparata and the construction and completion of the walls of the city of Florence and of the fortifications of this city and of the other works of this commune";[4] like, finally, Andrea Pisano, architect of the Cathedral and involved in the fortification of the Porta S. Frediano; so too Brunelleschi, architect of the Cathedral dome and a man whose career was solidly linked with public undertakings, was entrusted with the work of strengthening the defences of the Signa area. The documents published so far do not mention him specifically in connection with Malmantile, but because the work on the fortifications there and at Lastra was decreed in the same act and entrusted to the same persons, and because certain parts of the design of Malmantile recall the solutions adopted at Lastra, it is logical to suppose that he functioned there as general supervisor at least, a position which the financial documents prove he held at Lastra.

For Malmantile we have a very interesting document whose relevance to architectural history appears to have been overlooked so far. It was published by Filippo Baldinucci as appendix to his life of Lorenzo Lippi and connected with that painter-poet's delightful heroico-comic poem, *Il Malmantile racquistato* of 1648-49.[5] The memorandum, copied "ad verbum", Baldinucci claims, "from his own ancient original" (evidently the specifications for the allocation of the contract for the work on the castle), is divided into two parts. The first is undated but assignable to a period immediately preceding the second, which is dated 16 September 1424. In the first it is affirmed that the Ten Purveyors of the cities of Pisa, Pistoia and Volterra, having established that the "castrum" or stronghold of Malmantile, "begun some time past and not yet completed", in view of the "periculis imminentibus" (probably the war with Visconti) recognize before the Priors of the Guilds that the village cannot be defended: "In the said *castrum* resistance is not possible because of the machicolations, merlons and towers that have not been built". It was then decided to call for tenders for the contract, inviting "anyone who wishes to complete it at small expense". The contract was won by "Ambrosium & Pierum socios", the partners Ambrogio and Piero, and the document registered by "Baldesis" and "ser Antonii". In the second part of the memorandum (drawn up by the notary Baldese Ambrosii with the notary Antonio di Puccino di ser Andrea as witness), Ambrogio di Lionardo and Piero di Curradino, identified as masters in Florence, received the assignment from the Ten Purveyors and pledged "to work on and complete the said stronghold in that height and form that will be decided and ordered by the said office [of the Ten] or their Purveyor", promising to "build and complete entirely, according to the standards of good masters, the walls, machicolations, small vaults, towers, vaults, and stairways". It is specified that for "the places with machicolations, if there is no other design, they intend to use as a model the stronghold of Lastra". Finally the partners commit themselves to constructing the moat of the fortress as well. A week later, as we have seen, the Priors turned over the supervision of the work to the Operai of the Cathedral.

Long before then, however, the villages of Lastra and Malmantile had been given regular plans, basically rectangular and with one or two axes of symmetry, typical of these walled "new towns".[6] While for Lastra, already inhabited for over three centuries, the line of the walls by and large goes back to 1377, for the "Castrum Malmantilis", probably founded by public decree in an uninhabited area, it is difficult to say to what period the earliest settlement belongs. The term "burgo" — village or town of modest importance — used in 1400 does suggest that at that date the place had not yet been fortified. In their work there Brunelleschi and the institution employing him implicitly confirmed the model, as well as the "utopian" aspect associated with it on the economic and social level, on which the first such communities had been organized in country areas, thus in a way taking up again the thread of a pattern several times interrupted but stubbornly returned to, whose initial impetus had come from the ideology of Arnolfo's time.

The basic geometrical form usual in such town plans — the "idea" — was kept clearly in mind, but it was modified to take advantage of the possibilities offered by the terrain and natural environment for defensive techniques. This is evident in the different manner in which the same formal conception was varied and articulated in the two localities of the Signa area.

347, 348. Plan and air view of Lastra a Signa. Key to the plan: 1, Porta Fiorentina, linked by the Via Pisana to 2, Porta Pisana; 3, Portone di Baccio; 4, Ospedale di S. Antonio; 5, Palazzetto Pretorio.

Malmantile

Malmantile stands on a hill and looks out to one side on a vast plain, to the other on narrow and quite steep gulleys. Despite the undulating terrain and elevated position, an almost perfectly rectangular plan was laid out, about 125 m (410 ft) long and 75 m (246 ft) wide. The Via Pisana constitutes the central axis in length, at whose ends are the only two gates in the walls. There are bastions at the corners of the rectangle and a tower in the centre of each long side. At certain points one can still see at the top of the walls machicolations of traditional Tuscan Trecento type, with closely-set corbels supporting the sentry-walk, making a compact band around the curtain walls [246] and the projecting volumes of the towers. The presence of those elements (specifically stipulated in the contract), the long stretches of wall not protected by towers, and especially the straight rather than curving course of the curtain walls as well as their relative thickness tell us that the defence relied on a predominantly vertical technique: the foe who contrived to get past the rain of arrows from the crossbows fired from above, and then succeeded in crossing the moat, could be crushed by projectiles dropped through the apertures between the corbels. This system of fortification is not designed to make use of or to protect the defenders against firepower, which was being developed at the time, particularly in northern Italy; though, as we shall see, the possibility of explosive mining may have been taken into account.

This apparent conservatism cannot be because Brunelleschi had no experience of techniques of military defence. The profession of his father would have brought him, since childhood, into contact with the world of the *condottieri* and mercenary militia in the pay of the Signoria. But it does seem that Brunelleschi reflected the eclecticism, to say nothing of the uncertainty or downright backwardness, of many Tuscan cities of the time when it came to firepower. Until after 1450 the new weapons were thought of as no different in kind or effect from the traditional ballistic engines (shown for instance in a famous fresco in the portico of the monastery of Lecceto near Siena). Unlike the city-states of northern Italy, Tuscany did not produce a school of technicians experienced in the use of modern artillery.

This had become plain already in the war with Pisa, when the Florentine Signoria had had to call on foreigners, appealing to the Prince of Achaia, who sent them "Magister Janninus de Vigono", and to the Doge of Venice, whom they asked for "Magister Dominicus" — an expert not unknown to them since, in the service of Giangaleazzo Visconti, he had burned the framework of a bridge built by the Florentines near Borgoforte.

During the same Pisan war, however, abundant use was made of gunpowder artillery. If we can believe the passages concerning the terrible siege of Vicopisano in the *Cronica Volgare* by an anonymous Florentine (attributed to Piero di Giovanni Minerbetti), firepower served for more than mere intimidation:

The Florentines having for a long time besieged the castle of Vicopisano, and having a number of times attacked with many suitable engines and not been able to take it, they so smashed the walls of the parapets with large mortars [*bombarde*] that no one could stand on them any longer, and again with the mortars and catapults they knocked down all the houses almost entirely, and many people died there, men and women and children who were inside, though almost all the citizens were living in the underground caverns...

In the siege of Lucca, while the dam devised by Brunelleschi was being constructed, mortars were "fired in trajectories 600 to 700 *braccia* from the city and brought down a great quantity of stones".[7]

Even Alberti, in the chapter of *De re aedificatoria* devoted to city walls, still speaks of building "buttresses of triangular base" (i.e. triangular spurs) as a defence against the damage produced by "catapulting weapons" or the "destructive violence of war machines", to which it is best to oppose the "softness of clay": these ideas, taken over from Classical Antiquity, would not be of much use in resisting the new offensive weapons. It is probably no coincidence that it was Siena, the only Tuscan city to train a group of masters capable of constructing and using artillery, and which equipped itself as early as 1438 with a good store of firepowered bombards, that later produced such a revolutionary in the use of technology as Francesco di Giorgio.[8]

It should be remembered that gunpowder was used not only for mortars and small firearms: it was equally important in the work of sapping, excavating long tunnels or mines under the enemy's walls, which were then made to collapse by setting fire to the wooden pit-props supporting the mine shafts. At the same time experiments were being made with blasting, detonating charges of gunpowder below foundation-level, with even more disastrous effects. There is a discussion of this practice in a somewhat later manuscript, made up of drawings and notes by Taccola, Valturio and perhaps Francesco di Giorgio (Venice, Biblioteca Marciana, Cod. Latinus VIII, 40, ff. 219-20):

Let the excavators of the mines burrow as far as the centre of the fortress and where they hear the sound of footsteps make a large underground chamber something like an oven; into this let them put three or four containers open at the top and full of mortar powder; then from the containers they are to extend a cord impregnated with sulphur and this is to be set afire after the entrance to the chamber has been blocked with stones, sand and cement; the fire will thus reach the containers which will burst into flame and destroy the core of the stronghold.

As a defence against this, moats could be made deep enough to force an enemy to dig deep down and run the risk of having his mines flooded, and the walls could be provided with broader escarpments that would buttress them more solidly. Yet, as Machiavelli would point out a century later, fortresses "sited on mountains not too difficult to climb are today, when it comes to artillery and mines, extremely vulnerable".[9]

Of all this traces can be found at Malmantile, and it is probable that the work done there under the more or less direct supervision of Brunelleschi may also have involved solutions that took into account the lethal use of gunpowder in underground mines along with the intrinsic weakness of the very positions considered most secure. Thus, despite its high situation, the walls were surrounded by a moat, and it is difficult to imagine that this could have held water: a dry moat suggests that more than the traditional technique of warfare was envisaged. More important, the walls of Malmantile were reinforced by batters, visibly more massive than at Lastra, which is located in the plain at a short distance from the Arno and therefore has a ground-water level high enough to make mining under the walls out of the question.

The other features of the fortifications at Malmantile are the standard ones for the time in Tuscany. The gates are placed in broad towers whose lower walls are provided with loopholes through which the defenders could shoot at an approaching enemy. The corner towers were linked to the main rectangle by narrow passageways easy to block and defend: should the enemy succeed in breaking through the walls, the towers would be autonomous units for a last-ditch defence.

Lastra a Signa

Lastra, from a town-planning standpoint, is rather more complex. It is situated at the foot of a hill, the Colle Gangalandi, and traversed on the north by the main road to Pisa, features responsible for the development of the distinctive T-plan of the streets within the walls, with the arms of the T oriented towards the most important topographical and strategic factors, the Arno to the west and the hills to the south and east [*347, 348*]. The course of the walls follows this orientation. On the north [*349*] they run parallel to the Pisa road, extending for about 200 m (656 ft); on the south-eastern side, however, they do not continue the line at right angles but bend towards the road descending from the hills to the south, covering a total distance of 250 m (820 ft). Where this southern road meets the walls there is a tall defensive tower, the Portone di Baccio [*351*], whose role as watchtower and position commanding the Colle Gangalandi is obvious. Two other gates are provided at either end of the Via Pisana. Here as at Malmantile — which as we know was modelled on Lastra — we are faced with defensive provisions which blithely ignored the threat and possibilities of cannon power. Without detailed documents it is difficult to establish even roughly what was done in Lastra in 1424-26 and to be any more precise about a direct or indirect involvement on Brunelleschi's part. The document that appointed him to estimate the amount to be paid for the new constructions speaks only of "laborerio facto et dato edifitio murorum portarum et antiportarum", with no other specifications.

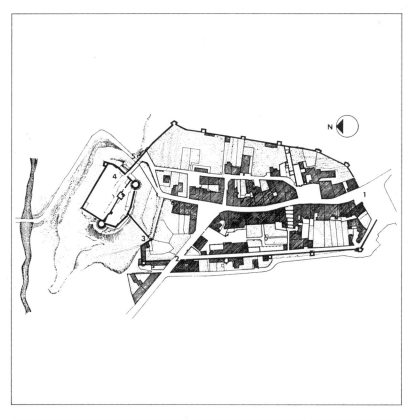

The Chianti area

The other strategic area for which the skill and experience of Brunelleschi in matters of fortification was called on was the triangle marked by the villages of Castellina, Rencine and Staggia, which constituted the farthest Florentine bulwark against Siena. There was good reason for this caution: throughout the first thirty years of the century it was precisely by way of the road from Siena that the armies of Giangaleazzo (which we have already seen in action in the Signa area) and of Filippo Maria Visconti effected their damaging incursions into the territory of the Florentine Republic. In the terrible war of 1397 all three strongholds were attacked by the ducal forces, and a glance at the chronicles of the time is enough to tell what destruction those armies brought: "And then", wrote Giovanni di Pagolo Morelli of the Milanese, "they swept across our country district and attacked Rencine for several days and with mortars tore holes in all the walls and smashed them; the folk of the village behaved valiantly and defended themselves." And Piero Buoninsegni: "On 19 March Count Alberigo, captain of the Duke, with all the people mentioned who were in Siena came down on our lands and first burned, then looted the village of Castellina."

After the Visconti finally withdrew, Florence was faced with the need to strengthen the three fortress-villages acquired and so tenaciously defended in the preceding centuries.[10] Thanks to the documents published by Gaye and Fabriczy the course of the work can be reconstructed with some precision. Losing no time, in April 1400 the Priors of the Guilds assigned to the Operai of the Cathedral the task of constructing fortifications at Castellina during the coming two years, and for that purpose appropriated 800 gold florins annually. In April 1402 the commission was extended for another two years, in 1404 for one more year. Despite this, it appears from a provision of the Signoria of 6 (actually 15) February 1431, in which there is no mistaking the note of ill-humour and impatience, that the *borgo* of Castellina "imperfectum remansit", though the emergency of the new war with the Duke of Milan made it urgent that it be completed with no further delay. The Priors in fact asserted the necessity "quam citius fieri possit" of fortifying the entire area: "castri et arcis castri castelline muros staggie et turris rencinis". Houses and buildings that might prove useful in facilitating the work were placed at the disposition of the Operai, along with an appropriation of 500 gold florins. That board in its turn resolved that Brunelleschi, with a companion and two horses, was to go to the three strongholds and see to everything necessary for the fortifications already decided on. Here again, as at Malmantile and Lastra, Brunelleschi found himself assigned to complete, or at the most improve, work begun by others.

Staggia

The curtain walls at Staggia, miraculously and marvellously well preserved, still surround the village with something of the shape of a lozenge, at one end of which, towards Florence, lies the castle [352-355]. The rectilinear course of the walls, the square towers, and the apparent absence of reinforcing escarpments along the walls suggest that subsequent rebuildings, of which at least two can be documented, substantially respected the initial plan. That design was made before the need arose to construct defences against the new artillery and it can only very hesitantly be attributed to Brunelleschi, because of the various building phases that preceded his.

The castle of Staggia is more complex in its arrangement. It stands on a natural rise, looming over a part of the village on one side, over the nearby stream on the other. Its ground plan is almost square, its walls are thicker than those around the village, and its interior is organized into separate defensible compartments. The entrance door leads into a vast outer bailey, a sort of parade ground, above which, on a natural escarpment, rises the inner bailey, which is itself overlooked by a square tower. The scheme is the standard one for castles in military areas where a large, fortified open space was required that could rapidly afford shelter for reinforcements, for contingents fleeing from other castles in the territory, or for one's own defenders should the enemy succeed in breaking through to the town below. In the direction of the most important strategic features of the site — the valley that would lead an invader to Florence, and the village — there are two large round towers accessible only from the inner bailey. In addition, the tower facing the village is placed so as to watch over and protect with ease both the entrance to the citadel and the gate between the two baileys. (The castle is now overgrown with vegetation: a modest programme of restoration and more diligent maintenance would be sufficient to return it to its original appearance.)

Clearly then, we have here a technique of fortification of remarkable quality, but it remains to be seen to what extent it is Brunelleschi's. By themselves, in the absence of more precise documents or of inscribed commemorative plaques or foundation stones, the masonry structures visible today do not seem attributable to Brunelleschi, or at least consonant with the idea of him as a military engineer that one gets from his earlier efforts in this field. In the first place, the walls of the castle lack the classic crown of machicolations found in most of the fortifications attributed to him. Or rather, these do appear, but only on the square central tower (which has been restored), which because of its protected position and its function as watch and control tower would have required fewer modifications than other structures more directly exposed to fire from outside [354, 355]. Also the walls have a massive escarpment, but only on the side towards the village, bounded by the two cylindrical towers.

This type of defence, differentiated and graded in importance between exterior and interior, was certainly no novelty in the fifteenth century. Not only was there the castle at Prato but also, among others, the great Hohenstaufen-Angevin castle at Lucera in Apulia which, for all its vastly greater dimensions, had an entirely comparable defensive structure: massive cylindrical towers defended the entrance gate and faced the town below, the great square keep or *palatium* lay just inside the gate, and escarpments were similarly positioned (though at a greater distance from the walls) towards the town.

The large cylindrical towers at Staggia are today — and it is reasonable to think were in the Quattrocento — distinctly higher than the curtain walls, so that they too would appear to have been conceived for a defence from above rather than as any serious obstacle to artillery fire which, as Francesco di Giorgio made clear, is best withstood by walls and towers more nearly the same height.

The only element that can be attributed with some degree of certainty to the second half of the fifteenth century would appear to be the band of stone that separates the zone of the batter from the vertical faces of the walls. This fact, combined with the uncertainties in the use of defences against artillery, could suggest that the external appearance is entirely due to Rosso di Niccolò di Antonio Ridolfi, who in 1451 was "sent on commission to Castellina in the Val d'Elsa and in the Val di Pesa... to supervise the fortification of the villages and castles existing in those places". Another possibility is that we are looking at modifications made during the war against Siena a century later.

For these reasons, and in the light of the documents published so far, it is even more difficult here than at Lastra to determine anything specific about the role of Brunelleschi and to distinguish early work from what was done in the second half of the century. The documents refer nowhere explicitly to the initiation of work at Staggia in 1400, but only, in 1431, to work on the "muros", and that without distinguishing, as in the case of Castellina, between the walls protecting the town and those of the castle. If the text is interpreted narrowly, Brunelleschi's activity would have been limited to the town walls, which, it must be said, are traditional in type, except for the peculiarity of having the corbels supporting the sentry-walk on the inside, and are too high to withstand firepower.

The urban form of Staggia is also traditional, no different from that of other walled "new towns". Its remarkably regular layout on an oriented longitudinal axis speaks of a settlement that grew up on either side of the road that led from Siena through the Val d'Elsa to Florence. Whatever else Brunelleschi may have done, he surely respected or perhaps rectified the line of the earlier town walls. The castle on the other hand is more progressive in its design, particularly for the Valdarno, and should new evidence prove that he was responsible at least for its overall basic structure, that would justify the eulogies of Gambacorti and explain the subsequent prestigious commissions that came to Brunelleschi for fortresses outside Tuscany.

Rencine

The case of Rencine [356] is perhaps simpler. It was damaged in 1397, and some repairs were probably already undertaken in 1400 in view of its close strategic connection with Castellina. The measure passed in 1431 speaks of "turris rencinis". It is likely that Rencine was a rather larger fortified complex, especially since Giovanni di Pagolo Morelli makes special mention of its walls and since the assignment received by Brunelleschi from the Opera del Duomo speaks of the "castrum" of Rencine. Not much remains of any such fortifications. In his *Diarj Sanesi* Allegretto Allegretti recounts that in 1478, during the war between the Florentines and Pope Sixtus IV, the Duke of Calabria and the Count of Urbino, who were allies of Siena, "on Sunday the 19th [of July] entered the field early at Rencine... and on the evening of the 23rd entered into Rencine and sacked and then burned it. And the Commune of Siena ordered all the houses and walls razed to the ground".

Of the walls there are now only a few scattered remains, overgrown and partly incorporated into a farmhouse. From the vestiges of the square batters of the towers and an occasional short stretch of straight wall it can be deduced that whatever Brunelleschi did was probably much like what we saw at Malmantile. That would also be likely because they occupy similar strategic positions, on the top of a hill overlooking two broad valleys.

Castellina in Chianti

The remains of the walls and castle at Castellina in Chianti [357], on the other hand, present the disheartening picture of what Ruskin termed "a destruction accompanied with false description of the thing destroyed".[11] Once it was surrounded by walls with two gates (according to the testimony of Repetti in 1833), but today one can only make out remains of walls which are partially incorporated into houses or churches and, above all, so scraped down, tidied up, and housewifed into nice order by what it is euphemistic to call "restorations" that any serious scholarly discussion of them is impossible. The most one can do is to note the volumetric and geometrical organization of what survives of the towers and the keep. This is all the more unfortunate because in what little documentation has been found concerning Brunelleschi's activity in the Chianti valley Castellina is the place most often referred to, and also because it was the administrative centre of one of the three districts into which the Chianti area had been divided by the Florentine Republic.

As at Rencine, the general pattern of the walls that are still visible recalls Malmantile, with hollow square towers which have broad scarped bases though not the typical crown of machicolations. Some interest attaches to the Via delle Volte, a street made from the old semi-underground passageway that ran along the walls where there were loopholes for defence by archers. But the justly more famous part is the keep, an extremely solid parallelepiped on a rectangular ground plan which seems very reminiscent of the tower-blocks in the Rocca Sismonda in Rimini. Here too, obviously, we may be seeing later remodellings: Castellina is the only place in which the presence in 1451 of Rosso di Niccolò di Antonio Ridolfi is firmly documented.

Conclusion

Of few works by Brunelleschi is our image as uncertain, even vague, as it is of some of the fortifications he projected or completed. Yet even here, by making cautious attributions and carefully attempting to distinguish between what was done earlier and what later, one can glimpse two complementary roles. One is the technician and engineer who, not always with equal success, sought to return to the grand technological tradition of the fourteenth century, and to test its capabilities, specifically with respect to the new ways of using gunpowder. (For this a study on his relations with Taccola that would take into account the technology of sapping and mining might prove extremely fruitful.) Brunelleschi's other role is as an architect firmly tied to public patronage. In Florence he contrived to get personal control over the most important projects for public buildings and squares: and in the surrounding territory his efforts were concentrated on the strongholds of entire strategic areas, such as those around Signa and the southern end of the Chianti valley, with whose overall reorganization he was entrusted by the Opera del Duomo. These undertakings would no doubt have included not only the fortifications but also a new plan for the lines of communication and water supply. What emerges from this is the fact that it had become necessary, indeed urgent, for the Republic to create a more centralized, more specific, and more technically oriented physical relationship with the territory around it. It may well be that the coincidence of such experiments with the institution of the *catasto* tax in 1426-27 was not accidental.

All these new ventures and undertakings point to the effort that Florence and the intellectuals most associated with the dominant oligarchy were making to move beyond the old Trecento approach of the Republic to administration, and to equip it with political and administrative structures more in keeping with the new extended holdings that resulted, among other things, from the conquest of Pisa. Rallying around it certain masters with a solid technical grounding, the Republic delegated to them the task of re-establishing entire parts of its territory. It is difficult to say whether this attempt to redefine the republican structures, whose triumph as regards architecture would later be attributed to Brunelleschi himself, proved socially positive in the further course of the Quattrocento. Certainly the delegation of such a conspicuous decision-making function provoked a dialectic of encounter and clash between the technocrats and the highest spheres of power. It is in the nature of an architect, and of Brunelleschi certainly, to desire to test directly, concretely, the possibility of transforming the city and the landscape according to the exigencies and indications arising from his own experience (and here surely also from hints and suggestions from Classical sources) or from the directives of the public body commissioning him. The Republic, however, had to ensure a political and administrative structure which would permit the effective realization of those objectives of "rebirth", of renaissance, that it had set itself. The emigration during the Quattrocento of certain people like Filarete or, even more, Leonardo (whose links to Brunelleschi are many and marked) to the most absolute and therefore most modern state in Italy, the Duchy of Milan, tells us that, for all the efforts and achievements, the polemical and innovatory ambitions of Florentine culture and, above all, of Brunelleschi himself had been only half realized.

16 Brunelleschi and literature

According to the Biographer, besides learning "to read and write the *abaco*" (a handbook for any of a number of disciplines) Filippo as a boy studied Latin authors "since his father was a notary and perhaps had in mind to have him be the same; because among those who did not intend to become a doctor or a notary or a priest there were few in those times who gave themselves, or were given, to humanities". What he seems to have received therefore was an education of pre-university secondary school level which exceptionally included Latin. Born in 1377, it seems that he was already an apprentice in the Arte della Seta in 1392, working immediately for some master or workshop.

His literary capabilities are attested to, directly or indirectly, in various ways but chiefly through a group of poems, some violently polemical, and an extremely subtle *burla*, a trick of diabolic ingenuity and complexity which became the subject of various verbal and written accounts, of which two versions have come down to us, one of them included in the same manuscript as the anonymous Biography (Florence, Biblioteca Nazionale, Cod. Magliabechiano II, II, 325).

Dante

Another biography, the *Libro di Antonio Billi*, alludes to Brunelleschi's Dante scholarship: "Pippo was learned in Holy Writ, and Maestro Paolo [Toscanelli], astrologer, used to say that when one listened to him speaking he seemed a veritable St Paul. He was an arithmetician and a geometrician. ... He was interested in the interpretation of the works of Dante and understood them very well indeed." At the time the *Divine Comedy* was attracting renewed attention for its political as well as cosmological content, and it became a custom for Renaissance architects — represented by such celebrated names as Giuliano da Sangallo, Bramante and Michelangelo — to write commentaries on Dante. Michelangelo made marginal comments and drawings in a manuscript, tragically lost in a shipwreck south of Livorno, and his opinions are recorded in Donato Giannotti's *Dialoghi* (1546), which also contains his hypothetical measurements of Dante's Hell.

It may be pure coincidence, but Antonio Manetti, who included a short but very specific biography of Brunelleschi in his *XIV Huomini Singhulari*, also drew diagrams of Hell, in the margins of a manuscript of the *Divine Comedy* dating from 1462 (Florence, Biblioteca Nazionale, II, I, 33) and in a copy of St Isidore's *Treatise on the Images of the World*. After Manetti's death, one of his close friends, Girolamo Benivieni, set down from memory his comments on Dante, subsequently published as *Dialogo di Antonio Manetti cittadino fiorentino circa al sito, forme et misure dello "Inferno" di Dante Alighieri poeta excellentissimo* (Florence: Filippo di Giunta, 1506). Manetti's studies had already been used by Cristoforo Landino in his short treatise, "De sito, forma e misura dell'Inferno", prefacing his large and lavish edition of the *Divine Comedy* with commentaries published in 1481.[1] Both Manetti and Landino lie behind Michelangelo's thinking on the subject. Benivieni takes a polemical stance against Landino, and apparently his *Dialogo* originated in his desire to correct erroneous interpretations.

It is interesting that Benivieni is thought to be the dedicatee of the anonymous Biography, which begins with the often-quoted words, "You desire, Girolamo, to hear who this Filippo was." If this identification is correct, and if we can presume an affinity of political and religious thought from the personal friendship between Brunelleschi and Manetti, and, through the latter, between Brunelleschi and Benivieni,

then there must have been a powerful current of anti-Medici dissent, desire for reform, and moral austerity.[2] One is tempted to detect the same attitudes in the circle of friends who gathered to listen to the aged Brunelleschi for something other, perhaps, than tales of his jests — friends like Antonio di Matteo dalle Porte, Michelozzo, Scheggia, Feo Belcari, Luca della Robbia, Antonio di Migliore Guidotti and Domenico da Michelino, who are named along with Buggiano at the end of the *Novella del Grasso Legnaiuolo* (see below). On the other hand, Brunelleschi is never mentioned in Benivieni's commentary on Dante, and presumably it will never be possible to prove in any concrete way that discussions with him underlay the ideas of Antonio Manetti, recorded only from memory and after Manetti's death.

This granted, the method followed by Manetti certainly recalls Brunelleschi, and in any case my concern is with the aims and means by which "one can now, beyond all shadow of doubt, comprehend the magnitude, the form, the structure, the measurements, and the admirable artifice of that (so admirable fabric) and by this penetrate in consequence into the intimacy of its marrow because therein reside, that is, in its very structure, form, artifice and measures, the seeds of many mysteries which lie concealed" (p. 33).[3] The apparatus of learning with which one must equip oneself is also carefully spelled out: "It is needful ... to have some little acquaintance with Geometry. Of Arithmetic I say nothing because I take for granted that those companions of yours would have as much as would suffice for this purpose. And thus it is necessary to grasp something of Astrology, at least to have seen the *Sphaera*. And of Cosmography the *Almagest* of Ptolemy and the *Charta da Navigare*, because one aids the other" (p. 40). These are all famous texts; the *Sphaera* is now ascribed to the humanist circle frequented by Brunelleschi, and specifically to Goro di Gregorio.

For certain geographical or other specific terms the writer advises seeking information from "men of practical experience, who are accustomed to go about the fairs and have had dealings with men in all walks of life" (p. 39). This, together with Ptolemy and the maps, can help us to pinpoint Jerusalem, beneath which Hell is said to open, or to identify the entrance used by Dante as in the neighbourhood of Cumae. For the general dimensions of the terraqueous globe [*358a*] we are referred to the computations of Boccaccio's celebrated teacher, Andalò del Negro.[4]

The basic image is one which Dante himself used to describe Hell — a gigantic amphitheatre sunk in the earth, with almost no arena space, below which another pit opens, that of Malebolge [*358c*]. One of the things said in the *Dialogo* to be especially difficult to draw or depict is the change in scale from one section of Hell to another: this necessitates not only a woodcut of the whole but four details on a progressively larger scale [*358c-g*]. Benivieni had these illustrations specially made for the *Dialogo*: Manetti is quoted as already referring to them, but it was necessary to have new ones made because of those Manetti knew only one could be found after his death [*358b*]. As Carlo Pedretti has pointed out, the diagrams in some ways resemble drawings by Leonardo. Here is Manetti's thinking, as reported by Benivieni:

These locations should be painted, and are much better understood through the pen and brush than with words [p. 81]. ... But I racked my imagination to puzzle out just how to put this site of Hell into a drawing, something most necessary to anyone wishing to understand it properly. Because for such things the eye serves much better than the ear. But to tell you the truth I simply cannot see any way that satisfies me to any extent, because it is not something that can be done to scale [*a miglia piccole*, with a reduced equivalent of miles] as on navigators' charts, because it is so far from the outer zones to the centre that you simply cannot make enough space adequately to show Malebolge, which calls for the expanse of ten great trenches in the stretch that exists between the outermost trench and the well, and that well must be made so that you can consign all those things to it proportionately. Nor do I speak of the Giants and their great stature, of the four concentric circles of the Traitors, of the tomb, and of Lucifer. In short, I think this something almost beyond doing. But if it could be done, or can be, one would as a result understand everything perfectly, because one would be able to mark in each place the measurements of the things and place before your eyes their exact form [p. 107]. ... And it could be done perhaps, but I do not know, and I do not believe that it can be done if one wishes to maintain the proper proportions, because the closer things are to the centre the more they diminish and become so tiny that few would be able to distinguish them [p. 108].

The solution, therefore, was to use four separate drawings to be read one beneath the other, these to be worked out by "someone skilled, either miniaturist or painter as you prefer". Manetti's reasoning is clear in this passage, where he suggests an overall view and five details:

First draw the entire body of the whole, and in it that part of its Inferno beneath the site of Jerusalem at its top simply in general form without marking the circles, because they could not be discerned [358a]. Then, in the other drawing [358c], put only that half of the Inferno that can be seen without the whole, and in it, because it can be made larger, distinguish all the circles as they are. In the third drawing [358d] depict (as has been said) the first part of that Hell down to the walls of the city of Dis. In the fourth [358e] put those walls with their cemeteries which form the sixth circle, and extend it to the seventh of the three great rounds, and put all that in this fourth drawing. In the fifth [358f] depict the eighth circle, which is Malebolge. In the sixth [358g] and last, the well, the four spheres of ice, and the tomb of Lucifer which make up the ninth circle and the eighth degree of distance as far as the other hemisphere. And it will be necessary to omit the Giants and Lucifer because they would muddle up everything [as regards proportions, because of their great size]. It would seem to me that this is how to do it should one wish to.

To simplify matters, and to make it possible to see them, in Benivieni's woodcuts the figures are all arbitrarily depicted much larger than they would be in proportion.

While the images give only a vague idea of the sort of visual solution Brunelleschi would have had to work on — *if*, to say it again, he ever did concern himself with these problems — in the text of Benivieni we find two specific points having to do with computation of the dimensions of Hell and its Giudecca region which may help in understanding Quattrocento methods of proportion and design. The first concerns the method of calculating the relative width of the first great circles of Hell. The two speakers in the *Dialogo* believe that Dante used a compass and set square, and there is a discussion (p. 99) about the reciprocal proportioning of circles by means of the "commutated proportion", this being "that relationship between one circumference and the other such as the arc of one has to the arc of the other ... presupposing according to the demonstration of the geometricians that, when a number of circles are formed having the same centre, one will include the other, and that two lines running from that centre will make, or include, an angle when extended to their circumferences". We can spare the reader the lengthy calculations that follow and which are exemplified in the plans of Hell [358b,g]. Easier to follow is the estimate of the size of the Giants and Lucifer. Proceeding from the assertion by Dante that the face of the first of the Giants "seemed to me long and large as the pine cone of St Peter's in Rome, and all the other bones were in proportion", the

speakers measure the enormous bronze pine cone, now in the great exedra of the Vatican Belvedere, and find it to be 5 1/2 *braccia* high. The Giant Nemboth will be eight times that height, or more than 44 *braccia* tall. For Lucifer Dante gives us only a vague reference to the length of his arm, but one can estimate his size in proportion to the Giants, and his arm as a third of their height. Painters and sculptors consider the well-proportioned man to be nine heads high, but "because men so proportioned are rare indeed, and in this matter we should (as it seems to me) proceed with that measure which is common to most people, we will assume that that man would be (as has been said) a full eight heads high and something more" (pp. 69ff.), that is, more than 1,936 *braccia* high.

Lucifer is seen only down to the waist. His sphere, Giudecca, as theoretically traced round his waist would measure 1,000 *braccia*, and this gives us a standard for the other circles [358g].

Even more vague, and desperately unconfirmed by texts or other sources, is the assertion by the presumed Antonio Billi that Brunelleschi had accomplished theological studies worthy of St Paul himself. The statement is so much the more strange in that he is said to have discussed such matters with Paolo Toscanelli, who was anything but a theologian.[5] Obviously this may be pure fantasy (but why attribute to an artist, of all people, this sort of interest?), and the reference to St Paul could be no more than an association with the Christian name of the great humanist mathematician. Still, there is one fact that cannot be ignored. In those times, normally, a sacred text was never discussed without taking some commentary as a basis, and it was precisely in the circle of Brunelleschi's most intimate acquaintances — in fact in the study of one of his patrons, Ambrogio Traversari — that the translation of St John Chrysostom's commentaries on the Epistles of Paul was being prepared, one group being completed in 1432.[6] Vespasiano da Bisticci recounts with what fluent ease Traversari dictated the Latin version of these exegetic texts to Niccoli, who repeatedly had to admonish him, "Ambrogio, go slower, I cannot keep pace with you."

The commentaries of St John Chrysostom are monumental, filling volumes of the *Patrologia Greca* series, and almost every possible question is cogitated and excogitated in them, so any induction must perforce be arbitrary. But we have had frequent occasion in this book to refer to liturgical problems associated with the type of basilica or central-plan church adopted by Brunelleschi, and it is not impossible that what Billi says refers only to this aspect, which, in the context, can be considered purely functional. Alessandro Parronchi finds in the Epistles references to optical experiments and has carried his argument further on the basis of the commentaries of Thomas Aquinas.[7] Considering the architect's friendship with Masaccio, it is interesting that the fresco of the *Tribute Money* in the Carmine can be read in the light of Romans 13:1-7 as counselling due deference to the civil authorities; though the fresco shows the tribute paid to an ecclesiastical authority, and it was perhaps the tithe that went into the coffers of Rome through Florentine bankers. These examples are adduced only to show both the infinite implications of the problem and the necessity of setting limits by referring to concrete documentary or philological evidence, which we hope someone will find in the future.

Verse

A group of poems which literary historians call "*Burchielleschi*", from the Florentine banker-poet Domenico di Giovanni, called Burchiello, include a handful which have sometimes been associated with Brunelleschi.[8] In examining them we must proceed with the greatest caution. We can begin with the easiest of them, a melange of pastoral and genre with perhaps a dose of *double-entendre* — though obscenity, so prominent in carnival songs, is fairly rare in the verse of Burchiello, however bizarre and grotesque that may be otherwise. For this poem, even more than for the others, the attribution to Brunelleschi is traditional and open to doubt.

> *Madonna se ne vien de la fontana*
> *Contro l'usanza con vòto l'orcetto,*
> *E ristoro non porta a questo petto,*
> *Né con l'acqua, né con la vista umana,*
>
> *O ch'ella ha visto la biscia ruana*
> *Strisciar per l'erba in su quel vialetto,*
> *O che 'l can la persegue o ch'ha sospetto*
> *Che stiavi dentro in guato la Beffana.*
>
> *Vien qua, Renzuola, vienne, che vedrai*
> *Una fontana e due e quante vuoi,*
> *Né dal padre severo avrai rampogna.*
>
> *Ecco, che stillan gli occhi tutti e duoi:*
> *Cògline tanto, quanto ti bisogna,*
> *E più crudel che sei, più ne trarrai.*[9]

(My lady comes from the fountain / Against her wont with empty pitcher, / And brings no comfort to this breast, / Neither with water nor friendly glance, // Either because she has glimpsed the spotted snake / Slithering through the grass along the lane, / Or that the dog has chased her, or that she half fears / That lurking there in ambush may be the bogey-woman Befana. // Come here, Lorenzuola, come and you'll see / A fountain or two and as many as you'd like, / Nor from your stern father need you fear rebuke; // Look now, how both my eyes are watering; / Take to yourself as much water as you need, / And the crueller you are, the more you will draw out.)

Whether this is really by Brunelleschi or merely in a style not too unlike that of other poems whose attribution is more plausible, to my mind it contains a singular concatenation of conceits or images (within a Petrarchism treated in anecdotal manner) and a notably symmetrical structure with strong forms: as far as possible each narrative episode, fantastic invention, or contrast corresponds to a single line of verse, with the result that a line can be read in isolation and understood independently of the others. Morever the physical localization of the episode (the street from fountain to house), the specific definition of the psychological situation (the father always prompt to reprimand the young and presumably beautiful Lorenza), the combination of the arcadian (the lane) and domestic and wild animals (dog and viper), plus a soupçon of mystery (the fear of phantasms, probably because the shades of evening are already falling) all contribute to defining the modest little tale in extremely precise, almost topographical manner. Then too there is a strong progression from the empty pitcher and the physical and psychological aridity to an almost Baroque profusion of outpourings, sensuality, effusions.

We have had occasion to mention the memorandum by Giovanni da Prato which attacked the change in curvature of the dome introduced by Brunelleschi and also the system of illumination devised for the lantern. We find the same writer associated with Ghiberti in a violent battle of sonnets with Brunelleschi — the dramatic prelude to a dispute which was obviously not limited to poetry and which became more and more exasperated. The core of the scandal this time was the shallow-draught boat for transporting stone along the Arno between Pisa and Florence, for which Brunelleschi obtained a rare patent in 1421. If that gives us a *post quem* date for the poems, then the *ante quem* must be 1425, the year in which the Dante lectureship held by Giovanni was suspended, an event to which he perhaps alludes in his sonnet. True, the "battello badalone", the dawdling driftabout easily stranded barge, did not prove commercially viable, and indeed it seems once to have capsized and dumped its entire cargo into the Arno. It never did come as far as Florence but, according to Pedretti, for decades it continued to ply from Pisa to Castelfranco and Empoli.[10] A late fifteenth-century sketch may depict it: that shows a broad-keeled boat supported at the sides by floats and moved by propellers, some of which revolved in the water, as in river steamboats, others apparently in the air. Its loading capacity, as calculated by Prager, would have been about four tons. (On the boat and the patent see Chapter 8, note 28.)

Giovanni da Prato is a personage of no small distinction. He was juridical consultant and archivist for Orsanmichele from 1414 onwards and thus was in contact with Donatello, Nanni di Banco and the other sculptors who made statues for the exterior of the building; from 1417 to 1425 he lectured on Dante at the University of Florence; in 1420, 1423 and 1426 he was consultant to the Opera del Duomo, representing Ghiberti, and came out of the no-holds-barred polemic with Brunelleschi well and truly trounced. Immediately afterwards he retired to a modest house in Prato, though the direct cause of that move was the suppression in 1425, for purely economic reasons, of his university post. He wrote a large-scale romance, *Il Paradiso degli Alberti* ("The Paradise-Garden of the Alberti"), dated by Hans Baron to 1425-26,[11] in which he expressed political ideas as well. Among the characters in his romance are not only humanists and lovers of the vernacular but also representatives of the medieval schools and therefore Aristotelians and Ockhamites.

SONETTO DI MESSERE GIOVANNI ACQUETTINI DA PRATO A PIPPO DI SER BRUNELLESCO

> *O fonte fonda e nissa d'ignoranza,*
> pauper *animale ed insensibile,*
> *che vuoi lo 'ncerto altrui mostrar visibile,*
> *ma tua archimia* nichil habet *possanza;*
>
> *la insipida plebe sua speranza*
> *omai perduta l'ha, ed è credibile:*
> *ragion non dà che la cosa impossibile*
> *possibil facci uom* sine sustanza.
>
> *Ma se 'l tuo Badalon che in acqua vola*
> *viene a perfezion, che non può essere,*
> *non ched i' legga Dante nella scuola,*
>
> *ma vo' con le mie man finir mio essere.*
> *perch'io son certo di tuo mente fola,*
> *ché poco sai ordire e vie men tessere.*

358. Illustrations from Girolamo Benivieni's *Dialogo di Antonio Manetti cittadino fiorentino circa al sito, forme et misure dello "Inferno" di Dante Alighieri poeta excellentissimo*, Florence, 1506.

a) The globe, with Jerusalem at the top, below which is Hell; on the opposite side is the mountain of Purgatory [*306*].
b) The circles of Hell in plan, with east at the top.
c) The circles of Hell in section, from Limbo to Cocytus.

d) The five upper circles of Hell, down to Dis.
e) From the walls of Dis down to (and excluding) Malebolge.
f) Malebolge.
g) The well of the Giants, the circles of the Traitors and the tomb of Lucifer, seen in section and plan. The Giants are not shown, but Lucifer appears at the centre.

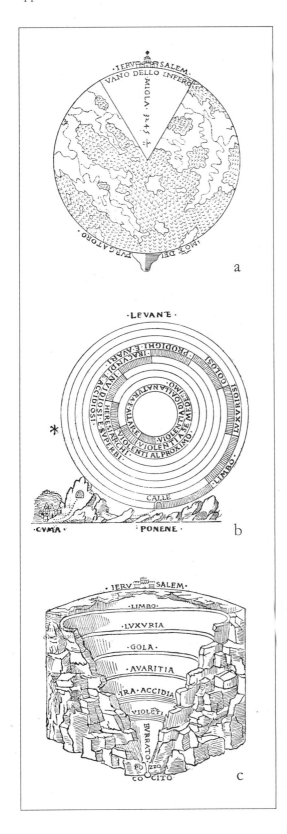

SONETTO PER RISPOSTA AL SOPRADETTO FE' PIPPO DI SER BRUNELLESCO

Quando dall'alto ci è dato speranza,
o tu c'hai efigia d'animal resibile,
perviensi all'uom, lasciando il corruttibile,
e ha da giudicar Somma Possanza.

Falso giudicio perde la baldanza,
ché sperienza gli si fa terribile:
l'uom saggio non ha nulla d'invisibile,
se non quel che non è, perc'ha mancanza.

E quelle fantasie d'un sine scola,
ogni falso pensier non vede l'essere
che l'arte dà quando natura invola.

Adunque e versi tuoi convienti stessere,
c'hanno rughiato in falso la carola,
da poi che 'l mio impossibil viene all'essere.

The two sonnets, where both authors do their best to turn each verse into a pithy aphorism, call for close reading line by line. The text is not clear: other transcriptions give different meanings, and many prose paraphrases have been made in Italian, none of them completely convincing.[12] For this reason, the best that one can offer here is a paraphrase, with due reservations.

Giovanni da Prato launches his attack by accusing Brunelleschi of being a deep and muddied well of ignorance, low even in the animal world, and incapable of understanding, trying to present as a truth that which is uncertain; but, says the accuser, his alchemy — false science —has no power. The wishy-washy ignorant plebs, having lost faith in other means, trust him. But they do not understand that an individual without facts in hand cannot transform the impossible into the possible: so if that barge which is to fly over the water should be perfected, which is impossible, I Giovanni will not only renounce my lectureship on Dante at the university but will take my life with my own hands, so certain am I that your mind is deranged: you are scarce able to set up the warp, let alone to weave.

The riposte by Brunelleschi contains noble affirmations of the transcendental value of knowledge. When there is some sort of inspiration from above (Parronchi somewhat exaggerates the mystical implication here, looking for a source in St Paul[13]), one arrives at the true core of man, free from the limitations of the corruptible physical world (whereas he, Giovanni, can only in outward image pass as a human being), acquiring a supreme power of judgment. At this point a second concept is brought into the fray. False judgment is easily defeated by experience, which is its terrible foe. For the wise man nothing is invisible except that which does not exist. [This verse is a quotation from St Paul: "invisibilia enim ipsius a creatura mundi, per ea quae facta sunt intellecta, conspicitur" (Rom. I:20)] The nonexistent is invisible and impossible (but, as we shall see, it can be transformed into something that does exist).

The *terzina* that follows seems obscure until one corrects the corrupt first line, as I have here, to read "fantasie d'un *sine scola*". According to Pellizzari and De Robertis, this stanza means: The imagination of a man without schooling (that is, a practical experimenter) is not understood by the mistaken thoughts of Giovanni, who does not know what art (in the broadest sense, like science), stealing the secrets of nature, can do.

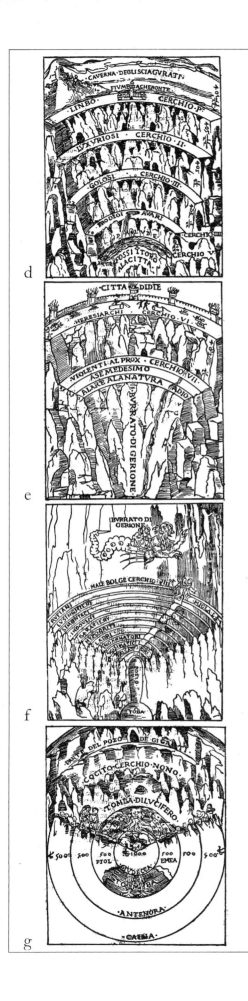

This is why Giovanni should begin to untwine the weft of his verses, which have provided a false, grunting tune to which others danced, because Brunelleschi's "impossible" is becoming reality.

The elements that go along with knowledge are quite well enumerated: illumination, abstraction of physical particularities, insistence on abstract reasoning, conviction that that reasoning coincides with experience and that therefore it can be taken as its verification, confidence in the knowability of everything that exists since reason and reality coincide. But there is something more: art, in its superior virtue, stronger than scholarship, is capable of wrenching secrets from nature and of entering into competition with her by creating existence out of imagination, the possible out of the impossible, even if unfortunately those not in the know, the non-initiate, cannot manage to understand that power. The final reference to music coincides with the belief in a harmonic structure in which knowledge and universe alike participate and which should constitute one more means of verification.

Another piece of verse, this one quite famous, should probably be understood as an encouragement to Donatello, perhaps upon his return from Rome which would be in 1433 — unless, of course, the poem is not by Brunelleschi, in which case it might apply to the sculptor's return from his more sensational successes in Padua.[14] In both cases we are presuming that "triumphs" refers to works in Florence. The theme is the contrast between the man who risks all in combat and the one who makes a great fuss and blows his own trumpet, with an affectionate invitation to lay down all quarrels and set to work in tranquillity.

> *Dimmi, Donato, senza alcun ritegnio*
> *chi più di loda è degnio:*
> *cholui che in lizza suona el serpentone,*
> *o cholui che più cozza a paragone?*
> *Ma tu, che sì ti gomphi*
> *De tuoi tanti triomphi,*
> *fà tacer quella gente sì loquace,*
> *et opera con pace;*
> *a lora sì coglierai a manate*
> *le lodi più presiate,*
> *poi che tu serai quel, che a te pertene*
> *te farai el tuo bene.*

(Tell me frankly, Donato, / who is more worthy of praise: / he who in the lists blows the trumpet, / or he who clashes most in the fight? / But you, who are so proud /of your many triumphs, / should also shut the mouths of that chatterbox crowd / and go on with your work in peace; / then you will gather great store / of the most worthy praises, / because then you will be what in truth you are / and do yourself most good.)

Unfortunately it is not possible to identify the bitterly polemical sonnet Brunelleschi is said to have written against Antonio Manetti Ciaccheri, concerning the model made in 1436 for the lantern of the Cathedral, which is known only from the Biographer: "And Filippo being informed of these things and having tried to stop him in several ways but to no avail, he made a sonnet which I heard in the past and cannot now put my hand on, the which he [Ciaccheri] remembered not only as long as Filippo lived but for as long as he lived himself".

An entertaining sonnet, "Panni alla burchia, e visi barbipiechi" (perhaps "Disorderly clothes, and faces with beards askew"), was formerly believed to have been written as an attack on Donatello and was then attributed to Burchiello himself. It is now again attributed to Brunelleschi, but it refers to a painter trying to imitate Orcagna (probably his *Triumph of Death*, in S. Croce).[15] From the collection of Burchiello verses, however, a poem can be singled out which, though it is difficult indeed to interpret (and to translate), throws some light on the situation of political and religious conflict in which Brunelleschi must have lived when work on the dome was nearing completion, the reference to Eugenius IV calling for the date of 1433 or later.

Innanzi che la cupola si chiuda
Certo sarà gran macco di starnoni,
Però che il Chericato, e i camicioni
Hanno messo i lor gufi tutti in muda;

E van così colla celloria nuda,
Come privati de' lor buon bocconi;
Fan' come quel che si castrò i coglioni
Per far dispetto alla sua dolce druda

E gli avversari lor van come savi,
Con gli assiuoli in pugno, ovvero Allocchi,
Che tanta autorità diè lor le chiavi.

A l'Agnusdeo par che se ne scocchi,
Che per volergli far del Duomo schiavi
Provò di far mugliar fino a' Marzocchi.

Credi, che siano sciocchi,
Di ciò portando invidia alla graticola,
Se Ugenio gli accetta a tal matricola?

(Before the dome is closed / In truth there'll be a great mash of young partridges, / Because the clerics and alb-wearers / Have put all their owls [*gufi*, also ecclesiastical hoods, almuces] to moult, // And thus go around with their topknots bare / As if deprived of their tastiest titbits [perhaps bribes, perquisites], / And act like the man who cut off his balls / To spite his fancy-woman, // And their adversaries go about like wise men, / With the horned or the tawny owls [*assiuoli*, also cuckolds, ignoramuses] in their grasp, / Something to which great authority gives them the keys [figuratively, the Keys of St Peter]. // At the Agnus Dei it seems the hour has struck / For him who, through wishing to make them slaves of the Duomo, / Even tried to make the Marzocco [the heraldic lion of Florence] roar. // Think you then that they are silly / When they try to imitate the conditions of a jail [*graticola*: the interpretation here is doubtful] / If Eugenius takes them on his payroll.)

What is odd in all this matter of poems and polemics is, as Tanturli observed at the 1977 Congress, that the decided reaction of the vernacular writers for or against the architect, in particular that of the "Burchiellesque" poets, was in no way matched by the humanists who, in their writings at least, ignored him until after his death.

"*La Novella del Grasso Legnaiuolo*"

Some day we shall understand better the way Brunelleschi used proportions, eliminating cubes and Golden Sections not only from our findings and drawings but also once and for all from the critical and historical literature. A pathway in that direction exists already, in the writings of Alberti himself, to whom we must return once again, as the faithful proponent of the ideas of Brunelleschi and his circle:

And to these things it should be added that opinion of philosophers and those who affirm that if the sky, stars, sea and mountains and all the animals and all

bodies [objects] became, should God so will it, reduced to half-size, the consequence would be that we ourselves would be entirely unaware of any diminishment. This is because large, small, long, short, high, low, broad, narrow, light, dark, luminous, tenebrous, and all such "accidents" (so called by philosophers because they may or may not be added to things) are of such nature that any cognition of them can only be by comparison. [*Della Pittura*, Book I]

The manipulation of accidentals, on the part of God or of the artist, is utterly and entirely free and unconditioned. What, however, preserves man from anarchy is the benevolence of God and also, in the thought of Alberti, the conviction that one precise and unchangeable measure does exist and persist: man. And man is, so to speak, the canon of the overall system of the universe, he being, like it, created in the image and likeness of God.

Now, in a famous trick, a *burla* reported in detail in two different versions under the title of *La Novella del Grasso Legnaiuolo* ("The Tale of the Fat Carpenter"), which belongs to the genre of "life-is-a-dream" tales except that in it the dreamer is fully awake, Brunelleschi denied in the most bold and bald manner that any such immutable and universal measure exists.[16] By manipulating the relationships around a man his personality, the personal identity of the onlooker, ceases to be a fixed measure and becomes entirely relative and variable. The joke appears to have been played on a historical character, Manetto di Jacopo Ammannatini, a master carpenter (the word *legnaiuolo* is sufficiently broad and vague to be translated as carpenter, model- and altar-maker, even furniture merchant), who later emigrated to Hungary and acquired considerable wealth, to judge from the tax rolls.[17] To pay this friend back for having absented himself from a convivial gathering, Brunelleschi, in 1409 not yet an architect, finding himself in "company of a number of men of good standing, government officials as well as ingenious masters of different arts and guilds, such as painters, goldsmiths, sculptors, and carpenters and similar craftsmen", came up with a system by which to make the unsociable carpenter believe himself to be someone else, a very well known man called Matteo. Il Grasso — the Fat Man — is arrested as a debtor and spoken to and treated in every respect as if he were the real Matteo, even by the other prisoners who attempt to console him. His "brothers" — the brothers of Matteo — pay the debt and have him released from confinement, then take him to their house where he is made to undergo a psychological treatment administered by the priest of their parish, S. Felicita. Of the many who take part in the jest in one way or another, some are perfectly informed, and they are actors, while others are themselves taken in by the change in personality and so themselves become victims. By their combined pressures Il Grasso is brought to accept that he is Matteo and to promise "from that point forward to make every effort to desist from trying to make others believe him to be the Fat Man as up to that point he had done"; though certainly something still itched in his brain since he appended to that oath the remark that the pact would remain in force until "he goes back to being the Fat Man".

Convinced and accepting the situation, still in the house of Matteo, the poor man is put to sleep with a narcotic and carried back to his own house. But to prevent him from identifying himself with himself he is put to bed in reverse position, with his head at the foot, and the entire disposition of the furniture and of the tools in his workroom is changed about, so that "thinking back to all that had happened, and where he had gone to bed last evening, and where he found himself now, he was plunged immediately into a fantasy of ambiguity as to whether he had dreamed what had happened or was dreaming now, and he thought himself certain now of one thing, now of the other... And was in the greatest confusion again whether he had been in a dream or was in a dream now."

While the thoroughly confused carpenter, who is said to be a bit simple but certainly not stupid, is having a hard time putting two and two together, the second part of the *burla* is launched, this one devised to eliminate all further possible points of reference by rendering them equally ambiguous. Enter the brothers of Matteo, who had at first taken loving care of the Fat Man as if he were indeed their closest kin. Now they do not recognize him. Which could be proof for Antonio the carpenter that he is indeed himself and not Matteo. But they confide to him the strange thing that has happened to their brother, who suddenly began to behave as if he were Il Grasso and fled from the house in the morning, identifying entirely with what was happening to the carpenter while remaining physically Matteo. When the Fat Man meets up with Donatello and Brunelleschi, they tell him all over again the entire story of Matteo and how he has taken to believing himself Il Grasso. And at that point Matteo in person turns up (obviously in on the joke): in part he confirms the story told by his brothers and Filippo and Donato; he declares that he has been in his villa, has slept "one whole day and two whole nights without ever waking", and then, upon awaking, had the impression of having become someone else: "and it does seem to me that I am another this morning". Worse, he tells that he dreamed he was working as a carpenter in a workshop, as if he were indeed Il Grasso, "but it did not seem to me that the tools were in the places he would have them, and I had to arrange them in a different order". Which could appear a logical explanation for the confusion the carpenter had in fact found in his shop. And then, "I find I have paid a debt of a number of florins, and it seemed to me, when I was sleeping, that I was another: o! it is as certain as that I see myself here amongst you; but who knows if I dreamed then or dream now?"

The Fat Carpenter remains perturbed, even if he cannot bring himself to believe that he had become — for a time at least — Matteo and that Matteo had become him. He searches for some proof, some incongruity, and finally lights on it: Matteo (*sub specie* Il Grasso) remarked that he had dined with Il Grasso's mother, but the true Grasso learned that his mother was in fact not in Florence. At this point he begins to find it all too suspect and the whole cruel joke comes apart. Furious and ashamed, however, the poor man quits Florence for Hungary, where he enters the service — as secret messenger from Florence as well as craftsman — of the *condottiere*-Croesus Pippo Spano. Here again we find a connection with Brunelleschi since, as we have seen, it was money left by Pippo Spano that started the building of the Rotunda of S. Maria degli Angeli.

As the novella shows, even the most intimate and persistent core of personal identity, the link of the individual with his own history, surroundings, work and social existence, can be shattered by a thoroughly worked-out and well co-ordinated change in factors external to him, and this with more convincing rationality than Alice found in Wonderland.

The temptation to associate this brutal invention, psychological and physical at one and the same time, with perspective, the science of illusion, is strong indeed. Just as Alberti explained it, if the displacement of the horizon line, the distance point, and the viewer's position can change the entire system but nonetheless leave it co-ordinated and compact — on condition, of course, that the correct laws be applied — so too a global "side-slip" in the surroundings, by an analogous operation, may modify the viewer as well. In the same way as, looking through the hole in the rear of Brunelleschi's perspective panel, it was difficult to be sure whether one was seeing the Baptistery or its image reflected in a mirror, so too when the carpenter was displaced from his own perfectly coherent system into another which was parallel and just as complete and without anything to betray it, he could not help but ask himself if the dream came first or afterwards, nor, as happens at one point in the tale, could he resign himself to being Matteo in the house of Matteo and himself, Il Grasso, in the house of Il Grasso. But if this be admitted, then Brunelleschi was more slyly (and wickedly) mischievous than the most mischevous of the gods: his implacable logic and his laborious projecting of all the techniques needed were not the instrument of reality but quite the contrary, a mechanism of deceit so refined and subtle as to make the dreams of night no more than children's games and to destroy forever our hearty faith in the fact of day.[18]

Two early lives of Brunelleschi

From Antonio di Tuccio Manetti, "XIV Huomini Singhulari in Firenze dal MCCC innanzi" written between 1494 and 1497
(Florence, Biblioteca Nazionale, Cod. Magliabechiano XVII 1501: a book of lives of outstanding Florentines from 1300 onwards, written as an appendix to *De Civitate Florentiae famosis Civibus*)

Filippo di ser Brunellesco, architect, a man of admirable ingenuity, erected the dome of S. Maria del Fiore from the round windows upwards, and built the vaults of the tribune without centering, and also made the lantern which is on it with wonderful fixed and mobile scaffolding and construction machines that avoid damage to the corners of the marble and to the masons. He built the sacristy of S. Lorenzo in Florence and the transept [*croce*] of that church, [but] the main body was by other masters who in many particulars did not follow his design. He built a small chapel for the Barbadori in S. Felicita, the first on the right when you enter the church. He built the chapter house of the Pazzi in the first cloister of S. Croce in Florence. He built part of the palace of the Parte Guelfa, the unfinished hall and other things in it that are good. He laid the foundations and built up to where it is now, that is, to the base of the vaulting over the chapels, the Temple of the Angels [the Rotunda of S. Maria degli Angeli]. The loggia of the Foundling Hospital, to a great extent: many parts of the front and the interior were spoiled by presumptuous individuals. He built S. Spirito in Florence and left a very well made model of it, but the building was spoiled in many parts after his death by presumptuous individuals. He built the fortress or citadel of Vicopisano [and] two towers at the first bridge, that is of the new citadel, in Pisa. He built a castle, an admirable fortress, for the Lord Sigismondo of Rimini. He put in order part of the principal church of Milan, that is he did what little is good in it. It was he who rediscovered the Antique manner of building and of [designing] ornamentation. He was a marvellous sculptor. He found or rediscovered how to realize with precisely measured foreshortening the different planes that the painters show receding in a three-dimensional space, and thus greatly helped the painters to render things so that they appear true to life, and to sculptors he gave the same system of receding planes, a system not used by the Ancients. He was a master in casting, relief carving, and other things, and in all respects marvellous.

From the "Libro di Antonio Billi" written between 1516 and 1520
(Florence, Biblioteca Nazionale, Cod. Strozzino and Cod. Petrei, respectively Magliabechiano XXV 636 and XIII 89)

Pippo di ser Brunellesco, Florentine citizen, was learned in Holy Writ, and Maestro Paolo [Paolo dal Pozzo Toscanelli, the outstanding scientist-humanist], astrologer, used to say that when one listened to him speaking he seemed a veritable St Paul. He was an arithmetician and a geometrician. He rediscovered perspective, which had for so long been lost sight of. He was interested in the interpretation of the works of Dante and understood them extremely well.

He found the way to build without centering the Florence dome which had for many years remained unfinished because no one could be found who dared or knew how to vault it, and in Florence they had almost come to the decision to fill [the Cathedral crossing] with earth and to use that as a support [around which the dome would be moulded]. As associate he had Lorenzo Bartolucci [Ghiberti]. But when they were just about to vault it, Pippo pretended to be ill, and the said Lorenzo not being able to or knowing how to get along without Pippo, Pippo sent word to him that he himself could do perfectly well without Lorenzo; and thus the officials gave him the entire responsibility and removed Lorenzo, to whom in exchange they allocated the bronze doors of S. Giovanni [the Baptistery].

He made all the machinery and models needed to carry out that task, and left them in the Opera where, through negligence, some have been ruined and some lost.

He made the model for the lantern in a competition [where] even a woman made so bold as to come up with another model; he was ridiculed by certain masters who saw no stairs in it, the which however he then revealed to them as being concealed inside a pier.

He was of great worth in sculpture, as is seen in the bronze model that he made for the doors of S. Giovanni; that model is today on the front of the altar in the sacristy of S. Lorenzo. Nevertheless they [the doors] were allocated to Lorenzo Bartolucci, or Ghiberti, though the said Filippo, Donatello, Luca della Robbia and Antonio del Pollaiuolo all worked on them.

He made a St Mary Magdalen in S. Spirito which was ruined when that church caught fire, and this was in competition with one by Donatello which is in S. Giovanni.

He made the Crucifix in S. Maria Novella in competition with Donatello who had made another in S. + [Croce].

Allocated to him and to Donatello were two marble statues which are between the pilasters at Orsanmichele, that is, those of St Peter and St Mark, truly works of merit.

He made [painted] in perspective the Baptistery and Piazza di S. Giovanni and also the Palazzo della Signoria.

He made the model for the church of S. Spirito, an excellent work even if the arrangement he designed was not entirely followed, either in the [number of] doors [on the façade] or in the outer faces of the external walls which were to be shaped like their inner faces, nor in the altars of the chapels which were to be placed forward of the wall so that the priest would turn his face towards the church when saying mass, exactly the opposite of what happens now. Nor in its dome did they follow his dispositions, having raised too high the piers and capitals of the columns and the entablature above them, so that the dome became out of proportion, and the entire building turned out to be weaker and more in danger of ruin than if it had been built according to the original design, and there is another error made there by competitors, i.e. an arch that is wrongly placed.

He also made the model for the church of S. Lorenzo, though there again his design was not fully executed, in spite of which it is a very beautiful structure, and so too the old sacristy. Similarly he made a model for the chapter house of the Pazzi in the cloister of S. Croce, and the model for the house of the Busini.

He also made the model for the house and façade of the loggia of the Innocenti, which he made without centering, a model which was adhered to in many respects, except for an entablature made on the order of Francesco della Luna which is wrong and a contradiction in style. This came about because Filippo was at the time in Milan in the service of Duke Filippo Maria for the model of the fortress; seeing the error on his return he wished to tear it down, but the Operai prevented him from doing so with soothing words, and so he had to put up with that façade which departs from his model with an entablature made on the order of the said Francesco who thought he knew about architecture. And when Filippo asked him why he had done such a thing, he replied that he had taken it from the church of S. Giovanni, to which Filippo replied: "There was only one mistake in that entire building, and you copied it."

He made the model for the fortress of Vico Pisano and that of the port of Pesaro, and in Milan a number of things. And he used to say that if he had to make a hundred models for churches or other buildings he would make them all different.

He made a model for the house, or palace, of Cosimo de' Medici which was to be located in the Piazza di S. Lorenzo in such a way that the door of the palace would be exactly opposite the door of S. Lorenzo, and this palace would perhaps have had few rivals in the world today if the plan of Filippo had been carried out. But since to Cosimo it seemed to involve too lavish an expenditure, he did not proceed with that commission, though later he regretted it greatly, because Filippo had put into it all his ingenuity, regardless of the cost, saying that he had always wanted to create one exceptional work and it seemed to him that this was the opportunity he had been seeking and was capable of realizing. And it is said that he was never seen so happy as when he was constructing that model. Cosimo very much regretted not having executed it, and used to say that it seemed to him that he had never spoken with a man of greater intelligence than Pippo, and he reproached himself greatly.

He had a pupil whom he kept in his house, called Il Buggiano, whom he had make the marble lavabo of the sacristy of S. Reparata [S. Maria del Fiore], with infants splashing water. Also he [Buggiano] made the head of Filippo which is in S. Reparata [3] and made a lavabo in stone in the sacristy there.

Filippo also made many designs and models for various lords, including the fortress of Filippo Maria, Duke of Milan, and that Duke did everything to retain him, no matter what the cost.

He made the model of the port for the Lord of Pesaro, and for many others those of houses and various buildings, and the design of the monastery of the Angeli.

Chronology: Brunelleschi and his times

This chronology is based on the documents published by Guasti, Fabriczy, and later researchers, such as R. G. Mather (*Art Bulletin*, 1948, 1, pp. 51-53), and on the *Mostra documentaria Filippo Brunelleschi, l'uomo e l'artista*, Florence, 1977. It also includes the new findings of Anthony Molho, Jeffrey Ruda and Diane Finiello Zervas which appeared in 1977, 1978 and 1979 respectively, as well as material not yet published.

1352
January
The father of Brunelleschi, Ser Brunellesco di Lippo Lapi, applies to be named notary, declaring himself to have reached the minimim age of twenty (from which one can deduce that he was born *c.* 1331).

1359-1402
Ser Brunellesco is regularly listed in the tax rolls (*Libri delle Prestanze*) and frequently changes his dwelling. He is candidate for the Tre Maggiori Uffici in 1393 and1398.

1367
1 April
Ser Brunellesco is sent as emissary to the Emperor Charles IV of Luxemburg and stops in Ferrara and Padua on his way to Vienna.

In the same year he is chosen by lot as impartial consultant in a large committee to discuss what is to be done about the first vaults built over the nave of Florence Cathedral, which have proved defective; he recommends the use of iron tie-rods instead of external buttresses.

1368
Ser Brunellesco is sent on an embassy to Lombardy.

1373
Ser Brunellesco is sent to Romagna "and many other places".

1376
Further missions to Romagna and elsewhere.

1377
Birth of Filippo Brunelleschi. (Jacopo della Quercia's birth date is 1375, Ghiberti's 1378, Donatello's between 1383 and 1386; Nanni di Banco's is unknown.)

1379
Ser Brunellesco finally settles in the house near S. Michele Berteldi which Filippo will eventually inherit.

1384
Ser Brunellesco is again sent to Lombardy.
Florence acquires Arezzo from its *condottiere* head.

1388
Throughout Europe, beginning of a stern repression of popular risings.

1392
B., it seems, is already an apprentice goldsmith in the Arte della Seta.

1393
The niches on Orsanmichele are assigned to various guilds, but only two statues, one sponsored by the Arte della Lana, are executed before 1400.

1397
Birth of the scientist Paolo Toscanelli.
28 August (feast of St Augustine)
Defeat of the Milanese at Governolo.

1398
18 December
B. sworn as master goldsmith. (According to a new reading of the documents: previously it was thought that he began his apprenticeship in this year.)

1399
One of the masters to whom B. was apprenticed is among the architects of the Cathedral.
31 December
First contract for the Silver Altar in Pistoia Cathedral mentions "Pippo da Firenze".

1400
Florence ravaged by plague and wars.
The Operai of S. Maria del Fiore appropriate 800 gold florins annually for the reconstruction of the walls and fortifications of Castellina, a commission extended for two years in April 1402 and for a further year in 1404.
7 February
Second contract for the Pistoia Altar, mentioning "Pippo di ser Benincasa da Firenze". The specifications of the altar are changed to reduce expense.
February-May
B. is member of the Consiglio del Popolo: he misses a meeting, being in Pistoia.
14 April
The Florentine Signoria decides that Lastra and Malmantile are to be fortified. This phase of the works is completed on 23 July 1403.
1 May-30 June
Ser Brunellesco is notary for the Priors of the Guilds and the Gonfaloniere di Giustizia of the Commune of Florence.
June-September
Ser Brunellesco is elected to the Consiglio del Popolo, for the term June-September.
September-December
Filippo is member of the Consiglio del Popolo; he misses a meeting, being out of Florence.

1401
Giovanni d'Ambrogio is named *capomaestro* for the Cathedral.
B. has delivered a figure of St Augustine for the Pistoia Altar (the only element attributed to him in an inventory).
B. and Ghiberti, who returns from Pesaro specially, take part in the competition for the Baptistery doors.
January-April
Ser Brunellesco is elected to the Consiglio del Popolo.

1402
In the tax levy the sons of Ser Brunellesco appear for the first time, taxed along with their father (payment of 10 gold *soldi*).
The consuls of the Arte di Calimala award the commission for the Baptistery doors to Ghiberti.
3 September
Giangaleazzo Visconti's death from plague interrupts the war between Florence and Milan.

1403
Coluccio Salutati, on the basis of Carolingian relics and documents found in SS. Apostoli, proclaims Florence to be the authentic heir of ancient Rome. Already at the start of the thirteenth century an inscription had been falsified to make the foundation of this church date back to 805. Poggio Bracciolini goes to Rome and is commissioned by Coluccio Salutati to send him copies of ancient inscriptions.

1403-18
Poggio Bracciolini at the Roman Curia.

1404
June
B., his brother Tommaso and their mother figure in the tax register, the father now deceased, and are liable for 3 florins and 6 *soldi*.
2 July
B. matriculates officially as master goldsmith, having "served the art for six years".
10 November
B., identified as a goldsmith, serves with many other citizens (among them Ghiberti, who, in these years, has Donatello among his assistants on the Baptistery doors) on a consultative commission to consider the buttresses of the Cathedral apse, which are thought to be too high and are to be lowered. It also debates the height of the chapels, in relation not only to the nave but to the unbuilt dome, and decides that they should not be heightened. The commission functioned until 16 February 1406.

1405
May-August
B. is member of the Consiglio del Popolo. Later his name will disappear from the lists until 1418, probably because he was not continuously present in Florence.

1406
Florence conquers Pisa.
March
B. is taxed individually, for 2 florins, 4 *soldi* and 2 *denari*.

c. 1406
Ptolemy's *Geography* translated from Greek into Latin.

1407
Date inscribed on a bronze statuette of *St Christopher* (Cleveland Museum of Art), of uncertain attribution.

1409
Date of the *burla* or elaborate joke played on the "Fat Carpenter", instigated by Brunelleschi, Donatello and others.

1410
Francesco Datini leaves a large sum for the con-

struction of the Foundling Hospital; work will not begin until nine years later.
30 September
B. is paid 10 *soldi* by the Opera del Duomo for a supply of bricks, a sum that would pay an unskilled labourer for one day only, so what was involved was presumably samples of brick.

1410ff.
Construction of the octagonal drum of the Cathedral dome.

1410-11
Leonardo Bruni is Chancellor of Florence.

1411
Sigismund of Luxemburg is elected Emperor, putting an end to a crisis persisting since 1379.
3 April
Donatello commissioned by the Arte dei Linaiuoli, the Linen Drapers' Guild, to make a *St Mark* for a niche at Orsanmichele. The statue is completed in 1413; sixteenth-century sources say that B. also worked on it.

1412
The Bohemian reformer Jan Huss, having lost the support of the Emperor Sigismund, is excommunicated as a heretic.
2 February
B. pays tax of 3 florins and 2 *denari*, but not the penalty exacted from those who quit the city during the plague, so he must have remained there during that time.
Before 11 March
B., identified as *capomaestro* together with Nanni Niccoli, goes to Prato twice for consultations about the rebuilding of the Cathedral façade, involving also an internal passageway from the Chapel of the Holy Girdle to the external pulpit, where on certain feasts the Girdle of the Virgin was solemnly displayed. [1]
29 March
The Signoria decrees that the new cathedral in Florence is to be dedicated to Our Lady of Flowers, S. Maria del Fiore, perhaps implying some liturgical symbolism.

c. 1412
Birth of Andrea di Lazzaro Cavalcanti, known as Il Buggiano, who will be adopted by B. and will work as his assistant.

1413
According to Guarino Veronese, B. had a verbal encounter with Niccolò Niccoli, whom he accused of "arid erudition".
10 August
A letter from Domenico da Prato refers to "the perspective expert, ingenious man, Filippo di Ser Brunellesco, remarkable for virtues [skills] and fame".

1414
The death of King Ladislao of Naples frees Florence from the burden of war and leads to a decade of peace and prosperity marked by many new building undertakings.

1414-17
Council of Constance convened to abolish antipopes, restore Church unity, make necessary reforms and extirpate heresy.

1415
New statute of the Arte di Pietra e Legname (guild of master stonemasons and carpenters), with protective measures against competition from the Lombard guilds.

An official of the Cathedral is sent to the forest owned by the Opera to find trees to be used for scaffolding and, more especially, for the centering needed for the dome, but he dies during the journey.

Some sort of very close collaboration between Brunelleschi and Donatello seems to have occurred around 1415 and is documented in the case of a model for a gigantic statue to be covered with gilded lead, for the Cathedral. Difficulties must have arisen quite early, and Brunelleschi, defaulting, was ordered on 29 January 1416 to deliver to Donatello the lead he had received.
22 May
Order for construction of the fortified bridge in Pisa.

1417
Election of Pope Martin V, of the Roman family of the Colonna. Not until autumn 1419 would he succeed in entering Rome, which is in total political and economic chaos.

In Florence, after the death of Maso degli Albizzi, his son Rinaldo begins what was to be a highly successful career. He kept to the same domestic and foreign policy, supporting the economic oligarchy in power and continuing the wars against Pisa and Milan, exercising the authority of an absolute ruler while respecting the republican ordinances (which were being exalted for propaganda purposes by humanists like Bruni).

Giovanni di Gherardo da Prato begins to teach at the University of Florence.
February
Marble for the base of the tabernacle containing *St George* at Orsanmichele is sold by the Opera del Duomo to the Arte dei Corazzai (Armourers' Guild). The date of the statue is unknown: it may have been completed before this block was purchased. The marble relief on the base has been variously dated, from 1417 (sometimes even earlier, because of a faulty reading of the document) to as late as 1428 or 1430. It seems to be the first instance of the correct use of receding sculptural planes to render perspective.
May
B. receives 10 florins for drawings and projects for the Opera del Duomo, probably concerned with scaffolding and centering for the dome.

1418
15 June
Giovanni d'Ambrogio, *capomaestro* for the Opera del Duomo, has a wooden model made of the scaffolding and centering for the dome. Later in the year he is discharged because of his age.
19 August
A public competition solicits ideas for the centering of the dome, for the scaffolding, and for the construction machinery, with a prize of 200 gold florins to anyone whose projects are accepted, as well as compensation for any expenses contracted in preparing models (even for projects not accepted). B. apparently proposes immediately a highly unusual solution.
31 August
The Opera appoints four masters to supervise the

construction of B.'s model and to verify its practicability.
12 September
Filippo's name is drawn as one of the Dodici Buonuomini.
23 September
Ghiberti is assigned four assistants to help in making a model of the dome.
18 October
Filippo is elected (to 31 March 1419) to the Consiglio dei Dugento.
7 and 12 December
The commission meets in the Cathedral to judge the competition and names B. and Ghiberti jointly as winners.
13 December
Solemn assembly of the Arte della Lana and the Opera del Duomo to exhibit the competition models.
20 December
Money is appropriated to pay Masters Cristofano di Simone, Tuccio di Giovanni and Jacopo di Giovanni Rosso 4 *lire* each and Gherardo Bellacqua 6 *lire* for "viewing, examining, and advising on the model of Filippo di Ser Brunellesco and whether it would be possible to build the large dome according to the forms of the said model".
22 December
Matteo Dolfini, Prior of San Lorenzo, requests permission to take over neighbouring property in preparation for the work of enlarging the church by a huge transept.

Payments are made for other models for the dome of S. Maria del Fiore presented by eight masters.

1419
Suppression of the confraternities.

The Arte della Seta, with the funds left by Francesco Datini, purchases from Rinaldo degli Albizzi the land to be used for the Foundling Hospital.
26 February-8 December 1420
Pope Martin V has his seat in Florence.
20 May
Ghiberti, with the help of Giuliano d'Arrigo Pesello and Pippo di Giovanni, designs and builds a staircase for the papal apartments in the monastery of S. Maria Novella.
11-12 August
B. is paid for further work on his dome model, having added a lantern and a circular gallery around the drum and dome.
11 August
Contracts for the first foundations of the loggia of the Foundling Hospital. By October, 124 *braccia* are completed.
15 November
Another commission is appointed to deal with the construction of the dome.
20 November
From this date B. and Ghiberti are paid 2 florins each per month for work on the model of the dome. The final payment is made on 24 April 1420.
29 December
B., Nanni di Banco and Donatello are paid 45 florins "for their long work in making a model in bricks mortared without any centering".

c. 1419
Buggiano, aged about seven, begins his apprenticeship with B.

1419-20

Leonardo Bruni writes the preamble to the new statutes of the Parte Guelfa, praising its work in defence of that liberty ''without which no republic is possible and no one should live''.

1420

Eight masters are elected by the Opera del Duomo, presumably one for each of the sides of the dome. The official building programme, with numerous clauses, is established.

8 March-22 April
Minor payments to Ghiberti and assistants for the model of the dome.

27 March-3 April
Final contest between B. and Ghiberti for a model (a new one?) for the dome.

16 April
B. and Ghiberti are appointed, together with the *capomaestro* Battista d'Antonio, as supervisors of the construction of the dome, with a stipend of 3 florins each per month. (This was a modest fee: according to the figures published by Prager and Scaglia, the average wage of an unskilled labourer was 10 *soldi* per day, that of a carpenter or mason 1 *lira* per day or about 7 or 8 florins per month.) As his deputy B. has Giuliano d'Arrigo Pesello, and Ghiberti has Giovanni di Gherardo da Prato. On this occasion the masters swear to follow the approved model.

7 June
Half the foundations of the church of the Foundling Hospital are paid for.

20 June
Measures are taken to protect the financing of the work on the dome from possible cuts or reductions in funds.

30 July
The programme for the construction of the dome is solemnly approved: '' and it can and should proceed with the modes, dispositions and forms... according to the model''. Work begins in August.

6 August
The Ufficiali delle Torri authorize the use of 3 *braccia* of public land for the stairs to the Foundling Hospital loggia. The stairs will be built in stages over a number of years.

20 October
The first monolithic column for the loggia of the Foundling Hospital is brought to the site.

29 October
The Opera del Duomo pays B. and Ghiberti their salary for four months and ten days.

October-31 March 1421
B. is member of the Consiglio del Popolo.

1420-21

The ''stella della cupola'' is constructed, presumably a machine for hoisting building materials.

1421

The south transept arm of the Cathedral is completed.

Decision to lay out a public piazza between the church of S. Simone and the prison, as a small-scale imitation of Piazza della SS. Annunziata.

January
At the Foundling Hospital the first column of the loggia is put in place (in front of the door to the church).

January-April
B. is member of the Consiglio del Popolo; he misses a meeting, being out of Florence.

21 February
The Opera of the Foundling Hospital makes a first payment of 15 gold florins for drawings for the pilasters, doorposts, and door sills. The first end pilaster and pediments over two doors are built.

22 February
The will of Messer Matteo di Jacopo Corbinelli mentions a wooden statue of St Mary Magdalen for the family chapel in S. Spirito, a work ascribed by the Biographer to B.

March
Beginning of contracts from the Opera del Duomo for a large winch to raise heavy materials from the ground to the level of the drum.

1 May-31 April 1422
B. is Operaio of the Foundling Hospital, representing the Arte della Seta.

10 June
The four officials in charge of the dome are ordered to settle on the amount to be paid to B. for the project, the work, and the expenses of constructing a hoist to raise materials to the dome platforms. On 8 July they decide to give him 100 florins. The expenses for materials and workers are not paid by the Opera until 27 August 1423.

19-23 June
Coincidentally with the conquest of Livorno and projects for a Florentine state fleet, B. obtains a patent for a cargo boat to be used on the Arno. He is given special monopoly privileges for three years, with the right to keep his invention secret and to burn any boats which copied his.

7 August
Work on the dome begins: wine and food sent up for masters and workmen.

10 August
Solemn foundation ceremony for the rebuilding of S. Lorenzo.

October-March 1422
B. is member of the Consiglio dei Dugento.

1421-22

Execution of the first pair of chains for the dome.

1422

The Pope sends money to the Medici bank in Florence for investment.

Gentile da Fabriano in Florence.

March
First change in the building programme of the dome, providing for brickwork to be used at a lower level than had been planned.

16 March
At the Foundling Hospital 4,914 *braccia* of foundations and 4,253 *braccia* of walls above ground have been built.

13 November
Part payment to B. of 10 gold florins for work at the Foundling Hospital.

14 November
After a period of litigation and a compromise settlement on 16 October, there is a division of property between B. and his brother Tommaso, a goldsmith who will live only until January 1431. B. receives a house in what is now the parish of S. Gaetano: ''Unam domum cum volta sub terram puteo et aliis hedefitii positam Florentiae in populo Sancti Michaelis Bertelde in Via [not indicated]'' (a house with underground cellar, well and other annexes, in Florence in the parish of S. Michele Berteldi, in... street). His brother receives a house in Via Valfonda in the parish of S. Maria Novella, a plot of land with vines and olive trees at Buggiano in the Val di Nievole, and another at Colle.

1423

War declared against Milan. Pandolfo and Carlo Malatesta are named commanders of the troops; the military commissioners are Rinaldo degli Albizzi and Francesco Tornabuoni.

Birth of Antonio di Tuccio Manetti. (As the supposed author of a major biography of B., he is also referred to in these pages as the Biographer.)

A '' castle'' or scaffolding tower is constructed to aid in building the dome, and B. is paid 10 florins for its design.

Gentile da Fabriano paints *The Adoration of the Magi* (Florence, Uffizi) for Palla Strozzi, perhaps the most acclaimed post-Gothic painting produced in Florence.

April
The roof of the Foundling Hospital church is completed.

27 August
Ten florins are paid for '' certain oak corners needed for the chain of the main dome'', i.e. the wooden chain that survives.

September
B. is recalled from Pistoia, where he has perhaps been working on fortifications or the Ospedale del Ceppo, to supply designs or instructions for the work at the Foundling Hospital.

c. 1423-25

Tabernacle commissioned by the Parte Guelfa for Orsanmichele — attributed to B., Donatello, or Michelozzo.

1423-53

Poggio Bracciolini in the employ of the Papal Curia.

1424

Paolo Toscanelli returns to Florence.

Defeat of Florentine troops in Romagna and defection of Carlo Malatesta.

March
Arches of the Foundling Hospital loggia built.

19 April
The first doors by Ghiberti are hung in the east doorway of the Baptistery.

4 May
Contract for the vaults of the Foundling Hospital loggia.

May-October
Epidemic in Florence.

6 May
At the Foundling Hospital the architrave, cornice, and roundels are commissioned.

19 May
B. is paid 10 gold florins for work at the Foundling Hospital.

31 May
Along with 130 other Florentine citizens B. is summoned to present himself to the Signoria before 8 June, on penalty of a fine of 200 florins and exclusion from public office. The reason is unknown.

June-September
B. is member of the Consiglio del Popolo. He misses a meeting, being in Pistoia.

8 June
B. appears before the Signoria.

25 June
Fra Bernardino of Siena makes a great bonfire of '' profane vanities'' in the Piazza del Campidoglio in Rome.

21 July
B., working in Pistoia, is asked for instructions on how to continue the work at the Foundling Hospital, presumably the vaults of the loggia.
September
B. is again in Pistoia, perhaps for work on fortifications or the hospital.
16 September
Contract between Piero di Curradino and Ambrogio di Lionardo, and the Ten Purveyors of the cities of Pisa, Pistoia and Volterra, for additional fortifications for the ''castle and place of Malmantile''. This involved ''walls, machicolations, small vaults, towers, vaults, and stairways'', for which they would supply bricks, stone, ashlar, and sand; lime, lead and locks were to be provided by the Ten. Pietro and Ambrogio also undertook to make a moat around the castle, presumably as a defence against mining.
25 September
Brunelleschi to go to Pisa for fortifications.
25/26 September
Decree that the Opera del Duomo of Florence is to pay for fortifications at Lastra and Malmantile as well as for the walls of the citadel of Pisa.
22 November
The Ospedale del Ceppo in Pistoia, with which B. is perhaps involved, is granted all the privileges which will in future be granted to the Foundling Hospital in Florence.

1425
Diplomatic mission of Cardinal Brancacci to Florence.

Campaign by Giovanni di Gherardo da Prato, deputy to Ghiberti on the dome and lecturer on Dante at the University, against the lowering of the curvature of the dome proposed by B.

Execution of the second pair of chains for the dome.
2 January
Contract with Ghiberti for the second pair of Baptistery doors. He is paid 200 florins per year, and his collaborator Michelozzo 100.
May and June
B. is named Prior for the S. Giovanni quarter. It may be in connection with this appointment that he made the perspective painting of the Baptistery, which was the emblem on the arms of the quarter.
28 June
Ghiberti's stipend as supervisor of the dome is suspended as of 1 July.
16 August
Another foundation ceremony at S. Lorenzo, perhaps connected with the Medici double-chapel, or with support by Giovanni de' Medici for a new transept design.
September-December
Filippo is member of the Consiglio del Comune.

1425-33/35
Florence suffers an extremely grave financial crisis with a consequent severe drop in the number of commissions. Many artists are impelled to seek work elsewhere: Donatello goes to Prato, Pisa (where he works for Cardinal Brancacci of Naples) and Rome, and does work for Siena. In 1426 Masaccio works in Pisa with Donatello. In 1428 Masolino — who had previously worked in Hungary — quits Florence for Rome, and Masaccio follows him.

1426
The castle of Lastra is rebuilt at the expense of the Opera del Duomo of Florence.

New fortifications are decided on for Pisa.

Protective tariffs are instituted in favour of the Arte della Lana.

A league against the Visconti is formed by Florence, the Empire and Venice, joined later by Savoy, the Este, the Gonzaga and the Pope.

Donatello is in Pisa (the date usually given, 1427, comes according to Procacci from a misunderstanding of the Pisan calendar, which was a year ahead of our calendar), and Masaccio too is in Pisa.
24 January
Ghiberti, B. and Battista d'Antonio submit a report on the procedure to be followed in constructing the dome. This is the second change in the programme.
28 January
B. becomes the main Provveditore of the Dome.
February-May
B. is member of the Consiglio del Popolo.
4 February
The committee of the Opera and the consuls of the Arte della Lana accept the report. B. is promised a salary of 100 florins a year for his full-time work, while Ghiberti will work part time and receive 3 florins a month.
11-12 March
B. and Battista d'Antonio commissioned to continue work on the dome.
May
B. again Operaio of the Foundling Hospital.
9 August
Contract for foundations of the central cloister of the Foundling Hospital; the columns will be erected only very much later.
16 August
B. commissioned to heighten the walls of the Vecchia Cittadella in Pisa. In the next month he obtains brief leaves of absence to carry out work.
12 September
With Battista d'Antonio, B. estimates the value of the work done on the castle at Lastra.
24 September
B. obtains four days' leave from the Opera del Duomo to carry out a mission concerned with fortification, at the expense of the Ufficiali delle Carni.
5 November
B. consulted on the tabernacle for S. Jacopo in Campo Corbolini, which will be executed by Giusto di Francesco da Settignano between 13 May and 5 September 1427 (lost).
20 December
Ghiberti matriculates in the Arte di Pietra e Legname.

1426-27
Institution of the *catasto* (property tax).

1426-28
Arnolfini and perhaps Alberti are in the retinue of Cardinal Albergati.

1427
Milan defeated by the Venetians, under the *condottiere* Carmagnola.

Bruni again becomes Chancellor, an office he will hold until his death in 1444.

It appears that Martin V has invested ''a discrezione'', that is, in such a way as to earn interest, in a company organized by the Medici to produce woollen clothing.
16 January
Contracts at the Foundling Hospital for the tiled roof of the ward (completed on 24 March).

26 January
B. paid for the last time at the Innocenti, receiving 10 gold florins, the work begin taken out of his hands as of 1 May.
February
Pisa fortifications under construction.
28 February
B. and Ghiberti are re-elected for their tasks on the dome, with the same salary. Agreement with B. and Battista d'Antonio over the cost of the work done on the fortifications at Lastra.
4-14 March
B. is granted a ten-day leave of absence to supervise fortification works at the expense of the Ufficiali delle Carni.
2 April
Another leave, for four days. B. borrows from the Opera del Duomo a long rope to haul his Arno barge.
May-August
Filippo is member of the Consiglio del Popolo.
7 May
B. obtains a letter of recommendation to the syndic of Castelfranco di Sotto for permission for river transport.
14 May
He obtains an advance of 15 gold florins for the transport of marble from Pisa to Florence.
12 June
Another advance of 40 florins for the same purpose.
13 June
A final contract calls for the transport of 100 Florentine tons of white marble entirely at B.'s expense.
12 July
In his tax declaration B. states that he owns a house in the S. Giovanni quarter, and has in the Monte (that is, invested in bonds of the state treasury) 1,415 florins, plus another 420 florins in the Monte of Pisa. He keeps in his house Andrea di Lazzaro Cavalcanti, called Il Buggiano, who has been with him ever since childhood and is treated as if he were an adopted son, and he has a serving woman who does the household work for him. In addition he has debts of about 80 florins in connection with his work.
October-January 1428
B. is member of the Consiglio del Popolo.
October-March 1428
B. is member of the Consiglio dei Dugento.
13 November
B. perhaps goes to Volterra as consultant for the dome to be built over the medieval baptistery.[2]
29 November
B. called in by the six councillors of the Tribunale della Mercanzia, '' among the most notable and wise and experienced men of the five major guilds'', to advise on placing at the Palazzo del Saggio the coats-of-arms of the Università dei Mercanti.

1427
Masaccio paints the *Trinity* in S. Maria Novella.

1428
Death of Gentile da Fabriano and Masaccio in Rome.

Peace with Milan.

Solemn visit to Florence of Prince Pedro of Portugal who, together with Prince Henry the Navigator, has been encouraging the creation of a colonial empire. His relations with Florence continue for several decades, and the visit may have resulted in an exchange of geographical information and maps.

B. is entrusted with work in the Palazzo Vecchio, in the Ufficio del Monte.

Donatello and Michelozzo are commissioned to sculpt the outdoor pulpit of the Holy Girdle for Prato Cathedral. Work will not begin until 1434.

According to the Biographer, in this year B. has his first contacts with a committee for the reconstruction of S. Spirito; but there are no documents earlier than 1434 and the information may be wrong.

Date (meaning the year 25 March 1428-24 March 1429) scratched on the cone over the lantern of the Old Sacristy indicating its completion.

May-August
B. is member of the Consiglio del Comune.
2 May
B.'s barge transported the marble from Pisa to Empoli and Castelfranco but could not proceed farther, so the marble has had to be trans-shipped on small boats, with the loss of about 12 tons.
21 May
B. and Ghiberti are re-elected for the work on the dome.
30 June
A committee named to plan the remodelling of the Chapel of St Zenobius in the Cathedral includes both B. and Ghiberti.

1428-29
Presumed sojourn of Alberti in Florence.

c. 1428-30
Around this time, according to a document now lost but which confirmed what the Biographer reports, B. was paid by the Opera del Duomo of Milan for work on, presumably, the *tiburio* of the Cathedral. In this same period he may have supplied designs also for the remodelling of the castle there.

1429
Andrea dei Pazzi deposits in the Monte a sum of about 4,263 florins in the name of his sons Guglielmo and Piero under special conditions, presumably already intending that the interest be used for constructing a family funerary chapel in S. Croce (information from the tax report of 1430).

January-April
B. is member of the Consiglio del Comune.
7 January
B. and Battista d'Antonio are authorized to construct the third (?) masonry chain of the dome as designed by them and Ghiberti.
8 January
The houses of the canons and chaplains of the Cathedral are unified, replacing the separate entrances with a single entrance which can be kept under surveillance. The design approved is by Battista d'Antonio.
12 February
B. is among the citizens who swear to "forgive injuries, lay down all hatred, entirely free themselves of any faction and bias, and to attend only to the good and the honour and the greatness of the Republic, forgetting all offences received to this day through passions of party or faction or for any other reason".
20 February
Death of Giovanni d'Averardo (Giovanni di Bicci) de' Medici, who leaves to his son Cosimo an enormous inheritance.

23 February
The frame of a window in one of the chapels off the choir in S. Maria del Fiore is executed to a design by B., presumably by Buggiano.
28 February
B. is paid for his activity (presumably as *capomaestro*) for "the work of the Monte" on the basis of the decree of January 1428, which estimated an expense of 300 gold florins now paid entirely to him. His work involved a set of offices in the Palazzo Vecchio no longer identifiable.
April-September
B. is member of the Consiglio del Popolo.
21 July
The positions of B. and Ghiberti at the Cathedral are confirmed for another year at the same salary.
12 August
B. is included in the Libri delle Età, that is, among men who have reached the age of 50 and can be considered for higher public office. In another register he is stated to be over 45.
22 September
B. and Ghiberti are requested to make a complete model of the Cathedral, including the transept and façade.
23 November
B., "architect from Florence", is again in Prato as consultant, and is paid 1 new gold florin.

1430
The siege of Lucca, begun in 1429, continues. Military commissioners in the field against Lucca are Alessandro degli Alessandri, Neri Capponi, and Felice Brancacci (donor of the frescoes by Masolino and Masaccio in the Carmine).
January-April
B. is member of the Consiglio del Comune.
2 March
Letter from the Dieci di Balìa to Rinaldo degli Albizzi: "We are sending with this Pippo di s. Brunellesco... in order that he may put into execution a certain idea and design he has which he explains he has made for the honour of this our Commune and the despatch of our present enterprise."
5 March
"On this said day of the 5th Pippo di ser Brunellesco presented himself, who was viewed and honoured willingly as befits his qualities; and what he requests he will have entirely from us, according to his needs. Who, dispatched from here, returns to Your Excellency."
6 March
Letter from Rinaldo degli Albizzi: "Pippo di ser Brunellesco came here. He has worked out his design. Today he is dining with me, and then leaves to return to you."
1 May
Letter to Florence from the notary Ciaio in the camp before Lucca: "With Pippo di ser Brunellesco I have gone over his design a good deal and brought up with him my doubts that the dam will either leak or will not withstand the weight of the water. To everything he replies with arguments I cannot contradict, though I do not know if this is because I do not know more of this matter. Soon we shall see what will come of all this."
Andrea Billi, a Milanese in the enemy camp, calls B. "mirus haec aetate machinamentorum artifex" (wonderful creator of machines of this age).
June-September
B. is member of the Consiglio del Popolo.

12 June
B. leaves the field at Lucca to return to Florence.
14 June
B. is elected to the Consiglio dei Dugento.
B. is paid for a hundred days of work, beginning 5 March, at the rate of 1 1/2 florins per day as "master of the dam being made around Lucca"; his companions are Michelozzo and Donatello, who arrived in Pisa on, respectively, 20 March and 15 April "to set in order certain buildings against the Lord of Lucca". They were paid 1 florin per day. Other collaborators were Niccolò di Lorenzo and Domenico di Matteo. From the tax reports of 1431 it appears that B. had his quarters at Pontetetto near Lucca, and that during the war he lost a bed (or military tent?) which he rented.
December
43 masters working on the Cathedral dome are laid off. The date "1430" scratched on the fresh plaster, found by F. Falletti and L. Paolini ("Una nuova data per la cupola del Brunelleschi", *Prospettiva*, III, 1977, 11, pp. 57-58), may suggest that the work was interrupted by the war.
14 December
B. re-elected to direct work on the dome alone.

1431
Luca della Robbia begins his *cantoria* for the Cathedral.
24 January
Tax reports of B., who has 1,535 florins in the Monte of Florence (120 more than in 1427) and 1,052 in that of Pisa (632 more than in the preceding report). From his father he has inherited, in addition to his house, after division according to the will, 537 1/2 florins. He is in debt to the Opera of S. Maria del Fiore for the 55 florins received as an advance for the transport of marble on the Arno.
26 January
B. is commissioned to design iron chains to reinforce the unsafe vaults of the nave of the Cathedral. (The chains are installed in 1433-34.)
Together with the *capomaestro* Battista d'Antonio, his regular associate, B. is commissioned to make a model of the "forms and measures and ornaments" for the altar of St Zenobius, to be modelled on the altar of St John in the Baptistery (according to a document of 14 March). Ghiberti also prepares a model.
February
B.'s stipend at the Cathedral is reduced by 50 florins annually because of taxation for the war.
Thirty-nine masters are re-engaged for work on the dome.
6 (actually 15) February
The Priors complain that the work of fortification at Castellina has not been completed. The Operai of S. Maria del Fiore are ordered to complete as soon as possible the fortifications at Castellina, Rencine and Staggia in the Chianti Valley. B. and an assistant, with two horses, are sent to the area to supervise the construction.
20 February
Death of Martin V. On 3 March Eugenius IV is elected. Nine days later he summons the Council of Basel, but dissolves it on 18 December.
23 June
B. and Ghiberti are re-confirmed as directors of the work on the dome.
28 June
B., together with Battista d'Antonio, is commis-

sioned to construct a crypt beneath the altar of St Zenobius.

23 September
B. has his will drawn up by the notary Ser Bartolomeo di Maestro Antonio da S. Miniato.

November
Sigismund of Luxemburg enters Italy for coronation by the Pope. He receives the Lombard crown in Milan on 25 November.

1431-32
Pisanello in Rome, painting in S. Giovanni in Laterano.

1432
The Council does not accept the papal bull reconvening it after 18 months, challenges the Pope to present himself in Bologna, and receives the support of the King of France and the Emperor Sigismund.

Sigismund visits Parma, Lucca and Siena, receiving a triumphal welcome on his arrival in the latter on 11 July, and remaining there nine months awaiting his coronation in Rome.

Once again B., Ghiberti and Battista d'Antonio are reconfirmed in their positions at the Cathedral.

Date (meaning the year 25 March 1432-24 March 1433) incised on the altar in the *scarsella* of the Old Sacristy.

January-April
B. is member of the Consiglio del Comune.

January-June
B. is member of the Consiglio dei Dugento.

22 February
Competition announced for a reliquary of St Zenobius for the Cathedral.

3 March
The reliquary of St Zenobius is commissioned from Ghiberti, the altar from B.

18 March
B. and Ghiberti are paid for their models for the reliquary of St Zenobius.

2 April
B. asks for leave of absence. He goes to Mantua at the invitation of Giovanni Francesco Gonzaga, and is called to Ferrara by Nicolò III d'Este.

27 June-12 August
B., Ghiberti and Battista d'Antonio are to make a model (or models?) for the closing ring of the dome, to be shown as round or octagonal.

22 August
B. and Ghiberti are re-confirmed in their positions at the Cathedral.

30 October
B. to make a model for the closing ring of the dome, showing the lantern as well.

9 December
B. is commissioned to make marble cupboard alcoves and a lavabo for the north sacristy of the Cathedral. The payments for the lavabo, executed by Buggiano, go on until 30 April 1440.

B. is commissioned to remodel a house with garden owned by the Opera del Duomo to accommodate offices, meeting rooms and workshops.

Other documents refer to transport of wood and to new scaffolding to be made for the Cathedral, doubtless in connection with the lantern.

December
End of the agreements made in 1427 for transport of marble: the undertaking has resulted in a grave financial loss for B.

1432-33
War against Milan.

Donatello and Michelozzo go to Rome.

1433
Peace of Ferrara.

Cosimo de' Medici is arrested and condemned to exile, the Barbadori and Peruzzi are banished for ten years and deprived of their civil rights for twenty years, Palla Strozzi is exiled to Padua for five years.

Although among the first candidates named in his quarter, Brunelleschi is no longer admitted among those eligible for office in the Signoria and the Colleges.

Filarete settles in Rome.

Project prepared for Piazza S. Lorenzo.

Donatello begins his *cantoria* for the Cathedral.

Taccola completes his treatise, *De ingeneis*, to which is appended an interview with B.

Andrea dei Pazzi pledges *c.* 11,120 florins for six years for his chapel.

3 April
In S. Maria del Fiore, the wooden partition between the nave and the area covered by the dome is dismantled.

21 April
Decision to do without a tie-rod in the crossing arch of the Cathedral which, according to a statement by B., is unnecessary. The level of the presbytery is lowered, seemingly abandoning the plan for a raised presbytery which would have involved a considerable change in level and probably a flight of steps.

April-May
Donatello returns to Florence from Rome.

31 May
Coronation of Sigismund as Emperor in Rome where he will remain until 14 August, visiting the monuments with Ciriaco d'Ancona as guide. When he finally leaves, the city falls prey to disorder and military attacks.

Tax declaration of B.: he now has 5,354 florins in the Monte of Florence, but there is no mention of a sum in Pisa. He further states, "I must pay Andrea di Lazzaro di Cavalcante, master carver, for a sepulchre and altar plus other works that he has done for Cosimo de' Medici and other citizens, and also in S. Reparata [S. Maria del Fiore], which money has been received by [has been advanced to] myself, Filippo Brunelleschi; this comes to 200 florins". The works mentioned have been tentatively identified as the sarcophagus for Giovanni d'Averardo de' Medici and his wife in the Old Sacristy of S. Lorenzo, with the altar in the *scarsella*, and the lavabo for the Cathedral commissioned in 1432. The "other works" have not been identified.

June
The Priors and Gonfaloniere di Giustizia agree to concede to the friars of S. Spirito part of the revenues from the salt tax, though this does not take effect until April 1436.

September
An anti-Medicean government takes over in Florence. Felice Brancacci, representing the S. Spirito quarter, is one of the Magistracy of the Two Hundred who banished Cosimo de' Medici.

9 September
Ser Filippo Pieruzzi, collector of scientific manuscripts, calls for the appointment of a magistracy to restore order to the city.

15 December
Pope Eugenius IV is forced to recognize the Council of Basel as supreme authority.

30 December
B. is requested to give the measurements for the blocks of marble to be used for the *cantorie* by Donatello and Luca della Robbia.

1433-34
Michelozzo follows Cosimo de' Medici into temporary exile in Venice.

1434
Defeat of the Florentines by the Milanese at Imola.

19 January
A committee is organized for the rebuilding of S. Spirito. They are to find the funds and to decide "eo modo et forma et prout et sicut" for the construction of the church.

25 March
Following a change in alliances, Eugenius IV appoints Francesco Sforza his vicar in the March of Ancona, as Gonfaloniere of the Church.

2 April
The Arte di Calimala, executor for the heirs of Pippo Spano, having contracted with the monastery of S. Maria degli Angeli to build a chapel dedicated to the Virgin and the Apostles, deposit 5,000 gold florins in the Monte.

May
Florence is in a state of economic crisis and is unable to pay the stipend due to Francesco Sforza, who had entered the service of Florence and Venice on 25 March 1434.

29 May
Insurrection in Rome.

3 June
Decision at S. Lorenzo on the plan of chapels flanking the nave.

4 June
Dramatic flight from Rome of Pope Eugenius, who sails from Ostia.

12 June
The dome is closed.

After a perilous journey the Pope disembarks at Livorno whence, with his closest associates, among them Alberti and Cardinal Giordano Orsini, he will finally reach Florence.

Before 20 August
B. is arrested for default, having failed to make due enrolment in the Arte di Pietra e Legname.

20 August
The Operai of S. Maria del Fiore decide to have the consuls of the guild arrested for the wrongful imprisonment of B. One of them is arrested: he will be freed, with B., on 31 August.

28 August
Defeat of the alliance of Florence and Venice led by Nicolò da Tolentino and Gattamelata.

1 September
A pro-Medici government is established in Florence.

28 September
A magistracy of 350 citizens assumes emergency powers. The Medici, the Pucci and Agnolo Acciauoli are recalled, and the Alberti also return.

2 October
The Albizzi are exiled, together with Palla Strozzi and Felice Brancacci.

6 October
Cosimo de' Medici returns to his villa at Careggi.

23 October
Eugenius IV intervenes with a papal bull to request Queen Giovanna of Naples to send back to Florence Buggiano, who has fled to Naples with money and jewels taken from his master.

1 November
New Medicean administration under Giovanni Minerbetti.
31 December
Ghiberti is paid 12 *lire* for a design for the choir enclosure of the Cathedral.

1434-36
Alberti in Florence.

1435
Death of Gregorio (Goro) di Stazio Dati, one of the promoters of the Foundling Hospital and perhaps also of S. Spirito.

B. is rejected from the Consiglio del Comune because of delinquency in the payment of tax.

Alberti writes *De pictura* (the original Latin version), dedicated to Giovan Francesco, Marchese of Mantua.

Operai of Florence Cathedral go to Vicopisano to decide where and how the fortress there is to be built.
January
Cosimo de' Medici becomes Gonfaloniere of Florence.
6 May
A new committee appointed to see to the tomb of St Zenobius.
27 May
"Fortress of the Porta al Parlascio of Pisa to be built."
28 June
B. and Battista d'Antonio are sent to Pisa.
29 July
A commission of five citizens is appointed for the construction of a fortress in the castle of Vicopisano.
5 October
A letter from the Florentine captain Giovanni di Astore, in Volterra, to Cosimo de' Medici mentions a visit of B., presumably sent by Cosimo to inspect the copper mine at Serrazzano near Volterra. The mining master Stefano di Valone was sent for the same purpose, and after the departure of B. made an attempt at fusion to see if the undertaking could be profitable. Minable vitriols (copper sulphates) are reported as present in Volterra in Biringuccio Senese, *Pirotechnia*, Venice, 1540, Book II, Chapter 5. This indication of Brunelleschi's capacities or interests in mining was unknown and not even suspected before the publication of the relevant document by Molho in 1978 (Florence, Archivio di Stato, Fondo Mediceo avanti il Principato, XII, 122). After his death, vases with verdigris were found in his house.
15 November
B. and Ghiberti are commissioned to design the new altars in the three apses of the Cathedral.
26 November
The Operai discuss the projects for the new Cathedral choir submitted by B., Ghiberti and Agnolo d'Arezzo. The commission includes Paolo Toscanelli and Francesco della Luna.

1436
Alberti dedicates to Brunelleschi the Italian translation of his *De pictura*.

Foundations are laid on the north side of the choir of S. Lorenzo.
24 January
B. is ordered to go to Pisa and Vicopisano to inspect fortifications.

9 March
B. submits a design for the long elevated wooden passageway to be built between S. Maria Novella and the Cathedral — across almost half the city — for the solemn pontifical procession on the occasion of the dedication of the Cathedral.
25 March
The Cathedral, with its dome almost completed, is dedicated by Pope Eugenius IV. Among those present is Sigismondo Malatesta.
30 March
Papal bull against the theft of ancient marbles and jewellery from the basilicas of Rome.
3 April
B. requests twenty days' leave to go again to Ferrara and Mantua. According to Vasari, one of the purposes of the journey to Mantua was to build dikes on the Po River.
30 June
Final payment to Ghiberti for his collaboration on the dome of the Cathedral.
14 August
Ghiberti has made a model for the lantern in competition with B. and others.
30 August
"On 30 August, at the third hour, the oculus of the dome was closed and all the bells rang and the Te Deum was sung and the divine office was sung thanking God." (*Diario* of the notary Ser Reccho di Domenico Spinelli)
15 October
B. and Battista d'Antonio are commissioned to make the supports necessary for the new *cantoria* by Luca della Robbia.
26 October
B. is commissioned to roof with terracotta tiles the three apses of the Cathedral. The work is to take six months; the expense is estimated at 400 florins (100 more than requested for the work by Brunelleschi himself), and he is to receive for one year a salary of 100 gold florins.
31 December
For the lantern the model submitted by B. is selected.

1437
Another war against Milan.

This date scratched on the exterior of the Rotunda of S. Maria degli Angeli presumably indicates when work stopped (i.e. between 25 March 1437 and 24 March 1438).
15 January
B. and Battista d'Antonio are sent to the quarries at Campiglia Marittima to select marble for use in the lantern.
5 April
Another trip to the same quarries by B. and Battista d'Antonio.
26 April
The Dieci di Balìa decree that the goods of the rebels of the city and countryside of Pisa are to be confiscated and used towards building two fortresses, one at the Porta del Parlascio in Pisa and the other at Vicopisano.
9 December
Death of the Emperor Sigismund.

1437-46
Construction of the Castello Sismondo in Rimini (officially founded on 22 March 1427).

1438
A gallery in the form of a loggia is built on top of the Palazzo Vecchio.
8 January
Cardinal Albergati reopens the Church Council, now at Ferrara. Later, plague in Ferrara and conflicts between Milan and Venice will lead the Council to leave.
27 January
Eugenius IV goes to Ferrara for the Council.
4 March
The Byzantine Emperor John VI Palaeologus attends the Council.
14 March
B. and Battista d'Antonio are authorized to cut away part of a pier of the Mass Sacristy to make room for the new *cantoria*, a task completed in August.
18 March
Albert II Habsburg, who is indifferent to the problems of Italy, becomes King of the Romans.
19 April-7 May
B. and Battista d'Antonio again examine marble for the lantern in the Campiglia quarries. The vein proves defective, and on 12 November they order marble from Carrara.
28 August-22 October
B. goes to Rimini to give advice and perhaps designs for the castle and fortifications in Romagna. He may also accompany Sigismondo Malatesta to Montefiori, Fano, S. Giovanni in Marignano, Cervia and Cesena. Except at Cervia, important for its salt works, documents indicate the building of walls in connection with fortifications.

1439
B. experiments with new systems of pumping air for the organ being built in the Cathedral, one more undertaking that earns him a derisive sonnet by Burchiello.
10 January
Eugenius IV orders the transfer of the Council to Florence.
22 January-7 March 1443
Eugenius IV in Florence. On the occasion of the Council, several churches present elaborate religious plays using complex stage machinery. In at least one, at S. Felice, B. is personally involved in designing the equipment for special effects.
28 January
Stairs built to the crypt below the altar of St Zenobius in the Cathedral.
27 February
Decision that the exedrae to be built around the dome of the Cathedral should follow B.'s design and be "round".
8 March
Final step towards the construction of the exedrae: decision that the niches are to be flanked by half-columns rather than pilasters.

A commission of eminent citizens concerned with the shrine of St Zenobius decides on the vaulting of the crypt, and the design of the altar above, which is to frame the head-reliquary of the Saint, commissioned from Ghiberti.
26 April
Eugenius IV and John VI Palaeologus solemnly inter the body of St Zenobius in the crypt constructed by B.
2 June
A second stairway to the crypt is to be built.
30 June
Choir enclosure of the Cathedral enlarged in pre-

paration for the great concluding ceremony of the Council of Florence.
August
B. and Battista d'Antonio are sent by the Opera to Carrara to check the quality of marble blocks being prepared for the lantern in accordance with B.'s instructions. The work goes slowly, so much so that on 18 January 1443 part of the first order for 50 (or 48) tons has to be assigned to another quarryman.
21 August
Final inspection at the quarries of Campiglia Marittima, with negative results.
27 October
Death of Albert II Habsburg.

1439-43
Alberti in Florence.

1440
Niccolò Piccinino, in the service of the Visconti, threatens Florence: the Dieci di Balìa are elected, among them Leonardo Bruni.

Work in the port of Pesaro directed by an engineer, Piero da Pozzo.

B.'s name does not appear among those eligible for the Three Major Offices.
31 January-29 February
B. now has in the Monte 2,226 florins, 15 *soldi* and 8 *denari*, to which are added later 290 florins, 5 *soldi* and 1 *denaro*.
22 February
The lavabo carved by Buggiano is installed in the Cathedral sacristy.
23 March
It is decided to send B. to inspect the fortifications at Vicopisano. He is also "to go to Pisa to work out the site and form of certain fortresses to be built in that city by commission of the Commune of Florence". These are the Porta del Parlascio, reinforced at this stage by iron tie-rods, and the Cittadella Nuova.
17 May
Work to be done on the Cittadella Nuova in Pisa.
13 June
B. sent to Pisa for work on the Cittadella Nuova.
29 June
In the battle of Anghiari the Florentines defeat the Milanese *condottiere* Piccinino.
5 August
B. again sent to Pisa.
20 November
Meeting in the Old Sacristy (not yet finished) to concede the high altar chapel, or chancel, of S. Lorenzo to private patronage.

c. 1440
The chronicler Giovanni Cavalcanti distinguishes stylistically between B. and Ghiberti on the basis of the "different will" that each manifests, and applies this also to Pesello and Gentile da Fabriano.

1441
Peace with Milan.

1442
Large sums are set aside for completing the unfinished Palazzo di Parte Guelfa.

In the Florentine Monte the Pazzi have over 12,000 florins, the interest to be devoted for another six years to building their chapel at S. Croce.
2 June
Alfonso of Aragon conquers Naples, whose titular king, René of Anjou, flees to Florence and then proceeds to Provence.

21 July
A second lavabo, for the south sacristy of the Cathedral, is commissioned to be executed by Buggiano. The final payment will be on 23 December 1445.

Cosimo de' Medici pledges to have the work resumed in S. Lorenzo at his own expense. He deposits 40,000 florins in the Monte, the interest to be paid to the Chapter for six years, a concession subsequently renewed several times.
3 August
Eugenius IV proclaims Francesco Sforza to be a rebel and demands the restitution of the territories belonging to the Church. He names Piccinino his gonfaloniere against Florence and Venice.
13 August
Concession of patronage of the high altar chapel and nave (as far as the old high altar) of S. Lorenzo to Cosimo de' Medici.
28 September
In his tax declaration, B. claims "I am old and can no longer profit by my industry" — obviously to be understood as a mere tax dodge. In the Monte he has 3,091 florins, with an annual income of 134 florins and 7 *soldi*. His declaration is submitted almost a month late, perhaps because he had been absent from Florence.

1443
Donatello goes to Padua. He will return to Florence only in 1454 or 1456.

Maso di Bartolommeo is cited before the court of the Mercanzia in consequence of a conflict with the board commissioning the grille for the Chapel of the Holy Girdle in Prato Cathedral. Cosimo de' Medici has B. and Cola d'Arezzo appointed as his expert witnesses, and they consult with Ghiberti and place at his disposal in Florence the model of the grille, a frame, and a panel that is already finished.
7 March
Eugenius IV leaves Florence temporarily.
24 March
First payment of interest on the 40,000 florins deposited by Cosimo de' Medici to benefit the chapter of S. Lorenzo. Work begins on the crossing piers of that church.
April
Church Council summoned to meet in Rome on 7 May.
12 April
B. appointed superintendent (*provveditore*) for the lantern, an appointment confirmed on 7 December.
30 April
Payment for a marble tabernacle for the Chapel of St Anthony or of the Parte Guelfa in the Cathedral, executed by Buggiano (lost).
May
B. and Cola d'Arezzo go to Prato at the start of the month to appraise the bronze grille by Maso di Bartolommeo.
10 May
Date written in red ochre on the left-hand outer wall of the Pazzi Chapel.
31 August
B. is paid 1 large florin for the wooden model of the pulpit in S. Maria Novella, to be made by Buggiano.
September
The Pope returns to Rome after an exile of seven years.

1444
The wooden tower or "castle" designed by B. for construction of the lantern is being built.

7 January
Eugenius IV dines in a temporary chamber built on the walls of the Pazzi Chapel, which is under construction.
8 January
B. witnesses a contract for work on the fortifications of Pisa.
8 March
Death of Leonardo Bruni.
19 May
B. and Ghiberti are called to Prato for consultation on the work in progress on the grille of the Chapel of the Holy Girdle.
16 August
B. returns to Prato to review the designs for the bronze grille, and perhaps reports the opinion of Ghiberti who is unable to join him.
Autumn
B. is perhaps asked to produce a design for a rotunda for SS. Annunziata similar to that of S. Maria degli Angeli.
16 September
B. is sent to Pisa to reinforce the banks of the Arno near Porta S. Marco.
10 October
After a series of battles and political intrigues, Francesco Sforza succeeds in having his possession of a major share of the Marches confirmed.
10 November
At Varna, the Turks repulse a crusade backed by the Pope, composed mainly of Hungarians and Venetians, and win a toehold in Europe.

1445
25 January
Formal opening of the Foundling Hospital (still unfinished).
20 March
The stonecarver Giovanni di Piero del Ticcia undertakes to see that the Carrara quarries supply marble for twelve half-columns for the exedra above the Mass Sacristy, according to B.'s designs, to be delivered in Pisa for transport to Florence at the end of April.
23 April
Renewal for twenty years of the concession of four-fifths of the salt tax to the construction of the new church of S. Spirito, on which a considerable amount of work is reported to have been done already.

1446
The Pazzi have 16,000 florins in the Monte, of which the entailed interest on *c.* 11,000 is designated for several years more for the construction of the chapel/chapter house at S. Croce.

Work in progress on the transept chapels at S. Lorenzo, though some will be begun only two years later.
5 April
The first monolithic column is brought to the site at S. Spirito.
15 April
B. dies in the night of 15-16 April.

The Opera del Duomo subsequently pays his salary up to 15 April. An inventory of his possessions is made immediately after his death (reprinted in Chapter 1, note 9). To his heir, Buggiano, B. leaves about 3,430 florins and his house.[3]
17 April
B. is buried in Giotto's campanile.

Completed at the time of his death are the Old Sacristy and the two adjacent chapels in S. Lorenzo, and the loggia of the Foundling Hospital with the upper storey (the latter built in simplified form).

Unfinished are the exedrae of the Cathedral (except perhaps the one on the north) and the lantern (only the base of which is built), S. Spirito (of which, according to the Biographer, B. was able only to "lay the foundations for some chapels and erect part of the walls"), and S. Lorenzo, where his plan had by then been entirely altered.

The Palazzo di Parte Guelfa and the Rotunda of S. Maria degli Angeli are unfinished and will remain so.

(For useful diagrams, see F. Borsi, G. Morolli and F. Quinterio, *Brunelleschiani*, Rome, 1979.)

June
In accordance with the will of Francesco Galeotti, who died on 28 May 1443, his heirs initiate the necessary bureaucratic procedures for the construction of the Oratory of the Madonna di Piè di Piazza (SS. Pietro e Paolo) in Pescia. The design is attributed to Buggiano, though there is no documentary evidence.

11 August
Michelozzo is elected *capomaestro* for the Cathedral dome and lantern.

30 December
The consuls of the Arte della Lana decide to provide a worthy tomb for the architect who had served them so well.

1446-52
Michelozzo directs work on the lantern and is probably also involved in the continuing work at S. Lorenzo and the Pazzi Chapel.

1447
February
Tax declaration by Buggiano, now master of the house in the parish of S. Michele Berteldi.

18 February
It is decided to bury the body of B. beneath the floor of the Cathedral, with the inscription "FILIPPUS ARCHITECTOR".

23 February
Death of Eugenius IV.

19 May
Approval of the inscription by Marsuppini for B.'s monument.

1451
Date of the dedicatory inscription of the Cardini Chapel in S. Francesco in Pescia, which is attributed to Buggiano.

August
The spur-buttresses of the lantern are built; decision that the volutes will not be monolithic.

14 October-April 1453
Payments for bronze ingots and glass for the windows of the Old Sacristy.

1452
16, 25 August
Michelozzo is discharged from the Opera del Duomo because the workers are not "happy with him".

Antonio Manetti Ciaccheri is appointed *capomaestro* for the lantern and dome as well as other undertakings. To him are no doubt due the volutes of the lantern buttresses, "drawn... on paper" by him (mentioned on 23 October).

1454
The Peace of Lodi ushers in another period of prosperity, during which many aristocratic palaces are built.

23 May
The first column is raised in S. Spirito.

1456
Work begins on the Badia at Fiesole (completed in 1466-67).

1457
Giovanni di Domenico da Gaiole mentions in a letter the model made by B. for S. Spirito.

1459
6 August
Last mention in documents of Buggiano, who acts as witness for a bequest connected with the Federichi monument by Luca della Robbia in S. Trinita.

11 October
Date inscribed on the main dome of the Pazzi Chapel.

1461
Date (meaning the year 25 March 1461-24 March 1462) inscribed on the small cupola of the portico of the Pazzi Chapel.

1462
26 August
Bernardo Rossellino is named *capomaestro* for the Cathedral dome and lantern.

1462-63
Pagno di Lapo working at S. Lorenzo.

1463-65
At S. Lorenzo, chapels off the aisle are under construction on the side next to the cloister.

1465
The old campanile of S. Lorenzo is demolished, which means that the lengthening of the nave has begun.

1466-68
The stained glass windows are made for the lantern of the Cathedral.

1468
19 January
"The structure of the lantern has been finished and completed to perfection with every adornment just as was ordained in the past."

10 September
The globe to crown the lantern is commissioned from Verrocchio.

1471
3 May
A letter from Giovanni di Domenico da Gaiole mentions criticisms by B. of the rotunda designed by Michelozzo for SS. Annunziata.

1477
4 November
Project by Antonio Manetti Ciaccheri for marble facing on the drum below the dome.

1482
S. Spirito is substantially complete, except for the façade, which will have three doors instead of the four planned by B.

1485
First printed edition of Alberti's *De re aedificatoria*, which owes so much to the ideas and practice of B.

1496
5 October and 29 November
Remarks under these dates in the *Libro di Ricordanze* of Vittorio Ghiberti indicate that he inherited drawings showing machinery by B. and the technical instruments of his father, Lorenzo Ghiberti.

Notes

Key sources that occur a number of times are referred to by author's name and date of publication. Full information will be found in the Bibliography.

Foreword and acknowledgments

1. Farulli wrote under the pseudonym N. Castrucci. His text, though late, was based on original documents. See *Vita del Beato Ambrogio Traversari di Portico di Romagna Generale Perpetuo di Camaldoli*, Lucca, 1722, p. 57.

Introduction

1. *The tomb and inscriptions*. The significance of the inscriptions and their location needs perhaps to be stressed. The building in which they are placed was of the highest civil and religious importance, and Carlo Marsuppini, author of the epitaph, held an important political position. Something like six months of discussion preceded the installation of the epitaph. Various other projects to honour Brunelleschi were put forward and rejected (see Poggi 1930, pp. 533-40). The delay is another proof of the existence of a strong anti-Brunelleschi party in Florence.

Marsuppini's epitaph was in all probability the model for the equally famous epigraphs added by Vasari to the end of each of his biographies of artists, and the ensemble may have been the stimulus for the inclusion of a portrait with each biography. (See D. Frey, *Der literärische Nachlass Giorgio Vasaris*, Munich, 1923; L. Sorrento, *Giovan Battista Strozzi*, Strasbourg, 1909; A. S. Barbi, *Madrigali di G. B. Strozzi*, Florence, 1899.) The phrase "arte daedalea" appears in the third line of the inscription: "daedaleus" was a fairly common term of praise indicating technical and architectural ability, found for example in the *Chronicle* of Lambert d'Ardres (*Monumenta Germaniae historica scriptores*, XXIV, 1879, p. 624), where it is applied to the carpenter Louis de Bourbourg.

The epitaph recalls Landino's eulogy in the "Proemio... Fiorentini Excellenti in Pictura et Sculptura" of his *Commento... sopra la Commedia di Dante Alighieri poeta fiorentino* (Florence, 1481): "Filippo di ser Brunellesco, architect, was of considerable merit in painting and sculpture as well: he had the utmost understanding of perspective, and some affirm that he was its rediscoverer or inventor: and in one art as in the other there are excellent things made by him." (See O. Morisani, "Art Historians and Art Critics, III", *Burlington Magazine*, XCV, 1953, pp. 267-70, and for Landino's close relations with Alberti, see the comment by P. Murray, ibid., p. 392.)

Brunelleschi's appearance [3-7]. According to Charles Seymour (1967, p. 36), Brunelleschi's death mask shows him, "so far as such a macabre document can, a generous, witty individualist, slight of stature and small-boned, full of energy and courage, hard on himself and, if one can judge from the anecdotes retailed by his biographer, by no means sparing of others".

Not even the story of the death mask is simple and uneventful. It is a plaster cast taken from the mask moulded on the cadaver. The earliest documentary reference to it is perhaps that of 8 January 1521, when Monte di Giovanni del Fora was paid for "a painted plaster head [which] must be the image of Pippo di Ser Brunellesco". Obviously this could be a second cast from the original mould or a copy of the one made immediately after his death.

G. Bottari, in a note to his edition of Vasari (Rome, 1759, I, p. 462, note 1), speaks of the mask as preserved "in the storeroom of the audience chamber of the Operai of S. Maria del Fiore". In 1930 Poggi recommended that it be placed in their museum, and since then it has been listed in the various catalogues of the Opera del Duomo (see especially that of 1970, ed. L. Becherucci and G. Brunetti, II, pp. 214-15).

The author of the mask is unknown. Fabriczy's suggestion (1892, p. 389) that it is by Buggiano, because he was commissioned to do the bust now in the Cathedral, is logical but cannot be proved. The similarities between mask and bust are not absolute, in part because of the intentional idealization in Classical terms introduced by Buggiano into the monument. Another bust in the vestibule of the Cathedral museum (see Poggi 1930, and Becherucci and Brunetti, op. cit., I, p. 211) has an inscription with the erroneous death date of 1444 and itself dates from the sixteenth century.

Further portraits of Brunelleschi, in addition to the bust by Buggiano, a painting in the Louvre which should be attributed to the School of Uccello, and Vasari's woodcut [3-5], have been proposed. The Uccellesque portrait bears some resemblance to the portrait of an unknown man in the museum at Chambéry, which bears a motto that might well apply to Brunelleschi: "EL FIN FA TUTTO" (the goal is everything). P. Meller ("La Cappella Brancacci", *Acropoli*, 1960-61, pp. 304-06) maintains that the figure at the extreme right of Masaccio's fresco depicting St Peter enthroned portrays the architect. J. Paoletti ("Donatello and Brunelleschi: an Early Renaissance Portrait", *Commentari*, XXI, 1970, 1-2, pp. 55-60) claims to recognize him in the relief by Donatello of the *Presentation to Herod of the Head of John the Baptist* on the baptismal font in Siena. Although in both cases Brunelleschi's friendship with the artists makes it possible that he might be portrayed in their works, it does not seem to me that the likeness is sufficient to justify the identification. At the 1977 Congress Giulia Brunetti suggested that Donatello's beardless Prophet is a portrait of Brunelleschi. For the portraits of artists in Vasari and that of Brunelleschi in particular, see W. Prinz, "Vasaris Sammlung von Künstlerbildnissen", *Mitteilungen des Kunsthistorischen Instituts in Florenz*, XII, 1966, addenda. The portrait attributed to Uccello is reproduced in colour in E. Sindona, *Paolo Uccello*, Milan, 1957, pl. 81.

Brunelleschi's skeleton was examined by the Institute of Anthropology of the University of Florence under the direction of Dr Edoardo Pardini. They found that he was somewhat below average height (1.63 m, or 5 ft 4 in.), and had rather small bones; that he had a slightly brachycephalic skull with above average cranial capacity (1,590 cc, or 97 cu. in.); and that his blood type was 0. See Pardini 1974, pp. 37-38, with illustrations, and by the same author, "Le ossa di Filippo Brunelleschi", *Archivio per l'Antropologia e per l'Etnologia*, CII, 1972, pp. 153-66.

2. The polemic against Gothic had its roots in a much earlier time and is probably not to be understood without reading the fourteenth-century literary sources. The question could be traced to the discourse — in a decidedly anti-Italian key — of the ambassadors of King Charles V of France, who in April 1367 attempted to dissuade Pope Urban V from leaving Avignon to return to Rome. The harangue has come down to us, incomplete, in a manuscript in the Bibliothèque Nationale, Paris (Fonds Lat. 14644) (see M. Prou, *Étude sur les relations politiques du pape Urbain V avec les rois de France Jean II et Charles V*, Paris, 1887, pp. 64 ff.). Petrarch replied vigorously to the accusations against Italy (*Lettere senili volgari*, ed. Fracasetti, Florence, 1869-70, p. 9). In the letters from Coluccio Salutati to Petrarch (1891-1911, I, pp. 74-75) one can see the reaction thus touched off, from which it can be deduced that, among other things, the French criticized Italian music and boasted of their theological school — in Paris, obviously — and their mechanical arts.

A close relationship can be established between Brunelleschi (and others working along his lines) and the literary historians of his time. They saw a watershed between the ancient and modern worlds and they stressed the total and rapid decadence that had occurred: "There came about such great misfortune and such great changes" in the wake of which appeared a few writers, "but it is not possible to compare them with those ancient and medieval writers" (ibid., III, pp. 86-88). Admiration for Antiquity is admirably expressed in this virtually warrior-like personification (ibid., pp. 79-80):

> Antiquity maintained its unsurpassed rank and remained in the field with banners steadfast and immovable [ibid., p. 78]... And in whatever manner modernity may seduce with sophisticated subtlety, believe me, it [Antiquity] wins out in wisdom and eloquence; nor do we succeed in discerning in anyone in our time knowledge as great and significant as the greatness and significance we have beheld in the Ancients.

The most elaborate of a number of attempts to link Brunelleschi's "anti-Gothic" stance with the cultural nationalism induced by Fascism is the article by Carlo Delcroix, an eminent speaker of the time, in *La Nazione*, LXXVIII, 1-2 November 1936, p. 3, on the occasion of the celebrations of the five hundredth anniversary of the dome of Florence Cathedral.

3. Hersey believes that the strips of parchment used by Brunelleschi and Donatello for their archaeological drawings were intended for a general system of proportions of Neoplatonic origin (*Pythagorean Palaces, Magic and Architecture in the Italian Renaissance*, Ithaca and London, 1976).

4. As far as is possible, we have tried throughout to calculate the measurements of Brunelleschi's buildings in the old unit of the *braccio* as well as in metres (measurements in feet given in this edition are to be taken as approximate conversions), though understandably this gives rise to various difficulties. To begin with, the length of the *braccio* is neither certain nor constant, as was shown also by L. Benevolo, S. Chieffi and G. Mezzetti in their study of S. Spirito (1968).

When the official conversion to the decimal system was made in 1808 the following equations were established:

1 *canna* = 5 *braccia* = 2.918 m (9 ft 7 in.)
1 *passetto* = 2 *braccia* = 1.167 m (3 ft 9 3/4 in.)
braccio da panno (cloth measure) = 0.5836 m (23 in.)
braccio a terra (ground measure) = 0.5512 m (21 3/4 in.)

These are late, though traditional, standards, and in fact the length of the *braccio* given by Scamozzi in his comparative table is slightly different. If the module used in S. Spirito was 11 *braccia*, the *braccio* as figured by Brunelleschi would come to 0.5860 m (23 1/8 in.); but in fact it is impossible to arrive at any secure conclusion by measuring this or other edifices. Because of approximations in the course of construction, and also through the wear of time, the measurements we make now of elements indicated with precise measurements in the contracts (the round opening in the Cathedral dome, for instance) differ considerably, though the *braccio* remains more or less in the vicinity of 0.5836 m (23 in.). A newly discovered document of 1434 concerning S. Lorenzo mentions the width of the *paraste*; when this was checked against the building the *braccio* was found to be 0.5966 m (23 1/2 in.). It can be supposed that different measuring instruments were used from one building to another, and that all were in some sense imprecise. The traditional drapers' measurement of the *braccio da panno* does seem the most common.

An important observation made by Benevolo and his collaborators is that one finds, consistently, regular subdivisions of the *braccio* in the form of fractions such as 1/3, 1/2, 2/3 and 3/4 and also 1/8, 5/12 and 5/6. Since the *braccio* was further divided into the *crazia* (1/12), the *soldo* (1/20), and the *quattrino* (1/60), such units may have been used as modules for decorative elements.

On measurements see also L. Bartoli 1977.

1 Brunelleschi and his world

1. The Biography is available in two excellent editions, one (Manetti 1970) with introduction, notes and critical text prepared by a major Brunelleschi scholar, Howard Saalman, and an English translation by Catherine Engass, the other (Manetti 1976) with text transcribed from the manuscripts by the philologist Domenico De Robertis and an introduction and notes by the literary historian Giuliano Tanturli, both of these constituting an enormous advance over the earlier publication by E. Toesca (Florence, 1927). The Saalman edition offers a diplomatic transcription of this extremely thorny text, while the De Robertis edition attempts to reconstruct meaning where there is uncertainty and, in consequence, offers many valuable variants. All excerpts cited in English in the present book (as also all quotations from other Italian and Latin sources, including Alberti and Vasari) have been especially prepared by the translator, Robert Erich Wolf, in collaboration with the author, who has revised his translations, taking into account alternative readings and interpretations. The folio numbers identifying the quotations throughout the text of the present book refer to Cod. Magliabechiano II, II, 325.

De Robertis (1974) and Tanturli (1970, 1975, 1976) (and see also Manetti 1976) adduce ulterior proofs in favour of identifying the Biographer as Antonio Manetti. Among his papers they have found an autograph copy of the statutes of 1420 for the construction of the Cathedral dome, and observe that the most reliable manuscript of the Biography includes five sheets in the same hand but with other paper and ink which replace four preceding folios, concluding from this that such a major interpolation proves that author and transcriber were the same.

The internal chronological evidence in the Biography is quite solid, and points to a date after 1482. Paolo Toscanelli, who died in 1482, is spoken of as having been dead for some time, his conversations being always referred to in the past tense: "according to what he used to say", "as he used to say". To move the date back to 1480, proposed for various reasons by G. Marchini (1961, p. 218; 1965, p. 181) and by Tanturli (1975), the latter on the basis of the chronology of the decorative work in the Palazzo Vecchio, is not convincing. It was only in 1489 that the frescoes in the new halls were completed and in place, as the Biographer himself states explicitly.

In any case, there are two decidedly contrary opinions as to the reliability of the Biography: an extremely positive acceptance by U. Procacci which he finds confirmed by archive material, and a rather emotional rejection by Renato Bonelli, both presented at length at the 1977 Congress.

Saalman (Manetti 1970, p. 32) saw in the Biography a manifesto of the anti-Alberti tendency in the Florence of the 1470s and 1480s, signalling various examples of fundamental differences in the method of architectural projection. His interpretation has been well received, and there is no doubt that the Biography is polemical. Manetti's divergences from Alberti are underlined by R. Krautheimer ("The Beginnings of Art Historical Writing in Italy", *Studies in Early Christian, Medieval and Renaissance Art*, London and New York, 1969, pp. 257-73). One of the Biographer's informants, we are told, was Luca della Robbia, and another must have been Giovanni di Domenico da Gaiole. The "adversaries" are numerous: Donatello, Michelozzo, Antonio Manetti Ciaccheri, and others, many of them collaborators and friends of Brunelleschi with whom he eventually quarrelled, often irrevocably. Still others simply replaced Brunelleschi on a project after having been appointed by the patrons. The polemics that echo in the Biography were obviously fuelled by the fact that construction of most of the buildings was still slowly proceeding.

To my mind, however, one should speak not of a precise current to which a name can be pinned (as Saalman, Tanturli, Bruschi and others hold) but rather of a series of compromises or incapacities chiefly practical in nature. As for Alberti, he is respectfully remembered by the Biographer as a theorist who was concerned with "general matters", and is associated with the writers of Antiquity. Nor should the dedication to Brunelleschi of Alberti's treatise on painting be overlooked, nor the implicit references to his works in the *De re aedificatoria*, these being proof of a cultural rapport well above the wrangling and arbitrary shifts and dodges that characterize the men assigned to complete the projects of Brunelleschi. In any case, the Florentine situation at the time the Biographer was writing is well exemplified in the voting for or against the four doors originally envisaged for the façade of S. Spirito.

2. For the attitudes to Gothic and Antique art see above, Introduction, note 2.

3. For instance, Fabriczy's suggestion, based on the Biography, that the Palazzo di Parte Guelfa must date from around 1420 was almost immediately supported by the discovery of documents showing that in 1422 the use of interest on very large sums was authorized in order to hasten the completion of the construction, by then well under way.

4. A date cannot be assigned to the interview with Taccola: it is found in an appendix to his *De ingeneis* in one manuscript alone (Munich, Bayerische Staatsbibliothek, MS Lat. 197), for which only a *terminus post quem* can be established—after 1433, the year of the writing of the fourth and final book. In the manuscript one finds such dates as 1438 and 1441.

For the relations between Brunelleschi and Taccola, see G. Scaglia (1955-56 and 1966) and F. D. Prager (1968-A). Before the recent editions, graphic documents were published by M. Berthelot ("Pour l'histoire des arts mécaniques et de l'artillerie vers la fin du moyen âge", *Annales de Chimie et de Physique*, ser. V, XXIV, 1891, pp. 433-521), A. de Laborde ("Un manuscrit de Mariano Taccola revenu de Constantinople", *Mélanges offerts à M. Gustave Schlumberger,* Paris, 1924, II, pp. 494-505), G. Canestrini (*Arte militare meccanica medievale*, Milan, 1946), and L. Michelini Tocci ("Disegni e appunti autografi di Francesco di Giorgio in un codice del Taccola", *Scritti di storia dell'arte in onore di Mario Salmi*, Rome, 1962, II, pp. 203-12).

One of the basic studies on Taccola is that of Lynn Thorndike, "Marianus Jacobus Taccola", *Archives Internationales d'Histoire des Sciences*, VIII, 1955, pp. 7-26. Biographical material is found in J. H. Beck, "The historical 'Taccola' and Emperor Sigismund in Siena", *Art Bulletin*, L, 1968, pp. 309-20. For the most scrupulous presentation of the philological problems see P. L. Rose ("The Taccola Manuscript", *Physis*, X, 1968, pp. 337-46), who recognizes as autograph MS Palatinus 766 in the Biblioteca Nazionale, Florence, MS Lat. 28800 in the Bayerische Staatsbibliothek, Munich, and the collection of drawings and notes in MS Lat. 197 in Munich. The first of these was published in part by J. H. Beck, *Liber tertius de ingeneis ac edifitiis non usitatis*, Milan, 1969. See also F. D. Prager and G. Scaglia (1972): G. Scaglia has also published the *De Machinis, The Engineering Treatise of 1449*, Wiesbaden, 1971, with introduction, Latin text, description of engines, and technical commentaries.

For the passage in the Biography see above, p. 79.

5. F. D. Prager (1968-B) gives the currently available documentation on Brunelleschi's experiments with clockwork, along with various hypotheses, suggesting a date around 1398-1405 on the basis of the chronological position within the Biography of the following passage: "and having in the past taken pleasure in and occasionally made clocks and alarm clocks in which are various and diverse types of gears [*mole*], whose efficacy is multiplied by a great many ingenious contrivances all or most of which he had experience of [*aveva vedute*]". This quite precise statement has been variously glossed, for example by A. Simoni ("A New Document and some Views about Early Spring Driven Clocks", *Horological Journal*, 1954, pp. 591 ff., and *Orologi* *dal '500 all'800*, Milan, 1965, pp. 32-36), and E. Morpurgo (*L'origine dell'orologio tascabile*, Rome, 1954, p. 24, and "Ruote o molle", *La Clessidra*, 1965, pp. 31-32). While the system of gearing (*mole*) is certainly the basis of the hoisting machines invented by Brunelleschi, no documentation on these mechanisms survives except in a British Library manuscript (Add. MS 34113, f. 156r), which is certainly later than 1450, and it seems to me arbitrary to correct the text of the Biographer (as do Prager in this article and C. Engass in her translation of the Biography) from *mole*, meaning gears or wheels, to *molle*, meaning springs and specifically clockwork springs — especially in view of the context which refers to groups of gears.

6. In Salutati we find the socially-oriented call for an entirely outward-looking morality, rooted in life and action (1891-1911, III, p. 302):

> And if you provide for your family and children, for your relatives and friends, for the State that you embrace with your whole heart, and serve them and concern yourself with them, you cannot but raise your heart to matters celestial nor fail to please God.

Salutati was associated with the natural scientists of the re-established Florentine Studio, that is with Marsiglio of S. Sophia, Biagio Pelacani and Jacopo da Forli, who went to Florence between 1388 and 1394, and derived from them the theory of impetus. See R. G. Witt, "Salutati and Contemporary Physics", *Journal of the History of Ideas*, XXXVIII, 1977, pp. 667-72.

For the polemic by Salutati and other humanists against Gothic and in favour of Antiquity see Introduction, note 2.

7. For the knowledge of Antique monuments in the fourteenth century, see W. S. Heckscher, *Die Romruinen. Die geistigen Voraussetzungen ihrer Wertung im Mittelalter und in der Renaissance* (Hamburg University dissertation), Würzburg, 1936. The key names are Petrarch, Cola di Rienzo, Dondi, Boccaccio, Fazio degli Uberti, and in Florence especially Niccolò Niccoli. For the visual arts, see Gombrich 1967 and Janson 1968.

8. See J. H. Beck 1978, which was generously lent to me in manuscript before its publication. On the Palazzo del Saggio see also Chapter 2, note 27.

9. The fact that Brunelleschi and Ghiberti were both wealthy was stressed by Martin Wackernagel (*Der Lebensraum des Künstlers in der florentinischen Renaissance*, Leipzig, 1948) and, for Ghiberti specifically, by the Krautheimers (1956/70, I, pp. 7-9), who equate his annual income at the peak of his career with that of the director of an agency of the Medici bank. In 1427 Ghiberti had over 700 florins on deposit in the Monte; four years later this had risen to 1,307, with an additional 500 by 1446, a sum successively invested in land and houses, and he also received such property in payment for his work.

The most complete edition of Brunelleschi's tax declarations is in the forgotten essay by R. Graves Mather, "Documents mostly new relating to Florentine painters and sculptors of the fifteenth century", *Art Bulletin*, 1948, 1, pp. 50-53.

Although everything indicates that by mid-life Brunelleschi had become a relatively wealthy man, the inventory of his possessions made immediately after his death — found recently and published by

Anthony Molho (Molho 1977) — suggests that his life was modest indeed, with no books (i.e. manuscripts) in his house other than an old and large manuscript of part of the Bible, though that is something not often found in the hands of a bourgeois or even an artist.

The inventory describes a two-storeyed house with a cellar. The furniture and blankets are modest; the clothes on the other hand are varied and rich. In addition to an incomplete manuscript of the Bible comprising the four major Prophets, there is a small painting of the Virgin, and an organ without pipes. In the room of a helper, Domenico di Pietro, there are drawings, 'several figures in plaster', and tools for carving. In the attic there is 'a building with iron instruments' (perhaps an architectural model), and a copper alembic, perhaps to produce the verdigris preserved in 46 vases. In the cellar there are tree military shields, an iron ball, and a further 50 vases for verdigris. Note too in the list the mention of a drawing on parchment of the Palazzo Vecchio.

No attempt will be made here to translate the inventory: archaic words present too many cruxes, and one would be forced to make guesses and interpretations. The reference for the document is Florence, Archivio di Stato, Notarile Anticosimiano, P 247 (1440-63), II, ff. 8r-9r.

f. 8r:

In primis in scriptorio existentia
Una panca pro sedendo et unum scanum et unum scanellinum cum tribus petiis assidum supra caput.
Unam partem Bibbie, voluminis magnis, all'anticha, IIII or propheti maiores.
   In camera
Una lectica bracchiorum quattuor et dimidii ingessata cum una cultrix
duo primaccia et una materassa
unum par lintiaminum
unus pannus rubeus, bucatus in medio
una cultrix alba
una panca circa lectum, unus lectuccius, una capsecta ad unum serramen, una alia capsa ad unum serramen, plena scripturarum, duo forzeria antiqua, una capsetina, unum cappellinarium parvum, una tabuletta Nostre Domine, duo enses, duo paria bisacciarum, duo paria savalium, unum descussium da parto
una cioppa nigra cum manicis apertis, foderata de taffettà rubeo
una clamis nigra ad eius dorsum, unum par caligarum nigrarum solatarum
unum capputeum nigrum, unum sciugatoiettum grossum, unum guarnelletum album, unum lintiamen ad tria tela cum dimidio, quattuor camisie fracte, duo canavacci tristes a manibus, una farsata pro elmetto drappi gialli, duo supravestes valesci et drappi, due banderuze valesci et drappi
unum farsitium album ab homine, unum gamurrinum bianchette, unum capputeum nigrum, unum par caligarum nigrarum factarum, aliqui censi azurri cum una berretta azurra, una camisia a puero, unum dimidium lenzuoli, una cappellina,

f. 8v:

duo paria chaligarum nigrarum fractarum et tristium, unum par caligarum bigellarum solatarum, unum par forfichum a sartore, unum petium tovagliacce, una cioppetta nigra cum manisis artis, duo cappelli beveris nigri et unum cappellum palearum, unum par calcearum, unum tappettum brachiorum trium, triste.
   In sala
Una sechia a puteo, una sechia ab aquario, tres panche regolate, una tabula cum duobus trespolis, unum designum corii cum disegno palatti Dominorum, una seggiola, unum tappetuzum triste prope murum.
   In secundo palco
Una catena ab igne, unum par mollarum, unum alare et unum tripedem, una paletta, unum schidoncinum, tres lucerne, tres schidones inter magnos et parvos, una

padella, quinque petia carnium salatarum, una stadera, unus orciolus ramis, una grattugia, viginti taferia, sex lentiamina tristia, una camisia, tres mantiletti tristes, una birretta alba cum duobus cuffionibus, unum celone vetus, una seggiola et una predella, una capsapancha as duos serramina, una panchetta senex cum duobus schannis, unum bariglione, sex fiaschi, unum deschettum.

   In camera superiori, que dicuntur esse Dominici
   Pieri, qui stabat cum eo in eius domo, reperiuntur
Unum lectum fulcitum materassa, saccone, copertorio, primaccio et uno pari lentiaminum, una capsapancha ad tria serramina, unum schannum, plures carte disegnate et plures fighure gessi et cum pluribus ferramentis pro laborando.
   In palco et camera superiori
Quadraginta sex vasa cum verderame, una lectica brachiorum 40r, una coltricetta cum uno primaccio et materassino chapechi et uno copertoietto triste, tria vasa a bucato, unum coppum ab oleo, unum paiolettum, una schala a pivolis, una seguccia, plures stoviglie terre et plura legnamina, unum hedificium cum pluribus ferramentis, unum mortarium, unum organum sine sufolis, una carriuola a puteo, unum candellaerium ottonis, una boccia ramis pro stillando.

f. 9r:

   In sala terrena
Unam catastam lignorum
tres palvesi, unum catinum ramis, una palla ferri
   In stalla
V salve lignorum pro ardendo.
   In volta
Duo botticelli, unum vacuum et unum cum quasi una salma vini, unum urceum ab olio, una pevera.
   In camera terrena
Unum urceum ab oleo, una veges cum aceto, 50 tegamina terre pro tenendo verderame, unum molendinum a secco, unum circulum ferri.

The connections between Brunelleschi and the political élite of Florence are impressive. He was elected to the councils of the city 22 times between 1400 and 1432. The councils were the Consiglio del Popolo, on which he served four-month terms voting on bills presented by the Signoria; the Consiglio del Comune, on which he again served four-month terms voting on the same laws; and the Consiglio dei Dugento, concerned with military and international affairs. His name disappears from the lists between 1405 and 1418, and again after 1432. The chronology suggests a close relation with the Albizzi party, and the opposition of the Medici party.

10. Brunelleschi's relations with Milan remain uncertain: indeed, one suspects that it was precisely the brilliant, if unsuccessful, proposal to use water against Lucca (for which see Chapter 11) that aroused Milanese admiration. See in particular the letter of Andrea Billi, correspondent of the Duke of Milan, in our Chronology under the date 1 May 1430.

11. See C. Gilbert, "The Earliest Guide to Florentine Architecture, 1423", in *Mitteilungen des Kunsthistorischen Instituts in Florenz*, XIV, 1969-70, pp. 33-46.

2 Goldsmith and sculptor

1. F. Hartt, "Art and Freedom in Quattrocento Florence", *Essays in Memory of Karl Lehmann*, ed. Lucy Freeman Sandler, New York, 1964, pp. 114-31.

2. According to a new reading of the documents: see A. Guidotti, "La 'matricola' di Ser Brunellesco orafo", *Prospettiva*, III, 1977, 9, pp. 60-61. Brunelleschi's oath as master was sworn on 19 December 1398; his official matriculation was delayed until 2 July 1404.

For the suggestion that Brunelleschi was away from Florence see J. T. Paoletti, "Nella mia giovanile età mi partii ... da Firenze", 1979.

3. Salutati is quoted here from L. Gai, "Frammenti di un codice sconosciuto di Coluccio Salutati", *Motivi di Riforma tra '400 e '500* (Memorie domenicane, no. 3, n. s.), 1972, pp. 302-06.

In the following paragraph, for Cennini I refer to *Il libro dell'arte o trattato della pittura di Cennino Cennini*, ed. G. and C. Milanesi, Florence, 1859, p. 2, and for Sacchetti to *Le Novelle*, ed. O. Gigli, Florence, 1860-61.

4. I accept the date of 1386 proposed by Milanesi in his edition of Vasari, II, Florence, 1906, pp. 330, 396.

5. For the situation of the goldsmith's art when Brunelleschi was young see two exhibition catalogues, *L'Oreficeria nella Firenze del Quattrocento*, Florence, 1977, especially for the documentary contributions by A. Guidotti; and *Lorenzo Ghiberti, "materia e ragionamenti"*, Florence, 1978-79. For sculpture and goldsmiths' work certainly or traditionally attributed to Brunelleschi see the exhibition catalogue, *Brunelleschi scultore*, ed. E. Micheletti and A. Paolucci, Florence, 1977. The early stages of his career are discussed by Guidotti.

Brunelleschi's metalwork and sculpture pose an extremely complex problem, partly because we lack information — most of what he did having been lost — but also because of the multiplicity of currents and influences in Florence in his early years. Virtually every European style was reflected there, or so concludes an illuminating overall study by Claudia Freytag (1973). For Giovanni d'Ambrogio see M. Wundram, "Der Meister der Verkündigung in der Domopera zu Florenz", *Festschrift für H. R. Rosemann*, Berlin and Munich, 1960, pp. 109ff. According to Ghiberti (1947 ed., pp. 40-41) a famous sculptor from Cologne, Gusmin, was active in Italy (about whom, see G. Swarzenski, "Der Kölner Meister bei Ghiberti", *Vorträge der Bibliothek Warburg 1926-27*, Leipzig, 1930, pp. 22ff., and R. Krautheimer, "Ghiberti and Master Gusmin", *Art Bulletin*, XXIX, 1947, pp. 25ff). Another German, Pier Giovanni Tedesco, was active in Florence where he arrived in 1366 and worked for fifteen years for the Cathedral. Yet another Northerner was the Lombard-Venetian Urbano di Andrea, though he is documented only for 1400-01.

For the relationship between architecture and the other arts see the still fundamental work of W. Paatz (1937) and for painting, still not thoroughly studied, see M. Boskovits, *La pittura fiorentina alla vigilia del Rinascimento, 1370-1400*, Florence, 1974; for drawings, see B. Degenhart and A. Schmitt, *Corpus der italienischen Handzeichnungen*, Berlin, 1968 *et seq.*

6. The Biographer writes that "certain figures in silver of good size on the altar of St James in Pistoia, which is very rich, ... [were] allocated to him to do, and he did them with his own hand, being at that time a master though very young." Vasari (*Vite*, ed.

Milanesi, II, p. 330) is more specific about the scope of the task: "half-length figures in silver of two prophets placed at the top of the altar of St James in Pistoia, and considered to be very beautiful", thereby showing himself acquainted with what was probably a local tradition.

7. The archive material began to be explored early in the nineteenth century, notably by S. Ciampi (*Notizie inedite della Sagrestia dei Belli Arredi*, Florence, 1810, p. 80), though his quotations came from the papers of Francesco Tolomei who published them himself subsequently (*Guida di Pistoia per gli amanti delle Belle Arti*, Pistoia, 1821, p. 24). At the end of the century the documents were studied again, and in 1899 the altar figures were brought up again in connection with the discussions of the relief plaques by Brunelleschi (A. Chiappelli, 1899, pp. 454 ff., and 1925, pp. 143-58, 191-201; G. Beani, 1899; P. Bacci, 1905). German art historians of the turn of the century generally rejected the attribution, including the most eminent among them, Fabriczy (1892, pp. 9-17; 1907, pp. 7-10).

8. "Beneencasa" may have been Brunelleschi's master as goldsmith; Fabriczy (*Brunelleschiana*, 1907, p. 9) identified this man as Benincasa Lotti, one of those who worked on the grille around Orcagna's tabernacle in Orsanmichele; his son, Manno, became an inlayer.

The Silver Altar was removed from Pistoia Cathedral in 1943 by the Soprintendenza alle Gallerie of Florence and stored for safety during the war. At that time the embossed panels and silver reliefs were disassembled, as well as the wooden framework that had supported the metalwork ever since a late transformation of the ensemble in 1787. Restoration, begun immediately after the war, was almost entirely completed early in 1950, and the most important elements, not yet reassembled, were then shown in an exhibition in Pistoia catalogued (anonymously) by the restorer, G. Marchini. No written report of the restoration exists, though some information is given by S. Ferrali (1956, pp. 14-17). The notes made during the various phases of restoration by the restorer Salvestrini were destroyed in the flood of 1966 in Florence, but there is good documentation in the Soprintendenza photographic archives, including photographs of the original wooden support of the altar. In October 1975 a photographic exhibition with fifty-seven panels illustrating the altar was held at the Istituto Statale d'Arte P. Petrocchi in Pistoia under the sponsorship of the Ente Provinciale per il Turismo.

After the 1950 exhibition the question of attribution was reopened by the restorer himself (Marchini 1950, pp. 12-14). The arguments, initially presented only sketchily, were taken up again in 1966 by Marchini (1972), and there have also been contributions by P. Sanpaolesi (1953), C. L. Ragghianti (1954), and E. Steingräber, "The Pistoia Silver Altar: a re-examination", *Connoisseur*, November 1956, pp. 152-54. [L. G.]

9. In the contract of 31 December 1399 (Archivio di Stato di Pistoia, S. Iacopo, 5, c. 114v) the Operai commissioned the two sides of the reredos not from the executant goldsmiths, who were from Imola and Florence, but from two companies of Pistoiese goldsmiths, each headed by two exponents of the art who were to have overall responsibility for the execution of the work. To the first company, whose

representatives were Niccolao di ser Guglielmo and Atto di Piero Braccini, was assigned the side towards the sacristy: they "are to make there... on the side, below, two half-length figures of prophets and, above those prophets, St Jerome and St Ambrose, Doctors, and above those figures two Evangelists in half-length, that is, St John and St Mark, and above those Evangelists a rosette according to the design made by the said Lunardo". To the second company of goldsmiths, represented by Lunardo di Mazzeo Ducci and Piero di Giovannino, was assigned the side towards the chancel, comprising "on the side, below, two half-length figures of prophets and, above, St Gregory and St Augustine, Doctors, and above those figures St Luke and St Matthew Evangelists in half-length, and above a rosette according to the form of the design made for them". The work administratively allocated to the first company was to be carried out by the goldsmith Domenico da Imola, that of the second by "Pippo da Firenze", both of whom, according to the document, were to remain in Pistoia.

After work had begun, however, the allocation was modified in order to save silver and perhaps also for other reasons not stated in the documents, taking into account that the side of the altar towards the Cathedral was the most exposed to view and therefore the most important. On 7 February 1400 another contract was drawn up which called for not only a reduction in the total amount of silver to be used but also some iconographical changes (A.S.P., S. Iacopo, 5, c. 115r). To the company of Niccolao and Atto was assigned the side towards the chancel, with the responsibility to make "two half-length prophets and St Jerome and St Gregory full length and in relief, and above those figures St John and St Mark Evangelists in half-length, with such frieze and floral patterns as may appear fitting and pleasing to the said *Operarii*". The other company, that of Lunardo and Piero, was given the side towards the sacristy "on which face they are to have made two half-length prophets and St Augustine and St Ambrose in full length and half-relief, and above them St Mark and St Luke in half-length with those friezes that will be specified by the said *Operarii*". The goldsmiths Domenico da Imola and "Pippo di ser Beneencasa" were to consign the completed work at the end of April of that year. That deadline was not met, however, nor was the work finished, and the reasons for this are not known. [L. G.]

10. According to the contract of 7 February 1400, for each side of the altar not more than 16 *libbre* (12 lbs) of silver was to be used. Yet, on 15 May of that year Atto and his companions consigned 13 *libbre*, 5 *once* and 4 *denari* of worked silver — which would mean the figures and reliefs — and on 16 June "the rest of the work" to the weight of 11 *libbre* and 6 *once lorde* of worked silver: thus, a total of 23 *libbre*, 9 *once* and 16 *denari* of worked silver. Lunardo and companions consigned on 15 May a total of only 6 *libbre*, 10 *once* and 22 *denari* of worked silver (A.S.P., S. Iacopo, 756, c. 79 v).

Clearly, then, the first company consigned more than was due, the second less. Yet the total weight of worked silver is fairly close to the 32 *libbre* foreseen, despite the fact that on 5 May, according to another document, "the aforesaid Atto and Lunardo said that they had in their workshops unworked silver of the said table to the value of about two hundred florins" (A.S.P., S. Iacopo, 5, c. 115 v).

The description of the altar in an inventory of

1401 makes quite clear the state of the work when interrupted (Beani 1899, pp. 32-35):

> On the side facing out towards the Cathedral, at the bottom two half-length prophets, and above the prophets is St Jerome and then [also] above is St Gregory, both in silver in full relief, and above them is [are] St John [and] St Matthew in half-relief and half-length with surrounding frieze with coats of arms bearing squares and shells along with a large flower above the said column... and then on the other side of the column [towards the sacristy] four tabernacles with enamelled pavilions. In the first, St Augustine; in the others for the present there is nothing.

A fact confirmed by later documents which need not be cited here is that since the work was not completed for the side towards the sacristy, an attempt was made to complete at least the other side, the one most visible, and all the available figures were set up there. It was only later, between 1447 and 1456, that the right side was completed, by Piero d'Antonio of Pisa. [*L. G.*]

11. Any consideration of what Brunelleschi as sculptor might possibly have learned in Rome, and of what possible impact he may have made there, must keep in mind what the city was — and was not — in his time. Its political and cultural revival had only fairly recently come about under the French pope Urban V (1362-70), who restored the Lateran Basilica, S. Paolo and St Peter's and set to rights their religious ceremonies — for a deeply moved report see the letter sent to Petrarch on 3 April 1369 by Coluccio Salutati (1891-1911, I, x, pp. 80-84) — and that process was intensified under Martin V (1417-31). See L. C. Gabel, "The First Revival of Rome, 1420-1484", and R. W. Kennedy, "The Contribution of Martin V to the Rebuilding of Rome, 1420-1431", both in *The Renaissance Reconsidered, A Symposium* (Smith College Studies in History, XLIV), Northampton, Mass., 1964, pp. 13-25 and 27-52.

The problem of Brunelleschi's origins is connected with those of what is known as Florentine humanism. To correct the idea that this was a purely local phenomenon one must recall the very close relations of many Florentine humanists with the papal court in Rome and the attempt to open a university there. The inaugural discourse of that university was read by Bruni, and contains the same concepts later used by him to eulogize Florence. It seems that the intellectuals linked with Brunelleschi and the other great Quattrocento Florentine artists may have sought in Rome a base for their activities as well as a forum for the dissemination of their ideas, and from the documents one gets the impression that it was only at a later phase that they settled for Florence.

Yet the names of neither Brunelleschi nor Benincasa Lotti, his presumed master as goldsmith, appear in the registers of artists and artisans in Rome at the time of Martin V and Eugenius IV compiled by A. M. Corbo (*Artisti e artigiani in Roma al tempo di Martino V e di Eugenio IV*, Rome, 1969), nor did anything that could be associated with Brunelleschi come up in the research that culminated in the exhibition, "Tesori d'arte sacra di Roma e del Lazio dal Medioevo all'Ottocento", Rome, 1975 (catalogue ed. by C. Pietrangeli, L. Mortari *et al.*).

Among the works commonly made by goldsmiths were small replicas of buildings, sometimes faithfully copied from Antiquity, as in the reliquary of the hairshirt of Mary Magdalen in the treasury of S. Giovanni Laterano which is dated to the second half of the fifteenth century and derives from an ancient relief depicting the Temple of Vesta in the Roman Forum (see the above catalogue, no. 148, entry by Maria Andaloro). This is an interesting demonstration of the connection between goldsmiths work and architecture.

12. The identification of particular saints is not always easy: see G. Kaftal, *Iconography of the Saints in Tuscan Painting*, Florence, 1952, I, col. 21, no. 12. [*L. G.*]

13. For Brunelleschi's relations with Giovanni Pisano, see among others E. Ybl (1946). [*L. G.*]

14. The plague of 1399-1400 is documented in *Cronache di ser Luca Dominici*, ed. G. C. Gigliotti, I, "Cronaca della venuta dei Bianchi e della morìa (1399-1400)", Pistoia, 1933. [*L. G.*]

15. Impressive photographs of the two panels, from the sides and below, have been published by G. Mantovani (1973); and what one might call structuralist analyses of the panels are to be found in the same article and in C. L. Ragghianti 1972, pp. 187-96.

16. Seymour 1967, p. 36.

17. Krautheimer 1956/70, pp. 31-50.

18. Although no document survives with the instructions given to the competing sculptors, they must have anticipated some of the precepts formulated by Leonardo Bruni in 1424 for the third set of doors for the Baptistery, Ghiberti's "Gates of Paradise":

> I consider that ... the scenes on the new door ... need to have two main qualities: one, that they be splendid, the other that they be significant. By splendid I mean that which can provide good nourishment to the eye with variety of design; significant I call that which has importance worthy of being kept in memory. ... He who has to draw the story needs to be well instructed in it so that he can maintain properly both the necessary persons and actions, and he needs to have such refinement as to know how to ornament it well. ... Now, I do not doubt that this work, as I have sketched it out for you, will prove to be of the highest excellence. However I should very much like to be alongside anyone who has to design it, so as to make him grasp every significance that the story implies.

(Copy of a letter of 1424, Florence, Archivio di Stato, coll. Gori A. 199, ff. 140-41, transcribed in Krautheimer 1956/70, II, pp. 372-73)

19. A highly detailed survey of the iconography of Abraham and Isaac can be found in the *Lexicon der christlichen Ikonographie*, ed. E. Kirschbaum, Rome, 1968, I, especially pp. 25ff.

For the portrayal of character in these reliefs see P. P. Fehl, "On the Representation of Character in Renaissance Sculpture", *Journal of Aesthetics and Art Criticism*, XXXI, 1973, pp. 291-307.

20. In the play as in the reliefs the main theme is the testing of Abraham: at the message of the angel he opens his eyes wide and stares (as in the Brunelleschi relief), "kneeling with great reverence", and has "his desire in all disposed to do the deed laid on him"; but nevertheless his reason and his emotions shrink from the command. Feo, indeed, emphasizes the cruelty of the divine message:

> Consider a moment the very words of that commandment with all its meanings; needful was it not, after "thine only son", to add "Isaac whom thou lovest", unless it were to give him greater pain and dolour, opening every lock of the coffer of his heart.

Equally cruel is the meek obedience of the boy and his logical questions about the purpose of the journey:

> Those words of Isaac were a knife deep wounding the heart of the holy Abraham, thinking as he was of his gentle and fine son whom with his own hand he must bring to death. So many things there were that tempted him not to obey a lot so harsh.

When finally Abraham, "having great thirst to serve his God, wished to obey, as you shall hear", having received the absurd command he tries to convince himself that it is only an apparent test and resorts to a bit of psychological blackmail on the Lord:

> Thou art the Creator Omnipotent and canst make come to pass whatever Thou speakest; and so I can but think and hope that, once dead, he will be resurrected.

In the *sacra rappresentazione* there are two further episodes which, in a crescendo, underscore the injustice of the divine decree: the lament of the mother, Sarah, and the consternation of Isaac upon learning his fate, the latter made even more poignant and pertinent by his certainty of his complete innocence and by his plea for ultimate forgiveness not for any sins of intent but only "if ever it chanced that I, unwitting, in some way vexed you, I pray you have my sins forgiven".

The difference in interpretation is peculiar, and perhaps the interval of forty years does not suffice to explain it. Underlying the different emphasis are disturbing theological changes in attitude and perhaps too in the problem of grace.

21. G. C. Argan 1968, pp. 90-91, and also 1955, pp. 23 ff.

22. The small relief ornamenting the altar on Brunelleschi's panel was vaguely understood by A. Venturi (1908, pp. 129-30) as an Annunciation, "conscious of the symbolic significance of the sacrifice of Isaac which recalls the allusion of S. Paul to the patriarch Isaac as a symbol of the Redeemer". In seeking for typological concordances Venturi thought also that the Classical poses of the two servants were meant to indicate a contrast between the pagan world, represented by them, and the upper part of the plaque with its Christian allusion. However, the relief on the altar does not depict the Annunciation, as was already recognized by Marquand Allan (1914), who saw it instead as a biblical episode of presentation in the Temple, perhaps Abraham presenting Isaac to the Virgin, whereas A. Parronchi ("L'Arcangelo Gabriele con la barba", *La Nazione*, CXIX, 18 August 1977, p. 3) reads it as God announcing to Sarah the birth of Isaac. More convincing is C. Gilbert, who suggests that it shows Elias raising the son of the widow of Zarephat, or Abraham and Isaac coming back to Sarah ("The smallest problem in Florentine iconography", in *Essays presented to Myron P. Gilmore*, ed. S. Bertelli and G. Ramakus, II, Florence, 1978, pp. 193-205).

For the iconography of the angel in flight, see H. W. Janson, "Nanni di Banco's Assumption of the Virgin on the Porta della Mandorla", in *Acts of the Twentieth International Congress of Art Historians*, Princeton, 1963, II, pp. 98-107.

23. Examination of the back of Brunelleschi's plaque shows that the base is entirely flat and of identical thickness throughout. Several bolts are used to fasten the relief sections to the base, and these bolts are more frequent near the edges: four hold the body of Abraham; the angel, Isaac, and the goat are anchored by one each; and three are required for the servant bending over on the right and the *Spinario*.

On the back of the plaque Bearzi also found four holes used for fixing the panel to a support, probably wooden, and two broad vertical slits whose purpose is not clear. All of these were quite ingeniously hollowed out in areas on the edge of the relief of the mountain and tree. There are two other smaller holes piercing the plaque at the top and bottom, at the tips of the cusps of the frame. Two prominent studs, which are also present in Ghiberti's plaque and are therefore surely original, must have constituted the basic system for fixing the elements together.

Bearzi's findings are recorded in Krautheimer 1956/70.

24. This was proposed by Emma Micheletti, in Micheletti and A. Paolucci, *Brunelleschi scultore* (exhibition catalogue), Florence, 1977, p. 26. A less convincing suggestion was made by Giuliano Ercoli in his paper at the 1977 Congress: Brunelleschi's aim was to renounce Antique naturalistic illusionism in order to "link background and figures in a systematically rationalized space".

25. According to the Biographer (f. 296v),

He made a crucifix in wood, life-size, in full relief, and coloured by his own hand, which is in S. Maria Novella in the crossing of the church in the arm towards the old piazza [the present Piazza dell'Unità d'Italia], supported on the pier in the middle between the two small chapels that face the same way as the high altar, and it is the opinion of connoisseurs that in sculpture, and especially among crucifixes, there is nothing of such excellence in the world.

Not a single piece of documentary evidence connects that Crucifix with the one now in the church, but nevertheless the identification has been universally accepted.

The historical sources were collected by Paatz (1940-54, III, p. 711 and note 243, not 234 as erroneously indicated in his text). Opinions as to the dating, for which so far there is no documentary evidence, vary greatly. A considerable group of scholars, among them most recently M. Lisner (1970), judge it to be a youthful work, whereas others like Reymond and Wackernagel have placed it around 1430-40, that is, under the influence of Donatello.

The Crucifix was restored in 1932 by Ferruccio Vannoni and again in May 1977 by Pellegrino Banella working under the direction of U. Baldini. It is in pearwood, made from a single piece except for a small addition to the inner side of the right leg. The polychromy of the original has been restored, with reddish blond hair, brown beard, red streaks of blood, and a "luminous" flesh tint like that in Domenico Veneziano or Fra Angelico which leads A. Paolucci (Micheletti and Paolucci, op. cit., pp. 33-38, and "Il Crocifisso di Brunelleschi dopo il restauro", *Paragone*, 329, 1977, pp. 3-6) to suspect that Brunelleschi was also active as a painter.

While considering the story of a contest with Donatello to be an invention based on the legendary

rivalry between Apelles and Protogenes related by Pliny, Lisner (1968, pp. 128-29) believes that it may have some kernel of truth. In another essay as well (1969) she stresses the importance of the presentation of the nude body, the return to the type created by Giotto in the preceding century, the tranquillity and nobility of the figure, and the "fine treatment" and "ingenious and highly skilled manner" praised by Vasari. She dates it after the Crucifix by Donatello in S. Croce and before Masaccio's *Trinity*, where the same type appears again [103].

26. The proportions advocated by the two principal theorists with whom Brunelleschi was in contact, Alberti and Ghiberti, were based on the male figure either standing or with legs spread wide (as the famous schema inscribed in a circle found in Francesco di Giorgio and Leonardo da Vinci) and therefore may be not at all applicable to the Crucifixus position. The proportional canon laid down by Alberti has, in any case, become more understandable thanks to a drawing in Oxford (Bodleian Library, MS Canon. Misc. 172), published by Cecil Grayson in his edition and translation of the *De Pictura* and *De Statua* (Alberti 1972). Ghiberti gives two canons, one which he calls perfect (in that it was followed by the Classical sculptors) and another, with which he concludes his treatise, which is based on a squaring whose unit is the size of the head. By that he means, however, only the face from the beginning of the hairline to the chin. But those measures do not agree. In the first case we have 9 4/15 faces (combined with the unspecified length of the neck) and *la natura*, the sexual organ, is not in the exact centre. In the second case of 9 1/2 faces, although the upper half is identical a half-module is added to the thigh (though the reading is in fact uncertain).

An elegantly elaborated, but perhaps too clever, geometrical analysis of the structure of the Crucifix by Ornella Casazza and Roberto Boddi, with an introduction by Umberto Baldini, was published in *La Critica d'Arte*, XLIII, pp. 160-62, July-December 1978, pp. 207-12.

27. The most general survey on Andrea di Lazzaro Cavalcanti called Buggiano is in Franco Borsi, Gabriele Morolli, Francesco Quinterio, *Brunelleschiani*, Rome, 1979, pp. 247-59 (documents, by F. Quinterio), and figs. 22-125. The book also contains an uncritical biography by Borsi (pp. 25-33), and a purely descriptive essay by Morolli (p. 182ff.). Concerning Buggiano's style, see Ursula Schlegel, "Ein Sakramentstabernakel der Frührenaissance in Sant'Ambrogio in Florenz", *Zeitschrift für Kunstgeschichte*, XXIII, 1960, 2, pp. 167-73, and "Vier Madonnen-Reliefs des Andrea di Lazzaro Cavalcanti genannt Buggiano", *Berliner Museen*, XII, 1962, 1, pp. 4-9, which is followed by a note by Arthur Kratz, "Restaurierungsbericht über drei Madonnenreliefs des Buggiano", pp. 10-12.

For Buggiano as architect, see the thesis by F. Quinterio (1975), who directed a meticulous programme of measurement and survey, together with a review of all the literature, on the two small chapels in Pescia — the Oratorio di SS. Pietro e Paolo (also known as the Madonna di Piè di Piazza) and the Cardini Chapel. Their authorship cannot be documented. They date, respectively, from after June 1446 and 1451, thus after Brunelleschi's death, though work on the Cardini Chapel may have begun earlier (the date 1451 comes from the dedicatory inscription). See Padre E. Nucci, *Piccola Guida*

Storico-Artistico della Chiesa di San Francesco a Pescia, Pescia, 1914; E. Nucci, *La Madonna di Piè di Piazza*, Pescia, 1936; *La Chiesa di San Francesco. Notizie e memorie per la solenne riapertura*, Pescia, 1930, with a discussion of the Cardini Chapel by Giuseppe Calamari on pp. 27-30; G. Calamari, *Andrea di Lazzaro Cavalcanti detto il Buggiano e la sua opera in Pescia*, Pescia, 1923; other writings, mostly exegetic, by Giulio Bernardini, "Progetto di restauro della Chiesa della Madonna di Piè di Piazza", in *Ricordi di Architettura*, VIII, 1885, fasc. X; Alfredo Melani, "Pescia: Una questione d'arte", *Arte e Storia*, XI, 1892, p. 88; B. Bruni, "Andrea di Lazzaro Cavalcanti detto Buggiano e i suoi capolavori in Pescia", in the daily newspaper *Il Messaggero* (date not known).

28. On the statue of the St Mary Magdalen, the Biographer's statement is corroborated by a reference, which does not mention Brunelleschi's name, has, in the will made by Messer Matteo di Jacopo Corbinelli on 22 February 1420, i.e. 1421 (Florence, Archivio di Stato, Conventi Soppressi, CXXII, fasc. 75, Libro di Contratti e Testamenti, f. 77v) where it is said to be in the Chapel of St Matthew constructed by that citizen and endowed for masses and prayers to be said continually for his soul ("et ibi missa assidua dici et divina officia, et sacrificia celebrari legavit". Although presumably not on the main altar, the *Magdalen* nonetheless had a perpetual light in front of it. The date 1421 can serve as *terminus ante quem*. The information was published, without details, by C. Botto (1931-32). (He gives an incorrect fascicle number, which has been kindly corrected by the Direction of the Archivio di Stato.)

The statue of St Mark was commissioned from Donatello on 3 April 1411 for a niche of Orsanmichele, and occupied him until 1413. Billi (*c.* 1516-20), the Codex Magliabechiano (1537-42) and Gelli (*c.* 1550) state that Brunelleschi collaborated on this statue, something which is possible but not ascertainable through any stylistic analysis (see Janson 1957, I, pls. 17-20, II, pp. 16-21), and also ascribe to the two the *St Peter*, now thought not to be by Donatello.

The perspective decoration of the niche for the *St Peter* was ascribed to Brunelleschi by A. Venturi (1908, 1, pp. 113-14) who was followed in this by others, including H. Kauffmann, *Donatello*, Berlin, 1936, p. 205. For M. Salmi (*Paolo Uccello, Andrea del Castagno, Domenico Veneziano*, Milan, 1938 and later edns) the decoration is more likely to be by Ghiberti (see also Janson 1957/63, p. 224), while for M. Wundram (*Donatello und Nanni di Banco*, Berlin, 1969, p. 31) the marble inlay decoration as well as the niche could be fourteenth-century, a proposal which I think must be rejected except, perhaps, for the vault. In any case, such geometrical and perspective decoration is entirely exceptional at Orsanmichele and, in fact, in Florence as a whole in that period.

During the autumn and winter of 1415-16 an important experiment was conducted by Brunelleschi and Donatello together for sculptural decoration for the Cathedral. This involved "a small figure in stone covered with gilded lead... as trial-piece and demonstration of the large figures that are to be placed on the buttresses [*sproni*] of S. Maria del Fiore", with an agreed payment of 10 gold florins. Brunelleschi, who is identified as *intagliatore*, carver, was found in default on 29 January 1416 and threatened with imprisonment if by 5 February he had not consigned to Donatello the worked lead promised, presumably the drapery that would cover the image, with all the gilding agreed on. There are no further notices concerning this undertaking, and no trace of the model has ever been found. The documents were published by Guasti (1887, pp. 302, 316), republished by Fabriczy with a commentary (1907, p. 11), and have been discussed in all important studies on Donatello.

The tabernacle in Orsanmichele was commissioned between 1423 and 1425 by the Parte Guelfa. It has been variously attributed to Michelozzo (O. Morisani, *Michelozzo*, Turin, 1951, pp. 27, 86), Donatello (Janson 1957, II, pp. 45-56), and Brunelleschi. Bruschi's comment occurs in his "Nota sulla formazione architettonica dell'Alberti", *Palladio*, sez. 3, XXV (XXVII), 1978, 1, pp. 6-44. See also Marchini 1965.

A. Parronchi (1964, pp. 156-81, pls. 41-65) has attempted, courageously, to fill out the corpus of earlier works of the master by attributing to him, for example, the Cross of the Pisans (exhibited in the "Mostra di Arte Sacra dal VI al XIX secolo", Lucca, 1957, catalogue ed. L. Bertolini and M. Bucci), a work completed after 1424 and before 1436, as well as the *portafuoco* of the Parte Guelfa, dated tentatively to 1425.

The tabernacle for S. Jacopo in Campo Corbolini was commissioned by Fra Giuliano Benini. Brunelleschi recommended the purchase of a slab of marble weighing 720 *libbre* from the Opera del Duomo in a transaction witnessed by the *capomaestro* of the Cathedral, Battista d'Antonio. The slab was transported to S. Lorenzo (valuable evidence that some sort of sculptural activity was under way there, perhaps for the Old Sacristy), where it began to be worked on 13 May 1427 by the stonecutter Giusto di Francesco da Settignano. The church, which belonged to the Knights of St John of Jerusalem and was therefore associated with a hospital, was altered in the 1420s, when vaults and a new choir were constructed and the refectory and an adjacent room were also vaulted. The date of these alterations was inferred by Paatz, Lotz, and Siebenhüner from stylistic considerations, and it may be that the tabernacle was made in connection with this general renovation. Benini, who commissioned it, was buried in the choir, and his funeral tablet dated 1451 remains on the left wall. The tabernacle, however, was removed from the church at an unknown date and its present whereabouts are not known. See Fabriczy 1892, pp. 22-24; C. Carnesecchi, *Ricordo di una cena nuziale*, Florence, 1899, p. 7; A. Cirri, *Note*, in *Firenze*, II, 1933, pp. 17 ff.; Paatz 1940-54, III, p. 406, and note 41, p. 410. At the 1977 Congress Parronchi suggested that this tabernacle may have given rise to the new Renaissance type.

On 29 November 1427 Brunelleschi was called in as consultant by the six counsellors of the Tribunale della Mercanzia to advise on the placing of a number of coats of arms in and on the façade of the Palazzo del Saggio. Apparently the decision was that one escutcheon should be placed in the centre of the building between two arches, another at the entrance, and a third in the centre of a vault on the *piano nobile* with the emblems of the five major guilds around it. The escutcheons, described by Vasari as "a lily above a bale which has around it a festoon of fruit and leaves of various sorts so well made as to appear natural", were executed by Bernardo Ciuffagni, who was paid in 1428. Ciuffagni

was sufficiently established not to need drawings or suggestions from Brunelleschi, and James H. Beck, who has published the document (1978), suspects that it refers to a remodelling of the fourteenth-century building opposite the Mercato Nuovo — that Brunelleschi's commission, while it involved positioning the decoration, was primarily architectural.

R. Longhi ("Fatti di Masolino e di Masaccio", in *Critica d'arte*, 1940-41, pp. 161-62) attributed to Brunelleschi a plaque in the Louvre with a very elaborate frame of geometrical motifs drawn with the compass around a scene with the miracle of the possessed woman, in the background of which is an imposing basilica in early Florentine Renaissance style. Salmi and Sanpaolesi favoured instead an attribution to Donatello. Parronchi (1964, pp. 245-49, pls. 92a-b, 93) restored the attribution to Brunelleschi with rather more considered arguments, for the frame as well. He also shows a schematic reconstruction of the plan of the architectural setting in the plaque which is very close to that of S. Lorenzo (about which see also Sanpaolesi 1948, p. 6, and our discussion of S. Lorenzo in Chapter 9).

A wooden Crucifix in S. Giorgio Maggiore in Venice is inscribed with the name of Brunelleschi and the date 1430 (see E. A. Cicogna, *Delle inscrizioni veneziane*, IV, Venice, 1834, pp. 258-59, 312ff., note 144). The inscription and attribution were rejected by P. Paoletti (*L'architettura e la scultura del Rinascimento in Venezia*, I, Venice, 1893, pp. 82-83); G. Lorenzetti (*Venezia e il suo estuario*, Venice, 1926, p. 728, and later edns); G. Fiocco (in *Dedalo*, VIII, 1927-28, p. 448) who proposed instead a Lombard follower of Michelozzo and suggested Niccolò Lamberti; V. Moschini (in *L'arte*, n.s., IV, 1933, p. 278) who found in it a "realistic harshness based on anatomical study in a Northern manner"; W. Körte (in *Kunstgeschichtliche Jahrbuch der Bibliothek Hertziana*, I, 1937, p. 13) who saw it as German; and N. Rasmo (in *Arte Atesina*, 1950, p. 140, and in *Festschrift Karl M. Swoboda*, Vienna and Wiesbaden, 1959, pp. 237ff.) who related it to the work of Hans von Judenburg who was active in Bolzano. M. Lisner (1969) has related it in iconography and style to the wooden Crucifixes in S. Lorenzo in Florence and S. Michele in Bosco in Bologna.

Finally there is a bronze statuette of St Christopher in the Cleveland Museum of Art whose authorship has been shifted from one to the other of the great masters of the early Tuscan Quattrocento with successive attributions to Donatello, Ghiberti, and currently to Nanni di Banco, though it really has nothing to do with those sculptors. From the Biographer we know that Brunelleschi "made other things in bronze and other materials, very beautiful according to the report of his contemporaries" (f. 296v), though it appears that this usually reliable informant had not himself seen them, a fact suggesting that they were either in private collections or not in Florence. While I recognize that it is difficult to establish a convincing comparison with the relief plaque for the Baptistery doors, and that since the statuette is in bronze and not silver and produced with a very difficult technique it cannot be compared directly with Brunelleschi's work for the Pistoia Altar, I think it is important to mention it here, because to the best of my knowledge it has never been discussed in connection with Brunelleschi. Although I certainly do not propose to put forward any attribution, or to claim it as an autograph work by Brunelleschi, the similarities with the facial types

and beards of the Pistoia saints and prophets, and with their gestures, are striking.

The statuette is in solid bronze without added elements in the body. It is incomplete, lacking the Christ Child on the shoulder, for which one can see the holes for attachment, and also the rest of the staff below the hand. There are few traces of engraving, and none of gilding. The date incised in Arabic numbers on the sole of the left foot is definitely to be read as 1407, which makes this the very earliest known bronze statuette of Renaissance character. A connection with the art of goldsmithing is provided by the fact that it was cast in bronze, at the time a specific prerogative of that art. No light is shed by the history of the object. Until 1912 it belonged to a Hungarian family. In 1911 it was exhibited in the Budapest Museum as South German work of the sixteenth century, obviously because of the marked Northern influences that characterize it. It was published in 1925 by S. Meller in his monograph on Peter Vischer the Elder as a work by that great master, but on the basis of an erroneous reading of the date as 1497. The date was corrected by Georg Swarzenski (in *Vorträge der Bibliothek Warburg*, VI, 1929, pp. 34ff.). The closest iconographical precedent is a miniature in the *Boucicault Hours* (Paris, Musée Jacquemart-André), but the subject is rare among bronze statuettes. Other names proposed for the work include Matteo Raverti and Niccolò Lamberti, both of whom were active in Venice. See especially G. Swarzenski, "A Bronze Statuette of St Christopher", *Bulletin of the Museum of Fine Arts*, Boston, 1951, pp. 84-95.

3 The Foundling Hospital

To the publications mentioned in these notes the following should be added: Francesco Bruni, *Storia dell'I. e R. Spedale di Santa Maria degl'Innocenti...*, Florence, 1819, 2 vol.; Luigi Passerini, *Storia degli Stabilimenti di beneficenza...*, Florence, 1853; Fabriczy 1891; Gaetano Bruscoli, *Lo Spedale di Santa Maria degl'Innocenti dalla sua fondazione ai giorni nostri*, Florence, 1900; C. von Fabriczy, "Per il Portico degli Innocenti", *Rivista d'Arte*, I, 1903, pp. 210-11; B. Marrai, "Per l'Arco degli Innocenti", *Rivista d'Arte*, II, 1904, pp. 23-24 (disagreeing with Fabriczy's article of 1903); Ugo Chierici, *L'assistenza all'infanzia ed il R. Spedale degli Innocenti di Firenze*, Florence, 1932.

1. Krautheimer 1956/70, I, p. 262.

2. Brunelleschi's neat façade covered a sordid story, according to the figures analysed by Iris Origo ("The Domestic Enemy: the Eastern Slaves in Tuscany in the Fourteenth and Fifteenth Centuries", *Speculum*, XXX, 3 July 1955, pp. 321-66, especially 346-47):

> of the 7,534 children registered in the ninety years covered by the books of the Spedale degl'Innocenti and that of San Gallo (1395 to 1485), 1,096 (i.e. fourteen per cent) are specifically mentioned as having slave mothers, while this may well also have been true of others whose parentage is not specified. And at Lucca, at the beginning of the fifteenth century, no less than one third of the foundlings (55 out of 165) were the children of slaves.

Foundlings were presented by top households, like

the Adimari, Bardi, Capponi, Cerretani, Medici, Della Stufa, Pitti, Rucellai, Salviati, Strozzi, Tornabuoni and Vespucci, and not only by the lower social classes, mostly as a result of illegitimate pregnancies. A slave lost value when she became pregnant, but she could be hired out as a wet nurse. The newborn children, who belonged to the owner of the slave, "as a calf belongs to the owner of the cow", gained considerable advantages by being sent to a foundling hospital: "they were considered, in spite of their parentage, free and legitimate 'since the Hospital is their free and legitimate father'." The hospital safeguarded the future of the children, should they be adopted, with a full notarial deed, and also opened the way to important careers.

3. The history of the Hospital is amply and precisely documented in the account books now transcribed by Don Attilio Piccino and Dr Enzo Casetti, and we are indebted to the former for particular enlightenment. At present only a selection of the relevant material has been published: it is to be hoped that the entire corpus of documents will follow as rapidly as possible, since a partial culling is no basis for a reliable historical reconstruction of the facts. This is all the more desirable because for once, to our good fortune, competence in dealing with archive material was accompanied by the opportunity to follow the restoration and to have certain tests and investigations made in the foundations, walls and ceilings which invariably proved scientifically productive.

The archives were explored and in part published by F. L. Jochem as early as 1936, with an impressive and thorough social analysis of the relationship between cost of materials, labour costs, etc. Saalman (1965, p. 43, note 47) also announced a forthcoming publication of the relevant documents in collaboration with Father A. Cardoso Mendes. Other documents concerning the Hospital were published by Attilio Piccini in the introduction to *Il Museo dello Spedale degli Innocenti a Firenze*, ed. Luciano Bellosi, with contributions by Piccini and Grazia Vailati Schoenburgh-Waldenburg, Milan, 1977. What follows is a chronology based on documents, mostly published, compiled by my student Marcello Mascagni and drawn also in part from the volume by Guido Morozzi and Attilio Piccini (1971), with corrections for which I am indebted to Don Attilio.

All the material is housed in the Archives of the Foundling Hospital. LM = Libri di Muraglie (Archive Series VII), with separate volumes identified by letters; LDC = Libri di Debitori e Creditori (Archive Series CXX), with similar identifications; LR = Libri di Ricordanze (Archive Series XII), LC = 1° Libro dei Conti, A.

1410

Foundation of the Hospital, in the will of Francesco Datini, dated 31 July 1410. (Lapo Mazzei, *Lettere di un notaro a un mercante del secolo XIV*, ed. C. Guasti, Florence, 1880, II, p. 275).
The first account book dates from 1419-20.

1419

The Arte della Seta acquire from Rinaldo degli Albizzi the land for construction of the Hospital, an area of "staio 70 achorda" (70 *stai* measured by cord lines) (LM, A, *carte fine*). In the second half of this year work begins (No. 1, LDC, 167).
1 May Appointment of the Operai.
6 August Preparation of the foundations (excavation

and filling with gravel and rubble) is commissioned from Ambrogio di Leonardo, and on the following day transport of the materials is contracted for.
October The first foundations are laid for the area of the colonnade, and also the first stretch of foundations where the doors of the loggia will be placed (a length of 124 *braccia*).
November Payment of the first instalment of the 1,000 florins left by Datini, a transaction contingent on initiation of work.

1420

24 March Payment of a total of 592 *lire* and 4 *soldi* for the foundations of the loggia (LC).
7 June Payment for the foundations of the part of the church towards the city, a length of 106 *braccia* (LC).
6 August The Ufficiali delle Torri give permission to build a stairway in front of the loggia that will occupy 3 *braccia* of public land (Ser. IX, no. 1, *Testamenti e Donazioni*, 1411-1574, 21).
17 August Contract with Jacopo d'Agnolo di Bono for transport of columns and hewn stone for the doors (LC).
20 October The first column is brought to the site (LC). The Hospital receives another instalment of the Datini bequest.
20 December Eleven "pilasters" (plinths under the columns) set up in an area of 120 square *braccia* (LC).

1421

4 January The raising of the first column allocated (LC).
29 January The first column — the one in front of the door of the church — is erected (No. 1, LM, 1419-20, 14) (payment on 1 February). A few days later the second, third and fourth columns are raised, of which only one has a capital (ibid., 55).
21 February First payment to Brunelleschi: 15 florins for drawing of the pilasters, doorposts, and sills for the doors (the models in walnut and poplar executed by Giovanni d'Agnolo) (No. 2, LM, B, 1;. Raising of the first pilaster "6 *braccia* long" that closes off the façade (LM, B, 1421-35, 6-24). The first pediments over the doors towards the church of SS. Annunziata are set in place (ibid., 4). Decision of the Signoria to concede to the hospital the same rights as other charitable institutions.

1422

The church is given its ashlar windows-frames (No. 1, LDC, 51). Consignment of half-capitals or corbels and other elements for the loggia (No. 2, LM, B, 24).
16 March By this date, 4,914 *braccia* of foundations and 4,253 *braccia* of walls above ground had been built, of which 160 *braccia* were demolished to accommodate five large doors, each of 32 square *braccia*, plus 46 *braccia* for entrances and windows (above ground) (LDC, 1421-35).
May Brunelleschi no longer listed as Operaio; from April 1421 to April 1422 he appeared among the Operai of the Silk Guild "as representative of the mercers and goldsmiths" (No. 2, LM, B, 1).
7 July Work allocated for the church and the roof of the childrens' ward (LDC, B, 1421-35).
8 July All the columns of the loggia are in place, and the first portion of the shed roof of the church is paid for (No. 2, LM, B, 176).
September Work done by this date comprises the piercing of 5 large doors (3 opening off the loggia of the Hospital and 2 low ones at the entrance to the

ward), 2 small doors, one at each end of the loggia, 10 columns of the loggia complete with base, capital and abacus, 10 corbels inside the loggia, 4 pilasters with capital, base and abacus flanking the two outer bays of the loggia (LDC, 1421-35).
13 November Ten florins are paid to Brunelleschi "for part of the work he has done and is doing in building the Hospital" (No. 1, LDC, 1421-35, 35).

1423

March Foundations are laid for the two small rooms on either side of the entrance corridor leading to the cloister (LM, B, 175) [*30d*]. The stone ornamentation of the first door is installed (LM, B, 31).
April Notations in the account books for 4 door jambs, 2 doorposts, 2 sills "for the two small doors to be made for the small rooms that are in the corridor of the entrance to the cloister". These "are wrought on the same model as the two at the ends of the portico" [*39, 40*]. The balance of the account for the roof of the church is paid (No. 1, LCD, 79). Payment is made for the bricks of the crowning cornice below the roof (No. 1, LDC, 58).
September Brunelleschi is called back to Florence from Pistoia (No. 2, LM, B, 86).

1424

March Arches and centering for the loggia begun (No. 1, LDC, 80).
4 May Contract between the Operai and Romolo di Lorenzo for the loggia vaults, according to decisions by Brunelleschi (No. 2, LM, B, 177).
6 May The stonemasons Albizio di Piero and Piero d'Antonio are commissioned to make the architrave, cornice, and roundels to be placed above the arches of the loggia as in the design by Brunelleschi. The 10 roundels are to be large enough to touch the upper moulding of the arches as well as the architrave [*42*]; their structural character is stressed by the fact that they are concave. The architrave is to be 1/4 *braccio* high (14.4 cm or 5 5/8 in.) and 2/3 *braccio* broad (37.8 cm or 14 7/8 in.) (No. 2, LM, B, 177); above it is the cornice, 3/4 *braccio* high (43.5 cm or 17 7/8 in.). Today one can still see that the original large slabs of the cornice do not correspond to the smaller stones of the architrave which rests directly on the arches.
19 May Brunelleschi is paid in cash as an independent self-employed architect (No. 1, LDC, 90).
9 July Allocation of work on the walls for the children's ward which will be completed on 19 June 1426 (LDC, B, 1421-35).
21 July Contacts with Brunelleschi again in Pistoia (No. 1, LDC, 96).
September The shallow domes of the loggia are under construction, and therefore postdate Brunelleschi's stay in Pistoia. The first dome constructed is that in front of the church (No. 1, LM, B, 177r).
4 October-22 November The chains (tie-rods) for the ten columns of the loggia are made. (There is also mention of eight square chains to be put around the vaults) (LC).
1 December The furnishing of material for the vaults is completed (No. 1, LM, B, 177r).

1425

30 April-4 May 5 roundels of ashlar above the colonnade of the loggia, and 61 *braccia* of cornice and architrave, likewise in ashlar, are paid for and put in position (LDC, B, 1421-35). A further 61 *braccia* of cornice and architrave, along with another 5 ashlar roundels, are installed and a different person is paid

for them (LM, B, 96r). The 9 arches plus the end bays framed by pilasters come to a total length of 121 *braccia*.
10 August 1,433 square *braccia* of rough temporary roofing and tiling done above the vaults of the loggia (LDC, B, 1421-35).

1426

May Brunelleschi is again among the Operai of the Hospital (No. 1, LDC, 138r).
19 June Children's quarters completed (LDC, B, 1421-35).
9 August Work allocated for the first square of the foundations of the central cloister, or men's cloister (LDC, B, 1421-35).

The 28 brackets in walnut and the 14 cross beams for the wooden ceiling of the ward are ordered [*48*] (LM, B, 181).

1427

16 January Allocation of the work on the tiled roof of the Hospital (LDC, B, 1421-35).
26 January Brunelleschi is paid 10 gold florins for the balance of his salary (No. 1, LDC, 146). The total sum received by him between 21 February 1421 and 26 January 1427 is 45 gold florins.

In the act recording his replacement there was also provision for the enlargement of the Hospital by lateral extension, and it was on that point that an irreconcilable conflict must have risen. The crisis can be dated between 26 January and 1 May 1427. In January the situation was as follows [*32*]. The ground plan was U-shaped, consisting of the front range, church and ward. The loggia comprised 10 columns, 4 pilasters (2 at each end), 10 roundels between the 9 arches, 122 *braccia* of architrave and cornice, 3 large doors in the loggia, 2 doors equal in size to them between the pilasters on the sides at the level of the piazza, and 2 small ones at the ends of the loggia. The church was roofed, the walls of the ward built, the two small rooms flanking the central entrance were almost ready, but the central cloister had only been excavated. The upper storey with windows did not yet exist; the roof of the loggia rested on the cornice and above it the gable-ends of the church and ward were visible. In 1427, when Brunelleschi was paid for the last time, the vaults of the loggia were covered by a rough roofing (timberwork and tiles). According to the documents this roof was supported by 26 small pilasters in masonry on the side of the eaves (in all 38 *braccia* long and 1/2 *braccio* wide) and a further 31 pilasters on the opposite side.
24 March The roof of the ward is completed (LDC, B, 1421-35).
27 April 353 square *braccia* of wall built in the cloister, to serve as foundation for the colonnades (LDC, B, 1421-35).
1 May First appearance of the name of Francesco della Luna, which remains in the documents until 1430 (LDC, B, 1421-35). Foundations begun on the garden side for the infirmary, lavatorium, granary, kitchen, and refectory (LM, B, 160, 164).

1429

11 May Payment for roof and chimneys for the church and loggia (LDC, B, 1421-35).
18 October 3,531 square *braccia* of foundations are laid, on one side extending from the central cloister towards the garden, on another to the south [*30d*, right] of the ward and adjoining the second cloister (the women's cloister) (LDC, B, 1421-35).

1430

15 May Allocation of work on the addition to the south end of the façade (LDC, B, 1421-35).

1431

10 March 2,000 roof tiles are required to cover all or part of the extended children's and women's quarters (LDC, B, 1421-35).

1435

17 June Paving bricks are supplied for the rooms, together with roofing tiles (LDC, B, 1421-35).

1436

Slabs are supplied to face the wall of the basement below the two pilasters of the addition at the south end of the façade. The stonecutting work was perhaps finished earlier (LM, D).
23 March Women's refectory roofed (No. 3, LM, D, 71).

1437

February Francesco della Luna authorizes the working of 19 round columns with base and capital plus 4 columns for the corners (for the women's cloister) and a hollow one with superimposed rings to be used as a drain (No. 3, LM, D, 103). The rooms between church and dormitory are roofed for a total of 42 *braccia*. The outer face of the wall above the loggia is partly dismantled to make room for an additional cornice.

1438

26 January 15 pieces of cornice are made and set on the façade above the loggia, to run below the windows (LM, D).
14 March 24 columns with base and capital erected in the women's cloister (No. 3, LM, D, c. 84). Construction of a covered balcony or gallery (*verone*) for the women and of two *veroni* at the end of the children's ward (No. 2, LM, D, 167-93).

1439

May Payment for white and red marble for the coat of arms of the Silk Guild (No. 4, LM, E, 23).
12 August Payment for the wood for the large roof of the façade range (LM, E).
3 November Stonecutting work for the storey above the loggia: stones are hewn to make window surrounds, the frieze above the windows, the pediment above those windows, the cornice for the front wall of the ward and the cornice beneath the consoles supporting the roofs on the façade, completed in its present form (LM, E).

1440

February Wood is supplied for the floor above the loggia and the gutters on the piazza side (No. 4, LM, 43, 47, 53, 57).
March Work is resumed on the church (No. 4, LM, E, 73, 75, 83).
August Allocation of contract for paving the central cloister and the women's cloister (No. 4, LM, E, 59).

1441

Women's cloister paved (No. 4, LM, E, 85-89).

1444

20 December Allocation of 20 columns with base and capital, 26 (or 24) corbels to be placed opposite the capitals of the columns, 4 imposts for the arches above the columns, and a moulding for the arches

facing inwards in the cloister (No. 4, LM, E, 119).
12 December Planks and battens are prepared for the centering of the arcades of the central cloister (No. 4, LM, E, 119).

1445

25 January Formal inauguration of the Hospital, though the work is not yet finished (Ser. V, no. 1, *Liber Artis*, P.S.M., 49).
10 March Allocation of 120 *braccia* of architrave for the central cloister (LM, E). The name of Francesco della Luna appears for the last time (1445?).

To construct the "Prior's quarters" the loggia range is heightened on the cloister side, with access by a new stairway in a corner of the cloister near the church (No. 4, LM, E, 209). This is another major alteration to Brunelleschi's plan: with the addition of an extra storey the first two one-light windows of the church and the children's dormitory opposite are blocked (No. 4, LM, E, 112-90).

1449

The central cloister is paved (No. 4, LM, E, 205). Work in progress on completion of the church (No. 4, LM, E, 209).

1451

April 2,030 large floor-tiles (*mezzane campigiane*) are acquired for paving beneath the church, that is, the crypt divided by a row of piers along its length (No. 4, LR, 12).

1457

20 August Bernardo di Matteo (Rossellino) is commissioned to plaster the entire façade, and to complete the steps and paving of the loggia (No. 4, LR, 159-60). The approach to the loggia is raised by two steps from five to seven, probably in connection with work on the piazza itself.

Rossellino is paid for redoing and raising the foundations between 5 columns of the loggia and for masonry work between the large steps. This means that the front wall between the piers on which the 5 columns rested was not strong enough.

1458

Consecration of the open cemetery "on the side of the confraternity"; administrators of the Hospital are to be buried in the floor of the loggia in front of the church, transformed into a burial ground (No. 4, LR, 193).

1459

The fresco in the arch over the door of the church is executed by Giovanni di Francesco (No. 4, LDC, 158, 168, 175).

1466

A "new" dormitory is constructed beside the church.

1467

The Hospital is responsible for 600 children, and houses 200 orphans, foster mothers or wet-nurses, and men.

1470

The second violation of Brunelleschi's plan: galleries (*verone*) with windows are built "above the loggia of the cloister of our Hospital" by Stefano di Jacopo Rosselli [*49*] (No. 1, LR, 181, 195, 202ff). It is interesting that many of the stones used in this work, as well as many *braccia* of ornamented cornice, were brought from the Ospedale di S. Gallo (No. 6, LDC, 222-36).

1487

28 August Antonio di Marco della Robbia is paid for helping to install the glazed terracotta medallions of swaddled infants in the roundels of the façade (No. 10, LDC, 343, 361, 450).

1488

Matteo di Giovanni is ordered to build the men's refectory (No. 10, LDC, 368). The Renaissance nucleus around the two cloisters is complete.

1493

The large loggia (for hanging out laundry) above the children's ward is completed (No. 11, LDC, 135).

1540

The living quarters in the Hospital are enlarged, by adding a large wing in Via dei Fibbiai, to the south, to house wet-nurses and others (Ser. III, no. 17, Giornale, 93).

1552

A large loggia is built in the women's garden, the court farther south, towards Via degli Alfani (demolished at the end of the nineteenth century), and the edifice on Via degli Alfani is completed.

1557 (according to Fabriczy, 1599-1600)

The Prior of the Hospital, Vincenzo Borghini, submits a request to the Capitani di Parte for their consent to make a vaulted passageway under the left side of the façade to provide access from one garden to the other (Florence, Archivio di Stato, Capitani di Parte, Suppliche 1556, no. 143). An arch was cut through and vaulted, leading to Via della Colonna, and one of the side doors was moved to the extreme left, outside the arcade (No. 19, LDC, K, 358f.).

1605

The main entrance door and the two doors at the ends of the loggia are altered [*35, 36, 40*] (Ser. XIII, no. 23, Giornale 1605-06, 23).

1615

First remodelling of the interior of the church (Filza no. 82, 198).

1660

Another wheel for receiving abandoned infants is built on the left side of the loggia (in *1699* the window was provided with an iron grating through which only newborn infants could be passed).

1662

Paolo Squarcialupi, Prior from 1648 to 1677, sees to the making of underground jar-like grain receptacles under the loggia at the dormitory end (found recently when the flooring of the loggia was reconstructed, and now marked by small inset stone slabs) (Ser. CXXII, no. 214, Entrate e Uscite, 65).

1759

Major transformations of the Hospital are made, in both its organization and its fabric, with embellishments that conceal even more of the original structure. To create more room, the women's cloister is much altered, and part of its northern walk and the balcony above it are destroyed [*30b, c*].

1781

Project drawn up for remodelling the large room on the upper floor of the children's ward (which is subdivided horizontally) to house the archives. The covered balcony in the women's cloister is replaced by a windowed gallery, and the roof of the gallery is raised.

1785

The architect Bernardo Fallani is put in charge of the church. He proposes various alterations on which work begins after May (Filza no. 91, 225ff.).

1795

Restoration of the steps on the Piazza della SS. Annunziata. Fallani opposes replacing their *pietra forte* with *pietra serena*, as had been proposed in order to make them harmonize with the later steps on the opposite side of the piazza (Filza no. 101, 1).

1831

The ground-floor room of the ward is transformed into the bookkeeping office, with new windows opening onto the main cloister. The central well is eliminated and the cloister given a new pavement and new bases for the columns.

1832

The arches on the south side of the women's cloister are filled in and the north side is almost entirely demolished in order to provide better light for the bookkeeping office (Filza computisteria, 1833, no. IV, 158, 170, 269).

1843

The architect Leopoldo Pasqui presents a project for completing the façade and a report on the state of the loggia, with particular regard to the consolidation of the columns.

Work is begun and some of the column shafts are replaced. In the right-hand bay a composition is inserted which consists of two columns supporting an arch with a lunette window, and the original motif of the pedimented door and roundel now appears one bay to the right (Filza no. 205, part. 2).

1846

The entire space underneath the church is transformed into a storage cellar (Filza computisteria, 1845, 53, 83, 86).

1865

Alterations are made, intended originally to affect only the kitchens and the women's dormitory (Filza computisteria, 1865, 522-38).

1872

The hospital temporarily transfers the use of the two wings overlooking Via degli Alfani and Via dei Fibbiai to the Ospedale di S. Maria Nuova (returned to the Foundling Hospital in 1966).

1896

A major alteration to the Renaissance ensemble: an attic storey is built at the front to house staff (Filza giustif. 1896-99, no. 930). It was removed during the recent restoration, but can be seen in old photographs.

4. Ecclesiasticus 32:6, "Like a signet of emerald in a gold setting is tuneful music with good wine" (see Guy de Tervarent, *Attributs et symboles dans l'art profane, 1450-1600*, Geneva, 1958, p. 155).

Robert Erich Wolf suggests a rather different explanation of the name. Agatha would indeed refer to the saint's day but Smeralda, instead, to the half of a ring or piece of jewellery that it was customary for the mother to leave with the infant she was abandoning. Thus, should she wish to reclaim the child at some future time it sufficed for her to present herself at the hospital and establish her right to it by the evidence of the year, date, and her half of the jewel or bauble (one cannot help thinking of the many recognition scenes in Cinquecento comedies!). For each child the information and evidence was kept in a carefully filed box, and great numbers of such boxes survived until the flood of 1966 when many were destroyed or lost.

5. For other Tuscan hospitals, see A. Barbacci, "Cronache d'arte: La Loggia di San Matteo a Firenze e la sua liberazione", *Bollettino d'Arte*, XXXII, 1938, 2, pp. 65-73, and "Osservazioni su alcune logge ospedaliere toscane", *Le Arti*, IV, 1941-42, pp. 225-26, as well as Heydenreich and Lotz 1974, p. 8 and fig. 3. For an even more general survey (though it should be remembered that the Innocenti was primarily a training school and residence, not a hospital) see John D. Thompson and Grace Goldin, *The Hospital: A Social and Architectural History*, New Haven, 1975.

That the Innocenti was not Brunelleschi's sole undertaking of the sort has become more probable with new information that may link him with the rebuilding of the hospital in Pistoia (see L. Gai, "Interventi rinascimentali nello spedale del Ceppo di Pistoia", *VII Centenario dello Spedale del Ceppo in Pistoia*, Pistoia, 1977, pp. 71-155, and the study by Francesco Gurrieri in course of publication). Comparison should be made less with the present appearance of the Pistoia hospital than with that recorded in an eighteenth-century inventory (formerly in the hospital archives but now known only from a photograph, reproduced in the 1977 volume cited above).

6. The Biographer's text is on f. 297r:

It is said that, wishing to build at Petraia, the owner asked the advice of Filippo and built the tower that is there with his counsel; some people have spoken highly of that tower to me, but I have never seen it except from a distance. The construction was not carried further because of reverses in fortune.

Since *torre* can also mean fortified villa the basic plan of the house today, despite the reconstruction by Buontalenti and more recent alterations, may still be that of the Quattrocento as is suggested by the presence of the cryptoporticus, which is not matched by anything in the plan of the ground floor. It should be noted that various investigations of the Medici villas generally attributed to Michelozzo have shown that in every case earlier masonry was put to use, which means that if Brunelleschi did build the foundations at Petraia they must survive below ground.

On the Villa della Petraia, see Ferdinando Chiostri, *La Petraja, Villa e Giardino, settecento anni di storia* (Accademia Toscana di Scienze e Lettere La Colombaria, Studi, XXV), Florence, 1972. In the tax register of 1427 La Petraia figures among the property owned by Palla di Noferi Strozzi and consisted of a small palace (*palazzetto*) and rustic living quarters, the latter being a peasant's house. During the exile of Palla Strozzi the property was confiscated, but in 1447 Alessandra de' Bardi, wife of

Lorenzo Strozzi, bought it back, with additional land. Subsequently the "chasamentum, palatium sive fortilitium Petraiae... cum turri et domo pro domino" (dwelling, palace, or fortress of Petraia... with tower and quarters for the master) was sold to Agnolo di Nerone Nigi in 1463.

Explorations underneath the villa have revealed that building was done at various times, and Chiostri considers the older elements to be remains of the old fortress of the Brunelleschi family (not related to the architect), but so far no adequate study of the ensemble has been carried out. Ground plans made recently are in the archives of the Soprintendenza ai Monumenti of Tuscany.

7. The theory that a formal plan was envisaged for the piazza on which both the Foundling Hospital and the church of SS. Annunziata face is supported by a historical item reported by Arcangelo Giani, historian of the church and of the Servite order, who died in his seventies in 1623:

> For the part depending on the Florentine monastery, that is the matter of completing the restoration and embellishment of the church of SS. Annunziata according to what had already been established by the Pope with the consent of the government of the city, the architects called in were Leon Battista Alberti for the new dome and choir [the rotunda], and Antonio Manetti Ciaccheri, commissioned to make a model of the other part of the church with a porch and a piazza [platea] to be laid out square according to what had already been designed by the illustrious Filippo Brunelleschi in his time; and after the ground had been broken for the foundations of the domed choir, Ludovico Serampo, Archbishop of Florence... on 18 October, St Luke's Day, blessed the first stone with solemn rites, in the name of Pope Eugenius, in the presence of the Florentine Senate, and laid it in the foundation of the choir that was to be built.

(A. Giani, *Annalium sacri ordinis Fratrum Servorum B. Marie Virginis a suae institutionis exordio centuriae quatuor*, Florence, 1618-22; quoted from the second edition, Lucca, 1719-21, I, p. 469). According to P. R. Taucci (1936) Giani would seem to have made use of a mid-sixteenth-century manuscript entitled *Memorie della chiesa e del convento della SS. Annunziata*, paraphrasing its statement that "the piazza with the two loggias in the manner of a theatre, laid out on a square, was to a design by Filippo Brunelleschi".

In reality, however, we have here a much more direct piece of evidence, because Giani himself states in a note that "a very old architectural model in wood, before it was eaten away [by woodworm], was seen by the author when he was an adolescent with his own eyes, and this model was made in accordance with the advice of the said men [Alberti and Manetti]". This means that between, say, 1560 and 1570 Giani saw the wooden model of both the choir and the remainder of the church and was given information by, presumably, the archivists of the order or the Operai of the church fabric concerning the parts due to Alberti and to Antonio Manetti Ciaccheri. That model included also a portico in front of the church and a piazza to be laid out on a square plan.

It is worth checking rapidly whether the other information given is reliable. Piero Roselli collected with great care the principal documents (included in the volume with measured drawings of the rotunda published in Pisa in 1971), and his Document 8 shows payment on 3 July 1447 to Antonio Manetti Ciaccheri, woodworker, who was making "the model of the church on the order of the Prior". Meanwhile a model, or at least an architectural drawing, of the rotunda must already have existed: preparations must have been made as early as 1444-45, since on 13 October 1445, St Luke's Day and a Sunday, the first stone was blessed and "the ground had been broken for the foundations of the domed choir". In any event, it was only quite late that steps were finally taken to observe the decree of the Pope, approved by the city, to restore and adorn the church. What the edifice looked like at the time was reconstructed by A. Biancalani and C. Lisi for the exhibition "Il luogo teatrale a Firenze" (catalogue, 1975, pp. 55f.), on the basis of studies by A. Sabatini ("La chiesa della SS. Annunziata in Firenze prima della ricostruzione Michelozziana", *Rivista d'Arte*, XXII, 1940, pp. 229ff.) and E. M. Casalini (*Il Chiostro grande della SS. Annunziata di Firenze*, Florence, 1976).

From the passage by Giani it seems that what was done was primarily to regularize and enlarge the church. But from whose designs? On that point the Latin text is ambiguous, declaring that the model was made "secundum quod olim designasset excellens Vir Philippus Brunelleschus", that is, after his death in 1446 but from designs made possibly much earlier. The choice of Antonio Manetti Ciaccheri to execute the model is understandable, since the Biographer says, "for Filippo during his lifetime this person [Antonio Manetti Ciaccheri] worked in wood with great precision and with diligence and was most clever... he had him make most of his models" (f. 370v). (In short, the situation is much like what we shall find in the work on S. Lorenzo and the Cathedral lantern.) Further, Giani may be taken to refer to the entire complex except for the rotunda or just to the portico and piazza. Indeed, the word *platea*, which we have read as piazza, could even mean merely the Cloister of the Vows, the atrium immediately behind the present façade of the church. A narrower interpretation is contradicted, however, for the present at least, by two important indications: one is a comment by the Biographer (f. 309r) which suggests that Brunelleschi was asked (presumably by or for Gianfrancesco Gonzaga) to duplicate the Rotunda of S. Maria degli Angeli "elsewhere" (see Chapter 12, note 32); the other is the attack launched by Brunelleschi himself on the design proposed for the rotunda of SS. Annunziata, referred to in a letter of 3 May 1471 from Giovanni di Domenico da Gaiole to Lodovico Gonzaga:

> It was designed by Michelozzo and in such manner as to be damned by Filippo, our master, for several reasons: first of all because it was erected so close up against the church that there remains no proper crossing for the nave and the body of the church. And neither altar nor choir can be placed there nor can the chapels [around it] be used. And there is nothing good, either *per se* or in the whole, which is why this work is condemned in its entirety.

It would appear from this that Brunelleschi was not a consultant called in from outside but was more intimately involved, and the church seems to be the result of a combination of two projects, one by Michelozzo and the other by Brunelleschi. At a later date Alberti corrected Michelozzo's project and ordered a special model for the rotunda (the one seen by Giani), while for the nave and chapels Brunelleschi's model continued to be followed, though with all too obvious uncertainties. Whence the legitimate conclusion that Antonio Manetti Ciaccheri begins to look rather more like the executor of other men's projects — and sometimes a fairly poor one — than himself an inventor.

Brunelleschi's name was also associated with the sacristy of SS. Annunziata by R. Taucci (1936) because of payment orders in favour of a mason named Filippo ("Filippo muratore") who, with one Benedetto Cera as helper, was paid for supplying bricks and for days of work between 1438 and 1441. It should be noted, incidentally, that this sacristy served also as a safe deposit place for the Parte Guelfa and its treasury.

In the present piazza, an important element is in any case the portico in front of the church, which already existed in the fifteenth-century model seen by Giani. Then too the intention of regularizing this open space goes back at least as far as 1421, as we know from a document (Florence, Archivio di Stato, Provvisioni, filza 114, 1421) reported by Gaye (1839, I, p. 549):

> The friars of SS. Annunziata request a subsidy for the completion of the paving of the piazza, desiring that people come in great numbers to the church for reverence to God and His most saintly Mother and for the devotion due her image in the act of the Annunciation which is painted in their church.

Another indication that would seem to support the whole idea of laying out a piazza here is the drawing by Filarete for the market square in his ideal city of Sforzinda (Florence, Biblioteca Nazionale, Codex Magliabechiano XVII, I, 30, f. 75), already associated with the portico of the Foundling Hospital by W. Lotz (1956, p. 198).

A fine sequence of depictions of the piazza in paintings and drawings of the sixteenth and seventeenth centuries has been published by G. Fanelli (1973, figs. 637-39, 1124-26, 1293-1307) in his splendid volume which should be consulted also for sensitive and well-informed presentation of all Brunelleschi's buildings. For the state of the piazza at the start of the sixteenth century we have a famous drawing by Fra Bartolomeo, which is however more picturesque than historically accurate (see the discussion by G. Miarelli Mariani in Marchini, Miarelli Mariani *et al.*, 1977, pp. 37-40). In it the Foundling Hospital is partially concealed behind the Servite monastery and is, as it were, only an epitome of itself, with the length of its façade and the number of its arches and windows much reduced. The atrium in front of the church is visible but unfortunately only from the side.

Certainly there can be no doubt that by its size and energetic character the front of the Foundling Hospital conditioned — in its proportions at least — the unorganized area in front of it. If one could accept the notion of G. C. Argan (1968, p. 104) that "the proportion between the two volumes is expressed, on that diaphragmatic plane, by the measurement of the round-headed arches, by the relationship between their opening and the height of the columns", it would be possible to reconstruct a Quattrocento programme for laying out the piazza.

A good start for such a study would be the extremely accurate plan of the piazza by M. Baldi, C. Bonanni and G. Degl'Innocenti (*Problemi Brunelleschiani* 1977), which shows it as an irregular trapezoid with sides which are not aligned and are oblique with respect to the streets leading to it, and differences in level of as much as 1.80 m (5 ft 11 in.). Klotz (1970, pp. 103-04) pointed out the correspondences in axiality and orthogonality between the church, the hospital, and the streets leading to them, but unfortunately his plan (on which our *fig. 30a* is based) is arbitrarily regularized. The irregularity of the piazza's plan, which makes splendid sense both optically and illusionistically, has already been stressed by E. N. Bacon (*Design of Cities*, New York and London, 1967, pp. 94-95). For the historical development of the area, see *Firenze. Studi e ricerche sul centro antico, I, L'ampliamento della Cattedrale di S. Reparata, le conseguenze sullo sviluppo della città a nord e la formazione della Piazza del Duomo e di quella della SS. Annunziata*, Pisa, 1974.

8. If this was the well-known merchant and political leader of that name, who was Gonfaloniere di Giustizia in 1418, he could only have been an administrator at the Hospital: see Martines 1963, pp. 341-42. His tax declaration in 1427 was for 34,987 florins (p. 372), which places his among the wealthiest houses of Florence, in third place in the S. Maria Novella quarter.

9. That the Baptistery was the prototype was also noted by G. B. Gelli (*I capricci del Bottaio*, Florence, 1546; Ragionamento V, p. 95 of the 1548 edition). Brunelleschi's comment is there reported as "You have imitated it only in what is ugly".

10. The phases of building, as revealed in the documents published by Fabriczy and Paatz, were accurately distinguished and schematized two decades ago by Saalman (1958-A, pp. 120-23). A first graphic schema of the phases of the loggia was published by Klotz (1970, p. 99), who devotes his entire fifth chapter (pp. 98-117) to that construction.

An excellent idea of the state of the Hospital before the restorations is given by the plan of 1819 by Francesco Bruni (reproduced in Fanelli 1973, fig. 1292).

On the façade as we see it now and the loggia as it was originally designed, see Giorgio Simoncini (*Architetti e architettura nella cultura del Rinascimento*, Bologna, 1967, with diagram on p. 242). He comments: "One cannot point to the existence of a dominant element that might serve as focal point for the composition". A hierarchy of height (now lost) was in fact intended for the doors, on a second optical level, within the shady loggia [35]. Simoncini (p. 243) thinks that one should speak of "co-ordination of the various parts" rather than of "reduction of the organism to a single spatial unity as was later attempted".

As for proportioning, the interaxis of each arch of the loggia comes to 10 *braccia*, while the height of the arch from the pavement is about 3/4 *braccio* less, as has already been stated (Benevolo 1968, pp. 83-90). Thus, to have a relation of 1:1 the moulding around the arch has to be counted in. Moreover, the columns constitute independent elements. Nor are the measurements of height linked with those of the ground plan in a clear geometrical relationship (see also R. Beltrame 1972). Subdivisions of the *braccio* — the *crazia*, *soldo* and *quattrino* (see Introduction, note 4) — may have been used as modules for the decorative elements.

Only by working on detailed photogrammetric measured drawings could one, following the lead of what Benevolo and his collaborators did at S. Spirito, compare the modules with a few formalized metrical units. So far no definitive conclusions have been possible for the Foundling Hospital.

For the recent restorations, see G. Morozzi (1964), M.A. Cardoso Mendes and G. Dallai (1966)

and G. Morozzi and A. Piccini (1971). Except for numerous newspaper articles that cannot be listed here, there has been rather limited discussion of that work, though see, especially, Charles Randall Mack, "New Look at the Hospital of the Innocents", *Southeastern College Art Conference Review* (University of South Carolina), VI, 1973, 1, pp. 12-15. A critical comment on the restoration appeared in *The Burlington Magazine*, CXII, 1970, no. 813, pp. 789-90, and Benedict Nicolson's editorial was published in translation in *Paragone*, XXII, 1971, 257, in a special issue devoted to conservation problems.

11. "A basket was placed by chance above an acanthus root... in that way the root, pressed down by the weight, put forth curled stems in spring; they grew along the sides of the basket, and at the corners of the tile (with which the basket was covered) were pushed outwards by reason of the weight and forced to curve the ends of their tendrils" (IV, 9).

The best published documentation on the capitals, photographic as well as historical, is given by Saalman (1958-A), Gosebruch (1958) and Luporini (1964, pp. 170-98, figs. 284, 285), and they have been analysed also by Klotz (1970, pp. 19-20, 98 ff. etc.) and Cadei (1971). They have been studied for this book by Riccardo Pacciani and E. Rodio.

Paraphrasing Saalman (1958-A), Cadei (1971, p. 189) distinguishes Brunelleschi's Corinthian capitals from the Classical type thus: "elimination of caulicoles with *folia projecta*, flattening of the caules with scarcely perceptible swelling of the calathos and fusion into a single nexus of the pair of continuous volutes".

The Foundling Hospital capitals have been, and still are, at the centre of discussion, adduced by some as proof of Brunelleschi's total dependence on the local medieval style, by others as examples of what he learned in his archaeological studies. The arguments so far have proved neither the first nor the second thesis but decisively rule out, I think, any local derivation not involving the Baptistery — which, in any case, was considered not medieval but Roman. The closest comparison is one proposed by Klotz (1970), though it is on an octagonal pier. Gosebruch (1958, p. 80), however, connects these capitals with those in the atrium of Pistoia Cathedral, which, though reconstructed in 1459, is said to have re-used capitals of much earlier date. But the relationship is really not all that close and the point of reference is untrustworthy. We are rather more inclined to see in them a deliberate return to Classical principles.

Vitruvius and Brunelleschi and the Foundling Hospital capitals (by Riccardo Pacciani)
Even if there may be late medieval prototypes for the Corinthian capital introduced in the Hospital by Brunelleschi, it is more than probable that the manner of delineating its volumes and components was new, at least insofar as it had a more rationalized basis. The working hypothesis that follows takes into account the necessity of relying as much as possible, for the study of the architectonic elements and their proportioning, on both contemporary and Classical treatises rather than on arbitrary empirical schemes arbitrarily selected. One thing of which we can be sure is that there were in Florence at the time manuscripts of Vitruvius; and at least one, the copy left by Boccaccio to the monastery of S. Spirito, was accessible to Brunelleschi. Further, we can also

safely presume that the methods of delineation he used were to some extent taken over or carried further by later architects. It thus seemed best to look at the treatise of Serlio, who shows a wide interest in the Florentine experiments; he also quotes Vitruvius but is nevertheless in some ways quite independent of him.

On the one hand, Brunelleschi did not follow the Vitruvian formula of making the height of the capital equal to the diameter of the base of the column ("Let the height of the capital with its cushion or abacus be the same as the thickness of the column at its foot"). Brunelleschi's capitals in fact exceed the diameter of the base by a variable number of centimetres. Moreover, the height of their abacus is not one-seventh of the total height of the capital as Vitruvius prescribed, with the result that the whole is considerably more slender than the models he proposed.

On the other hand, in the middle and lower parts of his capitals Brunelleschi followed Vitruvius faithfully, grouping the tendrils or volutes, the middle leaves and the lower leaves in three superimposed bands, all of the same height.

Viewed in plan, the abacus as designed by Brunelleschi reveals notable similarities with the plan specified by Serlio (Book IV, Chapter VIII):

> The width of the abacus on a diagonal from one corner to the opposite will be that of two diameters of the column at the base: if it [the column] is placed within a square and a large circle drawn around it that touches all four corners, and if outside this large circle is drawn another square divided by diagonal lines, those lines will prove to be as long as two thicknesses of column just as the text of Vitruvius says.

This geometrical method, expounded by Serlio as early as his Book I, was certainly in wide use and indeed very like what was done in Gothic workshops. With it one can obtain a circle of a diameter twice that of a given circle or, if desired, a square whose diagonal is twice the diameter of the given circle. Applying this method to the capitals at the Foundling Hospital one arrives at exactly the positioning of the corners of the abacus blocks. Note that this type of construction is not described explicitly by Vitruvius, who limits himself to saying that "the width of the abacus will thus be given its rationale in that whatever the height [of the capital] the diagonal will be twice that".

Vitruvius thus instituted a close linkage between dimensions, one that applies from the base to the very top of the order: the diameter of the base is to equal the height of the capital, the diameter of the abacus is to be twice that height. Brunelleschi, however, by altering the height of the capital eliminated the factor that would allow one to correlate the diameter of the abacus with that of the column. Thus, while accepting the individual linguistic elements he put no emphasis on the internal and general law that presides over the measurements of the volumes. This may have been either because he was chiefly attracted by the correlation between capital and *caput*, and therefore by the desire to give that architectural element its own independent tripartite structure, or else because he simply was not truly familiar with Vitruvius: we know he was taught at least the rudiments of Latin, but (as for others before and after him) this gave no guarantee of fluency. The latter in fact does seem to be confirmed by his use of incorrect bases for his columns, which are Roman Doric rather than Corinthian [45].

The method of tracing the curve between the

corners of the abacus may also contain vestiges of the medieval practice. That curve, says Vitruvius, should be as deep as "the ninth part of the width of its front". Serlio suggests drawing "a perfect triangle" on the segment that unites two corners, then subdividing into four equal parts the segment of radius comprised within the circular corona that derives from the preceding construction of the abacus: the arc of circumference having as radius the distance between the exterior angle of the triangle and the third and more interior subdivision of the radius within the circular corona will represent the curvature according to which the abacus is to be hollowed out. But that scheme does not correspond to the curvature found on the Foundling Hospital capitals, whose depth is, instead, one-sixth of the width of the front. On the other hand, a system that does give results very close to their particular profile involves tracing a square in which the centre of the sides is tangent to the corners of the outermost square used for the construction of the abacus. This method of drawing complex architectural elements based on the "doubled square" was much favoured in traditional Gothic designing. If one then draws the arc of circumference with its centre at the corners and radius equal to one-third of the diagonal, the result is a profile which, as we have said, is practically identical with the real one.

[The procedure outlined here was put to the test by my students Crussi, Gruenieri, Marchetti and Temperani using a careful full-size rubbing of a capital in the loggia. The method proved exactly applicable, with the difference that the diameter of the column, to be used as the point of departure, had to be taken at the top rather than the base of the shaft. Moreover (differing in this from Serlio) with the compass set at the apex of the equilateral triangle the outermost quarter was used to delineate the curve of the abacus.

A very accurate drawing of this construction method was published on the front page of *Problemi brunelleschiani: Sagrestia Vecchia e San Lorenzo*, Rome, 1977, comparing it with the curves proposed by Alberti, Serlio, Vignola and Scamozzi. — *E.B.*]

4 The Palazzo di Parte Guelfa and Florentine private palaces

1. The palace has undergone heavy-handed alterations, and that some parts are obviously late nineteenth-century appeared from student group investigations led by Beppe Cruciani. An adequate study of the building has never been made, and the documents concerning its construction and administration have been published only in part.

Listed among other possessions in 1322 in a register of property belonging to the Parte Guelfa is "a palace which has been built and completed recently to house the councils of the said Parte, in which there is only a large and handsome hall with a beautiful double row of benches and railed speaker's platform [*aringhiera*], and it is entirely vaulted along with a side consulting parlour or sacristy". The palace adjoined the old church of S. Maria sopra Porta (very close to S. Biagio, now the library of the Università Popolare), the piazza in front of the church, and the Via delle Terme, and it occupied the area of a house purchased by the Parte Guelfa in 1318 for 200 florins (information from U. Dorini 1898).

Some idea of what the palace was used for can be got from the statutes of 1335 (published by F. Bonaini, 1857-58). It served principally as headquarters for the six Captains and the Council of the Fourteen of the Credenza who were elected, two for each quarter of the city, every two years and who, in view of their small number, could meet comfortably in the "consigliatoio", the small consulting parlour. The Priors were expected to meet every Friday.

To take decisions concerning matters not settled by the statutes it was necessary to resort to a general council of sixty Guelphs elected every six months, while financial questions were dealt with by another council, this one of a hundred numbers elected annually whose decisions required an affirmative vote of at least eighty. These larger councils obviously met in the "large and handsome hall, with benches and a platform reserved for the Six and the Fourteen".

In addition to such meetings concerned with political and economic administration, the palace served for various types of ceremonies such as the election of new knights and festive gatherings on holidays like St John's Day, when every member was required to participate in the public procession with a candle after first assembling in the party headquarters.

This and the other buildings that were rented out served also as investments of capital, the statutes specifying that "every year there is to be spent in buying possessions and houses the greatest part of the funds that can be gathered" (Chapter XVI, Statutes of 1335). Though later statutes modified the organization of the Parte they brought no substantial changes.

The statutes of 1420 (of which I have not been able to find the publication by U. Dorini, "Notizie storiche sull'Università della Parte dei Guelfi", *Bull. dell'Associazione per la Difesa di Firenze Antica*, fasc. III, 1902, pp. 23-61), and the construction of a new hall and council room councided with a period of renewed power. At the same time the Parte commissioned from Donatello the statue of St Louis in homage to the French monarchy as protector of the Guelphs. Among the other public manifestations there was a grandiose tourney in Piazza S. Croce to celebrate both the conquest of Pisa and the French monarchy (the victory had taken place on the feast of St. Denis). An image of the French Saint, with two angels at the sides and the city of Pisa in the background, was painted by Gherardo Starnina on the front of the palace facing Piazza S. Biagio. A solemn offering was also made on St Augustine's Day in gratitude for the Florentine victory over Giangaleazzo Visconti on that feast day in 1397, the same victory that was to be commemorated years later in the rebuilding of the church of S. Spirito.

2. This dating was proposed by G. Marchini (1961) and M. Salmi (1951). On the basis of the known documents I do not think one can accept the thesis of H. Saalman (1965, and his edition of Manetti, 1970, p. 144, note 125) that Brunelleschi's involvement came late in his career, around 1422. In fact the Biographer, who associates this undertaking with the works done for the Barbadori, states that he was called in to complete the palace after its rebuilding had reached the level of the *salone*, and as one can see from the drawings published here [*52, 57-59*] Brunelleschi came in with decidedly different ideas and methods. As for the date 1442, it probably refers only to a resumption of work on the large *salone* itself and its elaborate interior decoration.

3. Among the parts where things went wrong, according to the Biographer, is one of the corners of the building (ff. 308v-309r):

And in order that he not be blamed for matters in which he should be praised, and lest anyone follow this bad example, I shall say something more here. Among other things Filippo ordered those flat [unfluted] pilasters on the exterior in such a way that every visible corner of the palace above the sills was to be included between two of the aforementioned pilasters; and at the only two corners that are visible — noting more of what was done in the time of Filippo — the pilasters are well built and placed properly. But on the side towards the Terma [the Via delle Terme, now covered by a later addition] it was later decided that there should be a different type of corner, as can be seen above the silk shops where one finds the architrave, frieze and cornice all bending at 90 degrees. And there it can be seen that the pilaster in position there is not well placed and that the individual who had it placed there did not understand correctly what Filippo had in mind and did not even think to look at how the other corners had been built. Responsible for this by no means slight defect was a citizen of good reputation who fancied he understood such matters and, being much concerned with things of that sort, put himself forward. And this was the same man who was responsible for violating all of his [Brunelleschi's] plans for the portico and façade of the Foundling Hospital [that is, Francesco della Luna]. I have mentioned these things so that whoever sees them in the future, having behind them as they do the authority of Filippo's name, and believes that they were due to him, will not make such errors again, or consider them justified.

4. Burns 1971, fig. 6c.

5. Here is a summary description of the state of the palace in 1431 (quoted in Dorini 1898):

A palace entirely vaulted over. The first storey [*primo palco*] with a painted and covered staircase and with a large hall, painted and frescoed [*storiata*], with three tiers of benches for the Captains and two tiers for the members of the College, and painted wooden backrests around the hall, with a platform [*ringhiera*] and several benches for seating, and a door that gives access to the corridor in which are the new chancellery office and audience chamber and office and that gives on to the balcony leading to the *agiamenti* [lodgings?].

The description may refer to the old hall on the ground floor, with the upper storey perhaps reserved for offices and lodgings. Alterations, among them those done by Vasari in 1557, as well as the fire in 1566 which destroyed most of the archives of the Parte Guelfa, make it difficult to understand both the description quoted here and the present state of the building, whose ground floor is now divided into offices, but consists basically of independent pre-Renaissance houses, divided by narrow alleys and unified at a later date.

6. Recently discovered documents show that the Palazzo Piccolomini is earlier, and Alberti is unlikely to have been responsible for a copy, unless he also designed the Pienza palace.

Domestic architecture in the Quattrocento. Limited as it was to a few families who probably constituted exceptional cases of initiative and success, the "boom" in domestic architecture in the Quattrocento is by no means proof of an economic expansion. On this point, partly through lack of adequate studies and documentation and despite the evidence of considerable social mobility and of highly profitable investments abroad, the opinions of historians differ greatly. In manufacturing, the decline in the production of wool was being successfully compensated for by silk weaving, and the system of public investments represented by the Monte seems to have transformed the city into nothing less than a gigantic corporation (see Louis F. Marks, *The Development of the Institutions of Public Finance at Florence during the Last Sixty Years of the Republic, ca. 1470-1530*, doctoral dissertation, Oxford, 1954). Yet it should be remembered that every investment in houses or land meant a future stagnation, because of the low income it afforded, compared with a manufactory or a commercial or banking enterprise.

Despite the importance of the subject, there are numerous popular or tourist-oriented publications but very few serious studies on the social, economic, and artistic significance of Florentine private palaces. Ingenious as it is, the essay by P. Francastel is too generalized (''Imagination et réalité dans l'architecture civile du Quattrocento'', *Hommage à Lucien Febvre: Eventail de l'Histoire vivante*, Paris, 1953, II, pp. 195-206), while for all its extensive documentation that by R. A. Goldthwaite (''The Florentine Palace as Domestic Architecture'', *American Historical Review*, LXXVII, 1972, pp. 977-1012) is dramatically negative in its recognition of the lack of significant studies, though for a meticulous account of the building processes see the article by the same author on the construction industry in Renaissance Florence (1973).

H. Saalman (1965) has prepared a detailed list of the Quattrocento palaces and villas in Florence and puts forward the convincing hypothesis that many dwellings supposed to date from the fourteenth or even thirteenth centuries are in fact fifteenth-century.

For a masterly study of the relations between economy, political structure, concept and evolution of the family, and construction of palaces, see the paper by Nicolai Rubinstein in the proceedings of the 1977 Congress.

The greatest expansion in building came after 1489: see Caroline Elam, ''Lorenzo de' Medici and the Urban Development of Renaissance Florence'', *Art History*, I, 1, March 1978, pp. 43-66. For a general picture see M. Bucci and R. Bencini 1971, 1973.

For the design of these private residences, we have Alberti's comments and, in a rather similar vein, a note on a Quattrocento drawing of a palace façade in the style of Brunelleschi, found in a manuscript compiled by Bartolomeo Neroni, known as Il Riccio (Siena, Biblioteca Comunale, Cod. S. IV 6):

Note that if you wish to make a façade for a dwelling, first take its diameter, that is, its width, and distribute the doors that you think will be needed. You should know that every dwelling needs one door or three or five or seven or nine or eleven, and with this when you make the windows correspond above them you should place void above void and solid above solid, noting that the solid needs to be the equal of the void and that in dimensions every window or door should be twice as high as it is wide, and that means two squares. Also you will make the thickness of the wall diminish every ten *braccia* [as it rises] according to how much space is available in the edifice, and this diminution should occur at the level of the imposts of the vaults or the ceilings

(translated from the transcription of the manuscript in Prager and Scaglia 1972, p. 202). The 10 *braccia*, understood as module for the height of a storey, are equivalent to 5.836 m or slightly over 19 ft. Another general law that was very scrupulously observed is that of Francesco di Giorgio (*Trattato*, ed. Maltese, Milan, 1967, II, p. 412):

a very general rule to be observed without exception... And that is, that all empty spaces should be above empty spaces: voids above voids and filled-in spaces above filled-in, upright above upright, column above column, and that in general every support or its equivalent should be in a straight line directly on axis above its analogue.

Work in the Palazzo Vecchio. Among the civil works said to be by Brunelleschi are two halls in the Palazzo Vecchio (the council hall and the audience chamber), along with ancillary rooms, though nothing survives that can be connected with him. At the time the Biographer was writing these halls, which he specifically credits to Brunelleschi and praises, were in part virtually completed and decorated '' and lacking nothing except the paintings and gildings''. On 28 November 1480 Giovanni d'Antonio, goldbeater, was paid 34 *lire* for 1,100 pieces of gold leaf used in the lower part of the door of the audience chamber and in the windows of the council hall, and payments were made at the same time to Bartolomeo di Antonio (30 *lire* and 16 *soldi*) and Clemente di Lorenzo, the latter for having applied the paint. This was done, it should be noted, on architectural elements we usually think of as finished properly when they are in simple monochrome. These were the final tasks taken care of in a series of payments for scaffolding, doorposts, and architraves begun in 1475 (for this latter phase, see Gaye 1839, I, pp. 572-83). Very recently a document of 28 February 1429 was discovered which shows payment of 300 florins for work on the Uffizi del Monte, and this large sum suggests that Brunelleschi not only supplied the project but acted as *capomaestro*.

It should be remembered that the inventory made after Brunelleschi's death refers to a drawing of the Palazzo Vecchio (see Chapter 1, note 9).

Palazzo of Apollonio Lapi. The Biographer tells us (ff. 296v-297r) that ''Filippo did a good deal of work there, and it can be seen that inside there is much that is beautiful, comfortable and pleasing. But in those times the manner of building was very rough and crude''. The house, located between the Canto de' Ricci and the Mercato Vecchio, was inherited by Bartolomeo, the son of Apollonio, and donated by him to the Ospedale di S. Maria Nuova though he continued to live there. The Lapi were related to the family of Brunelleschi.

The house survives and has been identified (by G. Carocci in *Arte e Storia*, XVIII-XIX, 1899-1900, p. 135 and by Saalman in his edition of the Biography, p. 130, note 15) as the building on the Via del Corso now occupied by the Grandi Magazzini Duilio 48, a department store. Saalman (1965, pp. 1-2) considers that its octagonal pillars and the capitals and their waterleaf consoles are in the style of the circle of Michelozzo and can be dated to some time between *c.* 1415 and the 1450s, and that the part Brunelleschi had in this building, if any, and its exact date remain an open question. Yet it is entirely possible that the association of the name of Brunelleschi with this building has no more basis than a family relationship with the Lapi: the overemphasis on such aspects of tradition and nobility is in any case a commonplace in the Florentine histories of the time (see Martines 1963, p. 44 *et passim*).

Palazzo Lenzi Quaratesi. This palace on Piazza Ognissanti (now occupied by the Institut Français) was owned from the outset by the Lenzi family, then acquired by the Busini in 1647 and by the Quaratesi in 1765, and should not be confused with the Busini palace attributed to Brunelleschi by Milanesi in his

edition of Vasari (1878, II, p. 379) and which, it would seem, is the present Bardi-Serzelli Palace in Via dei Benci. According to G. Marchini (1968, p. 243) the capitals and corbels of the staircases are identical with those in the Palazzo Ducale in Urbino and were unusual in Florence, and he therefore proposes attribution of the Palazzo Lenzi Quaratesi to Maso di Bartolomeo (for the origins of this problem, see G. Carocci 1887, p. 153, and see also L. Ginori-Lisci 1972, I, pp. 289-93). An idea of the extent of the remodelling can be had from the engraving in G. Zocchi, *Scelta di vedute di Firenze*, Florence, 1744, pl. IX.

Casa Giuntini (by Riccardo Pacciani). The attribution of this family dwelling to Brunelleschi goes back to Vasari: he ''...made the design for the house of the Giuntini on the piazza of Ognissanti along the Arno''. In a footnote in his 1878 edition (II, p. 379) Milanesi stated that it had probably been incorporated into the onetime Geri, later Martellini, Palace. The exact location, however, could not be pinned down since the piazza had undergone great changes in the nineteenth century when two large hotels were built over or made from various old palaces, notably the Hôtel de la Ville (now Excelsior, at no. 3) and the Grand Hotel (at no. 1) on opposite sides of the square. G. Carocci (1911) was able to identify the Grand Hotel as the building that arose on the site of the houses of the Giuntini family of Signa, of which all trace had been lost during the various alterations. However, going on to examine the origins of the building housing the Hôtel de la Ville, which occupies the entire east side of the square, he noted that at the start of the fifteenth century that stretch was occupied by the houses of the Aliotti, Boccacci di Signa, and Del Teglia families which faced directly on the piazza, while those of the Giuntini and Bartoli were at the corner of Borgo Ognissanti. In time all these were united into an edifice that belonged successively to the Pontenani, Della Rena, and Martellini families, and it is probably the latter that Milanesi had in mind. See also Girolamo Gargiolli, *Description de la ville de Florence et de ses environs*, Florence, 1819, I, p. 225; *Guida di Firenze e d'altre città principali della Toscana*, Florence, 1820, II, p. 296.

Palazzo Capponi. If we were to imagine a palace transitional in style between Trecento forms, already emended and regularized, and those of Brunelleschi, with all the traits of rigorous planning, scenographic disposition, nobility and decorum that one can expect from him even in youthful works or in those where he was not truly free to do as he wished, it would certainly be the palace at 36, Via de' Bardi, erected before 1424 by Niccolò da Uzzano and his brother Angelo and which later passed to the sons of Piero di Bartolomeo Capponi, descendants of Niccolò da Uzzano on their mother's side. The attribution of its design to Lorenzo de' Bicci, as proposed by Vasari (ed. Milanesi, 1878, II, p. 54), is unproven and perhaps unprovable. The uniform rustication of the entire lower storey looks forward to that of the Palazzo Medici-Riccardi, though it is sculpturally less aggressive; the windows of the principal storey, though smaller, anticipated those of the Palazzo di Parte Guelfa and are like those of buildings in the backgrounds of Masolino and Masaccio's frescoes in the Carmine. Access to the central court is by an axial corridor with service rooms on either side, just as in the Foundling Hospital, though as we see it now the court itself is not regular, a considerable part of the riverfront side of the palace having been shaved off obliquely to make room for the present Lungarno (see Bucci and Bencini 1971-73, II, pp. 47-53).

Palazzo Pitti. The historical sources rule out any possibility that the design of the Palazzo Pitti could have been, as Vasari claimed, by Brunelleschi. Scipione Ammirato, in Book XXIII of his *Storie Fiorentine*, written well along in the sixteenth century but following the lead of Machiavelli in Book VII of his *Istorie Fiorentine* completed in 1525, points to the year 1458 as the moment of greatest glory for Luca Pitti (glory acquired repressing the conspiracy of Girolamo Machiavelli and Niccolò Barbadori) when he decided to begin two buildings, "one in, the other outside the city, more in the manner of a king than of a private citizen", in explicit rivalry with the Medici. This source was used as far back as 1887, in a lecture by C. Conti. Subsequently K. H. Busse ("Der Pitti Palast, seine Erbauung 1458-1466 und seine Darstellung in den ältesten Stadtansichten von Florenz, 1469", *Jahrbuch der Preussischen Kunstsammlungen*, LI, 1930, pp. 110-32) confirmed the deductions already made by Fabriczy concerning the absence of any reference to the palace in the tax reports of 1458, whereas a document of 1461 attests to the acquisition in that year of land alongside that construction, this being the last in a series of acquisitions begun in 1451. Moreover, "the new house, which I built and am currently building for my habitation", was first declared in the tax report for 1469. In fact, the work appears to have been interrupted by a sudden political and economic crisis for the Pitti, and this was most likely in 1466, the date found by Ammannati in 1560 on the courtyard façade: "The year when the old wall was raised by the said Messer Luca Pitti was found carved there by B. Ammannati, that is, 1466" (Gaye 1839, III, p. 73, no. LXXV). That date is given also in the *Diario* of Agostino Lapini (Florence, Biblioteca Laurenziana, Cod. Ashburnhamiano 527, f. 104), as well as by Vasari and Ammirato. All this reinforces the attribution of the building to Luca Fancelli, who was sent to Florence from Mantua in 1458 (see G. Braghirolli, "Luca Fancelli scultore architetto", *Archivio Storico Lombardo*, III, 1876, pp. 613 ff., and for later documents, F. Morandini, "Palazzo Pitti, la sua costruzione e i successivi ingrandimenti", *Commentari*, Ser. II, V (XVI), 1965, 1-2, pp. 35-46).

The original ground plan of the palace can be easily deduced from the drawings of the ground floor and first storey published by J. Furttenbach (*Architectura Civilis, Architectura Ricreationis, Architectura Privata*, Ulm and Augsburg, 1628, 1640, 1641, repr. Hildesheim, 1971, pls. I-III).

U. Procacci (in *I Tesori: La Reggia di Palazzo Pitti*, Florence, 1967, and in his article in the 1968 Donatello Congress report), while admitting that before 1446 Luca Pitti simply did not have the financial means to request a design from Brunelleschi (and, we must insist, did not yet even own the land on which to build his palace), presumes that as a token of gratitude he may have obtained from Cosimo de' Medici the designs for the Medici Palace prepared by Brunelleschi but never built (see Chapter 9): the sole proof adduced is that the proposed Medici Palace which would have faced S. Lorenzo was frontal in design, not a corner building, and that the Palazzo Pitti is likewise frontal.

P. Sanpaolesi (1968) has come up with a last-ditch defence of the traditional notion that makes Brunelleschi the architect of the Palazzo Pitti, pro-

posing that the property may have already belonged to the Pitti as far back as 1428 and that the lack of any indication that they owned a palace in their tax declaration of thirty years later can be explained, simply, by supposing that it was not yet habitable. I really do not think the documents lend any support to such a thesis, though Sanpaolesi's essay remains essential reading for the structural history of the building and for various stylistic analyses.

For the Palazzo Pitti see also R. Redtenbacher, *Studien über verschiedene Baumeister der italienischen Renaissance*, Frankfurt, 1882; Cosimo Conti, *Il Palazzo Pitti. La sua primitiva costruzione e successivi ingrandimenti*, Florence, 1887; Giuseppe Boffito and Attilio Mori, *Piante e Vedute di Firenze*, Florence, 1926; Italo Gamberini, *Per un rilievo integrale di Palazzo Pitti*, Florence, 1947; Anna Maria Francini Ciaranfi, *La Galleria Pitti. Guida e Catalogo dei Dipinti*, Florence, 1956; *Mostra documentaria e iconografica di Palazzo Pitti e Giardino di Boboli*, exhibition catalogue, ed. F. Morandini, Florence, 1960.

Palazzo Strozzi. A Parronchi ("Il modello del Palazzo Strozzi", *Rinascimento*, IX, 1969, pp. 95-116) has suggested that the Strozzi Palace also goes back to Brunelleschi's project for a Medici Palace facing S. Lorenzo.

Interestingly, though, the Strozzi had already had contacts with Brunelleschi, but this was in connection with the remodelling of the Villa della Petraia (see Chapter 3, note 6).

5 The Old Sacristy of S. Lorenzo

1. Until a monograph is written, a good profile of Giovanni di Averardo de' Medici (1360-1429) is that by Raymond de Roover in his *The Rise and Decline of the Medici Bank, 1397-1494*, Cambridge, Mass., 1963, pp. 51ff. Giovanni withdrew from the Medici bank in 1420, after organizing it fully, and left it to his son Cosimo (1389-1464). Significantly, his retirement took place at almost the very moment when he pledged to build the sacristy. At his death he left 180,000 florins, and while it is said that he refused to make a will, perhaps for tax reasons or else to evade an accusation of indulging in usury, among the documents of S. Lorenzo there is a reference (though of later date) to a bequest made on his deathbed.

As to the taste of this early Medici, little can be learned from the inventory of his possessions made in March 1471. The titles of the manuscripts in his library indicate, among other things, some interest in ancient history and in Cicero and St Augustine, but the very few paintings he owned are listed, room by room, only by their subjects, which were invariably religious with, as one would expect, Madonnas, Crucifixions, and the Medici patron saints Cosmas and Damian, though there was also a "painted tourney cloth". (I derive this information from filza 129, cc. 54-78, in Florence, Archivio di Stato, Fondo Mediceo avanti il Principato, kindly called to my attention by the Direction.)

An unpublished document, for which I must thank Francesco Quinterio, gives the name of the *capomaestro* responsible for building the Old Sacristy. Filippo di Giovanni, who worked on the dome of S. Maria del Fiore with both Brunelleschi and Ghiberti, was aged fifty, and in his *portata al catasto*,

or tax return, of 1427 he declared that he had an income of 70 gold florins, to be divided with other men, working "al muramento di Giovanni de Medici in san Lorenzo che s'abattono" — on the building now rising under the patronage of Giovanni de' Medici in S. Lorenzo.

2. *Analysis of the foundations (by Emanuela Antoniacci, Andrea Cappelli and Pietro Gelardi).* The foundations are structurally distinct and the two basement rooms do not intercommunicate. Beneath the main chamber there is an approximately square room of 11.13 by 11.29 m (36 1/2 by 37 ft) with a central pier and groin vault, an entrance from the cloister, but no windows. The difference in level from the cloister is 2.57 m (8 ft 5 in.), from the upper storey 3.90 m (12 ft 9 in.), so knowing the height of the keystone of the vault, it is possible to establish its minimum thickness as 33 cm (13 in.). The surrounding walls have a uniform thickness of 1.20 m (3 ft 11 1/4 in.).

Beneath the *scarsella* and service rooms there is a wide barrel-vaulted rectangular chamber of 3.66 by 11.40 m (12 ft by 37 ft 5 in.), now reached from the right-hand service room, though that access is probably not original since the barrel vault was cut in order to insert the stairway.

Taking as point of reference the level of the cloister, this semi-basement is 1.78 m (5 ft 10 in.) lower than it and therefore 79 cm (2 ft 7 in.) higher than the other room. The minimum thickness of the vault remains 33 cm (13 in.).

The oblong crypt below the *scarsella* is not only shallower than the large square crypt, but its walls are thinner: this can be deduced from the fact that while the two crypts are aligned on the outside, on the inside the oblong room is 27 cm (10 5/8 in.) longer — 11.40 as opposed to 11.13 m.

If, as we have noted, all the surrounding walls of the large crypt are 1.20 m (3 ft 11 1/4 in.) thick, and the wall between the two rooms is 1.50 m (4 ft 11 in.) thick, this can be explained only if the construction occurred in two phases: in the second phase, alongside the existing wall another was raised only to support the new vault.

The diversity of structural solutions utilized and, even more, the disparity in levels suggest that the phases of building were entirely distinct. If the foundations had been dug at the same time the builders would not have chosen an arrangement which, due to the different depths and the juxtaposition of unlike and distinct structures, invites static problems. And the surrounding walls would surely have been built in line and with a uniform thickness.

Another problem is posed by the presence of a well inside the wall common to both chambers. Alberti (Book III, Chapter III), writing about the technique of foundations, mentions the custom of digging wells before proceeding to the actual construction, in order to determine

> just how able every stratum of the terrain is to support or not to support the edifice. Moreover, the water found below ground as well as that gushing forth at the surface is useful for many functions; and opening an outlet for the underground vapours will render a good service to our work, protecting it from noxious exhalations. Thus in digging a well, cistern, sewer or any other deep opening one discovers the otherwise concealed stratifications in the terrain and can select the one best adapted to support the construction.

Here and there throughout the church of S. Lorenzo and in the Cappella dei Principi there are other wells which may have been made and used during the building, but this one in the Old Sacristy is unusual in that it is within a wall.

Its depth of 9.20 m (30 ft 2 in.) goes very far below the level of the crypt, and it is wedged in between the left-hand pilaster of the large arch, the wall hollowed out by the door niche, and the side wall of the altar alcove, as if its position had been skilfully foreseen and calculated without the possibility of even minimum errors.

But what is problematical in any case is its very presence. Even if it had existed outside the building before the *scarsella* and side rooms were built, it would have been right on the edge, since the figure of 110 *braccia* cited for the total length of the new transept at its foundation (Chapter 9, note 8) would take one to exactly this point. (At S. Lorenzo 1 *braccio* = 0.5966 m, so 110 = 65.626 m, or 215 ft.) However, it is even more unlikely that the well was dug later. It must have been encased during the second phase of building, when the barrel-vaulted basement chamber was built: the well would have been enclosed in the thickness of the wall supporting the vault — and its course, one should note, is not perfectly straight. [E.A., A.C., P.G.]

Further confirmation that the *scarsella* and service rooms were added later comes from the fact that the 110 *braccia* envisaged in the original project correspond almost exactly (with only a few centimetres difference) to the actual distance between the outer walls of the square chamber of the Old Sacristy and the New Sacristy, in both cases excluding the altar alcove. Evidently the Medici were able to purchase additional land for the first sacristy and extend it outwards. Certainly at the New Sacristy the *scarsella* and two service rooms were built on land acquired later, their foundations being laid in 1519 (see Werner Goetz, "Annotazioni zu Michelangelos Medicigräbern", *Festschrift für Harald Keller*, Darmstadt, 1963, pp. 235-36). For the measured drawings, here discussed, see *Problemi Brunelleschiani: Sagrestia Vecchia e San Lorenzo*, Rome, 1977, figs. 1, 2, 4.

Thus the Old Sacristy would appear to have been built in three main stages: it was first projected as a cube and foundations laid accordingly; then three chambers were added (for liturgical purposes that were perhaps not originally foreseen); and finally the ensemble was encased to make it harmonize with the transept. For drawings by Francesco Quinterio illustrating this hypothesis see now, F. Borsi et al., *Brunelleschiani*, Rome, 1979, figs. 201, 202.

3. This date, seen by Sanpaolesi but lost in the rebuilding of the dome, may be connected (since the Florentine calendar began the new year on 25 March) with the solemn burial of Giovanni di Bicci, who died on 20 February 1429. That ceremony cost over 3,000 gold florins: "He was carried to the sepulchre exposed to view", wrote Ammirato, "with the body followed not only by Cosimo and Lorenzo, his sons, but by twenty-eight members of the Medici house, dressed in brown, all the ambassadors of the Emperor, of the King, and of Venice and other potentates." Some of the money may have been put towards the purchase of more land for an extension of the sacristy.

4. For the document of 1434 see Chapter 9, especially note 13. The sacristy was pronounced "celeberrima" and "jam fere perfecta" as early as the deliberations of 20 November 1440, when the

right of patronage of the chancel of the church itself was ceded to private citizens (Chapter 9, note 15). An assembly was held in the sacristy on that occasion as well as later (for example in 1442, when Cosimo de' Medici committed himself to carrying on the work in the church), which indicates that it served as a true chapter house.

Payments made in 1451-53 refer to the treatment of the oculi in the dome. A document of 14 October 1451 refers to bronze ingots; on 8 July 1452 bronze ingots weighing 13 *libbre* and 8 *once* were paid for, and on 17 July additional *libbre* were paid for (1 *libbra* = 0.3395 kg, or just under 12 oz). In April 1453, payment was made for glass for one or more windows " of the sacristy of the *chappola* [chapel or dome] of S. Lorenzo". Isabelle Hyman (1968, pp. 363-64) interprets these payments (which amounted in all to a little less than 50 *lire*) as connected with work on the oculi. The doubts I still entertained were dispelled by information from Ettore Bencini, who could say from personal knowledge that each roundel in the dome weighs 8 or 9 kg (18 or 20 lb), whereas the round-headed windows weigh 15 kg (33 lb) and have iron, not bronze, frames. Weight also rules out the possibility that the bronze was intended for grilles on the outside of the windows of the sacristy or transept, where deep notches indicate that such grilles did in fact exist. The bronze ingots were used for the splendid geometric pierced tracery in the oculi (for two of the patterns see Parronchi 1964, pls. 94a, b). In the original plasterwork around the oculi there are traces of graffiti with ornamental patterns (oral communication from Francesco Gurrieri).

That the sacristy was still not complete at the end of the 1450s appears from a poem in praise of Cosimo and his sons and of the public honours paid to the Pope and to the son of the Duke of Milan when they visited Florence in 1459 (1458 Florentine style). For the text of the poem see Chapter 9, and see also note 25 to that chapter.

5. That the chapel of the Medici Saints attached to its ritual western side was not part of the same scheme is demonstrated by the absolute disparity between the two elevations: the chapel wall blocks some of the sacristy windows, and the two systems of orders are on different scales. The presence of the sacristy, moreover, affected the positioning of interior access doors for the transept, which had to be symmetrical when seen from the crossing, but occur somewhat awkwardly in corners inside the Old and New Sacristies.

6. *The roofs of the Old Sacristy (by Riccardo Pacciani)*. From the small room to the left of the *scarsella* a stair leads to the upper storeys, at the level of the cornices and vaults.

Upon arriving at the level of the windows that stand directly on the entablature of the lower order of the sacristy one can see the well-preserved remains of a roof with its ridge at about the height of the imposts of the arches of the *scarsella* [76]. It is easy to deduce that the windows of the *scarsella* originally transmitted light directly from outside, so that much more light was concentrated on the altar area than on the rest of the chapel. It is clear that at an early stage the exterior of the sacristy was not as we see it now — a parallelepiped surmounted asymmetrically by the conical dome [63, 64] but instead a kind of montage of several distinct elements: the cube of the sacristy chamber, the small structure

of the *scarsella*, the two lateral service rooms, and the cylinder of the drum topped by the conical roof of the dome. This impression is confirmed by examining the outer surface, the extrados, of the small cupola over the *scarsella* as seen from the upper storey [77]. On the former outer wall of the sacristy one can make out clearly the signs of another pitched roof which covered the *scarsella* on the outside.

7. The connection between the two buildings was already suspected by K. Bauch (*Abendländische Kunst*, Düsseldorf, 1952, p. 183), but was denied by H. Keller (*Die Kunstlandschaften Italiens*, Munich, 1960, p. 336). Not only their plan forms but also their dimensions coincide exactly, both being squares of about 20 *braccia* per side (about 11.5 m or roughly 37 ft 8 in.), and even their elevations are similar in dimensions. Burns (1971, p. 279) hypothesizes that the derivation from the Padua Baptistery was intentional and requested by the patron, Giovanni di Bicci, who had been Florentine ambassador to Padua and Venice (see. B. Dami, *Giovanni Bicci dei Medici*, Florence, 1899, p. 28, and R. Cessi, " Gli Alberti di Firenze in Padova: Per la storia dei Fiorentini in Padova", *Archivio Storico Italiano*, ser. 5, XL, 1907, p. 84; and for architectural history in particular, G. Fiocco, " La Casa di Palla Strozzi", *Memorie dell'Accademia Nazionale dei Lincei*, ser. VIII, V, 7, 1954).

On the basis of our investigations, however, the relationship to Padua becomes less conclusive or at best partial, in that, if at all, it is to be seen only in the main chamber, whose correspondence in measurements might well depend, in any case, on an analogous use of simple multiples of the standard unit of linear measurement.

8. These terracotta tubes or vases are about 20 cm (roughly 7 in.) in diameter, fitted into each other and solidly fixed in superimposed rows by a lime mortar. They were discovered by a research group led by F. Gurrieri. See now his article, " La volta della ' sacrestia vecchia' ", in *La Nazione*, CXIX, 30 June 1977, p. 3.

9. The Ridolfi Chapel is known through the Biographer (f. 303v):

Schiatta Ridolfi having to build a small chapel in S. Jacopo in Borgo Oltrarno, and Filippo getting to know of this, he said that he would show them in that chapel just how to go about it. And this he did, and it was the first in Florence to use that form that is still called with crests and sails [a creste ed a vela], built with the help of a cane [canna] or pole [pertica] which is fixed at its lower end and is then revolved in a circle, little by little getting shorter the higher it goes, touching continuously with its movable end the bricks and half-bricks [mezzane] that are being put in position, until the dome is finally closed. This is a chapel open on two sides, which is beside the chancel and the campanile.

Though seemingly precise, the description has a number of points open to question, if not actually strange, which have created no end of confusion for scholars. It is probable that the chapel was at the end of an aisle and entirely open on two sides, like the Barbadori Chapel which does survive (see Chapter 6). But it is less certain that its vaulting was of the " crests and sails" or rib-and-web type [78] normally used only over spaces much larger than 4 by 4 m (13 by 13 ft), the dimensions of an average chapel, which would mean that here one would have to presume a perhaps exceptionally large chamber in what is only a modest-sized church.

On the other hand, this sort of dome could only with difficulty be extended to the dimensions of that on the Cathedral, and in fact its construction was never attempted for spaces larger than those of a chapel, or at most the crossing between nave and transept. The Ridolfi Chapel dome has occasionally been proposed (even by scholars in our time) as a model for the vast dome of the Cathedral: but there was no need for such an experiment, because a masonry model for that dome, to scale, was constructed by Brunelleschi himself beside the campanile, and similar models of brick were made by others.

It may be that what Brunelleschi did try out in this chapel was a system of internal chains or tie-beams which would do away with the need for visible horizontal ties in the space beneath the arches like those which, certainly because of its absence from the site, were introduced in the Foundling Hospital loggia after the first small vault constructed showed cracks. An analogous expedient was resorted to when cracks appeared in the great vault over the nave of the Cathedral.

Apart from the type of dome itself (which if anything may have served as model for the cupola of the Old Sacristy), the reference to the system of marking out the measurements remains unclear. In order to be fixed in place at one end, the rod would have to rest on a stable support and, specifically, a high scaffolding until the base of the vault was reached (something entirely impossible in the Cathedral, if only because of the expense and of the difficulty of moving such a contrivance). Moreover if the rod was shortened as it rose, then the vault must have been of depressed form, since, had it been perfectly round, the rod would not have had to be shortened, and, if it were pointed, it would have had to be lengthened.

For the history of the Ridolfi Chapel and the church, radically altered in 1709, see Paatz 1940-54, II, pp. 385-86, note 4 on p. 395, and note 16 on p. 396. An attempt at a conjectural reconstruction of the chapel on the basis of the Old Sacristy and the Pazzi Chapel was made by Sanpaolesi (1936, pp. 334-35). The date of the construction is unknown and 1418 has been tentatively suggested, on the basis of the position of the account of it in the Biography and also with reference to the projects for the Cathedral dome.

10. The Roman origin of the system of ribs used by Brunelleschi was put forward and discussed in particular by W. Sas-Zaloziecky (1959). The alternative thesis, to which I give my entire approval, that the rib-and-web dome derives from the solutions evolved for Gothic buttressed apses, was put forward, though without success, by both Folnesics and Fontana. The Roman examples adduced might explain, if anything, the complex ribless umbrella vaults much used in the Lombard Renaissance. It is true that a drawing by Francesco di Giorgio (Turin, Biblioteca Reale, Cod. Saluzziano, f. 90v) shows as an umbrella dome the covering, already then largely destroyed, of the Canopus in Hadrian's Villa at Tivoli, but this drawing is an inaccurate rendering of the monument; and such a structure was in any case extremely rare in ancient buildings, whereas it was common in Gothic design. For similar reasons — the difficulty of finding suitable models at hand, weighed against the availability and abundance of

later and more local models such as Gothic vaults — I think we can rule out Islamic mosques as a prototype, proposed by Sanpaolesi.

Although oculi are found in Tuscan architecture before Brunelleschi, and the immediate precedent may be the drum of the Cathedral dome [113], the result in the Old Sacristy is singularly akin in appearance (and probably in symbolism as well) to the crossing tower and west tower of the Carolingian abbey of Centula.

11. The Biographer is uninformed on the various initial changes in programme for the church as a whole, even confusing the moment when the Medici took over general responsibility for it. But of the walls flanking the *scarsella* he writes (f. 310r):

> Because it had not yet been decided whether the small doors of the sacristies that flank the [altar] chapel, one of which leads to the water fountain and well and the other to the place where the candles are kept, should be made in wood or in another material [bronze] as they are at present, they still remained to be done; likewise the walls were left roughly keyed [*addentellate*] and with nothing but the opening and the relieving arch at the top.

That the walls with the doors were left "roughly keyed" indicates that the openings were only provisional; the arches over them may mean that the wall originally had windows, which were then extended at the bottom so as to serve as doors. Donatello was in fact entrusted with redoing those walls entirely, and without consulting Brunelleschi he made the large reliefs and the doors below them entirely in his own manner. The Biographer makes it explicit that the conflict between the former friends concerned "those narrow stretches of wall with the small doors between pilaster and pilaster, from the *scarsella* to the corner of the walls", and in this context refers to sonnets written on this occasion by Brunelleschi attacking Donatello, none of which seem to have survived or at any rate been identified. The scurrilous "Panni alla burchia, e visi barbipiechi" is no longer attributed to Brunelleschi (see Chapter 16, note 15).

The doors designed by Donatello for the lateral service rooms are faithful imitations of ancient Roman models, either the portal near the Torre de' Conti which was drawn by Giuliano da Sangallo (see Burns 1971, ill. 12 facing p. 273, from Cod. Barberini 4424, f. 38v) or the door of the Pantheon. The triumphal arch resting on a markedly projecting entablature in the Old Sacristy derives from the design of the area around the inside of the doorway of the Pantheon — a design which, as H. W. Janson has stressed (in "The Image of Man in Renaissance Art: from Donatello to Michelangelo", *The Renaissance Image of Man and the World*, Columbus, Ohio, 1966, pp. 77-103), served also as the model for such humanist tombs as that of Leonardo Bruni by Bernardo Rossellino.

12. The altar, the astronomical painting on the vault, and the structure of the outer walls all present difficulties in interpretation.

The date 1432 is deeply incised at the back of a cavity in the altar, closed now by a wooden door but formerly by Brunelleschi's relief of *The Sacrifice of Isaac*. This cavity may originally have housed a reliquary. The Prior of the church, Padre G. Setti, pointed out to me that not the whole altar but only its central part is consecrated, still covered as the liturgy requires by a waxed cloth and with a relic in its centre. The date might refer to the completion of

the altar with its relief decoration, to its placing in the *scarsella*, or even to the time when relics were placed in it. This altar may also have been brought to the Old Sacristy from somewhere else: one must remember that when the *scarsella* was built the sacristy already had an altar, in the centre. That altar was consecrated in the normal way: at its four corners it has hollows which may have held the regulation four crosses engraved on bronze roundels.

The vault of the *scarsella* was the subject of a famous essay by Aby Warburg ("Eine astronomische Himmeldarstellung in der alten Sakristei von S. Lorenzo in Florenz", in *Mitteilungen des kunsthistorischen Instituts in Florenz*, II, 1912-17, 1, pp. 34-36, and *Gesammelte Schriften*, I, Berlin, 1932, pp. 165-72) which marked the start of the study of the relationship between astrology and Renaissance architecture and visual arts. As the most likely date for this representation of the night sky he proposed 14 July 1422, on the basis of the report by Ludovico Antonio Giamboni in his *Diario Sacro... di Firenze*, Florence, 1700, of a consecration of the high altar in S. Lorenzo. That report, however, in fact concerns the foundation (or re-foundation) of the new transept, which took place on Sunday 9 July 1422. Later, on the basis of the demonstration by F. Saxl (1934) that the Pazzi Chapel also has a hemispherical vault over the altar showing the night sky in July, and taking into account the dates which at the time were still assigned to that chapel, Warburg opted instead for 6 July 1439, date of the solemn conclusion of the Council of Florence.

Now, it is necessary to review step by step all the phases of his research, in which he had the assistance of Dr Graff of the Hamburg Observatory. In the fresco over the altar of the Old Sacristy the sun is clearly depicted in Cancer, thus between 21 June and 22 July. The moon is in Taurus and waning. With his unique competence in astronomical and astrological texts, Warburg could establish that this represents the twenty-third day after the solstice, and that the moon is in about the fourth night before the new moon. On the basis of the first element he determined the day and month to be 6 July and, working from the recurrences of the lunar phases between 1420 and 1440, the possible years to be 1422, 1423, and 1439. To obtain the exact date, one had only to subtract four days from the date of the new moon.

Professor Giuseppe Caprioli of the Rome Observatory has had the rare kindness to supply me with the dates of the ecclesiastical new moon according to the Julian calendar from 1400 to 1499, thus broadening the research done in Hamburg. These tables call for radical changes in the computations made by Warburg. What is most questionable is the method of computing the twenty-three days after the solstice. It is evident that Warburg counted them on the basis of the astronomical solstice, which was moved forward to 12/13 June. From this it was possible to deduce the date 6 July. But it is very probable that in the liturgical calendar, which is the only one that is relevant here, the solstice continued to be reckoned as 21 June. The twenty-third day after it would therefore be 14 July. Moreover, the dates of the lunar phases for 1420-40 supplied to Warburg by the Hamburg Observatory do not match those computed by the Rome Observatory (and I must thank Professor Caprioli for his extensive discussion of this point). For the periods of 10 July and 18 July, the astronomical and liturgical dates, we have the following recurrences:

8 July	10 July	12 July
1407	1415	1423
1426	1434	1442
1445	1453	1461
1464	1472	1480
1483	1491	*1499*

16 July	18 July	19 July
1409	1417	1406
1428	1436	1425
1447	1455	1444
1466	1474	1463
1485	*1493*	*1482*

A further reduction of the possibilities is given by the consideration that, as was the case for example with the foundation of the transept of S. Lorenzo or of the rotunda of SS. Annunziata, the liturgical event was commemorated on a Sunday, there being no solemn non-Sunday festivities in July. Now, 6 July was a Sunday in 1483 and 1499; if we include 5 and 7 July, then we can consider also the years 1415, 1426, 1461, 1464, and 1472. For 14 July, which I maintain to be the most probable, there were Sundays in 1409, 1482, and 1493, and for 13 and 15 July, in 1425, 1436, 1455, and 1466.

We see then that on the basis of the data utilized by Warburg the vault fresco in the Old Sacristy proves to be of very little help indeed for any sure chronology and, it must be stressed, he himself worked from external documents. Moreover, the event commemorated could just as well be earlier than the building, or even related not to it but to its patrons. We can rule out any connection with the dates of their death or burial.

In the matter of symbolism, the vault painted with astrological subjects would appear to represent a baldacchino, and as F. Saxl and A. Beer have shown for the zodiac at Qusayr 'Amra in Syria (in a contribution to K. A. C. Creswell, *Early Muslim Architecture*, Oxford, 1932-40, I, pp. 289-94), the use of such astronomical figurations is of Arab origin, though obviously by the early fifteenth century such images were treated entirely in a Renaissance manner (see J. Seznec, *La Survivance des dieux antiques*, London, 1940, trans. *The Survival of the Pagan Gods*, New York, 1953; and F. Saxl, *Lectures*, London, 1957, especially ''The Revival of late Antique Astrology''). The reason for the choice of such an unusual subject at S. Lorenzo is still not clear.

The third element that has been put forward for the dating of the Old Sacristy, the encasing of the *scarsella* and service rooms to form a unified block, gives only a remote date *ante quem*. Examination of the walls added in that operation shows, in fact, that the body of the *scarsella* and the service rooms was plastered over and then exposed to rain for some years. When the sacristy was joined to the transept the operation was carried out somewhat carelessly, or at any rate joints and gaps are plainly evident. The fact that on the exterior of this part, as on the Medici Chapel to the left of the transept, there is a handsome terracotta frieze with cherubs and the gridiron of the patron saint of the church, St Laurence, means nothing more than that the Medici took special pains when it came to their private chapels. Correctly understood, this certainly does not point to an earlier phase than that of the other parts of the entire complex. As we shall see in Chapter 9, it was only in the contract of 1442 that Cosimo de' Medici was granted permission to have both the chancel and the nave substantially altered, and it was only in 1449/50 that the upper part of the transept was built

and roofed (document from Isabelle Hyman). The original system of individual roofs resting directly on the vaults was later replaced over the aisles by a single monopitch roof, so the frieze, whose function was to mask the differences in the roofs, would be contemporary with that alteration. The date of the rearrangement is unknown, but it must be after 1452, when a new overall plan was drawn up for the entire church.

13. I find quite convincing the suggestion by Lando Bartoli (1971, especially p. 132, figs. 6 and 7) that the proportions of the internal elevations of the sacristy are based on a square module of 2 by 2 *braccia*. Up to about the point of juncture with the dome the walls are clearly divided in half by the entablature, which is itself one modular unit (2 *braccia*) high, giving rise to a sequence of $5 + 1 + 5$ ($= 11$) units. The height of the room is thus one unit more than the width, which is equivalent to 10 units. The dome adds another 5 units to the height. (The main chamber is thus not, as is usually said, a cube (though the dome is a hemisphere); the addition of an extra unit to the height may have been an optical corrective to compensate for foreshortening as one looks up from below, but there is no evidence of such expedients elsewhere.) The width of the windows and the centrepoint of the roundels does not fit into the square grid: to be applied there, the unit would need to be halved, to 1 *braccio*.

But even a half-unit of 1 *braccio* cannot account for the proportions of the *scarsella*, which were apparently worked out independently, nor is it applicable to the end wall with its decorations by Donatello, where the grid only roughly establishes the width and position of the windows and the two side doors, the line falling sometimes inside and sometimes in the centre of their frames. The discrepancy in proportional system between the main room of the sacristy, the *scarsella*, and the end wall, is further evidence that they were designed separately.

The validity of Bartoli's research is, however, lessened by the fact that he made use of Geymüller's old measured drawings, which recent investigations have shown to be unreliable. Sanpaolesi's drawings, reproduced here [60, 61], derive from the same source, and would therefore not be suitable for the close scrutiny that Wittkower recommended as essential to the understanding of the proportional principles underlying humanist architecture. A corrected ground plan with a vertical section, considerably more accurate than those usually reproduced, was published by E. Antoniacci, A. Cappelli and P. Gelardi in the proceedings of a meeting at the Accademia di S. Luca in Rome in 1977 (*Problemi Brunelleschiani: Sagrestia Vecchia e San Lorenzo*, Rome, 1977), and new measurements by F. Gurrieri will be published in the acts of the 1977 Brunelleschi Congress.

14. The two rooms thus correspond to the *prothasis* and *diaconicon* of Eastern churches. In the overall design for the new transept of S. Lorenzo a similar sacristy-cum-chapel was to stand at the end of the opposite arm, repeating the theme of the two *pastophoriae*, though on a scale large enough for them to be independent *sacella* (a traditional arrangement). Such *sacella* imitate the Holy Sepulchre, and are therefore particularly appropriate for a funerary chapel (see G. Bandmann, ''Über Pastophorien und verwandte Nebenräume im mittelalterlichen Kir-

chenbau'', *Kunstgeschichtliche Studien für Hans Kauffmann*, Berlin, 1956, pp. 19-58; for Brunelleschi in particular, pp. 55-58).

For the *scarsella* plan and the Holy Sepulchre, see R. Krautheimer, ''Introduction to an 'Iconography of Medieval Architecture' '', *Journal of the Warburg and Courtauld Institutes*, V, 1942). For the niches as segment of a single circle see H. Burns 1971; A. Grabar, *Martyrium*, Paris, 1946, I, especially pp. 102-19; E. Baldwin Smith, *The Dome*, Princeton, 1950, pp. 120-24; S. Sinding-Larsen, ''Some functional and iconographical aspects of the centralized church in the Italian Renaissance'', *Acta ad Archaeologiam et Artium Historiam Pertinentia*, II, 1965, pp. 228-29, 243-44, and ''Palladio's Redentore: a Compromise in Composition'', *Art Bulletin*, 47, 1965, pp. 431-37; H. Windfeld-Hansen, ''L'hexaconque funéraire de l'area sub divo du cimetière de Prétextat à Rome'', *Acta ad Archaeologiam et Artium Historiam Pertinentia*, IV, 1969, pp. 61-93.

Another reference to the Holy Sepulchre is the spirally-grooved roof of the lantern of the Old Sacristy [62], which resembles that on the shrine in the Cappella Rucellai in S. Pancrazio, itself an explicit copy of the Holy Sepulchre (see L. H. Heydenreich, in *De artibus, opuscula XL, Essays in Honor of Erwin Panofsky*, ed. M. Meiss, New York, 1961, I, pp. 219-29). Some writers have associated the spiral-crowned lantern with Islamic pinnacles. The sacristy/chapel may have been deliberately linked with the Holy Land, pilgrimages and crusades, but the allusion (if any) seems to have been purely devotional, and unassociated, as far as is known, with any current political programmes.

For architectural symbolism in general, see F. Möbius, *Bauornament im Mittelalter, Symbol und Bedeutung*, Vienna, 1974.

15. A fairly painstaking analysis has been made by M. Dezzi Bardeschi (1974, in particular pp. 46-48), who among other things has examined the cosmological significance of the two vaults, the smaller one divided into 36 segments, the larger into 108 by the knots in the twisted sailcloth motif around their bases, while ''the four pendentives celebrate the four parts of the nature of the world... Each 'segment' is divided, through the presence of a central oculus, into three equal parts, two of shadow, one of light.''

Support for this interpretation comes from Honorius of Autun (*De gemma animale*, in Migne, *Patrologia Latina*, CLXXII, cols. 586 ff.) who, writing before 1130, says: ''The transparent windows that keep out inclement weather and let light enter are the Doctors who resist the tempest of the heresies and pour light on the teaching of the Church.'' Moreover the windows, especially if shaped like oculi, ''twinkle like the lights of the sky'' (''ut luminaria in coelo micant''). (For the symbolic value of oculi in Italian medieval architecture see W. Ranke, *Frühe Rundfenster in Italien*, thesis, Berlin University, 1968, chapter II, pp. 52-128).

16. This is lucidly stated in the famous letter to Pope Leo X concerning architecture, compiled by Baldassare Castiglione though inspired or dictated by an unknown master who has been variously identified. According to this text, architectural drawing is different because its aim is to enable one ''to understand all the measurements and to know how to determine all the elements of a building without error", and it consists of plan, elevation and section with corrections of all the fortuitous alterations due to pre-existing structures or a difficult site. The space covered by the plan

> must be levelled and one must take care that the line of the base so levelled and on a precise level plane be parallel to all the planes of the building... so that all the walls of the building will be in plumb and perpendicular above it. Once the plan, round or square or of whatever shape, is drawn and articulated in all its elements considering their widths, always measuring everything with a metric scale [that is, maintaining the same scale], one must draw the line that marks the width of the base of the entire building, and from the middle one must draw another straight line which will create right angles on either side of it, and this will be the central axis of the building [and thus the elevation will be constructed in parallel with the central or longitudinal axis]. And all this is to be done with lines parallel to the line of the plane of the building.

As a final aid there is "the inside wall", that is the section, which "shows half of the building inside as if it were divided in the middle". In the case of a circular building the section and elevation must avoid perspective foreshortenings, rendering the walls as if they were developed in a single flat plane, the plan itself sufficing to indicate their curvature together with "the precise measurements in palms, feet, fingers and grains, right down to its very least parts", clearly given and easy to use. In addition, because everything is based on right angles, the compass and square are indispensable tools for the designer and for the construction worker, whether stonecutter or mason: we do in fact see the latter equipped with them in illustrations dating from the second half of the Quattrocento.

The structure of such centralized chambers as the Old Sacristy was interpreted thus by Pierre de Rossy in the twelfth century: "square... at the base and rises to the cone, thereby figuring the unity of the Church, as in the ark of Noah, contained completely in one cubit". Or, again according to Honorius, in the face of the pessimistic theme of persecution it would represent triumph: "Those built round in the form of a circle show that the Church is constructed along the circuit of the globe so as to become the circle of eternity by means of love".

Numerological speculations, especially relative to the number 3 and drawn from geometry (the triangle, the three dimensions of the cube), mathematics (the number 9), mythology and astrology are found in the correspondence of Coluccio Salutati (1891-1911 ed., IV, 1, pp. 48-52, 228-29), still in the wake of the medieval tradition.

This approach could be extended to all the elements and typologies and was, in any case, considered an essential aspect of the architectural semiotic. In the Pazzi Chapel the number 12 is associated with the element one can call literary — narrative even, in a sense — of the twelve doors and windows. Besides, there are more ways than one to link a symbolical content to an architectural function. To simplify, there are essentially two approaches: either one conceals the code or else one expresses and accentuates it so that its very conspicuousness becomes a kind of key. Let no one doubt that Brunelleschi was perfectly explicit, at least as much as Borromini two centuries later. It may be that we have difficulty in evaluating his aggressivity simply because the means he used most — the classicizing vocabulary and syntax — are by now largely taken for granted.

6 The Barbadori Chapel in S. Felicita

In addition to the works mentioned in these notes, see L. Balocchi, *Illustrazione dell'I. e R. Chiesa parrocchiale di Santa Felicita*, Florence, 1828. New photographs are in F. Borsi et al., *Brunelleschiani*, 1979, figs. 30-35.

1. According to information in the *Istoria dell'Antichissima Chiesa e Monastero di Santa Felicita in Firenze* by Domenico Maria Manni of 1750, a manuscript which has long been known (Florence, Biblioteca del Seminario Maggiore), the chapel was endowed by Bartolomeo Barbadori, who was condemned to death in 1379 accused of high treason. The chapel would therefore have been remodelled by his sons Giovanni and Niccolò, more particularly the latter, who was a dominant figure in the Florentine oligarchy from 1417 on but was banished in 1434 shortly before the return of Cosimo de' Medici from exile. The 1427 tax register shows him to have been among the eighteen wealthiest Florentines (see the article on him, with documents, by I. Walter in the *Dizionario Biografico degli Italiani*, VI, 1974). In the light of that wealth, however, the chapel seems on the face of it decidedly modest. Family interest in the church continued, and in 1435-38 a second Barbadori Chapel, dedicated to S. Frediano (St Frigidian) was built using money left by Donato, son of Bartolomeo, by Michele Barbadori, Rector (*spedalingo*) of the Hospital of S. Maria Nuova. (That chapel is not associated with Brunelleschi.)

The information given by Manni is not to be trusted because he merely borrows from Vasari (ed. Milanesi, II, 1878, p. 350), at least for the name of Bartolomeo Barbadori, while Vasari himself, except for the name of the patron, borrows word for word from the Biographer.

The Barbadori Palace, which has not survived, was said to have been built on a cramped and awkwardly shaped site. It is thought to be the one referred to in the tax registry of 1427 by Giovanni Barbadori as "a house situated in Florence at the foot of the Ponte Vecchio for my use and habitation... with four workshops on the ground floor". It stood alongside the Torre de' Rossi; the area was thoroughly disrupted by German mines in the last war. Although the palace was never completed, as we know from the Biographer, Brunelleschi seems to have resolved various difficult spatial problems in it.

2. Capponi was active in Rome under Julius II and Leo X: see F. M. Clapp, *Jacopo Carucci da Pontormo, his Life and Work*, New Haven and London, 1916, p. 279, doc. 279. For the donation of the chapel, see the deed drawn up by Ser Battista da Firenzuola on 1 July 1525 (Florence, Archivio di Stato, Notarile Antecosimiano, B. 955, cc. 332 ff., quoted by J. Shearman in *Pontormo's Altarpiece in Santa Felicita*, Newcastle-upon-Tyne, 1971, note 6).

Pontormo's dome fresco is known from drawings: see J. Cox, "Pontormo's Drawings for the destroyed Vault of the Capponi Chapel", *Burlington Magazine*, XCVIII, 1956, pp. 17-18, and J. Cox Rearick, *The Drawings of Pontormo*, Cambridge, Mass., 1964, pp. 253-56.

3. P. Fontana 1919-32.

4. For this tradition see Shearman, op. cit., and H. Saalman, "Further notes on the Cappella Barbadori, S. Felicita", *Burlington Magazine*, C, 1958, pp. 270-74.

5. This type of "compound pier" has been convincingly traced back by Klotz (1970, with a good photograph as fig. 42) to the tabernacle by Orcagna in Orsanmichele.

6. Here I am using Erik Forssman, *Dorico, ionico, corinzio nell'architettura del Rinascimento*, Bari, 1973, pp. 12-13 (original, *Dorisch, Ionisch, Korinthisch: Studien über den Gebrauch der Säulenordnungen in der Architektur des 16.-18. Jahrhunderts*, Stockholm, 1961) though disagreeing with him as well as with Klotz (1970, pp. 21 ff.) that these orders were used deliberately in a conscious quest for variety. Forssman however refers to the women's cloister in the Foundling Hospital, but this was built after Brunelleschi had left, and does not appear to have been designed by him.

7. Klotz 1970, fig. 13.

8. F. L. Del Migliore, *Firenze città nobilissima illustrata*, Florence, 1684, p. 17.

9. Niccoli's report (1938) is extremely precise, even if the elements studied were limited in number. The reduced corner pilasters terminate at the top abruptly and in an unsystematic way. This feature, he concludes,

> seems cut off and reaches different heights, starting from the abacus of the Ionic capitals, in the various corners. We must deduce that, at least in Brunelleschi's intention, it should have continued up to an entablature on the inside wall, upon which, in turn, there would have stood half-arches, pendentives and a dome... Having demolished a floor [the flooring of the loggia above the chapel], around the extrados of the eighteenth-century vault we found part of a brick dome springing from the same level and perfectly hemispherical.

How Niccoli could have judged the dome to be hemispherical from examining only its springing is difficult to say, and in his drawings he does not specify the exact height from which the dome would have sprung. Still, one must praise his prudence in not attempting to produce a schematic reconstruction drawing of it. (Sanpaolesi's alteration of Niccoli's drawings, with no indication at all that he had altered them, is misleading.) Moreover, Niccoli himself was uncertain whether those remains of a dome (which do not match up with the original prolongation of the corner pilasters) were to be ascribed to Brunelleschi or to the builder of the sixteenth-century vault, and indeed rather favoured the latter.

Other evidence of alterations is the way in which the surrounding brick walls are scraped away at the height of the original heavy cornice, as well as the recomposition of the stone ring around the dome, re-set to form a ring with a different diameter. Niccoli found also "a fragment decorated with a plaited moulding of lesser dimensions but in a design analogous to that adorning the soffits" and supposed this, with some doubts, to have been part of the frieze of the interior entablature.

Shearman found traces of blue and gold on the pilasters in the Barbadori Chapel, as did my students. Niccoli believed these to be the heraldic colours of the Barbadori family; but they are also found on the portal of Alberti's S. Andrea at Mantua. The

10. The reconstruction is partly based on observations made by my students Giuseppe Arcidiacono and Giuseppe Di Giovanni. It is substantially developed from Niccoli and Shearman's observations, but differs from the former in including an architrave of the same height as that on the exterior. We were not able to explore the space above the vault to check the findings of Niccoli.

11. The Barbadori Chapel, like the Ridolfi Chapel in S. Jacopo sopr'Arno, cannot be considered a trial run for the great dome of the Cathedral (see Chapter 5, note 9); not only was there a masonry model for that dome, but the model itself was larger than this chapel. If the chapel served as a model for anything — which I doubt — it could have been for the Foundling Hospital loggia, which is on the whole the work most like it, especially if one thinks of the roundels there in their original concave form [33].

For Saalman the capitals, paralleled in Donatello's, niche for his *St Louis* completed around 1423 (see Janson 1959, II, pp. 45-46), give grounds for dating this chapel between the Foundling Hospital and the Old Sacristy. The altar, however, might be later in view of the difference in style of its capitals (though they could also be merely by another hand), and for them Saalman (1958-B) proposes a date around 1433. The elements favouring an attribution to Brunelleschi and an earlier date are only the references in the Biography to this chapel and to the Ridolfi Chapel.

What stylistic analogies there are with Masaccio's *Trinity* and Donatello's niche can be turned the other way around since, as U. Schlegel has pointed out (1959, 1963), if the chapel was in fact by Buggiano, for example, and of late date — which would then agree with documents concerning other undertakings under the patronage of the Barbadori between 1435 and 1438, date of an altarpiece they commissioned — it would have to be read not as a prototype but as a free derivation.

As Schlegel views it, the elements weighing against an early date and an attribution to Brunelleschi are: the compound piers which are more advanced than those in the *Trinity* and therefore of later date; the acanthus leaves of the capitals with long rather than short stalks; the defective conclusion of the abacus which has only a weak rectangular profile; the lack of three-dimensional unity between tondo and rosette, the tondo being too flattened; and the architrave with small roundels that separate the horizontal bands and conclude it below as in the Palazzo di Parte Guelfa. There are no such small roundels in the Foundling Hospital loggia, but they are present in the Tabernacle of the Mercanzia by Donatello. Where Schlegel's argument proves fragile is in its too mechanical comparison with Masaccio's fresco and in its failure to take sufficiently into account the active collaboration between Brunelleschi and Donatello. The sculptural details could very well have been executed by some assistant. For Buggiano, born about 1412 (see pp. 247-59 in F. Borsi et al., *Brunelleschiani*, 1979), the earliest date would be around 1430, and that is in fact what Schlegel proposes.

A. Cadei (1971) also remains uncertain when it comes to the Cappella Barbadori: see below, Chapter 7, note 4.

7 Experiments with perspective

Basic studies of perspective are those by Decio Gioseffi, *Perspectiva artificialis: Per la storia della prospettiva*, Trieste, 1957; "Complementi di prospettiva", *Critica d'Arte*, n. s., IV, 1957, 24, pp. 468-88, and V, 1958, 25-26, pp. 102-39; and two articles in the *Encyclopedia of World Art* — "Optical concepts", in vol. X, cols. 757-70, and "Perspective", in vol. XI, cols. 183-221 (New York, Toronto and London, 1965 and 1966); and those by A. Parronchi, most of them republished in his volume of 1964. For a review of the material, see Marisa Dalai Emiliani, "La questione della prospettiva, 1960-68", *L'Arte*, n.s., 1968, 2, pp. 96-105.

Among general works, see Miriam Schild Bunim, *Space in Medieval Painting and the Forerunners of Perspective*, New York, 1940; John White, *The Birth and Rebirth of Pictorial Space*, London, 1957; Samuel Y. Edgerton Jr, *The Renaissance Discovery of Linear Perspective*, New York, 1975.

An extensive bibliography of treatises and studies on perspective has now been published by L. Vagnetti: "De Naturali et Artificiali Perspectiva", *Studi e Documenti di Architettura*, 9-10, Florence, March 1979. Another bibliography, by Kim Veltman, will be published in the second volume of the proceedings of the first International Congress on Perspective in the Renaissance (held in Milan in 1978).

For the reconstruction of Quattrocento perspective techniques see the *Manuale di Restituzione Prospettica di dipinti rinascimentali con rappresentazioni di architettura*, ed. G. Degl'Innocenti, Florence, 1975-76, with a full bibliography, pp. 29-35, and the proceedings of the International Congress on Perspective, of which the first volume has been published (Florence, 1979).

For Brunelleschi's experiments, in addition to the general works see Edgerton 1973 and Beltrame 1973.

1. It should not be forgotten that in the Byzantine tradition perspective had been a constant subject of discussion ever since the Hellenistic writers. Proclus in particular had defined *skenographia* in his commentary on Euclid as "the practice that teaches the artist how to proceed so that nothing in his work will appear distorted because of the distance and the height", basing himself on the optical corrections suggested to sculptors by Geminus (see G. Mathew, *Byzantine Aesthetics*, London, 1963, p. 5). Among other relevant Hellenistic texts are the minor treatise on astronomy by Pappus, which includes four initial definitions of the rays and visual cone, and the commentary by Anthemius of Tralles, the architect of Hagia Sophia, on the *Catoptrica* of the pseudo-Euclid and of Hero of Alexandria.

The best way of understanding at a glance just how diverse are our codes of interpretation of perspective, and therefore our ways of reading it, is to consult the "transcriptions" of Quattrocento frescoes proposed by Sven Sandström in *Levels of Unreality*, Uppsala, 1963 (with, on p. 29, the *Trinity* of Masaccio viewed laterally).

2. According to the inventory made at the death of Lorenzo the Magnificent, a picture on "wood painted with a view [*prospettiva*] with the Palazzo de' Signori and the Piazza and Loggia and houses just as it is" was in the "room with two beds" in the Palazzo Medici on Via Larga, and a "picture on wood, painted with the Duomo [sic] of S. Giovanni" was in the room of "Bartoldo, or of the men servants" (Florence, Archivio di Stato, Archivio Mediceo avanti il Principato, CCXV, f. 11, cited by Milanesi and by Saalman).

3. The most complete and scientific attempt at a reconstruction of the methods of perspective in use in the Quattrocento was that carried out by Giovanni Degl'Innocenti in collaboration with Franco Luchini and Silvano Salvadori in the History of Architecture programme of the Faculty of Architecture, University of Florence. (See the bibliography, above.) Degl'Innocenti and Salvadori have supplied the following account of their research on Brunelleschi's first perspective panel.

Puzzled as to just how Brunelleschi used his method involving mirror, glass and grid (see the comment on *figs. 101-103*), and aware of the enormous difficulties inherent in a procedure that is only apparently empirical (Filarete too reminds us that Brunelleschi's method was based on geometrical "reasoning"), we planned a systematic programme (using a computer in the later stages) to explore all the possible ways of realizing such a geometrical construction. After scrutinizing critically all the hypotheses put forward up to now by historians, and redrawing for ourselves the associated diagrams, we were able to establish models for all the solutions available to artists of the Quattrocento when they tried to represent buildings in foreshortening. If late medieval theories of perception grew out of a medico-physical theory of visual rays, the limpid geometrical reasoning of Brunelleschi — perhaps deliberately polemical because of his own equally intellectualistic theory — must surely have constituted a radical change. Indeed Brunelleschi turned the whole theory upside down, and he did it with demonstrable, tangible proof, placing, as it were, a kind of screen between eye and brain.

In re-enacting the experiment in perspective that the Biographer tells us Brunelleschi carried out, the only unknown factor in the geometrical data we had (either drawn from the sources or derived, for the first time, from precise measurements of the buildings and site) was the height of the ideal observer's eye. This was unknown partly because the question of the original level of the Cathedral pavement is very complex, and partly because we did not know how tall Brunelleschi himself was. But since the recent discovery of his skeleton proved his height to be 1.63 m (5 ft 4 in.) and his skull to be brachycephalic, we can suppose that his eye was 1.56 m (5 ft 1 in.) above ground-level. And the recent excavations of S. Reparata have made it possible to ascertain the original floor level.

If Brunelleschi took up a position — as the Biographer says — 3 *braccia* behind the central doorway of the Cathedral, he would have been standing on ground that was 90 cm (2 ft 11 3/4 in.) below the present level. At that point the doorway itself would have been like a window, framing the field of vision.

If he indeed stood at that level, which is very different from the height at the top of the steps now, this would have simplified the quantity of data he would have had to take into account; instead of the slightly foreshortened view that one now gets looking down at the base of the Baptistery he would have seen the plane horizontally. Under such conditions the only problem was to realize the foreshortenings of the oblique walls of the Baptistery and to give their inlaid compartments correct proportions. To reconstruct the operations presumably done by Brunelleschi, however, one must also put into foreshortening the base of the Baptistery seen from a higher point, as this has been taken for granted by all, or almost all, writers who have dealt with the problem.

The diagrammatic graphic reconstruction of the experiment involves three operations that must be co-ordinated. In the first, after measuring the piazza accurately the true dimensions must be incorporated to scale in the plan and elevation. In the second, the plan and elevation must be foreshortened according to correct perspective. Following the prescription of Piero della Francesca (Book I, Theorem XVI) we inscribed the octagonal form of the base of the Baptistery in a square, then connected the various points that corresponded, and thereby obtained the figure inserted into a regular grid of squares, which is the indispensable basis for a correct rendering in foreshortening.

After this, we established *a priori* the height of the observer as 3 *braccia* (see Alberti) and considered his position either at the level of the present pavement or 90 cm (2 ft 11 3/4 in.) lower, at the level of the old collapsed pavement of the original church of S. Reparata. In this way the horizon line should fall at about 2 or 3 *braccia* above ground level and the vanishing point will be within the first storey of the Baptistery and inside Ghiberti's Gates of Paradise. It should be noted that the viewpoint coincides with the point where the diagonal of the square within which the octagon is inscribed meets the horizon line and is 60 *braccia* distant from the nearest face of the Baptistery and 3 or 3 4/5 *braccia* (or more precisely 2.22 m) behind the outer sill of the central door of the Cathedral. (These new measurements are slightly different from those given by Krautheimer and White.)

The third phase of the procedure followed by Brunelleschi probably involved rendering the lateral faces of the Baptistery in foreshortening. Still utilizing the elevation of the east face, again the plane of projection is reversed as if hinged at the sides of the façade, and with that façade at 45 degrees one gets the perspective of the other sides, keeping in mind that the viewpoint coincides in this case with the vanishing point (as geometrical locus of the flight of all the straight lines at 45 degrees).

For the difficult execution of the foreshortening of the ornamental elements on the oblique faces of the building, and particularly for the correct perspective rendering of the arches of the second order, a modular grid is required which, we have seen, can be derived from the elevation of the east façade. The module is arrived at by dividing the pilaster strips of the topmost order of the Baptistery into two parts. This gives the relationship of 3:10:2:10:2:10:3; thus four large modules of 10 ft each represent the division of the east face of the Baptistery (and since the other faces are similar, their division is the same). In height the large module recurs eight times, so if we inscribe the elevation of the east face in a square its outermost line will coincide with that of the square that circumscribes the base.

In the final step we combined all these phases in a coloured painting in tempera on wood whose final result was, as the Biographer says, a perspective depiction made "with such care and accuracy and the colours of the black and white marble were so faithfully reproduced that no miniaturist ever excelled

him'' (f. 297v). However, Brunelleschi's aim of obtaining an image that could stand in for the reality was not yet achieved. The image arrived at with this procedure is a mirror-image, and to give a full illusion of reality one must use a mirror to correct it, adding other illusionistic tricks such as silvering the sky on the panel as Brunelleschi did (see *figs. 97-100* and their captions).

4. See especially Janson 1967. On Brunelleschi as the possible designer of the architectural background of the *Trinity* I share the caution of Cadei (1971): ''The affinities between the *Trinity* and the Barbadori Chapel do not in fact restrict us to the hypothesis of a single author but fit into a sort of *koinè* of classicizing neophytes among the Florentine artists of the 1420s.'' Cadei presents photographic comparisons with Donatello's doors in the Old Sacristy, which do show affinities in both the treatment of the Ionic capital and the type of horizontal members.

8 The Dome of S. Maria del Fiore

1. The numerous studies on the dome that have appeared since the original Italian edition of this book fall into two large groups, one concerned only with its physical structure, the other with its genesis. To the first belong the reports on measurements such as those begun in 1968 by Mario Fondelli using very modern systems of photogrammetry; to the second, the analyses carried out by our own Dome Study Group, by certain graduate students who worked with Professor Di Pasquale, and by Italian and foreign scholars including P.A. Rossi, T.B. Settle, and Gherardo Gurrieri. The two approaches have produced, so far at least, contradictory findings and a good deal of confusion. It was impossible to use the long awaited book by H. Saalman, since its publication coincides with the printing of this translation. What follows is a summary of the relevant publications since the turn of the century.

For the basic documents on the Cathedral, see Guasti 1887, Poggi 1909, Crispolti 1937, and Paatz 1940-54 (III, pp. 320-612).

For specific studies on the dome, see Bernardo Sansone Sgrilli, *Descrizione e Studj dell'insigne fabbrica di Santa Maria del Fiore*, Florence, 1733; Giovanni Battista Nelli, *Piante ed alzati interiori ed esterni dell'insigne chiesa di Santa Maria del Fiore*, Florence, 1755; C. Guasti 1857, presenting the archive material; Aristide Nardini Despotti Mospignotti, *Filippo di ser Brunellesco e la Cupola del Duomo di Firenze*, Livorno, 1885 (reviewed by Fabriczy in *Repertorium für Kunstwissenschaft*, IX, 1886, pp. 481-85); A. Doren 1898-99; Paul Wenz, *Die Kuppel des Domes Santa Maria del Fiore zu Florenz*, Berlin, 1901; Frederick R. Hiorns, "Brunelleschi and his Dome", *Journal of the Royal Institute of British Architects*, XXXI, 1924, pp. 489-98; Enrico Lusini, "Arnoldo e il Duomo di Firenze", in *Miscellanea di Storia dell'Arte in onore di Igino Benvenuto Supino*, Florence, 1933, pp. 99-111; the *Atti del I Congresso Nazionale di Storia dell'Architettura (1936)*, Florence, 1938, with contributions by Gustavo Giovannoni ("La cupola della Domus Aurea neroniana in Roma'', pp. 3-6), Roberto Salvini ("Arnoldo e la cupola di Santa Maria del Fiore. Tentativo di fondare un'ipotesi'', pp. 25-36), P.

Sanpaolesi ("Le cupole e gli edifici a cupola del Brunelleschi e la loro derivazione da edifici romani'', pp. 37-41), Carlo Roccatelli ("Le cupole di Brunelleschi e la tradizione costruttiva italiana'', pp. 43-51), and Luigi Crema ("Romanità delle volte brunelleschiane'', pp. 129-38); P. Sanpaolesi 1936; W. Paatz, *Werden und Wesen der Trecento-Architektur in Toskana*, Burg, 1937; P. Sanpaolesi, "Il rilievo della cupola del Duomo di Firenze'', *Rivista d'Arte*, ser. 2, IX (XIX), 1937, pp. 79-83; Opera di Santa Maria del Fiore 1939; William Barclay Parsons, *Engineers and Engineering in the Renaissance*, Baltimore, 1939; P. Sanpaolesi 1941 (reviewed by J. Coolidge in *Art Bulletin*, XXXIV, 1952, pp. 154 ff., and G. De Angelis d'Ossat in *Le Arti*, III, 1941, p. 386); F. D. Prager 1950; B. Lowry, "Letter to the Editor'', *Art Bulletin*, XXXI, 1953, pp. 175-77 (critical of both the Sanpaolesi book and the Coolidge review); Guido Guerra, *Statica e tecnica costruttiva delle cupole antiche e moderne*, Naples, 1958; Andreas Grote, *Das Dombauamt in Florenz, 1285-1370*, Munich, 1959; Gottfried Kiesow, "Zur Baugeschichte des Florentiner Domes'', *Mitteilungen des Kunsthistorischen Instituts in Florenz*, X, 1961, pp. 1-22; Decio Gioseffi, *Giotto architetto*, Milan, 1963; Wolfgang Braunfels, *Der Dom von Florenz*, Olten, 1964 (includes an essay by Rolf Dammann on the Dufay consecration motet); H. Saalman 1964; P. Sanpaolesi 1965; J. White 1966; A. Romanini 1969; R. J. Mainstone 1969-70; David Hupert, "Speculations on the Construction of the Dome of Florence Cathedral'', *Journal of the Society of Architectural Historians*, XXIX, 1970, p. 264; H. Klotz 1970, pp. 74-95; F. D. Prager and G. Scaglia 1970; W. Ferri, M. Fondelli, P. Franchi, F. Greco 1971; P. Sanpaolesi 1972; L. H. Heydenreich and W. Lotz 1974; H. Saalman 1975; B. Daddi, *Contributi alle ricerche sulla cupola del Brunelleschi*, Florence, 1977; S. Di Pasquale, P. L. Bandini and G. Tempesta, *Rappresentazione analitica e grafica della cupola di Santa Maria del Fiore*, Florence, 1977. For the graphic documents, see also Marchini, Miarelli Mariani et al. 1977, pp. 5-33, figs. 1-16.

A closer look at the actual structure of the dome characterizes some recent studies: several remarkable essays by Paolo Alberto Rossi, *Brunelleschi, Vera Cupola*, Florence, 1977; *Le otto piattabande curve. I segreti costruttivi della cupola del Brunelleschi*, Florence, 1977; "Principi costruttivi nella Cupola di S. Maria del Fiore'', *Critica d'Arte*, XLIII, 1978, 157-59, pp. 85-118, with splendid plans and drawings; also T. B. Settle, "Brunelleschi's horizontal arches and related devices'', *Annali dell'Istituto e Museo di Storia della Scienza di Firenze*, III, 1978, 1, pp. 65-80. Both authors consider the positioning of the bricks along curved lines a device to achieve a better connection with the ribs at the corners. And see also R. J. Mainstone, "Brunelleschi's Dome'', *Architectural Review*, September 1977.

For Gothic architecture in general, see P. Booz, *Der Baumeister der Gotik*, Munich and Berlin, 1956; Jean Gimpel, *Les Bâtisseurs de cathédrales*, Paris, 1958; J. H. Acland, *Medieval Structures: The Gothic Vault*, Toronto, 1972; J. Harvey, *The Mediaeval Architect*, London, 1972.

The complex prehistory of the construction of the Cathedral is expounded most convincingly by Saalman (1964), but see also Prager and Scaglia 1970, and for the respective differences in interpretation see the review of their book by Saalman in *Journal of the Society of Architectural Historians*, XXXI, 1972, pp. 241-43.

The essential problems in the construction of the dome — the relationship with the programme of 1367, the modifications of 1420, those in the years immediately following and again in 1426 when important innovations were introduced, together with a conjectural reconstruction of the initial design of the lantern as well as the circular gallery from vestiges of work done under Brunelleschi — were discussed by Herbert Siebenhüber on the basis of partially unpublished documents and of diagrams, in a lecture in Florence in 1937, of which only a half-page summary was printed in *Mitteilungen des Kunsthistorischen Instituts in Florenz*, V, 1937-40, p. 434. Although his studies were never published, he supplied data and notes to Howard Saalman for the latter's fundamental research on the dome and on Brunelleschi in general. A few pertinent remarks of his are to be found also in an article in *Zeitschrift für Kunstgeschichte*, VIII, 1939, p. 90, and in *Kunstchronik*, VII, 1954, pp. 129-31, and some of his drawings were published by Mainstone (1969-70).

Professor Saalman has now examined hundreds of previously unknown documents to add to those collected by Guasti, and these should clarify the principal problems still unresolved. He and R. J. Mainstone have also been able to effect certain measurements with laser beams and other scientific instruments. For the time being I have had to rely on numerous scattered references and brief reviews to supplement his very important article of 1964 and the notes to his edition of the Biography, often referred to in these pages. As an example of the method he has been pursuing in his recent research, see his article of 1975 as well as that of 1969-70 by Mainstone.

2. The date of foundation of the Cathedral is certainly 1296. There was generous funding until 1302, the year of the death of Arnolfo di Cambio. The following year, due to serious financial difficulties, the work was entrusted to the Arte di Por S. Maria, the merchants' guild, and after 1330 to the Arte dei Tessitori di Lana, the wool weavers' guild. Not until 1359 was work begun on the interior, the old church of S. Reparata having been not only preserved but even, since it was in regular use, restored.

I share with A. M. Romanini (1969, especially the notes on pp. 133-34) the opinion that Arnolfo must have prepared a model for the dome as well as for the rest of the church. A clearer idea of Arnolfo's project came out of the excavations of 1965-74: see F. K. Toker's report, "Florence Cathedral: The Design Stage", *Art Bulletin*, LX, 1978, pp. 214-31, and now, after excavation on the right side near the crossing, his paper at the Symposium "Roma nel Trecento", May 1980.

In 1360 an ingenious decree ensured that work would be continued on the Cathedral despite the expenses of war and the consequent economic crisis. To be set aside for that purpose were not only 6 *denari* of every *lira* entering the communal treasury but also 10 per cent "of every *denaro* paid out to the soldiers and that is drawn from the general treasury" (cited by Marchionne di Coppo Stefani, *Istoria Fiorentina, anno 1360*, published by Guasti, 1887, doc. 82, p. 141).

The first explicit documentary mention of a proposed dome over "the chapels at the rear", meaning the choir, is in a collegial decision of 18 June 1357, when work was resumed on the nave and, as has been convincingly suggested by Saalman among others, a system of vaults was substituted for the original covering with a timber roof. This deliberation established the eventual length of the nave as a mere three bays (164 *braccia*), and immediately afterwards the land was measured out for that purpose. Concerning the termination of the nave it stated: "In the part of [with] the chapels at ground level beneath the place where the dome is to come, the net width of the chapels [is to be] 62 *braccia*" (Guasti 1887, doc. 70, pp. 94-95). If a dome was envisaged in the earlier projects, its position and dimensions must have been substantially modified at this time, and in fact there were solemn ceremonies for the beginning of the construction of the first pier intended to support the vaults, almost as if it were a matter of a new foundation.

The problem of the dome had to be faced again when it came to deciding the form of the piers at the end of the nave that were intended to support it. At the same time it was proposed to increase the number of bays in the nave from three to four. Evident too were the difficulties in connecting the nave and aisles, now growing longer, with the ensemble of the apse, so much so that in a consultation on 13 July 1366, at which goldsmiths and painters sent by the Arte della Seta and the Arte degli Speziali took part, it was proposed to stop work on the nave and to concentrate instead on finishing to its maximum height the "chappella maggiore", the crossing terminating in three apsed chapels with sacristies, which was to be covered by the dome. Probably one of the reasons for these difficulties was the decision to use for the nave "round openings and not windows to provide light on the walls of the large vaults, placing an oculus in each vault", as stated in the deliberation of 20 December 1364 (Guasti, 1887, doc. 126).

3. In August 1367 there were discussions concerning the strength of the supporting piers at the end of the nave and also a possible enlargement of the area of the chapels and sacristies, and it seems probable that before 28 August the present drum and the curvature to be given the dome were proposed, altered and approved on the basis of various discussions and criticisms. Although we have no documentary confirmation, this can be deduced from the fact that the decision of 1367 was subsequently considered not subject to any change whatsoever, and the architects in charge of the work had to swear to abide by it. Among the citizens who gave their opinion for this decision was the father of the future builder of the dome, but this is perhaps no more than an oddity of history.

4. At least if we are to judge by the very large prize of 115 gold florins awarded to Giovanni di Lapo Ghini in 1371 for his "inventione... factam circa armaturam fiendam de volta cupole ecclesie" ("invention made in designing centering for the dome of the church") (Guasti 1887, doc. 231, p. 224).

5. For the former, perhaps the best early technical description is that by Giovanni da Prato in the *Paradiso degli Alberti* (ed. Wesselofsky, 1867, III, pp. 232-33):

Just look at that temple of exceptional beauty and, in form, of truly ancient construction in the Roman manner and style; the which, looked at and considered minutely, will be judged by everyone, not in Italy alone but throughout Christendom, to be the most highly noteworthy and singular work. Look carefully at the columns which in the interior are all uniform, with architraves of finest marbles supporting with the greatest skill and ingenuity such a great weight as the vault of the first level (over the lateral openings), which succeed in making the floor area more spacious and lighter. Look at the piers and walls supporting the dome above, with the passageways excellently constructed between one vault and the other. Look with minute attention inside and outside and you will judge it useful, pleasing, and everlasting, and fully worked out and perfect for all centuries to come, the most glorious and highly fortunate ones.

The Baptistery dome is a double-shell structure, and although the space between its shells is only partial it does allow for spacious passageways on the sides and also a convenient stairway which ends directly on the marble roof. Similar lateral interspaces are found in other Romanesque baptisteries, for example in the similarly octagonal one in Cremona.

Alberti speaks of the question of the double shell with the sort of considerations that must certainly have been at the basis of the decision of the *capomaestri* for the Cathedral (see the quotations in the text). The Baptistery was also the source for the idea of replacing stone, used for the lower third of the dome, with brick in the upper two-thirds, as pointed out in a fine study by Cadei (1971, p. 205), who also reminds us that the vault of the Pisa Baptistery is pyramidal on the exterior, having sixteen faces "with corners that match up with the radial arches of the gallery which are concealed by the support of the walls carrying the hemispherical dome covering it" (ibid., figs. 31-35).

6. Prager and Scaglia 1970, p. 89.

7. Brunelleschi's model, according to Vasari, was destroyed through "the insufficient care and diligence of the person governing the Opera of S. Maria del Fiore in years gone by" (ed. Milanesi, I, p. 292).

The interpretation of this whole episode given here may have to be modified in the light of material to be published by Howard Saalman. He has unearthed more than a hundred previously unknown documents relating to this particular period.

8. That there is a symbolic aspect to domes in general and this one in particular is no longer contested, and it is closely related to the symbolism associated with the Coronation of the Virgin and with influences from the Song of Songs. One finds the Church itself identified with the Madonna when Honorius of Autun writes: "Everything that is said of the Church can be understood as applying to the Virgin herself, bride and mother of the bridegroom" (*Patrologia Latina*, ed. Migne, CLXII, col. 494).

Other prescriptions on the symbolism of religious architecture and its elements can be found, for instance in Günter Bandmann, *Mittelalterliche Architektur als Bedeutungsträger*, Berlin, 1951, Otto von Simson, *The Gothic Cathedral*, New York, 1956, and Gerhart D. Ladner, *Ad imaginem Dei: The Image of Man in Medieval Art*, Latrobe, Pennsylvania, 1965. Numerous texts liken the dome to the human head and to the sky ("the supreme round form"), while the arms "like the other parts of the world are located between the sky and the depths of the earth". See, e.g., Honorius of Autun's *Elucidarium* (*Pat. Lat.*, CLXXII, 1116-B *et seq.*), the *Liber divinorum operum simplicis hominis*, Pars I, Visio IV, of Hildegard of Bingen (*Pat. Lat.*, CXCVII, pp. 807ff.), the *Philosophia* of William of Conches (ed. C. Ottaviano, Naples, 1935, p. 21), and the *De *mundi universitate* of Bernardus Silvestris (ed. C. S. Barach and J. Wrobel, 1876, p. 64), all based on Antique texts.

But the dome, in its imitation of the cosmos and the human head, is said, on the basis of Plato (*Laws* 745 B, 848 D), to be "like the citadel of Pallas, sited at the highest point of the city", and the transepts dominated by it are "in truth arms placed there as prudent and strong defences for the citadel". In a correct interpretation of the rigid hierarchical system characterizing the medieval city, there is a decline in "dignity", from the dome, and especially the lantern, to the lower and therefore inferior parts of the structure which can be associated with the human body: "The belly and knees are the vulgar women and artisans of that same city; the thighs and legs are the merchants running here and there; and the feet, finally, are the peasants" (quoted by Ladner, note 90).

The fascination exerted by the symbolism of the crown, to which the dome was related, is very well expressed by Coluccio Salutati in a letter to the King of Naples (1891-1911, II, p. 46):

And to speak briefly of the crown, what else would be prefigured by that turreted double circle of gold, as is now the custom, set upon the head, or by that delicate cloth studded with most precious gems which in the past was wound around the hair of the king, if not that the royal mind whose seat is in the head must be refulgent with the light of every virtue as the crown is with the splendour of the precious stones? Nor is it any wonder that the royal virtues themselves are characterized by those precious and rare gems. Indeed every stone, if we are to believe what has been written in the treatises on this subject, possesses the utmost power and virtue, so that each can easily be compared with a virtue itself.

See E. Battisti, "Il mondo visuale delle fiabe. In appendice: Giannozzo Manetti Oratio", *Umanesimo e Esoterismo: Atti del V Convegno Internazionale di Studi Umanistici, Oberhofen, 1960*, Padua, 1960, pp. 310-20, and W. Braunfels 1963-65. On the symbolism associated with the Coronation of the Virgin, see P. Wilhelm, *Die Marienkrönung am Westportal der Kathedrale von Senlis* (dissertation, Hamburg University, 1937), Hamburg, 1941. For the influence of the Song of Songs, see G. Zarnecki, "The Coronation of the Virgin on a Capital from Reading Abbey", *Journal of the Warburg and Courtauld Institutes*, XIII, 1950.

Further Marian symbolism is revealed in the consecration motet by Guillaume Dufay: see below, note 16.

A precise definition of the cosmological and political function of the dome, on the basis of a subtle exegesis of contemporary sources, was presented by G.C. Argan in his discourse at the 1977 Congress.

9. *The resolution of 1420*

Here we shall make a memorandum with particular reference to all the parts contained in this model made as example for the main dome.

1. First, the inner dome is [to be] curved according to the acute fifth [*quinto acuto*] in the corners, and at the impost is [to be] 3 3/4 *braccia* thick. And it continues [is to continue] narrowing upwards [*piramidalmente*] so that where it terminates in the eye at the top it remains of a thickness of 2 1/2 *braccia*.

2. Another, external, dome is to be made over this one to protect it from humidity and to make it more magnificent and swelling, and this is to be 1 1/4 *braccia* thick at its impost, and to narrow as it rises to the eye at the top where it remains only 2/3 *braccio* thick.

3. The space remaining between one dome and the other is to be 2 *braccia* wide at the impost; in this space are to be put the stairs for inspecting everything between one dome and the other, and at the eye at the top this space will terminate with a width of 2 1/3 *braccia*.

4. Twenty-four spurs [*sproni*: external ribs or buttresses] have been [are to be] made, that is, eight in the corners and sixteen on the faces; each corner spur is 7 *braccia* thick on the exterior at its impost, and in the middle between those corners on each face are to be two spurs, each 4 *braccia* thick at the base, and these link together the two vaults, and [are to] rise pyramidally to the summit of the eye in the same proportion.

5. Those twenty-four spurs with those shells are [to be] girdled by six circles of long hard sandstone blocks [*macigni*] well riveted with soldered iron [*ferro stagnato*]; and over those stones, iron chains [tie-rods] that gird the said vaults with their spurs. It is to be built solid up to the height of 5 1/4 *braccia* at the start; and then only the spurs should be solid and the shell should be divided [i.e. double].

6. The first and second circle are [to be] 2 *braccia* high; the third and fourth, 1 1/3 *braccia*; the fifth and sixth circles, 1 *braccio*. But the first circle at the base is, in addition to this, to be reinforced with long stones [*macigni*] transversally placed so that one shell and the other of the dome rests on those stones.

7. And at the height of every 12 *braccia* or so of those shells are [to be] small barrel vaults running from one spur to the other [to serve] as passageways through the domes; and beneath those small vaults, running from one spur to the other, are [to be] thick chains of oak beams that tie the spurs and gird the shell within, and over those oak beams an iron chain [tie-rod].

8. The spurs are [to be] built entirely in *macigno* [hard sandstone] and *pietra forte* [another type of sandstone, beige in colour], and the mantles or faces of the shells entirely in *pietra forte* bound to the spurs to the height of 24 *braccia*, and from there upwards the masonry is to be done in bricks or porous stone [*spugna*] according to what is decided best by the person who will at that time have to execute it, but [it must be] a lighter material than the stone.

9. To be made is an exterior passageway, above the eight round windows of the drum, which is to be supported from below by consoles [*imbeccatellato*], with openwork parapets about 2 *braccia* high, harmonizing with the small tribunes below; or better two passageways, one above the other over a quite ornate cornice, and the upper passageway to be unroofed.

10. The water running down the dome will end up in a steeply inclined marble drain 1/3 *braccio* wide, and the water is to run off into *pietra forte* gutters built beneath the cornice.

11. There are to be eight marble crests [large external ribs] over the corners on the surface of the outer dome, as thick as necessary and 1 *braccio* in height above [the surface of] the dome, moulded and sloping [*scorniciato e a tetto*], 2 *braccia* wide above so that it will be 1 *braccio* from the ridge to the gutter in all parts and rising pyramidally from the impost up to the end.

12. The dome is to be erected in the manner stated above, without any scaffolding whatsoever, to a maximum height of 30 *braccia*, but with suspended platforms, and from 30 *braccia* upwards in the manner that will be deemed best and decreed by those masters who will have to build it; and from the height of 30 *braccia* upwards according to what will be deemed best at that time, because in building it is experience that teaches what has to be done.

I have used the version first published by Doren (1898-99) of this document which is extremely difficult to read and understand and, even more, to render into another language. The translation here embodies my own interpretation. There have since been other readings, and a number of different interpretations, especially of points 5 and 7. The internal linkages, such as the stone and iron chains, mentioned in those paragraphs are not in fact visible, and only an examination with electronic instruments could give some idea of what something like the chains of stone with superimposed iron chains are really like. The results of such investigations have not yet been published. Prager and Scaglia (1970) think chains are present in both shells and that they are associated with the internal hooks, intended for the framework that would support mosaics, which visibly continue on the exterior at the level of the circular gallery. The "chain" can be understood as a system of bonding of adjacent stones by means of dove-tailed plugs, perhaps even in cast iron (something suggested by the electronic engineers), or in the literal sense of a superposed chain analogous to that consisting of wooden tie-beams. It is not impossible that at a later council meeting it was decided to dispense with such a chain. Note that the internal galleries built with transverse stone slabs also served as chains.

According to Saalman and Mainstone, about 4 m (13 ft) of the external stone chain may be visible along the stairway to the second internal landing. Cadei (1971, p. 207) has observed that to call the *sproni* mentioned in points 4, 5 and 8 "large ribs" or, even worse, "buttresses" is to miss the utter newness of the structure, which has its bonding and structural elements entirely incorporated into its interior to become what the Biographer calls its "order of limbs and bones". The translation here therefore simply uses the literal equivalent, "spurs", in preference to any attempt to interpret a point still under discussion.

For an extensive commentary on this document, with diagrams, see C. Verga, *Dispositivo Brunelleschi 1420*, Crema, 1978.

10. *The resolution of March 1422*

[It is resolved] that sixteen *sproni* [spurs], that is, two for each face of the dome, specified earlier to be 4 *braccia* thick on the inner face of the outer dome, are each to be 3 *braccia* thick on the inner face of the outer dome in order to eliminate superfluous weight.

And that the shells, previously determined to be built in stone to the height of 24 *braccia*, in order to reduce the excessive load and weight, are to be made in stone up to the ceiling above the impost over the doors [*i cardinali degli uscioli*] which are to be built presently [in the passageways between the shells], that is to a height of about 12 *braccia* from the base of the dome; and from there upwards they are to be built with *quadroni*, that is, large bricks.

11. *Supplementary decision of January 1426, as foreseen in point 12 of the resolution of 1420*

1. Firstly, that along the second passageway of the dome, where the stone chain has been built presently on each face of the dome is to be made a round opening of the diameter of 1 *braccio* for the convenience of setting up scaffolding for the mosaic which is to be made, or for other work, and to permit a view into the temple, and for many other reasons. ... And that the corridor to get to that opening be 1 1/8 *braccia* wide and no more. And nonetheless, for greater safety for the present, that passage is to be bricked up again solidly but in such a way that, when the time is right, it can be unblocked so as to be used for those purposes.

2. Likewise above the impost over the doors that are in the second corridor, in order to complete the circle that runs around the outer shell, so that the live arch [*arco vivo*] be entire and not interrupted, the ceiling should be built up in the form of an arch of the same thickness as the outer shell and to the height of about 1 *braccio*. (And should it appear that this addi-

tion looks clumsy [*rustica*] to the eye or blocks the access to the stairs, once the dome is completed one can dismantle that addition so that with more security one can build the dome to its conclusion.)

3. Likewise in each face of the dome there are to be built two stone chains of the width and height of 3/4 *braccio* or less that will have a length corresponding to the width of both the shells, and these chains are to be built over the two spurs that rise on the faces. And over each of those stone chains is to be put an iron chain [tie-rod] for each which is to be as long as the stones.

4. Likewise to be made are large bricks weighing 25 to 30 *libbre* [roughly 19-22 lbs] each and no more which are to be walled up in that herringbone [pattern] that will be decided by the person who will have to carry it out.

5. And on the side of the inner shell, toward the inside, planks are to be placed as parapet so that the masters can oversee everyone for their greater safety, and the bricklaying is to be done with the *gualandrino* [see below] with three ropes, both on the inner side and on the exterior.

6. Nothing is said here concerning lighting because it is thought that there will be light enough from the eight round windows below [in the drum], but if indeed at the end it is seen that more light is needed, it can be increased from the upper part easily, on the sides of the lantern.

7. Nor is it ordered that the dome should have centering: this would have given the work more strength and more beauty, but since it was not begun that way, it seems that to use centering today would be inconsistent with what has already been built and that it would give a different shape; and also it would be difficult to centre without scaffolding because right from the start centering was dispensed with only in order not to have to make scaffolding, etc.

8. And if the things stated above are taken in hand promptly, the work can go ahead in March.

The "*gualandrino* with three ropes" of point 5 was, we believe for etymological reasons (it is from *calandre*), a safety belt for the masons working unsupported at a great height and not, as Mainstone considers, a measuring instrument. For the use of herringbone brickwork (point 4), more useful than the often published drawing by Antonio da Sangallo (Florence, Uffizi, Disegni arch. 900) is the description from an eighteenth-century source printed as note 25, below.

12. The democratic management of the Opera del Duomo is commented on particularly by G.M. Pugno, "Nasce la più democratica delle cattedrali, S. Maria del Fiore", *Atti e rassegna tecnica della Società degli Ingegneri e degli Architetti in Torino*, n.s. IX, LXXXVIII, 1955, 2, pp. 47-57.

13. Heydenreich 1974, p. 5.

14. Additional information comes from the payroll of these masters and their wealth. Ugo Procacci reported to the 1977 Congress that in 1427 for one year Brunelleschi was taxed 53 florins, 12 *soldi* and 6 *denari*, thus five times the tax set for Ghiberti, over thirteen times that of Donatello, and fifteen times that of Battista d'Antonio, who as *capomaestro* of the Cathedral had a fixed salary and no private real estate holdings and so was liable for only 3 1/2 florins per year. The master masons employed by the Opera received 15-20 *soldi* per day. The most Brunelleschi received was 27 2/3 *soldi* per day, which, as Procacci remarked, was barely 1 *soldo* more than the *capomaestro*, and about 8 more than a good master mason. (In the same year 1427, Palla Strozzi paid 507 florins tax, and Giovanni de' Medici 398 florins 3 *soldi*.)

15. It seems to me, moreover, that here even the curvature of the dome becomes more conspicuously flattened, though my young friends who made the actual examinations have repeatedly shown that the variation of inclination is less than appears to the eye. When the upper part was built Brunelleschi's authority was, if not absolute, certainly great, as shown by the praise thenceforth regularly heaped on him in the deliberations that accepted his proposals.

16. This motet is a remarkable work which deserves further research both for its architectural and musical interest and as a link between these two arts.

> *Nuper rosarum flores*
> *Ex dono pontificis,*
> *Hieme licet horrida,*
> *Tibi virgo coelica,*
> *Pie et sancte deditum*
> *Grandis templum machinae*
> *Condecorarunt perpetui.*
>
> *Hodie vicarius*
> *Jesu Christi et Petri*
> *Successor EUGENIUS*
> *Hoc idem amplissimum*
> *Sacris templum manibus*
> *Sanctisque liquoribus*
> *Consecrare dignatus est.*
>
> *Igitur, alma parens,*
> *Nati tui et filia,*
> *Virgo decus virginum,*
> *Tuus te FLORENTIAE*
> *Devotus orat populus,*
> *Ut qui mente et corpore*
> *Mundo quicquam exoravit,*
> *Oratione tua*
> *Cruciatus et meritis*
> *Tui secundum carnem*
> *Nati domini tui*
> *Grata beneficia*
> *Veniamque reatum*
> *Accipere mereatur.*
> *Amen.*

(Of late the blossoms of roses, / a gift from the Pope, / despite the cruel cold of winter / adorned the great edifice of the Cathedral / dedicated in perpetuity / to thee, Virgin of Heaven, / holy and sanctified.
Today the Vicar and successor / of Jesus Christ and Peter, / EUGENIUS, / will with his own holy hands / and consecrated oils / dedicate this immense temple. Therefore, Mother, source of life, / born of thine own Son, / Virgin honour of Virgins, / thy people of FLORENCE / devoutly pray to thee / that those, being pure in mind and flesh, / call on thee for aid / made manifest through thy intercession, / and the merits of thy Son made flesh, / be granted gracious favour / and forgiveness of their sins. / Amen.

The motet makes reference to special indulgences for this festival, and for regular attendance in the Cathedral. For an essay on it see R. Dammann in Braunfels 1964.

17. L. Bartoli, in a paper at the 1977 Congress, argued that the curve of the "acute fifth" was used only for the inner shell, the interspace and outer shell being instead shaped on the "acute fourth", in which the diameter is divided into four equal parts. But the problem is extremely complex, since the thickness of both shells diminishes with height. The measurement must always have been taken on the basis of the inner curve, and the interspace was based on the configuration assumed by the inner shell.

18. Alberti's text reads: "angularem quoque testudinem sfericam, modo per eius istius crassitudinem rectam sphericam interstruas, poteris attollere nullis armamentis".

For Mainstone's comments see Mainstone 1977, p. 166, notes 19, 20.

19. Mainstone 1977, and also his contribution to the 1977 Congress.

Ideally a circular dome is composed of a series of superimposed rings of cones, and both Mainstone and Di Pasquale (1976) have carried out measurements that seem to confirm that the curved layers of bricks were laid conically, their courses varying in height according to the distance of the radius from the imaginary centre. This was one of the most important results of our investigation of the dome, and the only point where theory and the reality of the building seemed to coincide; though the actual construction was still not explained.

The problems of control over the placing of the bricks during construction, and their rationale, have yet to be faced. T. B. Settle (1978) believes that the horizontal arches between the spurs serve as a control device: he may be close to the truth. On the contrary Mainstone, Di Pasquale (especially 1976) and Verga (1978) seek their explanations in two instruments that I cannot think adequate to the task. The first is the *gualandrino* which they, following Braunfels, take to be a measuring instrument with three ropes serving for triangulation and not, as we have seen, a safety belt to be used when working at dizzying heights. The second is a mobile pole resting on a central (or lateral) support and acting as a mobile pointer, a device we have already encountered in connection with the Ridolfi Chapel (Chapter 5, note 9), where we found that it simply could not be utilized to lay out a rib-and-web dome, let alone an octagonal one of large dimensions, and even if it could one would have to fantasize an enormous trunk of California sequoia hoisted onto a central tower or suspended platforms. It is far more likely that the means used were those inherent in the project itself, based on verification of what was being built by reference to working drawings of the various parts and aided by such on-site expedients as reduction in the number of bricks of the same size to be used, oblique vertical lines established in the herringbone patterning, and so on. At the most, and then only in a simplified manner, something like the pointer-pole of the Ridolfi Chapel (of which the Biographer's description is most difficult to interpret) might have been used for the scale model of the dome, whose small dimensions would have permitted the operation described by a contemporary of the Biographer, Bartolomeo Scala, in his *De Historia Florentinorum* (I, pp. 23-24): "Nam centro invento signatoque filum a centro duxit ad circumferentias; quod in girum ferens quo ordine, quoque orbe lateres caementaque ducenda collocandaque essent a fabris, per parietem terminabat." ("For, when the centre was pinpointed and marked, he hauled a cord from the centre to the circumference [of the dome]; which [cord] running around, tracing the order and the circuit in which bricks and mortar were to be carried and placed by the mason, determined the position of the walls.")

Just as one must distinguish between a theoretical model of the dome and its realization, so too one must distinguish between the project and its actual construction. Our information is scanty on all three levels, the statics of brickwork structures remain to be explored, the geometrical and mathematical knowledge possessed by Brunelleschi is still to be deciphered, and the dome itself conceals, presumably, in its innermost fabric the secrets of the men who erected it, those "limbs and bones" that transformed it virtually into a living organism.

As regards the statics of the dome, P. A. Rossi in several important publications (see note 1, above) firmly denies that Brunelleschi thought in terms of circular domes or their static behaviour. In particular he considers that the herringbone masonry, permitting the formation of brick "wedges" gripped tightly between the ascending courses of bricks, forms a series of flat arches or architraves. Moreover, by laying the bricks using as guide a slack cord (*corda blanda*) it becomes possible to connect the webs with the spurs without sharp corners or projections that would have to be rounded off. He also believes that there are stone chains anchored together by metal braces running around the external shell, but the investigations made by engineers using magnetic detectors have ruled out the presence of continuous metal chains.

The fact that the bricks were laid in courses determined by a slack cord has been interpreted by Di Pasquale as proof of the use of a sighting apparatus located in the centre of the dome, and, because of the octagonal shape of the dome, the layers of bricks are said to form a set of successive circumferences of cones. The interpretation of Di Pasquale does not explain the constructional technique. Rather than the abstract geometry of the superimposed tiers of cones one should see instead a physical system of superimposed rings of diminishing diameter. I dare to suggest that because there is no place, in section, for such a ring (the interspace in which it would lie is empty); the rings would have to have taken a three-dimensional configuration as undulating bands. The undulation would have been produced at one and the same time by the "lay" of the bricks positioned with a slack cord and by the vertical blocks of the herringbone masonry. In this way Brunelleschi would have realized the geometrical miracle of making an octagon match a circle, in plan as well.

20. We were able to test just how difficult that feat was by checking a number of points of reference close to each other on the ribs themselves. We found that a divergence of millimetres at that distance from the centre, that is, around 22 m (slightly over 72 ft) in the void, results in errors of almost one hundred times that amount. Moreover, for all that the ribs were accurately planned, with a different cut of the material depending on the height and inclination, they cannot be thought of as perfect geometrical lines since they inevitably have imperfections which make any attempt to measure them in detail extremely difficult.

21. P. Sanpaolesi (1972) adduces splendid examples of Seljuk herringbone masonry, which is decorative as well as functional. The presence in Florence of a large number of Muslim slaves with special skills is documented in Iris Origo, "The Domestic Enemy, Eastern Slaves in Tuscany in the Fourteenth and Fifteenth Centuries", *Speculum*, XXX, 1955, pp. 321-66, but we do not know masons among them.

The old myth of the "Romanness" of Brunelleschi's conception has been largely exploded by studies of the local building tradition and of techniques used in Europe and, more particularly, in the Mediterranean region. An exemplary — and provocative — discussion of the question is that by H. Klotz (1970, pp. 74ff.).

22. Nelli's explanation (recently republished by Sanpaolesi) of the procedures involved in constructing vaults and domes without centering seems virtually a paraphrase of the kind of technical document that one might expect from Brunelleschi himself, despite the three centuries separating the two architects, and his remarks on the organization of the work-force are probably equally applicable. It is the *Discourse on the manner of vaulting domes without using centering* (from *Discorsi di Architettura del Senatore Giovan Battista Nelli*, Florence, 1753, pp. 53-74, in particular pp. 65-67).

The technique that the masons will use to make the body of the dome will produce such and so powerful a construction that persons of understanding will have no doubt that such a method of building a dome is the most obvious way to do it. First, one should not begin to close up the entire first layer of work if one has not first laid three entire courses of bricks [*mezzane*] in thin mortar [*sottil Calcina*]. While laying this layer, every 4 *braccia* there are to be placed crosswise as many pairs of upright bricks through all the thickness of the wall, and these will constitute so many clamps [*morse*] to be continued until the dome is entirely closed. And as for the skill needed in closing up the layer with the three full courses of brickwork it will be this: that the closing up [of the diameter] must be done simultaneously for every 10 *braccia* of distance.

Having made the 3 *braccia* of solid masonry, leaving open the little doors [*usci*] that give on to the gallery inside and outside, having also taken care of the exits of the stairways that come from below through the base [the drum], built the steps, and arranged for light from the outside through slits in the wall, one will go on with the fabric divided into two shells. Giving to the inner shell the thickness of 1 *braccio*, to the outer one that of 2/3 *braccio*, there remain 5/6 [*braccio*] of empty space within which, every 5 *braccia*, there will be a spur [*sprone*] 3/4 [*braccio*] wide, and all of these circling around to finish at the level of the lantern. These spurs will so link the two bodies of masonry that it will seem rather as if a single body had been formed by them.

The *capomaestro* and likewise that mason he will have chosen to be his assistant will have observed those among all the masons who are the most diligent and most resolute, and will keep them on until the entire fabric is completed; this is because, once the work on the dome reaches a third of the height, it draws in more with each new day and the circle of masonry becomes correspondingly reduced, so that one has to lay off a large number of masons and manual labourers — the ones who are least useful — giving to each the pay due to him. It should be remarked of the second time when there must be a reduction in the ranks of the workers (and this will be the last time) that it is doubly convenient in the very difficult tasks to use the masons themselves to help one another in place of the unskilled labourers, for which reason more unskilled labourers are laid off than other men.

When the valiant masters will have arrived at that height of the dome where the curved masonry, to advance further, calls for another manner of working so that the work will not collapse, with their expertise they will have discovered by themselves just what to do next. Since at the start upright bricks used as clamps had been inserted every 4 *braccia*, at this height the distance will be reduced to less than 2 *braccia* — and who is to prevent them from being reduced to less even than 1 *braccio* apart? If the bricks are narrow, thin, of the correct type, and either whole or halved, they [the masons] will close up [the ring] after every two courses of masonry; they can now close up at every course, setting up vertically narrower bricks which will wall it

up successfully without using any other means of support right up to the end.

Another way to achieve the same goal is to lay the first course, at the inner surface of the dome, with a row of single bricks, setting into mortar two of the thick bricks and two of the thin, one of the narrow and one of the wide; in that way one ends up by making a continuous inset for the first course thanks to the two thin bricks. All the bricks having wedge-shaped tops [*a capo di bietta*] and being set into mortar in those interlocks or, if you will, clamps, they simply cannot slip. And you will see that, by using thick bricks continuously, the interlocking bricks that have been started will follow along naturally in order. Changing places, you set one of the wide ones above one of the narrow ones, [then] above the wide ones [you set] narrow ones. So by making use of the long ones and the narrow ones the brickwork will be fully bonded and of powerful solidity throughout. Operating in this manner, the masons can state categorically, and the architects back them up, that any massive curved structure can be raised from the ground to any height whatsoever without support from centering or scaffolding.

23. Heydenreich 1974, p. 5.

24. On the revival of mosaic in Florence, and the project to decorate the dome with mosaic in Brunelleschi's time, see W. Haftmann, "Ein Mosaik der Ghirlandaio-Werkstatt aus dem Besitz des Lorenzo Magnifico", *Mitteilungen des Kunsthistorischen Instituts in Florenz*, VI, 1940-41, 1-2, pp. 98-108.

25. The external gallery should be compared diagrammatically with the gallery along the battlements of the Palazzo Vecchio, which was begun in 1439 by Giovanni di Piero del Ticcia, perhaps from designs by Brunelleschi himself (see. A. Gotti, *Storia del Palazzo Vecchio*, Florence, 1889, pp. 80-82). For this master, see *Brunelleschiani*, 1979, pp. 313-16. Too sketchy for our purposes, unfortunately, is the gallery depicted in a painting ascribed to the School of Masaccio (perhaps Francesco d'Antonio), in the Johnson Collection, Philadelphia, where a basilica is topped by a dome identifiable as that of Florence Cathedral.

26. For Brunelleschi as technician and engineer, see C. Guasti, *Commissioni di Rinaldo degli Albizzi per il Comune di Firenze del MCCCXCIX al MCCCCXXXIII*, Florence, 1867-73, III, pp. 440-515; F. D. Prager 1950; P. Sanpaolesi, "Ipotesi sulle conoscenze matematiche, statiche e meccaniche del Brunelleschi", *Belle Arti*, II, 1951, pp. 25-54; Eugenio Garin, in "Brunelleschi", *Encyclopedia of World Art*, London, 1960, II, 1958, cols. 663-65; G. Scaglia 1961; Ladislao Reti, *Tracce dei progetti perduti di Filippo Brunelleschi nel Codice Atlantico di Leonardo da Vinci*, Florence, 1965; G. Scaglia 1966; F. D. Prager 1968-B; and F. D. Prager and G. Scaglia 1970.

We now have an important and unusual study by W. von Stromer, "Brunelleschis automatischer Kran und die Mechanik der Nürnberger Drahtmühle. Technologie-Transfer in 15. Jahrhundert", *Architectura*, VII, 1977, 2, pp. 163-74, which is based not on drawings but on surviving instruments, and has finally shifted the research on this subject to an experimental and historical plane. P. Sanpaolesi also pointed out at the 1977 Congress that the winches are constructed with an iron screw and that the matrix in which the screw moves is bronze, which indicates that it was known that a metal moves more easily on a different metal because of the different coefficient of friction.

27. For the hoisting machinery, at the 1977 Congress Tanturli cited a little known first-hand account by Sozomeno: "Mirabilius fuit quod unus aut duo boves circuendo quibusdam archis textis ligneis et fune lapides septem milium librarum et ultra ascendere faciebat usque as testudinis altitudinem". ("It was a wonderful thing that one or two oxen going round in a circle with the help of [a structure of] intermeshing wooden wheels [literally, wooden arches] and of a rope could raise to the summit of the dome stones weighing 7,000 *libbre* [*c.* 2,400 kg] and more.") (*Sozomeni Pistoriensis Presbyteri Chronicon Universale*, in *Rerum Italicum Scriptores*, XVI, Città di Castello, 1907-08, p. 23.) The description confirms that the famous drawing reproduced here [*128*] is related to Brunelleschi's invention.

As for the theory on which Brunelleschi's mechanical devices were based, one needs to look thoroughly at a manuscript treatise on "loads, levers and hauling" (*Dei pondi, leve e tirari*) (Florence, Biblioteca Laurenziana, Cod. Ashburnham. 361; Milan, Ambrosiana, Cod. 191; Rome, Biblioteca Vaticana, Cod. Chigi M. VII; Turin, Biblioteca Reale, Cod. 148), whose attribution to Alberti by Mancini has been rejected by Cecil Grayson.

The writings of Archimedes had been partly published by Giorgio Valla in *De expetendis et fugiendis rebus*, Venice, 1501, from a manuscript of the ninth or tenth century in his possession which had been copied in 1491 by Angelo Poliziano for Lorenzo de' Medici. Previously a Master Paolo, perhaps Albertini (1430-75), had owned this or another manuscript in Venice or had made a copy of it, and in 1468 a manuscript entitled *Diversa opera Geometrica* was in the library of Cardinal Bessarion. Certain Arab writers claimed that Archimedes wrote a work on "tangent circles and others", but this is unproven. As early as 1423 a manuscript entitled *De instrumentis bellicis et aquaticis*, believed to be by Archimedes, was in the hands of Rinucci da Castiglione (see the correspondence of the humanist Giovanni Aurispa, Rome, 1931, p. 161).

The history of technology in the fourteenth and fifteenth centuries remains in large part to be written, especially since two basic surveys have totally changed our way of looking at the problem: Lynn Thorndike, *A History of Magic and Experimental Science*, 8 vol., New York, 1923-58, of which the first six volumes deal with ancient, medieval and Renaissance sources; W. B. Parsons, *Engineers and Engineering in the Renaissance*, Baltimore, 1939; and Bertrand Gille, *Les Ingénieurs de la Renaissance*, Paris, 1964, though the fact that Gille does not cite Thorndike is sufficient reason to make one look critically at every point he makes. There is also now a major collection of the existing treatises and drawings on microfilm in the Institute of Fine Arts, New York University.

For scientific libraries in Italy, see P. L. Rose, "Humanistic Culture and Renaissance Mathematics: The Italian Libraries of the Quattrocento", *Studies in the Renaissance*, XXI, 1973, pp. 46-105, especially pp. 53-73.

28. On the basis of a drawing by Taccola, C. L. Ragghianti (1977, pp. 263-64) suggests that it was the sort of barge depicted in Codex Palatinus 766, ff. 40 v and 41 r: "platforms joined to floats, barrels or rowboats, which recall boats described by Pliny and floats like those of Guido da Vigevano (1328) and perhaps also Giacomo Fontana (*c.* 1393-1455)".

As we shall see in our discussion of Brunelleschi and literature (Chapter 16), from the outset violent polemics with Giovanni da Prato accompanied the project, which must indeed have been technologically revolutionary if as early as 19 June 1421 its inventor took steps to obtain a special patent — one of the first of its kind — that would protect him from competitors and threaten with destruction any imitations of its mechanisms attempted during the ensuing three years. The patent moreover was quite certainly extended for some years more. The importance of that document for legal history was recognized in Italy by Giulio Mandich ("Le privative industriali veneziane (1450-1550)", *Rivista del diritto commerciale e del diritto generale delle obbligazioni*, Milan, XXXIV, 1936, 1, pp. 511-47), and by R. Franceschelli (*Trattato di diritto industriale*, Milan, 1960, I, pp. 292-93). Outside Italy, M. Frumkin (in 1943) was the first to point out the importance of this patent, after which the entire matter was studied thoroughly and effectively by Prager (1946) and Prager and Scaglia (1970, p. 111) by means of analyses of costs, of its technical efficiency as a means of transport, and of the profits and losses to its inventor.

There are documents to do with various administrative procedures and on-the-scene inspections undertaken by the architect in the spring and summer of 1426 and 1427 in order to obtain transit permits and tax exemptions. He was given the considerable advance of 55 florins by the Opera del Duomo, and the value of the marble to be transported has been calculated by Prager at 125 gold florins. The price of transport with his new boat was expected to be 4 *lire* and 14 *soldi* per Florentine ton as against the 7 *lire* and 10 *soldi* required for conventional river hauling or the 9 *lire* and 16 *soldi* overland. (1 ton = 1,000 *libbre* = 339.5 kg). To make any profit Brunelleschi would have had to transport 100 Florentine tons. From a document of 2 May 1428, however, we learn that the barge got as far as Empoli but then the load had to be brought to Florence in small boats in the usual manner, and that through some mishap about 12 tons of marble were lost overboard. The contract was dissolved four years later. If it is true that Leonardo made a sketch of this unusual boat, then it must have continued to ply for decades along the lower course of the Arno and been not quite the failure that Brunelleschi's foes would have it.

29. Concerning the dome's stability, we have an important and highly detailed document in the report made by Giovanni Battista Nelli on 6 December 1695, when it was found that the cracks in the structure were becoming worse. The course of that process was followed through the spring, summer and winter of that year and with precise reference to a specific unit of measurement. The findings ruled out the possibility that the movements in the structure were due to temperature changes (see Guasti 1857, doc. 391), but these cracks were much older and had already been filled in.

There has been much debate over the cause or causes of the cracks in the structure. These expand and contract with the daily and seasonal changes in temperature, and are growing ever wider, yet their origin is not thermal. However, as was recently again pointed out by B. Daddi (1977), we lack studies on the behaviour of brickwork structures, and the investigations proposed on the occasion of the 1977 Congress, to be carried out by the Institute of Science of Construction of the University of Florence, will require many years of study, verification, and formulation. What is needed is a good small-scale model or an elaborated mathematical model of the static forces involved in the dome, which would permit simulation of such exceptional conditions as, say, earthquakes.

The most recent report is probably that by Salvatore Di Pasquale, Pier Luigi Bandini, L. Paolini and G. Strigelli, *Elaborazione dei dati concernenti il quadro fessurativo della cupola di S. Maria del Fiore*, Florence, 1978. The problems seem ever more complex, and the situation is worsening; the research has been inconclusive.

30. Brunelleschi's fame as builder of the dome has not extended to the other tasks he undertook for the Cathedral, which have until recently been little studied. However, see now G. Morolli, "Gli 'arede' del Brunelleschi", *Brunelleschiani*, Rome, 1979, pp. 182-232. What follows is a summary of his activities: more detail will be found in the main Chronology.

Brunelleschi in 1429 designed a window frame in a chapel off the choir, which was probably executed by Buggiano. He designed the crypt containing the body of St Zenobius and the altar above it, which took the form of a marble slab resting on four colonnettes and eventually displayed the head-reliquary of the Saint, by Ghiberti (commissions in January and June 1431, inauguration in 1439). He was commissioned in December 1432 to remodel a small house belonging to the Opera, to serve as offices, meeting rooms and workshops, and to furnish at least one of the sacristies with marble cupboard alcoves and lavabo. (The lavabo, carved by Buggiano, was installed in 1440; its importance in reviving Antique forms, such as the Classical temple front, was noted by Hilda Weigelt in "The Minor Fountains of Florence", *International Studio*, XCIV, 1929, 391, pp. 87-90 and 122.) For the *cantorie* by Donatello and Luca della Robbia he had to prescribe the size of the marble blocks (December 1432), build the supporting vaults and arches (October 1436) and cut away part of a pier of the Mass Sacristy to make room (March-August 1438). He and Ghiberti were asked to design new altars for the chapels in the three apses, and he submitted proposals for the arrangement of the choir directly beneath the dome, which were discussed and rejected (November 1435). He designed a long raised wooden walkway between the papal apartments at S. Maria Novella and the Cathedral, to be used by the Pope for the dedication of the new Cathedral in March 1436.

Giovanni di Cino Calzaiuolo gives a precise description of the walkway with precise measurements: it was to be 900 *braccia* long, 4 wide, and 2 high with at every 6 *braccia* a column (perhaps a half-column attached to a pier) 8 *braccia* tall. This is the only example of a proportional system chosen by Brunelleschi without any external restrictions (other than the length of the walkway): the module is 2 *braccia*, that is roughly 1.18 m, or 3 ft 7 in. The proportioning is praised as "chiaro" and "pronto" — clear and (probably) immediately evident or effective. (*Capitolo della Congregazione di S. Maria del Fiore fatto per Giovanni di Cino Calzaiuolo, la quale consagrò Papa Eugenio IV a dì 25 di Marzo 1436 in Domenica mattina, e aveva seco molti Cardinali. Fu una degna cosa a vedergli venire*: MS quoted in Lami 1756, pp. 216-17).

On the measurement of the Cathedral dome (by the Dome Study Group — F. Cecconi, S. Maniatakos, A. Peggion, R. Rinaldi, E. Rodio, P. Scatigna and G. Themelis)

[The following note was compiled by the Dome Study Group, made up of Italian and Greek students in my classes in Florence who assiduously (and often at the risk of their necks) surveyed a side that is one-eighth of the dome above the Loggia del Grillo, so as to have at least one fully reliable sampling as a basis for discussion, and to list and analyse every single variation from the building programmes that they could detect. The research was supported by the Pennsylvania State University and by the University of Florence. - E. B.]

The precise measurements of the dome and its static situation are still open questions. The latter is worrying: cracks [174] continue to undergo variation due to a number of causes, among them wide changes in temperature, sagging, and vibration from traffic.

This is not the place for a history of the measured drawings, but one can summarize their development. They began with the drawing by Giovanni Battista Nelli in 1695, which was schematic and contained various errors in interpretation; they continue with Molini and his copies of the drawings and then with the scientific measurements by Durm in 1887 and by Geymüller and Stegmann in 1885-93. On 12 January 1934 a commission was appointed by the Opera di S. Maria del Fiore to study the static condition of the structure, and for it the surveyor G. Padelli, under the direction of the engineer F. Rossi, using precision optical instruments executed a survey in 1936 whose results were subsequently published in book form (1939). This survey revealed that the sides of the octagon vary from a minimum of 16.617 m (54 ft 6 1/8 in.) to a maximum of 17.240 m (56 ft 6 11/16 in.), a disparity of as much as 62.3 cm (24 1/2 in.). The plane of the surrounding gallery proved to be "entirely inclined to one side", and the curvatures of the segments along the centre line were found to be not an arc of one circle but polycentric.

The drawings published by Sanpaolesi in 1941, though to scale, are not true measured drawings, and his famous axonometric projection, since reprinted in every text and handbook, is only an interpretation of the static and constructional factors. But even more schematic and interpretative are those by Prager and Scaglia (1970) and by Mainstone (1969-70), even if the latter are based on drawings by Siebenhüner that were never published. Only in 1969 was it possible to establish minutely detailed charts, thanks to a survey promoted by the University of Florence with the collaboration of private industry and public bodies — the Officine Galileo of Florence, the EIRA, the IBM Computer Centre of Pisa, and the Istituto Geografico Militare — under the direction of M. Fondelli, with photogrammetric work by W. Ferri and calculations by P. Franchi and F. Greco. When those findings were published in the *Bollettino di Geodesia e Scienze Affini* of the Istituto Geografico Militare between 1971 and 1974 they touched off a decidedly heated debate, conducted especially by G. Birardi and P. Sanpaolesi in the pages of *Antichità Viva*. The results of this research were published in English in the proceedings of the Symposium on Close-Range Photogrammetry, Urbana, Ill., 1971, and of the Twelfth Congress of the International Society for Photogrammetry, Ottawa, 1972. But difficulties in taking measurements and in elaborating data were admitted by Fondelli himself (1973). In 1974 Benvenuti, Cagnola and Fondelli announced a new programme, this time using laser apparatus capable of measuring the lateral shift of 1/1000 mm in a crack, while ultrasonic means can detect differences of density in the dome and thermovision can help to establish a map of difference in temperature.

[Their research confirmed basic asymmetries, deformations of the structure, etc. For instance, not only do the eight sides have different measurements: the octagonal base itself is highly irregular in plan, and therefore differs considerably from the octagon that can be inscribed in and circumscribed by a circle. (See P. A. Rossi 1978, fig. 89.) In certain respects, however, Fondelli and his colleagues have been led to over-hasty conclusions by neglecting historical data and making do with incomplete information. Thus they have defined the curve of the dome as an ellipse, not measuring it at the corners where, for all its variations and errors, it does follow the curve of the "acute fifth". (The ellipse was in any case unknown to fifteenth-century architectural practice, being introduced only well along in the next century after the invention of a special type of compasses.) They misunderstood the important passage in which Alberti states that a dome *a padiglione* on a polygonal plan can be erected without centering on condition that "in its thickness a spherical vault is inserted", deducing from this too literally that the dome of the Cathedral was constructed as a spherical vault (*cupola di rotazione*), without considering the technical difficulties. Moreover, by misusing the description of the system used in the Ridolfi Chapel (see Chapter 5, note 9), they have come up with decidedly fanciful ideas about the methods used.

S. Di Pasquale proposes an enormous central pole with a movable horizontal beam resting on it for measurement and checking, while C. Verga imagines a kind of sextant resting on the scaffolding (see also note 19). - E. B.].

A particular difficulty in all these types of measurement, and especially in their interpretation, has to do with the curvature in the angles formed by the intersection of the webs (*vele*) with the external ribs. For Fondelli this is an ellipse, for Birardi and Sanpaolesi a circle, for Brogi a catenary curve; while from the documents we know that it was begun as an "acute fifth", and our measurements show that it was subsequently modified by means of two small proportional shifts in the geometrical centre of construction [141, 142].

Our own investigation of a segment of the dome, reported here and documented with diagrams and drawings that are quite without precedent, was carried out with modest technical means but with the deliberate aim of respecting to the utmost what the monument itself communicates in order to avoid all interpretative arbitrariness and preconceived conclusions.

If in some respects, such as the use of photogrammetry and laser-beam measurements, the more elaborate surveys of the dome made and published so far do mark a notable advance, in others they suffer from an equally notable deficiency. The space between the two shells in particular, one of the most distinctive elements of the Florence dome, has been simply excluded from those analyses. Deeming the study of this interspace essential, we had to face up to the problem of choosing between the various available methods and techniques.

Photogrammetry makes it possible to reduce to a minimum the direct measurements that need to be taken, replacing them with equivalent photogrammetric measurements effected on the stereoscopic model obtained by an appropriate pair of photogrammes executed with special optical photographic apparatus. Since a single photogramme furnishes up to 200 million points, it is clear that with it one can determine the lines of the real form with no need whatsoever for any interpolation, so that — when one can apply it correctly — it does give the most precise system of measurement.

Which is fine, except that the space between the two shells, of prime importance in our judgment, presents insuperable obstacles to this very modern technique. Given the spatial configuration within which one must operate, the great quantity of small fractional areas into which the operation would have to be divided in this method sets up a handicap right at the start, to which must be added the difficulties in linking those various fractions among themselves and, above all, the need for a general and complex system into which to order them. Then too, in certain fractional areas there is no or insufficient light. The dimensions likewise present difficulties and are decidedly unfavourable to photogrammetry as concerns the b/h (base to height) relationship. But what entirely rules out its use is the impossibility of photographing in a single exposure sufficiently large and homogeneous zones of the interspace itself.

A comparatively scientific method is the topographical, based on geodetic measurements made with optical instruments of great precision such as the tachymeter, the laser theodolite, and level. These provide an exact correlation of points, that is, they relate the angles read on the instrument to the distances from the points. But with this method there are much the same difficulties as with photogrammetry when, as in our project, the precision instruments must be applied to extremely short sides or their optical rays, by their nature, cannot reach large enough portions of the interspace. Because of this it is only partially usable, as a verification and for occasional measurements in points not reachable otherwise.

The direct method for which we opted (and not unwillingly nor, we believe, without reason) follows the same practice used by the builders of the dome. As a means of measurement and guide we could make use of the double decametre (a 25 m tape measure), plumb-line, and level and for the final plans and drawings the usual compass and T-squares. The only essential requirement of this method is direct access to every point to be measured, a handicap that could be overcome in the interspace, though with great difficulty and sometimes danger, by improvised and temporary scaffolding. We found, then, that despite the advances of modern science only the traditional direct method could cope with the problems of the interspace, helped out for a few measurements by the topographical techniques.

With direct measurement one can only determine isolated points, which are then used for interpolating the various lines of plane and space that delimit the individual structures, an operation that leads to a hypothetical representation of the monument based on simple and determinate geometrical lines and surfaces and with a well defined position within three-dimensional space. Hence, the more numerous and the better selected the points, the more the representation will conform to reality.

Keeping in mind that the dome itself was almost certainly designed and executed with the same matter-of-fact instruments — as a composition of simple figures even if it ended up in reality as something far more complex — then interpolations effected on sufficiently close points are perfectly acceptable and legitimate.

For our direct measurements we used principally three techniques: triangulation, the Cartesian co-ordinates, and the polar co-ordinates. Given the nature and limitations of the space between the two shells, triangulation was preferred as the basic technique because it is more effective in dealing with curving lines and also, being more rapid, affords the possibility of taking a greater number of points. Also we often resorted to the technique of the Cartesian co-ordinates, especially as a verification and as a means of relating the various parts to each other.

Once one has allowed for theoretical error in this method, which is inherent in the inevitable discontinuity of the points taken as bearings, and has established an adequate grid, the technique can go astray in three ways only, all of which can be checked and corrected: an erroneous reading of some partial measurement, which can be corrected by checking against the total measurements; a transposition or erroneous placing of points, detected only when the data are put together, which can be corrected by returning to the site and re-measuring the portion in question; and variations in measurements due to the use of different tape measures which may differ from each other or vary when put under tension by stretching, but these can be set to rights with overall optical measurements.

Faced with the enormous dimensions of the dome and the extremely long time that an overall survey with this method would require, it was clear that we would have to select only a portion, but one as complete in itself as possible, and this would have to be one of the eight segments in its entirety. On the advice of Ingegnere Rossi we chose the segment above the so-called Loggia del Grillo, partly because it has the most serious cracks but also because in various particulars it offered the possibility of comparison and collation with the survey of 1936. Our work, which went on for more than four months, was made possible by the administrative arrangements made by E. Settesoldi and Ingegnere Sabatini thanks to the intervention of Ingegnere Rossi and the kindness of Ingegnere Boldrini, President of the Opera del Duomo, who with generosity and understanding granted the necessary permits. There was no end of friendly help from the custodian, Fernando Ballini, who himself took an active part in our work thanks to his unrivalled familiarity with the Cathedral.

Having through exterior points of reference clearly defined the sectors of the segment we wished to deal with, we were faced with the problem of how to reach all the points, most of them at a considerable height and very often in awkward positions. There was no choice but to use ladders and planks, but carrying them up through the very narrow interspace was far from easy or simple. The winding stairways permit no objects taller than 1.90 m (6 ft 2 3/4 in.), and every angle to be negotiated passing from one segment to the next is yet another obstacle. Even with the ladders we did manage to bring up we could not reach all the necessary places: in the areas where the small and almost flat supporting arches occur, given the curvature of the two shells and the presence of those roundish structures we could climb only to a certain height and then had to use planks wedged between the small arches and the inner dome. We were, however, able to reach every part of the structure, whatever the inconvenience, and even if we had to depend for light on electric torches. Not infrequently we found ourselves working in very strange positions and conditions, to say the least, for example at 14 m (almost 46 ft) above the floor in a structure already 70 m (almost 230 ft) above the ground, perched somehow or other on two inclined planks propped against the inner wall, unable to see the corridor from which we had climbed to this point, with sunlight coming from 5 m (16 1/2 ft) below us. Because of the curving lines and surfaces and the peculiar visual conditions under which we were working, it was necessary to take a very great number of points. For this, especially in certain areas, a grid of points was formed at intervals of 50 to 70 cm (roughly 1 1/2 to 2 1/4 ft), and at every eight or ten of these partial measurements a total was taken, thereby setting up another control grid of about 4.50 m (14 3/4 ft) on which were further superimposed the maximum dimensions measurable for each part.

For general verification we used a tachymeter positioned in the interspace opposite each internal opening on the midline of the web between the corner ribs, and in addition a double decametre lowered from the upper opening to the one taken as a reference position for the tachymeter. This gave the Cartesian co-ordinates of the openings in the interior of the dome which served not only for positioning the findings on the three levels but also for determining, through differences, the thickness of the floors themselves.

Another factor of value in this sort of direct technique is the close daily contact with the structure under study whereby one comes to know at first hand and intimately a vast body of details that would otherwise escape one.

The type of drawing that we made, as well as the choice of scale, were guided by the principle enunciated by Hans Foramitti (*La conservation et la restauration*, UNESCO, 1973):

> the precision with which one can determine the real form is limited in practice by the dimensions of the drawing (the smaller the scale the more one is obliged to omit details in the interests of legibility). The ideal method consists in showing totally the real form, then executing the necessary plans, sections and elevations, accompanied by the pertinent information.

The curve that results from measurements of the median sector of the web is polycentric, with centres of curvature lying on the diameter of the circumference inscribed around the octagon [142]. The distance of those centres from the web itself proved to be, in *braccia*, 5/6 + 1/4, 5/6 + 1/3, and 5/6 + 1/2 of the diameter; and the curvatures relative to those radiuses follow the same sequence, from the bottom upwards. The first curve begins at the third internal gallery, therefore above the drum, and ends at the level of the second internal passageway. In this first stretch it is noteworthy how the distinctive notchlike indentations that occur at the same point inside the two shells are aligned with the centre of curvature (see also [144]). The ceiling, also, is inclined with respect to the floor level of the first passageway. In the second stretch, corresponding to the radius of 5/6 + 1/3 *braccia*, there are other elements inclined in a similar manner: the first is a notch on the inner wall of the external shell, the other is represented by a double indentation, probably the product of an error in construction, in both the inner and outer shells. The floor of the second passageway, on the other hand, has a drainage slope towards the exterior. In the third stretch there are no important elements oriented towards the centre of curvature except the bricks, which are always so aligned.

Measurements compared with those in the documents of 1420 and 1422 (above, notes 9, 10). Taking as a standard measure 1 *braccio* = 0.5836 m (1 ft 11 in.), we found the following discrepancies. (The measurement stipulated in the document is always given first).

Corner spurs at the base: 7 *br.* = 4.085 m (13 ft 1 7/8 in.); found: 3.60 m (11 ft 9 3/4 in.)

Intermediate spur: 4 *br.* = 2.334 m (7 ft 1 7/8 in.); modified in 1422 to 3 *br.* = 1.7508 m (5 ft 8 7/8 in.); found: 1.70 m (5 ft 6 7/8 in.)

Height to which the stone spurs extend: according to the resolution of 1420: 24 *br.* = 14.0064 m (45 ft 11 3/8 in.); modified in 1422 to 12 *br.* = 7.0032 m (22 ft 11 3/4 in.); found: 5 m from the circular gallery of the drum (16 ft 4 7/8 in.)

Thickness of the inner shell at the base: 3 3/4 *br.* = 2.1884 m (7 ft 2 1/4 in.); found: 2.22 m (7 ft 3 3/8 in.)

Thickness of the inner shell at the top: 2 1/2 *br.* = 1.4582 m (4 ft 9 1/2 in.); found: 1.30 m (4 ft 3 1/8 in.)

Thickness of the outer shell at the base: 1 1/4 *br.* = 0.7294 m (2 ft 4 7/8 in.); found: 0.96 m (3 ft 1 3/4 in.)

Thickness of the outer shell at the top: 2/3 *br.* = 0.3890 m (1 ft 3 3/8 in.); found: 0.40 m (1 ft 3 3/4 in.)

Width of space between shells at the base: 2 *br.* = 1.167 m (3 ft 10 in.); found: 1.21 m (3 ft 11 5/8 in.)

Width of space between shells in the upper part: 2 1/3 *br.* = 1.361 m (4 ft 5 5/8 in.); found: 1.480 m (4 ft 10 1/4 in.)

Height of marble revetment of the main ribs: 1 *br.* = 0.5836 m (1 ft 11 in.); found: 1.40 m (4 ft 7 1/8 in.)

Maximum width in cross-section of a main rib: 2 *br.* = 1.167 m (3 ft 10 in.); found: 1.75 m (5 ft 8 7/8 in.).

Particularly notable are the reductions in measurements of the spurs and also the fact that the thickness of the inner shell was similarly reduced, thereby allowing a roomier interspace in which to work.

9 The basilicas of S. Lorenzo and S. Spirito

1. The quotations are drawn from A. D. Frazer Jenkins, "Cosimo de' Medici's Patronage of Architecture and the Theory of Magnificence", *Journal of the Warburg and Courtauld Institutes*, XXXIII, 1970, pp. 162-70. On the idea of magnificence, see now R. Pacciani, "Brunelleschi e la magnificenza", *Ricerche Brunelleschiane*, Florence, 1977, pp. 203-18. On the liturgical function of the two churches discussed here, the best contribution is that of R. Zeitler (1959), equally applicable to S. Lorenzo.

2. Isabelle Hyman, in a recent study (1975), has added new information to what she had already published. She confirms the date of the decision, and that the project was intended to favour the Medici.

The advantage to other landowners is exemplified in a letter from Ugo di Lorenzo Lotteringhi Della Stufa to Giovanni de' Medici on 30 April 1434: "I think you have heard how our Lorentingo [Lotteringhi] has been to the Signoria and the houses that were opposite us have been razed to the ground and we now have a fine piazza in front of the door, so you can see how things are going." This member of the Della Stufa family must have had no small part and very considerable personal interests at stake in the "slum clearance" operation if in 1435 he had to reimburse the Chapter of S. Lorenzo for the lost income from the houses torn down; and this was followed by a law suit during which, in 1437, he was even excommunicated. Here certainly a religious undertaking was exploited shamelessly for a high-level speculation involving public land. (See Hyman 1975, pp. 108-09.)

3. For illustrations of the piazza see Fanelli 1973, figs. 1308-13. A measured plan is published in *Problemi Brunelleschiani*, 1977, plate 13. The earliest and most faithful view is in a miniature in the Book of Hours of Laodamia de' Medici: see my text p. 195, and note 28 below.

We know something of the buildings that originally surrounded the church from Luigi Zumkeller, "L'isolamento della Basilica di San Lorenzo e la questione della parte tergale della chiesa", *Firenze*, VII, 1938, pp. 377-81, and Caroline Elam, "The Site and Early Building History of Michelangelo's New Sacristy", *Mitteilungen des Kunsthistorischen Instituts in Florenz*, XXIII, 1979, 1/2, pp. 155-86.

A careful survey of Early Christian and medieval churches in Florence is given by G. Vannini, in *Scritti di Storia dell'Arte in onore di Ugo Procacci*, Milan, 1977, I, pp. 51-61. The area is included in the study of the entire historical centre of the city by Professor Sanpaolesi and his group, of which the first volume has now been published. The first mention of the church is in 393 (foundation by St Ambrose): it was totally transformed around 1060.

For the townscape value of Brunelleschi's buildings, see the topographical plans by M. P. Sette published by G. Miarelli Mariani in 1977. According to Paolo Sica (*L'immagine della Città da Sparta a Las Vegas*, Bari, 1970, pp. 133-35), Brunelleschi was even more innovative as a town-planner than as an architect, trying to substitute a rationalized structure for the spontaneous growth of cities by accretion.

4. See Chapter 5, note 4.

S. Lorenzo

5. The thorough examination of the church made for this publication would have been impossible without repeated visits, surveys, measurements, and even wall samplings, in all of which we had the extremely patient and courteous co-operation of the Prior, Giancarlo Setti, and the "Operaio" Ettore Bencini, superintendent of the fabric, who for many years has been most intelligently pursuing its restoration. To Paolo Mazzoni of the Opificio delle Pietre Dure I am deeply endebted for an analysis of the stone elements of the building.

Three detailed surveys with measured drawings have been published: one complete with elevations and details by Stegmann (in Stegmann and Geymüller 1885-93, Ia and Ib), another with a plan by Folnesics (1915, p. 36), and yet another plan, this one quite accurate, by Gamberini, published by Sanpaolesi (1962, fig. 45). (Professor Gamberini, when questioned, declared that he did not recall ever making this plan, or having it made for him, and had no copy of it.)

In this latter plan the difference between the left and right arms of the transept is particularly evident, something which our survey confirmed. Thus, in the right transept the chapels adjoining the chancel have a constant width of 6.10 m (20 ft), whereas those in the left transept, towards the Old Sacristy, vary between 5.90 and 6.00 m (19 ft 4 in. — 19 ft 8 in.), and the floor levels are also different. This discrepancy almost certainly has to do with the foundations due in all probability to Matteo Dolfini: one should not forget that beneath S. Lorenzo there is another, enormous, subterranean church [*182*]. Further, as the result of at least two changes in the project, on the left there is a vast filled-in space between the "western" chapel of the Medici double-chapel and the present access to the cloister, a space which presumably corresponds to part of the old street that ran behind the apse of the medieval church. Other incongruities, due to the impossibility of incorporating the Old Sacristy into the general system with any sort of neatness, have been discussed in connection with that structure (Chapter 5).

Considering the numerous restorations undertaken, in the nineteenth century in particular, an investigation of the archives for that period might well produce significant and unexpected results but has not been attempted so far. Only the projects of Poccianti have been carefully examined (see G. Miarelli Mariani, "Il Neoclassicismo fiorentino e il 'restauro' dei monumenti del Rinascimento: il caso esemplare di San Lorenzo", *Pasquale Poccianti, Architetto, 1774-1858* (catalogue of the exhibition in Bibbiena), Florence, 1974, pp. 25-34). Otherwise only scattered and insufficient information can be gleaned from Emilio Burci and Pietro Fanfani (*Guida artistica della città di Firenze*, Florence and Rome, 1875, p. 132) about the work done around 1865, and from Pietro Franceschini in the articles in his periodical, *Il Nuovo Osservatore Fiorentino*, 1885-86.

6. The history of S. Lorenzo has been reconstructed, though fragmentarily, on the basis of archive material known already in the nineteenth century but not studied systematically until the 1968 dissertation of Isabelle Hyman (published in New York, 1977); the appendix contains only a selection of the documents, though full publication is promised and will presumably also cover the building history from 1441 to 1452. Dr Hyman's ideas concerning what was completed in Brunelleschi's lifetime were immediately challenged by Marco Dezzi Bardeschi ("Brunelleschi e il meeting di Boston", *Necropoli*, 1969, 2-3, pp. 97-98), who attempted to defend the notion that the work went on continuously under Brunelleschi between 1421 and 1441, but had no documentary evidence for this.

The archives of S. Lorenzo, long inaccessible, are now open and in order. The fifteenth-century documents were not available during the original preparation of this volume, but in the English edition some of the new findings can be discussed.

Essential for the history of the church is Paatz 1940-54, II, pp. 464ff. The pioneer work on the various phases of building, and still a model of method, is Saalman 1958-A (especially pp. 123-26), derived from his Master's thesis of 1955 (New York University), which is of course much more extensive. While documents that have subsequently come to light have necessitated some modification to the schema he proposed, his general judgment has been confirmed. A parallel study, though more limited in its aims, is Gosebruch 1958. That there were several phases of work, of differing quality and design, is asserted also by Luporini (1964, pp. 43-56), with shrewd comments on how the foundations begun by Dolfini conditioned the work done thereafter, and his book includes excellent photographs of the transept, nave and capitals (figs. 67-84) along with all the early graphic documentation (figs. 340-42). Another important contribution is that of V. Herzner (1974), who makes full use of the published sources; he adduces new evidence to refute Sanpaolesi's theory that the building of the church began with the façade and worked toward the ritual east. Among recent publications, see the interesting observations by R. Scarchilli (1977), and for the graphic material, Marchini, Miarelli Mariani et al. 1977, pp. 43-82, figs. 18-28. G. Zander (1977) has convincingly discussed the relationships between the plan of the new transept of S. Lorenzo and the plan types favoured by the mendicant orders. Many of the ideas expressed in my monograph were embodied and illustrated in an essay by G. Morolli, in *Brunelleschiani*, 1979, pp. 76-140, figs. 170-91.

7. *The petition of 28 September 1417* (Cianfogni 1804, p. 22):

It is herein set forth, with all due reverence, to you, Magnificent and Powerful Gentlemen Priors of the Guilds and to the Gonfaloniere di Giustizia of the People and Commune of Florence, on the part of Master Matteo [Dolfini], Prior of the church of S. Lorenzo in Florence and also in the name of the canons of that church, that the election of the Prior of that church pertains by norm of canon law to the aforesaid canons with the approval of the Bishop of Florence, although it can be effected principally by the Supreme Pontiff himself whenever it is initiated by the consent of His Holiness; and that for some time now this election has been made by the Roman Curia; and that because the Supreme Pontiff cannot be informed as to the true facts concerning each individual when the appointment is to be made, these causes have ruined the said church beyond and against the will of the said Supreme Pontiff.

And holding as they do that it would be more salutary for the said church, which is among the most ancient in the city, to have and to obtain the protection of your authority, for above all they wish to proceed more cautiously in administration and also in such appointments and in many other things, they maintain that this church and its goods will receive daily many advantages and favours from that; though without claiming in any way by that something which could be directed against the Roman Church or against its sacred statutes, or indirectly redound against it; rather they [desire to] choose a way which the prelates, their governors, had followed in the past with many ecclesiastical benefices and places, and accordingly they decided to make the following petition.

It is therefore most devoutly requested of you abovementioned gentlemen on the part of the aforesaid that, to the extent that it pleases you, you should deign to take steps opportunely and solemnly to effect a reform by which the said church of S. Lorenzo in Florence, with its buildings and goods and every right, should be understood to be under and in fact be under the protection and tutelage and defence of the People and Commune of Florence, those of the present as of the future. And that those same Gentlemen Priors and Gonfaloniere di Giustizia are to be and should be bound — whenever and however often they should be requested on the part of the Prior or of his canons, whether of one or a number of them, to defend, to preserve and to enhance the said church or to increase it or any whatsoever of its goods and rights — to offer every favour and assistance and to intercede in every way and to do everything promptly that they think may redound to the utility, advantage, prestige and increase and conversation of that church and of the aforesaid titles and rights, without neglecting anything that might assist towards that utility among all and each of the aforesaid matters except as they may consider that the aforesaid matters do not come under their competence or are rights of the quarter of S. Lorenzo or of one or more patrons, should there be any, or be something displeasing to some layman, or if they find defects in some [proposed] alteration or variation; and may these things be as they now are and should be in the future and [what is requested here] be effectively observed.

8. *Request for expropriations for the enlargement of the church, 22 December 1418* (Cianfogni 1804, p. 228):

It is here declared with all due reverence to you, Magnificent and Powerful Gentlemen Priors of the Guilds, and to the Gonfaloniere di Giustizia of the People and Commune of Florence, on the part of the Prior and of the canons of the Chapter of S. Lorenzo in Florence, that they, for the glory of God and the decorum of your city, had in mind to enlarge and transform by means of splendid constructions, with the aid of the citizenry, the existing body of the said church of S. Lorenzo. The body of that church, with the chapels and the sacristy and other appropriate places, must be extended at the rear [i.e. at the ritual east] for a length of 65 *braccia* and, as site for the chapels [of the transept], a width of 110 [*braccia*] in that part of the street known as the Via dei Preti [Street of the Priests] in which, as is known, live persons of the lowest class and of uncommendable repute and manner of living and for the most part foreigners, and also there is a piazzetta behind the belltower of the church and other things which are the property of the Commune of Florence. It is further declared that there are some small private dwellings which, should their owners put up any opposition to the intended work, would severely affect the remaining properties that are owned with full rights by the Chapter itself. And because the latter [the Chapter] fear that this work, so holy to God and to the world, so honourable for your dominion and so full of devotion, may not be brought to completion, fearing indeed that nothing can be done without the aid of your authority, they have resolved to place themselves at the feet of Your Greatness and to request with utmost devotion the good office set forth below, hoping that the clemency of your power will not fail them because it has ever been solicitous for the good of all the churches under your jurisdiction and also because this church, by singular favour of your councils, is under your protection with a special privilege granted by your Council. Therefore we humbly supplicate you Gentlemen to deign, to the extent you choose, to provide fittingly for this and to state officially that all and any real estate existing between the aforesaid borders, no matter who it may belong to or be held by, whether the Commune of Florence or some other association, corporation, confraternity or community, or individual person of whatever state or condition and quality, from henceforth and in perpetuity be understood to belong and in fact belong to and be the property of the aforesaid Chapter which may make use of those properties freely, as true master and owner of them, putting a stop in this manner to all opposition and contradiction and refusal. All this with the understanding that the Chapter itself be held to, and must, satisfy the owner or owners, except it be the Commune of Florence, by paying the value of those properties on the basis of the estimate of value to be made by the Ufficiali delle Torri of the Commune of Florence or by the two parties, even if the other party [not the Chapter] be absent or cannot be found or be present and

opposed or in some manner impeded, and that each of the parties must adhere to this declaration and be held to observe it without any exception whatsoever. And in order to remove any doubt, it is stated that for properties in the possession of the Commune of Florence, no money is to be paid to the Commune but that, instead, it be as a gift and by the liberality of the Commune of Florence and for the love of God and of St Laurence, and that thus the said construction will come about in honour of God and his saints and for the decorum of the city. Nothing should be paid or given or changed or be disturbed or molested *in perpetuo*, in the body of the church or its possessions in any way.

9. I am using the measurement 1 *braccio* = 0.5966 m, deduced from the measurement of a pilaster as mentioned in the document of 1434 concerning the chapels off the aisles (below, note 13). For 110 *braccia* that would give a width of 65.626 m; and the actual width of the foundations, without the *scarselle* of the Old and New Sacristies, is about 64.80 m. (The *braccio da panno*, = 0.5836 m, would give a width of 64.196 m, and the *braccio* = 0.5860 m, used by Benevolo for S. Spirito, 64.460.)

A drainage channel discovered between the vault and the roof over the aisles, which is now interrupted but which can be presumed to have extended "westward" as far as the early basilica, indicates as we shall see that the transept was intended to be three bays deep; the chancel was not originally intended to project beyond the transept. This arrangement would in fact give one a depth of exactly 65 *braccia* (38.78 m, or 126 ft 5 3/4 in.).

10. Information from the document of foundation, or re-foundation (Cianfogni 1804, p. 191):

On the 10th day of August [1421]. For ten *libbre* of *cialdoni* [pastry horns], for peaches, and fennel, and shelled nuts for the second collation that was taken in the house of Ser Neri; and present there were the Vicar and the Operai and the Masters, who went that evening after Vespers and [made a] procession; and everyone, both the Prior and canons, with olive branches in hand went behind the belltower and each in turn gave a blow with the mattock where the foundations were to be dug.

11. Building funds were frequently expropriated by the commune. The forced loans imposed on the entire citizenry reached 3 million in 1427 and 4.5 million in 1433 after the war against Filippo Maria Visconti.

12. The phrase is "conformes et ordinatas".

13. This document was discovered since the original edition of my book, and published by Jeffrey Ruda in *The Burlington Magazine*, CXX, June 1978, pp. 358-61 ("A 1434 Building Programme for San Lorenzo in Florence"). In the same issue of the magazine, pp. 361-64, is a discussion of the document by Howard Saalman. Here is a translation of the complete *Deliberation concerning the chapels yet to be built, 3 June 1434* (Florence, Archivio di Stato, Notarile anticosimiano, M 273, insert I, f. 321v):

In the name of Christ, amen. In the year 1434 of his Incarnation, 3 June. In Florence, in the parish of S. Lorenzo and in the sacristy of the church of the aforesaid parish, in the chapter house of the church, in the presence, as witnesses, of Agnolo son of Jacopo Cristofari from Castro Franco in the upper Arno Valley, and Antonio Palmieri from Fornace, in the Casentino, cleric of this church.

Because (as the undersigned Prior and canons of the aforesaid church of S. Lorenzo have announced)

some men and persons, devoted to this church, caring for and loving this church, declared their intention to build, in future days, or to have built in the aforesaid church chapels, where it will be possible to celebrate the divine offices and [which will be] in form similar to the other chapels already begun, or that are to be built in future in the aforesaid church. And having had — as they declare — talks, discussions and consultations with many suitable and intelligent masters, and having established among themselves with solemn deliberation, in all the ways [required by law], etc., stipulated, disposed and deliberated that the chapels to be made from now on and to be built in the aforesaid church should be made and built in the following way and in this form and order, that is, that each and every one of these chapels is to be 10 1/8 *braccia* wide, no more, no less, and to either side of these chapels is to be made and should be made a stone pilaster in hewn *macigno* according to the form and quality of the other pilasters made ready and erected on the upper side [i.e. in the transept], in other chapels of this church, of a width of 1 1/2 *braccio*. That the pilaster is in and must emerge from the wall towards the nave of the church and, though remaining joined to the wall, should project by 1/4 *braccio*, with bases and capitals according to the form already specified and also of the same height and material. Above the pilasters are to be made and should be made the architrave, frieze and cornice in the prescribed form, that is, that of the other chapels of this church already built or under construction. Over the cornice of each of these chapels is to be and should be made an oculus in hewn stone in the exact manner and form of the oculi in the chapel of Giovanni de' Medici [the Old Sacristy] and of the same quality, height and form. Above that oculus is to be made and arranged also a band of hewn stone in the form of an arch which will match the vault to be made over the aisle of this church. And that there be made and edified between those pilasters a tribune [the chamber of the chapel] in each and every one of the chapels, and above each of those chapels that are to be built, of a width of 7 *braccia*, which tribune is to be and should be of the depth of 3 1/2 *braccia* and of a height up to the top of the capitals of those pilasters. And also that there be and should be made, in the corners of the tribune, stone ornaments similar to those that are in the tribune of the new sacristy of this church [the *scarsella*]. And that in each and every chapel there are to be made three stone steps, two straight and one that will turn [curve] around the said tribune. And also that there be made in them and in their tribunes an altar for each of them, in *macigno*, set on five columns with a square painted altarpiece without a tabernacle and of high pictorial quality. And that in these chapels or tribunes there cannot be made any picture other than the aforesaid altarpiece without the express consent of the Chapter of the church. In the oculus mentioned above is to be made and must be placed a round window of glass or stained glass of excellent quality. And that the walls of the said tribunes or chapels on the exterior of the church or the outside of the chapels are to be and are perfectly straight and with a base below and a cornice above in the manner and according to the form used in the other chapels on which work has already begun. And that they are to be made and constructed of quarry stone or of stones of the same sort used in the outer walls of the aforesaid chapels and are to be of the same height.

The signatories are the Prior (the priest Nero di Andrea), Master Baldassare di Mastro Antonio, Master Bartolomeo di Andrea, Master Giovanni de Spinellinis, Master Bernardo di Giovanni, Master Antonio de Aleis, and Master Lorenzo di Lorenzo da Pisa.

14. Permission to concede these chapels to outsiders was granted to Piero de' Medici in 1465, but that does not mean work began on them immediately. See also below, note 27.

15. *Report of the assembly conceding to private citizens the right to build in S. Lorenzo, 20 November 1440* (Florence, Archivio di Stato, Protocol of Ser Angiolo di Cinozzo Cini; from Ginori Conti 1940, pp. 236-40):

Because, as was affirmed by the undersigned Prior Benedetto, in the year 1419 or thereabouts, in the time of Matteo Dolfini of venerated memory, then Prior of the church and most celebrated temple of S. Lorenzo, when the undersigned Sig. Benedetto, now Prior, was canon of the said church and temple, the foundation of the high altar chapel [= chancel, or crossing] of the aforesaid church and temple was begun with the purpose of enlarging the said church and temple in the most appropriate manner, considering that in ancient times, according to tradition, it was the most important temple of the city and it was and still is to this day the foremost in number and nobility of parishioners, and is illustrious for its college of canons and many other clerics; and because, in addition to this, there dwelt there for a long time, and died there and was for many years buried there, the eminent Zenobius, most holy bishop of this city, and with him very often dwelt in utmost devotion and charity Ambrose, Doctor of the Church, endowing the said temple and church in his memory with the bodies of three saints — St Mark Pope, St Concordia Martyr and St Amator Abbot — clearly manifest today in the said temple and church; and because after the death of the said Sig. Matteo, the venerable Benedetto, son of the late Matteo degli Schiattensi, who is Prior of the said church and venerable temple, always desired and still desires to bring to completion the high altar chapel and to exalt the said church and temple, to build up and enlarge it, granted that he could never do it nor hope to do it in the remaining years of his life because of the constant wars and the need for ever-repeated war taxations incessantly required not only from laymen but also from the Prior and canons of the church itself; and in view of the fact that it is now fifteen years, or almost, since any further building has been done in the high altar chapel and that that chapel and undertaking has been entirely abandoned for lack of funds. And from that there arises damage, imperfection, and delay not only to the building of the high altar chapel, as has already been said, but also to the most celebrated sacristy and chapel almost completed by the highly celebrated man Giovanni di Averardo de' Medici and by Cosimo and Lorenzo, worthy sons of the said Giovanni, as well as to other chapels begun but left unfinished by private citizens and persons of the parish of S. Lorenzo, which are on either side of the high altar chapel, all of which is a source of humiliation and shame for the entire population of the parish. The undersigned venerable, worthy, and prudent gentlemen — Bartolomeo son of the late Cinozio di Giovanni Cini, Gonfaloniere of the *gonfalon* of the Golden Lion, Mastro Bartolomeo di Cambio doctor in medicine, Sig. Domenico di Niccolò dei Martelli doctor in law, Cambino di Niccolò di Francesco captain of the Parte Guelfa, Antonio di Ser Ludovico della Casa, Panuzio di Zenobio del Bua of the Office of the Eight Custodians of this city, Francesco di Mastro Antonio di Mastro Guccio of the said Office of the Eight, Simone di Francesco dei Ginori of the Office of the Six of the Mercanzia, Lorenzo di Andrea del Sig. Ugone della Stufa, Ser Francesco di Ser Tommaso Masi, Andrea di Rainaldo dei Rondinelli, Federigo di Niccolò di Ghoro Ghori, Jacopo di Giorgio Aldobrandini del Nero, Ser Alberto di Ser Tommaso Masi, Jacopo di Tommaso Tani, Michele di Francesco di Ser Santi Bruni, Mariotto di Giovanni dello Steccuto, Andrea di Sinibaldo di Sommaria, Niccolò di Biagio di Ser Nello, Andrea di Francesco Cambini, Francesco di Pietro dei Ginori, Andrea di Giovanni della Stufa, Domenico di Giuliano dei Ginori, Francesco di Jacopo dei Guasconi, Domenico di Lorenzo degli Attavanti, Giovanni di Nuto di Bartolo, Zenobio di Pietro dei Marignolli, Giovanni di Giovanni dei Ghori, Jacopo di Tommaso degli Schiattensi, Antonio di Venero di Cino goldsmith, Vettorio di Nello di Bartolomeo di Nello, Antonio di Marco di Sostegno, Marco di Bartolomeo goldsmith, Manetto di Masino strongbox maker, Antonio di Ser Giovanni Buonaiuti, Francesco di Nerone di Nigio di Nerone, Bernardo di Jacopo di Ser Francesco (Ciai), Andrea di Lancillotto di Luziano, Niccolò di Francesco di Cambino, Niccolò di Zenobio Bonvanni, Niccolò di Zenobio Benintendi, Giovanni di Luca di Maccianghini, Nerio di Leonardo Grilli, Bartolomeo packsaddle maker, Filippo di Bartolomeo del Grigia, Giovanni di Mastro Antonio della Scarperia, Matteo di Antonio goldsmith, Jacopo di Antonio di Venero goldsmith, Antonio di Nerone di Nigio di Nerone, Bartolomeo di Lotto Albizzi, Francesco di Niccolò Cambini, Nigio di Nerone di Nigio di Nerone, Lorenzo di Giovanni della Stufa, Francesco di Baldino di Giovanni Inghirami, Jacopo di Ghero della Ressa apothecary, Ser Jacopo di Ser Filippo di Luziano, Giovanni di Ser Ludovico della Casa, Zenobio di Jacopo dei Bucherelli, Nello di Nello di Bartolomeo di Ser Nello, Zenobio di Tommaso dei Ginori, Filippo di Simone Banchi, Ser Lotto di Ser Francesco di Ser Tommaso — all Florentine citizens and of the parish of this church and temple of S. Lorenzo as well as of the said *gonfalon* of the Golden Lion, convoked and gathered together in the aforesaid chapel or sacristy already almost completed by the said Giovanni de' Medici and Cosimo and Lorenzo his sons, according to the usual convocation proceeding through a herald, and at the request of the aforesaid Bartolomeo Cinozzi, Gonfaloniere and at the request and instance of the aforesaid Sig. Benedetto and of his canons, as well as of the Operai now finally constituted by the Priors of the Guilds and the Gonfalonieri di Giustizia of the parish and aforesaid Commune and of its colleges, in charge of completing the works initiated in this church and temple of S. Lorenzo; [they] heard first among the aforesaid and undersigned the venerable Prior Benedetto, now in charge, who proposed in his name and that of the canons and explained to those citizens and inhabitants of the parish what has been written above, namely, that the high altar chapel, as has been said, begun in the past, could not be completed because of the straits in which the Prior and Chapter found themselves, and that this resulted in deterioration and incompletion and delay of all the works begun in the church by individual citizens, with utmost opprobrium and blame for the Prior mentioned and the canons and the entire body of the parish, thus the men and persons of the said *gonfalon*; and [the Prior] finally requested and exhorted the citizens of his parish that they should complete that chapel at the expense of the entire parish and carry it through fully to completion, and that the aforesaid and undersigned should provide, resolve, and freely decide in favour of completing that chapel, and that on the basis of his [the Prior's] offer he was prepared, and the canons likewise, to offer and concede that high altar chapel which has been begun, in order to have it built and finished, to that man or those men, among the aforesaid and undersigned of his parish, who would be pleased to do so, and to him or to those whom the aforesaid and undersigned men of his parish should consider fitting to elect and appoint.

When all the aforesaid had heard everything set forth and explained by the Prior, and held full and mature deliberation, and after anyone wishing to do so among the said citizens had given his counsel, proposed, and spoken, and then finally after having held many negotiations and decisions among themselves and arrived at unanimous agreement and concord and without the opposition of anyone, Bartolomeo the aforesaid Gonfaloniere together with the aforesaid gentlemen and persons and the aforesaid men and inhabitants of the parish, in representation and name of the totality of that parish, in every mode and form, way and right that they could best do so, discussed, deliberated, and established that any citizen whatsoever, one or more of the parish of S. Lorenzo, could build and would be permitted to build and have built in that high altar chapel and on any wall whatsoever of it, and that it could be continued and completed according to what pleases and seems best to that citizen in accordance with the manner and form agreed on and how he will and wishes to do.

16. *Act of concession of patronage of the high altar chapel and the church to Cosimo de' Medici, 13 August 1442* (Ginori Conti 1940, pp. 240-45):

Since it is now twenty-three years, or thereabouts, since the Prior and canons and Chapter and various men and illustrious Florentine citizens, parishioners of the said church of S. Lorenzo, began to construct and edify for the increase of the divine cult and the salvation of themselves and their souls, in honour of the blessed Laurence Martyr, the new church of S. Lorenzo from the upper end and the high altar chapel with other chapels and the sacristy and other facilities with labours of no small expense, assigning and reserving the high altar chapel and the nave in the middle of the church to the Prior and canons, and to any other citizens a portion to be built, by themselves in other chapels: among others the sacristy with two adjacent chapels to the late Giovanni di Bicci de' Medici, of blessed memory, to raise and construct at his expense, the said sacristy and chapels having then been perfected and completed by the said Giovanni and richly endowed as is more circumstantially stated by myself, Jacopo the notary undersigned, in AD 1428 in the month of February. They [the Prior and canons] assigned and reserved to the said Prior and canons the high altar and the nave of the church, where the choir is to be built, down to the old high altar of the [medieval] church; but because of the wars that have raged until now and still rage in parts of Tuscany, the income, revenues and proceeds of themselves and the church and the Chapter were and are so diminished that, far from sufficing to build and complete, they are scarcely enough to sustain their life; [and] this results in no small harm not only to themselves and the Chapter and the church and parishioners but also to the entire Florentine population. Desiring therefore to obviate the said situation and carry to completion, as much as possible in their own lifetimes, the high altar chapel and the nave and the church in the manner desired, they have had discussions and examined among themselves and with a great number of parishioners of the church the manner and form in which the desired project can be completed. Finally, at their request the Operai and parishioners of the church of S. Lorenzo met together again in the aforesaid sacristy constructed and edified by Sig. Giovanni and in his name; the Prior then expounded all and every thing of what has been said here, in his name and that of the Chapter, in order to have it dealt with and decisions taken to do and act so that this newly edified part of the church shall not remain incomplete and imperfect. Thus, after many conferences and negotiations between the aforesaid persons concerning these matters, they finally after all due consideration and after having examined every aspect assert that they themselves are weighed down with many and various burdens and vexed by those, above all by such as regard the Commune, and that they cannot themselves provide for the aforesaid construction and edification. They have therefore resolved that the said Prior and canons should take the steps that they consider best to hasten and complete the work. The requests of the Prior and canons to a great many parishioners found no response from anyone who would offer his own hands and his own help. Only a single noble and respected citizen, Cosimo, son of the late Giovanni di Bicci de' Medici of blessed memory, honourable citizen and flourishing merchant, because of that devotion that he and his forefathers had and have for the church of S. Lorenzo, offered and offers — on condition that the high altar chapel and the nave of the church as far as the old high altar is assigned to him and his own sons and successors together with every work in masonry and construction made therein — to build with the wealth given to him by God and to complete the whole within the term of six years, taking everything on his own charge and expense and under his own arms and insignia: thus in the said chapel and nave no other private arms or insignia can or may be placed, nor is anyone to be buried there but solely and absolutely the said Cosimo, with the exception of the tombs of the Prior, canons, and chaplains of the church. To effect what is said above he will pledge himself and his own descendants and heirs and all his movable and real property by means of a legally binding public deed. For this matter the two parties approached legal experts and consulted and the Prior treated with the canons, and the canons with the Prior, concerning what is said here. Finally, after many and lengthy negotiations among themselves and consultations and conferences, unanimously and in full concord, collegially and capitularly, in every mode, manner and form in which they could best do so, they decided that it would be best and most advantageous for themselves and for the church and Chapter that, in order that the church be brought to completion within their lifetimes, they should concede the high altar chapel and nave as far as the old high altar to the said Cosimo and to his sons and successors according to the manner and form stated above so as to have them built by him in the manners and forms agreed on. This notwithstanding, so that the negotiations between them and the Chapter of the church should not appear to have been carried out without due consultation, they have resolved to meet in Chapter at another time and to establish, decide and consider more thoroughly whether such actions will be for the good and advantage of the Chapter and the church. For which they requested me, the aforesaid Jacopo, to draw up the official contract for the matters stated here.

17. Because of the reduction of the depth of the transept, the area of the high altar had to be enlarged to accommodate the choir stalls and furnishings (Herzner 1972, pp. 118-19), but the modification of the chancel (mentioned by the Biographer) did not solve all the problems. In particular, from the documents of 1442 it appears that Cosimo assumed the responsibility of placing the choir in the extension of the nave under construction ''behind the high altar of the old church'', which means that the change in programme cited by the Biographer occurred after that date. However, the pulpits executed by Donatello in the 1460s and the choir stalls made after 1459 called for a return to the initial disposition, with the choir in the crossing beneath the dome. The presence of two pulpits, presumably recalling the double ambos of the ancient basilica, is explained, I believe, by the use of the Ambrosian liturgy with its alternating antiphons. In 1461 the dome was completed — to a design that was either an unhappy reworking of Brunelleschi's or completely new.

18. That the door which now leads to the New Sacristy originally led directly to the street is indicated by a passage in Giovanni Cambi's *Istorie* (see *Delizie degli Eruditi Toscani*, ed. Ildefonso di San Luigi, XXII, Florence, 1786, p. 161): '' In the year 1519, in the month of March at the close of that year [that is, March 1520], Pope Leo X ordered work to be begun in the church of S. Lorenzo on a sacristy towards the Via della Stufa where there was a small door for the convenience of the people going to the church.'' The main door on that side, however, was between the belltower and the new transept, where there was a small public piazzetta perhaps only partly expropriated.

19. Since the church was built on existing foundations no modular system due to Brunelleschi is ascertainable in the plan; and because of repeated alterations to the plan there is no proportional correlation in the elevations. Benevolo (1968, pp. 100-107) noted this, but at the same time attempted to find a way of rationalizing the overall result:

> Everything comes about... as if the second order had been superimposed on the first in order to provide an architectonic framework for the structures of the central crossing, without considering the planimetric consequences of that process of grafting... One might say that the pilaster strips are there only to justify the significance of the frame that establishes the height of coping of all the secondary structures, and in fact they could be removed from every place except in the pilasters of the crossing.

Similar incongruities have been noted concerning the relationship between the height of the arcades and that of the nave (a ratio of 7:11) and the lack of a homogeneous overall grid, only the Old Sacristy and the chancel showing the consistent use of a module. A new discussion of the proportional system is in R. Scarchilli, '' Il complesso Laurenziano: La chiesa'', *Controspazio*, June 1977, pp. 43-47.

Despite the modifications, in the transept one can glimpse a compositional system noted by G. De Angelis d'Ossat (1942) and later often stressed by Bruno Zevi as a virtual symbol of a fundamental anti-Classicism on the part of Brunelleschi — the absence of true axiality. For all the rigorous symmetry of the whole, the axis never leads to the centre of an empty chamber such as a chapel or to a window, but rather to a dividing pilaster or to a wall, that is, to a solid surface between two chapels requiring, for homogeneity, two windows in the upper zone, in accordance with the rule of void above void. Note also that at both transept-ends the doors are at the sides, not centrally placed. This system was applied with total consistency in S. Spirito where, however, in the end Brunelleschi's revolutionary proposal for a façade with four doors lost out to the traditional tripartite arrangement after a bitter debate.

S. Lorenzo does resemble S. Spirito in the simplification of its interior in relation to its religious functions, as well as in the symmetry and the diversity of the light sources which makes for a lack of homogeneity. To an even greater extent in the original project, before Cosimo de' Medici introduced his economies and changes, there was in S. Lorenzo a distinct suggestion of a central-plan building, focused on the choir in the crossing.

20. The eight original chapels consisted of four opening off the ''eastern'' side of the transept and two double-chapels at the ends of the transept arms. Between the Old Sacristy and the chancel are the chapels of the Ginori and Rondinelli families, while to the right of the chancel are the Lotteringhi Della Stufa and Ciai Chapels. The double-chapels are, on the left, that of the Medici (dedicated to their saints, Cosmas and Damian), and on the right that of the Neroni (originally Ginori).

The two additional chapels, inserted between transept and nave, are, on the left, that of the Operai (now Martelli), and on the right that of the Corsi family.

There are some difficulties about the original owners of these chapels, because of the Ginori, but Herzner (1974) has shown that the Ginori originally owned the Neroni Chapel — a conclusion deduced from the *Nota e memoria delle sepolture della chiesa di San Lorenzo della città di Firenze*, a manuscript dated 1463 known in a copy by Carlo Strozzi (Florence, Biblioteca Nazionale, Cod. Magliabechiano XXVI, 170, f. 360).

For the Chapel of the Operai, we have Ugolino Martelli's tax declaration of 1447 stating that work had gone on steadily (see G. Pudelko's article on Filippo Lippi in *Rivista d'Arte*, XVIII, 1936, p. 60, note 2), and the information that it was still unfinished in 1450 (Moreni 1816-17, I, p. 51). Work continued on the transept chapels for many more years. The chronology for the period between 1453 and 1457 has been revised by Orietta Superchi, in *Nuovi documenti per la storia della Basilica di S. Lorenzo in Firenze: contributi ed ipotesi*, thesis, University of Florence Faculty of Architecture, 1976-77; she used the ledger, *Entrata e Uscita di spese fatte per la fabbrica delle Cappelle Ginori, Cambini, Taddei, Neroni, Aldobrandini, Marignolle dal 1453 al 1466*, written by Piero di Michele.

In 1458 the work on the Rondinelli, Lotteringhi Della Stufa and Ciai Chapels had not yet been paid for; the Della Stufa Chapel was not consecrated until three years later, and the Neroni double-chapel was completed two years after that — later than the adjacent Corsi Chapel (as Riccardo Pacciani's study of the roofs has shown), though that was, in terms of the original plan, an afterthought.

21. Report to Lodovico Gonzaga from his representative in Florence, Giovanni di Domenico da Gaiole, 3 May 1471.

Some idea of the appearance originally intended for the transept, with its succession of deep chapels, may be given by Donatello's roundel of the Resurrection of Drusiana, in the Old Sacristy itself; the Classical architectural background there is fairly close to the Basilica of Maxentius as shown in drawings such as that in the Coner Codex, f. 39 (London, Sir John Soane's Museum).

22. Saalman 1958-A, fig. 21, capital 11.

23. It was already clear from the documents published by Fabriczy (1892, pp. 606-08) that the Badia, on which work began in 1456, perhaps in September, cannot be ascribed to Brunelleschi. It may possibly owe something to a project for S. Lorenzo with the nave flanked by deep chapels, and it is likely that Cosimo the Elder was directly involved in its planning, at least to the extent of exercising minute control. The church, the most fully developed and noteworthy part of the ensemble, and which has often been attributed to Brunelleschi, was begun in March 1461, fifteen years after his death; work on the façade was paid for in September 1463, and the roofing was done in 1466-67.

Luporini (1964, pp. 162-64, and for the relevant bibliography, note 314, p. 223) still insists on an attribution to Brunelleschi. Recalling that in 1439 Pope Eugenius IV took the Badia away from the Benedictines to give it to the Augustinians, he assumes that the reconstruction financed by Cosimo may have been initiated as early as 1441-42.

The relationship between the Badia and the work of Alberti has been penetratingly explored by L. H. Heydenreich ('' Die Cappella Rucellai und die Badia Fiesolana: Untersuchung über die architektonische Stilformen Albertis'', *Kunstchronik*, 1960, pp. 352ff.).

24. The resemblance to the Portico of Pompey, known from an anonymous sixteenth-century drawing, was pointed out by B. Lowry. The dosseret is a gesture towards the Classical norm of arches resting on piers rather than columns, reformulated by Alberti (Book VII, Chapter 15): "Arcuatis imitationibus debentur columnae quadrangulae". Alberti admits the solution used in S. Lorenzo.

The triglyph decorations begun on the exterior were never used by Brunelleschi himself. They surely come from Pisa, where there are very famous examples in the Cathedral, the Camposanto, and S. Paolo a Ripa d'Arno, in Romanesque work (see M. Salmi, *L'Architettura romanica in Toscana*, Milan and Rome, 1928, figs. 288-89).

25. The poem, given here in a simplified modern transcription, was published by Fabriczy (1907, p. 40). It comes from a manuscript whose title — added in another hand — makes it clear that these *terze rime* were written in praise of Cosimo de' Medici and his sons and of the public tribute offered in 1458 (Florentine style, that is 1459) to the Pope and the Duke of Milan on their visit to Florence (Florence, Biblioteca Nazionale, Cod. Magliabechiano VII, 8, 1121; formerly Strozziano 474). The expressions of admiration are less generic than appears at first reading, and correspond to the rhetoric current in the religious establishment. A similar manner, using more specific terms (partly because he was writing in Latin), was used later by Egidio da Viterbo in the *Historia vigenti saeculorum* concerning the rebuilding of St Peter's (see L. von Pastor, *History of the Popes*, VI, London, 1898, pp. 472, 655): "ad religionem facere ut templum ingressurus facturusque rem sacram non nisi commotus attonitusque novae molis aspectu ingrediatur... animos quoque affectum expertes immotos perstare, affectu concitos facile se ad templa arasque prosternere". The religious building should create emotion, surprise, immobility or violent devotional passion. In the same context see the acute observations of E. H. Gombrich ("Hypnerotomachiana", *Journal of the Warburg and Courtauld Institutes*, XIV, 1951, p. 120).

26. The expenses for S. Lorenzo, as far as our incomplete documentation permits us to know them, can be usefully compared with the total cost of over ten years' work at S. Marco in Florence, which came to about 14,941 florins (Florence, Archivio di Stato, Fondo Mediceo avanti il Principato, filza LXXXI, c. 435). From the memorandum on the estate of Giovanni di Bicci de' Medici in the same archive file (cc. 425-37), it appears that large sums were disbursed for S. Lorenzo: in 1476 a total of about 2,993 florins; in 1477 about 2,799 florins; in 1478, 660 florins; in 1479, about 117 florins — expenditures quite certainly for the reconstruction of the high altar chapel or chancel and the nave, though not necessarily for the side chapels, since they are not mentioned specifically. I am indebted to the staff of the Archivio di Stato for their kindness in calling this important document to my attention.

27. Both Argan (1955, pp. 84ff.) and Luporini (1964, p. 44) view the design of the side chapels very favourably. Herzner (1974, pp. 99-104), on the basis of the few documents available when he was writing, argued that these chapels were later because they block the windows of the chapels at the junction of nave and transept. He also argued that they were built before the nave, something I cannot accept. For their dating see Superchi 1976-77.

28. For the Hours of Laodamia de' Medici see H. C. Krinsky 1969.

What one sees in Giuliano da Sangallo and Leonardo's drawings is certainly unrelated to the lost drawings by Brunelleschi. The notion of S. Lorenzo covered with a series of domes rather than a flat roof, in the manner of St Mark's in Venice or the Santo in Padua, or even of Fra Giocondo's project for St Peter's, may well be due to Giuliano himself.

There may be some connection between S. Lorenzo and a small plaque of which two versions are known, one of silver in the Louvre, and one of bronze in the Kress Collection, Washington, probably derived from the first. It represents Christ exorcising a possessed man, with, in the background, an imposing religious building in the style of Brunelleschi. This small relief, attributed first to Pietro da Milano and then to Caradosso (see Migenon, in *Monuments Piot*, XII, 1905), was ascribed to Brunelleschi by Roberto Longhi (in *Critica d'Arte*, V, 1941, pp. 161-62) but considered by Mario Salmi (in his *Masaccio*, 2nd ed., 1948, pp. 226-27) to be closer to Donatello. Its subject suggests an interesting association with a painting by Masaccio mentioned by Vasari (ed. Milanesi, II, p. 290):

> He devoted exceedingly much study to methods of working, and was ingenious and admirable in the difficult problems of perspective, as can be seen in a narrative picture with small figures now in the house of Ridolfo del Ghirlandaio, in which, besides Christ exorcising the man possessed by a demon, there are very fine buildings in perspective drawn in such a manner that interior and exterior are shown simultaneously, for he has shown them not from the front but from an angle, just because that was more difficult.

The unusual oblique view recalls a painting in the John G. Johnson Art Collection, Philadelphia, now attributed to Francesco d'Antonio (Burton B. Fredericksen and Federico Zeri, *Census of Pre-Nineteenth-Century Italian Paintings in North American Public Collections,* Cambridge, Mass., 1972, p. 73). Diagrammatic reconstructions of the plan of the perspective in both the relief and the painting (which a recent restoration shows to be the central portion of an oblong composition) have been given by A. Parronchi (1964, pp. 256-57, figs. 93b, 93, 96), and a more fully worked-out reconstruction has been published by C. Verga (1978).

The plaque shows the façade of a basilica with a nave perhaps flanked by aisles, chapels resembling the Old Sacristy on all four sides of the building, and a large transept. Although John Pope-Hennessy (*Renaissance Bronzes from the Samuel H. Kress Collection*, London, 1965, cat. no. 280, fig. 12, pp. 80-81) finds that there is "no other work of applied art in which the direct influence of Masaccio and Brunelleschi is so manifest", the connection with S. Lorenzo remains problematical, because in Brunelleschi's time there was no question of any such façade, the initial undertaking being limited to an enlargement of the existing church at the ritual east end. A group of students — G. Del Mastio, A. Migliorini and A. Ungarelli — experimentally worked out a scale drawing of the façade on the relief; comparing it to the measurements of the present church, they found that the lateral doors shown on the plaque lead to spaces beside the church, and that only one door leads into the church itself.

29. P. Franceschini (1885-86, p. 229), writing on

the basis of the Biographer's text and the archive documents (those recently re-explored by Hyman), concluded, somewhat paradoxically: "Nothing of what we see up to the end of the nave and aisles was built by Brunelleschi; yet I think that no one will dare deny that this is the most beautiful part of the temple".

30. Hyman 1975.

31. The subsequent building history of the church is easily summarized. At the end of the fifteenth century the blind arcades on the exterior were completed (Paatz 1940-54, II, pp. 465ff.). In 1515/16 Leo X, the Medici Pope, visited Florence and decided on major changes in the church, cloister and neighbourhood of the family palace. Various projects were assigned to Leonardo (see C. Pedretti, *A Chronology of Leonardo da Vinci's Architectural Studies after 1500*, Geneva, 1962, p. 111ff., 129ff., and *Leonardo architetto*, Milan, 1978, pp. 251ff.). Subsequently the designing of the façade and library were entrusted to Michelangelo. In the discussion to which this commission gave rise Giuliano da Sangallo presumably presented the project that we know from his Sienese sketchbook (f. 21v), with a portico attached to the façade, and perhaps suggested covering the entire church with domes. The façade was never completed, and after 1520 the work came slowly to a stop.

In November 1519 two houses next to the wall of the church were razed to make room for the New Sacristy, on which work began on 1 March 1520. For all the vast and painstaking literature on the subject, it is still not certain whether the lower part of that sacristy already existed, as foundations or as walls above ground. It is possible that the houses were demolished to permit an extension like that which took place during the work on the Old Sacristy. Although Michelangelo proposed in 1524 to use the choir of the church as well for additional Medici tombs, those were executed by Alfonso Lombardi, Baccio Bandinelli and Antonio da Sangallo and eventually installed in S. Maria sopra Minerva in Rome. This tells us, though, that in 1524 a transformation of the choir was again under discussion.

In 1525 Pope Clement VII Medici requested Michelangelo to design a ciborium in the form of a stone baldacchino supported by four porphyry columns within which all the relics in the possession of the church could be brought together and given a place of honour in the centre of the choir. However, between 1531 and 1533 the relics were instead deposited in a pulpit-sacrarium designed by Michelangelo, placed on the inner side of the façade wall above the central entrance door. An exterior loggia connected with this was planned but never built. It would have clashed with earlier projects for the completion of the façade, but those were soon abandoned definitively.

S. Spirito

32. Essential for the chronology and architectonic analysis of S. Spirito are Paatz 1940-53, V, and Luporini 1964, which is in large part devoted to it; for architectural measurements and drawings an exemplary study, Benevolo, Chieffi and Mezzetti 1968; for its history, Padre S. Bellandi 1921, and also G. Richa 1754-62, IX, 1761, pp. 1-67, Stegmann and Geymüller 1885-93, Ia, Fabriczy 1892, and C. Botto 1931-32. An axonometric projection was published as early as 1899 by Auguste Choisy; the one reproduced here [206] is from the *Dizionario enciclopedico d'architettura e urbanistica*, ed. P. Portoghesi, Rome, 1968 (there misidentified as S. Lorenzo). For older graphic documentation, see Marchini, Miarelli Mariani et al 1977, pp. 85-106, figs. 31-34.

33. Bernini's visit almost certainly took place in 1665; his comment is recorded in *La Pittura in Parnaso*, Florence, 1725 (pp. 78-79), by Giovanni Maria Ciocchi, a belated theorist of the Counter Reformation who nonetheless admired the Baroque.

For Juvarra see L. Rovere, V. Viale and A. E. Brinckmann, *Comitato per le onoranze a Filippo Juvarra*, I, Turin, 1937, pp. 54, 115, pl. 5.

34. The church was founded in 1251 by the Augustinians, as a small building with the appellation "Ecclesia Beatae Mariae Virginis et Omnium Sanctorum et Sancti Spiritus", and a piazza created in front of it fifteen years later.

In 1397 official provision was made to commemorate the victory at Governolo, when the Visconti were defeated by the league of Italian communes to which Florence belonged, on the feast of St Augustine, patron of the founding order.

35. For the bequest, by Piero Velluti, see Botto 1931, p. 479.

36. General confirmation comes from a parallel but independent source, Michele Poccianti's *Vite dei sette Beati Fiorentini*, Florence, 1589, p. 184.

37. Piero di Ghirigoro d'Andrea was taxable in 1427 for 3,377 florins, Stoldo de' Frescobaldi and his brother Lamberto for 1,994 florins, placing them respectively in 77th and 121st place in the tax list (see Martines 1963, pp. 377, 388).

The quotation comes from the memoirs of Francesco di Tommaso Giovanni (Florence, Archivio di Stato, Strozziane, cc. 12, 13).

The assets of the six Operai were considerable: Lorenzo Ridolfi, an advocate, was taxable for holdings of 5,249 florins, Giovanni di Tommaso Corbinelli, for 7,125 florins, Sandro di Giovanni Biliotti for less than 1,400, Neri di Gino Capponi for 4,720, Francesco di Niccolò del Benino for less than 1,400, and Francesco di Tommaso Giovanni together with his brothers for 1,881.

38. Paatz 1940-54, V, p. 163.

39. The funds to be used for the construction, a considerable percentage set aside from the salt tax, had been turned over to the friars of S. Croce to enable them to complete their dormitory, and the wars against Lucca and Milan must have conspired to prevent any significant building at S. Spirito.

40. The earliest certain date for an altarpiece is 1471: it was painted by Neri di Bicci for the Cappella della Palla (now Detroit, Institute of Arts).

41. I owe this information to Francesco Quinterio. Also, according to him, the approval given to the three-door version in 1486 must have been merely formal, for the work must have been almost finished by then: in 1484, when building was interrupted, cut

stones for the central door and the two smaller doors were already being brought to the site.

42. Folnesics (1915) suggested a reconstruction in which the niches are carried across the inside of the façade wall to form a kind of atrium or loggia.

43. For the proportioning of S. Spirito, the theoretical studies by Zeitler and by Dorothea F. Nyberg (1954-57), made on the basis of the nineteenth-century measured drawings, have been completely superseded by the work of Benevolo, Chieffi and Mezzetti (1968), and now by Joseph Behles, *Das Gestaltungsprinzip Brunelleschis beim Bau von Santo Spirito in Florenz*, Frankfurt, 1978.

Yet however persuasive the proposal of Benevolo and his co-authors that there is a basic module of 11 *braccia* in the ground plan — the *braccio* here exceptionally measuring 0.5860 m, or 23 1/8 in. — their attempt to analyse the elevation in proportional terms is not completely convincing. It may be that for the elevation Brunelleschi used other key elements such as the diameter of the columns, which, multiplied by 11, gives the height of the order. Nor is it made clear, at least in their examination of the ground plan, in what way it might differ from the proportioning *ad quadratum* used by the Cistercians, which can also be defined as "a rationalization of the traditional system of establishing heights, not a mathematical construction superimposed on the operations of the workmen" (Benevolo et al., p. 1). Our *fig. 204*, from Benevolo, shows a grid based on the unit of a half-bay, that is 5 1/2 *braccia*.

44. This was already recognized in 1887 by E. Marcucci, during restoration work carried out for the Soprintendenza, and a further and better investigation was made by Stegmann and Geymüller (1885-93, Ia, pp. 27ff.). Heydenreich (quoted in Paatz 1940-54, V, p. 166, note 22) observed that the type of window sill on the exterior changes after the first three bays from the façade, which would indicate a change in plan, and this has been confirmed by later research.

The system of projecting semicircular chapels on a high base comes less from medieval buildings like Orvieto Cathedral than from the Triclinium Lateranense, where each niche was intended to contain a semicircular bench around a table.

45. If perspective was ever taken into account in architectural design it must have been at S. Spirito, if only because of the scenographic organization of the whole and the presence of a succession of stage-flat-like elements and fixed axes that direct the eye. Benevolo and his collaborators established at 33 *braccia* (6 modules = 19 2/3 feet) the probable viewpoint from which to appreciate the succession of arch-chapel-niche which is repeated throughout the interior, as shown in the schema derived from drawing XVI in their article, though the successive perspective schemes would have to be revised or redone since their aim was to investigate the curvature of the niches (original, we think) rather than general field of vision (in which the visual angle would assume particular importance).

46. The only study of S. Spirito in relation to liturgy and iconology, a key aspect, is that by Rudolf Zeitler (1959). He identifies the basic principles governing the architecture of this church as: application of

proportions, uniformity, the location of the choir beneath the dome (not uncommon), the orientation of the altars in the chapels towards the centre of the church, so that the officiant faces the congregation directly, a homogeneous system of illumination, and the centralized disposition of the building, the whole making for an "invisible" ordering which, Zeitler points out, is accompanied by a number of sense stimuli such as dark and light, movement and repose.

47. The *capomaestri* who succeeded Brunelleschi after his death were Antonio Manetti Ciaccheri (until 3 March 1460; d. 8 November 1460), Giuliano Sandrini (3 March 1460-February 1461), Giovanni di Domenico da Gaiole (until 1471) and Giovanni di Mariano known as Lo Scorbaccia. See F. Borsi et al., *Brunelleschiani*, 1979.

48. Sanpaolesi's idea, with which Benevolo perhaps too hastily concurred, that S. Spirito was covered by barrel vaults supported on large consoles, was not borne out by Francesco Quinterio's study of the structure of the walls.

49. *The recent restoration (by Robert Erich Wolf).* Perhaps out of enthusiasm for "Brunelleschi Year" (and the government funds made available for that event though not, through the decades, for the normal expenses of upkeep), the church was subjected to a restoration most charitably described as "radical cosmetics". The entire exterior was plastered, even stone features presumably meant to remain visible, and over this was spread a flat and lifeless off-white pancake-makeup, a synthetic paint guaranteed not only to keep out damp but also to retain it in walls which centuries ago had made their own adjustments to "breathing" and changes in humidity. Damaged stonework was not repaired or replaced, perhaps because of new anti-aesthetic notions of "probity" in restoration. The old curved brick-red roofing tiles, so much a feature of aerial Florence, were replaced with pale greyish-red flat machine-made octagons. The base and drum of the cupola, uncleaned, make a wry comment on what has been done. The unadorned façade now looms so ghastly white over the green piazza that even the authorities have had to resign themselves to the expensive job of setting up the scaffolding again and restoring some texture to the plastic-paint surface by meticulous (and costly) stippling. Its essential link with the colours and textures of the city destroyed, S. Spirito will appear more a monument to its restorers than its architect until perforce restored again in what, given the destructive nature of the paint used, is predicted will be no more than five years' time.

10 The Pazzi Chapel

1. For the documentary evidence we must still depend largely on the text by Jodoco Del Badia in R. and E. Mazzanti and T. Del Lungo, *Raccolta delle migliori fabbriche antiche e moderne di Firenze*, Florence, 1876-93, pp. 29-30; P. Fontana 1893; Fabriczy 1892, pp. 215-19; and the review and revision of the documents by Paatz (1940-54) and especially Saalman (1958-A, pp. 127-29, 136-37).

The investigations of G. Laschi, P. Roselli and P. A. Rossi produced some surprising results, published in 1962 ("Indagini sulla Cappella dei Pazzi",

Commentari, XIII, pp. 24-41). They revealed the dates 1459 and 1461 on the cupola and the atrium, proving those to be later than Brunelleschi's death, and they also confirmed that (a) the outer walls were already in existence on three sides, which means that the proportions, as concerns width, were imposed in advance; (b) the front wall was prepared for revetment, probably in marble, and therefore the present atrium cannot be part of the original plan; (c) the façade wall had a round window in its centre which must have lit the interior but is now blocked up; (d) on the opposite wall, above the altar, there is a similar blocked-up window, which proves that the *scarsella* was not envisaged with a vault like the one it now has. Drawings were made by P. A. Rossi [232]. Unfortunately it was not possible to re-explore the space between ceiling and roof.

The same investigations showed that the drum has always been reinforced with two circular "chains", one at the level of the passageway, the other at the large eaves cornice, just as in the Old Sacristy of S. Lorenzo. Again as in the Old Sacristy, hollow clay vases were probably used in the vaults.

2. The suggestion of a resemblance to Civita Castellana was already made by Fabriczy, and was taken up again by C. Bertelli ("La Cappella dei Pazzi e Civita Castellana", *Paragone*, VII, 1956, 77, pp. 57-64), but this is not the only precedent.

3. Its late date is deduced from the fact that it does not appear in the view of Florence by Claude Lorraine (Dresden, Staatliche Kunstsammlungen, Kupferstichkabinett), which clearly shows the lantern and a gallery around it as at the Old Sacristy.

4. The sum invested in the building of the chapel is often given as 13,000 gold florins, as reported by Fabriczy. Saalman (1958-A, pp. 136-37), agreeing with the arguments of Del Badia as to the ambiguity of the *catasto* tax declarations, proposed a corrected reading of the documents, but to my mind not even that is acceptable and in what follows I present — with due doubts — my own reading. The main outline is in my text; here are additional details.

The sum involved at the outset was quite modest, a matter of 2,262 florins and 19 *soldi* plus another 2,000 florins, deposited in the Monte in the names, respectively, of Andrea's sons Guglielmo and Piero for six years and with interest of 4 per cent which would have given about 170 1/2 florins per year. In 1433 Andrea pledged instead two instalments, deposited in his own name, of respectively about 9,263 and about 1,858 florins, computed totally (with a slight error) as 11,120 florins. The pledge was for six years beginning in 1433, to yield about 445 florins per year. In 1442 the pledge was renewed for a further six years.

The tax declaration of 1446 states: "And also there remain in the Monte in the name of Messer Andrea 16,000 florins which are set aside for several years more for the expense of building the chapter house of S. Croce, and from which for the present, as long as the building is going on, we cannot profit. In addition to those, we have to put out of our own pocket other hundreds of florins each year. What falls to me is the third part". Thus, of the 16,000 florins two-thirds, or about 11,000, were tied up in the pledge, besides the direct disbursement of hundreds of florins annually. By 1448 7,567 florins had been realized by Pazzi purely as interest.

5. For the report of this discovery, made by the former superintendents U. Procacci and G. Morozzi, see Renzo Chiarelli, "Architettura del Brunelleschi e di Michelozzo", *Primo Rinascimento in Santa Croce,* Florence, 1968.

6. The Signoria's letter was sent at the end of May to Carlo Federighi, then at the papal court. The relevant passage reads, in full:

> We have heard that for certain pieces of porphyry taken from holy places Antonio de' Pazzi has been brought before the Conservators of that noble city. You should certainly believe that, desirous of adorning a very beautiful sacristy of theirs, and finding these items of porphyry for sale, he purchased them because he did not believe this to be dishonest, especially since he desired them for a sacred and not a profane place, and he would certainly merit great regard for his honour both because of the house from which he stems and because he is himself a merchant.

I am grateful to Francesco Quinterio for having called to my attention this document, published by G. Milanesi (*Nuovi documenti per la storia dell'arte toscana dal XII al XVI secolo*, Florence, 1901, p. 91), and for having correctly connected it with the Pazzi Chapel in his thesis, pp. 178-79.

The affair must have caused quite a scandal. That the legal complications were not resolved is suggested by the fact that there is very little porphyry in the Pazzi Chapel today. While columns are the most likely object of Antonio's efforts, he may have been attempting to buy sarcophaguses, or the great basin in front of the church of S. Giacomo al Colosseo (see R. Lanciani, *Storia degli scavi di Roma*, 1902-13, I, and E. Müntz, *Les Arts à la cour des Papes*, Paris, 1879, I).

7. Little has been written about the symbolic aspects of this chapel, chiefly a brief but convincing essay by Paul Barolsky (1973), and a few pages on the Old Sacristy in a general analysis of the façade of S. Maria Novella by Marco Dezzi Bardeschi (1974). The two interpretations, in part interchangeable given the resemblance between the Pazzi Chapel and the Old Sacristy, are both cosmological and liturgical. Barolsky, proceeding from a suggestion by Millard Meiss (1963), refers to the Apocalypse: he associates the illumination through the round windows in the cupola with the Evangelists and with various references to the cherubim of the Temple and to the Heavenly Jerusalem: the intense luminosity of the chapel recalls the Lamb with the Seven Seals that radiates light.

I would add that the low "windows", open or closed (true windows or sunk panels), so unusual in Brunelleschi's *oeuvre*, may allude to the twelve gates of the City of Heaven, corresponding to the twelve Apostles, a notion supported by St Antoninus (*Summa*, III, 31, Chapter 8): "Et Apocalyp. 21 dicitur quod murus civitatis scilicet supernae Hierusalem, est habens 12 fundamenta et in eis 12 nomina apostolorum agni..."

8. Inconsistencies in construction indicate that the initial programme was drastically modified while the work was in progress. What was done in the final stages is certainly due to whatever architect replaced Michelozzo as director of the work in the monastery after 1453 (see G. Marchini, "Aggiunte a Michelozzo", *La Rinascita*, January-July 1944, p. 30, and especially H. Saalman, "Tommaso Spinelli, Michelozzo, Manetti, and Rossellino", *Journal of the*

Society of Architectural Historians, XXV, 1966, pp. 151-64).

On the problems created by a late dating of the Pazzi Chapel, especially for the upper part decorated by terracotta roundels with the Apostles, Evangelists, and St Andrew, see H. W. Janson 1973.

9. Studies on the systems of proportion such as those by Rolf Linnenkamp (1961) and Dorothea F. Nyberg (1954-57, summarizing a thesis oriented in an arbitrary manner and based on the unreliable drawings of Stegmann and Geymüller), are rendered suspect by their authors' unfamiliarity with the fourteenth-century fabric of the chapel and with methods of architectural design in the Quattrocento, by their unwarranted assumption of an overall stylistic uniformity embracing *scarsella* and portico as well, and by the myth that the architect was free to design whatever he might wish. As for the all-too-famous Golden Section, it involves a relationship of 1:1.618: in the Pazzi Chapel the relationship of width to depth is approximately 1:1.721, and not even a diagonal proportion will fill the bill.

Better than this is the approach of L. Benevolo (1968, pp. 110-112), who inquires into what system might have been possible for Brunelleschi, not on the basis of some theoretical freedom but within the range of pre-established limitations:

> It is entirely likely that he may have mentally sifted through a great number of schemes (the "hundred models... all varied and different" that he boasted of knowing how to invent) and have selected the one that matched up with the limitations of the area, thereafter playing on the small shifts possible within various treatments of details. ... The organism depends always on three measurements (two for the ground plan and one for the elevation), independent and expressible in whole numbers but proportioned in quite different manner. ... The interaxis between the pilasters at the corners of the main dome is almost identical to that of the pilasters in the same position in the sacristy of S. Lorenzo and amounts to 19 1/2 *braccia*; the diameter of the dome, however, is less because the four supporting arms turn out to be completely interpenetrated by the impost... Also the proportion between the two domed chambers is different because the interaxis of the pilasters that support the communicating arch measures 9 1/2 *braccia* rather than 8. ... The interaxes can be read on the pavement, in the visible form of thin strips of stone that divide up the terracotta flooring. ... The pilaster strip in the corner of the large chamber extends over on the long side for the entire width (1 1/4 *braccia*), and bends over on the short side for only 1/4 *braccio*. ... The order, measured from the seat along the wall, comes to 15 *braccia*, with 2 *braccia* for the capital and 13 for the pilaster. The relationship between the minor interaxis and the height is therefore 1:3.

If we do not consider the vaults above the main cornice, and limit ourselves to comparing the elevation below them with that of the Old Sacristy, we find to our surprise a proportional system entirely incompatible with it, much taller and more slender, with an approximate relationship of 5 (Old Sacristy) to 7 (Pazzi Chapel), and narrower at the sides and broader in the centre. These two new qualities — the tall, slender proportions and the irregular horizontal rhythm — may well be features of Brunelleschi's late style, but that cannot yet be proved.

Charles Seymour (1967, p. 114) compares the schemes of the elevations of the Old Sacristy and the Pazzi Chapel, reducing them to the same scale, and also points out various coincidences and differences in the relationship between culture and architecture.

10. In an interview with the company which carried

out the recent consolidation of the chapel we learned that between the medieval wall, next to the basilica, and the enclosing Renaissance walls there is a space about 10 cm or 4 in. wide which was filled in with rough irregular masonry.

11 Military works, I: Lucca, Milan, Pisa, Vicopisano and Rimini

1. For this survey of fortifications I have made use of the excellent bibliographical and critical study by Horst de la Croix (1963) and the exhibition catalogue, *Le Compagnie di Ventura: Mostra di Arti figurative e Armi*, ed. Valentino Pace, Narni, 1970. The chronological outline is drawn chiefly from the documents published by Fabriczy in his famous book (1892, pp. 379ff.) and his yet more important later appendix (1907, pp. 73-78).

2. Brunelleschi's fame as a military architect and engineer seems to have been no less than as a civil and ecclesiastical architect, to judge by the unusually high payment he received for missions to do with fortifications: 1 florin 10 *soldi* per day as "*capomaestro* of the dam being made around Lucca" (Donatello and Michelozzo, his collaborators, earned only 1 florin a day), 1 florin daily for his inspection visits in Tuscany, including the expenses for a horse and servant. Procacci (1968) has compared these payments with the 2 florins *per diem* allotted to an ambassador on mission attended by four persons on horseback, and it should be remembered that the subsistence minimum in Florence at that time, according to Staley, was 5 florins per year, though it is true that entrepreneurs were amassing net annual profits of tens of thousand of florins.

If, as is possible, Brunelleschi was a military architect from the start of his career, his type of technological culture would have been much like that of Guido da Vigevano (Paris, Bibliothèque Nationale, MS lat. 11,015), Konrad Kyeser (numerous manuscripts, mostly copies), Giovanni Fontana (Munich, Staatsbibliothek, Cod. icon. 242), and Taccola ([9] and Chapter 1, note 4). The drawings now attributed to Buonaccorso Ghiberti, and published only in part, seem to derive rather from the experience of Lorenzo Ghiberti. The Florence manuscript (Biblioteca Nazionale, BR 228, ex-Magliabechiana XVIII, 2) includes a section on geometry and theoretical arithmetic, as does that in Siena (Biblioteca Comunale, MS IV 6).

3. Missive della 2ª Cancelleria, 2, f. 120v, cited by Michael Mallett in "Pisa and Florence in the Fifteenth Century: Aspects of the Period of the First Florentine Domination", *Florentine Studies: Politics and Society in Renaissance Florence*, ed. Nicolai Rubinstein, Evanston, Ill., 1968, p. 421.

4. The idea of using flooding to support military actions and sieges did not originate with Brunelleschi. Six examples of the redirection of rivers for military purposes, either to deprive a city of water or to flood it, are reported in the *Stratagemata* of Sextus Julius Frontinus, written in the first century AD (Book III, par. vii) and Brunelleschi had at least one immediate predecessor. Curiously enough, this was

another Florentine engineer, of no small fame in the last years of the fourteenth century and the first of the fifteenth, Domenico di Benintendi, who, condemned to be beheaded, fled Florence in 1391 and pursued his career in Northern Italy in the service of the Visconti of Milan, the Venetians, the Paduans, and finally his own countrymen when they laid siege to Pisa in 1406. In 1393 he constructed for the Visconti on the Mincio River at Valeggio a great dike whose imposing remains can still be seen and which, had it been put into operation, would have raised the level of the river some 10 m (30 ft) and caused severe damage to Mantua. The project would appear not to have been completed because of difficulties encountered in cutting a run-off channel through a hill.

Since we know virtually nothing about the scientific and technological training and background of Brunelleschi, it would be extremely interesting to try to trace whether and how the efforts and achievements of Domenico, and of fourteenth-century engineers in general, had their part in his formation, if only through their pupils or followers. (See G. Fasolo, "Domenico di Benintendi da Firenze, ingegnere del secolo XIV", *Archivio Veneto*, ser. V, I, 1927, pp. 145-80; G. Sandri, "Domenico da Firenze, il ponte di Valeggio e la deviazione del Mincio (1393-94)", *Atti e Memorie della Accademia di Agricoltura, Scienze e Lettere di Verona*, ser. V, XVI, 1938, pp. 219-47; and A. Cassi Ramelli, "La diga-ponte di Valeggio sul Mincio", *Civiltà Mantovana*, XI, 1977, 63-64, pp. 153-71.) [*E. B.*]

In turn, Fabriczy (1897, p. 361) had already rightly seen Brunelleschi's undertaking as the model for the attempt by Leonardo to change the course of the Arno near Pisa; and the machines used for that project were probably similar. Parronchi (1963) also judged Brunelleschi's project favourably. [*Riccardo Pacciani*]

5. Capponi had argued, "If Pietrasanta or Camaiore is won, the war is won. If we linger on here, we shall win neither country nor castle." ("Commentarj di Neri di Gino Capponi di cose seguite in Italia dal 1419 al 1456 alle quali Imprese si trovò il detto Neri in persona", printed in L. A. Muratori, *Rerum Italicarum Scriptores*, XVIII, Milan, 1731, cols. 1169-70.)

The military operations against Lucca are described by Michelozzo in two letters to Averardo de' Medici, published by Fabriczy in "Michelozzo di Bartolomeo", *Jahrbuch der Preussischen Kunstsammlungen*, XXV, 1904, pp. 75-76.

My summary of Brunelleschi's scheme is based on the paper by Paola Beninghi and Pietro Ruschi at the 1977 Congress; they too suppose that the undertaking failed not only because of the disorganization of the Florentine army but also because the Lucchese may have made a sortie in which they prevented the imminent completion of the dam and at the same time caused the water to flood back on their attackers. [*Riccardo Pacciani*]

6. For the siege of Lucca, the negative judgment of the Florentine historians is, rightly or wrongly, generally accepted and repeated, something along the lines set by Giovanni Cavalcanti (*Istorie fiorentine*, ed. Polidori, Florence, 1838, I, p. 328, quoted by E. Garin, *Ritratti di umanisti*, Florence, 1967, p. 60):

> Some of our fantastical spirits, among whom was Filippo di Ser Brunellescho,... advised, and with their false and misleading geometry... demonstrated that the

city of Lucca could be flooded; and they drew this so effectively with their bad arts that the silly masses were led to cry out... we touch with our hands what these theorists draw for us, but you others wish the war to go on and on so as to ensure that you will remain in power forever!

There is evidence of the ferocious polemics that attended that foolhardy venture at the time in at least two poems in the repertory associated with Burchiello which attack or ridicule those responsible for the conduct of the war. The first reads:

> *Pian di Mugnon e suon di campanelle,*
> *e pian dell'Ormannoro e Campi e Brozzi*
> *han ragunato da noi tanti tozzi*
> *chè ciaschedun suo picciole scodelle,*
>
> *Perchè da Lucca son sute novelle*
> *che pe'l gran secco acqua non viene in pozzi,*
> *e se non fusse ch'hanno pieno e gozzi*
> *manicar non potrebbon più fritelle.*
>
> *Però, se Lucca non s'ha così tosto*
> *come vorresti, o popol fiorentino,*
> *e' n'è cagion ch'e' non vi si fa arrosto.*
>
> *San Barnaba e san Pier Gattolino*
> *vanno gridando: "Dateci del mosto",*
> *e tutti stanno col coraggio fino,*
>
> *Però ch'a San Martino*
> *vi si sballa tanta lana francesca*
> *per poter far a Lucca una bertesca.*

(From the plain of the Mugnone at the tocsin's sound / and the plains of Ormannoro and Campi and Brozzi / a swarm of country louts have gathered here, / each with his own little porridge-bowl, Because the news has come from Lucca / that with the great drought the wells have gone dry, / and if they didn't already have their gullets full / they'd have to give up wolfing their fried cakes. Still, if Lucca's not been done in as fast / as you would like, O People of Florence, / the reason is that there they don't cook roasts. S. Barnaba and S. Pier Gattolino / run about crying: "Give us this day our daily wine", / and everyone puts on a big show of courage, But at S. Martino [the Cathedral] / they're still unpacking so much French wool /they could use it to build a tower in Lucca.)

The poem can be read on many levels and the following interpretations are offered tentatively. Here, Burchiello satirizes the greedy, boorish peasants from the environs of Florence who, always eager to turn a fast penny, are now ready to rush to Lucca with bowls of water at news of the drought. Inside that city, water is so scarce that the Lucchese cannot even moisten the dough for their fried cakes. The passage also contains an ironic comparison between the Lucchese and the Florentines. The Florentines fail in their scheme to flood Lucca, which carries on its lucrative wool trade deterred by neither flood nor drought. They succeed in this, the poet implies, because, unlike their plotting neighbours, they are not easily deceived ("non vi si fa arrosto": they do not mistake the smoke for the roast) nor are they divided by internal quarrels. Meanwhile the Florentines themselves (S. Barnaba and S. Pier Gattolino were at opposite points of the city) talk big but wonder just what goes on, confounded as they are by their masters and their great plans. Interesting in a military context is the fact that the small tower which the poet says the Lucchese can build with their wool, a *bertesca*, is of the specific type, either fixed or mobile, from which projectiles were catapulted against attackers.

The second poem is much more difficult to interpret and translate, not only because of uncertainties in the text itself but also because it appears to be a tissue of double meanings and veiled allusions to specific people and facts, perhaps related to the intolerable burden of taxes placed upon the people in order to fund the war.

Albizo mio, se t'hai potenza in Arno
Trami della farsata a Fallambacchio,
A Lisco, Capirosso, e Zufolacchio,
che s'immolar tutti jersena indarno:

Attorno, attorno a Banchi mi cercarno,
E io pappava allor com'un'orsacchio,
Quivi in un magazin, col gran Cornacchio,
Le cui parole, e spalle mi fidarno:

E portandomi i Diavoli a Minosso,
E mi potrebbon bene esaminare,
Che mi trovasser una croce addosso:

Però, deh non t'increscria di pescare;
E se ti domandasser, com'io posso,
Di' lor, ch'un cieco i' non faria cantare:

Se stasera a cenare
Di pesci non m'arrechi pien la zucca,
Io fuggirò, per non morir, a Lucca.

(Albizzo mine, if you have power along the Arno / get me out of the hands of Fallambacchio, / Lisco, Capirosso and Zufolacchio, / who tried and failed to do themselves in last evening.
Around and around Banchi they sought me / while I was blissfully lapping it up like a fat baby bear / right here in a storehouse with the great Cornacchio / whose words and shoulders they trusted me with.
And should the devils whip me off to Minos / and check me over part by part, / they wouldn't find so much as a cross on me.
Still, don't you regret your fishing, / and if they should ask you how I can get by, / tell them the likes of me couldn't even make a blind man sing.
So if tonight at supper / you don't stuff my gut with fish, / I'll take myself off, so as not to starve to death, to Lucca.)

The bearers of three of the obviously pejorative nicknames in the first lines have been identified. Fallambacchio was one Domenico di Stefano who in 1427 was a tax collector, Zufolacchio was an employee (*messo*, a messenger, though perhaps with other less creditable responsibilities) of the Tribunale della Mercanzia, the guild court, and Capirosso (or Caporosso) is cited in sonnets by other authors as a companion of Fallambacchio and likewise a tax collector or *sbirro*, thus a police spy or thug. (See the short but important study by V. Rossi, ''Un sonetto e la famiglia del Burchiello'', originally published in 1900, now in *Studi sul Petrarca e sul Rinascimento*, Florence, 1930, II, pp. 359-69.) The sonnet can thus be interpreted as a protest against the taxes for the war with Lucca (the *fardata*, literally a blow from a broom), and the unfair enrichment of those conducting it (''non t'increscria di pescare...''). ''Banchi'' could refer to the tables of judges or bankers, or to the place in the city where they were located. We have, then, a possible allusion to the poet's financial difficulties (''I have no money, even to make a blind man sing''). Moreover, the threat of fleeing to Lucca, if Albizzo (supposed to be Rinaldo degli Albizzi himself) does not supply him with money (''fishes''), suggests a connection between the poet's financial plight and the attempt to flood that city. The use of water images throughout the poem is not accidental. ''Cornacchio'' could be the name of someone whose ''words'' and ''shoul-

ders'' temporarily rescued the poet from his persecutors, Fallambacchio and Zufolacchio. Dr R. E. Wolf suggests, however, that ''Cornacchio'' also meant a stone or a projectile used in artillery; in that case, ''parole'' and ''spalle'' could be read as ''passwords'' and ''catapult breeches''. In other words, the poet claims he took part in the siege and, having thus fulfilled his duty, deserves a favour from ''Albizzo''. ''Banchi'' in this context might be the earthworks of the besieging forces.

The text of the first poem is from Domenico di Giovanni detto il Burchiello, *Sonetti inediti*, ed. Michele Messina, Florence 1952, sonnet XXVI; that of the second, from the classical collection, *Sonetti del Burchiello, del Bellincioni e d'altri poeti fiorentini alla burchiellesca*, Lucca, 1757, p. 128. See also Renée Watkins, ''Il Burchiello (1404-1488) - Poverty, Politics and Poetry'', *Italian Quarterly*, 14, 1970, 54, pp. 21-57, and Vittorio Rossi, ''Un sonetto e la famiglia del Burchiello'', *Scritti di critica letteraria*, Florence, 1930.

The split in Florentine humanist society that was particularly marked during the war against Lucca appears also in a very hostile comment by Leonardo Bruni, who speaks of Brunelleschi, without mentioning him by name, as ''stultus'' (stupid). See ''Leonardo Aretini rerum suo tempore in Italia gestarum Commentarius, ab anno MCCCLXXVIII usque ad annum MCCCCXL'', *Rerum Italicarum Scriptores*, XIX, Milan, 1731, col. 935a.

7. A description of the works executed on the castle of Milan which is almost contemporary with Brunelleschi is in Pietro Candido Decembrio's *Vita Philippi Mariae, Tertij Ligurum Ducis*, Chapter 36. He speaks of a new wing added to the old fortress on the west, which he considers almost miraculous. Some comments on the possibility of identifying Brunelleschi's work on the castle are made by the editors of this text, A. Butti, F. Fossati and G. Petraglione, in *Rerum Italicarum Scriptores*, XX, 1, Bologna, 1925, pp. 195-200 (related to pp. 151-53 of the Latin text).

The rebuilt Castello Sforzesco was highly praised by Cesare Cesariano (Book VI, p. Cr), though he does not mention Brunelleschi's possible role as adviser on the previous castle:

Francesco Sforza and Bianca Maria, having become Dukes of Milan in tranquil peace, had the chief palace built. And up to its time, as regards the beauty [*symmetria*] of ornamental work as described by Vitruvius, there was virtually never [anything comparable], from the time of the Romans until that time in Milan, from the destruction wrought by Frederick Barbarossa right up to our own day.

8. Brunelleschi's trip to Milan is mentioned by the Biographer and documented by a list of architects active on Milan Cathedral, which unfortunately, however, lacks specific dates (in G. Franchetti, *Storia e descrizione del Duomo di Milano*, Milan, 1908, p. 21). The visit can be dated to around 1430, a time when a solution for the design of the *tiburio* was becoming urgent, since the work had apparently got as far as the closing of the vaults in both apse and transept and no architect could be found capable of coping with the tower. Tragically, the relevant documents were all lost in 1906 in a fire at the Turin Fair where volumes from the archives were being displayed. The consultation with Brunelleschi would seem to have come right at the start of a long debate over this far from easy problem which eventually also involved Filarete, Giovanni Solari, Luca Fancelli,

Francesco di Giorgio, Giuliano da Sangallo, Leonardo and Bramante.

Brunelleschi's summons to Milan came certainly from Filippo Maria Visconti and also, presumably, from the Bishop, Bartolomeo Capra (in office 1422-31). Perhaps there is an echo of Brunelleschi's project in Bramante's *opinio* suggesting the use of a dome (see A. Bruschi, ''L'intervento di Leonardo da Vinci: Lettera ai fabbriceri del Duomo di Milan'', in *Scritti Rinascimentali di Architettura,* Milan, 1978, pp. 113-126, and ''La Bramanti Opinio super domicilium magnum'', *ibid.*, pp. 127-37). For Brunelleschi's activity in Milan, and its consequences detectable in the drawings and notes of Leonardo, see C. Pedretti, *Leonardo architetto*, Milan, 1978, especially pp. 32-52, and his notes presented at the 1977 Congress.

Recent publications on Milan Cathedral have completely ignored Brunelleschi's involvement except for A. Parronchi, ''Brunelleschi a Milano'', *La Nazione* (Florence), CVII, 2 January 1965, p. 3.

9. For the political relations between Florence and Pisa, see P. Silva, ''Pisa sotto Firenze dal 1406 al 1433'', *Studi Storici*, XVII, 1909-10. For the walls of Pisa, see Emilio Tolaini, *Forma Pisarum*, Pisa, 1968; Livio Borghi, *Le mura urbane di Pisa*, 1970; Giancarlo Severini, ''Osservazioni sulla cartografia cittadina'', *Rassegna del Comune di Pisa*, 1968, 11/12, pp. 23-24.

10. The Porta del Parlascio was not only accurately measured and drawn but also subjected to a thorough historical study, including archive research, by a group of students — Sandro Baldassari, Carlo Raffaelli, Paolo Pardini, Niva Pasquinelli and Laura Toghetti. See now Sandro Baldassari and Carlo Raffaelli, ''Porta del Parlascio'', *Antichità Pisane*, II, 1975, 3, pp. 16-23, based on the sixteenth-century manuscript of G. B. Totti (Pisa, Biblioteca Universitaria, 595).

J. R. Hale considers the Pisa fortifications to have ''begun the investigation of how to exploit flanking fire from artillery embrasures'' (*Renaissance Fortification - Art or Engineering?*, London, 1977, p. 12).

11. Of the fortified bridge the Biographer writes (f. 312r):

And in those same times, before there was a project for a new citadel in Pisa, they were discussing how to strengthen the city, and Filippo was sent there to examine in what way it could be fortified. And he had the idea of fortifying that first bridge with the fortress of two towers, one on one side of the Arno and the other on the other side; and they were built as he recommended and, considering what the offensive power of those times was like, earned him much praise because they contained many excellent conceits and many intelligent ideas of a sort not used later in constructions of such great importance, either because others did not wish to do things as he did, as happens often because people wish to be masters before being pupils, or because they did not know about them.

A recently completed investigation has identified the vestiges of the tower Brunelleschi designed to protect the port and bridge, and we now know that the misleading reconstruction we see today was built on wrong foundations.

12. For the history of the Cittadella Nuova see especially Giancarlo Severini, *Architettura militare* *di Giuliano da Sangallo*, Pisa, 1970, pp. 47-54, figs. 68-76.

Sangallo was called in immediately after famine had forced the besieged population to surrender to the Florentines on 9 June 1509. His new citadel was to house a garrison of 1,000 foot soldiers. Work began promptly, and presumably followed the earlier contours but incorporated all the new devices brought in with the progress of artillery. Brunelleschi's square towers were replaced by cylinders with battered bases and machicolated crowns. The quadrilateral fort behind the old Porta S. Marco was incorporated by Sangallo into the bastioned enclosure to serve as the keep.

13. G. Scaglia, "The Torre del Marzocco in Livorno in a Drawing by Buonaccorso Ghiberti", paper presented to the Convegno Internazionale di Studi Ghibertiani, in the press in 1979.

14. For Vicopisano I have made use not only of the drawings published here for the first time but also of the diligent harvesting of historical data, part of which appears in what follows, by a group of students comprising Fabio Daini, Simone Giusti, Marco Marchetti and Paolo Poggetti.

The courtyard measures 15 m (49 ft) across. The walls are 11.20 m (36 ft 9 in.) high internally, but externally their heights vary with the fall of the land: on the south 11.60 m (38 ft), and on the north 13.10 m (43 ft). Their thickness is between 1.25 and 1.30 m (4 ft - 4 ft 4 in.).

15. Built entirely of stone from the Verruca region, the Torre dei Silvatici is well preserved, and has a small gate on the eastern (outer) side and a small arch on the west, communicating with the inner curtain. There is a window to the east and two gunloops on each of the outer faces. At a lower level there are lower and wider openings, no doubt intended for firearms of larger calibre. At the bottom the tower has a batter giving it the form of a truncated pyramid, and at the top it has five Ghibelline or butterfly merlons on each side, and an extension which is narrower, squared off, and massive. Inside there are traces of segmental vaults.

16. A thorough reconsideration of military fortification in Romagna and the Marche, with an accurate chronology of Brunelleschi's possible travels, deduced from Sigismondo Malatesta's movements, was appended to Gastone Petrini's contribution to the 1977 Congress, "Aspetti e problemi del progrediente affievolimento documentario nelle fabbriche rinascimentali in relazione ai fenomeni di degrado, agli interventi restaurativi ed alla storia dell'arte". On the fortifications in the Marche, see T. Scalesse, "Senigallia e Peschiera: Nuovi dati sulle fortificazioni roveresche", *Quaderni dell'Istituto di Storia dell'Architettura*, XXII, 1975, fasc. 127-32, pp. 55-74, and in particular note 5, p. 71, with bibliography.

17. For the Castel Sismondo in Rimini, see *Città di Rimini: Sigismondo Pandolfo Malatesta e il suo tempo*, exhibition catalogue, ed F. Arduini, G. S. Menghi, F. Panvini Rosati, P. G. Pasini, P. Sanpaolesi and A. Vasina, Vicenza, 1970, pp. 177-207, with bibliography.

Information on the foundation comes from Cesare Clementini, *Racconto istorico della fondatione di Rimini*, 2 vol., Rimini, 1617. For Piero's fresco see

E. Battisti, *Piero della Francesca*, Milan, 1971, I, pl. 9 and p. 66.

A drawing showing the original appearance of the castle was published in F. Mancini and W. Vichi, *Castelli, Rocche e Torri di Romagna*, Bologna, 1959, pp. 270-72. The model made by Professor Ugo Barlini under the direction of Pier Giorgio Pasini includes the polygonal bastions of the outer circle of walls as modified before 1526 to withstand artillery fire, and many other elements that are inevitably arbitrary.

Happily the restoration is now well under way, after many vicissitudes, and although it was virtually impossible to visit the site during the preparation of this book the building is now open to the public. See P. Sanpaolesi, *Progetto di restauro della Rocca Malatestiana di Rimini*, Florence, 1969, and Pier Giorgio Pasini, "Castel Sismondo", *Rocche e Castelli di Romagna*, III, Bologna, 1972, pp. 41-67. I owe my information about the use of clay between the foundations of the towers and the outer stone facing to Professor Sanpaolesi.

18. There is documentary evidence of work on the port of Pesaro in 1440 by an engineer, Piero da Pozzo. Although Vasari attributed the fortification turret to Brunelleschi, according to an inscription it was begun in 1474 and completed in 1483 by Cherubino Guardabasso: see Annibale Degli Abbati Olivieri Giordani, *Memorie del Porto di Pesaro*, Pesaro, 1774, Carlo Promis, *Biografie di Ingegneri militari italiani dal secolo XIV alla metà del XVIII* (Miscellanea di Storia Italiana, XIV), Turin, 1874, p. 13, and C. von Fabriczy 1892, pp. 371-72.

The Rocchetta at Pesaro, the small fortress opposite the Rocca Costanza, had exceptional architectural quality. A rare photograph, made before its destruction at the start of this century shows clearly its extraordinary geometrical simplification — a central cylinder with lower squared-off arms coming off at an obtuse angle (published in N. Cecini, *Pesaro*, Pesaro, 1973, p. 73, kindly called to my attention by M. Dezzi Bardeschi).

19. The Roman writers are Julius Caesar, Vegetius Renatus, Sextus Julius Frontinus and of course Vitruvius. The medieval sources are Alexander Neckham, who in 1190 wrote the first detailed description of a modern castle, Fra Egidio Colonna's *De Regimine principum libri tres* (c. 1285), Marino Sanuto Torsello's *Liber secretorum* (1321), Guido da Vigevano's *Thesaurus regis Franciae* (c. 1335), and Fra Bartolomeo Carusi's *Tractatus de re bellica* (c. 1350).

20. Horst de la Croix 1963, pp. 31-32. Christine de Pisan — Cristina da Pizzano — was the daughter of a professor of astronomy who emigrated to France when she was a small child. She discussed contemporary fortification in her *Faicts d'armes et de chevalerie* (translated and published by William Caxton).

Even in Northern Europe, the first theorist to be fully aware of the problems posed by artillery was François de Surenne, who in 1446 wrote a report on the fortifications of Dijon: see B. Gille, *Les ingénieurs de la Renaissance*, Paris, 1964.

Another factor is that the development of artillery depended on learning how to forge cannon with an alloy of bronze and iron. This took time, and it was only the campaign of 1494, in which the French proved their absolute superiority, that led to a general renovation of fortifications in Italy.

12 Late works; the Rotunda of S. Maria degli Angeli and the lantern and exedrae of Florence Cathedral

1. Essential reading for Brunelleschi's late phase is two articles by L. H. Heydenreich (1931) and A. Bruschi (1972), the latter of whom explains the change in style thus:

> The edifice is no longer thought of — in large measure at least — as *constructed* from a skeleton of architectural members laid out on the walls and forming a space. ... It is the space itself, the *void*, that acquires a function which is, so to speak, active, *formative*; and it is the space, the void itself in itself, and not the "structural" skeleton which is dialectically counterposed to the wall structures. The *void*, interior or exterior, acts therefore on the limits constituted by the walls and, as it were, hollows them out, shapes them by opening niches in them

— a process Bruschi ascribes to "a penetrating observation of the characteristics of Roman architecture in concrete".

As the text makes clear, I hope, I take a completely opposite view of the late works of Brunelleschi from the traditional interpretation as formulated by Dvorák, Frey, and Heydenreich. According to that, as paraphrased by Luporini (1964, p. 8), the development of his style is

> a process which leads from the empty space of the traditional Gothic construction to the solid, corporeal, static space [*Raumkörper*] typical of Antiquity and found again precisely in Renaissance building, that is, in the so-called Brunelleschian space of the late works.

I do, however, share the idea of Luporini (ibid., p. 34) that

> we must... propose to ourselves a Brunelleschi who is very much more problematic and polyvalent,... who... expresses in [these buildings] a multiplicity of trials, of experiments without precedent in the past, and displaying specific interests. Only by selecting the evidence and arranging it arbitrarily according to our own ideas of chronology can they be made to show a neat line of development.

The Rotunda of S. Maria degli Angeli

2. Pippo Spano was the fiduciary of King Sigismund of Hungary and his companion in dramatic events; he was rewarded with ennoblement (made count, *ispán*, whence his name Pippo Spano), large estates, administrative and military positions, and ecclesiastical honours for his relatives, two Scolari being made bishops of Zagreb, Magyvárad and Kalocsa. Pippo, famed in the arts for having called Masolino to Hungary and for his portrait by Andrea del Castagno, was among other things the administrator of all the State rock salt mines as well as being involved in the transport of their products. In 1411 he was military commander in the war against Venice. In short, an outstanding personality who was also responsible for a cultural exchange of immense significance: no wonder the Fat Carpenter of the novella, to escape the social consequences of that heartless joke, rushed off to Hungary, where he promptly won the patronage of his powerful countryman and soon also the consolation of relative wealth (see Chapter 16).

3. One came from Messer Andrea di Filippo di

Renzo degli Scolari, Bishop of Magyvárad (now Oradea in Romanian Transylvania). On his death on 24 January 1426, he left his wealth to Pippo Spano on condition that he build a Camaldolensian monastery on his lands at Vicchio, some 35 km (22 mi.) from Florence, in accordance with the rule of the Florentine monastery of S. Maria degli Angeli, specifying also that should Pippo not carry out these testamentary obligations, the responsibility was to devolve on the consuls of the Arte di Calimala, the merchants' guild.

The other bequest was that of Messer Matteo di Stefano Scolari, brother of Pippo Spano, who left him half of his wealth for the purpose of building in the palace of the testator, located in the parish of S. Stefano at Tizzana (in the present province of Pistoia), a monastery for ten Camaldolensian monks which would be dedicated to SS. Julian and Anthony, by the same will appointing the consuls of the Arte di Calimala to be tutors of his children and conservators of the future monastery. The same testament was made twice again in Hungary, and the final version was signed on 13 January 1426.

4. Petitioned by Pippo Spano on the grounds that the funds would not extend to two such projects, Pope Martin V authorized him to build a single monastery. However, when news came of the death of the *condottiere* the bull remained in Rome. At that point too a grave diplomatic crisis opened between Florence and King Sigismund of Hungary. The Florentine captain Niccolò Lamberteschi, after a defeat, was accused of treason in 1427, and the Florentine merchants and notables settled in Hungary shared in his disgrace. In 1427-28 an embassy consisting of Luca di Maso degli Albizzi and Piero di Luigi Guicciardini was sent there, and their manuscript report survives. Among other things, they attempted to recover the estate left by Pippo Spano which, we have seen, already included one of the bequests for a monastery; it was said to total 2,000 gold florins plus another 2,000 earmarked for the daughter of Messer Matteo. Sigismund, however, held all the funds forfeit to his State treasury on the grounds that the accounts of Pippo Spano, his administrator, were not in order at his death.

Evidently there were further and presumably successful negotiations if in 1430 the consuls of the Arte di Calimala could consign the property of both Andrea and Matteo to Filippo di Rinieri di Lippo degli Scolari and his brothers Lorenzo and Giovanni, holding back 5,000 gold florins to be used for the Camaldolensian foundation. During this period first Martin V and then Eugenius IV confirmed the permission to use the bequest to build a single institution only. Finally on 2 April 1434 an agreement was reached between the consuls of the guild and the monks of S. Maria degli Angeli that an oratory was to be raised on the land of their monastery. This document is included in filza XIII of the Arte dei Mercanti (see below, note 30).

5. See especially his *Latinae Epistolae*, ed. P. Cannetus and L. Mehus, Florence, 1759, and A. Dini Traversari, *Ambrogio Traversari e i suoi tempi*, Florence, 1912; G. Mercati, *Traversariana (Ultimi contributi alla storia degli Umanisti)*, Vatican City, 1939; Maurilio Adriani, "Note sulla cultura proto-quattrocentesca fiorentina", *Un'altra Firenze. L'epoca di Cosimo il Vecchio. Riscontri tra cultura e società nella storia fiorentina. Relazione generale di Pietro Ugolini*, Florence, 1971, especially pp. 492-508. For a less sympathetic interpretation, see Frederick Antal,

Florentine Painting and its Social Background, London, 1948. Most recently there is Charles Stinger, "Ambrogio Traversari and the 'Tempio degli Scolari' at Santa Maria degli Angeli in Florence", *Essays presented to Myron P. Gilmore*, ed. S. Bertelli and G. Ramakus, Florence, 1978, I, pp. 271-86, an excellent study of the relationship between Traversari and contemporary archaeology, humanistic and scientific studies, patrons and architects, with a list of classical treatises concerned with war machinery, fortifications, aqueducts, mathematics and geography.

6. The relevant documents are summarized by Giuseppe Canestrini, "Discorso sopra alcune relazioni della Repubblica Fiorentina col re d'Ungheria e con Filippo Scolari", *Archivio Storico Italiano*, IV, 1843, pp. 185-213; see also Arturo Linacher, "Il 'Tempio degli Scolari' ", *Atti della Società Colombaria Fiorentina (1918-19, 1919-20)*, Florence, 1921, pp. 609-27.

The political complexity of the time, which must be seen in the light of the general European and perhaps even world situation, is well presented in the exemplary article by C.M.D. Crowder, "Henry V, Sigismund, and the Council of Constance, a Reexamination", *Historical Studies*, IV, London, 1963, pp. 93-110. I do not know any similar studies for Florence, but the documents we do have are significant. And there is the fact that the Fat Carpenter, Manetti di Jacopo Ammannatini, after fleeing to Hungary (which also, to judge by the frequent mentions by Giovanni da Prato, must have been a veritable Mecca for artists), served as secret messenger to convince Sigismund to come to Italy and therefore to Florence: see C. Guasti, *Commissioni di Rinaldo degli Albizzi*, Florence, 1867-73, II, p. 590. (Much of this information is from the "Atti del Convegno italo-ungherese di studi rinascimentali, Spoleto, 9-10 settembre, 1964", *Ungheria d'oggi*, V, January-February 1965, especially pp. 34-37, 40-41.)

7. The designing and approval of the project, the construction of a model, the laying of the foundations, and the raising of the walls and orders to the height of the pilaster capitals took from spring 1434 to 1437, the graffito date on an outside wall which was discovered by H. Siebenhüner and communicated by him to W. and E. Paatz (1940-54, III, p. 130, note 3). That date corresponds to the interruption in the work.

The expenses for the building were covered by the interest from the bequests of Andrea and Matteo, deposited in the Monte, plus 1,300 gold florins from Filippo degli Scolari.

8. According to Agostino Fortunio, writing in 1579. G. Miarelli Mariani has perceptively pointed out the importance in town-planning terms of the chosen site, at the intersection of Via degli Alfani and Via del Castellaccio, and stressed Brunelleschi's effort here and elsewhere to have a corner view.

9. According to Vasari and his near-contemporary Agostino Fortunio, work on the church stopped because of the expenses of the war in the spring of 1437, and perhaps too because of the failure of the embassy. Work never resumed because interest in the project faded.

10. Notable progress in our knowledge of the Rotunda has come in the form of a catalogue of the

early graphic documentation painstakingly prepared by Patricia Waddy (1970-72), which grew out of a seminar by Professor R. Krautheimer, and along with this, studies by Gaetano Miarelli Mariani (1975, 1974-76, 1977). For the drawings in the Uffizi see Marchini, Miarelli Mariani *et al.* 1977, pp. 109-27, figs. 39-47. The quality of conjectural reconstructions has also been much improved, in publications by G. Marchini (1938), P. Sanpaolesi (1962, fig. on p. 87), and A. Bruschi (1972), the attempt in this volume [273, 274], and the even more recent ones by G. Miarelli Mariani (1974-76) and Carla Pietramellara. Miarelli Mariani's has the merit of being based on a general comparison of the measurements derived from drawings (mainly sixteenth-century) with both the ground plan and the elevation — for which he uses drawings by Lucilla Labianca — and the section that he proposes seems more accurate as to the height of the order than the one published here.

11. The earliest mention of drawings in the monastery is in Vasari (1550 edn, p. 327), who refers to "the sheets with the ground plan and the *alzato* [elevation]" as being there. When he refers to them again in the 1568 edition, it is to state that they are definitely from the hand of Brunelleschi and are now in his possession. There is no way of ascertaining whether he was speaking of two different sets of drawings or of a single set that he had been able to acquire from the monastery. It does seem, however, that that institution continued to hold some early documents related to their oratory.

12. Although Patricia Waddy in her chronological account of the drawings and related engravings (1970-72) had to hand more material than did previous scholars studying the building (Marchini, Pane, Sanpaolesi, Bruschi), she did not make a graphic reconstruction, and the entire problem has recently been taken up again by A. Bruschi (1972) and others. Miarelli Mariani (1976) painstakingly compared the four principal drawings of the ground plan (Vatican Library, Cod. Barb. Lat. 4424, f. 15v; Florence, Uffizi, 7982 A and 3184; Paris, Louvre, 681).

13. I differ from Miarelli Mariani in believing that the Sangallo drawing and the others, though they are less exact, may be copies of Brunelleschi's original project. What is needed now is a close examination and search for marks that may have been left by the compass and square, in order to learn the methods of diagrammatic construction used by these various copyists, who must have been at least influenced by the procedure used by Brunelleschi himself.

The discrepancy between the measurements marked on the drawings and those of the oratory itself — something even more evident after our careful new survey — cannot be explained away as the result of the restoration done between 1934 and 1940 but, instead, points to something much more serious: either to a reduction of the project itself by at least 0.5 m (19 5/8 in.) during construction or else to the use of a measuring rod of a length different from the *braccio* we take to be normal. There are in fact many doubtful points among the main measurements. Giuliano da Sangallo reports the height of the pilasters to be 11 1/3 *braccia*, whereas for Fortunio and in the other drawings it is 10 3/4, thus making a disparity of something between 6.60 and 6.25 m. (21 ft

376

7 in. as against 20 ft 6 in.). And the measurements of the interior today do not match those given on the drawings: from one corner to another there are 30 *braccia* (17.50 m = 57 ft 5 in.), and from side to side of the octagon less than 26 1/2 *braccia* (15.50 m = 50 ft 10 in.).

14. Book III, Chapter 19, pp. 128-31. Fabriczy's transcription of the Latin original was very kindly checked for me by Carlo Pedretti, and found to be entirely accurate. Here is the text that precedes and follows the passage that I quote:

Because the negotiation for the construction, in consequence of various urgent matters, produced no positive result, in the year 1434 by initiative of the general of the order. Ambrogio [Traversari], the Apostolic authority was petitioned to consent to modifying the [plan to build a] monastery into an illustrious temple. Thus the consuls of the Merchants' Guild purchased from the monks of the [monastery of the] Angeli a garden site at the crossroads of Campacio which had been acquired from Giovanni di Andrea Lippi. And because it was necessary to use the common thoroughfare for the foundations of the church, permission to do so was granted by decree of the Ufficiali delle Torri with the proviso that no one else was to be permitted to build there. But once the church was begun and the foundations laid, while the building was actually under construction, the supreme magistrate of the city allocated the money placed in the Monte to works of public utility. Thus the fabric remained unfinished, as one sees, up to the year 1503. At that time finally, at the request of the monks, the roof was laid on and made fast; so that the consuls three times each year, that is, every four months, celebrate in the church of the Angeli the anniversary in suffrage of the souls of the testators with the funds remaining and, at the expense of the guild, participate in the divine rites...

Cosimo de' Medici, Grand Duke of Etruria, in our time intended to complete the building, but because the fathers feared that the nature of the ancient observance would be blighted if they had to open the church to women, in infraction of the very ancient law of the place, he limited himself to giving advice on how to preserve the monument.

15. Indeed, as we have seen, he specifically speaks of "Philippi Brunelleschij insignis Architecti graphis" — "a drawing by Filippo Brunelleschi, the illustrious architect". On this drawing the distance between two opposite corners and two opposite sides of the octagon inside must have been marked as, respectively, 31 and 29 *braccia* (as found also in the drawings by Giuliano da Sangallo — Uffizi 7982 A and Louvre 681 — though through an error in transcription 29 appears in the latter as 20). The space of a chapel is measured as 10 1/4 *ulnae* (Latin for *braccia*), precisely as in the Sangallo drawings, and the passageway between the chapels is marked (only by Sangallo) as 1 1/2 *braccia* wide. By elimination, then, the model copied by Sangallo may well have been the same as that used by Fortunio. The height is derived from a section with the same measurement markings, though no known copy matches his indications. From the floor to the eye of the lantern would have been 46 1/2 *braccia*. On the exterior, the cornice above the chapels (i.e. the first eaves level) would have run at a height of 22 *braccia*; from there the building "rose with moderate slope as far as the second eaves". This second large cornice, connected to the covering of the dome, was at a height of about 35 *braccia*.

A reliable version of the drawing itself seems to survive in the engraving published by Giuseppe del Rosso in the third edition of Mario Lastri's *L'osservatore fiorentino sugli edifici della sua patria* (1821,

II, facing p. 167); at that time it was said to be the property of Sig. Gaetano Ceccherini.

Other authors such as Onofrio Boni (*Memorie per le Belle Arti*, 1786, II, p. 39) and Giuseppe del Rosso (*Descrizione di alcuni disegni originali di architettura ornativa di classici autori*, Pisa, 1818, p. 33) speak of the drawing formerly in the monastery of S. Maria degli Angeli as "because of its great age... partly lost" and "in some parts, because of its age, not very distinct". On the other hand Del Rosso was aware that this drawing was more trustworthy, so much so as to write concerning the engraving by Boni (see below, note 33) that "the copy referred to here and published in Rome is infinitely altered by Gherardo Silvani".

In the engraving made by Del Rosso, the drawing was subjected to two alterations, having been recopied and engraved and then incorrectly transferred in scale. While the ground plan, from corner to corner, corresponds to the 30 *braccia* indicated by Richa (1759, III, p. 173) — though, as we shall see, differing from all the markings on the drawings derived, presumably, from the prototype by Brunelleschi, which unanimously give 31 *braccia* — in the elevation the height from floor to dome scarcely reaches 41 *braccia*, and the treatment of the niches in the chapels, rendered as if they were as high as the chapel openings, is also definitely wrong. The elevation is therefore a purely imaginary reconstruction, and since we cannot presume that at that date there was any acquaintance with the sketch of the elevation made by Giuliano da Sangallo or with the drawing in Florence (Biblioteca Laurenziana, Cod. Ashburnham 1828), it must be considered to have drawn its inspiration from the drum and dome of the Cathedral. The drawing itself appears to have disappeared since it was last mentioned, by Fabriczy (1892, p. 241, note 1), as in the collection of Marchese Giuseppe Pucci in Florence.

16. A large colour reproduction of a detail is in Sanpaolesi 1962, pl. XX.

17. U. Procacci (in his comments to A. Sapori, *Compagnie e Mercanti di Firenze antica*, Florence, 1955, pp. xlvi, cvii) argues that what we have here is not the original design for the oratory but a reworking in Late Gothic style. Carlo Pedretti has written to me to say that he believes that the exterior of the oratory appears in a sketch by Leonardo which is extraordinarily advanced in style (Milan, Biblioteca Ambrosiana, Cod. Atlanticus, f. 202v, reproduced in his *A Chronology of Leonardo da Vinci's Architectural Studies after 1500*, Geneva, 1962, p. 54, fig. 10), but I suspect that drawing is instead simply a reworking of the same theme.

18. By B. Lowry in *Renaissance Architecture*, New York, 1962.

H. Burns ("Progetti di Francesco di Giorgio per i Conventi di San Bernardino e Santa Chiara di Urbino", *Studi Bramanteschi*, Rome, 1974, p. 296) attributes to the Urbino architect Muzio Oddi or one of his heirs the compilation of the Ashburnham manuscript, a collection of drawings which range from the late fifteenth to the early seventeenth century. (For Oddi, see L. Servolini, "Muzio Oddi, Architetto Urbinate del Seicento", *Urbinum*, VI, 1932, 6, pp. 7-27). Burns suggests that the author of the sketch depicting S. Maria degli Angeli might be Francesco di Giorgio (though what we have may be not his original but a copy made by him); and this

seems to be confirmed by its similarity to the view of S. Bernardino at Urbino in the same manuscript (App., f. 87), which shows specific connections with Brunelleschi.

Another drawing, unique for the technical information it gives on the arrangement of the dome, is the axial section in the Uffizi (3219 A; published in R. Pane 1954, fig. 21) though this is more likely to be connected with projects by Gherardo Silvani.

19. Since the dome was only slightly more than 31 *braccia* in diameter, I do not see why it should require buttressing, especially since we know that in the dome of the Cathedral itself Brunelleschi opposed those who called for sustaining arches and exterior buttresses Here he simply surrounded a central domed area with radiating chapels.

20. For central-plan buildings in general see R. Wittkower 1949/62, and W. Lotz, "Notizen zum kirchlichen Zentralbau der Renaissance", *Studien zur toskanischen Kunst: Festschrift Heydenreich*, Munich, 1964, pp. 157 ff.; also S. Sinding-Larsen, "Some Functional and Iconographical Aspects of the Centralized Church in the Italian Renaissance", *Acta ad Archaeologiam et Artium Historiam Pertinentia*, II, 1965, pp. 203-52.

21. Miarelli Mariani 1974-76.

22. R. E. Wolf has called to my attention the letters of 1 and 3 February 1563, from Giorgio Vasari and Vincenzio Borghini respectively, in which they report to the Grand Duke, then in Pisa, about the founding session of the Accademia which took place "nel capitolo degli Angeli", i.e. in the long-neglected oratory. If the Academy subsequently opted for the chapel in the cloisters of SS. Annunziata as their headquarters, it may have been partly because of the opposition of the "hermits", well explained by Fortunio (see note 14), on the basis of the *clausura* rules (see the catalogue, *Mostra di Disegni dei Fondatori dell'Accademia delle Arti del Disegno*, Florence, 1963, pp. 3f.).

23. Perhaps it is no coincidence that the plan of the Rotunda in Giuliano da Sangallo's manuscript (Barberini Codex, f. 15v) is immediately next to a plan of the baptistery of S. Francesco at Bologna, which is an octagon on the outside with niches or chambers pierced in its inner walls. The type seems to go back to rotundas like S. Costanza in Rome, with a circular ambulatory and a dome over the central space supported on columns or piers. In Brunelleschi's version, the coupled piers are linked with the strong curving walls to provide more solid supports for the dome, and the ambulatory was probably a simple passageway.

24. Wittkower 1949/62, pp. 1ff., 31.

25. Zander 1977.

26. See in particular, for his careful exposition of the problem, G. De Angelis D'Ossat, "Sugli edifici ottagonali a cupola nell'antichità e nel medio evo", *Atti del 1° Congresso Nazionale di Storia dell'Architettura, 29-31 ottobre, 1936*, Florence, 1938, pp. 13-24.

27. Heydenreich 1931, especially pp. 5-9.

28. See Horster 1973.

29. Describing the Cathedral that he built in his native town, Pius II rightly dwelt upon its radiating chapels arranged as a crown and stressed them as something remarkable. Here we have an interesting definition of this type of radiating chapel surrounding a chancel or centralized building ("pars... tamquam coronatum caput in aediculas... divisa, quae a reliquo corpore exterius procumberent") in which the ensemble is likened to a head crowned with aedicules acting also as divisions and projecting from the rest of the body of the church. One is reminded of another Marian church of two centuries later, S. Maria della Salute in Venice by Longhena, intentionally conceived as a great crown alluding to the idea of Mary as *Regina Angelorum* and powerful protectress of the city, a concept perhaps traceable to the influence of St Bridget and her *Revelations* (I, 31): "Videbat Reginam coeli matrem Dei habentem coronam inaestimabilem in capite suo" ("She beheld the Queen of Heaven, Mother of God, with a priceless crown upon her head"), though if that is really the origin of the Venetian dome there should have been seven lilies and seven gems or twelve stars. The insistent repetition of triangles in the Rotunda of S. Maria degli Angeli might also allude to the Virgin as *Templum Trinitatis*, an appellation found in a much-imitated hymn attributed to Theophilus.

More directly, however, we might look at the parish church of Mödling in Austria, which is exactly contemporary with Pienza Cathedral, was known to Pius II, and was undoubtedly his model: its ground plan shows the same unusual device of triangular vaulted spaces on either side of the apse. The main departure from it at Pienza is in the development of the apsidal system, devoted to Marian altars (and conceived in function of them), and the insertion of buttresses. See R. K. Donin, *Österreichische Baugedanken am Dom von Pienza*, Vienna, 1946, pp. 44-45. It should be noted that Pius had a friend in Mödling (see V. von Hofmann-Wellendorf, "Leben und Schriften des Doktor Johannes Hinderbach", *Zeitschrift des Ferdinandeums*, ser. 3, 1893, p. 243) and that the church there also has a crypt.

30. The exact date is unknown, but the document is inserted between those two dates in the registers of Ser Francesco Guardi for the years 1433-36 (Florence, Archivio di Stato, G. 701, fasc. 19): see Linacher 1921.

31. Interesting too are the liturgical prescriptions which rule out Heydenreich's theory (1974, pp. 14-16) that each small chapel contained two altars to make a total of twelve, thus enabling all the monks to celebrate mass at the same time. There simply would not be enough space; but in any case the same document states that only once were all the religious obliged to be present simultaneously, on the Marian feast of 8 September. On feast days they were required to recite at least five masses of which one was to be solemn; on other days, three, all low. Particular celebrations were to mark the feasts of St Anthony Abbot and St Julian.

From this one can presume that a single altar was envisaged, possibly in the centre beneath the dome and lantern, and that the oratory would serve also as a commemorative monument (though not funerary, since all three founders had been buried with high honours in Hungary).

Another provision in the contract had to do with storage of the liturgical vestments and hangings of the altar, a responsibility of the monastery itself for which obviously a special room was needed, perhaps placed symmetrically opposite the one with a circular staircase to the roof. In connection with that stair, Professor Miarelli Mariani has called to my attention that in the restoration by R. Sabatini in 1939-40 a new choir was constructed to the right of the side where the choir was intended to be, and the entrance for the public was also shifted round to keep it in the side opposite the choir.

32. An attempt to reproduce its structure elsewhere is reported critically by the Biographer (f. 309r):

> From that time on, since it appeared a fine thing, without understanding it they sought to persuade him [*persuaderlo*] to build exactly the same form as this church elsewhere, not knowing among other things that the church has no purpose in and of itself but only as part of something else [i.e. the monastery] to which it is attached, nor how the high altar chapel is disposed nor [or: in] the choir.

The key word here is *persuaderlo*. Although he considers the passage obscure, Saalman interprets it as referring to another commission (in no way documented or documentable) awarded to Brunelleschi. According to Tanturli, on the other hand, *persuaderlo* does not refer to the architect: the real meaning is that certain individuals sought to persuade potential patrons to build the same sort of building elsewhere, to raise another rotunda as adjunct to another church having a choir but without taking into account the difficulties in using that form either in itself or in relation to the nave of a church and, further, without solving the problem of how to arrange the choir in it. The type of commission suggests the church of SS. Annunziata, whose enlargement by means of a rotunda with eight chapels was designed by Michelozzo in 1444. The project for that was paid for on 3 October of that year; the earliest reference to it being a central-plan building is on 27 January 1445; work began on 13 October 1445 and the cornerstone was laid on 13 December 1445. Brunelleschi spoke out against it sharply, and in terms strikingly similar to those of the Biographer. Apart from the technical difficulties, which could perhaps be overcome, one suspects that Brunelleschi may not have approved of the symbolic theme of the rotunda as an imitation of the Church of the Holy Sepulchre in Jerusalem, an imitation explained quite convincingly by S. Lang ("The programme of the Santissima Annunziata in Florence", *Journal of the Warburg and Courtauld Institutes*, XVII, 1954, 3-4, pp. 288-300), who analyses with considerable acumen the complex problems of construction and documentation. Work on the rotunda of SS. Annunziata under the direction of Michelozzo was interrupted after 20 March 1446, but taken up again energetically in 1453 under the direction of Antonio Manetti Ciaccheri, who on 3 July 1447 was paid for a model of the church "on the order of the Prior". Manetti in any case was paid in May 1460 for other designs that seem to match up with the construction existing today, whereas the work done under Michelozzo was demolished. (Important new documents for the rotunda were presented at the 1977 Congress by Paolo Carpeggianti.)

The Biographer's attack would therefore seem to be directed against Michelozzo, who either adopted or imitated the design of S. Maria degli Angeli for this quite different purpose without knowing how to solve the problems of structure and ground plan. Also, it is not impossible that Brunelleschi himself may have furnished designs for the nave of that church (see Chapter 3, note 7). A corollary to this complex question (for which see the very detailed information in Pietro Roselli, *Coro e cupola della SS. Annunziata a Firenze: Rilievo a cura dell'Istituto di Restauro dei Monumenti dell'Università degli Studi di Firenze*, Pisa, 1971) is the presence in the workshop of Antonio Manetti Ciaccheri, at the time when he made his will, of a wooden model which he left to Giovanni Zati. The simplest explanation is that this was a model for the choir of SS. Annunziata, but since the Biographer says that the model for the Rotunda of S. Maria degli Angeli had gone astray this might be it.

A number of famous echoes of Brunelleschi's design for this oratory have been listed by A. Bruschi (1972). The unfinished building was above all an ideal model for the church of the Florentine colony in Rome, S. Giovanni de' Fiorentini, though the only close contact that can be established is with the monumental project of Jacopo da Vignola in the album of Vincenzo Casale (Madrid, Biblioteca Nacional), published by K. Schwager ("Ein Ovalkirchen-Entwurf Vignolas für San Giovanni dei Fiorentini", *Festschrift für Georg Scheja zum 70. Geburtstag*, Sigmaringen, 1975, pp. 151-78, fig. 1), whose ground plan, however, is oval, not round. The design for Rome could be better connected with a small drawing by Leonardo of a domed building with spur buttresses (C. Pedretti, *A Chronology of Leonardo da Vinci's Architectural Studies after 1500*, Geneva, 1962, fig. 17).

The continuing interest of the sixteenth century in S. Maria degli Angeli is shown in a statement by Benvenuto Cellini (in "Della Architettura", in *La Vita, i Trattati, i Discorsi*, ed. P. Scarpellini, Rome, 1967, p. 566): "And after [the dome of the Cathedral] S. Lorenzo and S. Spirito were built with his models and also the temple of Pippo Spano, which is a most marvellous work but was left unfinished." The discourse in which this appears seems to have been addressed to the "students" in the Accademia del Disegno which, as we have seen, was intended by Cosimo I about 1563 to have its headquarters in the completed Rotunda.

33. An engraving published by Boni in 1786 (II, facing p. 37) and criticized by Del Rosso as "altered" is a project in seventeenth-century taste for completing the building (as shown also by the enlarged choir), and it is known that it derives from a copy made by the Florentine architect Gherardo Silvani, probably in 1647 when he was working on one of the cloisters in the monastery. The same engraving was republished by J. B. Séroux d'Agincourt in *L'Histoire de l'art par ses monuments*, Paris, 1811-23, III, pl. L-16. Its most interesting feature is the spur buttresses that rise from the roofs of the chapels to the large cornice of the central octagon, but such things are not unusual in Baroque architecture.

34. Francesco Renard, of the architecture department of the Accademia del Disegno, tried to derive ideas and designs for the completion of the Rotunda from other buildings by Brunelleschi before the project was given up. See *Gazzetta di Firenze*, 130, 29 October 1831, pp. 4-8.

35. Linacher 1921.

36. Miarelli Mariani 1976; Bencivenni presented a paper at the 1977 Congress.

The lantern of Florence Cathedral

37. The deliberation of 30 October 1432 specified that "Filippo di ser Brunellesco is to make the model of the lantern as he sees fit". We have already noted that this was an exceptional mark of esteem, but it did not do away with the custom of starting a bitter competition for the commission, nor with the fact that there were a number of second thoughts on the part of both architect and judges which meant a series of variants which the documents do not report or, more accurately, do not specify in so many words.

The whole matter is complicated by the existence of two very different images which may represent two fundamental alternatives going back to the time when the form and nature of the dome itself were under discussion. The first appears in a drawing by Giovanni di Gherardo da Prato, Brunelleschi's chronic bugbear, made perhaps in 1426, where one also sees the dark interior of the Cathedral below the dome [*143*]. In this version the lantern is a fairly simple structure, without external supports, quite low, and with broad round-arched windows. That this illustration, though schematic, must give a good idea of the initial project for the lantern is made more probable by the fact that this lantern type reappears, with a more pointed conical roof, in the painting now attributed to Francesco d'Antonio in the Johnson Collection, Philadelphia (see Chapter 9, note 28). Moreover, Giovanni da Prato attributes the form to Brunelleschi himself. The fact that the lantern was subsequently altered and its windows elongated almost surely indicates a response to the criticism that it would provide insufficient illumination, as we shall see.

The second, alternative, image of the lantern is very well known: as the knop of the pastoral staff in Donatello's *St Louis*. This actually represents a group of choir stalls arranged radially, but it curiously anticipates certain features of the lantern as built, notably the shell niches and spurs.

38. Payments of a gold florin were made to Antonio Manetti Ciaccheri for "model and design" on 19 March 1436, and of 2 *lire* to Nanni di Domenico, an employee of the Opera, for brass crosses and balls on 9 July 1436, plus other payments and balances to both in July of the same year. On 31 December 1436 the decision was made on the basis of this model, though comparing it with four others, among them one by Ghiberti on which other carpenters had been working unceasingly, even on holidays, as urged in a document of 14 August. The final date for consigning models, whether requested or submitted to the competition uninvited, had been 11 July, then extended to 15 September. Besides Brunelleschi and Ghiberti, the contestants included Bruno di ser Lapo Mazzei, Domenico Stagnatarium and Antonio Manetti Ciaccheri himself. The latter fact may explain why Brunelleschi hesitated to indicate in detail his solutions for the most difficult points, such as the stairway giving access to the spire and globe.

Rather than the splendid purely architectonic

decoration of the internal supporting octagon [*300*], it was planned initially to introduce figurative elements in the form of gigantic heads, for which models were requested from Donatello and Luca della Robbia on 27 July 1434. The deliberations, presumably negative, that put an end to that idea are still unpublished.

39. Here is the deliberation of 31 December 1436:

> The models made up to now for the construction and architecture of the said lantern were given due consideration; they were thoroughly examined and reports on them were made by numerous architects, painters, goldsmiths and other competent citizens. After all the models had been examined it seemed to them that the model of Filippo di ser Brunellesco was best in form and had in itself the best characteristics of perfection for the said lantern, both because it is strongest and has greater inherent strength than the other models and because it is also lighter and in itself ensures greater lightness, besides which it has more illumination and is better protected from water, because water cannot cause any injury to the lantern. For these reasons and considerations it was decided that the said lantern should be built according to the model prepared by the said Filippo and under the direction of the same Filippo although with the following modifications: that the said Filippo is to accept the collaboration of others and is to use with them a proper language in speaking about these problems; that it please him to lay down all rancour and that he correct in his model that part requiring correction and that he emend it, since in fact there are a few things in it, though by no means serious, that must be corrected; that he therefore take whatever is good and useful found in other models and incorporate it into his so that the said lantern may prove perfect in all of its parts, taking to heart everything said here.

40. The search for the right marble had begun in January 1437 in the quarries at Campiglia Marittima near Piombino, and probably the architect at once began to work on what scaffolding would be needed. Brunelleschi went to the quarries again in the spring and summer of 1437 and 1438, but the marble proved unfit for the purpose, and on 12 November 1438 the blocks were ordered from Giovanni di Piero del Ticcia in Carrara. But the drawings and instructions sent there were not sufficient, so the architect had to go there too in person in August 1439. We know that a large quantity of blocks (though not the number specified in the order of 1438) were transported to Florence by boat and overland beginning in 1443.

41. In the spring and summer of 1444 there were expenses for scaffolding, specifically for planks sawed from two tree trunks and for four endless screws in elm wood needed for the "tower", that is the rotary crane. These screws, doubtless for the apparatus used to position the marble blocks, came to a total length of 10 *braccia* (roughly 4 m, or 13 ft) [*292*]. In the drawings of these machines one sees two or three of these endless screws in use: nothing tells us how long each was, and they were probably of different lengths.

42. The method of raising weights for which Brunelleschi opted, a system using a hook in the centre, corresponds to the advice given by Anthemius of Tralles, the famous architect of Hagia Sophia, to lift solid bodies such as a column mechanically by balancing them at the centre of gravity: when weights are not brought into balance, he explains, and not held at their centre, it is difficult to lift them because the uneven weight pre-

vents a balanced traction (see T. F. Mathew, *Byzantine Aesthetics*, London, 1963, who refers to G. L. Huxley, *Anthemius of Tralles*, Cambridge, Mass., 1959, and to the *Mathematici Graeci Minores*, ed. J. L. Heiberg, Leipzig, 1927).

43. Because the documentation published by Guasti is incomplete, and is unfortunately what we must still rely on, the detailed history of the construction of the lantern is uncertain, but there do not seem to have been any changes such as to require special consultations or commissions. The most obscure matter is the dismissal of Michelozzo on 25 August 1452, and his replacement by Antonio Manetti Ciaccheri who held the post until 26 August 1462.

In 1450 "a stone for the pilasters of the lantern" was readied at Carrara by two stonecutters under the personal direction of Michelozzo, which means it presented particular difficulties. Greater difficulties because of size were caused by the architraves topped by shell niches over the "doorways" in the spur-buttresses, since it turned out that these had to be made in two pieces rather than one, as decided in a meeting on 18 August 1451, which tells us that by that time the construction had reached the top of the spurs. (The document is correctly interpreted by F. Quinterio in his thesis, 1975, p. 143.) The scrolls above them were designed by Antonio Manetti Ciaccheri, and were carved in 1453-54; in June 1455 the platforms were erected from which they were to be set into place. Two years later the bronze steps were delivered for the internal stairway leading to the top of the lantern. In 1462 Bernardo Rossellino was appointed *capomaestro* for the lantern and dome, and though he died in the next year he did virtually complete the classicizing cornice (see C. Randall Mack, *Studies in the Architectural Career of Bernardo di Matteo Gamberelli, called Rossellino*, thesis, University of North Carolina, Chapel Hill, 1972).

On 31 December 1466 the lantern was judged "almost at its perfection, so that in a short time it will be adorned and completed", and therefore commissions were given out for the stained glass windows which were to have white circles with frames of roses and the arms "of the people and Commune and Parte Guelfa, Libertà, Mercantia and others". On 8 June 1467 Giovanni di Bartolomeo is recorded as having made the stud "to go beneath the globe". The globe itself was made in the following year by Verrocchio, "of eight pieces according to the form of the model given by him... and round, and soldered with silver, and perfectly formed". It was placed in position on 28 March 1472, and two days later the cross was set up on it.

44. The vicissitudes undergone by the model, according to the documents and the Biographer, make the problem even more difficult to understand. Most of all one cannot decide whether it was merely because of simplification in the model that the pilasters below the volutes differ so markedly from those above them: in the lantern as built, each of the paired pilasters has three flutings above and two below, whereas the model shows four above and one below (see also note 45). We have already noted that the arched window-openings are less elongated and the octagonal cornice is therefore lower. The volutes on the spurs lack the splendid decoration proposed by Antonio Manetti Ciaccheri and agreed to in the deliberation of 23 October 1453, which would make one date the model before that decision, but the explanation could equally well be that the model was only roughly and sketchily executed, and perhaps intended not as a guide to the builders but only as a sort of memorandum or commemoration.

However, a date was found lightly incised in the marbled paint on the model (this paint was partly destroyed in the 1966 flood), and that date, disconcertingly, was 1673. And indeed such documents as we have seem to point to this not being the original Quattrocento model. For one thing, as Stegmann and Geymüller had already observed (1885-93, I), the globe and cross were supposed to be of bronze, not wood. Further, Vasari (ed. Milanesi, II, p. 364) says that the model included the stairway space leading to the conical roof, but the model we have is solid with no interior compartments. Then too, the deliberation of 1436 ordering Brunelleschi to take into account the ideas of the other competitors would mean that the final model no longer represented only his original ideas but also incorporated those of his rivals. Now, the model we have, even though it is composed of three different sorts of wood, showed no discernible traces of restoration or alteration before the flood of 1966. What is more, had it already been available when the lantern was struck by lightning on 27 January 1601, the Grand Duke would not have needed to order his architects that, should they not have "in their archive the old design of the devastated lantern", they were to seek with

diligence among all the architects, sculptors and painters and designers that there are in Florence, because it seems impossible that there is not one among them who, to satisfy his own curiosity, might have worked out the plan and reduced to a drawing or model the entire dome with its correct measurements, so that it can be restored to its former condition with the utmost accuracy.

This observation by Luisa Becherucci (Catalogo del Museo dell'Opera del Duomo in Firenze, Milan, 1970, vol. II, pp. 211-14) is so convincing as to make one suspect that the present model may be only a late copy, precisely because it corresponds to the real lantern which we know was repeatedly altered by restorations.

Little can be learned from a direct examination of the model (which was not easily accessible when these pages were written) since, smashed by the flood of 1966, it was taken to pieces to facilitate drying and then glued together again (see Otello Caprara, in the exhibition catalogues, Soprintendenza alle Gallerie di Bologna: Acquisti e restauri, 1966, Bologna, 1967, and (with Arnaldo Boldrini), Catalogo della mostra di restauri e sculture e oggetti d'arte minore, Museo Nazionale del Bargello, Florence, December 1967-February 1968, no. 34, pl. XII. An important point to check would be whether the half-columns with their capitals and arches were altered later to fit the space available for the windows. Photographs taken before 1966 do in any case show a considerable difference in workmanship and style between the base, which represents the upper part of the dome, and the lantern proper. According to Sanpaolesi, who made a careful analysis of the model in 1956, three sorts of wood were used: a hard one for the base, a softer one for the cylinder of the lantern (which is made up of many pieces worked separately and then completed by capitals and niche-frames made of paste and then covered with wax), and walnut in a single piece for the cone at the top.

E. Settesoldi of the Opera del Duomo, in discussion with Luisa Becherucci, suggested that the model may have been constructed on top of an earlier and original model of the terminal closing of the dome. I am inclined to accept that theory and therefore to join the ranks of Fabriczy, Folnesics, Heydenreich (who developed his opinion at length in his article of 1931, p. 21, note 1), Coolidge (in his review of the book by Sanpaolesi, 1952), and Saalman. Sanpaolesi himself (1956), however, on the basis of a detailed study and measurement of the model, with sections drawn at different heights [283-85, 288, 289], defends its authenticity, making skilful use of the Biographer and Vasari and, above all, of splendid photographic details. Unfortunately the measurements of the lantern itself to which he refers for the elevation come almost entirely from Stegmann and Geymüller or from the engravings done in the eighteenth and nineteenth centuries by Nelli and his imitators, so one cannot really check the relationship between model and construction.

A more precise photogrammetric measurement of the model has now been published by Mario Fondelli: "Studio geometrico di un antico modello ligneo restaurato", Atti del Convegno di Studi sul restauro delle opere d'arte a dieci anni dall'alluvione di Firenze, Florence, 1978. We are still waiting for the publication of the photogrammetry of the huge marble lantern itself.

45. From the documents we learn that a major constructional change was made in 1451 because of the impossibility either of quarrying or of transporting upstream the enormous blocks of marble that were to make monolithic arms linking the spurs, and indeed even a superficial analysis of what was built shows that above the huge volutes, composed of a number of pieces, there is no logical conclusion to the whole: for example, the fluting of the pilasters changes in number of grooves and dimension (though the treatment of the pilasters above the consoles in the wooden model is even more awkward [282]). While taking into account the numerous reconstructions the upper part of the lantern has undergone because of frequent damage from lighting, this incongruity may more plausibly be imputed to another designer, someone who had to go on with the work precisely where Brunelleschi's wooden models and the drawings he made for the quarrymen and stonecutters gave no information, that is, above the volutes.

And it is there that the worst error deplored by the Biographer appears (ff. 311v-312r):

the capitals of the half-columns [pilastrj] at the corners, or rather the arches that are placed on them, are not good: to put it better, they come out of the vertical line of the half-columns, and the little arches are therefore not a half-circle but much more than that.

That is, in the very tall windows the arches above the unusual capitals project too far from the capital and half-column, forming a stilted shape between a horseshoe and a lancet (less so in the wooden model), and furthermore do not touch the architrave [282, 290, 303].

To correct this error it would be necessary either to make the half-columns even taller or to lower the capitals of the pilasters and thereby the architrave and thereby, too, the height of the lantern as a whole. Even then it might prove impossible to have round-headed arches. Probably the entire design would have to be modified — which means, in short, that the solution originally proposed by Brunelleschi is beyond recovery. These difficulties,

evident only on the exterior, make one suspect that in the initial proposal the half-columns may not have existed and the lantern may have been composed exclusively of pilasters and spurs. However, the construction followed the present form from the outset, with monolithic blocks making up the base and the various elements of each nucleus including half-columns, pilasters, and part of the spurs as far as the doorways, all of these juxtaposed with remarkable regularity.

Yet another observation: as in his criticisms of the half-pilaster which bends at right angles at the end of the façade of the Foundling Hospital, or of the doors introduced by Donatello into the Old Sacristy, here again the Biographer in censuring the capitals of the half-columns was rejecting an element of presumably Classical derivation. And in fact H. Burns (1971, especially p. 271) has shown how this particular design, due to Antonio Manetti Ciaccheri, derives from a Classicizing capital found recently in the excavation of S. Reparat. (for which see G. Morozzi, "Indagini sulla prima cattedrale fiorentina", Commentari, XIX, 1968, pp. 3-17).

The later history of the lantern is a saga of lightning bolts and earthquakes. Particularly grave was the damage on 5 April 1492, "which threw down more than the third of the lantern". A meticulous record of these mishaps was compiled by Ferdinando Rossi, to whom we owe the recent repairs and restorations which have practically saved the structure: see F. Rossi 1956 (which contains important photographs of the condition of the lantern and an account of the restoration completed in 1955). A drawing of 1601 by Alessandro Allori shows the damage done in that year (see G. Marchini, "Fulmini sulla Cupola", Antichità Viva, XVI, 1977, 4, pp. 22-25). On the basis of the repairs done then, Marchini attributed to Gherardo Mechini the famous drawing of the scaffolding erected for the lantern [291] (Marchini, Miarelli Mariani et al. 1977, pp. 9-13). While this drawing may be late, however, it cannot refer to that occasion: it was not then necessary to rebuild the conical roof, whereas in the drawing the windows of the lantern have not been completed and the roof is not even begun.

46. Giovanni di Gherardo da Prato's note merits quotation in full. It is here translated from the transcription by Howard Saalman (1959).

This demonstration [143] of that eye [in the dome] shows that the sun enters there and should not be interrupted by glazed windows, but on the opposite side with the piers it may break and give light by reflection; now everyone should consider whether that reflection will be strong enough to extend upwards more than 70 braccia; I believe, and it seems to me certain, that it would not, according to what all reason shows me, as you can find in the treatise de Speculis and in Prospettivis; or think then what light the round openings of the drum will give when the light is broken up by glass, of which you have an example in S. Liperata [Reparata, the old Cathedral] in the round windows of the anterior part [the front] above the doors. I, Giovanni di Gherardo Gherardi, make known and manifest that, having been here in the Opera requested to give my opinion concerning how the dome is to develop, I have this to say concerning it as an official statement. It seems to me, considering that from the windows of the drum to the lantern is a distance of about 60 braccia straight up, that if, following the present system of building the dome without window or aperture to provide light, nothing is done to provide it before the masonry goes higher, then it will be not only dark but murky and gloomy. And already five years and more have passed since I proposed my way of doing it, which is: twenty-four windows should be made above the gallery [*ballatoio*] in the middle [of the segments?], and my design for this is still in the Opera here. And if anyone counters by asking whether one must and can cut the vault, then it seems to me that he is speaking out of ignorance or only slight knowledge.

The document throws light on the way in which Brunelleschi and his contemporaries used the science of optics in working out the interior lighting of a building.

47. A document of 27 June 1432 (like the others, published by Guasti) must be given in the original and in translation:

Deliberaverunt quod Filippus ser Brunelleschi, Laurentius Bartoli, et Battista Antonii provisor Opere, sine eorum preiudicio et danpno, expensis Opere, fieri faciant unum modellum seu unam formam circularem seu angulatam, cum otto faciebus, de vano Lanterne magne Cupole.

(It has been resolved that Filippo Brunelleschi, Lorenzo di Bartoli, and Battista d'Antonio, purveyor for the Opera, without commitment or expenses on their part, at the expense of the Opera are to have made a model of a circular or angular form with eight faces of the structure of the lantern of the great dome.)

Everything turns on whether in the phrase, "unum modellum seu unam formam circularem seu angulatam", we are to understand *seu* as distinctive or explanatory. In the first case, because "model" and "form" are taken as coinciding, *seu* can be translated as "in other words": thus, a model or, in other words, form. In the second case, because "circular", and "angular" do not coincide, *seu* may make the distinction, implying the execution of two models, one round, the other polygonal. The term "circular" is in any case not Classical, and *circulus* can also means "circuit". In the decisive deliberation of 12 August 1432 there is talk of "circumferentia", which does suggest that the two terms could be equivalent.

It was the decisions taken regarding the closing of the dome which determined the form of the lantern: the round opening (if it had ever been envisaged) was rejected for the present octagon which nicely fits the external arrangement. Thus here the Baptistery continued to be imitated quite strictly, whereas in the Old Sacristy, a short time earlier (1428/29, according to the date on the building) Brunelleschi had opted for a cylindrical lantern. A cylindrical design also appears in the knop of the pastoral staff of Donatello's *St Louis*, which, as we have seen, is often compared to the lantern.

While the model made between 27 June and 12 August 1432 was concerned only with the dimensions of the oculus of the dome, on 30 October Brunelleschi was asked to prepare a model showing the lantern as well as the closing ring of the dome. On 25 June 1433 his idea of reducing the diameter of the oculus from 10 to 9 3/4 *braccia* won agreement.

48. Here is Alberti on that point (*De re aedificatoria*, I, 56-57):

The corners must be positioned in such a way as to be turned towards the point subject to the pressure from the weight of a mountain or masses of water or the violence of the winds; in that way the mass of the impact will be divided and dispersed so that the walls will be able to stand up to the danger with their sturdiest part and not with the fragility of their flanks.

The exedrae of Florence Cathedral

49. The bibliography is scanty. The documents have not all been published, and the only scholars to discuss these particular structures, other than Saalman (1958-A), have been Gosebruch (1958), concerning the capitals, and Heydenreich (1931), who stressed their importance in the stylistic development of Brunelleschi's late years and made important observations about the use of perspective and the novelty of the paired demi-columns. The Biographer does not mention them because, being such late works, they would have been included in the last part of the manuscript which has apparently not survived.

50. The document of 27 February 1438 (i.e. 1439) reads (Fabriczy 1907, p. 20):

The aforesaid Operai... decided that the small tribunes to be made above the sacristies of the Cathedral of S. Maria del Fiore are to be made round in accord with the design and model of Filippo di ser Brunellesco and have decreed that they will be built in this form.

The document of 8 March of the same year states:

For the final part of the four small cupolas over the sacristies and piers they declare that these go better with a round form than with one that follows the angles [or corners].

51. The exedrae were studied thoroughly, in all their decorative details, in relation to the chronology that could be drawn from the documents then known, by H. Saalman (1958-A, pp. 133-34). He identified the north-east exedra as the first to be built, and indeed completed in 1445, observing that there were already differences in the style of the capitals used there. Saalman agrees with the opinion of Fabriczy that the cornice above the capitals post-dates Brunelleschi's death. It seems that the north-east and south-east exedrae were completed by Antonio Manetti Ciaccheri, and those on the north-west and south-west by Rossellino, probably in the early 1460s.

52. There is explicit mention of a model for demi-columns 5 *braccia* high and with capitals in a contract of 20 March 1445, made with the stonecutter Giovanni di Piero del Ticcia which called for twelve demi-columns fully hewn to be delivered by the end of April; these were for the north-east exedra.

The motif of paired columns has been traced by A. Bruschi (1972, p. 109, note 11) to works done around 1420 by Donatello and Michelozzo, and the association with sculpture makes it likely that the common prototype was a sarcophagus or Antique relief, though Burns (1971, ills. 11a,b, between pp. 272 and 273) has proposed an equally convincing comparison with a Byzantine miniature showing architecture in the Royal Library, Copenhagen, and with similar features in S. Marco in Venice and also in Murano.

53. Heydenreich believes that their function is static, but Bates Lowry (*Renaissance Architecture*, New York, 1962, p. 116, note 37) asserts that

the lantern and the aediculae designed as part of the Cathedral dome probably owe their massive character more to the problem posed by their distance from the viewer than to a sudden interest on Brunelleschi's part in space and mass. Similarly, the central church of S. Maria degli Angeli becomes less of a strong, space-molding structure when envisaged in elevation rather than in ground plan or cross section.

On the other hand, A. Cadei (1971), who gives

an extremely favourable judgment on the exedrae, believes that here Brunelleschi

knew how to eliminate precisely those suggestions of plastic intensity that the semicircular plan with large niches and paired columns implied virtually inherently. ... But it is most of all the wide fillets running along the intrados of the arches of the niches and their perimeter at floor level which break the continuity of implicit plastic value between the convex course of the tribunes and the concavity of the niches, translating the latter [the concavity], with the neat design of the shadow projected into it and the clear-cut handwriting of the shell that decorates the vault, into the pure aspect of surface inflected according to cylinder and sphere, as spatial limit.

An alternative explanation is that they were added at this late stage as covered space in which to store materials at a high level, after the temporary storage places used during the dome's construction were removed.

54. On 26 October 1436 Brunelleschi received the assignment in his own name and therefore also as *capomaestro*,

to roof with terracotta three tribunes of the new construction at the price of 300 florins in the course of the next six months, on condition that that roofing should not alter the appearance of the tribunes and should last for the span of twenty-five years as he has promised.

As noted in the text, his estimate of 300 florins was generously extended officially by an additional hundred (though with some scepticism, since any cost beyond the estimated figure was to be paid for out of Brunelleschi's own pocket) — proof of a new type of experiment intended to cut down significantly the quality of material needed and the number of working hours as well as to afford greater protection from decay, fire and other damage. From an examination of the section of roof that survives at the Old Sacristy [76] and from a carefully detailed inspection of S. Andrea in Mantua as well as from an old description of that church, I think it can be deduced that the new method may have involved laying the tile roofing directly on the vault by means of a system of transverse drainage channels within the interspace which would draw off any water.

As a fee for directing this work Brunelleschi was paid 100 florins annually, though for one year only (Fabriczy 1907, p. 38).

13 The pulpit of S. Maria Novella

1. Besides the publications on the church itself (Richa 1754-62, III; Paatz 1940-54; Stefano Orlandi, "*Necrologio*" di Santa Maria Novella, 2 vol., Florence, 1955), see G. Poggi 1905. The documents for the pulpit were assembled by Borghigianni in the eighteenth century (*Cronica annalistica di Santa Maria Novella*, II, p. 418), and by Fabriczy (1907, pp. 12-13).

A drawing, erroneously attributed to the fourteenth century, was published in *Ricordi di Architetture*, I, 1878, IX, pl. iv.

2. In the *Borsario* of S. Maria Novella, Book 7, c. 144, we read: "Item, today 31 August, given to Filippo S. Brunelleschi, by the hand of Magister Geronimo, for the wooden model of the pulpit being made in the church, one large florin of the value of 4.15 *lire*, this year 1443".

3. The words are "bonus arismeticus... bone et grate conversationis". Fra Andrea di Donato Rucellai died in 1464.

4. Because the latter were unable to produce documentary proof of ownership,

> the said arbiters judged that the said pulpit with the arms of the Rucellai was rightfully placed there, on condition that if the said Minerbetti should at any time prove that that column is theirs, and make a pulpit as fine as, or finer than, that of the Rucellai family, it is to be removed and that of the Minerbetti is to be installed in that place

(Florence, Archivio di Stato, Spogli Strozziani, series 2, no. 77, c. 103)

14 Theatrical machinery

1. A basic source for this chapter is the splendid exhibition of theatrical activities in Medicean Florence that was organized by Ludovico Zorzi, *Il luogo teatrale a Firenze*, for which the models by Cesare Lisi reproduced here were prepared. The text of the catalogue (ed. M. Fabbri, E. Garbero Zorzi, A. M. Tofani Petroli and L. Zorzi, Milan, 1975) has now been incorporated, with extensive notes, in L. Zorzi, *Il Teatro e la Città: Saggi sulla scena italiana*, Turin, 1977 (pp. 63ff, and notes 25-36 on pp. 154-67).

The documents and literature on the subject were thoroughly sifted by A. P. Blumenthal (1966-67). Blumenthal also identified the illuminated mandorla in the *Zibaldone* of Buonaccorso Ghiberti [*333, 335*], an identification accepted by Prager and Scaglia, who published the manuscript (1970, p. 83; also Scaglia 1960, 1960-61-B). See also, by Blumenthal, "Brunelleschi e il teatro del Rinascimento", *Bollettino del Centro Internazionale di Studi di Architettura Andrea Palladio*, XVI, 1974 (1976), pp. 93-104.

The bibliography on this apparently marginal aspect of Brunelleschi's activity is unusually extensive, proof of a permanent and indeed growing interest. At the beginning stands Jakob Burckhardt, *Die Kultur der Renaissance in Italien*, Leipzig, 1859 (and later editions and translations); Alexander Wesselofsky, "Italienische Mysterien in einem russischen Reisebericht des XV. Jahrhunderts", *Russische Revue*, X, 1877, pp. 425-41; Francesco Torraca, *Il teatro italiano dei secoli XIII, XIV e XV*, Florence, 1885, p. 115; Alessandro D'Ancona, *Origini del teatro italiano*, Turin, 1891, I, pp. 231, 506-08; K. Manzius, *History of Theatrical Art*, London, 1903, II, p. 45; Oskar Fischel, "Eine florentiner Theateraufführung in der Renaissance", *Zeitschrift für Bildende Kunst*, LV, 1919-20, 31, pp. 11-20; Valerio Mariani, "Fantasia scenografica", *Vita artistica*, I, 1926, pp. 19-20; Valerio Mariani, *Storia della Scenografia italiana*, Florence, 1930, pp. 29-31, 42-44, pl. XI; Joseph Spencer Kennard, *The Italian Theatre*, New York, 1932 (repr. 1964), I, pp. 42-43; Virginia Galante-Garrone, *L'apparato scenico del dramma sacro in Italia*, Turin, 1935; D. M. Robb, "The Iconography of the Annunciation in the Fourteenth and Fifteenth Centuries", *Art Bulletin*, XVIII, 1936, pp. 480-526; "L''Ingegno' del Brunelleschi", *Firenze*, XI, 1942, pp. 95-96; Mario Apollonio, *Storia del Teatro*, Florence, 1946, IIb, pp. 32-33; Kate Trauman Steinitz, "A Reconstruction of Leonardo da Vinci's Revolving Stage", *Art Quarterly*, XII, 1949, pp. 325-338; Enrico Prampolini,

Lineamenti di scenografia italiana, Rome, 1950; P. Turchetti, in *Enciclopedia dello Spettacolo*, Florence-Rome, 1954-68, II, cols. 1197-99; John R. Spencer, "Spatial Imagery of the Annunciation in Fifteenth-Century Florence", *Art Bulletin*, XXXVII, 1955, pp. 273-80; H. Kindermann, *Theatergeschichte Europas*, Salzburg, 1957, I, pp. 335-36; Orville K. Larson, "Vasari's Descriptions of Stage Machinery", *Educational Theatre Journal*, IX, 1957, pp. 287-99; Cesare Molinari, *Spettacoli fiorentini del Quattrocento*, Venice, 1961, p. 40; John Shearman, "Correggio's Ceiling Painting", lecture at the Institute of Fine Arts, New York University, 20 November 1964, and at the International Congress on Perspective in Milan, 1978 (proceedings published in Florence, 1980).

2. New documents on performances of the Ascension play in the Carmine in 1422 and 1425 (with restorations by Masolino and others) show that Quattrocento theatrical experiments began earlier than was thought. The documents were published by Götz Pochat in *Art Bulletin*, LX, 1978, pp. 232-34.

3. The translation given here was made from the Italian version published by D'Ancona in 1891 on the basis of Wesselofsky's 1877 article (for both, see note 1), which L. Zorzi tells me is largely a paraphrase. The Russian original has now been published, with a Latin translation, in *Concilium Florentinum Documenta et Scriptores. Acta Slavica Concilii Florentini*, ed. J. Krajcar, XI, Rome, 1976, pp. 112-24.

A point still in doubt is where the choir singers were placed in SS. Annunziata.

4. See J. Gill, *Eugenius IV, Pope of the Christian Union*, Westminster, Md, 1961, p. 51, and Krajcar, op. cit. (note 3, above).

5. The inscription in the upper part of the drawing [*335*] explains the purpose of the iron crank: "This iron handle in order to make it go faster, which with the † [crank] would take too long". Beside the detail drawing of the iron tube that conceals a lighted candle until it is pushed up by the cords activating the pivot that moves it inside the tube is an inscription reading:

> This cannon is of tin-plated iron, attached to the throne, and inside it is a little lamp of copper which has an iron wire below it which, when a cord is pulled as you see drawn here, makes the lights shoot out of the cannon, and a cord pushes out six or eight of them so that, when the time comes, all eight emerge simultaneously.

It has been thought that this was one of the first applications of the springs described thus by Vasari: "These [small lamps], when a spring was pressed down, all disappeared from view inside the copper mandorla".

Zorzi (1977, p. 165) now thinks that these drawings have less to do with the contrivance invented by Brunelleschi than with the much improved later one by Cecca. For its various reconstructions see the very rich anthology of illustrations presented, along with his own proposal, by A. R. Blumenthal in "A newly-discovered drawing of Brunelleschi's stage machinery", *Marsyas*, XIII, 1966-67, pp. 20-31.

A system of lamps hidden in metal tubes and made to emerge automatically appears in the *Instrumentorum bellicorum liber cum figuris et fictivis literis conscriptus* (Munich, Bayerische Staatsbib-

liothek, Cod. icon. 242), which may be dated to the 1420s or, more probably, 1430s.

6. Although the date of the first performance of this religious spectacle is not known, we do know that it was repeated on 25 March 1471 in honour of Galeazzo Maria Sforza, on 23 November 1494 for Charles VIII of France, again in 1525 and 1543, and on 15 April 1547 it was recorded by Antonio da Sangallo. The apparatus in S. Felice was restored by Vasari on the occasion of the wedding of Francesco de' Medici and Johanna of Austria in 1566, when it was moved to S. Spirito.

7. See E. Battisti, "Spettacoli d'acqua, di fuoco e trasformazioni", *Bollettino del Centro Internazionale di Studi di Architettura Andrea Palladio*, XVII, 1975, pp. 69-99. The descent of the angel of the Annunciation, in particular, prefigures the *deus ex machina* which so often came at the end of revived Classical Roman plays. The first documented revival was that of Plautus' *Amphitryon*, in Ferrara, in 1487 and 1491.

Ragghianti (1977) stresses the connection with the theatre of automata, which is also Antique in origin: that would provide another link between Brunelleschi and clockmaking.

There is an interesting echo of these Florentine experiments in the mechanism which protects and at the same time displays the chief relic in Milan Cathedral, a mechanism which somewhat resembles that shown in the *Zibaldone* drawing [*335*]. See "Leonardo e la macchina del Sacro Chiodo del Duomo di Milano", *Ambrosiano*, XV, 1939, pp. 107-12; and, for illustrations, *Duomo di Milano*, a monograph produced by the Cassa di Risparmio delle Provincie Lombarde, II, pp. 29 and 35.

Another such machine permanently *in situ* was the Paradise on the inner wall of the façade of Prato Cathedral: see G. Marchini, *Il Tesoro del Duomo di Prato*, Prato, 1963, p. 63, note 97.

15 Military works, II: the Signa and Chianti areas

by Riccardo Pacciani

1. In most studies on Brunelleschi these and the similar works discussed in the preceding chapter on fortifications have been neglected, perhaps in the belief that such tasks were of small moment or that all evidence of them, whether in stone or on paper, had virtually disappeared. A notable and early exception, with interesting photographic evidence, was Lucy E. Baxter, who wrote under the name of Leader Scott (1901, p. 132, pl. XLI). Yet a number of documents concerning these fortifications were published as early as 1839 by Gaye and in 1892 and 1907 by Fabriczy. For the localities examined here, the essential references are in Repetti 1833-46 (I, pp. 555-56; II, pp. 652-56; III, pp. 32-33; IV, pp. 742-43; V, pp. 402-05, 455-59).

2. See M. Richter 1940, C. Higounet 1962, and E. Detti, G. F. Di Pietro and G. Fanelli, *Città murate e sviluppo contemporaneo*, Lucca and Milan, 1968, pp. 162ff. For a few interesting but not always convincing theories on analogies of plan between Romanesque geometrical decorations and the urban layout of certain *terre nuove* see E. Guidoni, *Arte e urbanistica*

in *Toscana, 1000-1315*, Rome, 1970, pp. 219-34. The idea that these geometrical town plans were based on regular subdivisions of the circle was put forward again, with a wealth of arguments, by D. Friedmann in "Le terre nuove fiorentine", *Archeologia Medievale*, I, 1974, pp. 231-47. For general view of attitudes and town-planning schemes in medieval Tuscany, W. Braunfels, *Mittelalterliche Stadtbaukunst in der Toskana*, Berlin, 1953, has not been superseded. Some thirteenth-century examples from Northern Italy appear in *Monumenti d'Italia. I Castelli*, ed. P. Marconi, Novara, 1978, pp. 74-84.

3. Gaye (1839, I, p. 550) published an item dated 26 September 1424 from the Florence Archivio di Stato (Provvisioni, filza 116) which states: "The fortifications of the castle of Lastra and Malmantile and other works for the walls of the Pisa citadel [are to be] at the expense of the Cathedral church", and this is confirmed by another notice (Spogli Strozziani, XX, f. 69): "1426, the Castle of Lastra is being built by the Operai of S. Maria del Fiore".

4. On the connection of Arnolfo with the *terre nuove*, see Francesco Gherardi Dragomanni, *Memorie della terra di San Giovanni nel Val d'Arno Superiore*, Florence, 1834, pp. 129-30 and note 3. The reference to Giotto as superintendent of the Florentine fortifications is from Gaye 1839, I, p. 482.

5. "Vita di Lorenzo Lippi, cittadino e pittore fiorentino scritta da Filippo Baldinucci, e stampata fra le sue notizie de' Professori del Disegno, nel decennale del 1640", in *Il Malmantile racquistato di Perlone Zipoli* [Lorenzo Lippi] *colle note di Puccio Lamoni e d'altri*, 2nd ed., Florence, 1731, pp. xxxix-xl. See also Repetti 1833-46, III, pp. 32-33.

6. When these "new towns" were laid out their precise geometrical disposition, linear profiles and orientation were specified and imposed in the contracts for their construction, as can be seen in an act of 27 February 1336, which refers to Firenzuola and states:

> the masters Talento and Francesco and any others among them are to redo the walls of the gate, already built by them, where they are unseemly because they are not in a straight line... so as to be efficient and in the right order... and the money already taken by them for the previous buildings is to serve for this [correction] and they are to do all... according to the agreements [already made].

(Florence, Archivio di Stato, Capitoli XXXV, c. 242, cited in Richter 1940, p. 384 and p. 376, note 83)

7. Contemporary evidence concerning the use of fire power is taken from C. Montù, *Storia della Artiglieria Italiana*, pt I, Rome, XII [1934], p. 146 and especially pp. 263-74 on the use of artillery in the Tuscan armies of the Quattrocento. From the same source (p. 265) come these lines dated 1408 by Giovanni di Ser Piero, *podestà* (mayor) of Castel Fiorentino, in his *Sei Capitoli dell'acquisto di Pisa fatto da' Fiorentini nel 1406*:

> Esser convenne a' nostri fare aiuto
> E buon maestrier forestrier presenti
> Subito fur trovati, ch'ordinaro
> Briccole da gettar ferocementi
> Pietre si grosse e grandi, che pesaro
> Ben più di libbre cinquecento.

(There being need to bring aid to our forces, / and immediately good masters from abroad were / found to hand, who ordered / stone catapults to be launched ferociously, / stones so thick and large as to weigh / even more than five hundred pounds.)

The account of the siege of Vicopisano was taken from "Cronica Volgare di Anonimo Fiorentino", ed. E. Bellondi, in L. A. Muratori, *Rerum Italicarum Scriptores*, XXVII, pt II, Bologna, 1918 (*anno* 1416, Chapter VIII), and the quotation concerning Lucca from the "Commentari di Neri di Gino Capponi". in the same compendium, XVIII, Milan, 1731, col. 1170.

8. The Republic of Siena in 1416, in the war against Bertoldo Orsini, still had to employ a foreigner, "Ildebrandinum Teutonicum magistrum bombardorum"; but forty years later, on 7 November 1457, Federico da Montefeltro could write to the Sienese:

> It happens that at present I have need of a master in launching bombards. And because I am informed that in Siena there is a good and adequate master who would quite satisfy my needs... I ask urgently... that to please me most particularly you will give him leave and indeed order him to depart immediately.

From the *Libro delle tre balestre* in the Siena Archives it appears that in 1438 the communes and castles of the Siena region had to supply 165 bombards and much other artillery material (Montù, 1934, pp. 270-72).

9. See A. Cassai Ramelli, *Dalle caverne ai rifugi blindati*, Milan, 1964, pp. 244-46. Sapping is known to have been practised in Tuscany at least as early as 19 October 1384, when Naddo da Montecatini reported that in Florence "for the said Commune were enrolled 150 crossbowmen and masters in wood and stone, in bombards, and in mines [*cave*]".

A specific reference to the technique occurs in the manuscript of Mariano Taccola (Munich, Bayerische Staatsbibliothek, Cod. Latinus 28800, f. 47v): "It was the desire of Robert to take the citadel on the mountain, and that was difficult. Robert had recourse to miners". It has been suggested that this may refer to the military theorist Roberto Valturio, known before 1449, or to his manuscripts. The significance of the remark was stressed by P. L. Rose ("The Taccola Manuscripts", *Physis*, X, 1968, pp. 337-46). The quotation from Machiavelli comes from the essay, "Dell'arte della guerra", in *Arte della guerra e scritti politici minori*, ed. S. Bertelli, Milan, 1961, p. 494.

10. Castellina, an old fief of the Trebbiesi, passed to the Republic of Florence at the end of the thirteenth century. With Rencine it constituted the advance post of the Florentine penetration towards Siena. Staggia, fief of the Franzesi, was purchased in 1331 for 18,000 florins. For all these places see Repetti 1833-46, and for Staggia and its remarkable castle see also A. Canestrelli, "La Rocca e le mure di Staggia", *Miscellanea storica della Valdelsa*, XV, 1907, pp. 129-31; G. Piranesi, "Staggia Franzesi", ibid., XVI, 1908; P. Bargellini, "Staggia", *Bullettino senese di Storia patria*, XXI, 1914; P. Marzini, "Antico Castello e terra di Staggia", *Miscellanea storica della Valdelsa*, XXX, 1922; and I. Moretti and R. Stopani, "Il palazzo fortezza dei Franzesi a Staggia", *Antichità Viva*, X, 1971, pp. 49-59, in which the construction of the stronghold and then its transformation into a sumptuous family residence are attributed to the Franzesi family and especially the famous merchant Musciatto Franzini. On the war of 1397 and Castellina, see the *Historia fiorentina di M. Piero Buoninsegni*, Florence, 1631, Book IV, p. 741. For Rencine and its destruction see "Diarj scritti da Allegretto Allegretti delle cose senesi del suo tempo", in L. Muratori, *Rerum Italicarum Scriptores*, XXIII, Milan, 1733, col. 784; and, for the siege of 1397, Giovanni di Paolo Morelli, *Ricordi*, ed. V. Branca, Florence, 1965, p. 355.

11. John Ruskin, *The Seven Lamps of Architecture*, 1852, Chapter VI, Aphorism XVIII. There is something disturbingly appropriate in the fact that this splendid formulation by Ruskin should be the occasion for the last note to these chapters on the buildings which are, or are said to be, by Brunelleschi — buildings which survive in some state or other, or have disappeared altogether, or, perhaps worse, have in so many cases been built or rebuilt or what is euphemistically (or cynically) called restored, in a way that Brunelleschi would have denounced or disowned, probably with more verbal and social violence than his Biographer. [*Robert Erich Wolf*]

16 Brunelleschi and literature

1. Other commentaries or polemical articles arising from Manetti's calculations were written by Alessandro Vellutello in 1544 (*contra*) and Galileo in 1592 (*pro*).

2. Commentaries on Dante could obviously give rise to theological discussions as well, but more significant is the fine red thread of political, reformist and social ideas that linked Antonio Manetti with Girolamo Benivieni; he in turn through his nephew Lorenzo was linked with Giambattista Gelli and Donato Giannotti, and therefore with Michelangelo. It can be presumed, though proof is lacking, that Brunelleschi was anti-Medicean. So far as I can learn, this cultural problem has had the attention only of A. Parronchi ("Brunelleschi e Dante", in *La Nazione*, Florence, 2 March 1966, p. 3, and "Come gli artisti leggevano Dante", *Studi Danteschi*, XLIII, 1965).

For Girolamo Benivieni (1453-1542) see the meticulous biography, based on largely unpublished material, by C. Vasoli in the *Dizionario Biografico degli Italiani*. For the text I used the original edition in the Pattee Library, Pennsylvania State University, from which the woodcuts reproduced here were taken.

3. The aims are clearly indicated in a marginal annotation in the manuscript (Florence, Biblioteca Riccardiana, 2245), collocated by G. L. Passerini for the edition prepared by Nicola Zingarelli in the collection, *Opuscoli Danteschi inediti o rari*, Florence-Città di Castello, XXXVI-XXXIX, 1897.

4. Concerning whom, see Antonio Enzo Quaglio, *Scienza e mito nel Boccaccio*, Padua, 1967.

5. For Paolo Toscanelli see the superb essay in Eugenio Garin, *Ritratti di Umanisti*, Florence, 1967, pp. 41-67.

6. Information from Agostino Sottili, "Autografi e traduzioni di Ambrogio Traversari", *Rinascimento*,

1967-68, pp. 3-15. The humanists' attitude to St Paul was studied by W. Dress, *Die Mystik des Marsilio Ficinos*, Berlin and Leipzig, 1929.

7. "Brunelleschi 'un nuovo San Paolo' ", in Parronchi 1964, pp. 415-28.

8. On the Burchiello poems see A. Lanza, "Polemiche e Berte letterarie nella Firenze del Primo Quattrocento", *Storia e Testi*, Rome, 1972.

A critical edition of four sonnets (not including "Madonna se ne vien da la fontana") has now been published by Giuliano Tanturli and Domenico De Robertis, Florence, 1977.

9. Published in G. Baruffaldi, ed., *Rime scelte de' Poeti Ferraresi Antichi e Moderni*, Ferrara, 1713, and in the *Scelta di Sonetti e Canzoni de' più eccellenti Rimatori di ogni Secolo*, 4th edn., Venice, 1739, I, p. 122; republished in *Sonetti del Burchiello, del Bellincioni e d'Altri Poeti Fiorentini alla Burchiellesca*, London [in fact, Livorno], 1757, and in G. Borghi (ed.), *Raccolta di Lirici e Satirici Italiani*, Florence, 1835, pt I, p. 155. For a critical edition by D. De Robertis see "L'esperienza poetica del Quattrocento", *Storia della Letteratura italiana*, ed. E. Cecchi and N. Sapegno, III, Milan, 1966, p. 407. The version printed in my text is based on the reprint of the 1739 edition with notes by Achille Tartaro, in his *Il Primo Quattrocento Italiano*, LIL 11, Bari, 1971, pp. 83-84.

The attribution to Brunelleschi of this sonnet, as well as of the madrigal "Dimmi Donato", was questioned by A. Tissoni Benvenuti ("Appunti sull'antologia dei poeti ferraresi di Girolamo Baruffaldi", *Giornale Storico della Letteratura Italiana*, 1969, 149, pp. 18-30), because of the presumed unreliability of the anthologist Baruffaldi.

10. Professor Pedretti, who suggested this to me, is studying a number of projects for navigation on the Arno, and will eventually publish more information on this particular experiment. For the boat see Chapter 8, note 28.

11. Baron, *Humanistic and Political Literature in Florence and Venice at the Beginning of the Quattrocento*, Cambridge, Mass., 1955, pp. 13-37.

12. On this battle of sonnets and Brunelleschi's conflict with Giovanni di Gherardo da Prato, see C. Guasti 1874; C. von Fabriczy 1892, pp. 388-93; A. Pellizzari 1919; and also A. Wesselofsky, *Il Paradiso degli Alberti, ritrovi e ragionamenti del 1389: Romanzo di Giovanni da Prato*, Bologna, 1867, I, pt II, pp. 70, 74-75. Wesselofsky's material is incomplete, and based on a transcription which is in parts very bad but in other parts more accurate than later transcriptions. More recently, see Prager 1946.

The best version of the text is that reconstructed by D. De Robertis: "L'esperienza poetica del Quattrocento", p. 407, reprinted by A. Tartaro with extremely useful notes (for both publications see note 9), and now the new critical edition by De Robertis and Tanturli, 1977, from which my texts of the two sonnets come. For the poem "O fonte fonda" see also Antonio Lanza, *Lirici toscani del '400*, Rome, 1973, p. 659.

13. See above, note 7.

14. Published by Baruffaldi (see note 9) and several times by A. Chiappelli, who takes it as an attack on Donatello (in *Nuova Antologia*, 1899, in his *Pagine d'antica arte fiorentina*, Florence, 1905, in *Nuova Antologia*, 1923, and in his *Arte del Rinascimento*, Rome, 1925). See also A. Pellizzari 1919, pp. 310ff.

15. It was attributed to Burchiello by E. Giovanetti (*Antologia Burchiellesca*, Rome, 1949, p. 129). For the most recent edition, with attribution to Brunelleschi, see De Robertis and Tanturli 1977.

16. The first printed edition, with woodcuts, appeared in Florence in 1576.

The version by Manetti was published in Antonio Manetti, *Operette istoriche edite ed inedite*, ed. G. Milanesi, Florence, 1887, pp. 1-67; in G. Bellonci, *Sette Secoli di Novelle Italiane*, Rome, 1953, pp. 400-424; in C. Varese, *Prosatori volgari del Quattrocento*, Milan and Naples, 1955, pp. 769-802; in A. Borlenghi, *Novelle del Quattrocento*, Milan, 1962, pp. 343-89; in G. Ponte, *Il Quattrocento*, Bologna, 1966, pp. 781-810; and most recently in an authoritative scholarly edition, together with the Biography, by D. De Robertis and G. Tanturli (Manetti 1976). In English it is found in Thomas Roscoe, *The Italian Novelists*, London, 1825, pp. 111-30, and Decio Petoello, *Great Italian Short Stories*, London, 1930, pp. 78-90.

For the other version, which is shorter, see Michele Barbi, "Una versione inedita della novella del Grasso legnaiuolo", *Studi di Filologia Italiana: Bullettino della Reale Accademia della Crusca*, I, 1927, pp. 133-44; Bernardo Giambullari, *Rime inedite o rare*, ed. I. Marchetti, Florence, 1955, pp. 19-21, 91-139 (verse version); and the scholarly edition by D. De Robertis, *Novella del grasso legnaiuolo, nella redazione del codice Palatino 200*, Turin, 1968.

An analysis of the novella aiming to establish concordances and indices of word frequency was made by the Accademia della Crusca. See Bruno Basile's highly informative "Rassegna Petrarchesca (1959-1973)", *Lettere Italiane*, XXVI, 1974, p. 201.

Comments on the novella quite similar to mine can be found in Decio Gioseffi, "Realtà e conoscenza nel Brunelleschi", *Critica d'Arte*, n.s., XIV, 1967, pp. 8-18, where the trick is compared to Brunelleschi's experiments with perspective, as another case of deceiving the senses. See also A. Parronchi, "La Burla del Grasso", in *La Nazione*, Florence, 27 January 1968, p. 3.

The most complete study from an art-historical point of view is the thesis written by Emily Jayne under the direction of Carlo Pedretti at the University of California, Los Angeles, in 1972: this contains an introduction and an English translation as well as a map of Florence in which the houses of the characters and their movements in the story are visualized.

But see also: Andrea Moschetti, "Antonio Manetti e i suoi scritti intorno a Filippo Brunelleschi", *Miscellanea di studi in onore di Attilio Hortis*, Trieste, 1910, II, pp. 807-29; Arturo Pompeati, "Un Pirandello per ridere nel Quattrocento", *Rivista d'Italia*, n.s. X (XXX), 1927, pp. 651-63; and Fredi Chappelli, "La Novella del Grasso Legnaiuolo", *L'Approdo*, I, 1952, pp. 79-82.

The novella makes use of the mechanism of the *beffa*, the often cruel and humiliating trick, of which there are many examples in Boccaccio's *Decameron* and elsewhere. For a detailed analysis see André Rochon, "Une date importante dans l'histoire de la Beffa: La Nouvelle du Grasso Legnaiuolo", *Formes et significations de la "beffa" dans la littérature italienne de la Renaissance*, Paris, 1975, and also D. P. Rotunda, *Motif-Index of the Italian Novella in Prose*, Bloomington, Ind., 1942.

17. The facts about Ammannatini were published by Milanesi in his edition of Manetti (see the preceding note).

18. Another literary work attributed to Brunelleschi, *Geta e Birria*, was published by C. Arlia in *Scelta di Curiosità letterarie*, disp. CLXIX, Bologna, 1879. Tanturli considers that at least part of this verse narrative may indeed be by the architect.

Chronology

1. In addition to the two visits in 1412, according to documents Brunelleschi visited Prato in 1429 for problems connected with the façade, and again several times in 1443-44 for the enlargement of the grille of the Chapel of the Holy Girdle, the work of Maso di Bartolomeo.

The new façade was simply built in front of the old one, allowing for a well defended covered passage between them, running across above the level of the main entrance door and leading from the Chapel of the Holy Girdle to the outdoor pulpit by Donatello. The static problems posed by that pulpit, which projects boldly out from the corner of the Cathedral, were not inconsiderable, and the solution found is remarkable.

The extent of Brunelleschi's involvement in the work on the façade and on the Chapel of the Holy Girdle has not been settled. He was associated first with the *capomaestro* Nanni Niccoli and then with Ghiberti.

Among modern studies see especially the following publications by Giuseppe Marchini: *Il Duomo di Prato*, Milan, 1957; *Il Tesoro del Duomo di Prato*, Milan, 1963; "Di Maso di Bartolomeo e d'altri", *Commentari*, III, 1952, pp. 108-27; "Maso di Bartolomeo", in the congress report, *Donatello e il suo tempo, Firenze-Padova 1966*, Florence, 1968, pp. 235-43. I am also endebted to Francesco Gurrieri for his comments on the subject.

2. The Baptistery, begun in the thirteenth century, was left unfinished without a dome in 1320 (Fabriczy 1907, p. 79). Klotz (1970) illustrates and describes the present octagonal dome, which subtly combines a pyramidal and a semicircular shape by means of changes in the curvature.

While Brunelleschi undoubtedly visited Volterra in 1435 or earlier, it is not certain that he did so in 1427. The expenses mentioned in the deliberation of 13 November of that year were small, only 4 florins (as pointed out already by A. Cinci in *Guida di Volterra*, Volterra, 1885, after the publication of the original document by G. Amide in *Delle fortificazioni volterranee*, II, 2nd edn., Volterra, 1864); and lead for the dome was not purchased until 1483.

G. Levi and M. Melchiorre, who made measured drawings of the building (published in *Rassegna Volterrana*, XLII-XLIII, 1977, pp. 101-13), have come to the conclusion that Brunelleschi was not involved.

3. Buggiano's heir, in turn, was his brother. See Fabriczy, "Nanni di Miniato detto Fora", *Jahrbuch der Preussischen Kunstsammlungen*, XXVII, 1906, Beiheft, pp. 70-86.

Bibliography

There are now more than 2,300 books and articles on Brunelleschi known to me or to Corrado Bozzoni and Giovanni Carbonara, compilers of the excellent two-volume annotated bibliography, *Filippo Brunelleschi, Saggio di Bibliografia* (Rome, 1977, 1979), which covers the period up to the end of 1978. Given such a vast amount of material, the list that follows concentrates on the latest publications, highlighting the problems; publications before 1960 are included when they have been referred to repeatedly (in abbreviated form) in my notes.

Serious interest in Brunelleschi is a relatively recent phenomenon. Following the pioneering efforts of Fabriczy (1892, 1907) there were before 1976 only three detailed monographs. That by Leader Scott (pseudonym of Lucy E. Baxter — 1901, reprinted 1908) included the fortifications, and gave a description of the then almost inaccessible crypt of St Zenobius in the Cathedral. The book by Folnesics (1915) made a major contribution in its reconstruction of the original plan of S. Spirito. That by Sanpaolesi (1962), the first to use modern measured drawings, served as a basic reference work for thousands of scholars, together with the article on Brunelleschi in the *Encyclopaedia of World Art* (II, New York, Toronto and London, 1960), by Sanpaolesi, Garin and Portoghesi. The situation as regards studies of Quattrocento architecture in Tuscany was no better, as a pioneer such as Howard Saalman well knows. The long-awaited chapter by Heydenreich (Heydenreich and Lotz 1974) proved to be more compilation than fresh research. Somewhat more accurate is the general history of Renaissance architecture by Benevolo (1968). Fanelli (1973) links matters of style with the urban and artistic history of Florence, but without reference to the already well-developed studies on the economy and politics of the city. Only Argan (1955) hinted at the political position of Brunelleschi, now fully documented by D. Finiello Zervas (1979). For the economic side, we await the new book by R.A. Goldthwaite.

Many documents remain to be investigated. Those already known were shown in 1977 and catalogued by Benigni (see *Ricerche brunelleschiane*, 1977), but new ones appear almost every month. The question of proportional theory is more obscure than ever, because we are beginning to have measured drawings of the buildings; a new discussion has been initiated by Hersey (1976, 1978). The present state of our knowledge concerning Renaissance perspective is portrayed in the two volumes of *La Prospettiva Rinascimentale, Codificazione e trasgressioni* (ed. Dalai 1980, and a forthcoming volume, by Veltman, which will be an immense bibliography). On statics and on technology see Prager, Sanpaolesi (1951), Mainstone (1969-70 and 1975), Prager and Scaglia (1970), the thesis by O. Sangiovanni, *Per una storia dello sviluppo delle conoscenze statiche in rapporto all'architettura dall'Antichità alla fine del secolo XVIII* (Florence, 1977), various essays by Di Pasquale and Rossi (1978), and the monumental new work by Saalman on the dome of S. Maria del Fiore

(1980). Unconvincing, but worth following up by other research, is Warren's publication on the dome and Dufay's motet (1973). Klotz (1970) suggested strong ties with the Middle Ages; his opinion is often unsubstantiated, but generally seems correct.

I would like to suggest reading, together with my book, that of C.L. Ragghianti (1977); for its 135 good colour photographs, that of Fanelli (1977); and, as an anthology of the arts surrounding Brunelleschi, the huge catalogue, *Lorenzo Ghiberti "materia e ragionamenti"* (1978). For the architects, masons and sculptors in the immediate circle of Brunelleschi see *Brunelleschiani*, by Borsi, Morolli and Quinterio (1979). The fireworks of the six-hundredth anniversary celebrations in 1977 produced few serious analyses of buildings by Brunelleschi; but to the classic research studies on the Pazzi Chapel by Laschi, Roselli and Rossi (1962) and on S. Spirito by Luporini (1964) one should now add the exhaustive monograph on the dome by Saalman, and a short book on S. Lorenzo by Roselli and Superchi (both 1980). These came out too recently for me to discuss them in my text: I shall conclude this introductory note with a few comments on them.

On the basis of 383 groups of new documents, in addition to those published by Guasti (1887) and Poggi (1909), Saalman gives a more logical chronology of the building process. The new data should be added to my chronology of Brunelleschi. Essential chapters are those on building machines (with their working models), quarries, forges and transport. Inside the structure, Saalman has clearly identified the elements and the position of the three stone chains, in both the outer and the inner shells. It is impossible to go into detail here on some points of basic disagreement, but I should at least like to mention them. The "gualandrino con tre corde", which my students interpreted as a safety belt (following the suggestion of the Opera workers), is considered by Saalman to be "a system of string control for the radial disposition of all building elements and the inclination of all elements toward their respective pointed fifth center of curvature". This instrument would, however, have been gigantic and weighty, and in practice impossible to use. The building strings referred to in the documents would, I believe, have served instead for measuring shorter sections, and as optical devices, as today, for general assessment. Comparing plates 20 and 20a with 2L, and plate 105 with 85 and 107, I feel again that the late drawings representing scaffolding derive from Brunelleschi, and not from St Peter's. Other divergences, in the translation of the fifteenth-century documents and in the measurements of the dome, should be judged by the reader.

Roselli and Superchi publish new technical observations and some new documents on S. Lorenzo. The decree of 16 and 18 March 1434, concerning the creation of a piazza beside S. Lorenzo, reveals opposition on the part of the Operai of the Cathedral and the threat of a heavy fine. The opposition was directed against the Medici, who were interested in improving the surroundings of their palace. Demolitions for the piazza had taken place before 30 April. The documents of 3 November 1449 and of 1480 (Ginori, 256) seem to refer to the Ginori family as patrons of a group of arches of the nave. The key word is "ponti", which surely does not mean scaffolding. Some of the lateral chapels, off the left nave aisle, were under construction before spring 1465.

ABBREVIATIONS

A.B.	*Art Bulletin*
Ant. Viva	*Antichità Viva*
B.C.S.A.P.	*Bollettino del Centro Internazionale di Storia dell'Architettura Andrea Palladio*
B.d.A.	*Bollettino d'Arte del Ministero della Pubblica Istruzione*
Burl.M.	*Burlington Magazine*
Comm.	*Commentari*
Cr.A.	*La Critica d'Arte*
Jb.Berl.Mus.	*Jahrbuch der Berliner Museen*
Jb.Pr.K.	*Jahrbuch der Preuszischen Kunstsammlungen*
J.S.A.H.	*Journal of the Society of Architectural Historians*
Kunst Chr	*Kunst Chronik* (Munich and Nuremberg)
Mitt.Flor.	*Mitteilungen des Kunsthistorischen Instituts in Florenz*
Münch.Jk.	*Münchener Jahrbuch der Bildenden Kunst*
Naz.	*La Nazione* (newspaper, Florence)
Par.	*Paragone*
Q.St.A.Roma	*Quaderni dell'Istituto di Storia dell'Architettura*
Rin.	*Rinascimento*
Riv.A.	*Rivista d'Arte*
Z.f.Kg.	*Zeitschrift für Kunstgeschichte*

Works published over several years, or written in one year and published in another, appear just before the *later* date.

1568
VASARI: see below, 1878-85

1579
[FORTUNIO, A.] *Historiarum Camaldulensium pars posterior*, Venice

1754-62
RICHA, G. *Notizie istoriche delle Chiese Fiorentine divise ne' suoi quartieri*, 10 vol., Florence

1804
CIANFOGNI, P.N. *Memorie istoriche dell'Ambrosiana R. Basilica di S. Lorenzo di Firenze*, Florence

1816-17
MORENI, D. *Continuazione delle memorie istoriche dell'Ambrosiana imperiale basilica di S. Lorenzo di Firenzo*, 2 vol., Florence

1821
[LASTRI, M., and DEL ROSSO, G.] *L'Osservatore Fiorentino sugli edifizj della sua Patria, terza edizione*, 8 vol., Florence

1839
[GAYE, G.] *Carteggio inedito d'artisti dei secoli XIV. XV. XVI. pubblicato ed illustrato con documenti pure inediti*, I, *1326-1500*, Florence

1833-46
REPETTI, E. *Dizionario geografico, fisico, storico della Toscana*, 7 vol., Florence

1857
GUASTI, C. *La Cupola di Santa Maria del Fiore, illustrata con i documenti di Archivio dell'Opera secolare*, Florence

1857-58
BONAINI, F. "Statuto della Parte Guelfa di Firenze, compilato nel MCCCXXXV", *Giornale Storico degli Archivi Toscani*, I, pp. 1-41; II, pp. 171-87, 257-83

1871
NARDUCCI, E. "Intorno ad una traduzione italiana fatta nel secolo decimoquarto, del tratto d'Ottica di Alhazen", *Bull. di Bibliografia e di Storia delle Scienze Matematiche e Fisiche*, IV, pp. 1-48

1874
GUASTI, C. "Un disegno di Giovanni di Gherardo da Prato, poeta e architetto, concernente alla Cupola di Santa Maria del Fiore", in *Belle Arti.*

Opuscoli descrittivi e biografici, Florence, pp. 107-28

1878-85
VASARI, G. *Le vite de' più eccellenti pittori sculptori ed architettori*, ed. G. Milanesi, 9 vol., Florence

1885-86
FRANCESCHINI, P. *Il nuovo Osservatore Fiorentino*. On The Old Sacristy see pp. 212-14, 221-24, 228-31, 234-40, 252-55; on the façade of S. Lorenzo pp. 317-20, 326-28, 333-36; on SS. Apostoli p. 210; on the Pazzi Chapel pp. 29-31; on Palazzo Antinori p. 216; on Palazzo Pazzi pp. 279-80.

1885-93
STEGMANN, K. VON, and GEYMULLER, H.F. VON *Die Architektur der Renaissance in Toscana. Dargestellt in den hervorragendsten Kirchen, Palasten, Villen und Monumenten*, 11 vol., Munich

1887
CAROCCI, G. "Il Palazzo dei Lenzi", *Arte e Storia*, VI, pp. 153-55
DURM, J. *Die Domkuppel in Florenz und die Kuppel der Peterskirche in Rom*, Berlin
GUASTI, C. *Santa Maria del Fiore. La costruzione della Chiesa e del Campanile, secondo i documenti tratti dall'archivio dell'Opera secolare e da quello di Stato*, Florence

1891
FABRICZY, C. DE "Lo Spedale di S. Maria degl'Innocenti a Firenze. Documenti inediti sulla storia della sua Fabbrica", *Archivio Storico dell'Arte*, IV, pp. 291-300

1892
FABRICZY, C. VON Filippo Brunelleschi. Sein Leben *und seine Werke*, Stuttgart

1893
[FONTANA, P.] "Rassegna bibliografica. Illustrazioni storiche di alcune fabbriche fiorentine per Jodoco Del Badia", *Archivio Storico Italiano*, XII, pp. 438-43

1898
DORINI, U. "Il Palazzo dei Capitani di Parte Guelfa ed i lavori del Centro di Firenze", *Naz.*, XL, pp. 1-2

1898-99
DOREN, A. "Zum Bau der Florentiner Domkuppel", *Repertorium für Kunstwissenschaft*, XXI, pp. 249-62, XXII, pp. 220-21

1899
BEANI, G. *L'Altare di Sant'Jacopo Apostolo nella Cattedrale di Pistoia, Descrizione documentata*, Pistoia

CHIAPELLI, A. "Due sculture ignote di Filippo Brunelleschi", *Rivista d'Italia*, II, pp. 454-70

1901
SCOTT, L. (pseud. of Lucy E. BAXTER) *Filippo di Ser Brunellesco*, London

1905
BACCI, P. *Gli orafi fiorentini e il secondo riordinamento dell'altare di San Jacopo*, Pistoia
POGGI, G. "Andrea di Lazzaro Cavalcanti e il pulpito di S. Maria Novella", *Riv.A.*, III, pp. 76-85

1907
FABRICZY, C. VON "Brunelleschiana. Urkunden und Forschungen zur Biographie des Meisters", *Jb.Pr.K.*, XXVIII, Beiheft, pp. 1-84

1908
VENTURI, A. *La Scultura del Quattrocento* (Storia dell'Arte italiana, VI), Milan

1909
[POGGI, G., ed.] Italienische Forschungen, II, "Studien über die Benutzung der Antike in der Renaissance", *Monatshefte für Kunstwissenschaft*, II, pp. 267-80

1891-1911
SALUTATI, C. *Epistolario*, ed. F. Novati, 4 vol., Rome

1911
CAROCCI, G. "Antiche case su luoghi degli alberghi fiorentini", *L'Illustratore fiorentino*, n.s., VIII, pp. 50ff

1915
FOLNESICS, H. *Brunelleschi. Ein Beitrag Entwicklungsgeschichte der Frührenaissance Architektur*, Vienna

1919
PELLIZZARI, A. "Filippo Brunelleschi scrittore", *Rass. Bibl. della Letteratura Italiana*, XXVII, pp. 292-315

1921
BELLANDI, Fr. S. *La chiesa di S. Spirito in Firenze. Una pagina di storia con illustrazioni*, Florence
LINACHER, A. "Il Tempio degli Scolari", *Atti della Società Colombaria Fiorentina*, Florence, pp. 609-27

1925
CHIAPPELLI, A. *Arte del Rinascimento (Ricerche e Saggi)*, Rome, pt 1, vols. X, XII, pt 2, vols. III, VI

1930
POGGI, G. "La 'maschera' di Filippo Brunelleschi nel Museo dell'Opera del Duomo", *Riv.A.*, XII, pp. 533-40

1931

HEYDENREICH, L.H. "Spätwerke Brunelleschis", *Jb.Pr.K.*, pp. 1-28

1919-32

FONTANA, P. "Die Cappella Barbadori in S. Felicita zu Florenz", *Mitt. Flor.*, III, 1919-1932 [1930], reprinted Amsterdam 1971

1931-32

BOTTO, C. "L'edificazione della Chiesa di Santo Spirito in Firenze", *Riv.A.*, ser. 2, III (XIII), 1931, pp. 477-511; IV (XIV), 1932, pp. 23-53

1932

CHERICI, U. *L'assistenza all'infanzia ed il R. Spedale degli Innocenti di Firenze*, Florence

1934

SAXL, F. "La fede astrologica di Agostino Chigi. Interpretazione dei dipinti di Baldassare Peruzzi nella sala di Galatea della Farnesina", *Reale Accademia d'Italia, Collezione 'La Farnesina'* I, Rome

1935

SABATINI, R. "La Casa del Mutilato e la Rotonda del Brunellesco", *Firenze*, IV, pp. 97-100

1936

JOCHEM, F.L. *The Libri dello Spedale of the Florentine Foundling Hospital, Sources of the History of Building in the Fifteenth Century in Italy*, PhD thesis, Univ. of Wisconsin, Madison

SANPAOLESI, P. "Il Concorso del 1418-20 per la Cupola di S. Maria del Fiore", *Riv.A.*, ser. 2, VIII (XVIII), pp. 321-44

TAUCCI, P.R. "Di un lavoro sconosciuto del Brunelleschi", *Firenze*, V, pp. 157-60

1937

CRISPOLTI, V. *Santa Maria del Fiore alla luce dei documenti*, Florence

PAATZ, W. *Werden und Wesen der Trecento-Architektur in Toskana. Die grossen Meister als Schopfer einer neuen Baukunst: die Meister von S. Maria Novella; Niccolò Pisano; Giovanni Pisano; Arnolfo di Cambio und Giotto*, Burg b. M.

1938

MARCHINI, G. "Un disegno di Giuliano da Sangallo riproducente l'alzato della Rotonda degli Angeli", *Atti del I Congresso Naz. di Storia dell'architettura*, Florence, pp. 147-54

NICCOLI, R. "Su alcuni recenti saggi eseguiti alla brunelleschiana cappella Barbadori in S. Felicita", ibid., pp. 139-46

1939

OPERA DI S. MARIA DEL FIORE, *Rilievi e studi sulla cupola del Brunelleschi, eseguiti dalla Commissione nominata il 12 gennaio 1934*, Florence (includes contributions by Nobili, Sabatini, Alfani, Vervi, Padelli)

1940

GINORI CONTI, P. *La Basilica di S. Lorenzo di Firenze e la famiglia Ginori*, Florence

RICHTER, M. "Die Terre Murate im florentinischem Gebiet", *Mitt.Flor.*, V, pp. 351-86

1941

SANPAOLESI, P. *La cupola di S. Maria del Fiore. Il progetto. La costruzione* (R. Istituto d'Archeologia e Storia dell'Arte, fasc. XI), Rome

1942

DE ANGELIS D'OSSAT, G. "Un carattere dell'arte brunelleschiana", *Saggi di Storia dell'Architettura*, I, Rome

1943

FRUMKIN, M. "Early History of Patents for Inventions", *Chambers Journal*, Jan. 1943, pp. 21ff.

1946

PRAGER, F.D. "Brunelleschi's Patent", *Journal of the Patent Office Society*, XXVIII, pp. 109-35

YBL, E. "Die zwei älteren Pisani und Brunelleschi", *Phoebus*, I, pp. 156-60

1947

GHIBERTI, L. *I Commentari*, ed. O. Marisani, Naples

1948

SANPAOLESI, P. *Brunellesco e Donatello nella Sacristia Vecchia di San Lorenzo*, Pisa (n.d.)

1949/62

WITTKOWER, R. *Architectural Principles in the Age of Humanism*, London (rev. edn 1962).

1950

[MARCHINI, G., ed.] *Mostra d'arte sacra antica* (exhibition catalogue), Pistoia

PRAGER, F.D. "Brunelleschi's Inventions and the Renewal of Roman Masonry Work", *Osiris*, IX, pp. 457-554

1951

SALMI, M. "Il Palazzo della Parte Guelfa di Firenze e Filippo Brunelleschi", *Rinascimento*, II, 1, pp. 3-11

SANPAOLESI, P. "Ipotesi sulle conoscenze matematiche, statiche e meccaniche del Brunelleschi", *Belle Arti*, II, 1951, pp. 25-54

1952

COOLIDGE, J. Review of P. Sanpaolesi, *La Cupola di Santa Maria del Fiore* (1941), *A.B.*, XXXIV, pp. 165-66

1953

SANPAOLESI, P. "Aggiunte al Brunelleschi", *B.d.A.*, XXXVIII, pp. 225-32

1940-54

PAATZ, W., and PAATZ, E. *Die Kirchen von Florenz*, 6 vol., Frankfurt a. M.

1954

PANE, R. "Un disegno del Brunelleschi", *Cr.A.*, n.s., I, pp. 22-32

RAGGHIANTI, C.L. "Aenigmata pistoriensia, I", ibid., pp. 423-44

1955

ARGAN, G.C. *Brunelleschi*, Verona (rev. ed. Milan 1978)

SAALMAN, H. *Filippo Brunelleschi: Capital Studies*, M.A. thesis, New York Univ.

1955-56

SCAGLIA, G. "Drawings of Brunelleschi's Mechanical Inventions for the Construction of the Cupola", *Marsyas*, X, pp. 45-68

1956

FERRALI, S. *L'altare argenteo di S. Jacopo nella cattedrale di Pistoia. Guida storico-artistica*, Florence

LOTZ, W. "Das Raumbild in der Italienischen Architekturzeichnung der Renaissance", *Mitt Flor.*, VII, pp. 193-226

ROSSI, F. "La lanterna della cupola di Santa Maria del Fiore e i suoi restauri", *B.d.A.*, XLI, pp. 128-43

SANPAOLESI, P. "La lanterna di S. Maria del Fiore e il suo modello ligneo", ibid., pp. 11-29

STEINGRÄBER, E. "The Pistoia Silver Altar: a reexamination", *Connoisseur*, CXXXVIII, pp. 149-54

1956/70

KRAUTHEIMER, R., and KRAUTHEIMER HESS, T. *Lorenzo Ghiberti*, 2 vol., Princeton (rev. edn 1970)

1954-57

NYBERG, D.F. "Brunelleschi's use of proportion in the Pazzi Chapel", *Marsyas*, VII, [1957], pp. 1-7

1957

SCHLEGEL, U. "La Cappella Barbadori e l'architettura fiorentina del primo Rinascimento", *Riv.A.*, ser. 3, VII (XXXII), [1959], pp. 77-106

1957/63

JANSON, H.W. *The Sculpture of Donatello*, 2 vol., Princeton (edn in 1 vol. 1963)

1958

GOSEBRUCH, M. "Florentinische Kapitelle von Brunelleschi bis zum Tempio Malatestiano und der Eigenstil der Frührenaissance", *Römische Jahrb. für Kunstgeschichte*, VII, pp. 63-193

SAALMAN, H. (**A**) "Filippo Brunelleschi: Capital studies", *A.B.*, XL, pp. 113-37

— (**B**) "Further notes on the Cappella Barbadori, S. Felicita", *Burl.M.*, C, pp. 270-74

1959

SAALMAN, H. "Giovanni di Gherardo da Prato's Designs concerning the Cupola of Santa Maria del Fiore in Florence", *J.S.A.H.*, XVIII, 1, pp. 11-20

SAS-ZALOZIECKY, W. "Kuppellösungen Brunelleschis und die römische Architektur", in *Studies in the History of Art, dedicated to William E. Suida*, London, pp. 41-46

ZEITLER, R. "Über den Innenraum von Santo Spirito zu Florenz", *Figura*, n.s., I, pp. 48-68

1960

FEDERICI VESCOVINI, G. "Problemi di fisica aristotelica in un maestro del XIV: Biagio Pelacani da Parma", *Riv. di Filosofia*, LI, pp. 179-220

FRANKL, P. *The Gothic. Literary Sources and Interpretations through Eight Centuries*, Princeton

GOMBRICH, E. H. "The Early Medici as Patrons of Art: A Survey of primary Sources", in *Italian Renaissance Studies. A tribute to the late Cecilia M. Ady*, ed. E.F. Jacob, London, pp. 279-311

GRAYSON, C. "The Composition of L.B. Alberti's 'Decem Libri de Re Aedificatoria' ", *Münch.Jb.*, ser. 3, XI, pp. 152-61

LISNER, M. "Deutsche Holzkruzifixe des 15. Jahrhunderts in Italien", *Mitt. Flor.*, IX, pp. 159-206

PANOFSKY, E. *Renaissance and Renascences in Western Art*, Stockholm

SCAGLIA, G. *Studies in the Zibaldone of Buonaccorso Ghiberti*, PhD thesis, New York Univ. (University Microfilms, Ann Arbor, Mich.)

ZEVI, B. *Architectura in nuce*, Venice and Rome

1961

ALESSIO, F. "Per uno studio sull'ottica del Trecento", *Studi Medievali*, ser. 3, II, pp. 444-504
    — "Testi e documenti. Questioni inedite di Ottica di Biagio Pelacani da Parma", *Riv. Critica di Storia della Filosofia*, XVI, pp. 79-110

BAYLEY, C.C. *War and Society in Renaissance Florence, The "De Militia" of Leonardo Bruni*, Toronto

BRUSCHI, A. "La teorica architettonica rinascimentale nella formulazione albertina", *Q.St.A. Roma*, VI-VIII, 31-48 (*Saggi di Storia dell'Architettura in onore del Prof. Vincenzo Fasolo*), pp. 115-30

DALAI, M. "La questione della prospettiva", in E. Panofsky, *La prospettiva come "forma simbolica" et altri scritti*, Milan

GARIN, E. *La cultura filosofica del Rinascimento Italiano. Ricerche e documenti*, Florence
    — "Gli umanisti e la scienza", *Riv. di Filosofia*, LII, 3, pp. 259-78

KLEIN, R. "Les humanistes et la science", *Bibliothèque d'Humanisme et Renaissance*, XXIII, pp. 7-16

LINNENKAMP, R. "Die Pazzi-Kapelle, S. Croce, Florenz. Ein unbekanntes Proportionssystem Brunelleschis", *Deutsche Bauzeitung*, pp. 277-79

MARCHINI, G. "Il Palazzo Datini a Prato", *B.d.A.*, XLVI, pp. 212-18

PARRONCHI, A. "Le 'misure dell'occhio' secondo il Ghiberti", *Par.*, XII, 133, pp. 18-48

RAGGHIANTI, C. L. "Lo spettacolo automatico", *Cr.A.*, VIII, 45, pp. 57-65

SCAGLIA, G. (**A**) "Drawings of Brunelleschi's Mechanical Inventions for the Construction of the Cupola", *Marsyas*, X, pp. 45-68
    — (**B**) "Studies in the 'Zibaldone' of Buonaccorso Ghiberti" (summary of dissertation: see 1960), ibid., p. 73

1962

BRUNETTI, G. "Note su Luca della Robbia", in *Scritti di Storia dell'Arte in onore di Mario Salmi*, II, Rome, pp. 263-72

FEDERICI VESCOVINI, G. "Le questioni di 'Perspectiva' di Biagio Pelacani da Parma", *Rin.*, ser. 2, I (XII), (dated 1961), pp. 163-243

HIGOUNET, C. "Les 'terre nuove' florentines du XIVe siècle", in *Studi in onore di Amintore Fanfani*, III, Milan, pp. 1-17

LASCHI, G., ROSELLI, P. and ROSSI, P.A. "Indagini sulla Cappella dei Pazzi", *Comm.*, XIII, pp. 24-41

LOWRY, B. *Renaissance Architecture*, New York

[MOROZZI, G.] *Firenze. Spedale di S. Maria degli Innocenti: studi e rilievi compiuti negli anni 1961-1962 sulla costruzione originaria brunelleschiana, progetto di ripristino*, Florence

PARRONCHI, A. "Il Crocifisso del Bosco", in *Scritti di Storia dell'Arte in onore di Mario Salmi*, II, Rome, pp. 233-62.
    — "Il 'punctum dolens' della costruzione legittima", *Par.*, XIII, 145, pp. 58-72

SALMI, M. "Aspetti del primo Rinascimento: Firenze, Venezia e Padova", *Rin.*, ser. 2, II (XIII), pp. 77-87

SANPAOLESI, P. *Brunelleschi*, Milan.

1962-63

BOSKOVITS, M. " 'Quello ch'e dipintori oggi dicono prospettiva'. Contributions to fifteenth century Italian art theory", *Acta Historiae Artium*, VIII, pp. 241-60; IX, pp. 139-62

1963

DE LA CROIX, H. "The Literature on Fortification in Renaissance Italy", *Technology and Culture*, IV, 1, pp. 30-50.

HEYDENREICH, L. H. "Strukturprinzipien der florentiner Frührenaissance-Architektur: Prospectiva aedificandi", in *Studies in Western Art. Acts of the Twentieth International Congress of the History of Art. New York City, September 7-12 1961*, II, *The Renaissance and Mannerism*, Princeton, pp. 108-22

JANSON: see 1957

KLEIN, R. "Études sur la perspective à la renaissance, 1956-1963", *Bibliothèque d'Humanisme et Renaissance*, XXV, pp. 577-87

LORENZONI, G. "L'attività padovana di Nicolò Baroncelli", *Riv.A.*, ser. 3, XI (XXXVI), pp. 27-52

MARCHINI, G. *Il Tesoro del Duomo di Prato. Con documenti inediti ritrovati da R. Nuti et R. Piattoli*, Milan

MARTINES, L. *The Social World of the Florentine Humanists. 1390-1460*, London

MEISS, M. "Masaccio and the early Renaissance: The circular plan", in *Studies in Western Art. Acts of the Twentieth International Congress of the History of Art. New York City, September 7-12 1961*, II, *The Renaissance and Mannerism*, Princeton, pp. 123-45

MURARO, M. "Pasquali Poccianti restauratore di monumenti fiorentini", *Riv.A.*, ser. 3, XI (XXXVI), pp. 79-87

MURRAY, P. *The Architecture of the Italian Renaissance*, London and New York

PARRONCHI, A. "L'allagamento di Lucca", *Naz.*, CV, 8 Sept., p. 3
    — "Storia di una 'Gatta malata' ", *Par.*, XIV, 157, pp. 60-68

SCHLEGEL, U. "Observations on Masaccio's Trinity Fresco in Santa Maria Novella", *A.B.*, XLV, pp. 19-33

TIGLER, P. *Die Architekturtheorie des Filarete*, Berlin

1964

BRAUNFELS, W. *Der Dom von Florenz*, Olten, Lausanne and Freiburg i. Br. (contains Dammann on the Dufay consecration motet)

HARTT, F. "Art and Freedom in Quattrocento Florence", in *Essays in Memory of Karl Lehmann*, ed. L. F. Sandler, New York, pp. 114-31

LUPORINI, E. *Brunelleschi, forma e ragione*, Milan

MASETTI, A. R. *Pisa. Storia urbana. Piante e vedute dalle origini al secolo XX*, Pisa

MOROZZI, G. "Ricerche sull'aspetto originale dello Spedale degli Innocenti di Firenze", *Comm.*, XV, pp. 186-201

Mostra documentaria e iconografica: La Basilica di S. Lorenzo e le cappelle Medicee (catalogue, ed. F. De Feo), Florence

New Cambridge Modern History, I, *The Renaissance*, Cambridge

PARRONCHI, A. "La costruzione legittima è uguale alla costruzione con punti di distanza", *Rin.*, ser. 2, IV (XV), pp. 35-40

Studi su la "dolce" prospettiva, Milan

SAALMAN, H. "The Authorship of the Pazzi Palace", *A.B.*, XLVI, pp. 388-94
    — "Santa Maria del Fiore: 1294-1418", ibid., pp. 471-500

1963-65

BRAUNFELS, W. "Drei Bemerkungen zur Geschichte und Konstruktion der Florentiner Domkuppel", *Mitt.Flor.*, XI, pp. 203-26

1965

BAUER, H. *Kunst und Utopie. Studien über das Kunst- und Staatsdenken in der Renaissance*, Berlin

FEDERICI VESCOVINI, G. *Studi sulla prospettiva medievale*, Turin

HART, F. *Kunst und Technik der Wölbung*, Munich

MARCHINI, G. "Ghiberti 'ante litteram' ", *B.d.A.*, L, 1965, pp. 181-93

MORANDINI, F. "Palazzo Pitti, la sua costruzione e i successivi ingrandimenti", *Comm.*, ser. 2, V (XVI), pp. 35-46

SAALMAN, H. "The Palazzo Comunale in Montepulciano. An unknown work by Michelozzo", *Z.f.Kg.*, XXVIII, pp. 1-46

SANPAOLESI, P. *La cupola del Brunelleschi* (Forma e Colore 16), Florence

1966

BELLONI, G. G. *Il Castello Sforzesco di Milano*, Milan

CARDOSO MENDES, M.A., and DALLAI, G. "Nuove indagini sullo Spedale degli Innocenti a Firenze", *Comm.*, XVII, pp. 83-106

COOLIDGE, J. "Further observations on Masaccio's 'Trinity' ", *A.B.*, XLVIII, pp. 382-84

DE SANTILLANA, G. "Paolo Toscanelli and his Friends", in *The Renaissance Image of Man and the World*, ed. B. O'Kelly, [Columbus], pp. 77-104

EDGERTON, S.Y. "Alberti's Perspective: a new discovery and a new evaluation", *A.B.*, XLVIII, pp. 367-78

JANSON, H. W. "The Image of Man in Renaissance Art: from Donatello to Michelangelo", in *The Renaissance Image of Man and the World*, op. cit., pp. 77-104

MORPURGO, E. *Gli Orologi*, [Milan]

PARRONCHI, A. "Brunelleschi e Dante", *Naz.*, CVIII, 2 March, p. 3

SAALMANN, H. "Michelozzo studies", *Burl.M.*, CVIII, pp. 242-50
    − Review of *Brunelleschi. Forma e ragione* (1964), in *A.B.*, XLVIII, pp. 442-45
    − "Tommaso Spinelli, Michelozzo, Manetti, and Rosellino", *J.S.A.H.*, XXV, pp. 151-64

SCAGLIA, G. "Drawings of Machines for Architecture from the Early Quattrocento in Italy", *J.S.A.H.*, XXV, pp. 90-114

SIMSON, O. G. VON, "Über die Bedeutung von Masaccios Trinitätfresko in S. Maria Novella", *Jb.Berl.Mus.*, VIII, pp. 119-59

WHITE, J. *Art and Architecture in Italy, 1250-1400*, Harmondsworth and Baltimore

1966-67

BLUMENTHAL, A.P. "A newly-identified drawing of Brunelleschi's stage machinery", *Marsyas*, XIII, pp. 20-31

1967

BEC, C. *Les Marchands écrivains, affaires et humanisme à Florence (1375-1434)*, Paris and The Hague

EDGERTON, S.Y. Jr Review of Parronchi, *Studi su la "dolce" prospettiva* (1964), in *A.B.*, XLIX, pp. 77-80

GOMBRICH, E. H. "From the Revival of Letters to the Reform of the Arts: Niccolò Niccoli and Filippo Brunelleschi", in *Essays in the History of Art presented to Rudolf Wittkower*, II, London and New York, pp. 71-82.

JANSON, H.W. "Ground Plan and Elevation in Masaccio's Trinity Fresco", ibid., pp. 83-88

LEHMANN, E. "Zur Entwicklung der kirchlichen Baukunst des 15. Jahrhunderts in Italien und Deutschland", in *Acta Historiae Artium Academiae Scientiarium Hungaricae*, XIII, pp. 61-68

Rapporto sui danni al patrimonio artistico e culturale, Florence

Il Rinascimento (Tesori d'Arte Cristiana, IV), Bologna

ROCKWELL, A.F. *Filippo's Dome*, New York (for children)

RUSSOLI, F. *Il Rinascimento* (Scultura italiana, III), Milan

SALMI, M. *Civiltà fiorentina del primo Rinascimento*, Florence

SANPAOLESI, P., and BUCCI, M. "Duomo e Battistero di Firenze", in *I Tesori di Tuttitalia, Cattedrali*, Florence, pp. 59-100

SEYMOUR, C. Jr *Sculpture in Italy, 1400-1500*, Harmondsworth and Baltimore

SINGLETON, C.S., ed., *Art, Science and History in the Renaissance*, Baltimore

TOLAINI, E. *Forma Pisarum. Problemi e ricerche per una storia urbanistica della città di Pisa*, Pisa

1968

ARGAN, G.C. *Storia dell'arte italiana*, II, *Il Trecento e il Quattrocento*, Florence

BECKER, M.B. *Florence in Transition: II, Studies in the Rise of the Territorial State*, Baltimore

BENEVOLO, L. *Storia dell'Architettura del Rinascimento*, I, Bari (English transl. *The Architecture of the Renaissance*, London, 1978)
    −, CHIEFFI, S., and MEZZETTI, G. "Indagine sul S. Spirito di Brunelleschi", *Q.St.A. Roma*, XV, fasc. 85-90, pp. 1-52

BEYME, K. VON "Architekturtheorie der italienischen Renaissance als Theorie der Politik", in *Sprache und Politik*, Heidelberg, pp. 209-33

BRANDI, C. *Codice e struttura nelle arti figurative con un corso monografico sul Brunelleschi* (University lectures), Rome

DEGENHART, B. and SCHMITT, A. *Corpus der italienischen Zeichnungen 1300-1450*, Berlin

GORI MONTANELLI, L. "Il sistema proporzionale dell'interno del Duomo di Firenze", in *Festschrift Ulrich Middeldorf*, ed. H. Kosegarten and P. Tigler, I, Berlin, pp. 64-72

GÖTZ, W. *Zentralbau und Zentralbautendenz in der gotischen Architektur*, Berlin

HYMAN, I. *The Palazzo Medici and a ledger for the Church of San Lorenzo*, PhD thesis, New York Univ. (University Microfilms, Ann Arbor, Mich.) (See also Hyman 1977)

JANSON, H.W. "Donatello and the Antique", in

Donatello e il suo tempo (proceedings of the VIII Convegno Internazionale di Studi sul Rinascimento, Florence and Padua 1966), Florence, pp. 77-96

LANG, S. "Leonardo's architectural designs and the Sforza Mausoleum", *Journal of the Warburg and Courtauld Institutes*, XXXI, pp. 218-33

LISNER, M. "Intorno al Crocifisso di Donatello in Santa Croce", in *Donatello e il suo tempo*, op. cit., pp. 115-29

MALLET, M. "Pisa and Florence in the Fifteenth Century: Aspects of the Period of the First Florentine Domination", *Florentine Studies*, pp. 403-41

MARCHINI, G. "Maso di Bartolomeo", in *Donatello e il suo tempo*, op. cit., pp. 235-43

MARTINES, L. *Lawyers and Statecraft in Renaissance Florence*, Princeton

MOLHO, A. "Politics and the ruling class in early Renaissance Florence", *Nuova Riv. Storica*, LII, pp. 401-20

POPE HENNESSY, J. "Donatello's Relief of the Ascension", in *Essays on Italian Sculpture*, London, pp. 37-46

PRAGER, F.D. (A) "A Manuscript of Taccola, Quoting Brunelleschi, on Problems of Inventors and Builders", *Proc. American Philosophical Soc.*, CXII, pp. 131-49
    − (B) "Brunelleschi's Clock?", *Physis*, X, pp. 203-16

PROCACCI, U. "L'uso dei documenti negli studi di storia dell'arte e le vicende politiche ed economiche in Firenze durante il primo Quattrocento nel loro rapporto con gli artisti", in *Donatello e il suo tempo*, op. cit., pp. 1-39

RUBINSTEIN, N., ed. *Florentine Studies. Politics and Society in Renaissance Florence*, London

SAALMAN, H. "Michelozzo Studies. The Florentine Mint", in *Festschrift Ulrich Middeldorf*, ed. H. Kosegarten and P. Tigler, I, Berlin, pp. 140-42

SANPAOLESI, P. "Il Palazzo Pitti e gli architetti fiorentini della discendenza brunelleschiana", ibid., pp. 124-35

SEVERINI, G. "Osservazioni sulla cartografia cittadina", *Rass. del Comune di Pisa*, 11-12, pp. 23-24

TENENTI, A. *Florence à l'époque des Médicis: de la cité à l'état*, Paris

1968-69

HYMAN, Isabelle, "Summaries of Dissertations. Renaissance Art. Fifteenth-Century Florentine Studies: The Palazzo Medici and a Ledger for the Church of San Lorenzo", *Marsyas*, XIV, pp. 90-91.

1969

BOEHM, G. *Studien zur Perspektivität. Philosophie und Kunst in der Frühen Neuzeit*, Heidelberg

BRUCKNER, G. *Renaissance Florence*, New York

CLARK, K. *Civilisation*, London

GADOL, J. *L.B. Alberti. Universal Man of the Early*

Renaissance, Chicago

GARIN, E. *L'età nuova, ricerche di storia della cultura dal XII al XVI secolo*, Naples

HARTT, F. *History of Italian Renaissance Art*, New York

KRAUTHEIMER, R. "The Beginnings of art-historical Writing in Italy", in *Studies in Early Christian, Medieval and Renaissance Art,* London and New York, pp. 257-73

KRINSKY, H.C. "A View of the Palazzo Medici and the Church of San Lorenzo", *J.S.A.H.,* XXVIII, pp. 133-35

LISNER, M. "Deutsche Holzkruzifixe des 15. Jahrhunderts in Italien", *Mitt.Flor.*, pp. 159 ff.

MASETTI ZANNINI, G.L. "Da Castel Sismondo a Castell'Urbano. Documenti barberiniani inediti", in *Rimini. Storia, arte e cultura*, pp. 115-29

MURRAY, P. *The Architecture of the Italian Renaissance,* London

ROMANINI, A.M. *Arnolfo di Cambio e lo "stil nuovo" del gotico italiano*, Milan

ROSE, P.L. "The Taccola Manuscripts", *Physis*, X, pp. 337-46

TAFURI, M. *L'Architettura dell'Umanesimo*, Bari

VINSON, R.J. "L'Hospice des Innocents bâti par Brunelleschi était devenu méconnaissable. On a pu retrouver son état originel", *Connaissance des arts*, 211, pp. 62-71

WESTFALL, C.W. "Society, beauty and the humanist architect in Alberti's De re aedificatoria", *Studies in the Renaissance*, XVI, pp. 61-79

WILINSKI, S. "La serliana", *B.C.S.A.P.*, XI, pp. 399-429

1969-70

GILBERT, C. "The Earliest Guide to Florentine Architecture", *Mitt. Flor.*, XIV, pp. 33-46

MAINSTONE, R.J. "Brunelleschi's Dome of S. Maria del Fiore and some Related Structures", *Trans. Newcomen Soc.*, XLII, pp. 107-26

Il Museo dell'Opera del Duomo a Firenze, ed. L. Becherucci and G. Brunetti, [Milan]

1970

Città di Rimini. Sigismondo Pandolfo Malatesta e il suo tempo (catalogue of exhibition in Rimini, ed. F. Arduini, G.S. Menghi, F. Panvini Rosati, P.G. Pasini, P. Sanpaolesi and A. Vasina), Vicenza

FRANCASTEL, P. *Études de Sociologie de l'Art*, Paris

HATFIELD, R. "Some Unknown Descriptions of the Medici Palace in 1459", *A.B.*, LII, 3, pp. 232-49

KLEIN, R. *La Forme et l'intelligible*, [Paris]

KLOTZ, H. *Die Frühwerke Brunelleschis und die mittelalterliche Tradition*, Berlin

LISNER, M. *Holzkruzifixe in Florenz und in der Toskana von der Zeit um 1300 bis zum frühen Cinquecento*, Munich

[MANETTI, A.] *The Life of Brunelleschi by Antonio di Tuccio Manetti* (intro., notes and critical text ed. H. Saalman, English trans. K. Engass), University Park and London

MOOS, S. VON *Kastell, Palast, Villa. Studien zur*

italienischen Architektur des 15. und 16. Jahrhunderts, Zurich

PAOLETTI, J. "Donatello and Brunelleschi: An early Renaissance portrait", *Comm.*, XXI, pp. 55-60

PRAGER, F. D., and SCAGLIA, G. *Brunelleschi. Studies of his technology and inventions*, Cambridge, Mass., and London

TANTURLI, G. "Per la paternità manettiana della 'Vita del Brunelleschi' ", *Rin.*, ser. 2, X, pp. 179-85

1971

BARTOLI, L. "L'unità di misura e il modulo proporzionale nell'architettura del Rinascimento. Riflessioni su i *Principi architettonici nell'Età dell'Umanesimo*, di Rudolf Wittkower", *Quaderni dell'Ist. di Elementi di Architettura e Rilievo*, pp. 127-37

BATTISTI, E. "Nota sulla prospettiva rinascimentale", *Arte Lombarda*, XVI, pp. 87-97

BECK, J.H. "Masaccio's early career as a sculptor", *A.B.*, LIII, pp. 177-95

BUCCI, M., and BENCINI, R. *Palazzi di Firenze*, Florence (1971-73)

BUDDENSIEG, T. "Criticism and Praise of the Pantheon in the Middle Ages and the Renaissance", in *Classical Influences on European Culture, A.D. 500-1500* (ed. R.R. Bolgar) Cambridge

BURNS, H. "Quattrocento Architecture and the Antique: Some Problems", ibid., pp. 269-87

CADEI, A. "Coscienza storica e architettura in Brunelleschi", *Riv. dell'Ist. Naz. di Archeologia e Storia dell'Arte*, n.s., XVIII, [1973], pp. 181-240

CASALINI, E. *La SS. Annunziata di Firenze*, Florence

Coro e Cupola della SS. Annunziata a Firenze. Rilievo a cura dell'Istituto di Restauro dei Monumenti (with critical essay by P. Roselli; Florence Univ.), Pisa

DAL CANTON, G. "Ipotesi e proposte per una lettura semiologica della prospettiva rinascimentale", *Arte Lombarda*, XVI, pp. 108-13

FERRI, W., FONDELLI, M., FRANCHI, P., and GRECO, F. "Il rilevamento fotogrammetrico della Cupola di S. Maria del Fiore in Firenze", *Boll. di Geodesia e Scienze Affini dell'I.G.M.*, XXX, pp. 158-222

FRANCINI CIARANFI, A.M. *Pitti. Firenze*, Novara

GORI MONTANELLI, L. *La tradizione architettonica toscana*, Florence

HOFFMANN, V. "Brunelleschis Architektursystem", *Architectura*, I, pp. 54-71

LARNER, J. *Culture and Society in Italy, 1290-1420*, London

MOLHO, A. *Florentine public finances in the early Renaissance, 1400-1433*, Cambridge, Mass.

MOROZZI, G. and PICCINI, A. *Il restauro dello Spedale di Santa Maria degli Innocenti 1966-1970*, Florence

PARRONCHI, A. "L'uovo di Brunelleschi", *Naz.*, CXIII, 16 April, p. 13

POLZER, J. "The Anatomy of Masaccio's Holy Trinity", *Jb.Berl.Mus.*, XIII, pp. 18-59

ROSSI, P. *I filosofi e le macchine (1400-1700)*, rev. edn, Milan

SANPAOLESI, P. "Strutture a cupola autoportanti", *Palladio*, n.s., XXI, pp. 3-64

[TACCOLA, M.] *De machinis, The engineering treatise of 1449* (intro., Latin texts, descriptions of engines and technical commentaries by G. Scaglia), Wiesbaden

1970-72

WADDY, P. "Brunelleschi's Design for S. Maria degli Angeli in Florence", *Marsyas*, XV, [1972], pp. 36-45

1972

ACKERMANN, J.S. Review of *The Life of Brunelleschi* (Manetti 1970), *A.B.*, LIV, 2, p. 208

ALBERTI, L.B. *On Painting and On Sculpture* (ed. C. Grayson), London

BAXANDALL, M. *Painting and Experience in Fifteenth Century Italy*, Oxford

BELTRAME, R. "Sul proporzionamento nelle architetture brunelleschiane", *L'Arte*, V, 1972 [1973], 18-19/20, pp. 105-20

BIALOSTOCKI, J. *Spätmittelalter und Beginnende Neuzeit* (Propyläen Kunstgeschichte, VII), Berlin

BOLACCHI, M., and CERAGIOLO, P. *Vicopisano nell'Architettura militare*, Pisa

BRUSCHI, A. "Considerazioni sulla 'Maniera matura' del Brunelleschi. Con un'appendice sulla Rotonda degli Angeli", *Palladio*, n.s., XXII, pp. 89-126

CLEUR, E., DILAGHI, S., and FONDELLI, M. "Analisi della discontinuità della Cupola di Santa Maria del Fiore in Firenze", *Boll. di Geodesia e Scienze Affini dell'I.G.M.*, XXXI, pp. 313-92

FONDELLI, M. "La curva attuale della cupola di Santa Maria del Fiore, Risposta ai professori Piero Sanpaolesi e Giuseppe Birardi ('Vecchie e recenti ricerche sulla cupola di Santa Maria del fiore . . .', *Ant.Viva.*, 2)", *Ant.Viva*, XI, 5, pp. 85-86

GINORI LISCI, L. *I Palazzi di Firenze nella storia e nell'arte*, 2 vol., Florence

HERZNER, V. "Die Kanzeln Donatellos in San Lorenzo", *Münch.Jb.*, ser. 3, XXIII, pp. 101-64

HEYDENREICH, L.H. *Eclosion de la Renaissance. Italie 1400-1460*, Paris

HYMAN, Isabelle, "Brunelleschi, Filippo", in *Dizionario Biografico degli Italiani*, XIV, Rome, pp. 534-45

JACOROSSI, M., ed. *I Palazzi fiorentini. Quartiere di San Giovanni*, Florence

LANZA, A. *Polemiche e Berte letterarie nella Firenze del primo Quattrocento. Storia e testi*, Rome

MARCHINI, G. "L'Altare argenteo di S. Jacopo e l'oreficeria gotica a Pistoia", in *Il Gotico a Pistoia nei suoi rapporti con l'arte gotica italiana. Atti del II Convegno Internazionale di Studi (Pistoia, 24-30 Aprile 1966)*, Pistoia, pp. 135-47

— *Il Battistero, il Duomo e il Museo dell'Opera del Duomo di Firenze*, Florence

MICHELUCCI, G. *Brunelleschi mago* (ed. M. A. Toscano), Pistoia

PRAGER, F.D., and SCAGLIA, G. *Mariano Taccola and his book De Ingeneis*, Cambridge, Mass., and London

RAGGIANTI, C.L. "Pertinenze francesi del Cinquecento", *Cr.A.*, n.s., XIX (XXXVII), pp. 3-92
— "Prospettiva 1401", in *Scritti in onore di Roberto Pane*, Naples, pp. 187-96

SAALMAN, H. Review of Klotz, *Die Frühwerke Brunelleschis* (1970), in *Kunst Chr.*, XXV, 5, pp. 132-38
— "Towards a History of Architectural Technology", *Architectura*, I, pp. 1-2

SANPAOLESI, P. "La cupola di S. Maria del Fiore ed il Mausoleo di Soltanieh. Rapporti di forma e struttura fra la cupola del Duomo di Firenze ed il mausoleo del Jlkhan Ulgiaitu a Soltanieh in Persia", *Mitt.Flor.*, XVI, 3, pp. 221-60
— "La curva attuale della cupola di Santa Maria del Fiore. Risposta al Prof. Mario Fondelli", *Ant.Viva*, XI, 6, pp. 75-76
—, and BIRARDI, G. "Vecchie e recenti ricerche sulla cupola di Santa Maria del Fiore e la interpretazione di un nuovo rilievo fotogrammetrico", *Ant.Viva*, XI, 2, pp. 39-52

SCHÄPPI-WITZIG, H. *Der Beitrag der Florentiner Humanisten und Künstler zur Ausbildung des bürgerlichen Selbsverständnisses im Florenz des frühen Quattrocento (Leonardo Bruni, Filippo Brunelleschi)*, thesis, Zurich Univ. (see *Kunst Chr.*, XXV, 1972, p. 246)

THOENES, C. "Sostegno e adornamento. Zur sozialen Symbolik der Säulenordnung", *Kunst Chr.*, XXV, pp. 343-44

ULMANN, B.L., and STADTER, P.A. *The Public Library of Renaissance Florence*, Padua

1973

BAROLSKY, P. "Toward an Interpretation of the Pazzi Chapel", *J.S.A.H.*, XXXII, 3, pp. 228-31

BELTRAME, R. "Gli esperimenti prospettici del Brunelleschi", *Atti dell'Accademia Nazionale dei Lincei. Rendiconti*, XXVIII, fasc. 3-4, pp. 417-68

BUCCI, M., and BENCINI, R. *Palazzi di Firenze*, II-IV, Florence

DE FUSCO, R. *Segni, storia e progetto dell'architettura*, Bari

EDGERTON, S. Y. Jr. "Brunelleschi's first perspective picture", *Arte Lombarda*, XVIII, 38-39, pp. 172-95

FANELLI, G. *Firenze, Architettura e città*, 2 vol., Florence

FONDELLI, M. "Nuove considerazioni sull'attuale curvatura della cupola di Santa Maria del Fiore in Firenze - Ulteriore replica ai professori Piero Sanpaolesi e Giuseppe Birardi", *Ant.Viva*, XII, 5, pp. 76-77
— "Recenti sviluppi del rilevamento fotogrammetrico di Santa Maria del Fiore in Firenze", *Boll. della Società italiana di Fotogrammetria e Topografia*, 2

— "Testimonianze storiche e ricerche sperimentali sulla curvatura della cupola di Santa Maria del Fiore in Firenze. Replica ai professori Piero Sanpaolesi e Giuseppe Birardi con le due relative risposte", *Ant.Viva*, XII, 2, pp. 73-77

FREYTAG, C. "Italienische Skulptur um 1400: Untersuchungen zu den Einflussbereichen", *Metropolitan Museum Journal* (New York), VII, pp. 5-36

GOLDTHWAITE, R. A. "The Building of the Strozzi Palace. The construction Industry in Renaissance Florence", *Studies in Medieval and Renaissance History*, X, pp. 97-194

HOLMES, G. "The Emergence of an Urban Ideology at Florence c. 1250-1450", *TRans. Royal Hist. Soc.*, ser. 5, XXIII, pp. 111-34

HORSTER, M. "Brunelleschi und Alberti in ihrer Stellung zur römischen Antike", *Mitt.Flor.*, XVII, 1, pp. 29-64

JANSON, H. W. "The Pazzi Evangelists", in *Intuition und Kunstwissenschaft, Festschrift für Swarzenski zum 70.* (ed. P. Bloch and T. Buddensieg), Berlin, pp. 439-48

MACK, C.R. "A new look at the Hospital of the Innocents", *Southeastern College Art Conference Review*, VI, 1, pp. 12-15

MANTOVANI, G. "Brunelleschi e Ghiberti. Osservazioni sulle formelle", *Cr.A.*, n.s., XX (XXXVIII), 130, pp. 18-30

SAALMAN, H. "Brunelleschi", in *Encyclopaedia Britannica*, IV, p. 305

SPULER, C. *Opaion und Laterne*, dissertation, Hamburg Univ.

THOENES, C. "Zu Brunelleschis Architektursystem", *Architectura*, 1, pp. 87-93

VAGNETTI, L. *L'Architetto nella storia di Occidente*, Florence

WARREN, C.W. "Brunelleschi's Dome and Dufay's Motet", *Musical Quarterly*, LIX, 1, pp. 92-105

ZERVAS, D. FINIELLO *Systems of Design and Proportion used by Ghiberti, Donatello and Michelozzo in their large-scale sculpture and architectural ensembles between 1412 and 1434*, PhD thesis, Johns Hopkins Univ. (University Microfilms, Ann Arbor, Mich., 1976)

1974

BATTISTI, E. "Il metodo progettuale secondo il 'De re aedificatoria' di Leon Battista Alberti", in *Il Sant'Andrea di Mantova e Leon Battista Alberti*, (proc. of conference, 1972), Mantua, pp. 131-56

BENVENUTI, R. CAGNOLA, F., and FONDELLI, M. "Ricerche geometriche sulla Cupola di Santa Maria del Fiore in Firenze. Applicazione del Mekometro ME 3000 e del Teodolite DKM 2A - Laser", *Boll. di Geodesia e Scienze Affini dell'I.G.M.*, XXXIII, pp. 105-36

BLUMENTHAL, A.R. "Brunelleschi e il teatro del Rinascimento", *B.C.S.A.P.*, XVI, pp. 93-104

BRANDI, C. *Teoria generale della critica*, Turin

BUSIGNANI, A., and BENCINI, R. *Le chiese di Firenze. Quartiere di S. Spirito*, Florence

CARPEGGIANI, P. "La crisi dell'umanesimo: Leon Battista Alberti e le opere mantovane", in *Il Sant'Andrea di Mantova e Leon Battista Alberti*, op. cit., pp. 211-21

DAL CANTON, G. "Per un lettura semiotica della prospettiva", *Op. cit.*, 29, pp. 5-35

DE ROBERTIS, D. "Antonio Manetti copista", in *Tra latino e Volgare. Per Carlo Dionisotti*, II (Medioevo e Umanesimo, 18), Padua, pp. 367-409

DEZZI BARDESCHI, M. "Sole in Leone. Leon Battista Alberti: Astrologia, Cosmologia e tradizione ermetica nella facciata di Santa Maria Novella", *Psycon*, I, pp. 33-67

EDGERTON, S.Y. Jr "Florentine Interest in ptolemaic Cartography as Background for Renaissance Painting, Architecture, and the Discovery of America", *J.S.A.H.*, XXXIII, 4, pp. 274-92

Firenze. Studi e ricerche sul centro antico, I, L'ampliamento della Cattedrale di S. Reparata, le conseguenze sullo sviluppo della città a nord e la formazione della Piazza del Duomo e di quella della SS. Annunziata, Pisa

GAI, L. "Per la cronologia di Donatello: un documento inedito del 1401", *Mitt.Flor.*, XVIII, 3, pp. 355-57

HERZNER, V. "Zur Baugeschichte von San Lorenzo in Florenz", *Z.f.Kg.*, XXXVII, 2, pp. 89-115

HEYDENREICH, L.H., and LOTZ, W. *Architecture in Italy, 1400-1600*, Harmondsworth and Baltimore

HYMAN, I. *Brunelleschi in Perspective*, Englewood Cliffs

KREYTENBERG, G. *Der Dom zu Florenz. Untersuchungen zur Baugeschichte im 14. Jahrhunderts*, Berlin

MANTOVANI, G. "Brunelleschi e Ghiberti, in margine all'iconografia del Sacrificio", *Cr.A.*, n.s., XXI (XXXIX), 138, pp. 22-32

MCNEAL CAPLOW, H. "Sculptors' Partnerships in Michelozzo's Florence", *Studies in the Renaissance*, XXI, pp. 145.75.

MIARELLI MARIANI, G. "Il Neoclassicismo fiorentino e il 'restauro' dei monumenti del Rinascimento; il caso esemplare di San Lorenzo", in *Pasquale Poccianti, Architetto, 1774-1858. Studi e ricerche nel secondo centenario della nascità* (catalogue of exhibition at Bibbiena), Florence, pp. 25-34

PARDINI, E. "Relazione dello studio antropologico degli inumati in Santa Reparata", in G. Morozzi, *Santa Reparata, l'antica cattedrale Fiorentina. I risultati dello scavo condotto dal 1965 al 1974*, Florence, pp. 37-38

RAGGHIANTI, L.C. *Il libro de' Disegni del Vasari*, 2 vol., Florence

SUNDERLAND, E.R. "The System of Proportion of Filippo Brunelleschi", in *Hortus Imaginum, Essays in Western Art*, I, pp. 65-72

TIBALDI, U. "Il maestro di architettura di Leon Battista Alberti", in *Il Sant'Andrea di Mantova e Leon Battista Alberti*, op. cit., pp. 299-300

TIBERI, C. *Poetica bramantesca tra Quattrocento e Cinquecento*, Rome

ZEVI, B. *Architettura e storiografia. Le matrici antiche del linguaggio moderno*, Turin

1975

BENEVOLO, L. *Storia della città*, Bari

BOSKOVITS, M. *Pittura fiorentina alla vigilia del Rinascimento*, Florence

EDGERTON, S.Y. Jr *The Renaissance Discovery of Linear Perspective*, New York

FOSSI, M. "Una 'ispezione' a Santa Maria del Fiore eseguita dall'Ammannati nel 1590", *Ant.Viva*, XIV, 4, pp. 58-59

HYMAN, I. "Notes and Speculations on S. Lorenzo, Palazzo Medici and an Urban Project by Brunelleschi", *J.S.A.H.*, XXXIV, pp. 98-120

KENT, D. "The Florentine *reggimento* in the fifteenth century", *Renaissance Quarterly*, IV, pp. 575-638

Jacopo della Quercia nell'arte del suo tempo (exhibition at Siena and Grosseto), Florence

LINDBERG, D.C. *A Catalogue of Medieval and Renaissance Optical Manuscripts*, Toronto

MAINSTONE, R. *Developments in Structural Form*, London

MIARELLI MARIANI, G. "I disegni per la Rotonda degli Angioli. Elementi per la ricomposizione del progetto di Michelangelo" [sic], *Ant.Viva*, XIV, 2, pp. 35-48

QUINTERIO, F. *Dopo Brunelleschi. Indagine sui cantieri incompiuti del Brunelleschi: collaboratori e continuatori*, thesis, Florence Univ.

ROSE, P.L. *The Italian Renaissance of Mathematics. Studies on Humanists and Mathematicians from Petrarch to Galileo*, Geneva [1976]

SAALMAN, H. "Michelangelo: S. Maria del Fiore and St Peter's", *A.B.*, LVII, pp. 374-409

SINDING-LARSEN, S. "A tale of two cities. Florentine and Roman visual context for fifteenth-century palaces", in *Institutum Romanum Norvegiae Acta ad Archaeologiam et artium historiam pertinentia*, VII, pp. 163-212

STROM, D.P. *Studies in Quattrocento Wooden Sculpture*, PhD thesis, Princeton Univ.

TANTURLI, G. "Per l'interpretazione storica della 'Vita del Brunelleschi' ", *Par.*, XXVI, 301, pp. 5-25

VALLERINI, F. *Il territorio Pisano*, Pisa

VELTMAN, K. *Renaissance Optics and Perspective: a Study in the Problems of Size and Distance*, PhD thesis, London Univ.

ZEVI, B. "Sull'anticlassicismo depone Brunelleschi", *ACS*, XX, pp. 608-09

1974-76

MIARELLI MARIANI, G. "Il Tempio fiorentino degli Scolari. Ipotesi e notizie sopra una irrealizzata immagine brunelleschiana", *Palladio*, n.s., XXIII-XXV, pp. 45-74

1976

[BARTOLI, L.] *Filippo Brunelleschi, L'Architettura*, Florence

CLEUR, E., FONDELLI, M., and GRECO, F. "Numerical Photogrammetry and Automatic Data Processing tn the Study and Preservation of Ancient Monuments. Experimental Research on the Dome of Santa Maria del Fiore", in *Fotogrammetria dei monumenti* (proc. of Simposio internazionale di fotogrammetria dei monumenti, Lucca, 1973) Florence, pp. 191-99

EDGERTON, S.Y. Jr "Linear Perspective and the Western Mind: The Origins of Objective Representation in Art and Science", *Cultures*, III, 3, pp. 77-104

HECHT, K. "Massverhältnisse und Masse der Cappella Pazzi", *Architectura*, VI, 2, pp. 148-74

HERSEY, G.L. *Pythagorean Palaces: Magic and Architecture in the Italian Renaissance*, Ithaca and London

LINDBERG, D.C. *Theories of Vision from Al-Kindi to Kepler*, Chicago and London

[MANETTI, A.] *"Vita di Filippo Brunelleschi", preceduta da "La Novella del Grasso"* (critical edn of text by D. De Robertis, intro. and notes by G. Tanturli), Milan

PEDRETTI, G. *Il primo Leonardo a Firenze: l'Arno, la Cupola, il Battistero*, Florence

RAGGHIANTI, C.L. "Liberare il Brunelleschi", *Cr.A.*, n.s., XXII (XLI), 145, pp. 67-70

ROMBY, G.C. *Descrizioni e rappresentazioni della città di Firenze del XV secolo*, Florence

SCHUYLER, J. *Florentine Busts: Sculpted Portraiture in the Fifteenth Century*, New York and London

TANTURLI, G. "Le biografie d'artisti prima del Vasari", in *Il Vasari storiografo e artista* (proc. of the Congresso Internazionale nel IV Centenario della morte, Arezzo and Florence 1974), Florence, pp. 275-98

1976-77

SUPERCHI, O. *Nuovi documenti per la storia della costruzione della Basilica di S. Lorenzo in Firenze: contributi ed ipotesi*, thesis, Florence Univ.

1977

ARGAN, G.C. "La cupola di Brunelleschi", *Nuova Antologia*, CXII, 532, pp. 17-24

BACCI, B.M. *Il cielo di pietra*, ills by U. Fontana (for children), Florence

BARTOLI, L. *La rete magica di Filippo Brunelleschi: La seste, il braccio, le misure*, Florence

BOZZONI, C. and CARBONARA, G. *Filippo Brunelleschi: Saggio di Bibliografia I, Schede 1436-1976*, Rome

BRUCKNER, G. *The Civic World of Early Renaissance Florence*, Princeton

Brunelleschi anti-classico - mostra critica (catalogue), Florence. See Capolei and Sartogo, "Editoriale - Letture Brunelleschiane", *ACS*, XXIII, 4/5, pp. 194-283

BRUSCHI, A. "Un incontro brunelleschiano all'Accademia di San Luca", *Studi Romani*, XXV, 2, pp. 294-95

CALABRESE, O. "Inchiesta sui mali della Cupola del Duomo di Firenze", *Casabella*, XLI, 421, pp. 61-69

"La Cupola del Duomo di Firenze", *Casabella*, 421, pp. 61-67

DADDI, B. *Contributi alle Ricerche sulla Cupola del Brunelleschi*, Florence
– "Un tentativo di verifica della cupola di S.M. del Fiore con il metodo grafico di J.W. Schwedler", *Boll. degli Ingegneri*, XXV, 5, pp. 13-18.

D'ALFONSO, E. "Filippo Brunelleschi o la costruzione di un nuovo fondamento del sapere e del fare", *Parametro*, VIII, 60, pp. 36-47

DEL BRAVO, C. "La dolcezza della immaginazione", *Annali della Scuola Normale di Pisa*, ser. 3, VII, 2, pp. 759-99

DE ROBERTIS, D., and TANTURLI, G. *Sonetti di Filippo Brunelleschi* (intro. by Tanturli, critical edn and notes by De Robertis), Florence

DE TOLNAY, C., ed. *Brunelleschi e Michelangelo* (catalogue), Florence

DI PASQUALE, S. *Primo rapporto sulla Cupola di Santa Maria del Fiore*, Florence
– "Una ipotesi sulla struttura della cupola di S. Maria del Fiore", *Restauro*, V, 28, pp. 1-77

DI PUOLO, M., and MARINI, G.L., eds. "Brunelleschi. L'architetto che inventò il Rinascimento", *Bolaffiarte*, VIII, pp. 13-25

FALLETTI, F., and PAOLINI, L. "Una nuova data per la Cupola del Brunelleschi", *Prospettiva*, III, 11, pp. 57-58

FANELLI, G. *Brunelleschi*, Florence

"Filippo Brunelleschi nella Firenze del '300-400", *Città di Vita*, XXXII, 3-4, pp. 143-295

Firenze, note di storia e di urbanistica, Florence (with English text)

FONDELLI, M. "I fondamenti della fotogrammetria nella prima esperienza prospettica di Filippo Brunelleschi", *Boll. degli Ingegneri*, XXV, 11, pp. 18-21

FRILLI, R. *Brunelleschi. Tutte le opere*, Florence

GALLUZZI, P. "Le colonne 'fesse' degli Uffizi e gli 'screpoli' della cupola. Il contributo di Vincenzo Viviani al dibattito sulla stabilità della Cupola del Brunelleschi (1694-1697)", *Annali dell'Ist. e Mus. di Storia della Scienza di Firenze*, II, 1, pp. 71-111

GARIN, E. "Brunelleschi e la cultura fiorentina del Rinascimento", *Nuova Antologia*, CXII, 530, fasc. 2118-20, pp. 11-23

GOLDTHWAITE, R.A., and REARICK, W.R. "Michelozzo and the Ospedale di San Paolo in Florence", *Mitt. Flor.*, XXI, pp. 221-306

HEIKAMP, D. "Un progetto di Luigi Ademollo per affrescare il Duomo di Firenze", in *Scritti di Storia dell'Arte in onore di Ugo Procacci*, Milan

HYMAN, I. *Fifteenth-Century Florentine Studies The Palazzo Medici and a Ledger for the Church of San Lorenzo* (PhD Thesis, 1968, with documents revised by G. Conti), New York and London

Jacopo della Quercia fra Gotico e Rinascimento, ed. G. Chelazzi Dini (proc. of conference at Siena, 1975), Florence

LEVI, G. and MELCHIORRE, M., "Il Battistero di S. Giovanni a Volterra", *Rass. Volterrana*, XLII-LIII, pp. 101-13

LOTZ, W. *Studies in Italian Renaissance Architecture*, Cambridge, Mass.

MARCHINI, G. "Fulmini sulla Cupola", *Ant.Viva*, XVI, 4, pp. 22-25
—, MIARELLI MARIANI, G., MOROLLI, G., and ZANGHIERI, L., eds., *Disegni di fabbriche Brunelleschiane* (exhibition catalogue), Uffizi, 1977; intro. by A. Forlani Tempesti, G. Marchini and G. Miarelli Mariani), Florence

MIARELLI MARIANI, G. "Brunelleschi e Roma, Un incontro fra mito e realtà", *Studi Romani*, XXV, 2, pp. 202-06

MICHELETTI, E., and PAOLUCCI, A. *Brunelleschi scultore* (exhibition catalogue), Florence

MOLHO, A. "Three Documents regarding Filippo Brunelleschi", *Burl.M.*, CXIX, pp. 851-52

MUCCI, E. "Brunelleschi e i mass media: il Kitsch e la cupola", *D'Ars*, 43, 85, pp. 124-29

PANE, R. "Come fotografare Brunelleschi?", *Restauro*, V, 28, pp. 82-83
[—] *Filippo Brunelleschi, Firenze 1377-1446* (600th anniversary exhibition)

PARRONCHI, A. "La designò sulla rena dell'Arno", *Naz.*, CXIX, 26 Aug., p. 3
— "L'operazione del levare della pianta nel trattatello albertiano 'De Pictura' ", *Rin.*, ser. 2, XXVII, pp. 207-12
— "L'uovo del Brunelleschi", in *Scritti di Storia dell'arte in onore di Ugo Procacci*, op. cit., I, pp. 209-14
— "Tabernacolo brunelleschiano", *Prospettiva*, III, 11, pp. 55-56
— " 'Una nostra Donna' del Brunelleschi", *Naz.*, CXIX, 15 Jan., p. 3
— "Una 'tavoluzza' contro il Maligno", *Naz.*, CXIX, 9 Oct., p. 3
—, and CASALINI, E. *Le due Cupole* (conference), Florence

PETRINI, G. *Per lo studio del progrediente affievolimento documentario nelle fabbriche rinascimentali in relazione ai fenomeni di degrado, agli interventi restaurativi ed alla storia dell'arte*, Florence

POTTINGER, G. *The Court of the Medici*, Totowa, N.J. (and London 1978)

Problemi Brunelleschiani: Sagrestia Vecchia e San Lorenzo (texts by E. Rodio and. R. Pacciani, measured drawings prepared under the supervision of E. Battisti), Rome

RAGGHIANTI, C.L. *Filippo Brunelleschi, un uomo, un universo*, Florence
— "Spettacolo a Firenze nel Quattrocento", *Cr.A.*, n.s. (XXIII), XLII, 151-53, pp. 238-40

Ricerche brunelleschiane (papers presented at 1977 Brunelleschi Congress by Acidini Luchinat, Belluzzi, Bencivenni, Benigni (on the exhibition of documents) and Ruschi, Borsi, Brandinelli, Conti, Degl'Innocenti, Ferrara, Moretti, Morolli, Pacciani, Poma, Quinterio, Rodio, Vasic Vatoveč and Zangheri), Florence

ROSSI, P.A. *Brunelleschi vera cupola*, Florence
— *Le Otto Piattabande Curve*, Florence

SAALMAN, H. "Documenti inediti sulla Cappella della SS. Annunziata", in *Scritti di Storia de' Arte in onore di Ugo Procacci*, op. cit., pp. 226-27
— Review of Hersey, *Pythagorean Palaces* (1976), in *A.B.*, LIX, pp. 282-84

SANPAOLESI, P. "Der statische Zustand der Florentiner Domkuppel", *Kunst Chr.*, XXX, 8, pp. 333-37
— *La cupola di Santa Maria del Fiore. Il progetto, La costruzione*, Florence

SCARCHILLI, R. "Il complesso laurenziano: la chiesa (prima parte)", *Controspazio*, IX, 1, pp. 43-47

[VANNI, B.] *Avvenimenti e discorsi di Bartolomeo Vanni Ingegnere mediceo (1662-1732)*, ed. L. Zangheri, Florence

VELTMAN, K. Review of Edgerton, *Renaissance Discovery of Linear Perspective* (1975), in *A.B.*, LIX, 2, pp. 281-82

Ventura Vitoni e il Rinascimento a Pistoia, Pistoia

WHITE, J. Review of Edgerton, *Renaissance Rediscovery of Linear Perspective* (1975), in *J.S.A.H.*, XXXVI, pp. 45-46

ZANDER, G. "Il luogo sacro brunelleschiano e i luoghi sacri del '3-'400", in *Filippo Brunelleschi nella Firenze del '3-'400*, Florence, pp. 93-116

1978

ARNHEIM, R. "Brunelleschi's Peepshow", *Z.f.Kg.*, XLI, I, pp. 57-60

BECK, J.H. "Brunelleschi, Ciuffagni and Il Saggio", in *Essays Presented to Myron P. Gilmore*, ed. S. Bertelli and G. Ramakus, II, Florence, pp. 3-10

BEHLES, J. *Das Gestaltungsprinzip Brunelleschis beim Bau von Santo Spirito in Florenz*, Frankfurt a. M.

BROGAN, R. *A Signature of Power and Patronage. The Medici Coat of Arms, 1299-1492*, PhD thesis, Florida State Univ.

BROWN, B.L. *The tribune of SS. Annunziata in Florence*, PhD thesis, Northwestern Univ.

Brunelleschi 1377-1446, oeuvres; and *Florence au temps de Brunelleschi* (exhibitions, 1978-79), Paris

BRUSCHI, A. "Nota sulla formazione architettonica dell'Alberti", *Palladio*, ser. 3, XXV [XXVII], 1, pp. 6-44
— "Prima del Brunelleschi. Verso un'architettura 'prospettica' e 'sintattica': Arnolfo, Giotto, Taddeo Gaddi", *Palladio*, ser. 3, XXVII, 3-4
—, MALTESE, C., TAFURI, M., and BONELLI, R., eds. *Scritti rinascimentali di architettura*, Milan

CASAZZA, O. and BODDI, R. "Il Crocifisso ligneo di Filippo Brunelleschi", *Cr.A.*, n.s., 43, pp. 160-62, 209-12

CAVALLARI MURAT, A. "Brunelleschi: intuizioni tecniche e immagini", *Atti e Rassegna tecnica della soc. degli Ingegneri degli Architetti in Torino*, n.s., XXXII (CXI)

DI PASQUALE, S., et al. *Elaborazione dei dati concernenti il quadro fessurativo della cupola di Santa Maria del Fiore*, CLUSF, Florence

I disegni antichi degli Uffizi (catalogue), Florence

EDGERTON, S.Y. Jr "The Art of Renaissance picture-making and the great Western age of discovery", in *Essays Presented to Myron P. Gilmore*, op. cit., pp. 133-53

[FERRARA, M., and QUINTERIO, F.] "L'ultimo costruttore di S. Lorenzo", *Paese Sera*, XXIX, 30 July, p. 16

FEUER-TOTH, R. "The 'Apertionum Ornamenta' of Alberti and the Architecture of Brunelleschi", *Acta Historiae Artium*, 24, pp. 147-52

FIORE, F.P. *Città e macchine del '400 nei disegni di Francesco di Giorgio Martini*, Florence

Ghiberti e l'architettura (papers of the conference, *Lorenzo Ghiberti nel suo tempo*), Florence

HERSEY, G.L. "Alberti's cubism", in *Essays Presented to Myron P. Gilmore*, op. cit., pp. 245-51
— Letter to the Editor (in reply to Saalman's review, 1977), *A.B.*, LX, pp. 192-93

HYMAN, I. "Towards rescuing the lost reputation of Antonio di Manetto Ciaccheri", in *Essays Presented to Myron P. Gilmore*, op. cit., pp. 261-80

KEMP, M. "Science, non-science and nonsense: the interpretation of Brunelleschi's perspective", *Art History*, I, 2, pp. 134-61

KENT, D. *The Rise of the Medici*, Oxford

Lorenzo Ghiberti, "materia e ragionamenti" (exhibition, Accademia and Mus. S. Marco), Florence

MARCHINI, G. *Ghiberti architetto*, Florence

Masaccio, The Documents, by J. Beck with the collaboration of G. Conti, New York

MORANDI, M. *L'architetto: origini e trasformazioni di un ruolo*, Trieste

MYERS, M.N. *Observations on the Origins of Renaissance Perspective: Brunelleschi, Masaccio, Petrus Christus*, PhD Thesis, Columbia Univ., New York

[PEDIO, R.] "Mostra 'Brunelleschi anticlassico' nei Chiostri di Santa Maria Novella a Firenze", *ACS*, XXIV, pp. 198-226, 274-75

PIETRAMELLARA, C. "Alcuni aspetti dell'arte tarda del Brunelleschi", *Ant. Viva*, XVII, 1, pp. 40-51

POCHAT, G. "Brunelleschi and the 'Ascension' of 1422", *A.B.*, LX, 2, pp. 232-34

ROSSI, P.A. "La cupola, parliamone ancora", *Pegaso*, III, pp. 18ff.
— "Principi costruttivi nella cupola di S.M. del Fiore", *Cr.A.*, fasc. 157-59, pp. 85-118

SAALMAN, H. "I Tatti in 1427", in *Essays Presented to Myron P. Gilmore*, op. cit., pp. 683-86

SANPAOLESI, P. *Scritti vari di storia, restauro e critica dell'architettura*, Florence Univ., pp. 21-22, 25-26, 57-71, 73-77, 97-103

SETTLE, T.B. "Brunelleschi's Horizontal Arches and Related Devices", *Annali dell'Ist. e Mus. di Storia della Scienza di Firenze*, III, pp. 65-80

THIES, H. Review of Edgerton, *Renaissance Redis-*

covery of Linear Perspective (1975), in Kunst Chr., XXXI, 10, pp. 411-21

TOKER, F.K.B. "Florence Cathedral: the Design Stage", A.B., LX, 2, pp. 214-31

"Una chiesa millenaria ritrovata sotto S. Lorenzo", Naz., 15 Sept.

VERGA, C. Dispositivo Brunelleschi 1420, Crema

WITTKOWER, R. Idea and Image, London, pp. 125-35

1979

BATTISTI, E. In luoghi di avanguardia antica, Reggio Calabria, pp. 33-39

BORSI, F., MOROLLI, G., and QUINTERIO, F. Brunelleschiani, Rome

ELAM, C. "The Site and Early Building History of Michelangelo's New Sacristy", Mitt.Flor., XXIII, 1-2, pp. 155-86

Florence au temps de Brunelleschi (Chapel of the Sorbonne and Ecole des Beaux-Arts), Paris

FRANCHETTI PARDO, V. "Culture brunelleschiane et construction dans la Florence du XV siècle", in Brunelleschi 1377-1446, Paris

HYMAN, I. "The Venice Connection: Questions about Brunelleschi and the East", in Florence and Venice: Comparison and Relations, I, Florence, pp. 193-208

KENT, F.W. "A Letter of 1476 from Antonio di Tuccio Manetti mentioning Brunelleschi", Burl.M., CXXI, 919, pp. 648-49

MARTINES, L. Power and Imagination. City-States in Renaissance Italy, New York

PARRONCHI, A. Ghiberti, l'antagonista. Ghiberti e la sua arte nella Firenze del '3-'400

ROSELLI, P. "Brunelleschi in San Lorenzo, Contributi alla cronologia dell'edificazione", Ant.Viva, 2, pp. 36-43

STINGER, C. "Ambrogio Traversari and the Tempio degli Scolari at S. Maria degli Angeli in Florence", in Essays Presented to Myron P. Gilmore, I, Milan, pp. 271-86

ZERVAS, D. F. "Filippo Brunelleschi's Political Career", Burl.M., CXXI, 919, pp. 630-39

1980

BATTISTI, E. Brunelleschi and the Avant-Garde of the Renaissance (proc. of Seminar of the group History + Theory of Architecture, Univ. of Technology, 1977), Eindhoven

DALAI, M. (ed.) La Prospettiva Rinascimentale, Codificazioni e trasgressioni, I, Florence

HATFIELD, R. "Some Unknown Descriptions of the Medici Palace in 1459", A.B., LXII

PARRONCHI, A. "Su tre crocifissi", in Donatello e il potere, Bologna, pp. 51-85

ROMBY, C. Per costruire ai tempi del Brunelleschi. Modi, norme e consuetudini del quattrocento fiorentino, CLUSF, Florence

ROSELLI, P., and SUPERCHI, O. L'edificazione della Basilica di San Lorenzo, una vicenda di importanza urbanistica, CLUSF, Florence

SAALMAN, H. Filippo Brunelleschi. The Cupola of Santa Maria del Fiore, London

In preparation

Proceedings of the Convegno Internazionale di Studi Brunelleschiani, Florence, 16-22 Oct. 1977

Proceedings of the Convegno Internazionale di Studi Ghibertiani, Florence, 18-21 Oct. 1978

Index

Figures in *italics* refer to pages on which illustrations occur and to the contents of the accompanying captions.

The letters a, b, c refer to columns, left to right.

Illustration credits

Most of the drawings were made for first-hand surveys and measurements by students and assistants in the Istituto di Storia dell'Architettura e Restauro at the University of Florence, and are reproduced here for the first time. The majority of the photographs were also specially taken for this book, chiefly by Paolo Monti, but also by the author, by Riccardo Pacciani, and by architectural students.

Other sources, in addition to those mentioned in the captions, are: Alinari, Florence 3, 20, 25, 26, 51, 108, 111, 112, 154, 156, 162, 169, 229, 231, 233, 234, 282, 297, 298, 302, 303, 305, 306, 315; Aurelio Amendola, Pistoia 12-16; Bruno Balestrini, Milan 21-24; Raffaello Bencini, Florence 331, 333, 334, 336-342; Istituto Geografico Militare, Florence 344, 348, 353, 356, 357; Soprintendenza alle gallerie, Florence 10, 11, 17, 103, 105, 176, 267, 268; Soprintendenza ai Monumenti, Florence 30b, d; Pepi Merisio, Bergamo 1, 80, 81, 113, 190, 197, 205, 211, 290; Paolo Monti, Milan 27, 28, 38, 39, 41, 43, 44, 46, 49, 54-56, 65, 68-74, 99, 100, 110, 114, 115, 118, 119, 125-127, 129, 130, 132-134, 139, 149-152, 155, 157-160, 163-167, 170, 175, 191-196, 198-201, 207, 208, 210, 212-216, 218, 220-222, 226, 227, 250, 252-257, 266, 281, 295, 301, 304, 309, 312, 313, 317-320, 322, 323, 328-330; Pietro Sarti, Mercatale di Vernio 228; by courtesy of the author 2, 5-7, 47, 48, 63, 64, 75-79, 101, 120, 121, 128, 140, 143, 177-179, 206, 232, 258, 259, 275, 280, 286, 296, 299, 300, 314, 316, 345, 346, 349, 350, 351, 354, 355.

Illustrations have also come from the following publications: L. Benevolo, S. Chieffi and G. Mezzetti, ''Indagine sul S. Spirito di Brunelleschi'', *Quaderni dell'Istituto di Storia dell'Architettura dell'Università di Roma* (XV, 1968, fasc. 85-90) 202-204, 217, 219, 223, 225; G. Degli'Innocenti (ed.), *Manuale di Restituzione Prospettica* (Florence, 1975-76) 94-96; E. Detti, G. F. di Pietro and G. Fanelli, *Città murate e sviluppo contemporaneo* (Lucca and Milan, 1968) 343, 347, 352; *Dizionario enciclopedico d'architettura e urbanistica*, ed. P. Portoghesi (I, 1968) 206; *Encyclopedia of World Art* (New York, Toronto and London, 1968, XI) 91, 92; M. Fabbri et al., *Spettacolo e Musica nella Firenze Medicea. Documenti e restituzioni, I. Il luogo teatrale a Firenze* (cat. of exhibition in Florence; Milan, 1975) 181; H. Klotz, *Die Frühwerke Brunelleschis und die mittelalterliche Tradition* (Berlin, 1970) 30a, 67; G. Laschi, P. Roselli and P. A. Rossi, ''Indagini sulla Cappella dei Pazzi'', *Commentari* (XIII, 1962) 78,232; A. Parronchi, *Studi su la ''dolce'' prospettiva* (Milan, 1964) 97; F. D. Prager and G. Scaglia, *Brunelleschi. Studies of his technology and inventions* (Cambridge, Mass., and London, 1970) 135; P. Sanpaolesi, *Brunellesco e Donatello nella Sacristia Vecchia di San Lorenzo* (Pisa, 1948) 60-62; P. Sanpaolesi, ''La lanterna di S. Maria del Fiore e il suo modello ligneo'', *Bollettino d'Arte* (XLI, 1956) 283-284, 288, 289.